POLITICS AND SOCIETY IN REFORMATION EUROPE

Sir Geoffrey Elton

Politics and Society in Reformation Europe

Essays for Sir Geoffrey Elton on his Sixty-Fifth Birthday

Edited by

E. I. Kouri
Professor of History
Oulu University, Finland

and

Tom Scott
Lecturer in History
University of Liverpool

St. Martin's Press   New York

First published in the United States of America in 1987

Printed in Hong Kong

ISBN 0–312–00537–7

Library of Congress Cataloging-in-Publication Data
Politics and society in Reformation Europe.
Includes bibliographies and index.
1. Europe—History—1492–1648. 2. Reformation—
Europe. 3. Elton, G. R. (Geoffrey Rudolph)
I. Elton, G. R. (Geoffrey Rudolph) II. Scott, Tom,
1947–   . III. Kouri, E. I.
D223.P65   1987   940.2′3   87–9562
ISBN 0–312–00537–7

Contents

Contents

Preface

The knighthood recently conferred upon Sir Geoffrey Elton acknowledges his unique contribution to the history of Tudor and Stuart England over more than thirty years and his unrivalled place in the first rank of British historians, to which his presidency of the Royal Historical Society and his appointment to the Regius Chair in Cambridge have already borne witness. His many studies on the Tudor polity and his broader reflections upon the historian's craft reveal the true affection in which Geoffrey Elton holds his adopted country; yet he has never disavowed the intellectual heritage of his Continental background.

The son of Victor Ehrenberg, the eminent historian of ancient Greece, Geoffrey Rudolph Elton was born in Tübingen in 1921 into a family which over the generations had established a modest scholarly and professional dynasty. In 1929 his father was appointed to the chair of ancient history at the German University in Prague, but the darkening menace of National Socialism brought Victor Ehrenberg and his family to England in 1939. The dislocations and privations of the war and its aftermath may have disrupted, but could not destroy, the single-minded determination with which Geoffrey Elton applied himself to historical research as a student, under Sir John Neale in London, in new and unfamiliar surroundings.

In his subsequent career as scholar, teacher, research supervisor and editor, briefly at Glasgow and thereafter as a Fellow of Clare College, Cambridge, Geoffrey Elton has been associated above all with the history of England. Although, as he insists, England is not part of Europe in its modern historical development, he has nevertheless maintained links of learning and of friendship with the world of Continental scholarship.

Among Geoffrey Elton's scholarly achievements, which include some twenty books, his works on the international history of the Reformation have always held an important place. In 1963 *Reformation Europe, 1517–1559* was published and has since remained no less a trusty textbook to generations of students than his *England under the Tudors*. So popular – and provocative – did it prove that it was translated into several languages including German and Japanese. In 1963 Geoffrey Elton also edited a collection of sources, *Renaissance and Reformation, 1300–1648*, now in its third edition, in the series *Ideas and*

Institutions in Western Civilization. The crown was set upon his contribution to European scholarship by the appearance in 1968 of the eagerly awaited second volume of *The New Cambridge Modern History*, entitled *The Reformation, 1520–1559*. As well as an Introduction of magisterial authority and magical concision, he wrote both the chapter on 'The Reformation in England' and a lucid survey of 'Constitutional Development and Political Thought in Western Europe'.

It was entirely fitting, therefore, that he should be invited to join the board of management of the internationally renowned *Archive for Reformation History*, in whose 1977 issue he contributed the portrait 'Thomas Cromwell Redivivus', a Continental clarion for the figure at the centre of his historical endeavours. Elton's mastery of both English and European Reformation history has found further expression in numerous other articles collected in his *Studies in Tudor and Stuart Politics and Government*, including his study in German on England and the Reformation in Upper Germany.

Published forays into his mother tongue do not stand alone. Who can forget Geoffrey Elton addressing the International Luther Congress in Erfurt in August 1983 in fluent and faultless German, without text or notes, and in language so pithy that it astonished the staid assembly of scholars and divines? The Luther quincentenary took Elton to other conferences in West Germany, where his iconoclasm and pricking of conceits were worthy of the great Reformer himself. With the same vigour he has presented problems of Reformation history to audiences in all five continents.

In honour of his sixty-fifth birthday this collection of essays on *Politics and Society in Reformation Europe* by friends and colleagues at home and overseas pays tribute to Sir Geoffrey Elton's standing beyond England's shores in the world community of historians. In bringing together scholars from many countries, the editors, whose own doctoral research, guided by Geoffrey Elton, was devoted to European history, have sought to convey the wealth of original and challenging scholarship in which the Reformation era now abounds. No single volume can do justice to every facet of current debate. The collection therefore concentrates upon two principal themes: the political conditions within Germany in the age of the Reformation and the interaction of religion and society; and the dissemination of Protestantism beyond the German-speaking lands, and its repercussions upon international relations and the development of the early modern state. Spanning these topics are introductory and concluding surveys which reflect upon the Reformation's impact on the modern world.

In his recent biography of F. W. Maitland, Geoffrey Elton stresses that the historian's graces can come only from hard work, hard thought and concentrated research. By their plurality of subject and approach the authors in this *Festschrift* seek to observe another of his fundamental maxims: that true historical understanding derives not from reverence towards established opinion but from the critical scrutiny of evidence and the courage to engage in controversy and debate. In their willingness to submit their arguments to one of the most trenchant critics of our time, they fulfil Sir Geoffrey's most earnest desire: to uphold 'the comity of scholars in a discommodity of nations'.

E. I. KOURI
TOM SCOTT

Acknowledgements

The editors acknowledge with gratitude the financial assistance of the Alexander von Humboldt Foundation in Bonn towards the publication of this volume. They also wish to thank Cambridge University Press for permission to reproduce the map of the Swiss Confederation on page 189. To the several translators and secretaries who have helped in the preparation of this volume goes the editors' profound gratitude.

E.I.K.
T.S.

Editors' Notes

For clarity, upper and lower case are used to distinguish between Estates (*Stände*; corporations) and estates (*Güter*; lands). The adjective *ständisch* is rendered as Estatal.

Place-names are rendered according to existing political frontiers, except where common English forms exist.

Personal names have been anglicised in the case of ruling houses and territorial princes, but the native style has been retained for all other names, including the ecclesiastical Electors.

E.I.K.
T.S.

Notes on the Contributors

Thomas A. Brady, Jr is Professor of History at the University of Oregon. As well as numerous articles on aspects of the Reformation in Germany he is the author of *Ruling Class, Regime and Reformation at Strasbourg, 1520–1555* and *Turning Swiss: Cities and Empire, 1450–1550*.

Henry J. Cohn is Reader in History at the University of Warwick. Besides articles on the German Peasants' War and anti-clericalism in the German Reformation, he is the author of *The Government of the Rhine Palatinate in the Fifteenth Century* and has edited *Government in Reformation Europe, 1520–1560*.

A. G. Dickens is Emeritus Professor of History at King's College, London, and former Director of the Institute of Historical Research. Among his many books on the English and Continental Reformations are *The Age of Humanism and Reformation, The German Nation and Martin Luther*, his collected essays *Reformation Studies* and, most recently, with J. M. Tonkin *The Reformation in Historical Thought*.

Hans R. Guggisberg is Professor of History at the University of Basel and Managing Editor of the *Archive for Reformation History*. He has published widely on aspects of the Swiss Reformation and the international diffusion of Protestantism. Among his books are *Das europäische Mittelalter im amerikanischen Geschichtsdenken des 19. und des frühen 20. Jahrhunderts* and *Basel in the Sixteenth Century*.

Knud J. V. Jespersen is Senior Lecturer in Early Modern History at Odense University, Denmark. His research on Scandinavian military and diplomatic history has appeared in several books and articles, most recently in *The Scandinavian Journal of History* and *The Historical Journal*.

H. G. Koenigsberger, Emeritus Professor of History at King's College, London, is currently President of the International Commission for the History of Representative and Parliamentary Institutions. Among his many publications are *The Practice of Empire* and *The Habsburgs and*

Europe. In 1986 his collected essays *Politicians and Virtuosi* appeared.

E. I. Kouri is a visiting Fellow of Clare Hall, Cambridge, and was recently appointed to a professorship of history at Oulu University, Finland. Among his books are *England and the Attempt to Form a Protestant Alliance in the late 1560s, Elizabethan England and Europe* and *Der deutsche Protestantismus und die soziale Frage, 1870–1919.*

Sven Lundkvist is Professor of History and Director of the Riksarkivet, Stockholm. His research interests have focused on Sweden's commercial, social and military history in the sixteenth and seventeenth centuries. His best-known book is *Gustav Vasa och Europa: Svensk handels- och utrikespolitik 1534–1557.*

† **Heinrich Lutz** was Professor of Modern History at the University of Vienna and President of the Historical Commission of the Bavarian Academy of Sciences. His most recent books included *Ragione di stato und christliche Staatsethik im 16. Jahrhundert, Christianitas afflicta, Reformation und Gegenreformation* and *Das Ringen um deutsche Einheit und kirchliche Erneuerung.*

Antoni Mączak is Professor of History at Warsaw University. His research has concentrated on commerce and international relations in the Baltic and on travel and travellers in early modern Europe, on which he has written *Między Gdánskiem a Sundem: Studia nad handlem bałtyckim od połowy XVI do połowy XVII w* and *Życie codzienne w podróżach po Europie w XVI i XVII wieku.*

Peter Marzahl is Lecturer in History at the University of Constance. His principal area of research is the Spanish colonies in America, on which he has published *Town in the Empire: Government, Politics and Society in Seventeenth Century Popayan.*

Bernd Moeller is Professor of Church History at the University of Göttingen and President of the Society for Reformation History. He has written on many aspects of German Reformation history, and his books include *Johannes Zwick und die Reformation in Konstanz, Imperial Cities and the Reformation* and *Deutschland im Zeitalter der Reformation.*

Gerhard Müller is Landesbischof of Brunswick, having until recently been Professor of Church History at the University of Erlangen-Nuremberg. Among his many publications are *Die römische Kurie und die Reformation 1523–34*, *Die Rechtfertigungslehre: Geschichte und Probleme* and *Reformation und Stadt: Zur Rezeption der evangelischen Verkündigung*. He has also edited several volumes of the *Nuntiatur-berichte aus Deutschland*.

Thomas Nipperdey is Professor of History at the University of Munich and an Honorary Member of the American Academy of Arts and Sciences. His many books include *Die Organisation der deutschen Parteien vor 1918*, *Reformation, Revolution, Utopie*, and *Deutsche Geschichte 1800–1866*.

Heiko A. Oberman is Professor of History at the University of Arizona. His research spans the late medieval origins of Reformation theology to the international diffusion of Protestantism. Most recently he has published *Masters of the Reformation*, *Luther: Mensch zwischen Gott und Teufel* and *The Roots of Anti-Semitism in the Age of Renaissance and Reformation*.

E. Ladewig Petersen is Professor of History at Odense University, Denmark. His research interests include the late medieval and early modern history of international relations. Among his many publications are *The Crisis of the Danish Nobility, 1580–1660* and *Fra domænestat til skattestat: Syntese og fortolkning*.

Volker Press is Professor of History at the University of Tübingen. He has published numerous articles on the constitutional and political history of the German Empire and its territories. His books include *Calvinismus und Territorialstaat: Regierung und Zentralbehörden der Kurpfalz 1559–1619* and *Kaiser Karl V., König Ferdinand und die Entstehung der Reichsritterschaft*.

Horst Rabe is Professor of History at the University of Constance. Among his many books are *Naturrecht und Kirche bei Samuel von Pufendorf, Reichsbund und Interim, Autorität: Elemente einer Begriffs-geschichte* and *Die Entdeckung der Kindheit*.

G. D. Ramsay is Emeritus Fellow of St Edmund Hall, Oxford, where for many years he was a Tutor. His most recent publications include *The City of London in International Politics* and *The English Woollen Industry*.

Konrad Repgen is Professor of History at the University of Bonn. His many books include *Die römische Kurie und der Westfälische Friede* (2 vols). He is general editor of the *Acta Pacis Westphalicae* (15 vols to date).

P. L. Rose is Professor of European History at the University of Haifa, Israel. Among his numerous publications on European intellectual history are *The Italian Renaissance of Mathematics: Studies on Humanists and Mathematicians from Petrarch to Galileo* and *Bodin and the Great God of Nature*.

Hans-Christoph Rublack is Professor of Modern History at the University of Tübingen and Managing Editor of the *Archive for Reformation History Literature Review*. Among his recent books are *Gescheiterte Reformation: Frühreformatorische und protestantische Bewegungen in süd- und westdeutschen geistlichen Residenzen, Stadt und Kirche in Kitzingen* (with Dieter Demandt), and *Eine bürgerliche Reformation: Nördlingen*.

Heinz Schilling is Professor of History at the University of Giessen. Alongside numerous articles on the history of the Reformation in northern and north-western Germany, he has published *Niederländische Exulanten im 16. Jahrhundert* and *Konfessionskonflikt und Staatsbildung: Eine Fallstudie über das Verhältnis von religiösem und sozialem Wandel in der Frühneuzeit am Beispiel der Grafschaft Lippe*.

Tom Scott is Lecturer in History at the University of Liverpool. He has published several articles on aspects of town–country relations and on the German Peasants' War. He is the author of *Freiburg and the Breisgau: Town-Country Relations in the Age of Reformation and Peasants' War* and the editor of *Die Freiburger Enquete von 1476: Quellen zur Wirtschafts- und Verwaltungsgeschichte der Stadt Freiburg im Breisgau im 15. Jahrhundert*.

Bob Scribner is a Fellow of Clare College, Cambridge and University Lecturer in History. Besides many articles on the social history of the German Reformation and popular culture he has written *For the Sake* *of Simple Folk: Popular Propaganda for the German Reformation* and *The German Reformation.*

Bernard Vogler is Professor of History at the Institut d'Histoire d'Alsace in Strasbourg, and is currently Vice-President of the International Commission for Comparative Church History. His recent books include *Le clergé protestant rhénan au siècle de la Réforme (1555–1619), Le monde germanique et helvétique à l'époque des Réformes (1517–1620)* and *L'Alsace au siècle d'or et pendant la guerre de Trente Ans (1520–1648).*

R. B. Wernham is Emeritus Professor of Modern History in the University of Oxford. His most recent publications include *The Making of Elizabethan Foreign Policy* and *After the Armada.* He is also the editor of *List and Analysis of State Papers, Foreign, for the Reign of Elizabeth I,* contained in the Public Record Office.

Part I

1 The Impact of the Reformation: Problems and Perspectives

Heiko A. Oberman

I. THE EVENT BETWEEN ACT AND IMPACT

The earliest and still unsurpassed history of the ancient Near East may seem a surprising point of departure, but its opening lines alert us to the ambiguity of our term 'event'. They will only do so, however, if we avoid the translation errors, typical of all modern German and English versions and perpetuated even by the properly influential R. G. Collingwood, who sees in the Preface to his history of the ancient Near East a simple declaration of Herodotus' purpose 'to describe the deeds of men'.[1] As I read it, Herodotus distinguishes quite carefully between two dimensions of his awesome task, namely the outcome or impact of events, and the events themselves. He says:

> Herodotus of Halicarnassus publishes herewith the results of his [historical] investigation in order that future generations will be reminded both of what was achieved [= unleashed] by man and of the great and amazing deeds [themselves], whether performed by Greeks or by barbarians.

Whereas classical research has emphasised appropriately enough the capacious world view of Herodotus and his moral courage in spanning the gap of cultural disdain between Greeks and barbarians, a second distinction has been overlooked: that between the *genomena* (*ex anthropōn*) and the *erga* (*megala te kai thomasta*) – the outcome or impact of an event, and the nuclear event itself. Important to note is that Herodotus acknowledges in 'the deeds of man' not only the great but indeed the 'amazing' dimensions, manifesting that mental attitude of the historian to which Geoffrey Elton summons our return.[2] Herodotus can do this precisely because he distinguishes between the processes unleashed by man and the amazing events: he does not allow events to be robbed of their contingency, does not force them

3

into those chains of causation and structural developments which modern social historians often tend to associate with that dangerous word 'process'. Unfortunately, Collingwood is not far off with his conclusion: 'Herodotus had no successors.'[3]

In the preface to the earliest history of the Reformation, in Heinrich Bullinger's description of *enderung der religion* and *anrichten Christlicher reformation*, covering the years 1519–32, the sentiment of amazement is retained but the distinction of Herodotus is absorbed in the expression *Händel und Louff*, which should be translated as 'act and impact', but has come to mean 'the course of events':

> *Dann diser iar Händel und Löüff, sind nitt nu wunderbar, vast frölich und ouch träffenlich trurig, sunder zu läsen lustig, und zu wissen nitt wenig nutzlich, darzu ouch nodtwendig.*[4]

The *Louff* concerns less the deeds of men than the acts of God, or as Cotton Mather would later put it, the *magnalia Christi*. In keeping with the Renaissance vision of the function of history as *magistra vitae*, the vocabulary of Herodotus is pushed into the background by that raised finger of the headmaster who points to the *Bildung* and erudition that can be drawn – and must be drawn – for the present age from the events of the past.[5]

Although I quote Herodotus and Bullinger at the outset, I am not interested in abstract speculations about past views of history, but rather in drawing attention to the present dangers implied in the impact of structuralism on contemporary Reformation historiography. When one looks at Rainer Wohlfeil's *Einführung in die Geschichte der Deutschen Reformation*,[6] or Hans-Christoph Rublack's sketch of the social history of the Reformation,[7] it is obvious that Bullinger's *Louff* has become *Ablauf*, a historical process which allows the reader to master readily his sense of amazement about past events, once they 'receive' their inevitable place in the chain of historical necessity.

Since this structuralist tendency is an over-reaction in the service of a *necessary* crusade against the long-extended hegemony of free-floating ideas, we would be ill-advised to insist on a return to the primacy of the history of ideas based on literary sources alone. Yet it must be possible to find a common path – between the sole analysis of structures and a singular belief in so-called 'leading ideas' – towards 'total history'. Such a history can be 'total' only to the extent to which it makes room for that kind of intellectual history, which is so well encapsulated in the words of Felix Gilbert:

Whatever one thinks of the forces that underlie the historical process, they are filtered through the human mind and this determines the tempo and the manner in which they work. It is the human consciousness which connects the long-range factors and forces and the individual event, and it is at this crucial point of the historical process that the intellectual historian does his work.[8]

Social history makes its special contribution to 'total history' only to the extent that Gilbert's 'human consciousness' is not bypassed.

II. THE FAILURE OF THE REFORMATION: '*DIE GESCHEITERTE REFORMATION*'

The thesis that the Reformation is a failure is admittedly of longer standing, and reaches as far back as Luther's earliest opponents. But the conclusion of Gerald Strauss is not based on a confessional stance. In *Luther's House of Learning: Indoctrination of the Young in the German Reformation*, he observes that

The Protestant message was pitched to the solid burgher . . . As for the great multitude of men and women, they could have found little survival value in doctrines whose framers made no attempt to integrate their precepts with the practical needs and aspirations of plain people.

Strauss is willing to grant that a meaningful and lasting response to the Protestant message may well have been evoked before 1530: 'Later in the century, one finds mostly apathy.'[9]

A whole avalanche of articles and monographs has sought to document the same thesis with respect to other areas in and outside of Germany. Thus, Manfred E. Welti's *Kleine Geschichte der italienischen Reformation* ascribes the failure of the Reformation in Italy primarily to its lack of roots in the people.[10] Henry Heller, in *The Conquest of Poverty: The Calvinist Revolt in 16th Century France*, explains the loss of France to Calvinism by pointing to the fact that 'the base of the Calvinist movement lay in the skilled craftsmen, merchants and notables of the towns'. Calvin himself, however, encouraged

the subordination of the Protestant movement to the aristocracy . . . The fact is that on the eve of the civil wars the Calvinist bourgeoisie was eager to subordinate themselves to the nobility. In contrast, in 1789 the bourgeoisie was not prepared to do so.[11]

Although later generations may well note with suspicion that in our day stocks and bonds in failure issues are rising with such spectacular speed that we tend to uncover them everywhere from 'the mission of Europe' to 'the rise of Christianity', this is no proof that our *Zeitgeist* may not have an edge, at times, on an historical truth beyond the vision of former, more triumphant times. But at this point, surrounded by so many recent reports of failure in the sixteenth century, we might be well advised to look first at what hitherto has been claimed as the period of success, the years 1521–25. I should like to start with a study, at once admirable and challenging, by Thomas A. Brady, Jr., *Turning Swiss: Cities and Empire, 1450–1550*:

> The Evangelical leaders were well-educated clergymen from urban backgrounds – sons of patricians, merchants, and artisans. They gained hearings largely because they offered answers to long-posed questions, and they sowed seed on long-prepared soil. Even where such answers and such seed were not, from the preachers' perspective, central to their gospel, they hoped that by addressing such questions – usury, tithes, clerical immunities, clerical indiscipline – they would win a hearing for pure doctrine. Luther showed the way by trying to touch every sensitive nerve of his day, at the price of sowing unclarity about his message, though not about his person. Some of his partisans came to see the world through his central message; others did not. But in these years their cause was a common one. The urban preachers sensed this and tried skillfully to adapt Luther's message to the hegemonic corporate-communal values of their fellow citizens.[12]

Brady's latest book is again an admirable achievement, in so far as it is both well written and well documented, and so solidly argued that a serious review would claim many pages in a learned journal. His book is admirable above all because it is an eloquent and, in my opinion, convincing argument against the thesis that the Reformation was a 'national tragedy' in slowing down the process of the German nation becoming a Bismarckian empire. The main title, *Turning Swiss*, reveals, and the footnotes document, a very different direction in which the Reformation could have had its impact both on Germany and, far beyond the German borders, on European history.

For our particular purposes, *Turning Swiss* is a challenge because it seems to offer the key to the question why the Reformation could be seemingly so successful in the early years when, as so many studies today assume, it was to lose its impact and power soon afterwards. The answer is this. The earlier success was only a superficial one. The city reformers, after all, sowed seed in long-prepared soil, but for their own ulterior purpose of opening the ears for their 'pure doctrine'. Luther did not hesitate to touch every sensitive nerve, whereas the urban preachers tried 'skillfully' to adapt Luther's message to urban values.

Though Brady does not himself draw this conclusion, which is not central to his own impressive line of argumentation, the consequence for our quest is obvious: the impact of the Reformation must have been only of a temporary nature, since Luther and the urban preachers in the so-called victorious years of the Reformation harnessed social and political aspirations with an alien message of 'pure doctrine'. Their rejection of the peasant revolt as their own revolution is, then, not so much the cause as the proof that the cohesion between doctrine and communal life was an artificial one, a mere instrument of communication and ultimately of agitation. The apathy which Strauss finds later in the century becomes understandable, particularly in view of the divorce between doctrine and life, documentated and bewailed in the visitation records. The same applies to the findings of Heller and Welti: Calvinism in France had to look for a coalition with the nobility, because the broader base of the countryside folk had been cut off in the 1520s; and the Italian Reformation never had a chance to grow outside limited urban areas: the Reformation had become an intellectual movement, obviously and explicitly separated from social and political concerns.

To summarise the prevailing failure thesis: after suffocating its own grassroots movement, the Reformation became a willing prey to the greedy princes; henceforth, the Protestant ruling elite could only survive in limited areas with state support and social control, or – as Erwin Iserloh put it in his history of the Reformation epoch – the movement which started as a genuine popular campaign for spiritual renewal aborted in the *Fürstenreformation*, a Reformation enforced 'from above':

Immer mehr nahm die Obrigkeit die Reformation in die Hand und nutzte sie aus, um die Untertanen in den modernen Staat einzugliedern. Wir können seitdem von der Epoche der Fürstenreformation sprechen. Statt eines Gemeindechristentums mit freier Pfarrerwahl kam die Landeskirche.[13]

So much for the *genomena ex anthropōn* of Herodotus. Act and impact thus became irreparably divorced – or so it must seem.

III. THE LOADED LANGUAGE OF SOCIAL ANALYSIS

In the foregoing summary I believe I have fairly presented the growing consensus of some of the major spokesmen in the field of sixteenth-century studies. Though the social study of the Reformation owes its present strength to emancipation from the hegemony of theology and the history of ideas, the ease with which the confessional view of Erwin Iserloh could be incorporated shows that there is an often hidden continuity between the old scholarship and the new. Yet the very terminology used calls for closer investigation of each clause. However self-evident the concatenation of clauses may seem in the rhetoric of historical evaluation, they lose their authority and credibility when looked at singly. Consider the five key expressions employed in the previous 'convincing' summary.

1. 'The Peasants War is claimed to be the Reformation's "own grass-roots movement".' Karl Marx has pointed out that the peasants' uprising *an der Theologie gescheitert ist.*[14] This may well be more true than originally intended: the revolutionary peasants were from the outset on a collision course with the Reformation. After all, it was Christoph Schappeler, the co-author of the Memmingen articles, which were to be copied throughout Germany in later peasant manifestos, who reported to his mentor Ulrich Zwingli, after the bloody disaster of May 1525, that the original impetus had been thwarted and that in the escalation of the uprisings the initial leaders had been overtaken from the left (*sinistre*).[15]

Peter Blickle's restrictive interpretation of the crucial concept *gemeiner Mann*, and extensive definition of 'communalism', obscure the distance between countryside, village and city, and ignore – as Hermann Rebel has so convincingly shown[16] – the social stratification within the peasantry itself. Blickle's new definition of these two concepts seems to confirm the old thesis of the peasant uprising as the Reformation's own grass-roots movement – a view which in turn may have a similar influence in the English-speaking world through the excellent and attractive translation by Thomas Brady and Erik Midelfort.[17]

From Zürich's perspective, there did indeed exist an initial hope of channelling the uprisings in and outside the cities by 'turning them Swiss', at least as far as the *Rotten* in Upper Swabia and Lower Alsace were concerned. Wittenberg, however, never enjoyed such short-lived hope with its subsequent sobering outcome. Already in 1518 and 1519, Luther had rejected the concept of revolt in the service of reformation. One of the most precious aspects of the rich works of Thomas Müntzer is exactly that he had both the training and the vision which enabled him to grasp and to formulate the difference in goals between the movement with which he became associated after 1524, and Luther's Reformation.

2. The next sentence in the above summary contains not one but two misleading terms: 'The Reformation became a willing victim to the greedy princes.' The first noun, *'the* Reformation' is a misleading, unclear collective cover-name for a whole series of movements. Under this broad umbrella hide at least two triads. First, the traditional triad: the Protestant Reformation, the Catholic Reformation, and the Radical Reformation. But then there is also that other triple-grouping *within* the Protestant Reformation which deserves our special attention if we are concerned with the question of impact: Luther's Reformation, the City Reformation, and the Reformation of the Refugees. This division thus highlights first the unique magnetism of Luther's programme, and secondly the short-lived Reformation in the cities, during that quarter century between the Edict of Worms and the Schmalkaldic War (1521–48); and thirdly, the diaspora of the Reformation from Geneva to Italy, France, and through the Low Countries, Poland and Hungary, Great Britain and the New World. The City Reformation never became a 'willing victim' of the princes but rather, initially at least, a most unwilling victim of the emperor. This turn of events marked the beginning of the third Reformation.[18]

3. As to the 'greedy princes', three warnings are in order: one senses here a democratic and perhaps even populist assumption that 'greed' is particularly partial to high places at the summit of the social hierarchy. More misleading, however, is the suggestion that the role of the *Fürsten* in the whole drama of the Reformation can be exhaustively described in terms of territorial expansionism under the mere *pretext* of piety and thirst for justice. This self-serving quest for gain is just what Schappeler and Müntzer chastised in the peasants *que sua sunt quererunt – iustitiae praetextu*! It may be safely assumed that self-interest belongs to the constant forces in history on all levels of society. The crucial question is how self-interest is channelled,

controlled and legitimised: undisguised, naked greed has no impact.

But more importantly, it is not just ideological blindness but historical error to situate the role of the princes only at the end of the Reformation movement, as an unfortunate finale, as Iserloh has put it. Reformation scholars around the turn of the century still knew that territorial reform *in sacris* stands at the beginning of the Reformation – indeed, is part and parcel of the fifteenth-century reform movement, and forms in electoral Saxony the very cradle of Luther's Reformation in the early and sustained protection of Observant monasticism.

The third warning concerns the unreflected assumption that the *Fürstenreformation* is the typically Protestant outcome of the Reformation epoch. When we look at the Habsburg empire as the most immediate political context, there is no way to avoid the conclusion that the turn toward 'absolutism' did not respect confessional boundaries. As Robert A. Kann has put it with respect to the Habsburg territories: 'the ascendency of the Church over forces of the Reformation was largely state-sponsored and state-controlled'[19] – applying the same tools as the Protestant princes through property control and visitations of churches and monasteries – in the whole period reaching from Ferdinand II to Charles VI. We may conclude that the expression *Fürstenreformation* to designate the outcome of the Reformation is misunderstood if not extended to include the '*Fürsten-Gegenreformation*'.

Two more ambivalent expressions must be addressed, which seemingly are too often used in our historical analyses as if they are crystal clear expressions, but loaded with egalitarian sentiment: 'ruling elite' and 'social control'.

4. I have no quarrel with the use of 'ruling elite' for Pericles' Athens or Cato's Republican Rome, or for the sixteenth-century imperial city, Strasbourg. If, however, with that term political suppression is implied, from the arrogantly high perspective of modern democratic achievements, it may be important to note that even in modern countries that understand themselves as democratically governed – whether in the German Democratic Republic or the United States – the centres of power are in the hands of a ruling elite, albeit under widely differing circumstances; in the one case because of the concentration of power in the party, in the other due to the low percentage of electoral participation. The real character test for any given ruling elite is the potential for upward social mobility: and it is exactly that which I am inclined to concede to those sixteenth-century

imperial cities which moved from central government by the *Kleiner Rat* of the aristocrats and large entrepreneurs to the increasing involvement of the *Grosser Rat*, which represented artisans, craftsmen and small businessmen. 'Ruling elite', therefore, is an acceptable term, provided it is used in a descriptive fashion, cleansed of anti-elitist sentiment.

5. The last terminological pitfall lies in the expression 'social control'. In vain one searches the works of Max Weber for this term. Though part of this historian's greatness was his discovery of the potential of sociological insights for historical investigation, he may well have sensed that 'social control' is a misleading expression for describing relationships in late medieval society. On first sight, the expression is appealing: when Thomas N. Tentler presented his views on 'The Summa for Confessors as an Instrument for Social Control',[20] it seemed exactly the right term to describe the hold of the Confessors on pre-Reformation society. The religious and social protest, however, which we find in such varying forms reaching from the Waldensians in the High Alps to the Hussites in Bohemia, is not directed against the too *heavy burden* of a moral codex enforced by the Confessors, but rather against its *leniency* and unequal application. They turn against the lack of a thoroughgoing requirement for full contrition as a pre-condition for receiving absolution, and generally insist on a higher quality of life. This trend, which I have described as 'the upsurge of Donatism', can also be described as 'semi-monastic', as Steven Ozment put it in his pertinent conclusion: 'Until the Protestant Reformation, lay religious practice remained an imitation of clerical religious practice.'[21] In this very 'imitation' lurks the spark of fiery protest.

Such a critique is not confined to the heretical fringes. It comes from within, as is eloquently documented by the impressive Dominican, Robert Holcot († 1349), who in his widely disseminated commentary on the Book of Wisdom, exposes the '*Klassenjustiz*' of the Confessors: '*prelati moderni non divites et nobiles peccatores, sed pauperes ecclesiastica censura castigant.*'[22] The confessional – seemingly so private and secret; in effect, very public – functions as long as it corresponds with the communal, 'semi-monastic', moral consensus. I am inclined to regard the very vehemence of popular critique as an index of the success of this institution for a long period of time, in extended areas, as a sensitive and sensible tool for the support of social cohesion.

However, the term 'social control', in its *restrictive* sense, is fully appropriate for the analysis of the three conditions under which Reformation and Counter-Reformation managed to survive into the Confessional Age. For Lutheranism and Habsburg Catholicism, it means *Landesfürst* as Lord Protector by means of government support through legislation and visitation; for Calvinism it is the creation of independent congregations 'under the cross' by means of the consistory and its *censura morum*; and for the Italian Counter-Reformation, the reintroduction of the Inquisition.

To this institution we must now turn, since the effect of the Inquisition is directly related to our search for the impact of the Reformation.

IV. HOW TO COMBAT PROTESTANT HERESY: A VATICAN INSTRUCTION TO ALL INQUISITORS

Having exposed the hidden ideological assumptions on the contemporary historical battlefront, we are in a better position to return to the real fights of the sixteenth century. And battle is exactly the theme and centre of a revealing treatise, by Sylvester Mazzolini, called after his birthplace Prierias. On closer scrutiny, the treatise proves to be a pseudepigraphic satire in two distinct parts.[23] The first is dated Rome 1553, and assigned to Prierias, professor of Thomistic philosophy in Rome from 1514 until his death in 1523; from December 1515, Prierias was *Magister sacri Palatii*, chief inquisitor, and responsible for preparing the Roman process against Reuchlin and Luther.

The satirical tone itself must make the reader dubious about one further point of information on the title page, namely that the 1553 edition is a revision of an earlier instruction which Prierias had sent out to all inquisitors in 1519, a manual to detect and convict Lutherans: *in martini Luteri perditionem et eius sequacium*. But indeed, the satire was published in 1519, in Augsburg, Basel, Cologne and perhaps in Wittenberg itself.[24] Whereas the Augsburg version is dedicated to Sylvester Prierias by an imaginary younger Dominican under the name of Logumenus (= *loquax* or verbose?), a later edition, printed by Eduard Böcking in the first supplementary volume of his Hutten edition,[25] is assigned not to Prierias but to an unnamed canonist, and directed not against Lutherans but against heresy in general – this time dedicated to both Prierias and the German chief inquisitor Hochstraatèn. Böcking believes the satire to have been written by Rubianus Crotus (†1545), in view of its obvious proximity to the style and tone of the *Letters of Obscure Men*.[26]

The second treatise – added, as its author says, merely in order not to leave precious pages blank (folios 26–40!) – is dedicated to Esprit Rotier (Spiritus Roterus), the French Dominican who functioned from 1523 until 1547 as the vicar-general of his congregation in France, and from 1547 until his death in 1564 (or 1569) as chief inquisitor in Toulouse. This treatise is to be found on the index of Benedict XIV (1758) and assigned to Pietro Paolo Vergerio. Meeting Luther as papal nuncio on 7 November 1535 in Wittenberg, Vergerio had regarded the reformer as the devil incarnate. But afterwards increasingly open to the Reformation and despairing of the sincerity of papal reform efforts he converted, ending his life as a Protestant professor in Tübingen, 1565.[27]

What we have here before us in the edition of 1553 is a double plot to ridicule the Inquisition, of which the earlier 1519 treatise presents a more lightfooted sample, completely in keeping with the *Letters of Obscure Men*.[28] The second treatise is a much more embittered defence against Rotier's attack on the Genevan Reformation, which Rotier four years earlier in a book published in Toulouse in 1549 had identified as 'the new Babylon'. The first satire – divided into twelve so-called 'rules', perhaps a take-off on the four *Fundamenta* which Prierias had attached to his 1518 *Conclusiones* against Luther[29] – shows such precise information about theological terminology of the day that one may be inclined to assign it to one of Luther's students or younger colleagues, such as Johann Lang (1487–1548). The Inquisition is ridiculed by having Prierias send out from the Vatican an urgent warning 'to all Dominicans and inquisitors in Italy, France, Spain and elsewhere':

They should stop interrogating these heretics in public, because of their infectious good faith and convincing knowledge of the Scriptures. They should be killed before it comes to a hearing – on the basis of the 'old saw' that the one who sets the fire is always wiser than the one who is burned: *quia semper combustores sunt doctiores combustis*. If only the princes had allowed Reuchlin to receive his due, this thesis could have been wonderfully documented: the German heretic would have been burned; and to be wiser than Reuchlin really means something (*duodecima Regula*) . . . a beautiful feather in the cap of the Inquisition.

The final question raised is why the Holy Church did not burn any heretics in the first 1300 years, until the Council of Constance (1414–1418), yet cannot rule today without burning heretics galore? Answer: I wonder that people can be so stupid that they ask such a question! It is obvious that they have not yet studied their Thomas. I say, therefore, that the solution is short, and, well, thus: at that time, there were not yet inquisitors. If they had been around in the early Church, surely the heretics would have been exterminated by fire. Just as the truth grows over the course of time, so does also the purgation of the Church increase. In the Early Church, there were not yet so many gifted students of scripture as there are today thanks to the tutelage of Aristotle. I sincerely believe that if St Jerome and St Augustine were alive today – or even the Apostle Paul himself – they would not so easily escape the fires of the Inquisition, because the inquisitors have become real experts today: *bene tibi, Paule, quod vixisti illo tempore, quando non erant subtilia ista ingenia.*

The second satire, edited and added in 1553, follows another procedure: a young respectful trainee of the great French inquisitor Rotier reports a long series of formidable problems he has encountered in defending the opinions of his master. Finding himself gutted time and again by the sharpness of the arguments of the opposition, he is unable – indeed, helpless – to defend Rotier without immediate advice and support. This time, it is not the infallibility of the Pope which is carried *ad absurdum*, but Rotier's insistence on the Vulgate and directives against Bible translations. The inquisitor had published a book in Toulouse in 1548[30] to prove that Holy Scripture should not be translated into the vernacular, with the argument that then 'the living spirit is converted into the killing letter':

How then to deal with the feast of Pentecost when the Gospel was proclaimed in all languages? Do not think, great master, that in the debate about your thesis I succumbed. Thereby you would underestimate my long breath. However many convincing passages they showed me, they never silenced me. If you think that, you have forgotten my brashness. But it was difficult to argue against their solid proofs of structural weakness in your books, both in grammar and dialectics – especially the difficulty you have in grasping an argument of the opposition and reporting it fairly: how fortunate it is that you have a terrifying, powerful institution behind you which scares readers of heretical books from touching them and from comparing them with yours. When they turned to such basic issues as sin and forgiveness, I found it hard to discover a passage in Thomas which could help me. But I hit on the right kind of solution to escape the force of their arguments: I could slither away under the pretext that one is not allowed to debate matters that have already been decided.

At this point, I break off my report on the second treatise. It is just as much a satire as the first one, though different in strategy. Here, the young inquisitor reports his embarrassment and thus reveals the weakness of the arguments of his master, instead of the master himself prescribing antidotes for an 'obviously' formidable challenge. The power of the Inquisition is ridiculed as a mirror of the disintegration of that Roman Church which sets itself up as infallible and hence as unassailable, and yet can only defend itself with external force.

Amidst all similarities, a crucial new element should not be overlooked in the second treatise. The Inquisition is not merely a ridiculous Roman affair – that faraway, unpredictable court before which the great Reuchlin trembled, and where even Paul and Jesus would have had no chance: the Inquisition is now the direct and very present threat to the Genevan Reformation. Thirty-five years later, the struggle dramatically escalates: whereas Geneva is accursed as the New Babylon, the inquisitors are now unmasked as the soldiers of the anti-Christ. There is not just a difference in time – some thirty-five years – and a difference in locality – from German Lutherans to French Calvinists – but also a difference in a heightened sense of the diabolic power of the opponent: battle has grown out of banter. Behind the shift from irony to sarcasm we discern the growing awareness of the formidable obstacles on the path to reformation: its very impact is threatened.

V. THE NICODEMITES: COURAGEOUS ALTERNATIVE TO THE REFUGEE

From haughty banter to harsh battle – this escalation reflected indeed the course of events. From its staging area in Geneva, the third Reformation had sought to close ranks with endemic evangelism and to infiltrate the main bastions of Roman Catholicism in Italy and France. But just as it seemed that the evangelical dreams of such disciples of Valdés (†1541) as Bernardino Ochino and Peter Martyr

Vermigli under the patronage of Reginald Pole – in touch with Giberti, Contarini and Cortese – could be translated into structural reform, and just at the time when Viterbo, Modena and Lucca had become centres of what the Council of Trent would later define and condemn as heresy, the Roman Inquisition was established in July 1542.

Cardinal Caraffa – the later Counter-Reformation Pope Paul IV (1555–59) – gained control of what he fashioned into a powerful and feared institution.[31] Shortly afterwards, in August 1542, Ochino and Vermigli, symbolically just at the time when Contarini was lying on his deathbed, decided to burn their Roman bridges behind them. They were the first in a long line of refugees going the arduous road of emigration over the Alps to Switzerland, and in the case of Vergerio, ultimately all the way to Swabia.

Were these refugees faint-hearted or clear-sighted? Less than a decade later, by papal order of 12 August 1553, the Talmud and other rabbinical books were condemned to burning; in the next few months across Italy possibly hundreds of thousands of Hebrew books went up in flames.[32] The *spirituali*, in full accord with the rising tide of anti-Semitism, did not read the signs of the times, ignoring the medieval sequence 'first the Jew, then the heretic'.[33]

The index of forbidden books of 1549 was enhanced in 1554 to include works by Dante, Valla, Boccaccio, Machiavelli and Erasmus.[34] Three years later, Caraffa – now Pope Paul IV – started to round up the *spirituali* in high places. Sanfelice and Soranzo were arrested, Morone sent to the dungeons of St Angelo, and Pole was recalled from his mission as Papal Legate in England in order to allow the Curia to start proceedings against him. Erwin Iserloh called this crucial period from 1551–59 the *Durchbruch der katholischen Reform*.[35] Actually, it was a time of failure for *Catholic* reform and the beginning of the *Roman* Catholic Counter-Reformation.

The refugees could not but feel confirmed in their decision. Those who had stayed behind and clung to the hope for reform from within – peculiarly dubbed, for lack of a proper designation, the *spirituali* – drew the wrath of the refugees, who regarded them as 'timorous Nicodemists',[36] as Vergerio designated Cardinal Reginald Pole.

But if Pole had acceded to the papal throne when, on St Martin's Eve, the Holy See fell vacant through the death of Pope Paul III (10 November 1549) – on that fateful morning of 5 December Pole needed only one more vote in the conclave! – the *spirituali* would have been in charge of reform from above, and allowed to act so publicly that the charge of Nicodemism would never have arisen. Vergerio's charge is nothing but a red herring: understandable though his 'name-calling' may be, it is deceptive, and has indeed deceived scholarship in its search for the roots of Nicodemism. The learned Tübingen professor, by applying a current pejorative term to Italian evangelism, suggests a connection between Nicodemism, cowardice and spiritualism, which most certainly does not apply to Nicodemism as it had emerged ten years earlier in France.

The enigma of Nicodemism is not due to the dissimulation of its adherents, but to the confusing reaction it has evoked among its interpreters, all the way from John Calvin to Carlo Ginzburg.[37] It has been generally recognised that a crucial, but unknown, phase in the history of Nicodemism precedes the intervention of John Calvin.[38] What has not yet been highlighted is the positive connotations associated with Nicodemus, as propagated in late medieval theology,[39] piety,[40] and art.[41] The positive connotation of the term clearly puzzled Calvin: after all, according to the fourth Gospel, Nicodemus proved to be at the end one of the very few dedicated and steadfast disciples (cf. John 3 and John 19, 39). Originally, 'Nicodemite' may well have been an apologetic in-group designation to express the claim that though one cannot openly profess the Gospel, one comes like Nicodemus to the Lord, albeit by night. In this charitable sense, it is used by the reformer of Schwäbisch-Hall Johannes Brenz in a letter of 1 June 1529 to the lord chancellor of Brandenburg-Ansbach, Georg Vogler. Brenz expects the secret confession to become a public one.[42] But when Calvin, twice within one year (1543 and 1544), and in no uncertain terms, attacks the French Nicodemites as traitors and apostates, the leader of the third Reformation discredits a movement which would thus be encouraged to subvert, rival, and in certain respects eclipse his own impact on later history.

Thanks to a precious find by that eminent Strasbourg scholar, Jean Rott, we have recovered a missing link in the correspondence of Antoine Fumée (1511–68?), one of the leaders of French Protestantism in Paris. Long hidden in the library of Corpus Christi College, Cambridge, this letter sheds light on both the creed and the situation of the so-called Nicodemites in France. Writing to Martin Bucer and his colleagues in Strasbourg, Fumée reminds them of the fact that he is not in a position to teach the Gospel publicly: '*Scitote, fratres, non tam clare et diserte nobis licere, aut per infirmitatem, quam magnam in nobis agnoscimus, aut per assiduas improborum calumnias, docere*

justificationem hominis solius Dei gratiae esse, non operum.'[43] Fumée
proceeds to describe his theology in detail. Except for the invocation
of the saints – legitimate, he argues, provided it is done in the name of
God, and though not attested to in Scripture, not counter to it – it is
completely 'orthodox'. This new letter should be read in conjunction
with Fumée's earlier correspondence with Calvin.

Two points should be underscored. In the first place, 'Nicodemians'
have been erroneously confused with libertinists and epicureans.[44] Yet
it was Antoine Fumée himself who alerted Calvin to these very
dangers. Even more importantly, Fumée alerts us to the fact that the
refugee is not the only true Christian, or the only Protestant prepared
to suffer for his faith (after all, Calvin decided to flee); he takes no
risks in criticising those who dared to stick to their social and political
responsibility: *'hec te illic facile et predicare et monere posse, qui si hic
sis aliter forte sentires.'*[45] Almost exactly a year before, towards the
end of 1542, under an alias ('Capnius') Fumée had reported to Calvin
the tremendous pressure under which the young French evangelical
movement suffered through confusion in its own ranks and police
pressure from outside. This had taken on such extreme forms that he
expected shortly its *ruina*, and did not doubt *'nos diu hoc statu non
consistere posse'*.[46] And indeed, as the records show, the persecutions
had intensified since the late summer of 1542, with public burnings in
Bordeaux, Toulouse, Rouen and of course in Paris itself.[47]

It is at this point that the newly found letter of Antoine Fumée is of
such importance. A friend of Calvin's since the common study years
in Orléans and Paris, he was born into the ruling elite. His grand-
father, Paul Fumée, had been the personal physician of Charles VII
and Louis XI, ambassador to Rome and governor of Nantes; his
father, Adam Fumée, served as member of Parliament, as did Antoine
himself from 1536, at twenty-five years of age.[48] In complete agreement with Calvin as far as the rejection of libertinism is concerned, he
takes grave exception to Calvin's attack on those in France who have
to assume the posture of Nicodemites, and who do not give in to the
temptation to flee – as Calvin had done! – and therefore to make room
for people who will subvert the course of the Gospel in France.

At this early stage, it is certainly wrong to identify, as Carlo
Ginzburg has done, Nicodemism with spiritualism: spiritualism emphasises an interior religion which is indifferent to externals. Fumée,
however, makes it quite clear that he is critical of the spiritualising
interpretation of the Eucharist, as it has been reported to him about

Strasbourg. The confusion of the two movements, which finds support in George Williams' characterisation of Nicodemism as 'prudential spiritualism',[49] is understandable in so far as Calvin attacks often in one breath a whole series of opponents, from Libertines to Spiritualists and Nicodemians lurking about in all parts of Europe. In his report of 21 January 1545 to Martin Luther, Calvin makes quite clear that the Nicodemites who 'continue to defile themselves with the sacrilegious worship of the papists' are his own fellow countrymen in France. But these compatriots continue not only 'to defile themselves' but also to hold out and persevere – they have to give account of their faith under extreme duress.

Nicodemism is not some kind of abstract ideology which *a posteriori* applies what it first, *a priori*, culled out of the pages of a book, as Carlo Ginzburg has argued, when finding the bible of Nicodemism in Otto Brunfels' *Pandectae* (1527),[50] and constructing a school of Brunfels through Wolfgang Capito, Sebastian Franck, Johannes Brenz, Camillo Renato, and Lefèvre d'Étaples. Carlos Eire has convincingly pointed to Ginzburg's over-interpretation of the *Pandectae*; Pierre Fraenkel established that one of Ginzburg's so-called Nicodemite documents actually is a letter of Bucer,[51] and Olivier Millet recently uncovered that the Margarita, whom Ginzburg identified with Margaret de Navarre, is Margreth von Lodieuse, a French refugee in Strasbourg since December 1534. Strasbourg, with its influential preachers around Brunfels, particularly Bucer and Capito, is not a staging area for the export of Nicodemism to France, but rather its court of appeal. The Paris Evangelicals, under the high pressure of royal persecution, *and* simultaneously harshly assailed by Calvin, appeal to Strasbourg to intercede with Calvin and, if need be, to get in touch with Luther and Melanchthon to silence Geneva.

Calvin's sharp reaction is quite understandable in light of the fact that the sensitive point of his absence from the front line as a refugee is called into question. Yet at the same time, as commander-in-chief behind the front, he must keep the troops on the offensive. The impression he creates that the Nicodemists are uninterested in socalled 'organised' religion is sheer propaganda. Later, but only after Fumée's forecast had become all too true, the evangelical movement had met *ruina* under the pressures of the rising tide of the Counter-Reformation, the shift toward spiritualism occurs which Williams and Ginzburg see as its roots. When Calvin, some twenty years later, writes his *Response à un certain holandois* (1546) – successfully identified by George Williams as that enthusiastic follower of Sebastian Franck, Dick Volckertszoon Coornhert – Nicodemism has become that kind of ecumenism which pleads for a 'Christianity above confessional diversity' and which relativises or even dispenses with the visible church, its orders and sacraments.[52] In his creed, Fumée was explicitly a Protestant, and in his sense of priority of charity before faith he stands with Bucer and his colleagues. Yet in his rejection of vituperative and inflammatory attacks in confessional debate and in his insistence on the global Church of Love – which underlies his defence of the invocation of the saints – there are clear lines pointing to that development within the third Reformation, which we may best designate as 'irenicism'.[53] As anti-institutional ecumenism, this is still a force today.

Turning back once more to the situation in the 1540s, Calvin had to respond sharply for personal and programmatic reasons. Eire misinterprets Calvin's silence on the exact identity of his Nicodemite adversaries. Refuting Ginzburg, he holds that Calvin is so given to attacking persons by name that, if there had been an 'organised group' with a definite theology, Calvin would have made that explicit.[54] Whereas Eire justly criticises Ginzburg for assuming a theory which precedes practice, here he himself has lost sight of the historical realities. The Fumée case shows why Calvin could not possibly attack such a person by name. Under daily threat of exposure, Fumée had to write under the pseudonym of Capnius. The one occasion on which Calvin broke the seal of silence was in the horrible case of Michael Servetus; but then, Calvin no longer counted him as a member of the true Church. In short, the demarcation line does not run, as Calvin had put it, between the courageous confessor and the dissimulating coward; rather, the alternatives were the *courage to flee*, and become a refugee for the cause of faith, or the *courage to be*, to stay and endure the daily threat of prison and fire.[55]

Fumée's solution, as he so clearly saw, could only remain viable for a limited period of time – an interim, provided relief came soon. The success of the Counter-Reformation in France forced the steadfast soldiers of faith who, like the Nicodemus of the Gospel fought night battles under the cloak of darkness, to embrace a creed of man and his divine rights independent of structures, whether of a church state or a state church.

In this new form, the third Reformation was to have a profound impact, even though it would deviate from the vision of its main architect, John Calvin.

VI. LUTHER: THE POWER OF PROPHECY

Luther is not the father, but neither is he the son, of one single movement. He can – and should – be described as Augustinian, nominalist, humanist and biblical scholar. But all of this would be to no avail if the core of his being is overlooked: he is Luther the Apocalyptic. From the year 1519 onwards, he unquestionably understands himself as the forerunner of the coming great Reformation of God. As a Doctor of Holy Scripture, he must instruct the faithful by reopening the treasures of the Gospel; as a pastor, he is responsible for gathering the congregation of the faithful 'in these last days'.[56]

Though widely accepted, this recovery of the 'eschatological reformer' has evoked two substantial critical reactions which seem to neutralise each other. The first argues that this apocalyptic reinterpretation of Luther is too comprehensive, the second, that this interpretation is too limited and should be extended beyond Luther to the early leaders of the City Reformation generally. The first critique has been raised by the Hamburg Luther scholar, Bernhard Lohse, the second by the Göttingen church historian, Bernd Moeller. Lohse takes issue with the apocalyptic interpretation of the young Luther, for which he finds no evidence; where there is unmistakable evidence, he regards its interpretation as over-stretched. Lohse is prepared to admit that Luther regards the Reformation 'ultimately' as the work of God, but as he sees it this is from the beginning to the end for Luther *an historical, not an eschatological event.*[57]

This is not the place to debate the interpretation of single texts. As I see it, Lohse misunderstands the significance of crucial terms, such as the 'interim' before the 'Day of the Lord'; he renders Christ's *Zukunft* as 'future' instead of *Ankunft*, which means the 'advent' of Christ.[58] The basic issue is that Lohse feels that he has to opt for an historical *or* for an eschatological interpretation of Luther's understanding of Reformation. It is precisely Luther's point, however, that these last days have already started, and that therefore the 'last things' have commenced *in* our historical time, so that the eschatological clock has started to tick: '*demoliri coepimus Antichristi regnum*'.[59] Among a number of other things, this means that Luther, in contrast with the Nicodemite Fumée, does not regard the persecutions as a horrid sign of impending *ruina*, but as the hopeful sign of the recovery of the Gospel, since the devil is bound to assail the true Gospel and in these last days cannot but persecute its adherents: '*Sentit enim Satan potentiam et fructus . . .*'[60] Luther's sense of time is in keeping with

Revelations 20, 3, and with St Augustine's interpretation of the last phase of the Thousand Years of history, when – before the coming of the great Reformation – the devil will be loosed for a short time. When the first two martyrs of the Reformation are burned in Brussels in 1523, Luther is not surprised: instead, he is saddened that it is not granted him to sacrifice his own life in order to meet the onslaught of Satan.

From the opposite perspective, Bernd Moeller's criticism appears in an interesting article on the content of preaching in the cities in the early Reformation. He draws on some thirty-two so-called *Predigtsummarien* between 1522 and 1529 to show that in the towns throughout Germany a unified interpretation of the Gospel was proclaimed. Moeller documents his findings with references, but without quotations, and protects himself with the cautious provisos that these *Predigtsummarien* 'leave the impression' that across Germany 'more or less the same was preached'. One foremost characteristic, Moeller notes, is eschatological urgency: the Kingdom of God has drawn near, and the present is threatened by the Antichrist. There is no doubt that Luther's eschatological message was 'received' in a wide variety of ways, and well beyond the year 1525.[61] Though I do not dare to go as far as Moeller by claiming that Luther – on the basis of *this* evidence – can be claimed to be a 'figure of world-history', whatever that may mean, the implications of his apocalyptic view are far-reaching.[62]

Once it is clear, however, that Luther is to be regarded as the apocalyptic prophet, a number of conclusions can be drawn: in the first place, the understandable scepticism of the social historian that under the prophet's cloak the politician is hidden, and that by means of the Gospel social control is exercised, is groundless. Luther does not exploit sensitivities concerning usury, tithes, clerical immunities and clerical indiscipline: all these are rather signs of the end of time and the gruesome extent of the power of the Antichrist.

Furthermore, far from being one of the calculating *politiques*, the apocalyptic prophet is so much convinced that only the elect will hear his voice that he can concentrate on the content of his Gospel, without ulterior motives. The battle cry of *sola scriptura*, which in the City Reformation came to mean the replacement of Canon Law by Biblical Law, meant for Luther the preaching of the Gospel irrespective of political opportunism. As he put it, 'This is the time when we have to be prepared to live dangerously.'[63] The true Christian should not only be willing to endure persecution, but regard it as the sign of the extent to which we irritate Satan. For this reason, Luther criticises Melanchthon when the latter, during the Augsburg Diet in 1530, was prepared to enter into negotiations in order to gain political concessions in exchange for a less offensive formulation of the Protestant creed.

It is again the apocalyptic dimension which allows Luther to interpret the doctrine of justification by faith alone in a highly risky fashion, sacrificing the important impetus of reward for moral re-armament. And finally, once this apocalyptic stance is clearly seen, we can measure the distance which separates Martin Luther from a Nicodemite like Antoine Fumée. Though Luther's answer to Calvin has not been preserved, it is quite clear what he could and must have responded to Calvin's earnest question. After all, Fumée, the Nico-demite,[64] had become the most authentic *politique* of the century in protesting against all forms of sharp controversy, in the hope to avoid *ruina*, by courageously persevering with reform from within.

VII.   CONCLUSION

In trying to fathom the complex question of the impact of the Reformation, we must distinguish between the first, the second and the third 'Reformation', to ensure that our conclusions have the necessary precision.

First, as the history of Christianity shows, apocalyptic moods are not continuous but come in waves – at the time of St Paul, St John on Patmos, the churches under Roman persecution, or during the crisis of the Western schism. Thus also the apocalyptic climate which allowed Luther to speak and be heard passed away, re-emerging during the Thirty Years War and reappearing during successive crises ever since. In such times, the word of Luther is and will be heard afresh, and in this sense we can speak of the lasting impact of Luther. But also, Luther's single-minded, non-calculating investigation of the Scriptures would allow his voice to break through the cultural accretions to the Gospel, even when modern findings differ from his.

In so far as Luther was an active agent in the introduction of visitations, we can indeed speak of 'failure', albeit not on the basis of the moral deficiencies reported by the visitation records – proof of moral amelioration is not to be expected there, since the sources are intent on looking for deviation and depravity. But we may speak of failure in so far as Luther expected from the visitations '*Besserung*', a limitation of the greed of the ruling elite, which reached out to seize church goods. For Luther, the purpose of the visitations was not only to secure the teaching of Christian basics, but also to make sure that the secularisation of the church possessions would furnish ministers' salaries and the founding of good schools.

Luther had counted on another failure: namely, that the Gospel would not be victorious in Germany and hence would move elsewhere, like a *Platzregen* – a rainstorm. And finally, regarding the *Fürstenreformation*, whatever our critique may be concerning the development of the *Landesfürst* into the *Notbischof*, and of the prince into the leader of the territorial church in his own territory the Inquisition and the Index were unable to silence the voice of the apocalyptic prophet. Marjorie Reeves once observed that 'men's dreams are as much a part of history as their deeds'.[65] With Luther, the prophetic dreams themselves made history.

Secondly, as far as the significance of the second Reformation – the City Reformation – is concerned, we can be brief. It is a crucial *intermezzo* – an *intermezzo* in so far as it is limited to some twenty-five years until the free cities, which had already lost their economic power on the eve of the Reformation, lost also the last chance for spiritual revitalisation, when imperial troops marched in and enforced the Interim, in 1548 and 1549.

At the same time, it is *crucial*, for the *intermezzo* provided the Reformation with more than printing presses and Latin schools, the pulpits and the learning to understand, interpret and multiply Luther's voice; it also allowed the political space to experiment with what Bullinger called *enderung*, which encompasses the horizontal dimensions of the Reformation message. Within the city walls, the 'semi-monastic' tenets in late medieval lay piety could be translated into laws and a lifestyle which would be its – ambiguous – legacy to the third Reformation.

Thirdly, the impact of the third Reformation – the Reformation of the Refugees – is to be traced along two lines of development. The first is the victorious path of the Revolution of the Saints, who erected and extended the Kingdom of Christ wherever they could seize power and, where such seizure proved impossible, at least survived independently of town council and *Landesfürst*, as congregations under the cross. This Reformation failed to flower in the key territories of France and Italy, but was able to establish itself in many other areas north of the Alps, in Great Britain and beyond.

The second line of impact has its inauspicious beginnings with the Nicodemites of the 1540s in Paris. Wherever the victory of the Revolution of the Saints collapsed, whether in the Netherlands,

Scotland, England or the New World, the former Nicodemites could provide a new platform of unchurched ethics and voluntary societies – perhaps the stepchild of the Puritan ethic, but pervasive and adaptable to a new civic religion, which would make it a natural ally for socialism and ecumenism.

The subtitle of this paper is 'Problems and Perspectives'. The formidable task of measuring the impact of an ideology – in this case of a Christian reform movement – is a problem of perspective. John A. Tedeschi has characterised the impact of the Index and the 'devastating effects' of Roman censorship in these words: 'With the outlawing of Boccaccio and Machiavelli, the Renaissance had ended in Italy.'[66] A combination of Index, Inquisition and infantry spelled the end of the Reformation in Italy, France and the Habsburg territories. However, we would not dedicate our professional lives to the study of the Middle Ages, the Renaissance and Reformation if we held that in the case of Renaissance humanism, of Catholic reform, or of the Reformation, the 'end' is to be identified with ultimate failure. It may have been the end of the *erga*, the amazing events of the fifteenth and sixteenth centuries, but that does not spell the end of the *genomena ex anthropōn* – of what was unleashed by these events, their outcome and that heritage which Herodotus saw as being shaped by Greeks and barbarians alike.

Notes

1. R. G. Collingwood, *The Idea of History* (Oxford, 1946), p. 19.
2. G. R. Elton, *The Practice of History* (Sydney, 1967). See below, n. 55.
3. Collingwood, *The Idea of History*, p. 28.
4. J. Hottinger and H. Vögeli (eds), *Reformationsgeschichte: Heinrich Bullinger* (Frauenfeld, 1838; 2nd edn Zürich, 1984), p. 1.
5. Herodotus, too, sees the yield of history in keeping the past alive, but rather in the tradition of apportioning praise and blame he wishes later generations to know who was responsible for the outbreak and the course of war.
6. Rainer Wohlfeil, *Einführung in die Geschichte der deutschen Reformation* (Munich, 1982).
7. Hans-Christoph Rublack, 'Gesellschaft/Gesellschaft und Christentum, VI. Reformationszeit', *Theologische Realenzyklopädie*, vol. XIII (Berlin, 1984), pp. 1–13.
8. Felix Gilbert, 'Intellectual History. Its Aims and Methods', *Daedalus*, C (1971), pp. 80–97, 94.
9. Gerald Strauss, *Luther's House of Learning. Indoctrination of the Young in the German Reformation* (Baltimore, Md, 1978), p. 307f.

10.   M. E. Welti, *Kleine Geschichte der italienischen Reformation* (Schriften des Vereins für Reformationsgeschichte, CXCIII) (Gütersloh, 1985), p. 139.
11.   Henry Heller, *The Conquest of Poverty. The Calvinist Revolt in 16th Century France* (Studies in Medieval and Reformation Thought, XXXV) (Leiden, 1985), pp. 240, 243, 247.
12.   T. A. Brady, Jr., *Turning Swiss. Cities and Empire, 1450–1550* (Cambridge Studies in Early Modern History) (Cambridge, 1985), p. 153f.
13.   Erwin Iserloh (ed.), *Handbuch der Kirchengeschichte*, vol. IV (Freiburg im Breisgau, 1967), p. 145.
14.   Karl Marx, 'Zur Kritik der Hegelschen Rechtsphilosophie', *Deutsch-Französische Jahrbücher* (Paris, 1844) (Reclam edn, no. 542, Leipzig, 1981), p. 159.
15.   Cf. Heiko A. Oberman, 'The Gospel of Social Unrest', in Bob Scribner and Gerhard Benecke (eds), *The German Peasant War. New Viewpoints* (London, 1979), pp. 39–51, 48.
16.   Hermann Rebel, *Peasant Classes. The Bureaucratization of Property and Family Relations in Early Habsburg Absolutism 1511–1636* (Princeton, NJ, 1983), p. 13.
17.   Peter Blickle, *Die Revolution von 1525* (Munich, 1977; 3rd edn 1983); English translation, *The Revolution of 1525. The German Peasants' War from a New Perspective* (Baltimore, Md/London, 1981).
18.   For this distinction between the first, second and third Reformations see Heiko A. Oberman, *Die Reformation von Wittenberg bis Genf* (Göttingen, 1986).
19.   R. A. Kann, *A History of the Habsburg Empire 1526–1618* (Berkeley, Ca., 1974), pp. 133, 125, 134f.
20.   T. N. Tentler, 'The Summa for Confessors as an Instrument for Social Control', in Charles Trinkaus and Heiko A. Oberman (eds), *The Pursuit of Holiness in Late Medieval and Renaissance Religion* (Leiden, 1974), pp. 103–25; cf. Tentler's monograph *Sin and Confession on the Eve of the Reformation* (Princeton, NJ, 1977).
21.   S. E. Ozment, *The Age of Reform, 1250–1550. An Intellectual and Religious History of Late Medieval and Reformation Europe* (New Haven/London, 1980), p. 86.
22.   *Super Libros Sapientie* (Haguenau, 1494), Lectio 77 D.
23.   *Modus solennis et autenticus ad inquirendum et inveniendum et convincendum Luteranos valde necessarius, ad salutem sanctae Apostolicae sedis et omnium Ecclesiasticorum anno 1519 compositus in Martini Luteri perditionem et eius sequacium per venerabilem Monachum magistrum Sylvestrum Prieratem* [sic] *ex sacrosancto ordine Praedicatorum, Magistrum sacri Palatii et generalem haereticae pravitatis inquisitorem. Anno 1553 revisus et satis bene emendatus ab erroribus per Reverendissimos Cardinales ad officium sanctissimae inquisitionis depuratos* [sic] *per S. D. N. Papam Iulium III.* Romae, Per Iordanum typographum Pontificium [sic]. Anno 1553. (40 folios). Cf. *D. Martin Luthers Werke, Kritische Gesamtausgabe* (cit. *WA*), vol. I (Weimar, 1883), p. 605. I owe the exceptional gift of this rare copy to my colleague James Tanis, the librarian of Bryn Mawr College.

24. I am indebted to Professor K. Augustijn and to the librarian of the Free University, Amsterdam, B. Lau, for access to the version most probably published in Augsburg in 1519.

25. E. Böcking (ed.), *Epistolae obscurorum virorum* (*Ulrichi Hutteni ... opera ... omnia*, supplementary vol. I) (Leipzig, 1864; reprinted Osnabrück, 1966), pp. 489–99. This version probably printed in Cologne in 1519.

26. Cf. Otto Clemen in *WA, Briefwechsel*, vol. I (Weimar, 1930), no. 236, pp. 604–6. I doubt whether Clemen saw the 1553 treatise himself. Note his incorrect rendering of the title.

27. The author of the excellent monograph on Vergerio, Anne Jacobson Schutte, informed me in a letter of 17 February 1981 that she doubts Vergerio's authorship:

   Vergerio referred to the work only six years after its publication in Basel. In *Agli inquisitori che sono per l'Italia: Del catalogo di libri eretici stampato in Roma nell'anno presente 1559* (Tübingen(?), 1559), folio 42v, he said that he thought he owned a copy of this rare work and planned to have it reprinted. Since his references to books written and published by others and to books he himself issued are generally very accurate, my tentative conclusion would be that he was *not* responsible for the 1553 edition.

28. After a deficient bibliographical description, Friedrich Lauchert associates both parts with the *Epistolae obscurorum virorum*. In the first treatise Lauchert finds '*mehr Gehässigkeit als Witz*', citing particularly the irreverent treatment of papal infallibility: satire '*durch törichte Verdrehung*'. Lauchert, *Die italienischen literarischen Gegner Luthers* (Freiburg im Breisgau 1912), pp. 29f., 30, n. 1.

29. Heiko A. Oberman, 'Wittenbergs Zweifrontenkrieg gegen Prierias und Eck. Hintergrund und Entscheidung des Jahres 1518', *Zeitschrift für Kirchengeschichte*, LXXX (1969), pp. 331–58.

30. The following treatises of Rotier are alluded to:
   De non vertenda Scriptura Sacra in Fulgarem linguam, deque occidente littera et vivicante spiritu dissertatio (Toulouse, 1548); *Parergi sive tabellae tres similitudinum, quibus suis coloribus haeretici, vera Ecclesia vulgaresque S. Scripturae traductiones describuntur* (Toulouse, 1548 quarto; 1549 octavo); *Responsio ad epistolam civium novae Babylonis Gebennae a Mornero insigni apostata editam* (Toulouse, 1549).

31. Dermot Fenlon, *Heresy and Obedience in Tridentine Italy. Cardinal Pole and the Counter-Reformation* (Cambridge, 1972), p. 51.

32. Paul F. Grendler, *The Roman Inquisition and the Venetian Press, 1540–1605* (Princeton, NJ, 1977), p. 92. The Index of Paul IV is reprinted by F. H. Reusch, *Die Indices Librorum prohibitorum des 16. Jahrhunderts* (Tübingen, 1886), pp. 176–288.

33. Cf. Heiko A. Oberman, *Roots of Anti-Semitism in the Age of Renaissance and Reformation* (Philadelphia, Pa., 1984).

34. Grendler, *Roman Inquisition*, p. 95f.

35. Iserloh, *Handbuch der Kirchengeschichte*, vol. IV, pp. 501–10. Cf.,

however, Hubert Jedin: '*Die Regierung des Caraffa-Papstes war für alle Anhänger der Reform eine grausame Enttäuschung*', *Geschichte des Konzils von Trient*, vol. IV (Freiburg im Breisgau, 1975), p. 15. Jedin placed the *Durchbruch* after 1559: '*Der Pontifikat Pius' IV. brachte den endgültigen Sieg der katholischen Reform und den Abschluß des Konzils von Trient.*' Ibid., p. 18. Cf. Donald Nugent's evaluation: 'Paul's pontificate was a reign of terror rather than a reformation . . . Given all this, one can hardly insist that Paul IV launched the Counter-Reformation without allowing at the same time that he was destroying the Catholic Church.' Idem, *Ecumenism in the Age of the Reformation. The Colloquy of Poissy* (Cambridge, 1974), p. 29.

36. Anne Jacobson Schutte, *Pier Paolo Vergerio. The Making of an Italian Reformer* (Travaux d'Humanisme et Renaissance, CLX) (Geneva, 1977), p. 267.

37. A significant advance is made by C. M. N. Eire, 'Calvin and Nicodemism: A Reappraisal', *Sixteenth Century Journal*, X (1979), pp. 45–69.

38. Albert Autin, *La Crise du Nicodémisme, 1535–1545* (Toulon, 1917); cf. Francis Higman (ed.), *John Calvin: Three French Treatises* (London, 1970).

39. Cf. Gabriel Biel, *Canonis misse expositio*, Lectio 18 G; I. 157, 4; Lectio 34 L; II. 10, 22.

40. Jacobus de Voragine O.P. (†1298) elaborates on the significance of Nicodemus in his influential *Legenda Aurea* (1293). On the wide dissemination of the *Legenda*, see Sherry L. Reames, *The Legenda Aurea. A Reexamination of its Paradoxical History* (Madison, Wisconsin, 1985), pp. 197–209.

41. The account of the deposition in the *Gospel of Nicodemus* and in (Pseudo) Bonaventura's *Meditationes* – visibly represented and propagated in sculptures and paintings throughout Europe – usually presents both Joseph of Arimathea and Nicodemus as the *faithful* disciples who remove the nails from the crucified Christ. Cf. Wolfgang Stechow, 'Joseph of Arimathea or Nicodemus?', in W. Lotz and L. L. Möller (eds), *Studien zur Toskanischen Kunst* (Munich, 1964), pp. 289–302, 290, 292–6.

    I am indebted to Dr Jane Kristof for calling my attention to Stechow's article. In a paper not yet published Dr Kristof makes a good case for interpreting Michelangelo's Pietà in Florence Cathedral as representing himself as a Nicodemite. Via Vittoria Colonna Michelangelo belonged to the Viterbo circle of the *Spirituali*. The Pietà, begun about 1547, was mutilated and abandoned by him before December 1555; by that time the *positive* self-identification with Nicodemus might well have become self-incriminatory.

42. T. H. Pressel (ed.), *Anecdota Brentiana. Ungedruckte Briefe und Bedenken* (Tübingen, 1868), pp. 31–3, 32. Cf. Martin Brecht, *Die frühe Theologie des Johannes Brenz* (Tübingen, 1966), p. 55, n. 1.

43. Jean Rott and Olivier Millet, 'Miettes Historiques Strasbourgeoises', in P. Barthel, R. Scheurer and R. Stauffer (eds), *Actes du Collôque Guillaume Farel (Neuchâtel, 29 septembre – 1er octobre 1980)*, vol. I

(Cahiers de la Revue de Théologie et de Philosophie, IX, 1) (Geneva/ Lausanne/Neuchâtel, 1983), pp. 261–2, 264.

44. See Marc Lienhard (ed.), *Croyants et Sceptiques au XVIe Siècle. Le dossier des 'Epicuriens'* (Publications de la Société Savante d'Alsace et des Régions de l'Est, Collection 'Recherches et Documents', XXX) (Strasbourg, 1981).

45. A. L. Herminjard (ed.), *Correspondance des Réformateurs*, vol. IX (Nieuwkoop, 1966), p. 126.

46. Ibid., vol. VIII (Nieuwkoop, 1966), p. 231f.

47. Ibid., pp. 107, n. 18, 108, n. 20.

48. Ibid., p. 228, n. 1.

49. G. H. Williams, *The Radical Reformation* (Philadelphia, Pa., 1962), p. 598.

50. Carlo Ginzburg, *Il Nicodemismo. Simulazione e dissimulazione religiosa nell'Europa del '500* (Turin, 1970), pp. xiv, xvi, 154. Cf. Welti, *Kleine Geschichte*, pp. 50, 98.

51. Pierre Fraenkel, 'Bucer's Memorandum of 1541 and a "Lettra nicodemitica" of Capito's', *Bibliothèque d'Humanisme et Renaissance*, XXXVI (1974), pp. 575–87; Rott/Millet, 'Miettes Historiques Strasbourgeoises', p. 271.

52. Williams, *Radical Reformation*, p. 775.

53. See G. H. M. Posthumus Meyjes, 'Jean Hotman's *Syllabus* of Eirenical Literature', in Derek Baker (ed.), *Reform and Reformation. England and the Continent, c. 1500–c. 1700* (Oxford, 1979), pp. 175–93, 179–80.

54. Eire, 'Calvin and Nicodemism', p. 67.

55. As an eminent example of the power of narrative history in the service of historical analysis Geoffrey Elton wrote one of his finest vignettes 'Persecution and Toleration in the English Reformation', *Studies in Church History*, XXI (1984), pp. 163–87. Though the issue of Nicodemism as such is not treated, the case of John Fox against Thomas More serves to gainsay the assumption that toleration is the child of tired scepticism when, all passions spent, the sober shores of the eighteenth century have been reached. Elton disproves the contention that 'only the gradual evaporation of such passions produced a weariness with religious strife which made the return of mutual sufferance to early humanism à la More possible'. Ibid., p. 163.
   This thesis is not only unfounded because of More's explicit approval of and active support for persecution; more importantly, it is not 'weariness' and tired scepticism which lead to the ideal of toleration. Himself a victim of persecution, John Fox is shown to be an advocate of toleration on the basis of his personal experience. 'In a very real sense, he knew what he was talking about. Thus one result of the history of religious strife was that people came to experience persecution in reality: it jumped off the page into their lives.' Ibid., p. 179. Exactly the same transition from the experience of persecution to the defence of toleration marks the history of the 'forgotten' Calvinists.

56. Heiko A. Oberman, 'Martin Luther – Vorläufer der Reformation', in E. Jüngel, J. Wallmann and W. Werbeck (eds), *Verifikationen. Festschrift für Gerhard Ebeling zum 70. Geburtstag* (Tübingen, 1982), pp.

91–119. The extent to which this shaped Luther's development and thoughts from the beginning to the end is spelt out in Heiko A. Oberman, *Luther. Mensch zwischen Gott und Teufel* (Berlin, 1982; 3rd edn 1985).

57.   '*Vielmehr muß es u.E. dabei bleiben, daß Luther zwar die Reformation stets letztlich als Gottes Werk ansieht, daß sie für ihn jedoch auch in der Frühzeit ein innergeschichtlicher, nicht ein endzeitlicher Vorgang ist.*' Bernhard Lohse, 'Luthers Selbsteinschätzung', in Peter Manns (ed.), *Martin Luther. 'Reformator und Vater im Glauben.'* Referate aus der Vortragsreihe des Instituts für Europäische Geschichte Mainz (Stuttgart, 1985), pp. 118–33, 122; with p. 131f, especially p. 132, n. 22.

58.   Lohse, 'Luthers Selbsteinschätzung', p. 130, n. 6, 13, 16. The parallel between the use of 'interim' at pp. 130, n. 13 and 131, n. 22 is overlooked. To translate 'interim' by '*vorläufig*' in the sentence *una interim consolatio tua erit futuri dies* ('*Betont wird viel mehr der zunächst vorläufige Trost*', ibid., p. 133, n. 3) is to negate Luther's confident faith and *only* hope during the interim before the imminent end; as Luther's Reformation, the interim itself is '*vor-läufig*'! See further *WA*, vol. XL, 1 (Weimar, 1911), pp. 367, 13–15; 372, 18–32; 581, 23–25.

59.   Ibid., p. 583, 29. Commentary on Galatians 4, 6; 1531/35.

60.   Commentary on Galatians 3, 13; 1531/35; ibid., p. 444, 28f.

61.   Bernd Moeller, 'Was wurde in der Frühzeit der Reformation in den deutschen Städten gepredigt?', *Archiv für Reformationsgeschichte*, LXXV (1984), pp. 176–93, 184, 193. Before we lose ourselves in 'apocalyptic' vagaries, however, the different types of eschatological expectation in early modern times should first be established. One of the best known forms was the widespread expectation of cosmic upheaval. From the Tübingen astronomer Johannes Stöffler to the Nuremberg painter Albrecht Dürer the end of the world was calculated to occur sometime between 1524 and 1526. Present research indicates that this upheaval was frequently associated with the intervention of the Antichrist. Gustav Hellmann, *Aus der Blütezeit der Astrometeorologie. Johannes Stöfflers Prognose für das Jahr 1524* (Berlin, 1914), pp. 5–67; Lynn Thorndike, *A History of Magic and Experimental Science*, vol. V (New York, 1941), pp. 178–233; Dietrich Kurze, *Johannes Lichtenberger. Eine Studie zur Geschichte der Prophetie und Astrologie* (Lübeck, 1960); Paola Zambelli, 'Fine del Mondo o inizio della Propaganda?', in *Scienze Credenze occulte Livelli di Cultura* (Florence, 1980), pp. 291–368, 300. This 'astrological' eschatology can be used just as well as a weapon *against* the Reformation, and is structurally independent of Reformation theology. Cf. Max Steinmetz, 'Johann Virdung von Haßfurt. Sein Leben und seine astrologischen Flugschriften', in H.-J. Koehler (ed.), *Flugschriften als Massenmedium der Reformationszeit* (Spätmittelalter und Frühe Neuzeit. Tübinger Beiträge zur Geschichtsforschung, XIII) (Stuttgart, 1981), pp. 353–72. Equally, it has been used *against* Luther to 'unmask' him as the expected Antichrist. Though not convinced that the 'forecasts' can properly be divided into 'consolation literature' and 'apocalyptic warnings' since I regard their ultimate purpose precisely as consolation by placing the evils of

the time on the divine timetable, Paola Zambelli has noted the need to develop typologies in order to distinguish varieties of apocalyptic expectation:

    Ĝ *gꞥꞥꞥꞥ ꞥꞥ ꞥꞥ ꞥꞥꞥꞥꞥꞥ ꞥꞥ ꞥꞥꞥꞥꞥꞥ ꞥꞥꞥ ꞥꞥꞥꞥꞥꞥꞥ ꞥꞥ ꞥꞥꞥꞥꞥꞥꞥꞥꞥ ꞥꞥꞥꞥꞥꞥ* tori fra gli scrittori che restano fedeli al papato, e al contrario una inclinazione apocalittica fra quelli filo-luterani.* Idem, 'Fine del Mondo', p. 300.

62.   Moeller finds in the *Summarien* such a far-reaching consensus with Luther that he speaks of a *'lutherische Engführung'* which in turn made *'den Theologen Martin Luther zu einer Figur der Weltgeschichte'.* Idem, 'Was wurde . . . gepredigt?', p. 193.

63.   Oberman, 'Vorläufer der Reformation', pp. 115–18. At this point Moeller inserts a surprising aside: *'Heiko Obermans These, die eschatologische Orientierung unterscheide Luther von der übrigen Reformation, läßt sich anhand unserer Texte und also für die Frühzeit nicht verifizieren.'* This statement is all the more surprising when we learn that Moeller wishes to see his interpretation of the 'unified Reformation message' confined to the period up to 1525; in his documentation no reason for reducing the span from 1522–29 to 1522–25 is adduced. I have been concerned to show that Luther, in the name of a whole series of city preachers, insisted on the introduction of visitations, in complete agreement with Melanchthon. But whereas the latter expected the visitations to establish peace and good order, and ultimately to lead to reconciliation with the Papacy, Luther never left any doubt that the Reformation could not be introduced by visitations but only through an act of God announcing the end of the throes of this world. Melanchthon was supported in his view by such leaders of the urban Reformation as Bucer, Zwingli and to a certain extent also Calvin. By his valuable discovery of the genre of *Predigtsummarien*, Moeller has been able to convey the impact of Luther's eschatological theology, which was not to become characteristic of the urban Reformation; the apocalyptic vision should be seen as one of the hallmarks of the first Reformation.

64.   *Corpus Reformatorum*, vol. XII (Halle a.d. Saale, 1844), p. 7.

65.   Marjorie Reeves, *The Influence of Prophecy in the Later Middle Ages. A Study in Joachimism* (Oxford, 1969), p. 504.

66.   John A. Tedeschi, 'Florentine Documents for a History of the "Index of Prohibited Books"', in Anthony Molho and John A. Tedeschi (eds), *Renaissance Studies in Honor of Hans Baron* (Dekalb, Ill., 1971), pp. 579–86.

Part II

2 Martin Luther and the Political World of his Time*

Gerhard Müller

Luther lived in a society of Estates, in which considerable differences existed between the nobility, the burghers and the peasants. As a cleric and university teacher Luther lived in a city and thus should be classed among the burghers. This class had a comparatively modest influence, since it was the nobility which still formed the politically most important Estate. But the nobility itself was also marked by considerable differences and developments. Thus the princes carefully observed the exact order of rank among themselves, while at the same time the influence of the lower nobility waned considerably throughout the sixteenth century. Viewing Luther's social standing in the context of such developments, one would therefore expect to find that his political influence was very small indeed.

The reason why Luther dealt with political questions at all is explained by the close ties between church and state which enabled clerics to exercise an influence on political events. Through written and oral statements the university teacher Dr Martin Luther made much use of this possibility. He also reflected upon the very principles of church–state relations – a theory nowadays called the doctrine of the two realms. However, we are not concerned here with this theory about which there exists extensive discussion;[1] rather, we intend to look at Luther's actual conduct in the political world of his time. In particular, his attitude to and comments on rebellion, war, peace, and the right of resistance will be the subject of our investigation.

I. AGAINST RIOT AND INSURRECTION

Already at the beginning of the 1520s Luther realised that the impatience of many of his contemporaries threatened to erupt with the force of an explosion. The exasperation which had accumulated over the years – most of it directed against the church – resulted in a general mood of anti-clericalism which incited many to acts of violence against unpopular clerics. Such hatred of popery was, of course, already well established and was also directed against the monks who frequently had become so rich that they provoked the envy of the laity. If Luther had approved of revolution as a solution, he would have found it easy to make himself the mouthpiece of traditional prejudice and excite the masses into rebellion against bishops, unpopular clerics and monks. But already in 1521 he had rejected riot and revolution, and in 1522 he published a treatise with the title 'A Faithful Exhortation to All Christians to Beware of Riot and Insurrection'.[2] The verdict contained in it was unequivocal. No one yet assumed the possibility of a peasants' revolt. Towards the end of 1521, when Luther committed his thoughts to paper, he was convinced that no uprising would take place, but he wanted to 'instruct the hearts'[3] in order to point out what was now required of all Christians. He believed that his time was determined by God's wrath which was directed against all those who had ruined the church. God would himself take action and effect more than all mankind. In fact, it was the princes' duty to intervene – something which Luther had already demanded in his treatise 'To the Christian Nobility of the German Nation' of 1520.[4] But a year later he observed that they, too, could not be relied upon. In fact, they rather obstructed each other in the execution of their duties, some of them even actively supporting the cause of Antichrist, as Luther thought. If, however, the prince did interfere, this should be considered as the 'legitimate execution of power', not as riot. God himself would judge the princes on whether they had fulfilled their task in an appropriate manner. On the other hand, Luther wished to instruct the common man to abstain not only from all violence, but also from 'those desires and words which lead to riot'.[5] For this Luther had several reasons.

First, Luther held that it is God's punishment which ultimately matters. Consequently, there would not be a general uprising, because the enemies of the Lord did not deserve anything lighter than his very wrath. Furthermore, it would be sufficient to oppose the enemies of the Gospel with the spoken and written word; there was no need for butchery.[6] What Luther demanded was an intellectual conflict with those whom he considered the enemies of God. Physical violence should not be applied by the common man, whereas the princes ought properly to fulfil their duty by removing grievances. In this way they could at least in part prevent and appease the wrath of God. But, as this was rarely the case (at least in Luther's opinion), those who had no magisterial function should confine themselves to the spoken and written word.

An uprising would yield no profit, nor the necessary improvement. Luther declared:

> There is no sense in riot; it usually damages the innocent rather than the guilty. Therefore, riot has no justification, however justified its cause may be. Riot is wont to cause more damage than improvement, according to the common saying, 'From bad to worse'. Secular authority and its sword have been ordained in order to punish the wicked and protect the godly, that uproar may be prevented. But when Mister Omnes, the common man, rises, who is incapable of making or maintaining the distinction between good and evil, he will hit out indiscriminately, which cannot be without great and cruel injustice. Therefore take heed and follow the authorities; as long as they do not take action or give orders, restrain your hands, mouth and mind, and take no sides. If you are in a position to influence the authorities to attack and give orders, you may do so.

Luther sums up his opinion as follows:

> I hold – and always will hold – with that side which suffers riot, no matter how unjust its case may be; and I will oppose that side which causes riot, no matter how justified its case may be. For riot cannot be without innocent bloodshed and ruin.[7]

This shows that for Luther the momentum of revolution entails nothing but damage. The potential suffering of the innocent leads him to reject riot and insurrection outright.

Another point is that God himself has prohibited riot. He commanded: 'That which is just, carry out justly.' Furthermore, God said: 'Vengeance is mine and recompense.' Both these biblical passages (Deuteronomy 16, 20 and 32, 35) prohibit riot because it is nothing less than an attempt to take judgement and vengeance into one's own hands. This God will not suffer. Consequently a riot will always make things worse, for it is 'against God, nor does it have his support'.[8]

Luther believed that behind all thought of riot lurked none other than the Devil himself who, having become weak and feeble, now tried to discredit by riot the preaching of the Gospel which had received a loud and strong voice through Luther. He declared:

'Whoever reads and understands my teaching in the right way, will not create riot.' His name may be misused by many, but there is nothing he can do about that. But God will see to it that a general uprising, so urgently desired by the Devil, will not take place. Therefore Luther begged his followers to give the enemy no cause to slander the newly proclaimed teaching by associating it with riot and violence. He implored his friends to behave as he advised, lest 'the sacred word of God should bear our disgrace'.[9]

To the question of what a Christian should do if the authorities failed to take action, he replied that he has three duties. First, everyone should acknowledge and rid himself of his sin, by which God in his justice torments Christians in the church. Secondly, everyone should humbly pray against the reign of Antichrist in the church. Thirdly, everyone should let his mouth be 'a mouth of Christ's spirit'. As before, he advised Christians to proceed with the spoken and written word against wrong teaching and conduct. As Luther put it: 'The mouth of Christ must do it.' He dispelled evil more effectively than a hundred revolutions. 'With violence we will do no harm to Antichrist; rather, we will strengthen him . . . It is with the light of truth' that the enemy of God is defeated. Luther suggested: 'Look at me! Have I not with my mouth and without a single stroke of the sword done more damage to the pope, bishops, patrons and monks than ever did all the power of emperors, kings and princes?'[10]

Nevertheless, Luther's repeated pleas reveal that he did in fact fear the danger of violent action. Denying all justification for such action he demanded that the battle against whatever is felt to be unjust be confined to the weapons of the spoken and written word. This does not mean justifying the conduct of those princes who fail to take the necessary steps; on the contrary, they must be criticised. Yet, no individual Christian is permitted to justify use of violence by an appeal to Luther: that would indeed be playing the Devil's game. He ought rather to take Luther as an example of one who has achieved much more with the spoken and written word than all those who had previously proceeded with violence against Christ's enemies in the church.

It is important to realise that Luther adhered to these principles throughout his life. Each Christian is granted the right of critical comment, be it spoken or written. He is thus entitled to a place in the arena of intellectual conflict. On the use of force, however, Luther agrees with Romans 13 that this is a prerogative of the state. Whoever violates God's institution and makes himself the avenger puts himself in the wrong. Furthermore, the reformer believes that more injustice is created than removed by riot. If the individual Christian behaves as Luther directs, the next question is, of course, how the secular authorities ought to conduct themselves.

II. THE DUTIES OF THE SECULAR AUTHORITIES

The activities of Thomas Müntzer were soon to give Luther the opportunity to renew his warnings of riot. Müntzer had been unimpressed by these warnings; on the contrary, he demanded the destruction of the ungodly as it was envisaged in the Old Testament. In his open 'Letter to the Princes of Saxony Concerning the Rebellious Spirit' of 1524 Luther warned his territorial lords of Müntzer's machinations.[11] Müntzer, he suggested, should be allowed to preach as much as and against whom he liked. If the people were swayed by his sermons, that was regrettable but could not be helped.[12] However, the state should make sure that Müntzer planned no uprising. If he actively whipped up a riot or resorted to violence, the princes had the duty to reply with force. It was the word of God which mattered in the church; fist-fights were the least appropriate. As Luther put it: 'Our office is to preach and to suffer, not to fight with fists and put up resistance.'[13] To appeal, as Müntzer does, to Moses' law because it demands the destruction of idols, is a false argument. That order was once given to the Jews that they might have a sure commandment from God. It was wrong to apply this law to Christians as well, otherwise the entire Old Testament would be binding as a rule for Christian life, including circumcision and all the works of the Old Law. Here Luther is already clear that Müntzer's use of the Old Testament would lead to extreme consequences. If, on the basis of the Old Testament, someone demands the complete destruction of all false worship, he cannot stop at that, but must go on to bring about the extirpation of the ungodly as well, because the Old Testament commands it. As is well known, Thomas Müntzer was soon to draw that conclusion. Luther, on the other hand, argued in the opposite direction: 'The removal of offence must be brought about by the word of God.'[14] Carrying out purely external changes would soon necessitate further action. For Luther the most urgent tasks that faced the church at this time were not about external matters, but concerned the Devil's kingdom which had to be destroyed.

As early as 1525 the question arose whether the state ought not in fact take action against insurrection. The peasants' revolt (which also included craftsmen, burghers and even some of the nobility) proved that Luther had been right to warn of a development which, however, he was incapable of preventing with words alone. Were the peasants' demands for a fundamental change of rights legitimate?

At the beginning of the conflict Luther, whom the peasants had appointed mediator between them and the princes, immediately called for peace and demanded that both sides avoid offence and remove injustice.[15] Yet he was unable to prevent the Swabian League from proceeding with force against the rebellious peasants of southern Germany. In April and May it was above all Thomas Müntzer who stirred up the revolts of the insurgents in Thuringia – in Luther's immediate vicinity. The reformer's personal attempt at intervention to calm the peasants down was unsuccessful. Meanwhile, the fact that Elector Frederick the Wise lay on his deathbed had a paralysing effect on Saxon politics.[16] Luther took up his pen and wrote the short tract 'Against the Robbing and Murdering Hordes of the other Peasants'.[17] It is possible that by doing so he was supporting a faction at the elector's court which considered the state's interference essential. Because of the elector's state of health its members may have regarded an address to the public as the only feasible option.

In this treatise Luther addressed himself only to those who had resorted to violence. He exhorted the princes to proceed against the rebels. Again he referred to Romans 13, 4, according to which secular government was God's minister and servant. It had the duty to fend off evil, since the sword had been entrusted to it for that purpose. Not to carry out this office in such a dangerous situation would be as great a sin as an illegitimate claim to the sword. A government which now proceeded against evil did not become guilty before God, but was obedient to him. If princes were killed in their fight against the rebels, they nevertheless had carried out God's orders. Another important reason why the princes should step in was that the wicked among the peasants had dragged in many godly people. Luther asked the princes to exercise mercy towards these 'captives among the peasants', and to liberate them from the evil influence of Müntzer and his like.[18]

Thus in the uprising in Thuringia we see a clash of two theological principles. While Thomas Müntzer, following the example of the Old Testament, appealed to Gideon's sword by which the ranks of God's enemies were slain, Luther referred to the New Testament which concedes to the individual Christian no more than the preaching of

God's word and the suffering of injustice. The authorities alone are commissioned to use force, whereas insurrection by the common man is in Luther's eyes a wrong which ought to be put down as soon as possible, so that those who have been seduced into it may be liberated from the spell under which they have fallen.

While Müntzer set himself up in the place of authority, regarding himself as a messenger of God in the Old Testament sense, Luther drew a sharp distinction between the duties of the government and those of every individual Christian. It was not compassion which the reformer most urgently required of the princes, but the sort of action which would prevent an even greater disaster and separate the wicked among the insurgents from the misguided.

Luther's statements drew criticism in his own lifetime. One could argue in his favour that he had always warned of insurrection because of its damaging consequences for the progress of the Gospel. Yet, his short treatise is not without problems. It is true that the peasants' revolt had already been put down by the time Luther's statements appeared in print. Since they had not been committed to paper until the beginning of May they could have had no immediate effect on the princes' course of action. But since Duke George of Saxony and Landgrave Philip of Hesse had so relentlessly taken action against the rebels in Thuringia, it was possible to see a sinister connection between the bloodshed there and Luther's statements. To be sure, Luther reprehended the princes for the shedding of innocent blood.[19] But, as a matter of principle, he was convinced that force was a prerogative of the authorities; therefore the peasants had sinned against God, for they wanted to be judges in their own right.[20]

III. LUTHER AS ADVISOR

Luther served the princes as an advisor not only during the peasants' revolt, where he did so on his own initiative, but he was consulted by them about many issues.[21] In particular, his territorial lords, the Saxon electors, required him to utter a number of political judgements. Likewise, the last Grand Master of the Teutonic Order in Prussia, Albert of Brandenburg, consulted him when he planned to transform the Order's territory into a secular duchy. Of the many instances of Luther's advisory activity – which incidentally also included the magistracies of imperial cities – his counsel to the emperor's brother-in-law, Christian II, the exiled king of Denmark, may suffice for demonstration. On a visit to Wittenberg, the king made contact with Luther who himself wrote a letter which Christian signed. As under normal circumstances Luther did not occupy himself as a scribe, one may conclude that not only the text of this letter but even the whole idea originated largely from him.

The letter of 6 November 1523[22] contains plans of far-reaching consequence. In it Christian II addresses himself to Frederick the Wise with the request to secure from the former's brother-in-law, Archduke Ferdinand of Austria, a pension for himself and his family, since Christian, who was married to a sister of Ferdinand, was very short of money. The letter also indicates that the Elector of Brandenburg, Joachim I, had already turned down a request for asylum from the exiles. Therefore Frederick was being asked to plead with Ferdinand on behalf of his brother-in-law, sister, nephews and nieces. Should this request fail, Christian was prepared to transfer his kingdom to Ferdinand in return for the requested pension and protection.

This letter, written in Luther's own hand and signed by Christian in person, may serve as an example of the far-reaching political proposals which Luther was prepared to make. One might object that this plan was so utopian that it could only have been thought out by an unworldly theologian! For, what could Ferdinand ever hope to gain from a title to the Danish crown which would never be acknowledged there? On the other hand, Luther realised that Christian was in a situation of great need and that his wife's family had thus far been unwilling to grant the necessary support. He therefore saw the possibility of Frederick acting as Christian's intercessor with Ferdinand, and even went so far as to communicate the intention of exchanging the title to a whole kingdom for a pension.

There is much that indicates that this letter was the result of Luther's own ideas. It also demonstrates how naive his political judgement could at times be. For it is hard to believe that Christian was seriously willing to renounce his title to the Danish crown. At the same time, the letter demonstrates the sort of problems about which high-ranking politicians consulted the reformer. Although the present case shows Luther as a political amateur, his judgement was more realistic in other instances, as for example shortly before his death, when after difficult negotiations he reconciled the Counts of Mansfeld. Here Luther played a much more successful role, although even then he could not hope to solve the Mansfeld problem once and for all.[23]

IV. WAR AS A POLITICAL MEANS?

Military thinking demands being one step ahead of the enemy. For this reason the leading politician among the Protestant princes, Landgrave Philip of Hesse, planned to respond with immediate action to the news in 1528 that a few Catholic princes had formed an offensive alliance. Philip attempted to win over the elector of Saxony for his plan of a preventive war. In Wittenberg, however, news of an imminent offensive was received with scepticism. The rumours of preparations for military conflict also reached the imperial government. Therefore a mandate was passed on 16 April 1528, demanding all Estates to keep the peace. The mandate also referred to the principles of the *Landfrieden*, the imperial edict which called for peace throughout the empire, and which provided legal means for the settling of conflict.

Luther and Melanchthon were among those who viewed a military offensive with scepticism. Capitalising on the imperial mandate they exhorted Elector John by letter not to start a war. They believed it to be a contempt of God if the mandate were disregarded, because in it God had shown himself mercifully inclined towards peace. Furthermore, they pointed out that the imperial mandate had been issued by an authority which God had instituted and to which the elector, too, owed obedience. In this case obedience was even more necessary, since it was something good which was being sought and commanded: peace and the commonweal of the empire. If electoral Saxony and Hesse were to start a war now in spite of the mandate, they would have to be judged rebellious against God-given authority. Saxony and Hesse would rightly deserve the imperial ban; they could have no clean conscience before God and would lose their imperial rights as well as their esteem in the eyes of the world – 'a terrible and cruel prospect indeed'. The reformers were convinced that by such an act of disobedience the whole of Germany would be plunged into chaos and the Gospel finally extinguished. Behind Philip of Hesse's plans for war they suspected none other than the Devil himself.[24]

For this reason the Wittenberg reformers threatened to dissociate themselves from the elector, even to leave his territory if a war of aggression were to originate in Saxony. They would be forced to take this step for the sake of the Gospel, lest the innocent word of God be discredited by such a disastrous political action. For the Protestants' cause would be associated with war and bloodshed rather than with peace and good government. 'We who have and praise the word of

God ought to keep that suspicion even further away from us than the other princes who do not have the word of God.' For this reason Luther and Melanchthon advised the elector to assure the imperial government of his and Hesse's obedience to the mandate.[25]

This letter shows the two Wittenberg reformers anything but war-mongering. They begged the elector to consider that there was great danger behind the clever political schemes of the Landgrave of Hesse, a temptation into which Satan himself tried to drag the followers of God's word. A preventive war has no place in the Protestant view of church and state! Those authorities which commit themselves to the word of God must on no account cast suspicion on their political conduct.

Both Luther and Melanchthon remained faithful to this line of argument. They were disappointed when the landgrave mobilised his troops and marched against the enemy; they remained highly suspicious of him both then and later. That the Elector of Saxony did not allow himself to be dragged into rash military action may, in part, be credited to this letter by Luther and Melanchthon.[26]

Later comments show that this was not a unique statement of Luther's. In 1532, for example, he was asked whether electoral Saxony should become involved in the attempts by the electors of Mainz and the Palatinate to mediate between the emperor and the Protestant Estates. Luther's approval was unequivocal. He thought that the articles proposed by the opposite side were indeed acceptable. He even went so far as to recommend his elector to abandon a previously voiced protest against Ferdinand's election as Roman king. The election may indeed have been unjust; but, as things go in this world, trying to remove an injustice usually creates greater evil than retaining it. Furthermore, the reformer considers whether God may possibly have offered this agreement in order to advance the Gospel. To oppose it would mean to oppose God. That could result in war by which the proclamation of the Gospel might be impeded if not completely suspended. Luther referred to Romans 12, 18 where Christians are commanded to do their best to live in peace with everybody. This means that they may have to sacrifice their rights for the sake of peace. As Luther put it: 'Peace matters to me more than justice, indeed, than rights given for the sake of peace.' On no account, he warned, should the elector rely on other powers such as foreign kings or cities.[27] Here Luther defines peace as the highest political good. Even if justice suffers disregard, it should remain subject to peace. In fact, by its very nature justice should promote and preserve peace.

The reformer is also guided here by political considerations which support these more theoretical points. He pointed out, for example, that the Protestants form no more than a minority in Germany. Consequently, they cannot expect to win a war. Whoever relies on foreign kings – here Luther may have been thinking in particular of Francis I of France – may soon find himself betrayed. Moreover, one should not overestimate the power of the cities. The unexpected defeat of Zürich in 1531 had shown how unpredictably a situation can change. Thus Luther also advises against a war, because he considers it unwise both politically and strategically. The enemy would only be provoked into mobilisation, and one's own money would have been used up before the war even started. Consequently, the preservation of peace remains the best political solution.

In a letter of 16 May 1532, addressed to John Frederick, the new Elector of Saxony, Luther attempts to win also his support for this view.[28] He writes: 'This Your Princely Highness know, that no temporal good on earth deserves higher respect than peace.'[29] Concerning defence against the Turks Luther did not act as a war agitator either, but demanded repentance if Christians wanted to oppose the enemy with any chance of success.[30] Thus, even defensive wars have a purpose only if they are conducted by Christians who are penitent before God.

V. RESISTANCE AGAINST THE EMPEROR?

In 1530 Emperor Charles V summoned the imperial diet to Augsburg, where he intended to settle the religious issue as an arbitrator. Philip of Hesse intended to abstain from the diet since he expected no good from such arbitration. During the course of the diet his fears were confirmed. On 3 August, Charles V declared the confession of the Protestant Estates refuted and demanded their return to the sole church. His threat to carry out his duty as the church's steward if they did not return within six months prompted the Protestants to examine the question whether resistance to the emperor, who, after all, was their overlord, could in any way be legitimate.[31]

Philip of Hesse was of the opinion that an elected emperor was not an authority in the proper sense since he was bound by the law just as any other prince. If he waged war on the Protestants they had the right to defend themselves and were not obliged, as Luther thought, to suffer such an injustice. Philip himself made contact with Luther in order to persuade him of his views.[32] So far, as we have seen, Luther believed that no theological argument existed for resistance against secular authority. Even if imperial or other secular laws allowed for such a possibility, he could as a theologian concede no right of resistance against persons of higher authority. As long as they remained in power, their subjects had to suffer injustice patiently. Writing to the elector, Luther maintained that if the mayor of Torgau thought that the elector had acted against God and therefore need not be obeyed, the prince would find this most unacceptable. As long as the prince was in his place of power the municipal council had the duty to serve him. The same applied to the Protestant princes in their relation to the emperor. The only case in which they were not bound by obedience to the emperor was if he demanded their assistance for an unjust cause. Luther believed that if the Protestants were to offer resistance to the emperor, this could result in general uproar. But who would want to take the responsibility for butchery on such a large scale? It would be better for the princes to lose three principalities, indeed to be dead three times over! Luther hoped, however, that Charles V would not start a war at all. He recommended the princes to make concessions in all external matters as far as could be reconciled with one's conscience, so that the Protestants' enemies would find no cause to proceed against the adherents of the Reformation.[33]

The lawyers, on the other hand, even those from Saxony, took a different view. They maintained that a prince had a right to protect his subjects. Luther declared that as a theologian he was in no position to comment on this legal interpretation. In Nuremberg, where resistance to the emperor was considered illegitimate, Luther's comments were received with unease. To explain his attitude Luther wrote to Lazarus Spengler, the secretary of the city's court, that he was unable to contradict the lawyers if they interpreted resistance against the emperor as self-defence. However, as a theologian he persisted in his opinion that a Christian may not resist evil but should suffer everything. If, on the other hand, the lawyers maintained that a Christian could offer resistance not as a Christian but as a citizen, he had to accept this view.[34]

Luther solved the issue by means of his distinction between state and church. He declared that he was not competent to judge the legal aspects of the matter, but made it plain that the lawyers had to bear the responsibility for their interpretation themselves and therefore should see to it that they had right on their side. As a theologian he could not recommend a political alliance which was only the work of men and which demonstrated that one no longer trusted in God alone.[35] Yet Luther was not able to prevent the formation of the Schmalkaldic League, which after his death, as is well known, was unable to withstand the emperor's troops. Instead, Luther had tried to recommend to the princes a political rather than a military solution.

VI. THE FIRST COMMANDMENT FOR A PRINCE

When in 1542 military conflict between the two Saxon cousins, the Elector John Frederick and Duke Maurice, seemed to be imminent, Luther composed an open letter. In it he admitted that he was commenting on a secular matter about which a preacher was not in a position to pass judgement. On the other hand, the word of God had commissioned him 'to take care of the secular rulers and to pray for peace and tranquility on earth'. Moreover, he had the duty of upholding the word of God against the obdurate. Thus he only wished to fulfil his duty and to relieve his conscience 'before God' by preaching his word to the princes. Both princes professed the Gospel, both of them were Christians, i.e. they wished to 'hear and obey Christ's word'. Thus if he, Luther, preached the Gospel to them, it follows 'that he who hears me, hears God'.[36]

Luther's point of departure was the beatitude in Matthew 5, 9: 'Blessed are the peacemakers, for they shall be called the children of God.' From this he derived its antithesis: 'Damned are the haters of peace, for they must be called the Devil's children.' Thereafter Luther was very blunt indeed:

Such a saying, coming from God the Almighty, is valid for everyone, no matter how high-ranking they may be. On the contrary, as all men are subject to Him they are all commanded to preserve the peace under pain of eternal damnation. Therefore, this is the first commandment which Your Electoral and Your Princely Highnesses are bound to keep: above all to strive for peace in word and deed, if necessary at the cost of life and goods.

Luther then dealt with the immediate cause of the conflict. It concerned the town and district of Wurzen, a small but strategically important place, which up till then had been jointly governed but was now claimed by each of the cousins for himself. Luther maintained that the whole issue was not worth a war at all and that: 'Your Electoral and Princely Highnesses could not seriously continue in your rash anger and strife to break such a divine commandment without offence to your conscience or the danger of eternal damnation.'[37]

Luther anticipated the objection that 'one can only live in peace as long as one's neighbour permits it'. This may be correct, but Christians are bound by Paul's commandment in Romans 12, 18 which is of particular importance here: 'So far as depends upon you, live peaceably with all.' Thus both princes owed obedience to God, 'and by means of arbitration the one side must offer to the other peace and settlement'. The princes were warned not to be judges, let alone avengers in their own right. As Luther put it:

> Even if somebody were to kill my father or brother, I am not judge or avenger. What need is there for laws and authorities, what need for God, if everybody wanted himself to be judge, avenger, even God over his neighbour, especially in worldly matters?

For this reason the reformer exhorted the princes to put an end to their quarrel immediately, especially since

> the small town of Wurzen was not worth the expenses which had already been incurred, let alone the wrath of such powerful princes and splendid Estates. To sensible people the whole affair looks no different from two drunken peasants having a fight in a pub over a broken glass or two fools over a piece of bread. The danger, however, is that the Devil and his servants would like to fan this spark into a wildfire to the enemies' joy, the Turks' laughter and the disgrace of the Gospel.[38]

Luther believed that such a war was 'not war but, in fact, riot'. Since the princes were related to each other they would 'irreversibly drag their magnificent and praiseworthy Estates into disgrace and slander', if they engaged in war over the district of Wurzen. If one of the two sides were to refuse the other's offer of peace and arbitration, Luther himself would give his support to that side 'which offered arbitration and peace'.[39] Whoever used violence would thereby discredit his cause, no matter how just it may be. Consequently Luther exhorted the princes to keep the first commandment, *their* first commandment. In Luther's words: 'Above all strive for peace in word and deed, if necessary at the cost of life and goods.'[40] Here too, Luther advised against a war which in his eyes was, in any case, no more than a petty feud. The proper condition for which all men must labour is peace.

In his political world Luther thus declared himself against war and rebellion. Instead, he advocated intellectual conflict among men, conceding to the state alone, and then only in an emergency, the use of force. In such a case, however, the state has the duty to control the wicked and protect the good. Only then does the state act on God's behalf. Yet in most cases it is better to preserve peace than to assert one's rights with force, and so peace remains the highest political good.

Luther's political deliberations were not always shared by the politicians. His opposition to political alliances could not prevent the formation of the Schmalkaldic League. His reservations about resistance to the emperor were pushed aside with legal arguments. But it is true that, in 1528 and 1532 especially, he exercised a moderating influence on political decisions. Likewise, the feud over Wurzen was not settled by war; this was, however, not only to Luther's credit, but also thanks to the Landgrave of Hesse's mediation between the quarrelling cousins.[41] All in all, Luther showed himself a man who viewed political problems from a theologian's perspective, and for whom the decisive maxims were subordination to God and the resulting preservation of peace in the world.

Notes

*   This paper was translated by Gotthilf Wiedermann.
1.   See for example Niels Hasselmann (ed.), *Gottes Wirken in seiner Welt. Zur Diskussion um die Zweireichelehre* (2 vols, Hamburg, 1980).
2.   Printed in *D. Martin Luthers Werke. Kritische Gesamtausgabe* (cit. *WA*), vol. VIII (Weimar, 1889), pp. 676–87.
3.   Ibid., p. 679, 22–24.
4.   *WA*, vol. VI (Weimar, 1888), pp. 404–69.
5.   *WA*, vol. VIII, pp. 679, 31–34.
6.   Ibid., pp. 679, 36–680, 15.
7.   Ibid., p. 680, 16–35.
8.   Ibid., pp. 680, 36–681, 5.
9.   Ibid. pp. 681, 6–682, 9.
10.   Ibid. pp. 682, 12–683, 11.
11.   *WA*, vol. XV (Weimar, 1899), pp. 210–21.
12.   Ibid. pp. 218, 19–219, 4.

13. Ibid. p. 219, 15f.
14. Ibid. p. 220, 25.
15. Cf. his 'Admonition to Peace on the Twelve Articles of the Peasantry in Swabia', *WA*, vol. XVIII (Weimar, 1908), pp. 291–334.
16. See for example Heinrich Bornkamm, *Martin Luther in der Mitte seines Lebens* (Göttingen, 1979), pp. 314–53.
17. Thus the original title, cf. *WA*, vol. VIII, p. 345.
18. Ibid., pp. 359, 14–361, 35.
19. Cf. his 'An Open Letter on the Harsh Book against the Peasants', ibid., pp. 384–401.
20. Gottfried Maron, '"Niemand soll sein eigener Richter sein." Eine Bemerkung zu Luthers Haltung im Bauernkrieg', *Luther. Zeitschrift der Luther-Gesellschaft*, XLVI (1975), pp. 60–75.
21. Cf. Hermann Kunst, *Evangelischer Glaube und politische Verantwortung. Martin Luther als politischer Berater seiner Landesherren und seine Teilnahme an den Fragen des öffentlichen Lebens* (Stuttgart, 1976).
22. *WA, Briefwechsel* (cit. *WA, Br.*), vol. III (Weimar, 1933), p. 186f.
23. Arno Sames, 'Luthers Beziehungen zu den Mansfelder Grafen', in Helmar Junghans (ed.), *Leben und Werk Luthers von 1526 bis 1546* (Göttingen, 1983), pp. 531–600.
24. *WA, Br.*, vol. IV (Weimar, 1933), p. 448f.
25. Ibid., p. 449f.
26. Luther's influence on electoral Saxon politics was particularly great during the reign of Elector John. Cf. Gerhard Müller, 'Luther und die evangelischen Fürsten', in idem, and Erwin Iserloh (eds), *Luther und die politische Welt* (Wiesbaden/Stuttgart, 1984), pp. 65–83.
27. *WA, Br.*, vol. VI (Weimar, 1935), p. 260f.
28. Ibid., pp. 308–11.
29. Ibid., p. 307 maintains erroneously that the letter was sent to Elector John. The form of address 'Your Princely Grace' (e.g. ibid., p. 310, 62) makes it plain, however, that John Frederick was the recipient.
30. Rudolf Mau, 'Luthers Stellung zu den Türken', in Junghans, *Leben und Werk*, pp. 647–62.
31. Gerhard Müller, 'Luthers Beziehungen zu Reich und Rom', ibid., pp. 380–8.
32. *WA, Br.*, vol. V (Weimar, 1934), p. 660f.
33. Ibid., pp. 258–60.
34. *WA, Br.*, vol. VI, p. 56f.
35. Ibid., p. 57.
36. *WA, Br.*, vol. X (Weimar, 1947), p. 32f.
37. Ibid., p. 33.
38. Ibid., p. 33f.
39. Ibid., p. 34f.
40. Ibid., pp. 33, 35–7. Luther's open letter was only partially printed and not published. Ibid., p. 37f.
41. Cf. Günther Wartenberg, 'Luthers Beziehungen zu den sächsischen Fürsten', in Junghans, *Leben und Werk*, p. 571.

3 The Holy Roman Empire in German History[1]

Volker Press

One might use the old German Empire as a parameter to compare historical research in the German Democratic Republic with that of West Germany. If one also includes Austria and Switzerland in the comparison then it seems to me that a number of significant things emerge; at any rate the result is certainly not one-sided.

I cannot avoid making some introductory remarks. It is a well-known fact that the Germans find their history a difficult topic to deal with. The German monarchy had been elevated to imperial status ever since the high Middle Ages and linked with claims to a European 'universal monarchy', which was admittedly mostly felt to be more theoretical in character. This turned out to be a considerable problem for Italy, but perhaps Italy initially paid a higher price for this combination than Germany, whose central European location made it to a certain extent predestined for such a position. It is no coincidence that in Italian historiography since the *Risorgimento* the Roman Empire of the Germans appears as a form of foreign rule, Frederick Barbarossa as a tyrant hostile to the cities, Henry VI as a cruel despot and the Habsburgs as the very embodiment of foreign domination. It should be pointed out, however, that from Dante's picture of Henry VII to the modern analysis of the imperial fiefs in Italy there are overtones of another view of the emperor and the empire. The importance of both views to the development of Italy is a separate and intriguing topic, which has still received no exhaustive treatment to date.[2]

Seen in retrospect, Germany's position in central Europe makes the political solution which the old empire comprised appear far from inappropriate: an elastic system which was able – albeit decreasingly – to absorb the crises of Europe. True, the Germans were not really able to cope with their tradition. The old empire had to declare its bankruptcy in 1803 and 1806 with the revolutionary invasion of France; its last emperor, Francis II, since 1804 Francis I of Austria,

51

deliberately refrained from restoring the imperial association (*Reichs-verband*) in 1813–15, placing the power of Austria on a different foundation. The German League founded in 1814–15, with its combination of Austrian hegemony and conservative political tendencies, was entirely in the tradition of the old Empire.[3] But the League was not a national state; in fact it was subsequently declared to be its much maligned enemy.[4]

The subject of this paper is not why the attempt to set up a national state with Austria in 1848–9 failed, or why Prussia finally qualified as the forerunner of national unity in 1866 and 1871, thus putting an end to the continuity of 368 years of virtually unbroken Austrian emperorship. Thereafter, we in Germany tended to refer to Carolingians, Ottonians, Salians and Hohenstaufen, but for the centuries after 1250 Luther and Frederick the Great of Prussia were preferred to Charles V and Joseph II, who both wore the crown of Otto the Great. It was not simply a question of the un-German role of the House of Habsburg; rather, the development of the empire from the days of the Hohenstaufen is really seen as a period of continuous decline, whereas the age of the Hohenstaufen is celebrated in vague terms as the heyday of German national development. This 'little German' view of history determined the perspective for a long time, until both the collapse of Germany in 1945 as a national state and a power and the demise of old Prussia revealed the problematical nature of the little German interpretation.

After 1945 this situation changed in West Germany, too. Suddenly the old empire became a major theme, and this has a great deal to do with developments after 1945. For one thing, it is evident that with Swabia, Franconia and the Rhineland the Federal Republic possesses the traditional heartlands of the old empire, whereas since the late Middle Ages Thuringia had rather detached itself from the kingdom. There have certainly been tendencies in Germany since the war to overemphasise the importance of the old Empire instead of Prussia and the little-German empire. It seems to me that precisely the animated discussions of the last few years have favoured the sober analysis of the old empire, and have contributed to the development of an apparatus for researching a phenomenon which appears so utterly alien to the modern way of thinking. The problem of the interpretation of emperor and empire is thus closely connected with the sometimes erratic course of German history, but it is certainly high time it was pointed out that until 1806 the imperial association of territories formed the political framework of Germany – until it was eventually destroyed from within and from without, that is, by the collaboration between its larger territories and the heir of the French Revolution, Napoleon. It thereby became clear not only that the construction of the empire was obsolete, not only that it would be necessary to tame the revolution if there was to be co-operation between France and the German princes, but also it turned out that the traditions of the *Reich* were in many respects passed on to the nineteenth century.[5]

The collapse of the imperial association between 1803 and 1806 will continue to deter the historian from any romantic glorification. We must therefore investigate the problems which arise in connection with an interpretation of the imperial association, then attempt to sketch the development of the empire from the point of view of the emperor, and finally investigate the special features which the phenomena of emperor and empire entail for German history.

I

An indispensable tool for the interpretation of the old empire is the apparatus and work of the imperial publicists, which reached a peak in the eighteenth century. It set later historians on the track of a strongly judicial interpretation which is still influential to this day and whose justification is certainly not about to be questioned in this paper. But it must not remain the only perspective. Imperial history – particularly of the seventeenth and eighteenth centuries – has, for modern historiography, remained above all the history of the imperial constitution. Political history is being only laboriously linked with it, while the failures of the old empire in power politics are quite rightly being identified – I need only recall the imperial army's oft-quoted disaster at Roßbach against Frederick the Great in 1757. But this picture seems to me to be but one side of the coin, contrasting with the reality of the imperial association, particularly in the fragmented areas of Swabia, Franconia and the Rhinelands, but also in Thuringia and Hesse. In fact it is possible to observe a strengthened presence on the part of the emperor in north-west Germany. How can one reconcile these diverging interpretations?

The empire is undoubtedly an association that pre-dated states;[6] as an entity it was not fundamentally called in question, perhaps with the exception of the Swedish plans under Gustavus Adolphus and Oxenstierna, until the second half of the eighteenth century. It thus remained Germany's political framework. It can also be argued that the stalemate between the emperor and the imperial Estates which had emerged from the legacy of the Hohenstaufen towards the end of the Middle Ages was continued throughout the modern period and legally consolidated ever more strongly. This increasingly restricted the emperor's scope for action, but made possible entirely new manifestations of the imperial system, indeed its transformation and further development. But imperial rule over the empire was not uniform:[7] thus Thuringia was taken away from the emperor, the special position of the electoral principalities was qualified and the imperial presence in north-west Germany became clear, albeit in different ways under Charles V and again after 1715, after the acquisition of the Spanish Netherlands by the Austrian Habsburgs. All in all, the result was a partial levelling of the differences within the imperial association on the one hand; but, on the other, this was counteracted by the strong consolidation of the larger territories, which, as I have pointed out, eventually destroyed the empire.

This in itself shows quite clearly that the emperor's means of governing were 'pre-state'. The hereditary lands signalled a role conflict for the Habsburg emperor with his position in the empire. The elective character of the German monarchy was always bound ultimately to secure the primacy of the hereditary lands. There are any number of examples of this, from the imperial policy of Maximilian I, via the surrender of Württemberg by Ferdinand I in 1534 and the priorities of the imperial emissaries in Münster and Osnabrück in 1648, via the Pragmatic Sanction of 1713 to the imperial policy of Maria Theresa and Joseph II.[8] This development corresponds to the paradox that the special position of the Austrian lands as the hereditary lands of the emperor quite definitely promoted their emergence from the empire. The establishment of an Austrian emperorship in 1804 and the renunciation of the imperial crown by its last bearer in 1806 were an almost logical consequence of the same development.

The emperor's role conflict is certainly harder to see clearly in that it contrasts with the initial co-extension of hereditary and imperial authorities, and above all the unity of imperial action. On the other hand, the continuity of the Austrian imperial dynasty, with the short break from 1740 to 1745, facilitates the interpretation. The Viennese and the Prague Courts thus turn out to be the real centre of imperial rule.[9] The court represented not only the common umbrella for the authorities of the hereditary lands and the empire, but also the centre of interwoven personal, dynastic structures which were an important instrument of imperial influence in the empire. This ancient network, borne by the high aristocracy of the hereditary lands and the empire, continued to play a part until the end of the old empire – the imperial clientele under the empire was above all attached in the south to the Viennese Court, though it always deferred to the nobility of the hereditary lands – once again a clear indication of the self-evident priorities of Habsburg politics.

Because of this link with the imperial court large sections of the nobility comprising counts and knights remained true to the old church; on the other hand, the Reformation increasingly alienated the north and west German territories from the emperor. As a general rule the influence of the emperor was greater where the territories or cities were small or immediately threatened. Traditional imperial influences were linked with legal titles in respect of imperial cities, imperial princes and the imperial church. In other words, imperial authority was based on personal and family, regional, judicial and – from the sixteenth century on – religious ties. Modern techniques of government were only partially employed. The imperial fiscal system was still characterised by improvisation and imperfection; the legation as an instrument was only employed by the emperors after the Peace of Westphalia and was not used consistently until the eighteenth century. Traditionally it was the imperial subjects who had to come to the emperor, and not the imperial emissary to the vassals. This proved of considerable advantage to French diplomacy in particular, and did not help to keep the imperial court informed of events. An extension of imperial influence had produced a progressive juridification of the empire. It resulted from the stalemate within the imperial association of territories which was perpetuated by the turning points of 1495, 1555 and 1648, and reflected the imperial role of supreme feudal lord and judge of the empire. The emperor countered the attempts of the Estates to wrest the Imperial Court of Chancery (*Reichskammergericht*) away from him with the jurisdiction of the Privy Council (*Reichshofrat*).[10] True, there was always a link with the law, as this was the only way in which the Privy Council could function; but it was also a political instrument of great importance and was therefore very much opposed by the more influential Estates. The opponents came chiefly from the Protestant camp, as the Privy Council was all too firmly embedded in the Catholic system of the court. Moreover, its limitations were evident in the constraints resulting from its lack of executive powers: it was necessary to appoint imperial commissions. In the juridicised empire of the seventeenth century these were to play a considerable part among the smaller Estates in particular. The strongly legal character of the imperial association was definitely advanced by the Peace of Westphalia, but it was certainly not a result of it. The late medieval king's lack of power and the territorial structure of the empire had already done much to promote its legal character. Observation of these movements shows that between 1500 and 1800 there was a considerable and fundamental concentration of the empire, combined with imperial attempts to extend its influence to north Germany. The personal links were tightened; the legal developments adapted – even outside the areas traditionally close to the emperor the support of the emperor and imperial law were appreciated as a buttress against the larger imperial Estates' appetite and desire for hegemony. On the other hand, however, the stagnation of the system also became apparent. Increasingly the emperor had to stabilise his clientele from outside. The smaller lords and imperial cities immediately dependent on the empire were obliged to submit to repeated visits by commissions of auditors in their disastrous indebtedness; the emperor intervened in civil disturbances in the cities and territorial conflicts between subjects; the imperial association proved to be a conservative power for unviable entities which flocked together beneath the double eagle in growing numbers. Thus the empire eventually acquired an increasingly antiquated character.

This in turn was related to the growing consolidation of the larger territories: Saxony, Hesse–Kassel, Hanover, Württemberg, Bavaria, and particularly Brandenburg–Prussia. These territories increasingly acquired an advantage over the smaller ones, and also over the ecclesiastical ones, and were hence incorporated even more securely into the imperial clientele. Within the powerful ones, however, the forces were grouping which were eventually to destroy the imperial association.

The ecclesiastical territories did not manage to develop in this way. Certainly, the three ecclesiastical Electors – and in addition to them Salzburg and, at times, Würzburg and Münster – retained their position among the leading group of territories. But the ecclesiastical Estates were not able to keep up with developments. This was not simply due to the fact that their existence had been increasingly called in question since the end of the seventeeth century; as a substratum of the nobility they were unable to keep pace with the movements of the larger secular lords. Thus although the Elector of Mainz was the pre-eminent prince of the empire, his role was not based on the display of armed power but on a place in the imperial constitution. This is also true of the eminent Electors of Mainz from Berthold von Henneberg, Johann Schweikard von Cronberg and Johann Philipp von Schönborn to Karl von Erthal and Karl Theodor von Dalberg.

This, however, tended to qualify the importance of the Electoral College; through its participation in the empire in the fifteenth century it seemed at times to rise to the position of the emperor's sole partner.[11] Then with the extension of the Imperial Diet over princes and cities it became the most important of its curiae. But the emperor always retained the electors as his most important partners; in the crises of the Thirty Years War they even acquired renewed significance. Since the days of Maximilian the Imperial Diet[12] was an important platform for the empire, but it cannot be properly understood in isolation – the universal rules of the European corporative constitutions also applied to the Imperial Diet, those customs which Geoffrey Elton has described so aptly with his phrase King-in-Parliament. This means that the Imperial Diet was not empowered to act without the actions of the emperor, that the Viennese Court constituted its permanent partner. After 1663 Viennese policy was to exploit these possibilities brilliantly.[13]

The Imperial Diet, however, was founded on a sort of majority of the weak – not in the sense of a modern parliamentary majority, but on a protective function. Yet the weak were continuously growing in number; the decline of many imperial Estates in the struggle for priority in the empire was in the long run to undermine the system of the Imperial Diet.

This development, likewise, was a consequence both of the formation of the territorial state and also of the formation of regional hegemonic zones. Thus the second most eminent dynasty of the empire, that of the Wittelsbachs, proved not only to be a geographical barrier but also, from the point of view of imperial politics, a rival to the ruling house – it also sought to acquire a clientele. It is true, though, that the attempts of the two Wittelsbach lines to slow down the advance of the ruling house, in 1620 and 1742, were of short duration, and both ended in disaster.[14]

But individual Estates could still rise to a regional hegemonic position. From the fifteenth century on, the formation of the Imperial Circles (*Reichskreise*), which structured the empire and had defined regional duties of often considerable importance, favoured such developments, whereby individual leadership roles such as that of Württemberg in the Swabian district, or that of Brunswick–Lüneburg or Electoral Hanover in the Lower Saxony district, existed alongside complicated arrangements for maintaining balance. In order to take into account the special position of the hereditary lands, the ruling house had had its own imperial districts in Austria and Burgundy allotted to it, but in doing so it had emphasised the special status of the hereditary lands to the detriment of imperial policy, as the emperor was thereby at first driven out of the circles and was only able to regain this position with difficulty.

The primacy of the policy on the hereditary lands here proved to be a disadvantage, but it is pointless to discuss it, since it was indispensable for the position of the Habsburg emperor. This was also linked to the fact that the zones traditionally loyal to the emperor in south and west Germany were not significantly expanded, despite certain territorial gains in north Germany. After the acquisition of the Spanish Netherlands the north of the empire remained 'distant' from the emperor and displayed a growing tendency to become the Achilles heel of imperial policy.

Yet it always remained a major question how far the supreme head of the empire was able to slow down or prevent the hegemonic aspirations of individual princes. In the north the emperor's chances of exerting his influence were smaller than in the south. The most successful regional hegemonic policy, least troubled by any counterforce, was pursued by Prussia, which was eventually able to become a European great power, straining the imperial association to the limit. In many respects Prussian policy in the eighteenth century imitated Viennese techniques, thus playing a quasi-imperial role.

It was always Vienna's policy to create counter-balances. It recognised how dangerous were the advantages that the Great Elector Frederick William of Brandenburg had attained through the Peace of Westphalia, and how consistently he exploited them. This resulted in the co-operation between Vienna and Hanover, which was closely connected with the acquisition of the ninth electoral vote by the Guelphs. But the accession of the Elector George Louis to the throne of England totally undermined the calculations of Viennese policy. Hanover was increasingly taken in tow by the great power policy of England.

The rise of Prussia thus clearly pointed up, by contrast, the weakness in the position of the Habsburg emperors. The source of the imperial position – its family relations, the pull of the court, its judicial functions – proved to be predominantly conservative and aristocratic, maintaining an increasingly obsolescent social system. The modernisation of Austria itself was hampered by the imperial role of the ruling house, while the high aristocratic character of the Viennese Court was reinforced by it: the special role and the limits of Austrian reform were thus closely linked. The roots of Austria's special position in German history and its eventual departure from it are thus to be found deep in the early modern period. It should, however, be emphasised once again that the independence of Austria had not been prefigured since the days of Rudolph of Habsburg, nor was it an inevitable development.

II

In this section we shall attempt a chronological approach, in which the age of 'imperial reform', as it is known, assumes central importance, perhaps that of a watershed.[15] At that time the king and emperor Maximilian, attacking from a defensive position, succeeded in warding off and reversing the tendency to turn the empire into an empire of electors, or even of princes. Maximilian's father, Frederick III, the longest reigning head of the empire, had been drawn into the maelstrom of the patrimonial-Austrian options for south-east Europe, and had played a rather problematic part in the empire. True, the old emperor had for the most part codified the imperial rights, but the usual means of imperial influence inside the empire no longer worked if they were applied too much from its periphery. In the end the royal house of Bavaria threatened to take possession of the property of the second Habsburg line in Innsbruck, and a Wittelsbach empire seemed to loom ahead. Although the Habsburgs had succeeded to the inheritance of the House of Luxemburg, they were always bound to fear that the other surviving dynasties who were eligible to provide a king of the Romans aspired to their patrimony.

Then Maximilian's confrontation with the empire first entrenched the stalemate between the emperor and the imperial Estates which was to be decisive for the modern period. Even though Hermann Wies- flecker maintains in his comprehensive and thorough biography of Maximilian that the emperor did not bring together his empire with 'blood and iron', it was thanks to the emperor's statesmanship, his ability in handling the forces of the Estates, that the imperial association of territories was convincingly consolidated.[16] The Imperial Diet, having sprung up from various different roots, had by now partly supplanted the court, and became the platform for agreement between the emperor and the empire – the term *Reichstag* is first recorded in 1495.[17]

The bitter struggle between the emperor and the imperial Estates also gave the imperial constitution an institutional character which subsequently affected the entire modern empire: apart from the Imperial Diet we are particularly concerned with the Imperial Circles and the Imperial Court of Chancery. Maximilian engineered the demise of the Imperial Governing Council (*Reichsregiment*) which had been imposed on him by insisting on the inalienable royal prerogatives. But Maximilian succeeded in removing the imperial position from the clutches of the Estates – incidentally, the possibility cannot be excluded that a corporative council would have led to greater dynamism in developments than the stalemate enforced by Maximilian.

In the most controversial German electoral decision of the modern era, the imperial election of 1519, Maximilian's policies were crowned with a late success. His grandson, Charles of Spain, was elected. With his western European and Mediterranean power base, Charles V naturally reversed the polarity of the fundamental components of Maximilian's policies. He utilised the empire, with its traditional roots in Germany, to pose claims to European power. Italy and the Mediterranean were for him a priority; Spain was the heart of his European authority; the Netherlands his German patrimony. Charles V's imperial position turned everything that had comprised German politics since the Hohenstaufen on its head. There had, it is true, been absentee rulers as early as the late Middle Ages, such as Sigmund of Luxemburg and his Hungarian monarchy. But he had had nothing approaching the firmly constructed power base of Charles V – though this could not replace his presence in the empire, despite the awe of the German princes. On the other hand, the emperor's regular absence strengthened the institutions of the Estates – the Imperial Diet, the Imperial Court of Chancery and the Imperial Circles. Rapid institutionalisation took place under the distant emperor. The dramatic struggle of Charles V, who was tied to the old Church because of his extra-German possessions, with the Reformation, forms another essential component of German constitutional history. It promoted, in particular, the development of the Imperial Diet into a platform for agreement between emperor and Estates.

The emperor's priorities lay outside the imperial territory on which his empire was based. The struggle for Italy, sustained by a revived idea of the emperor, gave Charles' policies a Mediterranean centre of gravity; it also led in the long run to enmity with France. Despite family connections and thoroughly effective features of dynastic solidarity, the French king's fear of a potentially lethal threat and encirclement was simply too great. Relations with the Pope were also complicated by the imperial role. The different levels of imperial action in the empire (in the stricter sense) and in Europe continued to affect the problems of the Reformation, particularly with regard to the Pope. Because of his imperial plans, Charles V favoured stability in the empire and therefore he had to give the princes (and hence also the Reformation) their head.

This resulted from an obvious decision to leave the running of the empire to the electors and the princes, while protecting his prerogatives – a precondition for the success of the Reformation that should not be underestimated. While Charles V gave priority to the Mediterranean and western Europe, the German Reformation stabilised – by 1540 it had even begun to threaten Charles' position in the Netherlands.

Finally, then, the emperor was left with little choice but to proceed against the Protestants with force. Charles succeeded in gaining military victory, but not in overthrowing the imperial constitution, which had become stabilised in the clashes of the Reformation, nor in halting the Reformation itself. For it soon became apparent that the emperor could only employ his formidable display of power temporarily and locally. He was not able to hold the line set by the 'Imperial League' and the Interim. The 'Imperial League' was supposed to moderate the imperial institutions which were ruled by the princes, above all the Imperial Diet; the Interim was supposed to bring the Protestants slowly back to the old church with a tolerable compromise formula.[18] Both experiments foundered on the factors which had led to their creation twenty years before. Nevertheless, Charles V's importance to the empire should not be understated – without attaining his goals, he had consolidated the imperial office even against the Reformation, extending the stalemate of the constitution, as it were, into the religious sphere. The fact that Charles himself was not prepared to complete this development and left it to his brother to finish off should not blind us to this. The small Estates of the empire, the counts, the knights, the cities (even the Protestant ones) had by this time definitely been brought back to the clientele of the emperor for the duration of the empire.

With the Princes' Revolt of 1552, all plans for an alternating succession, and hence for a lasting link between German and Spanish Habsburgs, were thwarted. The end of Charles V's government and the now inevitable succession of his brother Ferdinand I, and thus the German Habsburgs, liquidated a multitude of experiments. The hereditary possessions in the Netherlands had already been detached from the *Reich* by Charles by virtue of his imperial office in Europe as a consequence of an older, independent development. They now passed to the Spanish branch of the Habsburgs. This was also a consequence of the emperor's policies in western Europe and Spain, despite all attempts to keep the situation in the empire stable and then actively to counter the Reformation. Most recently, Heinrich Lutz in particular has emphasised how uninterested the policies of Charles V basically were in Germany, how disillusioning for a national perspective. The logical consequence, however, was the rise of the German Habsburgs and Charles V's replacement by Ferdinand, who had long had to regulate the situation in Germany. An imperial lordship was now followed by what was virtually a national one. The line of continuity of the Habsburg authorities ran in any case from Maximilian I via Ferdinand to his son, Maximilian II; since his election as king, Ferdinand I had attained a position of his own and since the late 1540s increasingly dissociated himself from his imperial brother.

Ferdinand I's deliberate attempt to tackle the German problems was not only characterised by a stronger involvement in German conditions; in 1526, after the disaster of the Jagiellon dynasty Ferdinand had clutched at their patrimonial lands. This meant a shift of the centre of gravity towards the east, a greater measure of coolness towards the problems of the *Reich*, a retreat from the old heartland of Swabia. With Bohemia, Moravia and Silesia the king gained an advanced position against central and north Germany, against Saxony and Brandenburg. With Hungary, however, Ferdinand acquired the problem of the Turkish Wars, which were to exert a decisive influence on the history of the House of Austria for centuries. The watershed of 1526 was to polarise the spheres of interest of the two branches of the House of Austria and to make the help of the empire against the Turks a decisive question for the senior line. The Turkish Wars also became a central theme of the subsequent diets. Ferdinand's co-operation with the German Estates, especially the Catholic state of Bavaria and the Protestant Electorate of Saxony created the foundation of the system of religious peace of 1555. It rested on the consensus of all who were interested in the preservation of peace in the empire – which, incidentally, was also a precondition for the extension of the territorial state. In the process the Protestants traded the possibility of unrestricted expansion for legal security and a dogmatic attachment to Lutheranism typical of the development of the empire into a legal system. Faith was formally linked to territoriality in exchange for the maintenance of a peaceful order in the empire, and hence ultimately the stabilisation of the position of the territorial princes. At any rate, this system could be cemented by the co-operation between the Catholic and Protestant Estates of the empire.

The true emperor of religious peace was Maximilian II, who continued his father's policy more consistently, deliberately displaying a certain measure of religious ambivalence without finally leaving the old church. The relative religious permissiveness of Maximilian II favoured collaboration within the empire, which accorded with the religious peace and was most strongly supported by Bavaria, Saxony and Württemberg. But even his son, Rudolph II, was unable to balance the divergent forces any longer; his seat was in Prague, far from the centres of the empire. The revisionism of the Catholic and Protestant Estates with regard to the religious peace created growing tensions which the emperor was increasingly unable to absorb. Rudolph II was not in a position to play the imperial role fully. His vacillation between depressive quietism and aggressive Catholicism demonstrates a link between general tendencies and the personal problems occupying the emperor.

Protestant revisionism, embodied above all by the Palatinate, realised that the system of religious peace played principally into the hands of the Catholic side. Rudolph II's inability to make an appropriate reaction to the intensifying religious crisis led to a dual destabilisation: within the empire and inside the House of Austria. Towards the end of the sixteenth century the mediatory function of the central institutions within the empire diminished more and more; the Imperial Diet and the Imperial Court of Chancery were no longer able to carry out this function in the face of mounting religious antagonism. Here there might have been a chance for the emperor to fill the widening gap. He did not do so, though he was not devoid of insight into the problems of the development. But his Privy Council was unable to win the confidence which the other imperial institutions had lost. In fact, Protestants regarded it as particularly prejudiced in religious matters.

The Lutheran partisans of the religious peace from Electoral Saxony and Württemberg could no longer mitigate the effects of the uncontrollable crisis. But the aggressive tendencies were increasing on the Catholic side too, particularly as after 1605 the unifying factor of the Turkish Wars was gone. It culminated in the *Bruderzwist*, a fraternal struggle among the Habsburgs, an inner-dynastic revolt against an emperor who was increasingly felt to be a liability. The efforts of the brothers, headed by Archduke Matthias, resulted in a continuing diminution of the imperial position and met with success. Rudolph's final fall from power was anticipated by his death in 1612. The price was first of all a considerable decline of authority in the patrimonial lands and in the empire, which the next agnate, Matthias, could no longer stem. Again he consistently sought the renewed support of the other Habsburg line, the House of Spain. But the dual revolt by the Protestant sections of the empire and by the opposition of the Estates in the hereditary lands led to the disaster of the Thirty Years War which threatened to turn the empire upside down. Events in the empire were connected with the paralysis of the imperial institutions, those in the patrimonial lands with the crisis of authority engendered by the *Bruderzwist*. All this was overlaid by growing fears of an act of force by the Catholics, combined with a feeling of increasing inferiority, though fear of war was also mounting on the Catholic side.

A key role in all these developments was played by Bavaria. Since the Reformation it had enjoyed a splendid position between the solidarity that united the Estates against the emperor and the Catholic-inspired desire to side with him. The Bavarian position had reached its zenith on the eve of the Thirty Years War – in the crisis of 1618–20 Bavaria was able to cover the Habsburgs' deficit. But with the successes of Ferdinand II the imperial position acquired its own dynamic. The tragedy of Bavarian policy was that having helped initiate the revival of the Habsburg Empire, it was now outflanked by it. Swiftly Ferdinand II gained the upper hand, thanks largely to the successes of Wallenstein. The triumphal progress to north Germany changed the imperial position in the empire geographically, too. Ferdinand II established a presence in the north never equalled by any of his predecessors or descendants. With the Edict of Restitution of 1629, the restoration of the ecclesiastical institutions appropriated by the Protestant Estates in accordance with the strictly interpreted stipulations of the Peace of Augsburg, he sought to link the demands of the Catholic Church and those of a re-established ecclesiastical clientele. The confiscation of the lands of proscribed Protestant Estates and imperial knights and their distribution to Catholics was supposed to supplement this system. But by his clumsy conduct the emperor not only mobilised the Protestant Estates of the empire most directly affected, especially as his policy of restitution extended to the distant north, whose bishoprics had very largely come out on the Protestant side; in practice, Ferdinand aroused the opposition of the Catholics, too, since the predominant position of the emperor also seemed to be turning into a threat to them.

The Swedish intervention in the empire after 1630, provoked by imperial expansion to the North Sea and the Baltic, then destroyed Ferdinand's position. The plans of the Swedish chancellor Axel Oxenstierna in south Germany, culminating in the League of Heilbronn of 1633, constituted a reply to the expansionist policy of the emperor.[19] These plans were dashed, however, by the Swedish disaster at the Battle of Nördlingen in 1634. In view of the military balance between Sweden and the emperor, it seemed for a moment that a key role was about to fall to the Elector of Saxony. But Ferdinand II's retreat from the highest religious objectives in order to achieve a consolidation of the emperor's political position within the empire which was also acceptable to the Protestants, and was formulated in the Peace of Prague in 1635, came too late and did not go far enough in its offers of an amnesty. The French intervention, which was meant to support the flagging forces of the Swedes, then led to an increasing state of exhaustion which finally led to a peace of exhaustion. In the 1640s the Emperor Ferdinand II and his advisors realised that the war could no longer be won.

The Peace of Westphalia of 1648 appeared, in fact, to entrench this situation and to shift the balance between the emperor and the imperial Estates in favour of the latter.[20] It now seemed that the House of Austria would have to pay the price for its imperial plans. The *status quo ante* was laid down, with slight changes in favour of the Catholic side. The emperor was to become a *primus inter pares* with reduced rights, pushed back to the hereditary lands; France and Sweden were to oversee the preservation of peace and the imperial constitution. In return, however, the House of Austria received a free hand in the hereditary possessions; there was to be no revival of the dangerous opposition from the provincial Estates which had almost destroyed the framework of power in the hereditary lands prior to the Thirty Years War.

But this provided the House of Habsburg with the basis for a remarkable recovery. A further prerequisite was the increased juridification of the empire. The trauma of the great war had led to the attempt to list the points of dissension in the Peace of Westphalia and to settle them; behind this lay the continuing endeavour to replace the armed conflict by a judicial war. One result was the great importance which the imperial courts now assumed. The Imperial Privy Council, which was dominated by the emperor, swiftly obtained the upper hand over the Imperial Court of Chancery, controlled by the Estates. The consequences of this were far-reaching; the principle of clinging to the existing law conserved the corporative society and led to the ossification of the imperial constitution. True, the peace settlement of 1648 was fundamental and effective, but it increased the immobility of the empire and the corporative society. Yet at the same time the position of the emperor as judge and arbitrator had been extended.

All attempts to organise the empire without and against the emperor had failed. Although Bavaria lost a good deal of ground compared with its previous position as a result of the internationalisation of German politics, the premier Elector of the empire now tried to comply with the stipulations of the Peace of Westphalia and to organise the empire without the emperor. Johann Philipp von Schönborn failed – it turned out that the empire could not be organised without the emperor. His reliance on France as an alternative did not bring him the political freedom of action for which he had hoped: the pull of the rising European power was too strong. We shall return to the real alternative – the expansion of a strong territorial state – below.

Thus the second half of the seventeenth century was not the epoch of an entirely Estate-dominated empire, but that of the re-emergence of the Habsburg monarchy. Internal stabilisation, the role of arbitrator, the military efficiency increasingly demanded against the French and the Turks – all these factors allowed the position of the emperor under Leopold I and Joseph I to grow ever stronger, reaching its glorious apogee in the War of Spanish Succession, which, however, simultaneously revealed its fragility.[21] Above all, it was the period when the emperor was able to mobilise the empire once again: the struggles and reconciliations between emperor and empire revived the Imperial Diet after 1663 as the expression of a continuing stalemate and made it a permanent one.

One should not overestimate the importance of the Imperial Diet from a modern, parliamentary point of view, nor from a romantic one, but it proved to be an instrument of the advanced integration and concentration of the empire as well as a means of exerting the emperor's influence. With his clientele gathered in it and constantly increasing, the supreme head of the empire was able to exert a considerable influence. Above all, the Regensburg Diet of 1541 gave the apparently diffuse framework of the *Reichsverband* a clearer and more intelligible structure. The corporative tradition, the position of the emperor in, and in relation to, the Diet, gave him a considerable advantage; without the emperor the Diet was not able to act. The Viennese Court asserted this freedom of action as the opponent and the partner of the Diet simultaneously. Leopold I, Joseph I and even Charles VI exploited this position brilliantly. Certainly, the centre of gravity quickly shifted in favour of the patrimonial lands as a result of Austria's grandiose successes against the Turks. The emperor became more and more the head of a European great power, which qualified his attitude to the empire: the difficulties experienced by the representatives of imperial interests when facing the exponents of Austrian power politics at the court of Joseph II make this quite clear.

Yet because of the problems connected with the empire as an elective monarchy, the imperial office as such was constantly being called in question. The problems of succession, which had been increasingly in evidence since the early seventeenth century, reinforced yet again the importance of the hereditary lands as the true foundation of the ruling house, a priority which was, of course, an older one. Succession to the throne also required the consent of the Estates in the individual states of the hereditary monarchy. The fact that it could be attained without much difficulty showed the cohesion of the Habsburg lands – it was more difficult to obtain the assent of the empire and of the European powers. On the other hand, the Habsburgs' policy of succession after the Pragmatic Sanction of 1713 did more to weaken Austria's position than to strengthen it. So Charles VI's death in 1740 triggered off a German and European crisis.

Even so, it should be stressed that developments after 1648 also clearly showed the limits of the emperor's powers. We have already mentioned the predominance of the hereditary possessions; the legal role of the Imperial Privy Council kept the supreme head of the empire strictly tied to imperial law. There was a narrow dividing line between a cautious policy of protection and the observance of the norms which determined the Viennese Court's room for manoeuvre. Finally, the preservation of the emperor's zones of influence, which jutted out into the traditional heartlands of the empire, towards Swabia, Franconia and the Rhinelands, remained an essential prerequisite of the imperial office. The emperor's influence in the north had been strengthened by the acquisition of the Netherlands in 1715 and by the expanded system of imperial legations, but it was still faced by clear boundaries. Because of its central political role, the Catholicism of the Viennese Court had a deterrent effect on the Protestants, who saw their own chances diminishing under the system of imperial patronage and client states. Finally, the internationalisation of German politics continued, just as it had rapidly developed during the Thirty Years War, leaving scant room for any further extension of imperial power. This was linked with tendencies to ally German territories with foreign crowns: Brandenburg with Prussia, Saxony with Poland, Hesse–Kassel temporarily with Sweden, and not least the Electorate of Hanover (Brunswick–Lüneburg) with England.

In the final analysis the imperial deficit in northern and central Germany could never be balanced (though one should certainly not underestimate the influence emanating from the lands of the crown of St Wenceslaus). The dynastically based beginnings of a quasi-imperial policy in the two Wittelsbach territories of the Palatinate and Bavaria failed – as did short-lived Saxon ambitions. Prussia alone could fill the vacuum of the north German sphere, far as it was from the emperor. The beginnings of a quasi-imperial policy under the Great Elector led to the gradual formation of latent great power status, which was, in addition, favoured by the constellations around the Baltic, particularly the rise of Russia. By the time of King Frederick William I (1713–40) Prussia already had latent great power status.

Prussia was, in fact, the lever which brought the entire Austrian system to collapse. With an inspired instinct for power, King Frederick II sensed the crises of the monarchy, and in 1740 struck a blow against Austria at its moment of greatest weakness – only with the extinction of the Habsburg male line did the great power waiting in the wings enter the arena. The thrust was directed at Silesia, whose loss repulsed the Habsburg monarchy from central Germany. The fact that Frederick failed to champion his claims on the Lower Rhine but struck instead at the heart of the monarchy was a devastating change of direction as far as Austria's position in the empire was concerned; its isolation from north Germany was considerably increased. It is above all the judicial and political implications of this development for the empire that are interesting. The purely dynastically founded claim of the Bavarian Wittelsbachs to the imperial office coincided with Prussia's goal – which was also France's – of establishing a counterweight to Austria. It now turned out that the free suffrage of the electors was not sufficient to overthrow the

Habsburg system, which had evolved over the centuries. It had, however, entered into a disastrous crisis, from which it was never really to recover – thereby the importance of the patrimonial interests was once again strengthened.

The Wittelsbach experiment of 1742–45 failed.[22] It transpired that no other solution was feasible but that of a Habsburg empire. But with the establishment of a second European great power on the territory of the empire, the basic constellation had changed – and after Frederick II Prussia did not restrict itself to controlling the north German sphere but increasingly set about disrupting the Habsburg system. In this way Prussia successfully thwarted the last attempts to implement a deliberate Habsburg imperial policy under Joseph II.

The emperor had at first attempted by means of a visitation to gain control of the Imperial Court of Chancery in Wetzlar in the years following 1767. He had clearly recognised the central function of the imperial courts within the judicial system, whose activity had outlasted the crises of the Silesian Wars. But the move to take over Wetzlar failed, and at this, after the attempt to acquire Bavaria in 1778, an aim which despite every setback was never abandoned, Joseph followed the path of a realignment of the hereditary possessions, thus accepting the permanent break-up of the empire. Twice Prussia forced him to retreat.[23] The emperor had risked everything, irritating large sections of the traditionally loyal Estates to the limit of their endurance and thus enabling the King of Prussia, Frederick, to mobilise the imperial Estates against him in the League of Princes in 1785–86, which had last been attempted by the Archbishop of Mainz, Johann Philipp von Schönborn, in 1648.[24]

The growing tension within the imperial system did not at first curb the activities of the Imperial Court, the Imperial Court of Chancery and the Imperial Circles, but they increasingly assimilated the ideas of the Enlightenment, which found their way into the political disputes within the empire and the dispensation of justice by the imperial courts. However, a growing division into spheres of interest emerged, a growing tendency for the other German states to lose ground to both Austria and Prussia, which in the electoral capitulation of 1790 even tried to wrest the instrument of the Imperial Court of Chancery out of the emperor's hands; in the capitulation any intervention in the constitutional framework of the imperial towns was forbidden.[25] The traditional counterbalances of the empire continued to operate, albeit increasingly out of step with developments in the larger territories. The function of the Imperial Diet had changed under the conditions of German dualism: it was no longer able, especially after 1740, to play the part which it had come to play since 1663. The presence of a second German great power with its own association of client states disturbed the Diet. Inner tensions arose particularly when Joseph II's expansionist policy conflicted with the emperor's traditional role – the supreme head of the empire was thereby creating uncertainty among the old Austrian clientele. The signs that the emperor was finally giving priority to his European great power policy were multiplying, not least among them being his continued aim of gaining control of Bavaria. From 1778 on, even after the League of Princes, the policy of realignment was followed whereby the Wittelsbach Elector was to be compensated for Bavaria wholly or in part with the Austrian Netherlands, an operation which the empire would have found it hard to countenance. The disunity of the major German powers attracted the influence of the others to the empire. France and Russia had already participated in the Peace of Teschen in 1779 as guarantee powers and still retained this function. Great Britain had been represented since 1714 by the Electorate of Hanover, which had been completely drawn into the pull of English great power politics, thus forfeiting as far as Austria was concerned the function designed for it from Vienna's point of view when it was raised to an electorate: that of an effective north German counterweight to Prussia. This completed the internationalisation of German politics which had been reinforced by the reciprocal blockade of the two leading German powers. This state of affairs was only temporarily interrupted in the period between the Treaty of Reichenbach in 1791 and the Peace of Basel in 1795, when Prussia again departed from its policy of uniting with Austria adopted in 1791.

The conservative solidarity of the two German great powers in opposition to the French Revolution was thus relatively short-lived. Subsequently Austria engaged in a lone struggle against revolutionary France, a struggle which increasingly became a war waged by Austria as a great power. It had, after all, only the rump of an empire on its side after the north had broken off the war in Prussia's wake. There was now no mistaking the conflict of interests between the developed medium-sized states and the small territories for which the protection of the emperor had been a final support to fall back on. Certainly a slowing down of the Revolution with the Directory, the Consulate and the Empire was necessary before Napoleon's coalition with the medium-sized German states was possible. Incidentally, it was also evident that with few exceptions the *Reich* rejected radical revolution.

In a recent survey I have shown quite clearly that the conflicts between the imperial cities died down rather than escalated against the background of the French Revolution. It was only with the coming of the Directory that the old oppositional forces of the urban middle-classes on the left of the Rhine were won over to France, a manifestation of old, corporative habits of thought deeply rooted in the German mentality.

With Austria's last imperial war against France came the end. In 1795 Prussia had retired to its hegemonic zone; Austria's dwindling support in a south Germany still loyal to the emperor was not sufficient. The explosive forces of the territorial powers against the empire came to fruition at a time when Austria was in decline; the pushing back of the Habsburgs eastwards was the result of this process. The traditional priority accorded to the hereditary possessions was thereby asserted once and for all, even though the ruling house attempted covertly to save what was left of its old clientele.

III

Until recently, national historiography saw the universal *Reich* as having led down the wrong path, the more strongly territorial history hardly spared it a glance, while as far as social history is concerned – not only from a Marxist point of view – the empire often disappears entirely from its field of vision.

It nevertheless remains a fact that for centuries it was the undisputed political framework of Germany. For several hundred years it was obviously able to control the situation in central Europe, a loosely knit formation that was incapable of an aggressive foreign policy, though it often had to bear the pressure of expansion, particularly from the West. Its only expansionist constituents were the two leading powers, Austria and later Prussia. Thus the empire formed a reassuring zone of calm, much as people were always deploring the lack of any advances on the foreign front, for instance in providing support to the rebellious Netherlands. Moreover, it was so elastic as a political association that, though not unscathed, it was ultimately able to absorb the shocks that rocked the system of European powers. More recent experiences of a central European great power in a position of hegemony may well lead us to view some aspects of the empire in a kinder light.

Domestically, too, it formed a political framework which allowed a multiplicity of forces to live and thrive. The imperial constitution was characterised by a stalemate between emperor and princes that was handed down through the ages. In this way, the empire twice managed to overcome the crisis of religious schism, though on the second occasion only after the experiences of a disastrous war. The imperial ambitions of the emperors, above all Charles V and Ferdinand II – and perhaps Joseph II, too – were absorbed by the empire. For a while it was even able to endure a second European great power within its structure.

Out of this stalemate there not only developed a complex, regionally highly differentiated system of balances; a further consequence was the necessity of settling conflicts, which in turn caused a marked trend towards juridification, whose origins are of an early date. The Peace of Westphalia became a milestone of the juridification which shaped the later empire especially. The Viennese Court thereby exerted its influence in the territories, particularly the less powerful ones, right down to the level of the subjects and the conflicts between Estates.

The emperor remained respected, but in an empire in which the Estates had a determining influence his powers were limited. There was already talk of the 'rules of the game' under which he ruled. The special position of the hereditary lands, and thus the subsequent detachment of Austria, was a consequence of its ruler's imperial office. (This had been demonstrated earlier and more clearly in the case of the Netherlands, Charles V's patrimonial lands.) The emperor had to rule the empire according to a complicated system, complying with the traditional rules of the game, allowing for the graded zones of influence and taking into account the regional constellations. The judicial system of the empire offered the emperor advantages, and yet restricted him, too. Austrian policies, however, were quite able to exploit this situation, even if it was repeatedly necessary to balance the status of the hereditary possessions – and in the sixteenth and seventeenth centuries the very unity of the *Casa di Austria* – against the empire.

Of course, the Imperial House also had to pay a price: the linking of empire and hereditary possessions quite definitely reinforced the aristocratic nature of the Viennese Court. It allied itself with the old corporative and conservative client states in the empire, with the magnates of the patrimonial lands. This tended to perpetuate an obsolescent system which acted as a brake on more modern developments in the monarchy. It was on this system that the reforms of

Joseph II foundered. The imperial office was also a burden on Austria's position in the nineteenth century.[26]

Furthermore, a high aristocratic court as the focus of government and a legal system which inevitably tended to conserve an Estatal society were bound to support each other. Here a further aspect of development became evident. The political organisation of the empire conserved an old, corporative social order, though not in the sense of absolute rigidity. The judicial practice of the Imperial Privy Council and the Imperial Court of Chancery was quite capable of channelling developments, but its effect was always to stabilise the system. German freedom was a corporative freedom. The imperial association thus slowed down the process of territorial concentration and protected the small domains in their direct dependence on the empire, with all the economic and social consequences entailed by the large number of courts and governments, the small size of each economic unit and fragmentation, though there was admittedly a gain in cultural diversity. In the large territories the emperor acted as a restraint against absolutism.

Of course, he could not halt unconditionally the development of the large territorial states. They continued to develop the secular tendencies towards bureaucratisation, concentration, the preservation of peace, and the provincial police force, and fewer and fewer were able to keep pace. Since the late seventeenth century the financial crises of the imperial cities, the small territories and the knights made it plain that their existence was by now only stabilised from outside, that the emperor and the imperial law protected them from the clutches of the larger states. On the other hand, a group of medium-sized states had evolved in which the emperor's influence was comparatively small, and dwindling. This had resulted in a gap which put an increasing strain on the structure of the empire.

Another factor was more important for German history. The conservation of the old corporative order was a direct consequence of the foundation of a distinctive legal system. This led to relative immobility, above all in the conflicts between princes and Estates. It was quite evident from the civil disturbances in the imperial cities that, although repeated attempts were made to clear up the conflicts, to channel them off, and even to carry out a certain amount of cautious social modernisation, as the basic structures remained constant the causes were not eradicated. This did not always entail economic weakness: no city was so plagued by constitutional conflicts as Frankfurt (with the result that the Viennese Imperial Privy Council was almost part of its government), but the city was economically very stable. Nevertheless, the fact remains that the judicial system of the empire conserved not only an obsolescent political order, but also an obsolescent social order, which in the end was overdue for modernisation. That this system of Estates was no longer able to cope with the onslaught of the French Revolution was obvious. The development of the old empire was conceivable, but by 1800 it had finally reached its limits, so that the question which the age of Napoleon posed was how this politically highly sensitive sphere could be differently organised.

In the main, certainly, the empire could not prevent the modernisation of the more important and larger territories, or the special development of Prussia. Yet it must be recognised as a fundamental fact of German history that the expiring empire passed on to the nineteenth century a multitude of old corporative traditions.

All in all, the question of the reality of the empire in German history could be answered in the affirmative, at any rate from one point of view – that of its utopian character. But the question of utopia has another aspect. This has its roots in the old empire itself, in the Roman law's exaltation of a ruler, whose power was inherently limited by the Estates, as an absolute monarch, which continually led to discrepancies and has skewed a proper understanding of the reality of the empire to this day. Much more problematic, however, is the elevation of the concept of the universal empire since the age of Romanticism. It became dangerous to fill in this framework with an expansionist nationalist content and to embark on expansionist German policies in the footsteps of Barbarossa and Charles V. Herein lies the other, dangerous, utopia of the old empire, the problems raised by proceeding from justifiable pride in national history to staking a claim to Europe. Paradoxically, though, precisely such a view of the reality of the late empire has resulted in a considerable undervaluation of it. In many quarters experience of this cult of the empire seems to have aroused mistrust of the phenomenon itself. I have endeavoured to show that the analysis of the imperial body is no easy task. The conceptual difficulties involved should not, however, deter the historian, but rather should serve as a challenge to him to attempt a dispassionate analysis of the old empire, for without one there is no understanding German history.

Notes

1. Unabridged version of a lecture given in June 1983 at the Humboldt University, East Berlin, with the title 'Das Alte Reich – Utopie oder Wirklichkeit'. I am grateful to Manfred Rudersdorf (Tübingen) for assistance.
2. K. O. Freiherr von Aretin, 'Die Lehensordnungen in Italien im 16. und 17. Jahrhundert und ihre Auswirkungen auf die europäische Politik. Ein Beitrag zur Geschichte des europäischen Spätfeudalismus', in H. Weber (ed.), *Politische Ordnungen und soziale Kräfte im Alten Reich* (Wiesbaden, 1980), pp. 53–84.
3. Cf. most recently Heinrich Lutz, *Zwischen Habsburg und Preußen. Deutschland 1815–1866* (Berlin, 1985); W. D. Gruner, 'Die deutschen Einzelstaaten und der Deutsche Bund. Zum Problem der "nationalen" Integration in der Frühgeschichte des Deutschen Bundes am Beispiel Bayerns und der süddeutschen Staaten', in A. Kraus (ed.), *Land und Reich, Stamm und Nation. Festgabe für Max Spindler*, vol. III (Munich, 1984), pp. 19–36.
4. Volker Press, 'Das römisch-deutsche Reich – ein politisches System in verfassungs- und sozialgeschichtlicher Fragestellung', in Grete Klingenstein and Heinrich Lutz (eds), *Spezialforschung und 'Gesamtgeschichte'. Beispiele und Methodenfragen zur Geschichte der frühen Neuzeit* (Vienna, 1981), pp. 221–42.
5. See Volker Press, *Altes Reich, Rheinbund, Deutscher Bund – Kontinuitäten und Neuanfänge* (forthcoming).
6. Peter Moraw and Volker Press, 'Probleme der Sozial- und Verfassungsgeschichte des Heiligen Römischen Reiches im Späten Mittelalter und in der Frühen Neuzeit', *Zeitschrift für Historische Forschung*, II (1975), pp. 95–108; Press, 'Römisch-deutsches Reich'; Moraw, 'Wesenszüge der "Regierung" und "Verwaltung" des deutschen Königs im Reich (ca. 1350–1450)', in Werner Paravicini and K. F. Werner (eds), *Histoire comparée de l'administration (XIVe–XVIIIe siècle)* (Beihefte der *Francia*, IX) (Zürich/Munich, 1980), pp. 149–67; Moraw, 'Die Verwaltung des Königtums und des Reiches und ihre Rahmenbedingungen', in K. G. A. Jeserich *et al.* (eds), *Deutsche Verwaltungsgeschichte*, vol. I: *Vom Spätmittelalter bis zum Ende des Reiches* (Stuttgart, 1983), pp. 22–53; Moraw, 'Fragen der deutschen Verfassungsgeschichte im Späten Mittelalter', *Zeitschrift für Historische Forschung*, IV (1977), pp. 59–101.
7. Idem, 'Landesgeschichte und Reichsgeschichte im 14. Jahrhundert', *Zeitschrift für westdeutsche Landesgeschichte*, III (1977), pp. 175–91.
8. Volker Press, 'Die Erblande und das Reich von Albrecht II. bis Karl VI. (1438–1740)', in R. A. Kann and F. Prinz (eds), *Deutschland und Österreich. Ein bilaterales Geschichtsbuch* (Vienna/Munich, 1980), pp. 44–88.
9. O. von Gschließer, *Der Reichshofrat. Bedeutung und Verfassung, Schicksal und Besetzung einer obersten Reichsbehörde von 1559–1806* (Vienna, 1942); R. Smend, *Das Reichskammergericht*, part I (Weimar, 1911).

10. R. J. W. Evans, 'The Austrian Habsburgs. The Dynasty as a Political Institution', in A. G. Dickens (ed.), *The Courts of Europe. Politics, Patronage and Royalty 1400–1800* (London, 1977), pp. 122–40.

11. Peter Moraw, 'Von offener Verfassung zu gestalteter Verdichtung. Das Reich im späten Mittelalter 1250–1490', in *Propyläen Geschichte Deutschlands*, vol. III (Berlin, 1985).

12. The Imperial Diet is now at the centre of lively debate. Cf. most recently Heinz Angermeier, *Die Reichsreform 1410–1555. Die Staatsproblematik in Deutschland zwischen Mittelalter und Gegenwart* (Munich, 1984); Helmut Neuhaus, *Reichsständische Repräsentationsformen im 16. Jahrhundert* (Schriften zur Verfassungsgeschichte, XXXIII) (Berlin, 1982); Volker Press, 'Der deutsche Reichstag in der frühen Neuzeit', *Historische Zeitschrift* (forthcoming).

13. Anton Schindling, 'Die Anfänge des Immerwährenden Reichstags zu Regensburg. Ständevertretung und Staatskunst im barocken Reich' (Habilitationsschrift, University of Würzburg, 1982).

14. Volker Press, 'Bayern, Österreich und das Reich in der frühen Neuzeit', *Verhandlungen des historischen Vereins für Oberpfalz*, CXX (1980), pp. 493–519; idem, 'Schwaben zwischen Bayern, Österreich und dem Reich 1486–1805', in Pankraz Fried (ed.), *Probleme der Integration Ostschwabens in den bayerischen Staat. Bayern und Wittelsbach in Ostschwaben* (Sigmaringen, 1982), pp. 17–78.

15. Angermeier, *Reichsreform*. Cf. also Peter Moraw, 'Die Reichsreform und ihr verwaltungsgeschichtliches Ergebnis', in Jeserich, *Verwaltungsgeschichte*, vol. I, pp. 58–65.

16. Hermann Wiesflecker, *Kaiser Maximilian I. Das Reich, Österreich und Europa an der Wende zur Neuzeit*, 4 vols (Munich, 1971–81).

17. Peter Moraw, 'Versuch über die Entstehung des Reichstags', in Weber, *Politische Ordnungen*, pp. 1–36.

18. Horst Rabe, *Reichsbund und Interim. Die Verfassungs- und Religionspolitik Karls V. und der Reichstag zu Augsburg 1546/48* (Cologne, 1971); Volker Press, 'Die Bundespläne Kaiser Karls V. und die Reichsverfassung', in Heinrich Lutz and E. Müller-Luckner (eds), *Das römisch-deutsche Reich im politischen System Karls V.* (Munich/Vienna, 1982), pp. 55–106.

19. J. Kretzschmar, *Der Heilbronner Bund 1632–1635* (3 vols, Lübeck, 1922).

20. F. Dickmann, *Der Westfälische Friede*, 5th edn (Münster, 1985); Anton Schindling, 'Der Westfälische Frieden und der Reichstag', in Weber, *Politische Ordnungen*, pp. 113–53.

21. K. O. Freiherr von Aretin, 'Kaiser Josef I. zwischen Kaisertradition und österreichischer Großmachtpolitik', *Historische Zeitschrift*, CCXV (1972), pp. 529–606; Ch. W. Ingrao, *Joseph I. Der vergessene Kaiser* (Graz/Vienna/Cologne, 1982).

22. F. Wagner, *Kaiser Karl VII. und die großen Mächte 1740–1745* (Stuttgart, 1938); Volker Press, 'Das wittelsbachische Kaisertum Karls VII. Voraussetzungen von Entstehung und Scheitern', in Kraus, *Land und Reich*, vol. II, pp. 201–34; P. C. Hartmann, *Karl Albrecht – Karl VII. Glücklicher Kurfürst. Unglücklicher Kaiser* (Regensburg, 1985).

23. K. O. Freiherr von Aretin, *Heiliges Römisches Reich 1776–1806. Reichsverfassung und Staatssouveränität* (2 vols, Wiesbaden, 1967).
24. Idem, *Bayerns Weg zum souveränen Staat. Landstände und konstitutionelle Monarchie 1714–1818* (Munich, 1976), pp. 64–119; P. J. Bernard, *Joseph II and Bavaria. Two Eighteenth-Century Attempts at German Unification* (The Hague, 1965); Volker Press, 'Bayern am Scheideweg. Die Reichspolitik Kaiser Josephs II. und der Bayerische Erbfolgekrieg 1777–1779', in Pankraz Fried and W. Ziegler (eds), *Festschrift für Andreas Kraus zum 60. Geburtstag* (Kallmünz, 1982), pp. 277–307.
25. This reference is taken from the *Magisterarbeit* by Horst Carl, 'Die Aachener Mäkelei 1785–1792. Konfliktregelungsmechanismen im Alten Reich' (Magisterarbeit, University of Tübingen, 1983).
26. E. Wangermann, *Von Joseph II. zu den Jakobinerprozessen* (Vienna/Frankfurt am Main, 1960).

4 *'Comme représentant nostre propre personne'* – The Regency Ordinances of Charles V as a Historical Source

Horst Rabe and Peter Marzahl

I. THE REGENCIES OF CHARLES V[1] IN THE POLITICAL SYSTEM OF CHARLES V

No Holy Roman emperor after him – and few before – held such extensive claims to rule as did Charles V. These claims did not represent a coherent spatial complex; they included a multitude of countries, even leaving aside the American possessions. In kind and in intensity, the emperor's authority varied between countries as it depended upon constitutional arrangements, and on social, economic and ecclesiastical conditions. This absence of homogeneity within his dominions was one of the fundamental problems the emperor had to face, since his goals were not limited to the simple accumulation of claims to rule over countries with such diverse historical trajectories. In the emperor's view all his domains existed to serve his goals, the foremost of which were the restoration of his Burgundian inheritance, dominance over Italy as the key to imperial hegemony in Europe, and the internal reform of the Roman Church. A task of this magnitude would raise uncommonly difficult problems of co-ordination and communication; the attempt to solve them, through appropriate institutions and procedures, constituted a fundamental aspect of the political system of Charles V.[2]

Co-ordination and communication within this political system posed organisational and technical problems; the profoundly divergent structures and interests within the emperor's dominions, however, exceeded mere technical solutions. The emperor's frequent enforced absence from his realm, a consequence of its territorial fragmentation, added another dimension, as important as these divergences but less visible to us. Rule was as yet no abstract concept, no less than in the Middle Ages; it was not a body of rights and duties that could be delegated easily, independent of persons, least of all to an anonymous administration. Rule meant the concrete and personal demonstration of political power and authority. Therefore a ruler's absence potentially enfeebled or even endangered his authority, whether *vis-à-vis* aristocratic factions or *vis-à-vis* the Estates.[3] Other less traditional concepts of rule did exist, closer to the institutional shape of the modern state. These concepts go back to the Middle Ages and in the sixteenth century they began to be accepted in theoretical and practical terms.[4] And yet, even in relatively modern polities, the actual presence of the ruler remained a political fact of the utmost importance. Substitute arrangements were far too often uncertain and remained insufficient in character.

Charles' first years of rule in Spain demonstrated the shortcomings of any substitute arrangements. The specific purpose of his trip there in 1517 had been to secure his rule; only by appearing in person could he claim his inheritance. His renewed absence, when his coronation as newly-elected emperor required his presence in Germany, was one of the causes of the revolt of the *Comuneros* in 1520. When leaving Spain again in 1529, as he was entrusting the empress with the regency, the emperor took great care to justify his departure in detail and in public.[5] By contrast, the Low Countries never experienced as volatile a situation as did Castile. Here Chièvres had taken matters in hand after Charles had been declared of age in 1515, against the background of Margaret of Austria's difficult first regency. Margaret, who had been appointed regent after the death of Philip the Fair, had been unable to keep the turbulent aristocracy in check and instead had become an instrument of its factions.[6] With good cause, then, a ruler's absence was regarded with misgivings. Queen Mary of Hungary's powers of regency of 1531 reflected this fact, justifying the emperor's departure by pointing out the great and urgent affairs of Christendom and regretting the impossibility '*de faire continuelle residence . . . selon toutesfois que bien seroit nostre inclination pour la singulière affection que leur portons*'.[7] As regards the Austrian inheritance, the conflicts that broke out after Emperor Maximilian's death in 1519, whether caused by rivalries between the princely administration in Upper and Lower Austria or by revolutionary popular movements in the Tyrol, show the importance of the heir's presence in a situation of political and social unrest, a situation made worse by the uncertainty about who was to be the actual heir.[8]

Examples that demonstrate the weight of the ruler's personal presence can easily be multiplied; one taken from Charles' political correspondence may suffice here: in 1529 Margaret and Ferdinand insisted on Charles' coming to Germany; otherwise it would be impossible to solve the pressing problems, as in the matter of religion.[9]

The necessity of his presence in the countries he ruled represented a fundamental problem for the emperor's political system. A solution, or at least an approximation to it, could only consist in creating such institutions as could compensate for this fundamental defect – the lack of his personal presence. In practice this meant that the regimes to be instituted during his absence had to reflect his constitutional position as far as possible, both in their competence and in their place within a country's political structure; the regent had to appear as the ruler's *alter ego*.[10] And yet, despite the grant of authority required by a regency, the emperor had to retain his superior power of decision. How would he otherwise have been able to maintain the coherence of his policies that spanned Europe and beyond, and the integration of his countries into a cohesive political system?

To design a satisfactory political framework between these mutually conflicting demands was an extremely delicate task that could be accomplished only through a well-balanced compromise between the emperor's interests and those of his countries. During his reign the emperor nearly achieved this feat of squaring the political circle, an achievement also to the credit of the regents and the leading counsellors. Yet such a durable solution had not been in sight from the very beginning. Instead, the first years were characterised by a high degree of uncertainty and by serious failures in running the government through regencies.

The situation in the Low Countries had been handled with relative ease, perhaps because of the failure of Margaret's first regency which had been unable to prevail over the foreign-oriented factions of the nobility. It was this very experience that caused the energetic action of Chièvres who, after Charles' accession, managed to convert the fractious noblemen into the ruler's clients, thus basing his neutral foreign policy on general agreement. The policy's success became evident after Charles' departure in 1517, when the *conseil privé* functioning as a council of regency performed acceptably even though only a few years earlier it had been the focus of factional struggles.[11]

Margaret's position in this council under the presidency of Carondelet and on the same footing as everyone else, created a problem of
sorts: as the emperor's daughter, she could not easily be accommo-
dated as she was indisputably the highest ranking member.[12] Margaret's perhaps inevitable political degradation could easily have
become the cause of renewed conflict; her fundamental loyalty helped
avoid the danger. The death of Carondelet in the early summer of
1518 helped Margaret to regain her position;[13] by July 1519, when
Charles formally appointed her '*régente et gouvernante*' of the Low
Countries,[14] she had achieved her aim. A milestone had been reached.
Henceforth the political fortunes of Charles, especially as they transcended individual countries, were secured in dynastic fashion, a
solution that was to become the model for the emperor's other
regencies.

Substantial problems that should not be minimised remained under
Margaret's second and third regency. Mary of Hungary, Margaret's
successor and niece, found occasion to describe the situation she
encountered in the Low Countries in highly critical terms many years
later in a letter to her nephew Philip.[15] The emperor himself used
Mary's installation as regent in 1531 to reorganise the central councils
of the Low Countries, in particular their relation to the regent.[16]
While it was not until then that the regency of the Low Countries
acquired its final shape, the basic outline was settled by 1519.

Finding a successful formula for the government of Spain by
regency was a drawn-out process. At the beginning of Charles' reign
such a formula had seemed available, but the revolt of the *Comuneros*
demonstrated its inadequacy. After his return to Spain the emperor
first had to re-establish his own authority before he could consider the
problems surrounding a regency and their possible solutions. Clearly,
such considerations had been largely absent during Charles' first stay
in Spain.[17]

Why did the emperor and his advisers think that to entrust Adrian
of Utrecht, a Fleming and hence a foreigner, with the government of
Spain would suffice to keep the country under control once the
emperor had departed? It was a costly illusion, the consequences of
which were to shape Charles' attitudes toward the government of
Spain until the end of his reign. After the death of Ferdinand the
Catholic, Spain had been governed by Cardinal Ximénez de Cisneros,
in the name of Charles. His powers were so extensive as to be
practically unlimited, certainly not by any formal restrictions or
general instructions. For five months, in fact, the cardinal had

exercised power in Spain without possessing any formal empowering instrument and only by virtue of Ferdinand's will and Charles' consent.[18]

Cardinal Ximénez de Cisneros' regency was a success. It was easy to take this for granted and to see only the defects of the regency, the cardinal's independence of the court in Brussels and the difficulties the lack of co-ordination between the two parallel governments had created.[19] There appeared to be no reason why this success should not be repeated, especially since Adrian had been associated with the cardinal's government. The new regent's powers would have to be circumscribed in adequate fashion, with the previous regency and the contemporaneous experience in the Low Countries in mind, so as to keep control strictly in the hands of the emperor's distant government.[20] Not even during the crisis of the revolt when the Admiral and the Constable of Castile were made co-regents together with Adrian were these restrictions appreciably modified. When they perforce ignored them, their actions were taken as proof of the dangers posed by the grandees' participation in government.[21]

Had it been the grandees who had dissipated the crown's authority, or was this the regencies' doing? In a piece of unsolicited advice sent to Charles in 1522, upon his return, the Admiral of Castile disputed these contentions and placed the blame on the king's government.[22] When he began his rule, the admiral reminded the emperor, he was loved by all, and his coming was so much desired that Cardinal Cisneros governed the country, even without title to do so, while the king was still in Flanders. And even though there were many causes of trouble in the country, it held together.

> And if there was a change, it was on account of Your government ... now Your Majesty is at the same point [again]. You must turn Your eyes here, understand what needs to be done and know those who proffer good advice or bad ... Your Majesty will know that You are the Emperor and that perforce You will have to move around the world; what behooves You is to be loved more than to be feared.

For the modern reader the word love in this context needs to be translated to mean the result of a carefully calculated system of rewards administered by the emperor. The substance of authority resided in this 'love'. To regain it would take time and effort.

The emperor heeded the advice even though he may not have needed it any more. For the next seven years he stayed in the peninsula, rebuilding royal authority and fashioning the arrangements that would in the future allow him to depart with tranquillity and with the assurance that his commands would be obeyed.

The emperor's first priority was to create beyond his own person a dynastic presence that would support his rule instead of endangering it. It was Charles' marriage in 1526 and the birth of an heir a year later that secured the dynasty's hold over Spain. Its hold was reinforced by Charles' reorganising the government of Spain into a coherent framework; the work of an expanded congeries of councils was co-ordinated by the emerging state secretariat.[23] This reorganisation in itself was not enough to solve the problems posed by the extension of the emperor's regime over so many individual countries. A more coherent internal organisation might even make these countries less amenable to direction from outside. How then were policy choices to be discussed and to be sifted beyond their established confines? Neither a simple superimposition of governing institutions would do, nor their amalgamation, as could be seen from the preceding years' experience. The answer found would determine the future shape of the emperor's regime.

Two views clashed here, that of the Grand Chancellor Gattinara and that of the Castilians, foremost among whom were the royal councillor Lorenzo Galíndez de Carvajal and the secretary Francisco de los Cobos. The chancellor's proposals amounted to a more coherent organisation of the emperor's government at the top, with the Chancellor and the Council of State exercising a co-ordinating function beyond individual councils and countries.[24] Galíndez de Carvajals's proposals, adumbrated at the same time as Gattinara's in response to questions about the future organisation of a regency for Spain and its relation to the emperor's government, foreshadowed the solution that was actually later adopted.[25] Instead of distinguishing between levels of importance, with matters of policy to go to the Emperor's Council of State, these proposals relied on a clear separation of functions and competencies between a regent, the councils assigned to him, and the emperor's sphere. The emperor's visit to his realms of the Crown of Aragon in 1528 provided the opportunity to test in practice how a systematic separation of functions and competencies between a regency and the emperor would work. After extensive preparations that included the setting up of her court along Castilian lines, the Empress Isabella was entrusted with the government of Castile on a trial basis.[26] The success of this experiment allowed the emperor to plan his voyage to Italy in earnest. The adequacy of these arrangements was tested again in 1529, between the emperor's departure from Toledo in March and his actual departure for Italy in July, with the business of government handed over to Isabella in instalments. This was a proceeding which resembled the way in which authority over the Low Countries had been parcelled out to Margaret ten years earlier.

The emperor's early policies for running the empire through a regent failed less conspicuously than they had in Spain but the consequences were nearly as grave. For his Austrian dominions the Emperor Maximilian had established a governing body (*Oberstes Regiment*) in Augsburg that had been confirmed in its position by Charles, in the name also of his brother Ferdinand. This body was neither capable of settling conflicts with the Estates nor of dealing with regional revolts in Austria and the Tyrol. Matters improved only after Ferdinand had taken over the Austrian duchies as independent ruler, conceded to him in piecemeal fashion by Charles between 1521 and 1522.[27] In territories such as the Tyrol, where Ferdinand ostensibly served only as Charles' lieutenant, he ran into considerable difficulties. As a mere stand-in for his brother, his authority was deprecated.[28] It was in fact a grotesque situation: the agreement of 7 February 1522 had conceded the rule over these western territories of the Austrian inheritance to Ferdinand with the proviso of keeping this a secret for six years, or at least until Charles' coronation by the pope.[29] Ferdinand's governorship was hardly more than a facade with the purpose of maintaining the fiction of the emperor's rule. The construction proved untenable – creditors such as the Fuggers had to be told anyway – and Ferdinand soon began to press for an abrogation of the secrecy clause. By 1525 he was successful; in February the emperor publicly conceded the whole Austrian inheritance to Ferdinand,[30] a concession the more easily made as these countries remained within the emperor's political system, tied to it by Ferdinand's sense of obligation towards the *maison d'Autriche*, which he regarded as self-evident.

The problem posed by the emperor's absence from Germany was a question that was initially resolved in a wholly unsatisfactory manner. It was not until the emperor's second stay in Germany, when things had fallen into shape in Spain and were about to in the Netherlands, that a durable institutional framework was found, with Ferdinand's election as King of the Romans. In the tradition of imperial law, the institution of the imperial vicar *absente rege* existed, as a device to deal with the king's absence. The imperial vicar was subject to imperial mandates, yet the king could not select him at will. The Elector Palatine held the claim to this office in imperial tradition.[31] Charles in fact did not respect the claim, because he may have feared that the elector would do little to advance the emperor's goals, both dynastic and universal. Since the office had been a frequent focus of opposition to imperial policy in the past, the emperor looked for alternatives. In 1521 he made his brother Ferdinand his lieutenant in the empire; the Count Palatine Frederick, the elector's younger brother, was selected as deputy. The Estates of the Empire assembled at Worms agreed to the arrangement and the elector had to content himself with a formal reservation concerning his rights.[32]

Making Ferdinand his lieutenant did not imply that the emperor could make rules for the institution at will in order to suit his political purposes. As lieutenant Ferdinand was nothing more than the chairman of the *Reichsregiment*. Charles had been forced to agree to the establishment of this institution in his election capitulations of 1519; at the diet in Worms in 1521 it had been given its final shape. The institution of the *Reichsregiment* had originally been a part of the movement for imperial reform at the turn of the century, representing the Estates' attempt to impose their constitutional predominance over the emperor.[33] Such a notion was far removed from the way the *Reichsregiment* was designed in 1521, since it was to function only in the emperor's absence, rather than as a permanent institution. From the emperor's view this was quite obnoxious as he could not determine how affairs were to be handled during his absence and had to grant the Estates a decisive voice in running them. Furthermore Ferdinand, as the emperor's lieutenant, could not claim a superior authority *vis-à-vis* the Estates.[34]

The *Reichsregiment*, itself a potential opposition to the crown, could for its part also run into opposition from groups among the Estates of the empire, regardless of having been designed to represent the common good of the empire. Against such opposition it could not prevail since it depended upon the co-operation of the very Estates that were opposing it. No wonder that the latter years of the decade were years of increasing futility for the institution; upon the emperor's arrival in 1530 it expired without anybody taking much notice. Its positive accomplishments may have been minimal yet there is no doubt that it contributed to the delay in setting up a functioning regency in the empire.[35] The shortcomings of Ferdinand's position as lieutenant and the existence of the *Reichsregiment* kept the emperor from pursuing a coherent policy in and with Germany during the decade of the 1520s.

The absence of such a policy was a fact of great historical relevance. Recent research on the Reformation has emphasised that the emperor's absence was an essential precondition for the success of the Reformation in establishing territorially based churches, for the movement of the imperial knights, and even for the Peasants' War.[36] This judgement is not in itself false but must be modified: the decisive factor was not simply the emperor's absence but his inability to establish a functioning and effective regency for the empire.

One legitimate possibility existed for making Ferdinand Charles' deputy in the empire: to designate him the emperor's successor by electing him as King of the Romans. Such a proceeding would have dealt with the dissolution of the *Reichsregiment*, which had been in the offing since 1523: it would also have disposed of the Palatine claim to the post of imperial vicar since the imperial constitutional tradition had established the precedence of the designated successor over such claims. It does seem that Charles at their talks in Brussels in early 1522 had signalled his agreement in principle to Ferdinand's succession by having him elected as King of the Romans.[37] Since November 1522 Ferdinand had been pressing for the implementation of the project.[38] Within the empire there were voices favourable to this solution, even arguing that this would mean getting rid of the *Reichsregiment*.[39] There was also opposition. Most importantly, Charles himself had for years done nothing to advance the matter. In his testament of 22 May 1522 he did designate Ferdinand as his universal heir and successor in case of his death without issue, endowing him also with a series of privileges normally reserved for the king.[40] Yet his fundamental position during the 1520s was that he would push for Ferdinand's election only after he himself had been crowned emperor by the pope. In 1530 things fell into place. The situation in Germany demanded the emperor's personal intervention; *en route* there he was crowned emperor in Bologna; Ferdinand's election was then moved up on the agenda, with an appropriate financial outlay; early in 1531 Ferdinand was elected king. Almost at this same moment Ferdinand also became the absent emperor's deputy alone, without the shackles of the *Reichsregiment*.[41] Ferdinand's regency conformed in its substance to those of Isabella in Spain and Mary in the Low Countries. Notwithstanding Ferdinand's complaints about the restrictions imposed on him,[42] it proved to be a workable and durable solution.

II. POWER – RESTRICTION – INSTRUCTION: THE FORMAL SHAPE OF THE REGENCY ORDINANCES

The term 'regency ordinances' is defined here as the body of rules and regulations promulgated by the emperor for the regency governments of his countries at their inception[43] and for the duration of each regency.[44] The ordinances set down the fundamental rights and duties of the regent or regency council. In addition there commonly were also the powers and ordinances governing the relevant institutions of the territorial administration. This corpus of ordinances did not constitute a homogeneous kind of source; there is no contemporary concept of the 'regency ordinance' as such. Nevertheless, the documents possess an internal coherence based on their specific political function within the system of government of Charles V and as such they exhibit a characteristic structure in formal terms – as a trinity of empowering instrument, instruction and restriction.

This corpus of regency ordinances constitutes a group of sources of respectable dimensions that so far has received little attention from scholars.[45] A listing of all the regulations for the Low Countries which is probably incomplete comprises forty such ordinances; for Spain there are more than 100.[46] A comprehensive analysis of the regencies' functioning as a part of the emperor's political system would have to go beyond these ordinances; simply clarifying the relations between regents and emperor would necessitate consulting the emperor's political correspondence on a broad scale. Furthermore, the regency ordinances constitute a body of normative texts, necessarily at variance with prevailing practice. Nevertheless the ordinances serve to comprehend the essential matrix of imperial government, with the legal and political authority granted to regents on one side and the institutionalised aspects of the emperor's relations with these regencies on the other, modified according to country and yet exhibiting common characteristics. The regency ordinances hardly mirror the emperor's political system as a whole, yet they do allow us to grasp its important structural elements.

The regency ordinances had to address two major tasks, in line with the regencies' political functions: to equip a regent with the plenitude of power sufficient to warrant his functioning as the ruler's *alter ego*; and yet to limit these powers so that neither the emperor's superior authority nor his chance of formulating a coherent policy was endangered. The promulgation of these ordinances also offered the opportunity to clarify through concrete regulations the relation between the regent and the court and administration of 'his' country, thus providing an additional check upon a regency. After some initial false starts the ordinances developed a clearly delineated and differentiated pattern.

Each set of ordinances included the power to conduct the government during the ruler's absence and in his place. Such a power constituted the legal basis for conducting a regency; as such it was indispensable as the legal act of instituting a regent.[47] Such an appointment was a political step of great relevance, not merely an administrative act. This meant that the regent's powers had to take the form of public documents, giving pride of place to an extensive *narratio* justifying the emperor's departure. They tended to lose all procedural elements, and became, as it were, pure instruments of power. The exclusive political relevance of these powers and the intended effect meant that explicit limitations of a regent's authority tended to disappear altogether from these powers. Of course this did not mean that limitations whether expressed in obligatory ties to a territory's administration or reservations of the emperor's authority did not continue to exist; they were merely not included in the regent's power which represented him as the fully-fledged *alter ego* of the ruler in the country concerned.[48] Charles' earliest instruments of government of June 1516, confirming the regency of Cardinal Ximénez de Cisneros in Spain, already conformed to this type of 'pure' power,[49] which is seen more clearly still in Cardinal Adrian's power of May 1520 with the clause '*provea en nuestro nombre y como nos lo podríamos proveer todos y cualesquier oficios y beneficios de los dichos nuestros Reynos*';[50] the later powers for Isabella, Tavera, Philip, Maximilian, Mary, and, finally, Juana all conformed to the pattern thus established.[51]

The picture is less clear when one considers the early powers of government promulgated in the Low Countries or in the empire. When the *conseil privé* was instituted in 1517 as a council of regency for the Low Countries, its powers of government did not include a covering clause that would enable the *conseil privé* to exercise all those rights pertaining to the ruler himself; on the contrary, the listing of limitations upon its authority was more extensive than that stating its positive content; much of the document was taken up by procedural matters concerning the *conseil privé*.[52] This was not an impressive demonstration of confidence. What shone through was rather a strong concern about giving too much leeway to the regency and to Margaret as the former regent. Yet only one year later Margaret's authority was expanded;[53] in July 1519 the emperor formally appointed her '*régente et gouvernante*' of the Low Countries with authority '*de faire, ordonner et commander ... comme nous mesmes ferions et faire pourrions en nostre propre personne*', this time without any procedural matters cluttering the document and without any mention of limitations.[54] This document of 1519 became the model for those of 1520 and 1522, and even for those empowering Queen Mary of Hungary after 1531.[55] The power of government in its 'pure' form had arrived in the Low Countries, earlier even than in Spain.

In the empire, the situation was altogether different. Here the emperor depended upon the co-operation of the Estates of the empire in matters of substance as well as in mere formalities. The ordinances of 1521 instituting the *Reichsregiment* were hence the outcome of a struggle of many months between the emperor and the Estates, in which both sides had attempted to push through their respective claims.[56] In this situation it is hardly surprising that the ordinances would both specify the positive authority and dwell upon its limitations. Regulations concerning its composition, the recruitment of the members and the organisation of the *Regiment* were so extensive since they had been at issue in the preceding negotiations.[57] Even in purely formal terms, the ordinance was a half-hearted compromise, useless as a substitute for the emperor's absence.[58]. Quite different was the power granted by Charles to his brother Ferdinand after he had been elected King of the Romans. There was no mention any more of a *Reichsregiment*. In essence, this was a 'pure' power of the type already established elsewhere. Article V gave Ferdinand

> *nobis et sacro Romano imperio in Germania Superiori subditos omnimoda iurisdictione civili et criminali et quocunque alio mero et mixto imperio cum omnimoda gladii potestate nobis tanquam Romanorum imperatori de iure vel consuetudine pertinenti utatur, fruatur atque ea exerceat et iis uti, frui atque ea exercere valeat.*[59]

The second fundamental type of ordinance concerning the regencies was the instruction. Instructions related to how a regency was to be exercised, in particular to the running of the central administration; they also could summarise series of ordinances with administrative purposes for the benefit of a regent.[60] Instructions were an early feature of the regencies; for 1517 and again for 1520 there were instructions concerning the financial administration of the Low Countries.[61] After 1520, instructions became a constituent part of the regency ordinances in Spain and in the Low Countries; beyond finances they could refer to all spheres of administration. The earliest example of a comprehensive instruction is that for the Low Countries given to Margaret between April and May 1522;[62] it formed part of a general attempt at overhauling the administration; the *instruction particulière* for Mary in 1531 and 1540 followed this established pattern.[63] For Spain the sequence of general regency instructions began in 1520;[64] later on these general instructions[65] were complemented by specific ones for the central governing councils.[66] When Philip was made regent in 1543, Charles added to the instruction *'de la manera que asy en el govierno ... en general os aveys de guyar y governar'* another one *'secreta que sera para vos solo'* that would inform the regent about his councillors' strengths and frailties; in part this instruction resembled a veritable political testament.[67]

At the beginning of Charles' reign there were no instructions for the empire. The ordinance of 1521 instituting the *Reichsregiment* settled fundamental procedures; the emperor could do nothing unilaterally to effect changes or modifications; *ad hoc* negotiations could produce some leeway or, in an extremity, the emperor could intervene directly.[68] As the emperor's lieutenant, Ferdinand could have been given separate instructions but this was not done. For the emperor's part, the business of the empire was dealt with by correspondence. Only after Ferdinand's installation as King of the Romans was he given a set of general instructions that corresponded in general to those for Spain or the Low Countries.[69] An important divergence remained, since the *sommaire mémoire* of 12 February 1531 containing these instructions also dealt with other business. Mainly it included a formal restriction of Ferdinand's power. The content of these instructions was, by comparison, hardly as weighty as the others, some of it being almost trivial.[70]

Instructions were not public documents. Rather than letters patent *'a tous ceux qui ces presentes lettres verront'*, they were internal regulations for the regent and the appropriate administrative bodies.[71] Their political function, in precise contradistinction to the powers of government, consisted in holding the regent to specific procedures, especially in his relations with the administration; beyond this, they were designed to establish the general direction of affairs for a regent's benefit. In practical terms, they amounted to limitations upon a regent's action which remained an internal matter between the emperor and the regent. As limitations they were largely of a kind that the emperor himself would submit to, a fact indicated by the frequently reiterated formula of heeding the rules, just as he, the emperor, was wont to do.[72] The purpose of such proximate identity was to maintain continuity between the ruler and the regent, in their position *vis-à-vis* a country's administration.

Another kind of limitation affected a regent's powers in fundamental fashion. These more far-reaching limitations soon acquired a specific shape of their own. As restrictions they constituted the third type of regency ordinance. It was clear to all concerned that the 'pure' power of regency, as presented to the public, gave a regent more extensive powers than he was supposed to exercise. In practice such a power would have meant that the emperor gave up his right to rule, albeit temporarily, in favour of a regent. As such it was clearly incompatible with the emperor's aims and principles. Instructions could lessen the contradiction; the emperor's political correspondence could serve to co-ordinate the emperor's interests with those of the regent and the territory.[73] Yet to the emperor and to his advisors these precautions must have seemed insufficient. Hence the emperor, in clear contradiction to the powers ostensibly granted, reserved certain matters to himself and made others depend upon his explicit agreement. It was these specific limitations that appear together with the empowering instrument and with the instruction as separate ordinances when Margaret was made regent of the Low Countries and when Adrian was made regent in Spain; from then on they formed a permanent feature of the regency ordinances for Spain.[74] After 1529 they were designated explicitly as '*restriccion*' or as '*restriccion del poder*'.[75]

The restriction, like the instruction, tied down a regent only in relation to the emperor; it was not a public instrument. The difference between the two instruments was occasionally obscured by their formal similarity. The lack of distinction shows through clearly in the *sommaire memoire* for Ferdinand as King of the Romans: Ferdinand himself somewhat mislabelled it as '*moderaciòn del poder*'. In the Low Countries no distinction seems to have been made between instruction and restriction. The restrictions for Margaret of 1519 and 1522 and, it would seem, also that of 1531 for Mary were labelled '*instruction et mémoire*',[76] where the actual instructions of 1522 bore the label '*instruction et ordonnance*' or simply '*instruction*', and those of 1531 and 1540 were labelled '*instruction particulière*'.[77] The vagueness of nomenclature may be the reason why the special significance of these restrictions has as yet hardly been recognised.

The fact that restrictions were not public instruments was neither unimportant nor self-evident. It meant that the emperor, in line with his public grant of authority, had to recognise the validity of a regent's acts, even though they might contradict the restriction. He could, of course, dismiss a regent, but aside from such a radical solution this was obviously a fertile source of conflicts. It may not only have been desirable but even necessary to present a regent as the ruler's *alter ego*, yet to make this presumed identity work as intended the regent's loyalty was required in heeding the limits set by the restrictions. The restriction for Margaret of July 1519, and the peculiar form it took, furnished a telling example of the dilemma and of how it was faced.[78]

After the *conseil privé* had served as council of regency since 1517 with powers and restrictions publicly promulgated, Margaret was appointed '*régente et gouvernante*' of the Low Countries in 1519. Her authority derived from a 'pure' power; this instrument was complemented by an appropriate restriction. But this document was not intended to remain a matter between Margaret and her nephew only. Instead, Margaret had to send Charles a *lettre patente* with the restriction inserted and acknowledged by her. Its publication was held in abeyance for the time being but in case of a conflict it could be published without delay. Such a precaution bordering on mistrust proved to be unnecessary; when Margaret was reappointed in 1522, the emperor acted without requiring an analogous reservation concerning the restriction's publication.

The discussion has shown how the trinity of empowering instrument, instruction and restriction had already acquired its definitive shape during the 1520s. Henceforth its formal structure remained unchanged. The institutional-legal framework of the regime had acquired its appropriate form. One important change did indeed take place after 1531, indicating how much the regencies were tending to become routine arrangements in formal and even in political terms. Ever since his accession the validity of the regency ordinances had been strictly limited to the duration of the emperor's absence. The limitation was abandoned for the first time when Ferdinand was granted his powers of government in 1531.[79] In the Low Countries it ceased to be heeded in the 1540s aided, one may assume, by the continuity represented by Mary's long regency. There are no regency ordinances later than 1540 for Mary[80] though in theory new ones should have been promulgated upon each of Charles' departures, in January 1544, in May 1545, in March 1546 and again in June 1550. That such a renewed grant was indeed deemed necessary, although none had been issued since 1541, was explicitly stated in the ordinance of 8 March 1546 for the *conseil privé* in the management of its affairs.[81] Similarly the ordinance dealing with the Council of Finance of 22 February 1546 was still deemed sufficient in 1554.[82] No *argumentum e silentio* presents clear proof. Nevertheless, one may presume that Mary's regency had become a fact taken for granted by the emperor, the regent, the administration and the country to such an extent that no formal renewal of the ordinances was considered necessary, those already established coming back into force on the emperor's departure, and changes to be made only as changing circumstances might require.[83] Should this conjecture be correct, it would furnish an additional instance of those rationalising and modernising tendencies also observed elsewhere under the emperor's rule.

III.   TOWARDS A POLITICS OF THE EMPEROR'S REGENCIES

The early regencies established under Charles V had been simply superimposed on an existing machinery of government. No adjustments of this machinery were initially considered necessary since regencies were only a stop-gap, not a permanent solution. But even if a more than provisional perspective had existed, the capacity to effect changes in the organisation of government was necessarily limited during the emperor's first years of rule. The early regency ordinances reflected this situation: in so far as they dealt with the organisation of government they tended, as instructions, to codify existing practice. Yet, over the long haul, this was not quite enough. As the regencies changed from being temporary arrangements to becoming permanent fixtures they had to be made more responsive to the emperor's emerging regime. It is with these requirements in mind that we will consider some features of the regencies' organisation in relation to the emperor's regime.

These requirements can be stated succinctly. Foremost was the dilemma posed by the need for a kind of authority that could be delegated and yet be retained. Dynastic authority filled this need, but in itself it was insufficient. The emperor first had to assert his own authority in the manner related by Mary of Hungary who told how Charles had in 1531 devoted himself to restoring the Low Countries' government, 'by putting his hand to everything, reordering justice and finances'.[84] Only the emperor's personal presence and his effective action could establish the substance of this authority. Its semblance could then be granted fully, as power; its reality could be doled out in instalments, as access to patronage. The emperor's early years showed how quickly he had learned to husband authority. With supreme realism and parsimony he administered his capital by hedging and restricting its use by the regents, thereby maintaining his own capacity to reward service and to attract good people to his government.[85] The circumstances of the emperor's rule produced a pronounced need for expert advice that could easily create an impression of dependence upon others. After the years of tutelage under Chièvres the emperor was acutely conscious of the need to keep his own counsel, to be the master of his own decisions. This concern informs the secret instructions of 1543 to his son Philip with their stress on the quality of advice Philip was likely to get from the members of his court.[86] A regent had to be in charge as much as the emperor, or at least appear to be so. And yet, any ruler, especially a regent, had to be protected from precipitate or ill-considered decisions. Therefore the essence of the emperor's regency instructions for Spain resided in two matters: a firm admonition to hew closely to the formalities of the process of consultation in the same way the emperor did; and secondly, the selection of capable councillors to fill the gap left by those he took with him.[87] The selection of these councillors, together with his own and the regents' recognition of their qualities and frailties, was one of the emperor's principal achievements.

What kind of arrangement was capable of managing the increase in business produced by the emperor's regime? The Grand Chancellor's extensive claims to exercise a universal control over the despatch of business had never met the emperor's assent. In his stead Cobos and Granvelle had, by 1530, emerged as those in charge of the emperor's affairs.[88] Cobos' position rested on his having achieved control over the business of a number of councils in Spain in the course of the 1520s. When absent from Spain with the emperor, he farmed out his positions to deputies of his choosing, maintaining an extensive correspondence with them that paralleled the official correspondence between emperor and empress; it thus became an additional and vital channel of information for the management of the Spanish regency.

Granvelle's operation was founded above all upon a vast network of correspondence, but also upon a family clan which merged into a clientele. It was, however, less rooted in the bureaucratic soil of the Low Countries than Cobos' was in Castile's. The role of both men was fundamental in keeping the regencies on course, by running a system of communications that co-ordinated the emperor's flexible regime with the more formal operation of the regencies.

The definition and direction of affairs of state, the decision in matters of grace, continued to belong to the emperor. The regime of regencies was an instrument finely calibrated toward that purpose. The emperor's own government could remain a rudimentary operation that consisted of a limited number of councillors (hardly ever more than four or five on a permanent basis after 1531) who possessed the expertise in handling and despatching the kind of business the emperor had reserved for himself. Yet these councillors were not simply delegates from the emperor's territories, co-opted because of their expertise. They were the core element of the emperor's political system, as collaborators which he had selected for their capacity to serve him.[89]

The regents were the emperor's foremost collaborators. They formed a dynastic network. Other networks were those centred on the secretary Cobos and on Granvelle. The precise configuration and the functioning of these interlocking networks that sustained a framework of communications supporting the emperor's regime still needs to be established properly. The emperor himself in his secret instruction to his son Philip emphasised the factional character of some of these networks. Yet it was their very divisions, actual and potential, that made them valuable for a regime such as the emperor's that depended upon competition to generate a maximum flow of information.

The system of regencies of Charles V confronts us with an apparent paradox. The regencies' organisation displayed an institutionalising and rationalising tendency that seems to be contradicted by the very personal character of the emperor's regime at the centre. Conciliar government at the regencies' level was combined with a kind of cabinet government under the emperor that could produce the advantages of both, as long as the moving spirit at the centre persisted. Personal ties of allegiance and of dependence may have been the essential glue of politics, in the emperor's view, but whenever these looked like failing he could choose to make use of institutional devices, too. It is these that survived him, in the shape of conciliar government promoted by the regencies' establishment.

Notes

1. This paper stems from a research project at the University of Constance on the political correspondence of Charles V. In line with its emphasis the regencies for Spain, the Empire and the Low Countries, rather than those for the Italian and American territories, are discussed.

2. Horst Rabe, 'Elemente neuzeitlicher Politik und Staatlichkeit im politischen System Karls V. Bemerkungen zur spanischen Zentralverwaltung und zur Politischen Korrespondenz des Kaisers', in Heinrich Lutz and E. Müller-Luckner (eds), *Das römisch-deutsche Reich im politischen System Karls V.* (Munich/Vienna, 1982).

3. Peter Moraw, 'Wesenszüge der "Regierung" und "Verwaltung" des deutschen Königs im Reich (ca. 1350–1450)', in Werner Paravicini and K. F. Werner (eds), *Histoire comparée de l'administration (XIVe–XVIIIe siècle)* (Beihefte der *Francia*, IX) (Zürich/Munich, 1980), p. 160 states: '*Anwesenheit oder jedenfalls Erreichbarkeit des Königs und seines Hofes im Reich wurden aber im ganzen Zeitraum und darüberhinaus als notwendig angesehen ... lange Abwesenheit vom Binnenreich wurde scharf kritisiert und führte fast zwangsläufig zur Herrschaftskrise.*'

4. Gerhard Oestreich, *Geist und Gestalt des frühmodernen Staats* (Berlin, 1969); A. Kraus, 'Le développement de la puissance de l'État dans les principautés allemandes (XVIe–XVIIe siècle)', *Revue d'Histoire Diplomatique*, LXXXIX (1975), pp. 298–319.

5. J. H. Elliott, *Imperial Spain 1469–1716* (London, 1963), pp. 132–53. J. M. Jover Zamora, *Carlos V y los Españoles* (Madrid, 1963), pp. 49–72. The regency empowerment of 1529 is published in *Corpus Documental de Carlos V* (cit. *CD*), ed. M. Fernández Alvarez (5 vols, Salamanca, 1973–81), vol. I, pp. 143–7.

6. A. Walther, *Die Anfänge Karls V.* (Leipzig, 1911), pp. 66ff, 150ff.

7. *Recueil des ordonnances des Pays-Bas* (cit. *RO*), 2nd series: *1506–1700*, vol. III, ed. M. J. Lameere (Brussels, 1902), pp. 236–8.

8. Alphons Lhotsky, *Das Zeitalter des Hauses Österreich. Die ersten Jahre der Regierung Ferdinands I. in Österreich (1520–1527)* (Veröffentlichungen der Kommission für Geschichte Österreichs, IV) (Vienna, 1971), p. 81ff. As regards the Empire, Charles had even been forced to promise explicitly to reside there '*sovil muglich'. Deutsche Reichstagsakten, Jüngere Reihe* (cit. *RTA, JR*), vol. I, ed. A. Kluckhohn (Gotha, 1893), p. 876, no. 387.

9. Horst Rabe, 'Befunde und Überlegungen zur Religionspolitik Karls V. am Vorabend des Augsburger Reichstags 1530', in Erwin Iserloh (ed.), *Confessio Augustana und Confutatio. Der Augsburger Reichstag und die Einheit der Kirche* (Münster, 1980), p. 104ff. The high esteem of the emperor's personal presence can still be found in the negotiations concerning an imperial confederation in 1547. Cf. *Correspondenz des Kaisers Karl V.*, ed. K. Lanz (Frankfurt am Main, reprinted 1966), pp. 572–6, no. 586.

10. The *alter nos* formula occurs explicitly in the Brussels treaties of January and February 1522. See W. Bauer, *Die Anfänge Ferdinands I.*

(Vienna, 1907), pp. 247ff, appendices III, IIIa. The terminology changed in the later empowerments, but not the political meaning.

11. A. Henne, *Histoire du règne de Charles-Quint en Belgique*, vol. II (Brussels, 1858), pp. 182ff, 211ff; Walther, *Anfänge*, pp. 127ff.

12. *RO*, vol. I, pp. 578–81. Maximilian's appointment as superintendent of the council of regency did not really deal with the problem, since he was out of the country and was to be called upon in an emergency only.

13. Margaret's authority was considerably expanded in Charles' decree of 24 July 1518, ibid., p. 656f; see also the commentaries in Margaret's correspondence, in A. Walther, *Die burgundischen Zentralbehörden unter Maximilian I. und Karl V.* (Leipzig, 1909), pp. 203–5, appendix 5.

14. *RO*, vol. I, pp. 682–4.

15. Mary to Philip, 7 September 1558, in L. P. Gachard, *Retraite et mort de Charles-Quint au Monastère de Yuste* (Brussels, 1854), pp. 342–52, esp. p. 349.

16. The centrepiece of this reorganisation, the new institution and the reordering of the *conseil d'état, conseil privé* and *conseil des finances* (*RO*, vol. III, pp. 239–54), was to persist to the end of Habsburg rule and even beyond. Henne, *Histoire*, vol. V, pp. 164–72.

17. M. Giménez Fernández, *Bartolomé de las Casas*, vol. II (Seville, 1960), pp. 3–379 contains the most detailed discussion of this stay.

18. Ferdinand's testament is in Alonso de Santa Cruz, *Crónica de los Reyes Católicos* (2 vols, Seville, 1951), vol. II, pp. 342–92. Conde de Cedillo, *El Cardenal Cisneros, gobernador del reino* (3 vols, Madrid, 1921–28), vol. II, pp. 30–1. The power granted to the cardinal in Archivo General de Simancas (cit. AGS), patronato Real (cit. PR) 26, F. 9 (no. 2589) has apparently remained unknown until now.

19. Salustiano de Dios, *El Consejo Real de Castilla (1385–1522)* (Madrid, 1982), pp. 183–5.

20. AGS, PR 26, F. 17. Published in M. Dánvila y Collado, *Historia crítica y documentada de las Comunidades de Castilla* (5 vols, Madrid, 1897–99), vol. I, pp. 335–9, and in L. P. Gachard (ed.), *Correspondance de Charles-Quint et d'Adrien VI* (Brussels, 1859), pp. 237–42. A contemporary copy that also contains the hitherto unknown instruction in Real Academia de Historia, Madrid (cit. RAH), Colección Jesuítas, no. 9–3688, fos. 634v–637v.

21. 'We had the power to punish, but not to reward,' Adrian wrote to the emperor. Quoted in J. Pérez, *La révolution des 'Comunidades' de Castille (1520–1521)* (Bordeaux, 1970), p. 206; see also Dios, *Consejo Real*, p. 193.

22. Dánvila, *Historia crítica*, vol. V, p. 228.

23. Dios, *Consejo Real*, pp. 209–15; Rabe, 'Elemente neuzeitlicher Politik', pp. 167–9.

24. An example of these proposals is given in J. M. Headley, *The Emperor and his Chancellor* (Cambridge, 1983), appendix IV.

25. Fritz Walser, 'Spanien und Karl V. Fünf spanische Denkschriften an den Kaiser', in *Berichte und Studien zur Geschichte Karls V.*, vol. VI (Nachrichten von der Gesellschaft der Wissenschaften zu Göttingen, Phil.-hist. Klasse II) (Berlin, 1932), pp. 163–7.

26. Alonso de Santa Cruz, *Crónica del Emperador Carlos V* (5 vols, Madrid, 1920–22), vol. II, p. 357.

27. Bauer, *Anfänge Ferdinands*, p. 181ff; Lhotsky, *Zeitalter des Hauses Österreich*, pp. 119–31.

28. *Georg Kirchmairs Denkwürdigkeiten seiner Zeit 1519–1533*, ed. Th. G. von Karajan (Fontes rerum Austriacarum, I, 1) (Vienna, 1855), p. 459f. See also Ferdinand's complaint about his subjects: '*N'ont envers nous l'amour et l'affection qu'ilz devroient avoir a leur seigneur naturel, pensant, que ci pour le présent sent en notre gouvernement que si-après pourront devenir en cellui d'aultrui*' (W. Bauer (ed.), *Die Korrespondenz Ferdinands I.*, vol. I: *Familienkorrespondenz bis 1526* (Vienna, 1912), pp. 21–30, esp. p. 22f, no. 21). There were also increasing complaints about Ferdinand and his *entourage*, especially the greedy treasurer Salamanca. Lhotsky, *Zeitalter des Hauses Österreich*, pp. 131–45.

29. Bauer, *Anfänge*, pp. 136–61; the secret treaty of 7 February 1522 ibid., pp. 249–53, appendix IIIa.

30. Ibid., pp. 260–4, appendix VI.

31. W. Hermkes, *Das Reichsvikariat in Deutschland* (Karlsruhe, 1968). In line with the division of the vicariate *vacante imperio* between the Saxon and Palatine Electors, Saxony occasionally claimed it *absente rege* as well.

32. *RTA, JR*, vol. II, ed. A. Wrede (Gotha, 1896), p. 732, no. 101 (6); p. 939, n. 1, no. 239; p. 940, no. 241.

33. Heinz Angermeier, 'Die Reichsregimenter und ihre Staatsidee', *Historische Zeitschrift*, CCXI (1970), pp. 265–315.

34. Yet the emperor's relations with Ferdinand in the early 1520s were not free of suspicion. In 1523 the possibility of appointing another prince as the emperor's lieutenant should the *Reichsregiment* be dissolved was still under consideration; see Bauer, *Anfänge*, p. 206. The emperor's final decision was made on 20 February 1525, ibid., p. 234, n. 1.

35. Bauer, ibid., p. 156, emphasised correctly '*daß es für die Zukunft sowohl des Infanten wie des Regimentes bedeutungsvoll werden sollte, daß Ferdinands Einfluß auf die Politik des Reiches an den Bestand dieser obersten Behörde in Deutschland gekettet war, mit ihr stand und fiel*'.

36. Heinrich Lutz, *Reformation und Gegenreformation*, 2nd edn (Munich, 1982), p. 27.

37. At any rate Ferdinand claimed such an agreement by Charles in his long instruction to Bredam (Bauer, *Korrespondenz*, vol. I, pp. 147–95, esp. p. 161, no. 76).

38. Thus in the instruction for Hemricourt and Salinas, ibid., pp. 21–9, esp. p. 26. For the context of the negotiations about Ferdinand's election see E. Laubach, 'Karl V., Ferdinand und die Nachfolge im Reich', *Mitteilungen des Österreichischen Staatsarchivs*, XXIX (1976), pp. 1–51, and A. Kohler, *Antihabsburgische Politik in der Epoche Karls V. Die reichsständische Opposition gegen die Wahl Ferdinands I. zum römischen König und gegen die Anerkennung seines Königtums* (Schriftenreihe der Historischen Kommission bei der Bayerischen Akademie der Wissenschaften, XIX) (Munich, 1982).

39. For the vote of the imperial free cities cf. H. Baumgarten, *Geschichte Karls V.*, vol. II (Stuttgart, 1888), pp. 306–9; cf. also Laubach, 'Karl V. ... und die Nachfolge im Reich', p. 7. Ferdinand's analogous argument in the instruction for Bredam of June 1524 is in Bauer, *Korrespondenz*, vol. I, p. 158.

40. Lhotsky, *Zeitalter des Hauses Osterreich*, p. 115.

41. H. Wolfram and Chr. Thomas (eds), *Die Korrespondenz Ferdinands I.*, vol. III: *Familienkorrespondenz 1531 und 1532* (Vienna, 1973), pp. 25–40, nos. 457a, 457b. For continuing resistance to Ferdinand as King of the Romans up to 1534 see Kohler, *Antihabsburgische Politik*, pp. 203–373.

42. Chr. Thomas, '"Moderación del poder." Zur Entstehung der geheimen Vollmacht für Ferdinand I. 1531', *Mitteilungen des Österreichischen Staatsarchivs*, XXVII (1974), pp. 101–40.

43. During the first years of Charles V's rule fundamental changes in the content of the ordinances occurred during the period of regency itself: in Spain by the appointment of the Constable and the Admiral of Castile as co-regents with Adrian (22 September 1520, *CD*, vol. I, p. 83f); in the Low Countries when the council of regency established in 1517 was remodelled in favour of Margaret in 1518 (24 July 1510, *RO*, vol. I, p. 656f; 1 July 1519, ibid., pp. 682–4). These changes reflect the uncertainties characteristic of the early regencies. Later on, modifications amounted usually only to *ad hoc* amplifications of powers to mortgage or sell crown domains in the face of acute financial distress: these have largely remained unpublished. For the Low Countries see the ordinances of 4 May 1536 and 13 July 1554 in Michel Baelde, 'Onuitgegeven dokumenten betreffende de zestiende-eeuwse Collaterale raden', *Bulletin de la Commission Royale d'Histoire*, CXXXI (1965), pp. 141–52, 196–8, as well as the Spanish powers of 16 January 1530 and 18 September 1552, *CD*, vol. I, pp. 195–7; vol. III, p. 472f.

44. See below, pp. 90–2.

45. Practically no work, either chronological or comparative, seems to have been done on this topic, except in part for M. Fernández Alvarez, 'Las instrucciones políticas de los Austrias Mayores', *Spanische Forschungen der Görres-Gesellschaft*, XXIII (1967), pp. 171–88.

46. Many of these pieces are unpublished, while the existence of others can only indirectly be established. Mary's power for the Low Countries in 1540 seems not to have survived, but that such a power was granted is evident from specific references to it, e.g. in the *instruction particulière* of 14 October 1540 and in the ordinance for the *conseil d'état* of 16 December 1540 (Baelde, 'Onuitgegeven dokumenten', pp. 161–7, 167–71).

47. For the tacit abandonment of this principle, see below, p. 93.

48. Strongly formulated versions can already be found in Maximilian's power granted to Mary as regent of the Low Countries of 18 March 1509 '*comme représentant nostre personne*', *RO*, vol. I, pp. 79–81. This document already represents in formal terms the type of 'pure' power.

49. See above, n. 18.

50.   18 May 1520. AGS, PR 26, F. 17. Unsatisfactorily published versions in Dánvila, *Historia crítica*, vol. I, pp. 335–9 and Gachard, *Correspondance*, pp. 237–42.

51.   A special feature of these Spanish ordinances was the existence of additional powers which allowed the regent to exercise specific rights pertaining to the crown such as the administration of the knightly orders, war and peace negotiations, or the sale of crown domains, in the case of the emperor's capture. The general powers have largely been published in the *Corpus Documental*; the special powers, still unpublished, are in AGS, PR 26.

52.   *RO*, vol. I, pp. 578–81.

53.   Ibid., p. 656f.

54.   Ibid., pp. 682–4.

55.   Ibid., vol. II, p. 26f; pp. 167–9; vol. III, p. 236. The archival sequence demonstrates that the earlier powers served as the model for the later ones. See Haus-, Hof- und Staatsarchiv, Vienna (cit. HHSA), Belgien PA 1/2, fos. 42r–44v.

56.   *RTA, JR*, vol. II, pp. 173–232.

57.   Ibid., pp. 222–32.

58.   There is also the curious document of 20 February 1525 in which the emperor makes Ferdinand his lieutenant in the empire in the case of the dissolution of the *Reichsregiment*, Bauer, *Anfänge*, p. 234, n. 1. Such a lieutenancy would most certainly have encountered the resistance of the Estates, in particular that of the Elector Palatine as potential imperial vicar *absente rege*.

59.   Wolfram/Thomas, *Korrespondenz* (see n. 41), vol. III, pp. 25–33, esp. p. 28f, no. 457a. Article 22 implied a kind of limitation: reserving the right of future changes was obvious enough in itself, but not so obvious as to be included in the empowerment; those for the Low Countries and Spain dispensed with it.

60.   The *instruction particulière* of 7 October 1531 for Mary is an especially characteristic example, as it accompanies the three ordinances of 1 October 1531 for the *conseil privé*, the *conseil d'état* and the *conseil des finances*. *RO*, vol. III, pp. 239–54, 260f.

61.   The '*ordonnance et instruction*' of 18 August 1517 is in *RO*, vol. I, pp. 586–9, that of 19 October 1520 in ibid., vol. II, pp. 32–6.

62.   K. Lanz (ed.), *Actenstücke und Briefe zur Geschichte Kaiser Karls V.* (Monumenta Habsburgica, 2nd sect., vol. I) (Vienna, 1853), pp. 92–100. The dating of this piece to the year 1519 is erroneous. For its correct dating see Horst Rabe, Heide Stratenwerth and Christian Thomas (eds), 'Stückverzeichnis zum Bestand Belgien PA des Haus-, Hof- und Staatsarchiv Wien', part I, *Mitteilungen des Österreichischen Staatsarchivs*, XXIX (1976), pp. 437–93, esp. p. 453 (for no. 87).

63.   *RO*, vol. III, p. 260f; Baelde 'Onuitgegeven dokumenten', pp. 161–7.

64.   For this unpublished and hitherto unknown instruction for Adrian see above, n. 20.

65.   No such instruction seems to have been given to Mary, daughter of Charles, in 1550, aside from her empowerment, AGS, PR 26, F. 113.

Possibly the instruction for Maximilian and Mary of 29 September 1548 (*CD*, vol. III, pp. 31–6) was still considered valid.

66. When installing Philip as regent of Spain in 1543 the emperor promulgated separate instructions '*para los de la hacienda*', for the *contadores mayores*, for the council of the Indies, the council of the military orders and the council of Castile. F. de Laiglesia, *Estudios históricos 1515–1555*, 2nd edn, vol. I (Madrid, 1918), pp. 50ff.

67. Karl Brandi, 'Die Testamente und politischen Instruktionen Karls V., insbesondere diejenigen des Jahres 1543/44', in *Berichte und Studien zur Geschichte Karls V.*, vol. XII (Göttingen, 1935), pp. 46–69, 70–97; the Spanish text is also in *CD*, vol. II, pp. 90–103, 104–18. The special status of this secret instruction may have been due to Philip's position as heir in Spain; already when installing Tavera as regent in 1539 after the death of Isabella, the emperor had given Philip an '*instruction par forme d'admonicion, advis et conseil*' that belongs to the genre of the *testament politique*. *CD*, vol. II, pp. 32–43.

68. The interventions of Charles against the anti-monopolistic policy of the imperial diet and *Reichsregiment* may serve as examples. See Jakob Strieder, *Studien zur Geschichte kapitalistischer Organisationsformen*, 2nd edn (Munich, 1925) and Fritz Blaich, *Die Reichsmonopolgesetzgebung im Zeitalter Karls V. Ihre ordnungspolitische Problematik* (Schriften zum Vergleich von Wirtschaftsordnungen, VIII) (Stuttgart, 1967), esp. pp. 53–80.

69. Wolfram/Thomas, *Korrespondenz* (see note 41), vol. III, pp. 36–40, no. 457c.

70. See for example articles 5, 7, 14 and 15 of the *sommaire*.

71. That the instructions were not therefore secret documents becomes evident from the parallel instructions for Philip in 1543; only the second instruction was labelled as '*secreta*'.

72. The instruction for Tavera of 1539 provides especially telling illustrations. *CD*, vol. II, pp. 53–5.

73. The function of this political correspondence is discussed in greater detail in Rabe, 'Elemente neuzeitlicher Politik', esp. pp. 173–84.

74. The restrictions for Margaret of 28 July 1519 and 23 May 1522 are in Lanz, *Actenstücke*, pp. 100–3 and HHSA Vienna, Belgien PA 1/2, fos. 45r–46r; this latter piece – with marginal corrections in Granvelle's hand – probably served as the draft for the lost restriction of Mary's power of 1531, whose existence is attested by Charles' letter to Mary of 22 December 1538, ibid., Belgien PA 29/1, fos. 133r–136r. Adrian's restriction is in Dánvila, *Historia crítica*, vol. I, pp. 339–41; the sequence of restrictions for Spain after 1529 is in *CD*.

75. For the first time in the ordinance for Isabella of 8 March 1529. *CD*, vol. I, pp. 151–4.

76. The restrictions of 28 July 1519 in Lanz, *Actenstücke*, pp. 100–3; of 23 May 1522 in HHSA Vienna, Belgien PA 1/2, fos. 45r–46r. The restriction of Mary's power of 1531, for which that of 1522 may have served as a minute, was labelled a few years later by the emperor as '*restrinction*', ibid., Belgien PA 29/1, fos. 133r–136r.

77. The *'instruction et ordonnance'* of 1522 is in Lanz, *Actenstücke*, pp. 92–100; the *'instructions particulières'* of 7 October 1531 and of 14 October 1540 are in *RO*, vol. III, p. 260f and in Baelde, 'Onuitgegeven dokumenten', pp. 161–7.

78. Lanz, *Actenstücke*, pp. 100–3.

79. Wolfram/Thomas, *Korrespondenz* (see note 41), vol. III, pp. 25–33, no. 457a. This was not yet clearly expressed *'quamdiu nos abesse continget'* (p. 28), when Ferdinand was entrusted with the task; nevertheless, the notion seems to have taken hold that in every imperial absence the King of the Romans would stand in without needing a renewed empowerment.

80. For the power of 1540 see above, n. 46; the instruction of 14 October 1540, above, n. 77. It is likely but not certain that there was a separate restriction in 1540, but none has been found so far.

81. Baelde, 'Onuitgegeven dokumenten', pp. 179–81, 182. This ordinance derives from a *memoire* of the *conseil privé* produced on Mary's initiative, published in Walther, *Die burgundischen Zentralbehörden*, pp. 205–7, appendix VI (the year 1543 may be too early).

82. Baelde, 'Onuitgegeven dokumenten', pp. 196–8.

83. Explicitly stated in the ordinance for the *conseil privé* of 8 March 1546, where it is stressed that the state of peace with France necessitated arrangements different from those in time of war.

84. See above, n. 15.

85. The crucial character of access to patronage emerges from a request of Margaret in 1530. See H. G. Koenigsberger, 'Patronage and Bribery during the Reign of Charles V', in idem, *Estates and Revolutions. Essays in Early Modern European History* (Ithaca, NY, 1971), p. 168.

86. Brandi, 'Testamente'.

87. An example in the emperor's own hand is the selection in 1529 among the councillors of the crown of Aragon of those to stay and those to go, with pungent commentaries. AGS, Estado leg. 267, ff. 197–8.

88. See Rabe, 'Elemente neuzeitlicher Politik', pp. 165–72.

89. Michel Baelde, *De Collaterale Raden onder Karel V. en Filips II. (1531–1578)* (Brussels, 1965), pp. 140–5.

5 Police and the Territorial State in Sixteenth-century Württemberg

R. W. Scribner

Historians of early modern Europe have long been fascinated with the creative role of the state in social, cultural and economic affairs. This interest has taken many forms: sometimes a Whig view of the state's progressive and modernising role, sometimes a Marxian view of the state as a coercive means of ensuring class domination, sometimes an anthropological understanding of a process of 'acculturation', in which rural culture was eroded by a state directed by educated urban elites.[1] Central to all these views is an understanding of the territorial state as an entity developing, from the sixteenth century onwards, a bureaucratic, military, fiscal and policing apparatus increasingly exercising control over the lives of its subjects. Grounding itself on sixteenth-century theories of sovereignty, the state began to employ law codes and regulations which progressively extended its political control into all areas of life. It gradually enforced a general obedience to its will enabling it to create new forms of social order, which one recent work has summed up under the rubric of 'the well-ordered police state'.[2]

Such interpretations rest on a number of assumptions about the link between the territorial state, social order and the possibilities of political control which cannot be examined here in any detail.[3] However, it is noticeable how much they all concentrate on the observable structures of the state and its prescriptive legislation at the expense of close examination of the practical difficulties the state encountered in the pursuit of its own goals. Geoffrey Elton long ago pointed out the inadequacy of neglecting the realities of government in favour of examination of its structures and of how to confront the aims of state policy with the difficulties of enforcing it.[4] In this article I want to follow his example, and examine the problems of policing, law and order in sixteenth-century Germany through the example of

the duchy of Württemberg. The case in question may tell us something about the problems involved in assessing the positive role of the
state, and its role in the 'transformation' of early modern German
society.

In the three sections that follow I want to concentrate first on the
prescriptive view of the state and its major task of creating social
order; then to look at the structure of the territorial state in sixteenth-
century Württemberg; and finally to assess the difficulties of enforcing
'law and order' in that state to gain some idea of how prescription
matched reality.

I

It was a primary assumption of any state in sixteenth-century Europe
that it existed to further a condition of order embodied in the concept
of 'police' or *Polizei*. This term had quite different connotations from
those attached to modern usage, which associate it with the control of
crime, deviance or social pathology. The concept first turns up during
the last quarter of the fifteenth century, especially in urban statutes,
and has a twofold meaning. First, it denotes a condition of good order
in the public realm and in the commonweal; secondly, it denotes
regulations or statutes (*Polizeiordnungen*) directed at producing and
maintaining that good order. The beginning of the sixteenth century,
however, sees the term used in an increasingly extended form to
indicate one of the major tasks of government. A wider moral tone is
provided to the term by humanist thought about the 'common good'
(*res publica* or *Gemeinnutz*), which is further strengthened by evangelical thought during the Reformation.[5]

We can examine the full range of such meanings employed during
the sixteenth century through an informative example. In 1530
Johann Oldendorp, city syndic of Rostock, produced a treatise on
how good police should be maintained in towns and territories.[6] This
was probably not an influential work – it first appeared in a High
German edition in 1597 – but we may take it as expressing the
conventional wisdom of the age as seen through the eyes of a
humanist-jurist actively engaged in urban politics. Oldendorp distinguished between the private and the public realms and their
counsels. The first was concerned with private self-interest (in the
form of fields, houses, farms, money and other private goods), while
the second was concerned with the collective good, the welfare and
prosperity of the many, as opposed to the individual. Welfare and

prosperity were understood to involve both body and soul, and these were the main concerns of good police and good government (*Regiment*). Oldendorp sets his discussion within the characteristic moral framework of the sixteenth century: if the heart is in order, then all the rest of the body will thrive; so one should beseech God for his assistance, and be ruled through his Word and his Grace.[7] Oldendorp's positive reflections on how this is to be attained are rather banal and pious. The most interesting reflections in this part of the tract are found when he discusses why good police might not be present in a state. He singles out three causes for this: unbelief, greed and lack of understanding.[8]

The first cause pointed to the inadequacy of merely human laws. Where human laws do not suffice, Oldendorp believed it was necessary to rely on the laws of God. This was not possible without proper proclamation, and so required 'learned, experienced and loyal preachers'. The consequences, however, are to be found in the material realm: if God's word was not heeded it would lead to hunger, confusion and ruin; if it was observed, all streets and houses would be full of grain and money, and all worldly laws would be as strong as iron.[9] The second cause, greed, had two remedies: order and moderation. Order was created by the structure of laws and statutes to regulate trade, marketing and all commerce. Moderation was both internal and external. Goods acquired by trade should not be used to excess or for external things; modest needs would still allow commerce to flourish. Lack of understanding could be combated by the removal of ignorance through schools and universities. Printing had an important role in this, though it should not be used carelessly or without supervision: no one should be able to print what they liked, nor should schools be able to teach without proper supervision. Both should be under careful control of the government, which should foster the good arts and an earnest diligence.[10]

Oldendorp presents a sober evangelical vision of an ordered and moderate society, directed towards the common good by the rational arrangement of means to ends, under the benevolent protection of the divine Word. This is close to what has recently been called the 'well-ordered police state'. But whereas this phenomenon has been denied any existence in the sixteenth century, we can certainly perceive it as an integral part of sixteenth-century political thought. No less than its later variant, it was a rational structure aimed at the achievement of the common good, and anxious to 'release the creative and productive forces' of the citizens.[11] The only difference is the characteristic view of the sixteenth century that this occurred within a moral universe ultimately dependent on God's favour. Within this framework, government exists to create the optimum conditions for order, moderation and the flourishing of social and economic life. Although Oldendorp wrote from his experience of a city state, his views were just as applicable to the notions of 'police' pursued in a territorial state such as Württemberg.

II

Sixteenth-century Württemberg nestled in a triangle bounded by the Black Forest, the Danube and the line of the Neckar and the Jagst. It was a state of some 300,000 to 400,000 inhabitants who were predominantly engaged in primary production. It has been estimated that by 1618 only 4.2 per cent of the population were employed in industrial production. The economy rested on mixed arable farming, livestock farming and viticulture. The territory was rich in natural resources, with a highly developed marketing system, and a dense network of small towns. Stuttgart, with around 9000 inhabitants, was the only town of any substantial size. Regional economic life was dominated by imperial cities – Eßlingen, Reutlingen and Weil der Stadt within the territory, Heilbronn and Rottweil on its borders, and more importantly, Augsburg and Ulm, economically the most dominant towns in the region. Politically it was under the control of the Dukes of Württemberg, except for a brief interlude of Habsburg rule (1519–34), following the expulsion of Duke Ulrich by the Swabian League. This does not seem to have changed the basic structures of the state; the Habsburgs essentially ran the machinery they found on their arrival and it passed back, more or less intact, to Ulrich on his return.[12]

The administrative structure was based on the district (*Amt* or *Vogtei*), with between forty-five and fifty-eight *Ämter* in operation during the course of the sixteenth century. These varied in size, ranging from a single market town and its environs to a district covering more than seventy villages. Each *Amt* was based on a market town which served as a seat of local and district administration, and from which a district governor (*Amtmann* or *Vogt*) exercised jurisdiction over the countryside. Municipal government was run by a town council, aided by a town court which dealt with urban civil litigation, acted as a criminal court for the surrounding district, and served as a court of appeal from the village courts. The town council and the court were filled from the ranks of the local urban elite or *Ehrbarkeit*, and functioned under the control of the district governor, assisted by a secretary-scribe and the town mayor. The district governor was responsible for the administration of political, financial and legal affairs, and was directly answerable to the ducal administration in Stuttgart. Village government was run by a village mayor (*Schultheiß*) and a communal assembly, with a village court responsible for civil litigation and as a court of first instance in minor criminal matters. These bodies were made responsible to the district governor through an annual accounting. However, this did not create a genuinely two-tier system of government, for Württemberg was characterised by a high degree of interchange and continuity between town and country. This continuity had no doubt influenced the decision to locate the seats of district government in market towns, one of the real strengths of the Württemberg administration.[13]

Integration was further encouraged by the existence of representative territorial assemblies or *Landschaften*. Two representatives were usually sent from each district to the territorial assembly. The district governor was often one of them, and the urban elite made sure that they filled the other position at the expense of the countryside. The district governor was often drawn from the same social group as the urban elites, but he did not always merely echo their interests, and sometimes felt compelled to voice the concerns of the commons. From 1514 onwards, as a result of the upheavals around the Poor Conrad revolt, a second elected representative was sent to the territorial assembly, but this too quickly became the preserve of the urban elite, who by 1515 filled both positions. Real representation by the countryside was only won after a tough struggle throughout the course of the ensuing century.[14]

The structure of government was certainly simple and effective. The key to it was the functional role of the district governor. Towns and villages each had their own clearly defined administrative organs, while the person of the district governor linked the two to each other and to the central administration in Stuttgart. He was also in charge of defence, and in some districts commanded a castle with a small garrison.[15] The system was quickened by the legislation which flowed through its veins in the form of territorial statutes or *Landesordnungen*. Territorial and policing statutes were the common administrative and legislative forms throughout the sixteenth century. A notional distinction has been made between territorial statutes concerned more with general laws and constitutions, and policing statutes characterised by their concern with merely regulatory matters, but in practice the lines between the two were fluid, and there was little real separation over time.[16] The frequency of such legislation during the sixteenth century can be seen in those enacted for Austria between 1527 and 1577: no less than seven in the fifty-year period (1527, 1544, 1552, 1566, 1568, 1573, 1577).[17] Such legislation began to flow in Württemberg from 1495, when the first territorial statutes were issued, followed by others in 1515, 1521, 1536, 1552, 1567 and 1621. There were policing statutes issued in 1549, and thereafter there was a continuous stream of individual statutes in the form of general mandates and rescripts covering the areas of general police.[18]

The 1495 territorial statutes give a good example of what was covered by such legislation. Many sections have the tone of reactions to specific complaints, others show an attempt at active involvement by the state to shape the lives of its citizens. The various stipulations can be broken down into three major areas of concern: regulation and promotion of commerce; the inculcation of social discipline; and regulation of the 'common good'. Regulation and promotion of commerce ranged over such diverse matters as repair of roads, hospitality to visitors, observation of safe passage, prohibition of officials' engaging in commerce, prohibition of deception in retailing, and regulation of grain markets. Regulations concerned with social discipline involved stipulations about breach of the peace, prohibition of gambling, excessive drinking and drinking bouts, as well as prohibition of dealings with the Jews, regarded as the result of running into debt. Regulation of the 'common good' involved provision of supplies of fuel and building timber; checks on superfluous building; fire regulations; stipulations for the transmission of real property, inheritances, annuities, and bequests to pious foundations; regulation of begging; and regulation of the transmission of serfs. Regulation of begging involved the establishment of four common grain-chests for poor relief, an anticipation of the characteristic Reformation means of poor relief.[19] In their totality such territorial statutes were aimed at rational and systematic administration of economic and social life, but they were certainly set within the kind of altruistic moral framework described by Oldendorp. The moral cosmos they inhabited is revealed by the recitation in the 1515 *Landesordnung* of the evils that were held to flow from drinking contests and gambling: drunkenness, blasphemy, violence, murder, poverty and ultimately, because of blasphemy, the wrath of God over the entire community.[20] So private vices were to be moderated in the interests of the public good.

The 1495 ordinances also contained stipulations on how felonious behaviour was to be dealt with, and on how officials should conduct themselves. District officials and district courts were assigned key roles in both cases. The district governor had to ensure that offences were investigated and the offenders summoned before himself or the court. This official supervision also covered such non-criminal matters as supervision of traders, butchers, inn-keepers, weights and measures – indeed, anything that might lead to a complaint by a subject about commercial dealings. The coercive force at the district governor's command in this task was rather meagre. Usually he had only one or two constables, unless he was in command of a castle, when he also had charge of a small garrison, although this was not usually used as a policing force. In great part policing depended on policing by consent, through the co-operation of the community. In this difficult task, the officials could usually rely on two important legal instruments to compel compliance with the law: the *Gebot* and the *Urfehde*. Both of these, and especially the latter, were developed into very flexible instruments to coerce subjects to submission to the law.

The *Gebot*, or 'formal command', consisted of commanding the obedience of a subject on his or her oath of allegiance, so that a refusal involved a charge of perjury. It could be used to compel the performance of various feudal services, a complaint raised by rebels during the Peasants' War in territories outside Württemberg. Mostly, however, it was used as a policing measure, taking the form of a command to keep the peace, to desist from violence, to go to gaol, or to present oneself before an official or before a court. Refusal to obey incurred punishments of increasing severity.[21]

The *Urfehde* was an ancient legal instrument, founded on its basic notion of settling a feud through an agreement not to take revenge. Used as a legal instrument in Württemberg (and elsewhere) during the fifteenth and sixteenth century, it was a document issued on the release of a person from custody, by which he swore that he accepted the treatment accorded him, accepted any penalty imposed, and would not seek further redress, either within the law or outside it. Again, a breach of this agreement involved perjury.[22] However, this basic usage was further extended in several ways. It was used as a form of bail bond, enabling a suspect to be released on sureties pending investigation and trial; the sureties involved guarantors pledging on oath sums varying from 50 Gulden to 7000 Gulden in exceptional cases. It could also be used as a way of 'keeping a file open' for a suspect against whom nothing definite could be found or proven. A further usage was as a form of being 'bound over', essentially as a sworn pledge of future good behaviour. Here it could be effectively used in a personal dispute, where it was applied both to the innocent and to the party accused. Finally, it served as a form of criminal record, originally filed in the office of the district governor, although there were occasions on which the existing *Urfehden* were centralised in Stuttgart. *Urfehden* could be rewritten to change their terms or penalties, and could be returned and so effectively nullified (*kassiert*).[23] During the Peasants' War attempts were made to seize and destroy them as a hated record of previous bad behaviour.[24] They functioned, in short, as an essential form of social control.

The discussion so far has concentrated on the structure of the territorial state in Württemberg. This was simple but effective, given the minimal resources available to sixteenth-century rulers, and rested crucially on the social force of oath-taking as a means of legal compulsion. Let me now take one interesting example of how efficiently such a system of policing could work, the case of Hans Ziegler of Monsheim.[25]

On 20 December 1552 Cyriacus Horn of Stuttgart, an official in the Württemberg government, was sitting in an inn with his son-in-law, when they fell into discussion with two jurists, both assessors on the Imperial Court of Chancery. The jurists mentioned that two days earlier they had stayed overnight in a village inn, where they heard a man openly engaging in seditious speech. Among other things, he had said that within two months, when the ploughs were brought back into the fields, it would be time to strike the authorities dead; leaders had already been chosen, and he had warned the two jurists that they too would not escape. On 22 December, Horn reported this incident to Duke Christopher who asked him to go to the village named Mossa near Ditzingen, and to make discreet inquiries. Horn did so on 25 December, locating the inn from the description supplied by the jurists. He spoke in confidence to the inn-keeper, and identified the man in question as Hans Ziegler from Monsheim. Horn then went to see the village mayor, who told him that he did not take Ziegler too seriously: he had probably been drunk at the time of the alleged incident. However, Horn established that Ziegler had also said similar things when sober, and this was confirmed by others who had been present at the same table in the inn. The government decided that two men should be set to spy on Ziegler, while Horn made two visits to Ziegler's home town of Monsheim between then and 2 January, taking evidence especially from the village pastor. He said that Ziegler was fifty-five years old, a rather dotty old man, who was partial to a regular nightcap and inclined to be very chatty when in his cups.

When Horn's report was received in Stuttgart, attention switched to the two jurists. On 12 January the duke ordered another official to inquire further about one of them, Dr Johann Munsinger. (Perhaps there was a suspicion that they, or even Cyriacus Horn, had laid malicious information with the intention of stirring up trouble?) On 19 January Munsinger replied to this inquiry, confirming the story in all its essential details as Horn had given them, adding only that he had taken the matter as no more than idle gossip. On 6 February attention switched back to Ziegler, and a fuller inquiry about him was instituted in Monsheim: What kind of man was he? How had he behaved during the Peasants' War and since? What was his attitude towards authority? Did he engage regularly in seditious speech? How did he respond to commands (*Gebote*), and what was his attitude on religion? This was conducted by the steward or district governor in whose jurisdiction Monsheim lay. He made inquiries with eight different persons, including the mayor of Monsheim. The latter reported that Ziegler had not been active in the Peasants' War, and had always been obedient. Occasionally he had discussed with carriers the question of cartage fees, where he had always sided with the carriers' view. He was not refractory in religion, and went regularly to sermons. One of the suspect's neighbours reported that once when Ziegler had been ill, he had taken Communion under both kinds. Others reported some mutterings against the clergy and disagreements with the schoolmaster.

When all this evidence was assembled, Ziegler was arrested for questioning on 22 February (presumably unaware that inquiries about him had been going on for two months). He was confronted with the evidence and interrogated – the documents do not say whether with or without torture. In the end, the authorities seem to have decided that he was nothing other than as he had been described by the inn-keeper in Mossa, *ein voller, toller alter man*, a crazy and drunken old man, given to ranting over his drink. He was released on 5 March 1553, and bound over by an *Urfehde* to be of good behaviour in future. The only penalty imposed on him was perhaps the cruellest that could have befallen him: he was prohibited from visiting inns for life.

The case shows how remarkably efficient and thorough law enforcement could be in sixteenth-century Württemberg, but we should not be misled into thinking that policing was always such an easy task. The machinery of law enforcement depended crucially on the local knowledge of village and town mayors, the overall supervision of district governors and the co-ordinating efforts of central government in Stuttgart. It could function extremely efficiently once a suspect was identified and located. It was much less effective in detecting crime and tracing culprits. When warrants or wanted posters were issued for suspects or wanted criminals the system was singularly incapable of apprehending them.[26] It certainly functioned very well as an information gathering network, but was often very ineffectual in enforcing the law where it really mattered, at the grass-roots. Here it encountered considerable problems of law and order which often negated the apparent efficiency suggested by the structure.

III

Let us examine some of the problems of policing, law and order encountered in sixteenth-century Württemberg which support this judgement. My comments here are based on work in progress on the *Urfehden* issued in Württemberg district courts (*Vogteigerichte*) during the sixteenth century. The pattern of offences revealed in these records shows that the major problems of policing had less to do with serious crimes such as murder, grand theft and the like, but were more a matter of petty theft, breach of the peace, or mischief (*Frevel*), usually in the form of minor personal violence.[27]

'Breach of the peace' (*Friedensbruch*) was a carefully defined technical term: when disputes arose between two parties a third party could intervene and bid them 'to keep the peace' in the name of the prince. To avoid the peace-bidder being caught up in the dispute, the 1515 territorial statutes stipulated that it was not necessary for the peace-bidder to intervene physically – it was sufficient to do so from a safe distance.[28] Once peace had been proclaimed, penalties for breaching it could be severe: for breaching it with words, 10-Gulden fine; for a breach in deed, three fingers of the offender's right hand could be removed (the penalty for perjury), and in extreme cases even the right hand itself, although a penalty of such severity was rarely imposed.[29]

Breach of the peace was related to, and flowed from a series of forms of unruly behaviour: unseemly and unbecoming speech, threatening or slanderous words, 'suspicious' words (which usually had a hint of seditious speech), and unseemly behaviour. These were often the result of domestic disputes, quarrels between neighbours or with strangers, occurring in inns or on the streets, in the fields and on the roads. Sometimes it was the result of mere rowdiness, as in the case of Jörg Armhanns from Schwäbisch Gmünd, who abused an inn-keeper in the Brackenheim district for refusing to serve him wine after time had been called.[30] These disputes and quarrels often led to minor personal violence, exchange of blows or wounding. It was the constant fear of the authorities that such matters could escalate into disturbance on a larger scale, especially where kinship or friendship networks, or craft allegiance was involved. In 1527 Balthasar Meyer, the miller of Oberdigesheim in the district of Balingen, gathered several companions around him following a wedding, and 'invited themselves' to the wedding of the daughter of the mayor of Digesheim. Subsequently, Meyer summoned together a further thirty men from nearby villages and set about drafting letters, the contents of which are unknown, but which would certainly have been regarded by the authorities as potentially seditious.[31]

The fragility of law enforcement was most evident at this level: breach of the peace or mischief rarely led directly to an arrest. The offender was usually requested to present himself before the district governor or the local court, or else put on his oath by *Gebot* to present himself at gaol. In the latter case, the culprit was rarely imprisoned, but was usually bailed on his own assurances or with a guarantor to ensure that he would appear before the court in due course. However, the legal force of such undertakings on oath was sometimes not sufficient to compel compliance, and the response to a summons of this kind was sometimes to take flight. This was a sufficiently common solution for the law to recognise it implicitly as an understandable reaction to a serious charge. A more severe attitude was taken towards those who fled in response to a charge that 'did not involve life or limb', a tacit recognition that flight was at least understandable in the more serious case.[32]

The authorities had a good sense of the kinds of matters that led to breach of the peace: marital quarrels, family squabbles, and especially gambling, drunkenness and drinking contests. The last three were believed to lead to loss of control and reversion to indisciplined behaviour, and especially to blasphemy, violence and homicide. The moral view of policing characteristic of the time was doubtless built on such awareness. The whole area of breach of the peace underlines how far policing in our modern sense depended on communal consent and co-operation. The true measure of the task thus resided in the inculcation of moderation in habits of public and private behaviour. In short 'policing' in our modern sense depended on 'police' in the sense understood by the sixteenth century.

A second problem of law and order can be found in another feature of sixteenth-century life which directly undermined popular willingness to co-operate with the authorities: recalcitrance or *Widerspenstigkeit*. Recalcitrance was expressed in four different ways. First, there was downright disobedience to the commands of the policing authorities: refusal to heed a summons to the court, refusal to present oneself at the gaol, refusal to be bound over or to abide by bail conditions. In 1531 Hans Bider and Hans Ber resisted arrest and refused to present themselves at gaol in Böblingen; Claus Straubinger, a resident of Erpfingen in the Urach district in 1535 told the mayor that even if he was bound over seven times to keep the peace, he would still ignore it; and Michael Rörer from Schmier in the Maulbronn district, arrested in 1533 for intended desertion of his wife and family, said belligerently that as soon as he was released he would do as he pleased, and would observe no bail conditions imposed upon him. Often it was necessary to call upon bystanding citizens to come to the aid of officials – though not always with success: in 1537 Hans Bomler of Eltringen in Markgröningen not only refused to assist in seizing the murderer Hans Baldtreych, he actively helped him escape.[33]

This last example indicates the second form of resistance: direct and positive actions such as resisting or hindering arrest and aiding the escape of prisoners. Thus, in 1522 Hans Kurzmaul from Ingersheim in the district of Bietigheim was charged with resisting arrest and drawing a knife to do so; a few months later Bastian Kurzmaul of Ingersheim was charged with attempting to prevent the arrest of his son (possibly Hans Kurzmaul). In 1554 Michael Beck tried to hinder the arrest of Jacob Krauss in Ehningen in the district of Böblingen. Similarly, in 1558 Claus Sauberschwartz of Tübingen resisted arrest and cried out for justice, provoking a tumult. More spectacular was the action in Lauffen in 1483, when no less than eighteen men fell upon the district governor and the steward in Lauffen to release their prisoner.[34]

A third form of recalcitrance involved abuse of officials, especially of the district governor, his constable, forestry officials and their assistants, abuse of the town or village mayor and of the court. In the district of Bietigheim, such offences made up 10 per cent of the extant cases in the sixteenth century, typified by that of Ulrich Kurzweil arrested in 1565 following a brawl; he refused to recognise the judgement against him, wrote a letter abusing the district governor, mayor and court, and threw it into the cellar of the town constable. Occasionally such abuse was accompanied by accusations of partiality by officials or the courts. So Hans Stoll, resident at Glems in the district of Urach, abused the mayor of Glems in 1522, and charged that during the previous autumn he had cheated during the assessments; while Heinrich Kais, a citizen of Böblingen, in 1544 accused the mayor and court of having passed judgement in a lawsuit in which he was involved without having first heard his witnesses.[35]

Finally, there were direct attacks on officials, particularly on the district governors, their constables, and the mayors. Typical instances were Caspar Frembdysin from Holzgerlingen in the district of Böblingen, who in 1529 struck down the city constable from behind; Steffan Otthlin of Löchgau in the district of Bietigheim, who attacked the mayor in the public street in 1523; and Michel Hoylin of Gerhausen in the district of Blaubeuren, who twice attacked the district governor, in 1539 and 1548.[36] Long-standing personal enmities could grow up against such officials, who were pursued and attacked by their enemies even following their retirement. These forms of recalcitrance constituted a major category of offence during the sixteenth century.[37]

Such recalcitrance was grounded in social tensions in both town and country. There was often hostility to the urban court as a body representing the interests of the urban elites; village mayors and courts were often regarded as upholding the interests of rural elites. There could also be conflict between these elites and local officials, since the urban elites continually sought to gain greater freedom of political action and independence from ducal control. Their tactics sometimes took the form of discrediting a district governor with the central administration in Stuttgart as well as with ordinary citizens, which cannot have helped to foster a respectful attitude towards policing commands. Occasionally one finds a district governor who championed the needs and grievances of the commons against the elites.[38] Finally, there was a sufficient degree of negligence and deceit among Württemberg officials to lower public belief in their impartiality: cases of fraud and peculation were uncovered regularly throughout the sixteenth century. Typical examples were Burckhart Fraider of the district of Balingen, charged in 1531 with seventeen years of peculation from the tithe incomes; or Ludwig Riepp, charged in 1546 with embezzling 1600 Gulden from the incomes of the administration of the abbey of Bebenhausen. Charged alongside Riepp was Sebastian Waibel, grain-steward at Tübingen, who fell under suspicion of multiple irregularities involving a total of 1000 Gulden.[39]

Aggravating these social tensions was a constant undertone of political tension traceable throughout at least the first third of the sixteenth century. Opposition to Duke Ulrich kept Württemberg politics in a state of ferment up to his expulsion in 1519. The Habsburg period from 1519–34 was marked by regular activity of partisans of the exiled duke, who sought to stir up unrest that could be exploited to enable his return.[40] Following his restoration, there were alleged plots against him in 1535 and 1536, and for several years afterwards there was a mood of muted opposition to his rule, expressed in mutterings, abuse and ballads against him.[41] Added to this was peasant recalcitrance based in socioeconomic grievance. This broke surface in the Poor Conrad revolt of 1514, which found echoes in more urban communities than has been hitherto recognised in the general literature on the pre-1525 peasant revolts.[42] Following the upheavals of 1525, there was uneasiness in rural and urban communities for at least a generation. There was no major revolt during this time, but often unrest seemed to come close to it, and some communities such as Kirchheim were in a state of continual truculence.[43] It was only around the middle years of the century that these signs of restlessness seemed to become less frequent.

To sum up, law and order in sixteenth-century Württemberg was a delicate balance. Seen from above and from the outside, it was orderly and efficient, almost a 'well-ordered police state'. At the grass-roots, where policing really mattered, it was far more fragile. This accounts for the trouble taken over the case of Hans Ziegler of Monsheim. The effort invested in the investigation seems like a clear case of overkill, given the initial assessment of the local inn-keeper that he was harmless. But seen in the light of the fragility of law and order, it was a necessary preventive measure. In the long run, the orderly policing of the territorial state depended on the consent of its citizens, although this was often a grudging consent given only conditionally; sometimes it appears more like unwilling compliance than genuine consent.

Such a case study might well make us cautious about some of the recent interpretations of the development of the early modern state. It challenges, for example, views about its essentially repressive nature, and especially the 'acculturation' thesis advanced by Robert Muchembled. It also calls into question the view of the 'well-ordered police state' as a product of the seventeenth and eighteenth centuries. On the one hand, we find in the sixteenth century a view of the state no less regulated and rational than that of the later centuries. On the other hand, any attempt to argue from legislation alone is doomed as inadequate unless the actual working of that legislation is examined at the grass-roots. Moreover, later attempts at efficient regulation were probably as unlikely to succeed as those of the earlier period. Besides the upheavals of the Thirty Years War, there was the continual problem of recalcitrance and the inability of the authorities to deal with crime of all kinds. The 'well-ordered police state' was probably as ineffectual in the seventeenth and eighteenth centuries as it was in the sixteenth.[44] There were no doubt changes in the terms in which the state was legitimated and a certain secularisation of its perspectives. However, these matters tell us nothing about its practical workings at the level of daily life. To understand that we must explore the often grim contest for policy and police reflected in the court records.

Notes

1   For examples of these approaches see respectively M. Raeff, *The Well-Ordered Police State. Social and Institutional Change through Law in the Germanies and Russia 1600–1800* (New Haven/London, 1983); P. Anderson, *Lineages of the Absolutist State* (London, 1974); R. Muchembled, *Popular Culture and Elite Culture in France 1400–1750* (Baton Rouge, La./London, 1985).

2.   Raeff, *Well-Ordered Police State.*

3.   For a discussion where some of these assumptions are more explicitly laid out, see C. Tilly, 'Reflections on the History of European State-making', in idem (ed.), *The Formation of National States in Western Europe* (Princeton, NJ, 1975), pp. 3–83.

4.   See G. R. Elton, *Policy and Police. The Enforcement of the Reformation in the Age of Thomas Cromwell* (Cambridge, 1972).

5.   On the concept of *Polizei*, see A. Erler and E. Kaufmann (eds), *Handwörterbuch zur deutschen Rechtsgeschichte* (Stuttgart, 1971–85), vol. III, cols. 1800–3; and in more detail W. Kunkel (ed.), *Polizei- und Landesordnungen* (Quellen zur neueren Privatrechtsgeschichte Deutschlands, II, 1) (Weimar, 1969), introduction.

6.   Johann Oldendorp, *Van radtslagende, wo men gude politie und ordnunge ynn Steden und landen erholden moghe* (Rostock, 1530). This is cited

below in the High German edition: *Von Rathschlagen, Wie man gute Policey und Ordnung in Stadten und Landen erhalten möge* (Rostock, 1597), reproduced in facsimile edition (Glashütten im Taunus, 1971).

7.   Oldendorp, pp. 5–17 *passim*.
8.   Ibid., pp. 49–54.
9.   Ibid., pp. 55–6.
10. Ibid., pp. 66–72.
11. Cf. Raeff, *Well-Ordered Police State*, p. 171; cf. p. 179.
12. For a succinct but skilful recent sketch, see J. A. Vann, *The Making of A State. Württemberg, 1593–1793* (Ithaca, NY/London, 1984), ch. 1.
13. On *Ämter* and local government, ibid., p. 39f. and D. Sabean, *Power in the Blood. Popular Culture and Village Discourse in Early Modern Germany* (Cambridge, 1984), pp. 4–20.
14. Vann, *Württemberg*, pp. 41–4.
15. For example, in Asperg or Schorndorf.
16. On *Landesordnungen* and *Polizeiordnungen, Handwörterbuch zur deutschen Rechtsgeschichte*, vol. II, cols. 1405–12; vol. III, cols. 1803; the distinction between *Landesordnungen* and *Polizeiordnungen*, Raeff, *Well-Ordered Police State*, p. 5.
17. W. Brauneder, 'Der soziale und rechtliche Gehalt der österreichischen Polizeiordnungen des 16. Jahrhunderts', *Zeitschrift für historische Forschung*, III (1976), pp. 205–19, esp. p. 207.
18. These can be found in A. L. Reyscher, *Sammlung der württembergischen Gesetze*, vol. XII (Tübingen, 1841).
19. Ibid., pp. 5–15.
20. Ibid., pp. 18–19.
21. The notion of the *Gebot* (like that of the *Urfehde*) is not explicitly defined in the legislation, but can be inferred from the usage in sixteenth-century Württemberg, as reflected in criminal records. Its basic meaning is that of the power of command by virtue of the sovereign power of the prince, see J. and W. Grimm, *Deutsches Wörterbuch*, vol. IV, 1 (Leipzig, 1935), cols. 1804–5. There were complaints about commanding on oath, and the 1515 *Landesordnung* tried to correct this by stipulating that commands should be issued only on pain of a monetary fine, Reyscher, *Sammlung*, p. 21. However, my impression is that this was not always observed in practice, without being able to document this fully at this stage of my research on Württemberg.
22. Cf. for the basic medieval meaning of the *Urfehde*, J. and W. Grimm, *Deutsches Wörterbuch*, vol. XI, 3 (Leipzig, 1936), cols. 2410–11. According to the Grimms, this was replaced during the course of the sixteenth century by the notion of an oath either not to leave a specific territory or to accept exile from it, but this was only one of the many subtle uses to which it was put in early modern Germany.
23. The above discussion is based on analysis of the series of Württemberg *Urfehden* extant for the sixteenth century, held in the Hauptstaatsarchiv Stuttgart (hereafter HStASt), A44, nos. 1–7236, which are usually cited simply with the prefix 'U'. There is a further series of pre-1500 *Urfehden* designated with the prefix 'WR'. I intend to discuss these in

detail in a subsequent publication on crime and deviancy in sixteenth-century Württemberg. On the occasional centralisation in Stuttgart cf. U592b, in which the district governor of Böblingen in 1541 reports sending the *Urfehden* in his possession to Stuttgart, after having them recorded in a book.

24. See HStASt U5261: Ulrich Metzger, a citizen of Sulz, went to great lengths to get hold of his *Urfehde* and tore it up, saying as he did so that the lords and citizens of Sulz had done him great violence and injustice.

25. The case of Hans Ziegler of Monsheim is in HStASt A43, Bü. 38.

26. On the difficulties involved, see a memorandum prepared in 1557 for a joint meeting between the rulers of Württemberg, the Electorates of Mainz and the Palatinate and the County of Hohenlohe about how to deal with the problem of banditry in the Odenwald, HStASt A38, Bü. 15.

27. This is only an impressionistic judgement based on sample analysis of offences in selected districts in Württemberg. I intend to publish at a later stage the result of an analysis of over 7000 Württemberg *Urfehden* extant for the sixteenth century.

28. Reyscher, *Sammlung*, p. 21. On the technical sense of bidding the keeping of the peace, see *Handwörterbuch zur deutschen Rechtsgeschichte*, vol. I, col. 1288.

29. Reyscher, *Sammlung*, p. 21.

30. HStASt U652 (Armhanns).

31. HStASt U108.

32. Cf. HStASt U5479, where Jörg Metzger, a resident of Schlaitdorf in the Tübingen district was in 1522 charged for taking flight in an offence not involving risk to life or limb; also U1829 (1529).

33. HStASt U369 (Ber and Bider); U5862 (Straubinger); U6625 (Rörer); U1472 (Bomler).

34. HStASt U205 6 (the Kurzmauls); U421a (Beck); U5133 (Sauberschwartz); WR4022 (Lauffen).

35. HStASt U200 (Kurzweil); U5868 (Stoll); U374 (Kais); the figures for Bietigheim are eleven cases from the 112 extant *Urfehden*.

36. HStASt U433 (Frembdysin); U239 (Otthlin); U326,329 (Hoylin).

37. Cf. the district of Böblingen, where the *Urfehden* attest abuse of officials on eleven separate occasions 1512–1583, HStASt U363, 374, 426–7, 430, 439, 448, 471, 478, 483, 523.

38. For the best documented case of this kind, involving the district governor of Urach, Hans Wern, see my forthcoming article 'Magie und Aberglaube: Zur volkstümlichen sakramentalischen Denkart in Deutschland am Ausgang des Mittelalters'.

39. HStASt U116 (Fraider); U5391–2 (Waibel, Riepp).

40. There are fifty-eight cases of partisanship for Duke Ulrich in the *Urfehden* for this period.

41. Plots against Ulrich: HStASt U916, 4016, 4090; abuse: U805 (1537), 1532 (1535), 2961 (1544), 5389 (1544), 6553 (1552), 6563 (1536); ballads: U2182 (1543), 2183 (1551).

42. For example, in Brackenheim, Kirchheim, Leonberg, Schorndorf, Stuttgart and Tuttlingen, HStASt U629, 1932, 2633, 3869, 4263, 5706.

43. There were thirty cases of recalcitrance of various kinds in the district of Kirchheim up to 1572, including an attempt to raise a general disturbance in Owen unter Teck in 1533 (HStASt U2295).
44. See, for example, the view of the problems of the eighteenth century in C. Küther, 'Räuber, Volk und Obrigkeit. Zur Wirkungsweise und Funktion staatlicher Strafverfolgung im 18. Jahrhundert', in H. Reif (ed.), *Räuber, Volk und Obrigkeit. Studien zur Geschichte der Kriminalität in Deutschland seit dem 18. Jahrhundert* (Frankfurt am Main, 1984), pp. 17–42, esp. pp. 36–7.

6 Is There a 'New History' of the Urban Reformation?

Hans-Christoph Rublack

I

Following the impact of a generation of research on the urban Reformation,[1] it would seem appropriate to question whether a 'new history' has emerged. While it might be tempting to approach the question iconoclastically, that would surely be too narrow. Moreover, it would fail to take account of the shift in emphasis which has relativised the importance of the ideal of the 'corporate identity' of the citizenry.[2] This ideal has now been confined to the milieu of the petty artisan, while its development through evangelical preaching into a means of control valuable to and exercised by the ruling elite has been demonstrated. The resulting emphasis upon the social context of the Reformation reflects a marked change in historiographical approach.[3] No longer is the Reformation seen purely in terms of Luther, Zwingli or even Calvin, for it has been shown that the statement by the Augsburg ropemaker, Ott, 'We have always been evangelicals and we still are today . . . If we truly followed the Gospel we would all be brothers' demands at least equal consideration.'[4] The ropemaker is therefore a part, if not an integral element, of what we term the urban Reformation.

As a result, more recent research has been less concerned with iconoclasm than with the painstaking task of revealing the urban Reformation in all its complexity. A revision of the previous macroscopic view with its broad cultural, social and political interpretation has given way to a highly differentiated, though at times confusing, picture. Although we may regret the loss of the previous interpretation with its seemingly global clarity, we are, however, beginning to learn about the reception of Reformation ideas, even if we are still unclear why particular concepts and ideas appealed specifically to layfolk, whether citizens or peasants.

It has become clear that a simple transition from analysis to synthesis is no longer possible. In order to arrive at a new view of the

121

urban Reformation there are two basic facts which have to be considered. First, Reformation ideas had to appeal to cities with complex social systems. Secondly, not only was the Reformation not confined to an urban setting, it was also much more than an urban event.

The former proposition would concede that life in the cities was more multi-faceted than reflected by either the appeal or the effect of the Reformation gospel; the latter would set a limit upon the cities' contribution to the larger and more far-reaching process termed 'Reformation'. Hence the urban Reformation was but one formative element, albeit limited, in this process. Limitation does not imply elimination, but it leaves open the problem of how compatible these perspectives are. Thus the first proposition challenges an interpretation which can be termed that of the 'double renaissance'.[5] It was Luther's Reformation which rebaptised the German city by giving a genuine religious meaning to its social order and redeeming it from a feudalised church whose hierarchy was dominated by the aristocracy and whose religion was tainted with folklore and rural superstition. It ensured the restoration of the Christian aura of a sanctified civic life by granting the city a religious image compatible with its origins. Citizens were able to define their existence as imbued with the spirit of peace, concord and brotherly love. The city, by reverting to its communal origins, attained a religious status compatible with the city of God. It was absolved of conflict and not found wanting when set against the archetype of early Christian communal life. This vision differed from that of the nineteenth century which heralded Luther as a prophet of future bourgeois dominance, in that the religious core of the commune was taken seriously and that the metaphor of revitalisation was purely historical in character. Cities did not strive for modernisation but rather were restored to their ancien regime essence. This concept, which rested on the assumption of essential unity and harmony, faced the problem of conflict from the outset. Measured against the reality of social life in sixteenth-century German cities this interpretation can only convince if it accommodates the growing tensions in those cities. It is therefore unclear whether concord implies anything more than a conscious effort to produce consent within the city. In this respect religion assumed the function of averting total chaos. A younger historian has consequently turned the tables round by suggesting that one might as well start with conflict and end with integration.[6]

If this is true of Reformation religion, then its appeal to the egalitarian character of the commune would be only one of a number of such ideologies acting as instruments of integration. The obvious criticism of such an inverted concept is that there is adequate evidence that the ideas which determine social reality are not merely instrumental. What is misleading is to conceive of the relationship between ideas and social interests as strictly reciprocally determined.[7]

To argue for their disengagement is not to divorce religious ideas from their social roots or context. Secularisation was no part of the Reformation message. It does mean, however, that social and political life in sixteenth-century German cities cannot be viewed as entirely or totally dominated by evangelical ideas. This has recently been demonstrated in the case of corporate civic politics.[8] As for their social system, the pattern of social differentiation remained unchanged, with the exception of religious orders, whose laicisation reaffirmed rather than countered the existing social structure.[9]

Irrespective of the new poor laws Protestant cities continued to be faced with the problem of poverty. Patriarchal household rule continued, though more firmly controlled by the civic courts. Even the renowned Protestant work ethic has faced detraction in recent research, which stresses that the basic notion of labour, meaning drudgery, did not yield to a view of subduing the world by work alone.[10] We are left, therefore, with a picture of civic social systems purifying themselves of alien religious elements and cutting their intangible or burdening ties with an ecclesiastical system beyond their walls. But the achievement of bringing religion to bear directly upon the city was an ambiguous one. It enhanced the chances of the ruling classes to control the clergy and social morality, but at the same time they were confronted by a clergy whose self-consciousness had been roused through its role as proclaimer of God's word. It was no longer possible for a self-centred city to distance itself from such developments.[11] Religion continued to be the life force, more specifically the principal medium of truth as well as the only generally accepted symbol of the unity of society and government. Just as this discredits any attempt to reduce its impact to a secondary level, so, too, social concerns should not be regarded as ancillary to the Reformation mainstream. The complexity of civic social systems requires an analysis which takes religion and social action as mutual contexts. Such an approach needs to be flexible enough to accommodate the shifting interrelationships between religion, political and, indeed, economic power, in which various levels of action might thus converge or be loosely coupled. The analysis of the urban Reformation, therefore, should pursue two complementary lines at once – each as important as the other: one which examines the impact of Reformation religion, the other which examines how far urban life was affected or else remained untouched. The second proposition – the wider process of 'Reformation' – has a long history to which we need merely allude. Though it is one of the focal points of current debate, the princes' Reformation is merely one issue among many;[12] another is, of course, theological discourse; and a third is the movement towards higher educational qualifications. These issues serve to remind us that the notion that there is more to the Reformation than its urban dimension should not be seen as a relapse into the Rankean paradigm of religion and imperial politics, the founding myth of German Reformation history.

II

For a social corporation, however sacral, Luther's most original and focal idea of justification by faith implied at the least devaluation if not disintegration, since sacral power was reserved to God alone. It involved a clear demarcation over any secular or human agency. The radical impetus of what may be regarded as the doctrine of a monk deprived any religious qualities intrinsic in human actions of their sacral power.[13] Even if balanced and internalised by love of one's neighbour as the product of a pure faith the individual's confrontation with God's law as well as His sole grace conduced to isolation and psychological strain on the part of the common man within the community.[14] Instead of being exposed to faith alone by God's imputation, citizens rightly and of necessity adapted Luther's paradox of Christian liberty so that its second element – total subjection to God's will – became complementary to the first – freedom from human law – and thereby inverted this vertical relationship which dominated their earthly lives. It was, in Heiko Oberman's phrase, 'horizontalised'.[15] This inversion not merely reflected artisans' needs to subjugate the clergy but also the impossibility of reconciling a highly sophisticated doctrine such as that of the two realms with civic social reality, which was exposed to constant threats from irrational forces, both internal and external. That a community divided or 'driven by multiple conflicts'[16] would fall to ruin, just as peace and unity would strengthen it, was common traditional wisdom reaffirmed by experience.[17]

Equally, the egalitarian connotation of Luther's teaching of the priesthood of all believers and his conscious stressing of love of one's neighbour from around 1520 onwards[18] were difficult to implement in social systems whose principle of social differentiation was stratification. So brotherly love – as Ott's remark demonstrates – voiced the aspirations of subjects against their rulers in line with longstanding, if latent, communal traditions.

It was, then, the generalised nature of Luther's teachings which allowed both flexibility to changing situations and also at first left large areas of the social problems undefined. At the same time, his religious claim and political appeal were such that they urgently required detailed application. Thus a spectrum of divergent interpretations according to social station and time-scale unfolded containing the seeds of protest, which in any case were nurtured by a failure to strengthen the mediating role of the local magistracies and by a failure to control the sermons. Evangelical teaching was received by various groups in various ways, though the potential range of interpretation was restricted by concomitant authentic exegesis on the part of the reformers and their literate followers.

Given these options and choices there is no need to force this potential into one category, as Peter Blickle has done for the early Reformation.[19] His historical interpretation corresponds to what Hegel termed 'pragmatical'. Against the writing of history as a colourful presentation of details and external events, as in the novels of Sir Walter Scott, the pragmatical alternative sees the past as a necessary evolution through phases, which leads to reason, justice and the entrenchment of liberty, manifesting itself in a system of institutions, which comprises both the form of constitution and the content of its polity. 'In each phase there is not merely an exterior sequence and a necessity relation of events, but a necessity of the concept itself. That is the true subject.'[20] Blickle regards both the urban Reformation and peasant revolution together as a 'communal Reformation'. This he takes to be more than merely a new label since the commune reflected institutionalised reality. As citizens and peasants were brought into contact with various concepts of Reformation theology, contained in Luther's published tracts, such as transferring the right of electing ministers to what he called the congregation, seen as coterminous with the commune (*Gemeinde*), or rather the extension of Zwingli's communalism into the Rhineland, their preconceived aspirations of expanding communal autonomy at the expense of feudal lordship were sanctioned. Reception of the Gospel was thus filtered by social reality. Here the argument pioneered in Moeller's notion of 'sacral corporatism' is taken further by extending it to the country-side. As in the cities, Reformation theology, at least in part, was reshaped in the peasants' minds. A commune therefore is taken to be a group based on solidarity which minimises internal conflict. There are further similarities in the concept of sanctification[21] and the greater impact of Zwingli's and Bucer's theology on the popular mind. Blickle's argument, however, differs from Moeller's in import-ant respects. No longer is the commune held to be an ideal revived by theology; it is a living structure, the reality of which can be discovered no matter how obscured by the layers of traditional historiography. Moreover, Reformation theology is transformed into what can be more adequately termed a religiously inspired social philosophy of brotherly love and the common weal. From a vast mass of ideas printed or preached (though the sources tell us little about village preaching), peasants somehow instinctively[22] picked the one or two ideas relevant to their situation. It was their needs and aspirations which specified the pure 'Word of God'. This argument for selective reception would be tenable even if it risks reviving venerable suspi-cions only recently allayed that the peasants misunderstood the Gospel advocated by the reformers. That, however, is exactly what Blickle implies: Luther's Christ crucified was turned into a weapon against secular lords and given a religious meaning. There were, it appears, two Reformations, the one in Luther's heart, head and pen, the other in the peasants' minds and hands. If so, then the Reformation of the theologians may indeed stand in its own historical right, without the need to denounce a theological revolution which fails to live up to its social responsibility. There might even be three Reformations if Blickle were willing to concede the princes the same grace as he grants the ideals of liberty[23] in communal reform. Yet the princes' Reforma-tion stands deprived of any religious motives: theirs is a counter-revolution prompted by sheer striving for power. This neo-Whiggish view, partisan to the peasants' pragmatic quest for freedom, leaves essential problems unresolved. Is, for example, ideological incitement sufficient to direct a propensity to rebel into a revolution? Should peasants not be conceived of as having hearts and minds and capable of considering eternal salvation as well? What did biblicism mean to those who were not accustomed to handling the printed word, as Strauss has demonstrated with reference to the teaching of catechism.

As for urban reform one may with Blickle rightly complain that too many parochial studies have blurred a clearer pattern and that preoccupation with cities has led to a failure to consider rural communities. Admittedly, highly specialised research has raised analysis of the urban Reformation to a level of sophistication which at present admits of no clearcut model which can successfully reduce its complexity. Blickle's interpretation, however, suggests an inner dialectic of a communal-populist reform movement and the councils' function of control and ratification. Both commune and council, therefore, were necessary to achieve religious reform.[24]

It is this complex dialectic within the cities which does not allow us to press the urban Reformation into one particular pattern. Rather there was conflict within the commune about which pattern was to be imposed. As Brady has shown,[25] it was the power holders within the communes who ensured the partial success of the Reformation by controlling the popular movement. What mattered was who controlled the church's integration within the city. This localising of the universal church echoed the traditional policies of the magistrates, but now arose from disputed or negotiated positions which reveal a shifting constellation of interests dependent upon the degree of stratification and diversity of attitudes among the inhabitants. Blickle's nominalist approach may help to open the debate with a well-defined position, as did Bernd Moeller twenty years ago. The social appropriation of the Gospel can no longer be held to be historically illegitimate, as simply distorting Luther's ideas. But the 'communal Reformation' may turn out to reveal its reductive aspects as in the case of the magisterial Reformation, where the commune represents a segmentary mode of social differentiation into which modes of stratification had already been implanted as well as incipient elements of functional differentiation.[26]

III

As far as the transformation of theological ideas and religious impulses through a communication process within society is concerned, there is no need to reduce it to a one-dimensional perspective. Bernd Moeller has recently underlined the incongruities of Luther's ideas with those of his urban followers.[27] If Luther was alien to, indeed different from, his fellow citizens, it would be fair to acknowledge that citizens could be equally different. As Luther 'transcended' or 'superseded' social conditioning, urban appropriation equally went beyond his message. As Moeller understands this to be a 'creative process of elaboration' we have to regard it as something other than mere imitation, a reduction to simpler terms, or an inferred or implicit consequence. Moeller cites two concepts which rendered Luther's ideas partially adequate to the urban setting: his conception of God as not antagonistic to mankind[28] and his idea of justification by faith alone, which evolved into a stress upon love of one's neighbour. Moreover, the equation of laity and clergy proved especially attractive.[29] These notions obviously presented Luther's ideas of law and the Gospel, of faith and works in a way which could be assimilated by citizens, though the individual emphasis or accent may have differed. Religious comfort and social aspirations were not mutually exclusive categories. The process of communication is, as Moeller states, a complex one with paradoxical consequences, such as social disciplining and domesticating the clergy.[30] It seems more appropriate to call this, as Moeller does for medieval religion, a reshaping of the Christian message by social conditions, rather than an 'impoverishment', a judgement which takes Luther's standards as normative.[31]

A case in point is Lazarus Spengler, a committed Lutheran and city secretary of Nuremberg.[32] His interpretation of the 'Word of God' was, as Berndt Hamm has shown, biased towards the oligarchical necessities of civic order. Even to him Luther's subtle anthropological categories, *coram Deo* and *coram mundo*, which betrayed the anxieties of a spiritually attuned monk, proved alien. Spengler placed the church in a political context since politics were sanctioned by religion. The authorities were held directly responsible for salvation and not merely for the physical well-being of their subjects. As matters of conscience are elusive, their responsibility in matters of public religion allowed a pragmatic element. Yet the public profession of religion included the morality of Christians, which for city life meant that peace, concord and the commonweal were commanded by God: 'God's word promotes joy, peace and total concord, and it prevents any disturbance of peace, opposition, conflict and rebellion.'[33] What Berndt Hamm finds in Spengler is an obsession with civic order. This transformed egalitarian claims of the doctrine of all believers into a lay principle legitimising the magistracy's power over the clergy. Characteristically, controversies arose over the clergy's claim to interfere in Christians' lives. The Nuremberg council's refusal to concede any more than the institution of a general absolution met Osiander's opposition. He charged the council with usurping authority in ecclesiastical matters. To this Spengler responded by asking whether the authorities and the congregation had power to determine doctrine or not. Did Osiander believe that he was to be immune from control by the city fathers? The upshot, as Hamm concludes, was the subordination of the clergy to the council, which was assumed to be acting as the instrument of God's word but not as the servant of the ministers. This same theme was echoed most pointedly in Strasbourg where an attempt in 1574 to institute a pre-communion interview was rejected on the basis of a quotation from scripture: it was Aaron, not Moses, who had violated God's law by constructing the golden calf.[34] This may have even referred to Luther's bible, where the Wittenberg reformer had added a marginal note to Exodus 32 which interpreted the image as representing human traditions.[35] Control of Christian morality was not to be arrogated by the clergy who would then have to suffer unfair comparison with their unreformed predecessors.

The inclusion of the clergy in the citizenry was certainly one of the central civic achievements of the Reformation and mitigated some aspects of anti-clericalism by opening the path to domestication. That the ministers persistently aroused tensions by claiming the freedom of God's word shows that domestication by the magistrates remained incomplete even though a new pattern had been established. In several cases the civic magistrates were successful in domesticating the absolute claims of God's word as well, at least in so far as these threatened to disturb their own conception of morality. Martin Luther's spectacular ban on the Zwickau council is well known, but even he could not enforce a new priestly independence against the will of secular authority.[36] All this suggests that we have moved away from what Bernd Moeller in 1978 defined as a scholarly consensus in which the German cities were held to have adopted Luther's ideas exactly. The accent has now shifted to his second statement that Luther's ideas were developed and elaborated within the cities,[37] a view which echoes Brady's assessment of Moeller's original impact, 'that the civic society of Reformation Germany transformed Luther's gospel according to its own lights'. [38] Since the cities should be regarded as standing on an equal footing with the reformers there is as much need for local urban studies as for further research on the theology of Luther, Zwingli and other leading reformers.[39]

IV

The impact of the original concept may have stemmed from its stress on the essential unity of the city. Hence the 'Reformation was an urban event', or it was a double renaissance or a communal Reformation. The results of research on urban Reformations have in fact run counter to initial expectations, for it has been demonstrated that the concept of urban unity is too limited to encompass the diversity and complexity of the Reformation in the cities and that an alternative conceptual model is required if this diversity is to receive an adequate synthesis. Leaving aside the obvious fact stressed by Bob Scribner,[40] that it is self-contradictory to attempt to prove the popular character of the Reformation by pointing to its urban character since townsfolk were a minority in sixteenth-century Germany (and for that matter until the end of the nineteenth century),[41] Peter Blickle's concept of the communal Reformation as an anti-feudal movement has to face the paradoxical fact that those cities which were the most highly feudalised did not experience an urban Reformation at all, either communal or elitist. Equally, a Protestant movement was not necessarily accompanied by civic revolt. Apart from the celebrated stumbling block of Cologne, episcopal cities would have provided many reasons for anti-feudalism with their combined ecclesiastical and civil system of authority.[42] Here early reforming groups remained notoriously weak, however, and later Protestant movements peaceful, though in some cases these cities could invoke a respectable tradition of struggling for autonomy. Again, with the exception of Cologne, where civil control was greater than clerical dominance, this means that there was no automatic connection between religious conviction and social movements, either anti-feudal or anti-oligarchical, communal or elitist.

Secondly, the discovery of a number of 'late city Reformations'[43] has diminished the implied identity of Reformation and city from the outset, since they did not coincide with the Reformation proper, unless one is prepared to extend the duration of the urban Reformation to what Jane Abray calls the 'long Reformation'.[44]

To the sizeable number of sixty-five imperial cities which formed the basis of Moeller's original argument, some northern German cities with an effectively autonomous character could be added where the same interpretation of a Lutheran commune rising against reluctant oligarchies would apply.[45] There are, however, sufficient instances of other territorial towns where the urban Reformation was a princes' one.[46] It is clearly not appropriate to regard these as underdeveloped cities.[47]

Finally, even imperial cities have been shown to be restricted in their political autonomy, so that urban Reformations cannot be understood as autogenously generating new ecclesiastical systems.[48]

The diversity of the urban reforming movement is also evident in the varying pattern of its reception among rich and poor, literate and illiterate, citizens and non-citizens, councillors and commons, oligarchs and *menu peuple*. As Brady and Scribner have noted, the urban Reformation began within a social group which was middle-class but which had become jurisdictionally separate from the citizenry, that is, the lesser clergy.[49] This revolt within the clergy provided the springboard for the urban Reformation by its appeal to a popular audience as well as the magistracy for assistance. Brady reveals that the initial phases of urban reform proved to be highly disruptive, threatening peace and order. On the other hand, there are clear cases of early and successful co-operation between commune and council, for example in Zürich,[50] Berne, or even Nördlingen. This consensus stands in contrast to Hanover, where the Reformation ran parallel to the complete replacement of the ruling council and its subsequent exile.[51] Here Mörke's generalisation applies: 'The Reformation in Lower Saxony cannot be subjected to a unifying pattern.'[52]

There is also great diversity in Reformation discourse. The studies of the northern German cities suffer from a particular lack of pamphlet analysis which would help define specific theological or religious impulses in promoting opposition to the council. Thus Heinz Schilling posits the impact of the Lutheran doctrine of *sola fide* with its egalitarian connotations, as well as biblicism in general.[53] Mörke points to the slogans of Christian freedom, equality, the gospel and obedience to God's will.[54] In Hanover the demand was to read the pure gospel and God's word.[55] An equally significant fact is that in the pamphlets summarising sermons analysed by Moeller[56] the whole range of the Hanseatic Reformation is missing. All the slogans mentioned, though, are well covered in his sermon abstracts but, as Mörke confirms, although Reformation discourse did not specify an explicit social programme it did determine social action and everyday practice. This contrasts with the experience of southern German cities where the writing of pamphlets extended to the artisan class.[57] Again there is a difference in timing: the flood of printed Reformation propaganda subsided by 1525. Instead, more permanent bibles, available from 1522/3 onwards, took its place, as pamphlets for the less literate became the exception.[58]

V

In view of the recent works by von Greyerz, Brady and Scribner[59] a systematic summary is unnecessary. Instead, I shall try to identify those issues on which future research on the urban Reformation may usefully reflect.

1. Our awareness of the Reformation as an urban event underlines the importance of social actions which should rank equal to ideas. To illustrate this point we may conveniently turn to the litanies described by Brady in which the authorities expressed their dilemma to the emperor, empire and public at large.[60] What would follow from suppressing the common man's thirst for God's word was 'disturbances, rebellion, murder, bloodshed, yes, total ruin and every sort of evil'. The enforcement of the edict of Worms would cause 'serious uprisings, the destruction of law and order, and dissension between commons and regimes, and between clergy and laity', leading – again – 'to murder and bloodshed' and the ruin of the empire. These catalogues of 'uprisings, ruin, destruction, and bloodshed'[61] show how far the urban oligarchies had meretriciously sacrificed their civic pride to the emperor by 1524. That their fears chimed with the judgement of conservative princes and with Luther's attitude towards the peasants a year later is striking. But the point is that this catalogue of woe listed actions and not internalised beliefs. To the extent which it gave rise to specific actions, however, the Reformation could become an 'event', and may be investigated as collective action by thick description.[62] Incidentally, these oligarchic fears reflected a crisis of authority on the part of the ruling urban regimes. For Luther, potential and actual revolutions invoking the Gospel entailed a crisis of Reformation as well, by which the devil was trying to destroy peaceful reform. In that light conflict rather than consent emerges as the hallmark of the Reformation. The crisis of authority also implies that urban Reformations were never purely urban, since the regimes' dilemma sprang from external as well as internal pressures.[63]

2. It is equally true that the Reformation as an event interacted with discourse. In disputations, discourse took on the character of an event;[64] in pamphlets oral discourse might coagulate and be translated from a local level to a regional, national, and then international public, just as written discourse was transformed into oral and local communication by preaching.[65] As God's word entered oral and written communication it became effectively transformed as it enlightened the perceptions of the learned and unlearned. No matter how hard oral communication on the

level of common man may be to pin down, it should not be thought of as independent of the structures of authority, though Luther's 'Word of God' for a time certainly destroyed an established ecclesiastical monopoly. The more alert authorities tried to regain lost ground by controlling the channels of communication. Urban Reformations, accordingly, were never self-sufficient, and in that resides the importance of the reformers, both local and national, in writing and preaching. The more that learned discourse detached itself from popular discourse, moreover, the character of the urban Reformation changed.[66]

3. Discourse and actions determined the urban Reformation over time. The reforming process was neither precluded by Luther's ideas nor entirely exposed to contingence. In all its erratic flux it tended to adapt itself to the structural span of the *longue durée*. Even in the exceptional case of Hanover, oligarchical government was eventually restored.[67] In the end the urban Reformation consolidated as the princes' did. But within the traditional structures a new ecclesiastical subsystem was incorporated, depending on the varying pattern of reforming innovation. The initial consequence of a localised and domesticated church which catered for the needs of its individual urban congregations and stressed the role of preaching rather than sacramental rites was to open it to greater social and political control, but in the long term the outcome was to increase its chances of educating the laity. If we belittle the degree of social change in the 1520s, then we ought at least to consider the possibility of changes in mentality in the long run. If these accompanied adjustments in the social structure they did not automatically pave the way for modernisation. This raises the question of how long the Reformation process actually was. We may for clarity's sake limit it to a short period in which the new pattern of church and society was established, the so-called 'introduction' of the Reformation, in order to follow the longer process of the implantation of the new religion. Again, this should not be taken as a one-way process of education percolating downwards from on high, for as with longer-term structural transformation tradition was mingled with innovation. The secular thought of an Enlightenment before the event may have inspired imperial jurists,[68] but the simple folk were more persistent in their popular religious beliefs and their religious prejudices took some time to dispel.

The historical revision which sees both Reformation and urban Reformation as part of a more far-reaching process – either in terms of growing confessionalisation or of stages of Reformation – is in any case already under way.[69]

4. Urban social systems were themselves complex and related to complex environments. The commercial life of the cities might stretch to trade with Venezuela or be confined to the local market. Cities of the north saw themselves as Hanseatic; cities in the south wished to 'turn Swiss'. Some townsfolk regarded the nobility, others the rural commons as their neighbours. Some citizens wished to adapt the parish church to their religious needs, while others made their way to Wittenberg or Geneva. Great variations in mobility and in wealth existed. Some citizens possessed large specialised libraries, others merely pious stocks of catechisms, hymnbooks, prayerbooks, and possibly the New Testament, or parts of it.[70] Those who held that there was only one Lord might oppose the lords of the city who enforced 'civic righteousness'[71] in the name of the Lord. The assertion of a communal identity expressed in the annual convention of citizens to take the civic oath provided basic but minimal social cohesion. That claim was no illusion but a serious matter given a fragile social system under threat from rebels and rulers alike. Just as Luther himself, the city was torn 'between God and the devil', if perhaps under a different guise. Before we attempt to reduce historical complexity to neat categories we should take a longer view at the untidy battleground for survival, power and advantage. Both the pragmatic experience of the ruling magistrates[72] and the religious meaning imparted by the clergy sought to control this 'murderous' and sinful ground. It was their task, as they saw it, to grant order to make life possible. But those with a sense of communal civic values aspired to less hegemonial control from above and sought instead to establish more effective control of the authorities from below. As the urban Reformation progressed, the most tangible structural change was that of divine worship. This change, as in Zürich or Geneva, might lead to a change in the social system itself but elsewhere it might be minimal and susceptible to reversal by the Interim. Councils might submit to communal pressure or stoop to conquer. Internal pressure could be balanced by intimidating external pressure. Ideas might rapidly take root in people's minds, or else be quickly grasped, only to be forgotten or slowly assimilated

into society. Theological reading might convert into preaching, or petrify in slogans with an indefinite range of meaning such as 'God's Word', thus increasing the emotional appeal which explicit programmes would block. The varieties of the urban Reformation, however, were not indefinite, as social structures and beliefs delimited their spectrum. As the Reformation became reality in its progress through society it left a definite mark on towns, adding to traditions and preparing the way for changes to come.

Notes

1. For an analysis of recent research cf. Kaspar von Greyerz, 'Stadt und Reformation. Stand und Aufgaben der Forschung', *Archiv für Reformationsgeschichte*, LXXVI (1985), pp. 6–63. There is a concise exposition of the south German and Swiss urban Reformations in Thomas A. Brady, Jr., *Turning Swiss. Cities and Empire, 1450–1550* (Cambridge, 1985). I am grateful to Bob Scribner for showing me his manuscript 'Urban Culture and Religious Reform in Sixteenth-Century Germany'.
2. Thomas A. Brady, Jr., *Ruling Class, Regime and Reformation at Strasbourg, 1520–1555* (Studies in Medieval and Reformation Thought, XXII) (Leiden, 1978); Bob Scribner, 'Religion, Society and Culture: Reorienting the Reformation', *History Workshop*, XIV (1982), pp. 2–22, 6.
3. Lawrence Stone, 'History and the Social Sciences in the Twentieth Century', in C. F. Kelzell (ed.), *The Future of History* (Nashville, Tenn., 1977), pp. 3–40; Lawrence Stone, 'The Revival of Narrative: Reflections on a New Old History', *Past and Present*, LXXV (1979), pp. 3–24.
4. Quoted in Brady, *Turning Swiss*, p. 157.
5. My argument was first advanced in 'Martin Luther and the Urban Social Experience', *Sixteenth Century Journal*, XVI (1985), p. 15f. For clarity's sake the argument has been couched in its simplified ideal-type. For further comments on Moeller's interpretation cf. below, p. 127f. This concept echoes a tradition in German historiography which traces a phenomenon to its origins in order to locate the essential quality which determines its evolution.
6. Olaf Mörke, 'Der "Konflikt" als Kategorie städtischer Sozialgeschichte des 16. Jahrhunderts', in Bernhard Distelkamp (ed.), *Beiträge zum spätmittelalterlichen Städtewesen* (Städteforschung. Veröffentlichungen des Instituts für Vergleichende Städtegeschichte in Münster, Reihe A XII) (Cologne/Vienna, 1982), pp. 144–61.
7. That this only allows a limited range of interpretations has been demonstrated by Clifford Geertz, 'Ideology as a Cultural System', in D. E. Apter (ed.), *Ideology and Discontent* (London, 1964), pp. 1–76.

For a more general version cf. Niklas Luhmann, *Funktion der Religion* (Frankfurt am Main, 1982 edn), p. 184. '*Kein komplexes System kann es sich leisten, alles von allem abhängig zu machen.*'

8.   Georg Schmidt, *Der Städtetag in der Reichsverfassung. Eine Untersuchung zur korporativen Politik der Freien und Reichsstädte in der ersten Hälfte des 16. Jahrhunderts* (Veröffentlichungen des Instituts für europäische Geschichte Mainz, Abt. Universalgeschichte, CXIII: Beiträge zur Sozial- und Verfassungsgeschichte des Alten Reichs, V) (Wiesbaden, 1984); idem, 'Die Haltung des Städtecorpus zur Reformation und die Nürnberger Bündnispolitik', *Archiv für Reformationsgeschichte*, LXXV (1984), pp. 194–233.

9.   E.g. Ingrid Bátori and Erdmann Weyrauch, *Die bürgerliche Elite der Stadt Kitzingen. Studien zur Sozial- und Wirtschaftsgeschichte einer landesherrlichen Stadt im 16. Jahrhundert* (Spätmittelalter und Frühe Neuzeit, XI) (Stuttgart, 1982); Hans Füglister, *Handwerksregiment. Untersuchungen und Materialien zur sozialen und politischen Struktur der Stadt Basel in der ersten Hälfte des 16. Jahrhunderts* (Basler Beiträge zur Geschichtswissenschaft, CXLIII) (Basel/Frankfurt am Main, 1981).

10.   Thomas Fischer, *Städtische Armut und Armenfürsorge im 15. und 16. Jahrhundert* (Göttinger Beiträge zur Wirtschafts- und Sozialgeschichte, IV) (Göttingen, 1979); Max Safley, 'Marital Disputes and Marital Litigation in Basel, Freiburg and the Diocese of Constance: A Comparative Study, 1550–1600' (PhD Dissertation, University of Wisconsin, 1980); idem, *Let No Man Put Asunder* (Kirksville, Mo., 1984); Lyndal Roper, 'Work, Marriage and Sexuality: Women in Reformation Augsburg' (PhD Dissertation, University of London, 1985); Steven Ozment, *When Fathers Ruled. Family Life in Reformation Europe* (Cambridge, Mass., 1983); Konrad Wiedemann, *Arbeit und Bürgertum* (Beiträge zur neueren Literaturgeschichte, 3rd series XLVI) (Heidelberg, 1979); Paul Münch (ed.), *Ordnung, Fleiß und Sparsamkeit. Texte und Dokumente zur Entstehung der 'bürgerlichen Tugenden'* (Munich, 1984).

11.   Lorna Jane Abray, *The People's Reformation. Magistrates, Clergy and Commons in Strasbourg, 1500–1598* (Oxford, 1985).

12.   Heiko A. Oberman, *Werden und Wertung der Reformation. Vom Wegestreit zum Glaubenskampf*, 2nd edn (Tübingen, 1979); idem, 'Stadtreformation und Fürstenreformation', in L. W. Spitz (ed.), *Humanismus und Reformation als kulturelle Kräfte in der deutschen Geschichte* (Veröffentlichungen der Historischen Kommission zu Berlin, LI) (Berlin/New York, 1981), pp. 80–103. For the Rankean paradigm cf. Hans-Christoph Rublack, 'Forschungsbericht Stadt und Reformation', in Bernd Moeller (ed.), *Stadt und Kirche im 16. Jahrhundert* (Schriften des Vereins für Reformationsgeschichte, CXC) (Gütersloh, 1978), p. 9, n. 2.

13.   For a clearer exposition cf. Hans-Christoph Rublack, 'Reformation and Society', in Manfred Hoffmann (ed.), *Martin Luther and the Modern Mind. Freedom, Conscience, Toleration, Rights* (Toronto Studies in Theology, XXII) (New York/Toronto, 1985), pp. 237–78.

14. Markus Schaer, *Seelennöte der Untertanen. Selbstmord, Melancholie und Religion im Alten Zürich, 1500-1800* (Zürich, 1985), which deserves to be complemented by a study of Lutheran communities.
15. Cf. Rublack, 'Luther and Urban Social Experience', p. 16.
16. Scribner, 'Urban Culture and Religious Reform'.
17. Cf. Hans-Christoph Rublack, 'Political and Social Norms in Urban Communities in the Holy Roman Empire', in Kaspar von Greyerz (ed.), *Religion, Politics and Social Protest. Three Studies on Early Modern Germany* (London, 1984), p. 39f.
18. I have developed this theme in 'Luther and Urban Social Experience'.
19. Peter Blickle, *Gemeindereformation. Die Menschen des 16. Jahrhunderts auf dem Weg zum Heil* (Munich, 1985); idem, 'Die soziale Dialektik der reformatorischen Bewegung', in idem *et al.* (eds), *Zwingli und Europa* (Zürich, 1985), pp. 71–89; idem, *Die Reformation im Reich* (Stuttgart, 1982).
20. Georg Friedrich Wilhelm Hegel, *Vorlesungen über die Philosophie der Geschichte* (*Hegel Werke*, vol. XII) (Frankfurt am Main, 1970), p. 555.

   [*Ein Staat*] *geschieht in einer notwendigen Stufenfolge, wodurch das Vernünftige, Gerechtigkeit und Befestigung der Freiheit hervorgeht.* [*Es ist ein System*] *von Institutionen, a) als System der Konstitution, b) der Inhalt derselben ebenso, wodurch die wahrhaften Interessen zum Bewußtsein gebracht und zur Wirklichkeit errungen werden. In jedem Fortschreiten des Gegenstands ist nicht bloß äußerliche Konsequenz und Notwendigkeit des Zusammenhangs, sondern Notwendigkeit in der Sache, im Begriff. Dies* [*ist*] *die wahrhafte Sache. ... dies ist der Gegenstand und Zweck der Geschichtsschreiber, aber auch Zweck des Volks, Zweck der Zeit selbst. Darauf* [*wird*] *alles bezogen.*

21. Blickle, *Gemeindereformation*, p. 114: '*Weihe*'.
22. Ibid., p. 113: '*unbewußt gewiß, aber ihren Bedürfnissen entsprechend*'.
23. Ibid., p. 116.
24. The three case studies cited by Blickle – Erfurt, Kitzingen, Basel – do not in fact constitute a random sample. Moreover, Erfurt and Basel, which were strongly affected by peasants' movements, differed from cities which carefully tried to keep citizens and peasants apart, as in the celebrated cases of Nuremberg, Augsburg or Nördlingen, the latter a 'low profile' Reformation city. In this context I will omit Kitzingen, leaving it open whether Blickle has correctly interpreted the study by Dieter Demandt and Hans-Christoph Rublack, *Stadt und Kirche in Kitzingen. Darstellung und Quellen zu Spätmittelalter und Reformation* (Spätmittelalter und Frühe Neuzeit, X) (Stuttgart, 1978). A rather more suitable case would have been Rothenburg ob der Tauber, or even Nuremberg, which has recently been admitted to the series of cities susceptible to populist action. Cf. Günter Vogler, *Nürnberg 1524/25. Studien zur Geschichte der reformatorischen und sozialen Bewegung in der Reichsstadt* (Berlin, 1982).
25. Brady, *Ruling Class*; cf. idem, 'Göttliche Republiken. Die Domestizierung der Religion in der deutschen Stadtreformation', in Blickle, *Zwingli und Europa*, pp. 109–36.

26.   This theme cannot be treated fully here. Cf. Niklas Luhmann, *Soziologische Aufklärung*, vol. II, 2nd edn (Opladen, 1982), p. 153 for a concise version, as well as idem, *Funktion der Religion*, p. 188f. For a clear analysis cf. Erdmann Weyrauch, 'Über soziale Schichtung', in Ingrid Bátori (ed.), *Städtische Gesellschaft und Reformation* (Spätmittelalter und Frühe Neuzeit, XII) (Stuttgart, 1980), pp. 5–57. With regard to Luhmann cf. Weyrauch, *Konfessionelle Krise und soziale Stabilität. Das Interim in Straßburg (1548–1562)* (Spätmittelalter und Frühe Neuzeit, VII) (Stuttgart, 1978), pp. 33ff, esp. p. 45 on the modes of differentiation.

27.   Bernd Moeller, 'Luther und die Städte', in *Aus der Lutherforschung. Drei Vorträge* (Opladen, 1983), pp. 9–26, summing up on p. 17: '*Auch die Wirkung, die Luther ausübte, überstieg ja die sozialen Bindungen und Schichtungen*'; ibid., p. 26: '*Aber vielleicht hat es in einem Lutherjahr ja auch etwas beruhigendes an sich, wenn man feststellen kann, daß Luther in seiner Anhängerschaft nicht aufgeht.*' The notion of Luther's alienness from civic life is developed in Rublack, 'Luther and Urban Social Social Experience'.

28.   Moeller, 'Luther und die Städte', p. 23: '*angeeignet und schöpferisch weiterverarbeitet*'; ibid., pp. 18, 24.

29.   Ibid., p. 24.

30.   Ibid., p. 25f.

31.   *Verarmung*: ibid., p. 26.

32.   This follows Berndt Hamm, 'Stadt und Kirche unter dem Wort Gottes. Das reformatorische Einheitsmodell des Nürnberger Ratsschreibers Lazarus Spengler (1479–1534)', in Ludger Grenzmann and Karl Stackmann (eds), *Literatur und Laienbildung im Spätmittelalter und in der Reformationszeit. Symposion Wolfenbüttel* (Stuttgart, 1982), pp. 710–29.

33.   Ibid., p. 717: '*das wort gottes verursacht bei allen christen freud, frid und alle einigkeit, verhůt auch unfrid, widerwertigkeit, zanck und entporung.*'

34.   Abray, *People's Reformation*, p. 200. This book should be consulted for the other themes adumbrated by Hamm.

35.   Hans Volz (ed.), *Martin Luther: Biblia. Das ist die gantze Heilige Schrifft Deudsch auffs new zugericht*, vol. I (Munich, 1974), p. 183f: '*das bedeut/ das menschen lere dem volck furbilden/ was sie fur werck thun sollen/ da mit sie Gott dienen.*'

36.   The latest and most accessible account is in Eike Wolgast, 'Luthers Beziehungen zu den Bürgern', in Helmar Junghans (ed.), *Leben und Werk Martin Luthers von 1526 bis 1546. Festgabe zu seinem 500. Geburtstag*, vol. I (Berlin, 1983), pp. 609–11.

37.   Bernd Moeller, 'Stadt und Buch. Bemerkungen zur Struktur der reformatorischen Bewegung in Deutschland', in Wolfgang J. Mommsen *et al.* (eds), *Stadtbürgertum und Adel in der Reformation* (Veröffentlichungen des Deutschen Historischen Instituts London, V) (Stuttgart, 1979), pp. 25–39, here p. 27: '*Deutschland ... stellte in seinen Städten ... die Schauplätze bereit, auf denen die geistig-kirchlichen Impulse, die von Luther ausgingen, besonders genau aufgegriffen werden, ein besonders lebhaftes Echo finden und weitergeführt werden konnten.*'

38. Thomas A. Brady, Jr., '"The Social History of the Reformation" between "Romantic Idealism" and "Sociologism". A Reply', in ibid., pp. 39–43, quotation p. 43.

39. Cf. the summary of the seminar discussion at the International Luther Congress in Erfurt, August 1983, by Gottfried Seebaß, 'Martin Luther und die Anfänge der Reformation in den Städten', *Lutherjahrbuch*, 1985, p. 269.

40. Scribner, 'Religion, Society and Culture', p. 6.

41. Cf. Gerd Hohorst, Jürgen Kocka, and Gerhard A. Ritter, *Sozialgeschichtliches Arbeitsbuch. Materialien zur Statistik des Kaiserreichs 1870–1914* (Munich, 1975), p. 52, Table 15b.

42. R. W. Scribner, 'Why was there no Reformation in Cologne?', *Bulletin of the Institute of Historical Research*, XLIX (1976), pp. 217–41; Hans-Christoph Rublack, *Gescheiterte Reformation. Frühreformatorische und protestantische Bewegungen in süd- und westdeutschen geistlichen Residenzen* (Spätmittelalter und Frühe Neuzeit, IV) (Stuttgart, 1978).

43. Kaspar von Greyerz, *The Late City Reformation in Germany. The Case of Colmar, 1522–1628* (Veröffentlichungen des Instituts für Europäische Geschichte Mainz, XCVIII) (Wiesbaden, 1980), which discusses Essen, Dortmund, Aachen and Haguenau as well.

44. Abray, *People's Reformation*.

45. Heinz Schilling, 'Die politische Elite nordwestdeutscher Städte in den religiösen Auseinandersetzungen des 16. Jahrhunderts', in Mommsen, *Stadtbürgertum und Adel*, pp. 235–308; Olaf Mörke, *Rat und Bürger in der Reformation. Soziale Gruppen und kirchlicher Wandel in den welfischen Hansestädten Lüneburg, Braunschweig und Göttingen* (Veröffentlichungen des Instituts für Historische Landesforschung der Universität Göttingen, XIX) (Hildesheim, 1983); idem, 'Stadt und Reformation in Niedersachsen', in *Stadt im Wandel. Kunst und Kultur des Bürgertums in Norddeutschland 1150–1650* (Brunswick, 1985), pp. 75–87; for Hanover cf. Siegfried Müller, 'Stadt, Kirche und Reformation: Das Beispiel der Landstadt Hannover' (Diss. phil., University of Hanover, 1984); for Hamburg cf. Rainer Postel, *Die Reformation in Hamburg 1517–1528* (Quellen und Forschungen zur Reformationsgeschichte, LII) (Gütersloh, 1986); idem, 'Reformation und Gegenreformation, 1517–1618', in *Hamburg. Geschichte der Stadt und ihrer Bewohner*, vol. I (Hamburg, 1982), pp. 191–258.

46. Günter Vogler, 'Die Reformation und die kurmärkischen Städte (1517–1539)', *Frankfurter Beiträge zur Geschichte*, XII (1985), pp. 3–13.

47. Schilling, 'Politische Elite', p. 241; idem, *Konfessionskonflikt und Staatsbildung. Eine Fallstudie über das Verhältnis von religiösem und sozialem Wandel in der Frühneuzeit am Beispiel der Grafschaft Lippe* (Quellen und Forschungen zur Reformationsgeschichte, XLVIII) (Gütersloh, 1981), p. 139: '*die Vielzahl kleinerer und kleinster Städte, ... denen es ... an politischer Kraft und bürgerlicher Tradition fehlte, um unabhängig von Landesherrn und Territorium reformatorische Initiative und Beharrungsvermögen zu beweisen.*' That might apply to Wittenberg, as least in terms of persistence. For the south German Kitzingen it has

been shown that the urban Reformation was controlled by the prince from a very early stage. Cf. Demandt/Rublack, *Stadt und Kirche in Kitzingen.*

48. Brady, *Turning Swiss.*
49. Ibid., p. 153; Scribner, 'Urban Culture'.
50. The salient event being the colloquy of January 1523, which I have argued conformed to constitutional procedure: Hans-Christoph Rublack, 'Zwingli und Zürich', *Zwingliana*, XVI (1983), pp. 393–426.
51. Müller, 'Stadt, Kirche und Reformation'.
52. Mörke, 'Stadt und Reformation'.
53. Schilling, 'Politische Elite', p. 302f, as well as a 'communal theology of the Reformation', ibid., pp. 303, 239; idem, *Konfessionskonflikt*, p. 81 (*Gottes Wort*).
54. Mörke, *Rat und Bürger*, pp. 139, 150, 153, 157, 160, 269, 302.
55. Müller, 'Stadt, Kirche und Reformation', p. 112.
56. Bernd Moeller, 'Was wurde in der Frühzeit der Reformation in den deutschen Städten gepredigt?', *Archiv für Reformationsgeschichte*, LXXV (1984), pp. 176–93.
57. Paul Russell, *Lay Theology in the Reformation. Popular Pamphleteers in Southwest Germany, 1521–1525* (Cambridge, 1986); Miriam Usher Chrisman, *Lay Culture, Learned Culture. Books and Social Change in Strasbourg 1480–1599* (New Haven/London, 1982).
58. Heimo Reinitzer, *Biblia deutsch. Luthers Bibelübersetzung und ihre Tradition* (Ausstellungskataloge der Herzog August Bibliothek, XL) (Wolfenbüttel/Hamburg, 1983), pp. 118, 124.
59. The summary in A. G. Dickens and J. M. Tonkin, *The Reformation in Historical Thought* (Oxford, 1986) is less useful, since it is biased towards literature in English and fails to take account of more recent monographs.
60. Brady, *Turning Swiss*, pp. 168f, 173, 181.
61. Ibid., p. 181.
62. Cf. R. W. Scribner, 'Reformation, Carneval and the World Turned Upside-Down', in Bátori, *Städtische Gesellschaft*, pp. 234–64; Scribner, 'Volkskultur und Volksreligion. Zur Rezeption evangelischer Ideen', in Blickle, *Zwingli und Europa*, pp. 151–61.
63. Brady, *Turning Swiss.*
64. Bernd Moeller, 'Zwinglis Disputationen. Studien zu den Anfängen der Kirchenbildung und des Synodalwesens im Protestantismus', parts I and II, *Zeitschrift der Savignystiftung für Rechtsgeschichte, Kanonistische Abteilung*, LVI (1970), pp. 275–324; LX (1974), pp. 213–64.
65. Hans-Joachim Köhler (ed.), *Flugschriften als Massenmedium der Reformationszeit* (Spätmittelalter und Frühe Neuzeit, XIII) (Stuttgart, 1981); idem, 'Erste Schritte zu einem Meinungsprofil der frühen Reformationszeit', in Volker Press (ed.), *Martin Luther und seine Zeit* (forthcoming); R. W. Scribner, 'Oral Culture and the Diffusion of Reformation Ideas', *Journal of European Ideas*, V (1984), pp. 237–56; Rainer Wohlfeil, *Einführung in die Geschichte der deutschen Reformation* (Munich, 1982), pp. 123-33.
66. Chrisman, *Lay Culture, Learned Culture.*

67. Müller, 'Stadt, Kirche und Reformation'; for northern German cities cf. Schilling, *Konfessionskonflikt*, pp. 142ff; for south German cities cf. Brady, *Turning Swiss*, pp. 158, 165f.
68. Martin Heckel, *Deutschland im konfessionellen Zeitalter* (Göttingen, 1983); idem, 'Weltlichkeit und Säkularisierung. Staatskirchenrechtliche Probleme in der Reformation und im Konfessionellen Zeitalter', in Bernd Moeller (ed.), *Luther in der Neuzeit* (Schriften des Vereins für Reformationsgeschichte, CXCII) (Gütersloh, 1983), pp. 34–54; Heckel, *Korollarien zur Säkularisierung* (Sitzungsberichte der Heidelberger Akademie der Wissenschaften, Phil.-hist. Klasse, 1981, IV) (Heidelberg, 1981).
69. Here Abray, *People's Reformation*, is a case in point, as is Schilling's *Konfessionsbildung*, and von Greyerz, *Late City Reformation*; again, Scribner's discussion in 'Religion, Society and Culture' is relevant here. For a renumbering of Reformations cf. Heiko A. Oberman, 'Die Reformation als theologische Revolution', in Blickle, *Zwingli und Europa*, pp. 11–26.
70. Erdmann Weyrauch, 'Die Illiteraten und ihre Literatur', in Wolfgang Brückner *et al.* (eds), *Literatur und Volk im 17. Jahrhundert. Probleme populärer Kultur in Deutschland* (Wiesbaden, 1985), pp. 465–74.
71. Roper, 'Work, Marriage and Sexuality', pp. 1, 82ff.
72. The pragmatic sense of urban oligarchies is attested by Brady, *Turning Swiss*, and Scribner, 'Urban Culture'.

7 The Common Man and the Lost Austria in the West: A Contribution to the German Problem[1]

Thomas A. Brady, Jr

One of the persistent peculiarities of German history is 'the idea of a *Sonderweg*, or German historical aberration'.[2] The currently most prominent version of the idea holds that 'the central point about Germany's passage to "modernity" was the lack of synchronization between the economic, social, and political spheres', with the result that 'Germany did not have a bourgeois revolution of the normal kind associated with England, France, or the United States'.[3] There is another notion of a German *Sonderweg*, ideologically related to the first, which holds that Germany failed in the sixteenth century to imitate 'the growing signs of organised strength, the growing unity of national consciousness, the growing reality underlying the pomp of dynastic monarchy',[4] which may be identified in contemporary England, France, or Castile. The deficit attributed to this second *Sonderweg* is not the bourgeois revolution of the eighteenth century but the Protestant Reformation, sometimes in its guise as the 'early bourgeois revolution'. What is at stake in this notion of *Sonderweg*, again, is not the class character of the new Germany created in 1871, but its confessional character. The point was perfectly made by Adolf Stoecker, the Prussian court preacher, who exulted that 'the Holy German Evangelical Empire is now achieved', in which 'we can see the hand of God from 1517 to 1871!'[5]

The twentieth century has made a historical curiosity of the quarrel of *großdeutsch* and *kleindeutsch* over the shape of the German state. What survives is a myth of the German national *Sonderweg* in the sixteenth century. Two examples from very different corners may illustrate how widely it is held. The English historian A. J. P. Taylor has written:

The first years of Charles V were the moment of Goethe's phrase which, once lost, eternity will never give back. The moment for making a national middle-class Germany was lost in 1521 perhaps forever, certainly for centuries. By 1525, it was evident that the period of national awakening had passed, and there began from that moment a steady advance of absolutism and authoritarianism which continued uninterruptedly for more than 250 years.[6]

From another point of view Max Steinmetz, dean of the German Democratic Republic's historians of the Reformation era, contends that 'The early bourgeois revolution, which culminated in the Peasant War, represented the first attempt of the popular masses to create a unified national state from below.'[7]

Neither historian specifies the term 'national', though one suspects that each means Germany in something like the configuration of 1871. Neither specifies the political meaning of a national – as distinct from a patriotically-minded – 'middle-class' or the 'popular masses'.

There are at least two serious objections to the general view expressed by Taylor and Steinmetz. The first is that the 'national' states created in sixteenth-century Europe were, with the exception of the Netherlands, centralised, dynastic monarchies, which possessed of the attributes of absolutist states – civil bureacracies, taxation, standing armies, diplomatic corps, and claims to sovereignty – and which had war as their chief business. Far from being creations of 'middle-classes' or 'popular masses', such states represented 'the new political carapace of a threatened nobility', which now required the state's mediation for its extraction of the surplus.[8] In some parts of Europe, state-building forces also arose from the burghers and even the ranks of the peasantry. Such forces were strong in a belt of lands that stretched across the northern foot of the Central Alps, where they tended politically not toward absolutism but toward republics based on the representation of urban and rural communes.[9] It is conceivable that in regions of Germany where the nobles were weak, such forces might have combined under royal leadership to form a state which would have been monarchical but not absolutist.

A second objection to the statements by Taylor and Steinmetz concerns the concept of the 'nation'. A close examination of the Holy Roman Empire's structure at end of the Middle Ages reveals a system that was centred firmly in the South. Not only did the High Court and Governing Council, created in the reform era of 1495–1521, sit in the South, but the Imperial Diet was also predominantly southern in its meeting sites, membership, and attendance. The Habsburg dynasty, which ruled the empire continuously since 1440, had its dynastic lands entirely in the south. Austria stretched from the borders of Hungary to those of Lorraine, and it was never combined administratively with the Habsburg Netherlands except for the brief years of personal union between Maximilian I's death in 1519 and Archduke Ferdinand's assumption of rule over Austria in 1522. In the opening decades of the sixteenth century this dynasty was faced not with the creation of a 'national' Germany on a bourgeois, popular, or any other basis, but with the formation and consolidation of an Austrian system of lordship and clientage solid enough and rich enough to serve as a basis from which to strengthen its power over the rest of the empire. The creation of such a basis may well have lain within Habsburg grasp around 1520, but the chance was shattered by a combination of forces and events that doomed the basis that was then forming, Austria's kingdom in the west.

I

Shortly before Christmas 1519, a Brabantine nobleman named Maximilian van Bergen rode into Augsburg to negotiate with representatives of the Swabian League about the transfer of the duchy of Württemberg, which the League had conquered from its reigning duke, to King Charles of Spain, who was also King of the Romans and emperor-elect. 'Your Majesty should be thoroughly convinced', Bergen wrote to his master,

> that this land of Württemberg is a large and important territory, and that Your Royal Majesty can procure no greater advantage than to bring it into Your Majesty's hands. This is so because it lies in the middle of the Holy Empire and borders on some of Your Royal Majesty's hereditary Austrian lands. If Württemberg is added to them, then Your Royal Majesty would have, as archduke of Austria, adequate power *vis-à-vis* the disturbers of the peace in the German lands. Your Majesty should also consider that he could thus all the better maintain law and order in the Holy Empire, and that the common folk in Württemberg wish nothing more than to join the obedience of Your Royal Majesty and the House of Austria.[10]

The alternative, Bergen thought, would be the destruction of the Swabian League by the princes, who would

> shove the cities aside and enjoy a 'free government' in the Empire.

Your Majesty can well imagine how much obedience you would then command! Also, once the cities see what is happening, His Majesty can be assured that nothing less will happen than that all these cities will join the Swiss, and thereafter the whole land of Swabia and the Rhine Valley all the way down to Cologne would join as well. God grant that it might go no further! We are firmly convinced that the princes who thus intrigue do not sufficiently consider what they do; for if it develops so far in this direction, they will be expelled by their own subjects, who would then join these others; and in the end the whole German land would become one vast commune, and all the lords would be expelled.[11]

Bergen thus laid before his sovereign the two political paths that South Germany might reasonably take. The townsmen and other commoners might well support a strong House of Austria, if it could keep the peace in the South and provide good government. Otherwise, they would try to 'turn Swiss', that is, either to join the Swiss confederation or form 'new Switzerlands' in imitation of the old. Monarchism and communal federalism were thus not contrary policies but alternatives.

The wisdom of Bergen's comments in the winter of 1519–20 can be judged only in the context of the dead emperor's reign. Three years before he succeeded his father, Emperor Frederick III, in 1493, Maximilian became lord of Tyrol and Western Austria (*Vorderöster-reich*), a belt of lands stretching from Vorarlberg across Upper Swabia and the lands west of Lake Constance – the Hegau, Klettgau, and Breisgau – to the Sundgau in southern Alsace. Tyrol now became the pivotal point of Habsburg Austria, based on its control of the strategic Brenner Pass, its mining wealth, and its position as the bridge between the western and eastern parts of Austria. What Western Austria lacked were major cities and all the good things cities provided – guns and foodstuffs, credit and men – for although the neighbouring lands were, by Central European standards, relatively highly urbanised, most of the cities had acquired self-rule and owed obedience to Maximilian only as King of the Romans and later as emperor. Maximilian gathered them under the Austrian eagle's wings through two strategies: he made them Habsburg clients through membership in political federations he organised; and he offered the big merchant bankers very lucrative business through chartered monopolies, loans, and purveyance to the royal court.

The cities of the neighbouring lands, Swabia and the Upper Rhine

Valley, had exercised little military power since the princes had smashed the last German urban league in the Cities' War of 1449–53. The Swabian cities drew near the House of Austria with little resistance, for Maximilian knew what they wanted. In 1488 he organised the free cities, along with the free nobles and prelates of Upper Swabia, into the Swabian League, which only had to show its teeth through a mobilisation in the Lech Valley in 1492 in order to restore Duke Albert IV of Bavaria to good behaviour. The next year Maximilian corralled the Upper Rhenish powers, some of whom had refused to join the Swabian League on the grounds that they were 'too distant', into a league called the Lower Union. The reconstitution of the Lower Union was a cunning act. The original Lower Union formed in 1474 of Alsatian powers, the duke of Lorraine, and the House of Austria, and it allied with the 'Upper Union', the Swiss confederation, in the League of Constance against Burgundy in the same year. Together the allies caught and killed the Burgundian governor on the Upper Rhine, invaded and plundered Burgundy, and in 1475–77 smashed the Burgundian power in three glorious battles. The reconstituted Lower Union of 1493 formed the western, Rhenish wing of Maximilian's system of clientele.

Maximilian's South German system dominated the region from the earlier 1490s until well after the king's death in 1519. In 1492 it halted Bavarian expansion in Upper Swabia; in 1499 it fought a disastrous war against the confederation, from which it nevertheless emerged relatively unscathed; in 1504 it crushed the expanding power of the Palatine Wittelsbachs on the Upper Rhine; and in 1519, just after the old king's death, the Swabian League invaded Württemberg and expelled Duke Ulrich, its wild, reckless ruler. The humiliations of the Swabian War of 1499 aside, Maximilian's system was a most effective instrument of the free cities and Austria against the chief princely dynasties of the South. After the Swabian League expired in 1533, a Protestant Nuremberger lamented its demise: 'The Swabian League was the proper form of the German Nation. It was feared by many, and in many ways it protected and sustained the public peace and law and order.'[12]

Maximilian bound the urban rich to his person and his treasury through many types of connections. His legendary penury meant opportunity to the urban bankers, those of Augsburg in particular, to whom he owed about 3 million florins at his death, 1.3 million to the Fuggers alone. In return they got chartered monopolies for the import of foodstuffs into the alpine lands and for the exploitation of Tyrol's rich silver and copper mines and smelters. Of the 1.5 million florins his Tyrolean mines annually produced, perhaps a tenth remained unmortgaged and came to Maximilian. A very large portion of the commissions and orders for the court, ranging from clothes to books to paintings to gems to armour to guns to funeral monuments, went to the city folk, who supplied the notoriously slow-paying court on speculation. So dependent did he become on the urban merchants that in 1508, when the Italian Wars had ruined his finances beyond all hope, the king even tried to assume direct royal jurisdiction over the great firms of South Germany, just like his jurisdiction over the Jews.

Maximilian also showed himself in the cities, moving from town to town like a 'royal locust' and papering his progress with bad debts. He recruited personnel for his court in the towns – secretaries and councillors, humanists and poets, artillerymen and physicians. He bound many of the urban elite to his person through vassalage, honorary appointments, literary commissions, and familiar ties, such as standing godfather to the baby daughter of Claus Jörger, an upstart cloth merchant at Strasbourg. He did not inspire much awe. As a young prince, when he and his father had been unable to pay their bills in 1474, the good burghers of Augsburg threw dung at him in the streets. Here, at Augsburg in the Lech Valley, Maximilian's favourite route northward from Italy and Tyrol, the king was most at home; here he owed the most money, and here the big folk knew him best. When he died, the Augsburg merchant Wilhelm Rem wrote the king's epitaph:

> The emperor was Austria's lord, he was pious but not especially intelligent, and he was always out of money. In his own lands he had given away so many cities, castles, rents, and dues, that very little came to him.
>
> His councillors were genuine scoundrels, and they completely dominated him. Almost all of them grew rich, while he was poor. And whoever wanted a favor from the emperor, ... he had to pay bribes to the councillors, who got it done. When, however, an adversary came to court, they also took money from him and gave him charters which contradicted the earlier ones. The emperor stood by and let it all happen.[13]

Dr Erasmus Topler of Nuremberg, who lived for five years at court, put it more succinctly: 'for the nature of this court [is] dedicated to deals (*finanzen*)'.

The positive responses with which Maximilian's overtures and programmes were received among the urban ruling classes found their most lasting expression among the South German humanists, who propagated a monarchist and pro-Austrian ideology during Maximilian's era. At Nuremberg, Augsburg, and Strasbourg, the leading literary lights all did their part to spread the fame and glory of the House of Habsburg, men such as Jacob Wimpheling at Strasbourg, who lashed out with fury at those who suggested that Alsace had ever been ruled by Latins, and Conrad Peutinger of Augsburg, who spent his spare time composing Habsburg genealogies. It was for the glory of the Habsburgs that this generation of humanists stitched together the unbroken line of majesty from Maximilian right back to Augustus.

Behind this elegant hyperbole lay hard calculation. The oligarchies of this generation faced severe threats to their power and independence from both without and within the city walls. Without lay the great princes, who coveted the cities' resources and laid siege to their liberties, either individually through attempts to mediatise the cities and incorporate them into their territories – the fate of Mainz, Boppard, and Erfurt – or collectively in the Imperial Diet, where the princes staged in the early 1520s a whole series of attacks on commerce in general and the chartered monopolies in particular. Added to these political threats were the more straightforward predations of the robber-nobles, such as Cuntz Schott, who specialised in collecting hands from Nuremberg merchants, which heightened the already acute need for law and order.

Within the city walls, the fabric of hegemonic values – justice, peace, and unity in the service of God's honour and the common good – was beginning to unravel. The mounting wave of urban revolts during the first two decades of the century differed in some respects from earlier upheavals, for they arose less from political ambition and more from need. The economic boom that began in South Germany around 1470 lasted until about the middle of the sixteenth century, but despite the signs of urban wealth – it was the age of Holbein, Grünewald, Riemenschneider, and Dürer, of Jakob Fugger the Rich and the Welser colonisation of Venezuela, of the golden age of German printing and of the *Landsknechte* – despite such signs the cities witnessed a growing polarisation of wealth. Poverty's sharp claws reached much further up the social structure than the urban tax registers reveal, for above the actual poor were the potential poor, those threatened by the falling real wage. The consequence was that the ranks of the potentially poor embraced in many cities the bulk of the work force,[14] while at the same time the apprentices and wage-workers – up to a third of those gainfully occupied in some cities[15] – had few organisations through which to express their grievances.

Faced with such forces, the urban oligarchies drew ever nearer the monarchy, especially when, early in Charles' reign, the princes mounted their campaign against the great firms under the slogan of anti-monopoly. In the summer of 1523, they sent an embassy to the emperor at Valladolid in Spain, which begged Charles to assume direct rule in Germany, deposing the Governing Council and High Court and presumably bypassing the Imperial Diet, or to direct his brother, Archduke Ferdinand, to rule Germany in his place. The further development of this proposal was blocked for the moment by the envoys' lack of powers to commit their cities to direct financial aid to the monarch, but the proposal itself represented a direct development of the political partnership of cities and crown in Maximilian's time.

What was true of the free cities' oligarchies applied, *mutatis mutandis*, to the elites of the territorial towns as well. Or so Maximilian van Bergen alleged, and his view is confirmed for Württemberg, at least, by the strongly pro-Austrian sentiments among the small-town notables (*Ehrbarkeit*) in the duchy. Just as in the free cities, however, in Württemberg the elites had important ties to the Swiss confederation. Not only did their spendthrift duke, Ulrich, owe large sums of money to Swiss creditors, but Württemberg was one of the regions that regularly supplied the confederation with grain. Bergen expressly attributed to them the same motives he ascribed to the governments of the free cities: if Austria could not guarantee law and order, they would seek it from the confederation.

II

These were the tendencies and policies that brought Maximilian, as ruler of Tyrol and Western Austria, as head of the House of Austria, as leader of the Swabian League and Lower Union, and as King of the Romans and emperor, together with the South German burghers and especially those of the southern free cities. The tendencies were both objective – trade and security – and subjective – monarchism and Austrian feeling, and the policies groped toward an ever closer association of crown and cities. At the same time, there emerged a notion of forming Austria, particularly Tyrol and the western lands, into a more adequate basis both for the system of Austrian clientage in South Germany and for the domination of the Holy Roman Empire.

The relatively advanced state of Tyrolean administrative institutions made the land a reasonable base for state-building. Although the origins of a territorial administration built up of collegial bodies having specific competencies (finance, etc.) for the entire territory reached back well before Maximilian's time, and although the king himself, driven by the need to find money for his political schemes, destroyed nearly as much as he created, by the early 1500s Tyrol had the most advanced administrative bureaucracy in the German-speaking world.[16] The combination of a relatively efficient bureaucracy and abundant revenues from mining ought to have made Tyrol a powerful state, as it did the two Saxonies, had Maximilian not drained the country for his plans in Italy and elsewhere.

There is ample evidence that Maximilian none the less recognised the need for a stronger centralised government for Tyrol and the other dynastic lands. His first project, framed in 1516, was to transform Austria into a separate kingdom, to be cut out of Charles' fabulous heritage and given to Archduke Ferdinand as Austrian king, a plan which foundered on Charles' objections. Two years later, he broached to an assembly of envoys from all of the Austrian lands a plan for a central government for Austria and the empire. In the new State Council (*Hofrat*) would sit five councillors from Eastern Austria (the five Austrian duchies), four from Western Austria, and four royal nominees, plus five from the rest of the Holy Roman Empire. His purpose, as he explained, was to promote 'our own welfare and that of our lands and subjects' by establishing 'at the proper time and place, a neighbourly union, agreement, and league with the estates of the Holy Empire, or, if that is impossible, at least with the principalities and lords that border on our Austrian lands'.[17]

The emperor also promised to establish a central Austrian treasury and chamber of accounts at Innsbruck, plus separate provincial regimes at Vienna, Innsbruck, and Ensisheim in Alsace. Though approved by the wary deputies, the plan came to nothing, largely because the emperor's new defeats at the hands of the diet of Augsburg in 1518 were closely followed by his own death.

The consolidation plan of 1518, which foresaw a united, centralised Austria, flanked by the Swabian League, as a base from which to strengthen royal authority in the empire, was not just a passing fancy of Maximilian, a ruler admittedly given to fancies. A newly rediscovered document from the archives of the short-lived (1520–34)

Habsburg regime at Stuttgart repeats the vital parts of the Innsbruck plan and adjusts the Austrian part of it to make room for an Austrian Württemberg.[18] The plan may come from Bergen's pen, and it certainly fits his vision of the need for a strong, centralising hand in Austria as the basis for Habsburg domination of South Germany, lest the duchy turn Swiss, 'for the land of Württemberg lies near the Swiss, and should it join them and they admit it, then other lands – Tyrol and Inner and Outer Austria – would also be lost, and also all Swabia and the regions down to Cologne. Bavaria, too, would doubtless fall'.[19]

One way or another, Bergen believed, South Germany would evolve into a larger, stronger state. It may perhaps be forgiven a Netherlander that he foresaw neither the blockage of both Austrian and Swiss expansion nor its result: stable, long-term, domination by the territorial princes.

The potential Austrian state in the west can now be described. It was a political structure having its administrative head at Innsbruck and its financial heart at Augsburg. The Austrian dynastic lands, with their subsidiary centres at Vienna, Ensisheim, and Stuttgart, formed the system's core, surrounded by federations of clients, among whom the free cities played the most promising and most vital role. For the urban oligarchies feared the unstable social forces within their walls, while without they sensed a threat less from the aggressions of individual princely dynasties than from the collective effort to make the cities, and their resources, truly subject to the Imperial Diet. The oligarchies needed a stronger guarantee of the monarchy, but the Swiss confederation remained a strong second best.

III

What happened to the Austrian kingdom in the west? There are several traditional explanations of the political development of Germany in the sixteenth century. The first held that the Habsburg dynasty failed, because of its foreign attachments and engagements, to devote itself to the formation of a national monarchy in Germany, while its devotion to an alien, Roman, church deprived the Germans of their one chance for a national Lutheran religion. A second view held that the Reformation and the revolt of the Protestant princes against Charles V saved Germany from an absolutist monarchy in the Spanish style. A third view argued that by splitting the German people over religion the Protestant Reformation itself was responsible for the lack of a German national state. To these three traditional arguments we may add two more recent ones. One is Max Steinmetz's opinion that the failure of the Peasants' War in 1525 doomed the chances for a German national state because the German bourgeoisie betrayed the popular cause, just as they would again in 1848. Another attitude beams with favour upon the actual political evolution of the Empire, which it fondly calls 'the Old *Reich*', and it is not free of a certain nostalgia for the unsystematic, uncentralised, comfortably aristocratic politics of an age when the German burghers felt their strongest attachments to their own home towns. The events of the sixteenth century appear hardly to have disrupted the evolution toward this condition.

Each of these views suffers from a blindness toward the social basis of German politics in the age of the Reformation. The first traditional view rests on one correct perception, the preoccupation of Charles V and Ferdinand I with non-German engagements. The situation for a continuation of Maximilian's South German system looked very good in 1522, when Ferdinand arrived as Austria's new lord. The Württemberg notables rallied to the best government in the duchy's recent memory, and the Habsburg officials struggled with the territorial Estates to reduce Duke Ulrich's mountainous debts and restore solvency to the duchy. In Tyrol and the eastern Austrian duchies, which Ferdinand found in a state of revolt, he was able to satisfy some grievances and restore the lands to order. In January 1527, Ferdinand was even able to issue a decree for a unified Austrian government (*Hofordnung*), which in Maximilian's time had remained but a dream. Ferdinand was an extremely able prince, better educated, more thoughtful, and more tolerant than his elder brother, and in time he might well have become the creator of the Austrian kingdom in the west. What intervened, however, was the Turkish invasion of Hungary in 1526 and the death of his brother-in-law, King Louis, at Mohács. Thereafter his overriding political aim, the creation of a realm for his own descendants, came to centre on his two royal crowns, those of Bohemia and Hungary, for the defence of which he bled Austria white, and though he did become King of the Romans in 1531, his main achievement lay not in the government of Germany but in the creation of the eastward-looking Austria–Hungary of early modern times. Vienna, not Innsbruck, became this land's political centre.

As for Charles V, once he reluctantly surrendered the Austrian lands to Ferdinand, he regarded the Holy Roman Empire chiefly as a source of revenue and religious quarrels. The glue of his vast system was not military but fiscal, and he rarely used his moments of real advantage – Castile after the *Comuneros*, Italy after Pavia, or Germany in 1547–48 – to install genuinely absolutist political forms. This is a major objection to the second traditional view, that the Reformation saved Germany from a Latin-style tyranny. When Charles V did have the German opposition in hand, at the imperial diet of Augsburg in 1548 after his victory over the Schmalkaldic League, his plan of political reform looked nothing like an absolutist agenda. He proposed not strict centralism but a double system of federations under his own presidency, a plan which owed more to the Swabian League than to absolutist monarchy. His suppression of the guild regimes in a series of southern free cities between 1548 and 1552, which has also been cited as proof of his centralising aims, was also nothing of the sort. The direct model came not from Spain or Italy but from good, solid, loyalist, Protestant Nuremberg.[20]

The third traditional view suffered from an excess of nostalgia. Without some centralisation and bureaucratic efficiency, South Germany could hardly have been defended against the Ottoman Turks, and the centralisation occurred in Austria alone, because the Germans of the rest of the empire would not submit to it. A structure as large as the Holy Roman Empire simply could not have been governed according to the standards of western European monarchy without a genuinely imperial system of government, with its centralised bureaucracy which drew the surplus to the centre and exported force to the periphery.

The fourth view, that represented here by Steinmetz, derives, despite its Marxist dress, from the old Liberal notion that the chief historical role of the bourgeoisie was to create the centralised modern state. It appears in many forms, among them Fernand Braudel's thesis of the 'treason of the bourgeoisie'.[21] An Italian model would yield, of course, quite the opposite conclusion about the politics of the bourgeoisie. The very existence of a 'national bourgeoisie' in sixteenth-century Germany is a myth derived largely from taking too seriously the historicising effusions of such humanists as Jacob Wimpheling and Ulrich von Hutten.

The fifth view, that the institutional development of Germany was little influenced by the eruptions of the 1520s, suffers from a conservative myopia about the sources and directions of German politics in the sixteenth century. There existed in sixteenth-century South Germany an important tendency toward state-building in the western European style, which was frustrated partly by the failure of Habsburg leadership and partly by the massive intervention of the common man in South German politics in the later Middle Ages.

IV

The missing element in an explanation of Austria's failure in the west is to be found in the role as neighbour and model of Austria's most ancient foe, the Swiss confederation. The confederation represents the only successful European republic built upon an alliance of city-states with federations of free rural communes. It thus presented two faces to its northern admirers: its oligarchically ruled cities, such as Berne and Zürich, closely resembled their non-Swiss counterparts, such as Constance, Reutlingen, or Ulm; its rural federations, however, had no counterpart outside the confederation, and their freedoms exerted a strongly attractive power on the common people of South Germany, both rural and urban alike. To 'turn Swiss' meant to live without lords, as a songster wrote about the Battle of Leipheim in Upper Swabia in 1525:

> The peasants tried to learn
> Evil tricks from the Swiss
> And become their own lords,
> But we baptized them in a different faith,
> And whoever didn't get away,
> He was soon cut down.[22]

Reports that the common people wanted to 'turn Swiss' came from as far north as Franconia, and by 1500 it was proverbial that the whole of South Germany had at least the potential to join or imitate the Swiss. Ulrich Arzt, mayor of Augsburg and a president of the Swabian League, wrote to Conrad Peutinger in 1519 that he feared the old prophecy would come true, that 'when a cow stands on the bridge at Ulm and moos, she'll be heard in the middle of Switzerland'.[23]

Such reports do not mean that the farming populations of South Germany stood ready to pour into the confederation, or that they hated the House of Austria, but they do mean that reports had spread widely of people elsewhere who worked the land without lords and managed, and defended, their own affairs. Whether the free institutions of the Swiss upland stockmen could have survived among farmers on flatter terrain remains to be studied. The existence of such sentiments, however, corresponded to the objective peculiarity of the rural federations as one pillar of the confederation, and the extension of the Swiss model further northward, where the many cities already had their freedom, would have meant – if possible – the political and military liberation of much of the land. This, in turn, could well have threatened the economic, but not political, subordination of the land to the towns through market relationships. Whether or not the objective interests of the land conflicted with those of the urban artisans and wage-workers,[24] therefore, the very notion of giving the land its freedom ought to have made the urban upper classes more strongly monarchist and pro-Austrian.

The history of the urban front, which reached its pro-centralist peak just before it foundered on the religious question, reveals the importance of the early Reformation – and not just the Revolution of 1525 – as a massive, brief intervention of the common man into South German politics. Brief though it was, it was massive enough to force religious change far more rapidly than the oligarchs might have wished, if they wished for it at all, for it forced them to illegalities which estranged them from their monarch. The views of Charles himself, though he was no fanatic, naturally played a certain role. So did the varying political traditions of the major South German free cities. The correspondence none the less holds good that the stronger the popular Reformation movement the more radical an anti-Austrian and even anti-monarchist external policy the city's oligarchs were willing to consider. Zürich, Constance, and Strasbourg blazed the way. What they were not willing to consider, however, was that the rural folk should have the same freedom to respond to the Gospel that the burghers themselves claimed, the friendship between Zwingli and Michael Gaismair notwithstanding. The coming of the Reformation, therefore, did not alter the terms of South German politics sufficiently to bring the 'middle of Switzerland' any further north, much less to the bridge at Ulm, but it did disrupt the basis of Austrian influence in South Germany long enough to make that basis irretrievable. The Austrian paralysis, which spread like wildfire at Maximilian's death and reached a first peak in Archduke Ferdinand's helplessness during the Revolution of 1525, reached a second, fatal peak in 1534, when the Habsburg brothers allowed Landgrave Philip of Hesse to pluck Württemberg from the lifeless Austrian grasp.

The Austria in the west failed, not so much because it lacked the institutions of the early modern state, 'independent of the household, bureaucratically organized in national departments, but responsible to the crown',[25] but because, when the Reformation broke in upon it, time, fiscal need, and the quest for security had not yet begun to lead the South German burghers and petty nobles over the bridge of monarchist and pro-Austrian sentiment into the administrative arms of Austria itself. To have made anything lasting of this opportunity, the Habsburgs would have to have had a much freer hand than they had ever had, or Austria would have had to rank higher in their priority than it ever did. Their loss owed something, however, to the intervention of the common man.

An illumination of the early modern German *Sonderweg* does not explain the modern one. Neither, however, ought to be regarded, as each commonly is, in a too narrowly national context. The Reformation and its political consequences were but one force which 'helped to depose Germany from the place of first importance which it had intermittently held since the ninth century'.[26] The greater context is dominated by the fact that 'above all, in this age Europe was tilting away from the landmass to the oceans – to that open side where success awaited the enterprising few to the benefit of the many'. And, one might add, to the confusion, sorrow, and grief of many others.

Notes

1. This study draws on my recently published *Turning Swiss: Cities and Empire, 1450–1550* (Cambridge Studies in Early Modern History) (Cambridge/New York, 1985), where references will be found for statements otherwise unsupported here.
2. David Blackbourn and Geoff Eley, *The Peculiarities of German History Bourgeouis Society and Politics in the Nineteenth Century* (Oxford/New York, 1984), p. 10.
3. Ibid., pp. 6–7.
4. G. R. Elton, *Reformation Europe, 1517–1559* (New York, 1963), p. 304.
5. Quoted by Karl Kupisch, 'The "Luther Renaissance"', *Journal of Contemporary History*, II, 4 (October, 1967), p. 41.
6. A. J. P. Taylor, *The Course of German History* (London, 1945), p. 162.
7. Max Steinmetz, 'Theses on the Early Bourgeois Revolution in Germany, 1476–1535', in Bob (Robert W.) Scribner and Gerhard Benecke (eds), *The German Peasant War of 1525 – New Viewpoints* (London, 1979), pp. 9–18, here at p. 17.
8. Perry Anderson, *Lineages of the Absolutist State* (London, 1974), p. 18. For an illuminating case study of how this mediation worked, see Hermann Rebel, *Peasant Classes: The Bureaucratization of Property and Family Relations under Early Habsburg Absolutism* (Princeton, NJ, 1983).

9. See Peter Blickle, 'Communalism, Parliamentarism, Republicanism', *Parliaments, Estates and Representation*, VI, 1 (1986), pp. 1–13.
10. Quoted in *Turning Swiss*, pp. 107–8.
11. Quoted in ibid., pp. 110–11.
12. Quoted in ibid., p. 18.
13. Quoted in ibid., p. 87, and there, too, the following quote.
14. Robert Jütte, *Obrigkeitliche Armenfürsorge in den deutschen Reichsstädten der frühen Neuzeit. Städtische Armenfürsorge in Frankfurt am Main und Köln* (Kölner historische Abhandlungen, XXXI) (Cologne/Vienna, 1984), pp. 8–19.
15. Knut Schulz, *Handwerksgesellen und Lohnarbeiter. Untersuchungen zur oberrheinischen und oberdeutschen Stadtgeschichte des 14. bis 17. Jahrhunderts* (Sigmaringen, 1985), pp. 37–46.
16. Theodor Mayer, *Die Verwaltungsorganisationen Maximilians I. Ihr Ursprung und ihre Bedeutung* (Forschungen zur inneren Geschichte Österreichs, XIV) (Innsbruck, 1920; reprinted Aalen, 1973), pp. 57–63, 75–85.
17. Quoted in *Turning Swiss*, p. 90.
18. It is edited in ibid., pp. 235–41.
19. Quoted in ibid., p. 111.
20. The persistent belief that Charles suppressed twenty-eight guild regimes for religious reasons is laid to rest by Eberhard Naujoks (ed.), *Kaiser Karl V. und die Zunftverfassung. Ausgewählte Aktenstücke zu den Verfassungsänderungen in den oberdeutschen Reichsstädten (1547–1556)* (Veröffentlichungen der Kommission für geschichtliche Landeskunde in Baden-Württemberg, Reihe A XXVI) (Stuttgart, 1985), pp. 7–26, 335–9.
21. Fernand Braudel, *The Mediterranean and the Mediterranean World in the Age of Philip II*, trans. Siân Reynolds (2 vols, New York, 1973), vol. II, pp. 725–34. Braudel much softens this judgement in his *Civilization and Capitalism, 15th–18th Century*, vol. II: *The Wheels of Commerce*, trans. Siân Reynolds (New York, 1982), p. 594.
22. Quoted in Brady, *Turning Swiss*, p. 35.
23. This and the following texts are quoted in ibid., pp. 38–40.
24. A point made by Tom Scott in 'The Peasants' War: A Historiographical Review', *Historical Journal*, XXII (1979), pp. 957, 966.
25. G. R. Elton, *The Tudor Revolution in Government: Administrative Changes in the Reign of Henry VIII* (Cambridge, 1953), p. 425.
26. Elton, *Reformation Europe*, p. 324, and there, too, the following quote.

8 Church Property in the German Protestant Principalities

Henry J. Cohn

When the kings of England and Sweden seized church lands and revenues during the 1530s and 1540s, they were following in the footsteps of the major Protestant princes of the Holy Roman Empire. Since all the leading secular rulers in Germany, with the notable exceptions of the Austrian Habsburgs and Bavarian Wittelsbachs, sooner or later adopted the Reformation, they all benefited to some extent from a policy of secularisation. The transferred property came under secular control, even if a large part of it continued to be used for the purposes of the new churches. Secularisation in this sense was the fate in Germany not only – and not even principally – of monastic lands, but of church property in the wider sense, embracing also the lands and whole government of bishoprics that were incorporated into most north German Protestant principalities, the property of parishes in town and country, patronage to benefices, religious and charitable endowments, schools and universities, and by extension the ecclesiastical jurisdiction that had controlled all such property. Not surprisingly, the effects of such widescale transfer of ecclesiastical property were not limited to the financial sphere, nor were the major principalities, which will be considered in this survey, the only ones to benefit.

Catholic critics, beginning with the papal nuncio Aleander in 1521,[1] were quick to charge Protestant rulers with sheer materialism in their change of faith. Even some Protestant preachers later upbraided Protestant princes for using church property for themselves while taxing their subjects more heavily than before.[2] Yet Henry Brinkelow, alias Roderyck Mors, an English Protestant critic of Henry VIII's misuse of monastic properties, extolled by contrast 'the godly ... Christian Germans [who] divided not such goods and lands among the princes, lords and rich men, that had not need thereof, but they put them into the use of the commonwealth and unto the provision for the poor according to the doctrine of the Scripture'.[3] The

158

conflicting opinions of the sixteenth century on this issue have been reflected in the views of rival Catholic and Protestant historians ever since. The complex relationships between the introduction of the Reformation, the seizure of church property and the growth of the state may be considered under four heads:

1. Did the Reformation bring about a significant advance on previous control by the state over the church and its property, on those territorial churches (*landesherrliche Kirchenregimente*) that were well developed by the early sixteenth century?
2. To what extent were princes influenced to adopt Protestantism for their territories by the desire for ecclesiastical property?
3. How much did rulers benefit financially from their acquisitions, or did they fritter them away or alienate them to nobles and townspeople, much as happened in England? Did the new church, the schools, universities and charities receive many of these resources?
4. Was the state perhaps strengthened more by its other gains from the Reformation than by church property?

The trend towards territorial churches had accelerated since the fourteenth century, especially during the Schism and conciliar period, by means of unilateral princely actions backed by papal privileges, Concordats or at least tacit papal consent. Despite the occasional disagreements with a resurgent papacy in the later fifteenth century and the *Gravamina* of the German nation against Rome, control of their churches by the princes depended on co-operation with the popes and thus did not directly pave the way for the later breach with the papacy. In several states the pope found princely assistance essential to collect annates, papal tithes and crusade taxes from the clergy, and to sell indulgences to the laity, all in return for a share of the proceeds. Reciprocally granted papal privileges helped rulers to make bishops and cathedral chapters amenable to their will, to conduct visitations for both the spiritual and the economic reform of monasteries, and to push back the frontiers of ecclesiastical jurisdiction.[4]

The growth of territorial churches before the Reformation should, however, not be exaggerated. During the second half of the fifteenth century the bishops of Speyer and Worms were either officals and nominees of the electors Palatine or so dependent on them in conflicts with the cities of Speyer and Worms that they were unable to pursue independent policies and obliged to allow the Palatinate use of their castles and territories in wartime. Yet their territories made only limited contributions to the electors' finances in times of emergency and they remained independent rulers even after the Reformation, although no longer with spiritual authority beyond the frontiers of their own lands.[5] After the Reformation in Saxony the bishoprics of Meißen, Merseburg and Naumburg became secundogenitures governed by younger sons of the ruling house into whose lands they were eventually absorbed; similarly the sees of Brandenburg, Havelberg and Lebus were entirely incorporated into the electorate of Brandenburg. Yet in all six bishoprics the degree of control had fallen far short of this before the Reformation.[6] The bishops in Brandenburg even increased their territories and the large number of their vassals until the eve of the Reformation, thus removing some noblemen from membership of the elector of Brandenburg's Estates. As in Saxony, the castles and towns which these prelates owned were strategically placed on the frontiers between powerful secular neighbours. A wide gulf separated the authority which the Brandenburg rulers claimed as territorial princes over the bishops and that which the bishops would either admit in theory or concede in practice. Even though the bishops allowed the electors to levy taxes and military services on their subjects and were no longer represented at imperial diets, they still exercised numerous regalian rights, higher jurisdiction and economic control in their scattered lands, well beyond what Brandenburg monasteries and all nobles except the lords of Ruppin enjoyed.[7] In Saxony, lengthy conflicts with the see of Meißen at the turn of the century were followed by its steadfast refusal to accept the Reformation until 1561.[8]

By the end of the Middle Ages rulers were acting as territorial princes to a greater extent in their relations with monasteries than with bishops. Not everywhere did monasteries pay the property tax (*Bede*) and territorial tax (*Landessteuer*), as many did in Bavaria, Pomerania and Saxony,[9] but forced loans and more usual forms of credit were common. Monasteries provided not only the great majority of the carts that formed the baggage train of princely armies but buildings that could be used for defensive purposes.[10] The universal obligation of monasteries to give lodging and hospitality to itinerant rulers, their entourage, officials, hunters and hunting dogs was frequently commuted into a profitable money payment, which was additional to one for the protection of religious houses.[11] When rulers took the initiative in sponsoring reform by the Observant branches of monastic orders in dozens of monastic houses in each major principality, they sometimes went along themselves with the visitation commissions. The commissions in any case usually included lay officials appointed to set the finances to right and then provide ongoing audit and supervision. Particularly in Bavaria, where between a quarter and a half of all the peasants who paid taxes to the dukes were tenants of the great prelates, the economic well-being of monastic lordships was of utmost importance to the state, with the result that increasingly these ducal visitations were far more concerned with the economic than the spiritual regulation of monastic communities.[12]

Church property was coming even more under the purview of territorial administration in those parishes where rulers were patrons to the benefices. The terms of later Reformation church ordinances were foreshadowed in detail in an ordinance of 1499 in the Palatinate which provided for joint supervision of the parish records and finances by the priests and the local officials (*Amtleute*).[13] Local officials had similar functions in Saxony and Bavaria, while rulers in Franconia exacted an oath of loyalty from parish priests which extended to their pastoral duties and allowed in effect for a right of dismissal.[14]

Yet it may not be assumed that such practices were universal. Certainly the degree of success achieved by princes varied considerably in another and important sphere, that of ecclesiastical jurisdiction. In Bavaria, Württemberg and the Palatinate nearly all ecclesiastical causes, including those concerned with tithes, benefices and other church property, came before the princely courts.[15] Elsewhere the boundaries between the jurisdictions could remain more obscure, as is shown best in Saxony, where nine bishops shared ecclesiastical lordship, by no means all of them as pliant as the three whose territories lay entirely within the principality. For forty years until 1525 Frederick the Wise conducted without clear resolution a struggle against what he considered the misuse of ecclesiastical jurisdiction at all levels up to the episcopal courts.[16] The landgraves of Hesse had an uphill task against the archbishops of Mainz to secure jurisdiction over the clergy in secular matters; only in 1528, after the introduction of the Reformation, was the issue resolved to the landgrave's satisfaction.[17]

Princely church government was often a patchy affair[18] before the Reformation, but many historians have succumbed to temptation and strung together isolated instances of roughshod intervention, often at brief moments of weakness for the papacy, to build up an exaggerated picture of burgeoning state control. It was at the height of the papal struggle with the Council of Basel that Landgrave William III of Thuringia had his commission of lay and ecclesiastical advisors visiting all Benedictine monasteries also regulate the conduct of services in their incorporated parishes.[19] The often-quoted phrase 'The duke of Cleves is pope in his territories' was coined much later in reference to the five-year period from 1444 when Eugenius IV, in order to secure an advantage against the Council of Basel and the rival Pope Felix V, granted the duke merely temporary exemption from the ecclesiastical jurisdiction of the archbishop of Cologne by appointing the bishop of Utrecht as titular bishop for the Cleves lands.[20] *Ego sum papa in terris meis* or similar phrases were indeed put into the mouths of several fourteenth- and fifteenth-century rulers by contemporary chronicles. There is, however, no documentary evidence that any prince uttered such words, although a few, like Albert V of Austria (1411–39) did pursue deliberate and systematic policies of encroachment on the secular rights of the clergy which might have appeared to the superficial observer as challenging papal spiritual authority.[21] Precedents were set somewhere or the other for almost every kind of control established at the Reformation, but scattered precedents are not the same as progressive development. At the other end of the spectrum was Brunswick–Wolfenbüttel, where backwardness in the secular administration in the fifteenth century may have accounted for the failure to resist ecclesiastical courts or control church property, until the Catholic Duke Henry the Younger (1514–68) rapidly made up the ground at the same time as he modernised the government.[22]

The idea that church property might be secularised or placed under lay administration erupted from time to time in both learned and popular circles before the Reformation.[23] The most that rulers attempted was to limit clerical exemption from taxation and stem the flow of property by inheritance, sale and endowment into the dead hand of the church. Even so the few laws against mortmain and measures requiring princely consent for new endowments failed to halt the trend. The more drastic solution of secularisation was brought forcefully into the debate by Luther and Ulrich von Hutten during 1520. The fullest blueprint that most princes are likely to have seen before they embarked on the Reformation was drawn up towards the end of 1525 by Hans von Schwarzenberg for Margrave Casimir of Brandenburg–Ansbach and discussed at the Augsburg imperial diet.

It contained many suggestions similar to the later practice of Protestant principalities, but also one derived from Hutten that was less likely to attract the princes, for an imperial army of noblemen financed by the surplus left after using secularised church lands for other purposes. An elected government in each of the existing six circles of the empire should keep the peace in the manner of the Swabian League and administer church property, not the common man who had tried to seize it that very year in the Peasants' War. Bishops and prelates would have adequate pensions and cathedral chapters be left their possessions for the moment, but it was expected that all these incumbents would die out without replacement. Of the monastic houses, only a few convents would be left in each circle for young noblewomen. The first calls on the confiscated revenues were to be for new pastors, preachers, and bishops without secular rule, a university in each circle, and a tithe to support the poor.[24]

The first specific advice about church property which Luther gave, in 1523, was devoted to the use of redundant urban mass and other endowments in Wittenberg and Leisnig for common chests to support preachers and the poor. On that occasion he did also say that rulers had the responsibility to return rural monastic houses to religious purposes akin to those presumed to have lain behind their original endowments, in particular for charity towards the needy of every social class from nobles downwards. The monks should receive pensions to show that the true enemy of the monasteries was Christian belief, not greed for ecclesiastical property.[25] Some towns followed his advice that the houses of the mendicants be used for schools and that other buildings pass to the city councils, but princes still waited for a national decision and the emperor. Towards the end of 1525 concern in Luther's correspondence with the elector of Saxony shifted to the fear that ecclesiastical revenues were being dissipated through neglect and plunder; an immediate ordinance for the whole country was necessary to save the new church from further losses.[26] A year later he made it explicit that the ecclesiastical institutions belonged to the elector now that papal authority was at an end. Any resources left after paying for the clergy, schools and charity could be devoted to the needs of the state.[27] Luther was always ready to defend the Saxon electors from the charge of robbing church property for profane purposes, but after the Augsburg Diet of 1530 required the restoration of the monasteries the basis of his argument changed: once the needs of the parishes, church servants, schools, hospitals, poor chests and poor students had been met, then the prince deserved recompense for all his labour and expense in the service of the Gospel; he might also support poor nobles and use church property in moderation to build roads, bridges and defence works, since secular rule was also a service to God.[28]

By contrast Bucer, in a memorandum of 1538 for the Schmalkaldic League, insisted that church property belonged to the religious community and should merely be administered by rulers in a fund kept separate from their other resources. Subventions for government, the armed defence of the country against the Turks, and maintaining the families of noble founders could be made only from the income of the fund, not from its capital, and only after religious and charitable needs had been fully met.[29] Bucer sent both this opinion and his dialogue *Von Kirchengüter* (1540), which enlarged on its arguments, to Philip of Hesse.[30] Although the League of Schmalkalden in a declaration of 1540 assumed that church property would not be alienated, and only the surplus revenues be used by rulers,[31] the difference in emphasis between theologians from Wittenberg and those in south Germany remained unresolved on this issue as on others. Many princes were to respond with solutions close to either Luther's or Bucer's guidelines.

These alternatives only emerged during the 1530s, but meanwhile several of the larger principalities, even before they determined the pace or nature of secularisation, had adopted the Reformation for motives that were both various and complex. Quite a number of rulers were genuine converts and a few even sacrificed political interest to religious conviction. Frederick the Wise, neither a Protestant nor a seculariser, supported Luther out of a series of political and legal considerations arising from his position as territorial ruler and in the tradition of his predecessors: rivalry with the archbishop of Mainz and the Hohenzollerns, protection of an Augustinian monk at his own university against Dominicans of the rival order at other universities, and above all resistance to foreign ecclesiastical jurisdiction, now that of the papacy itself.[32] Even those for whom material gains were uppermost drew differing consequences. Albert of Hohenzollern contemplated seeking Luther's advice on secularising the Teutonic Order in Prussia in 1521, well before he was won to the Protestant faith by Osiander at Nuremberg in 1523; the political circumstances of his relationship with Poland prevented him from formally making East Prussia a Protestant secular state until 1525. Yet even he later composed and compiled Lutheran prayers, corresponded on matters religious with princes and theologians, and took seriously his duties as a Protestant ruler.[33] One can be more cynical about the motives of his brother Margrave Casimir of Brandenburg–Ansbach. The indecisiveness of his religious views contrasted sharply with a clear policy from 1520 to eliminate the authority of neighbouring bishops and strengthen his hold over church lands in the aftermath of the Peasants' War. Reformation principles and theology were only introduced under his brother George, a Protestant already before he succeeded in 1527.[34]

The Reformation often had to wait for full implementation until a member of the princely family fully conversant with its teachings came to power. If Henry VIII of England could study theology, so did many German princes, or at least they allowed themselves to be guided by their theologians or their pious wives or secular advisers. Long-standing study of the Bible and the works of the Reformers led to the conversion of the young Philip of Hesse in 1524, even before Melanchthon wrote a treatise for him in that year; no contemporaries doubted the sincerity of his convictions. His conversion matched the anti-Habsburg stance of his policies, but in 1524 it was politically disadvantageous to alienate his allies, the staunchly Catholic duke of Saxony and the electors of Trier and the Palatinate. At first Philip prevaricated about both religious reform and secularisation, until the Diet of Speyer, by leaving all to the discretion of princely consciences in 1526, gave some legal colour to a ruler reforming his territories. Whereas Philip's conversion arose out of conviction, his policies as leader of the Protestant party were increasingly dominated by political considerations until, in the débâcle after the battle of Mühlberg, he was prepared to forswear most Protestant tenets in the hope of release from captivity by Charles V.[35]

In marked contrast Philip's ally John Frederick of Saxony was prepared to make supreme sacrifices for his faith. Threatened by the emperor with the loss of his electorate, continued imprisonment (possibly even in Spain) and hints that the death penalty already passed might yet be implemented, all unless he abandoned the Augsburg Confession and submitted to the religious settlement still to be made by the Council of Trent, John Frederick stood fast and remained a captive for five years, a widely admired martyr to his faith. Eventually he was released through the good offices of his powerful relatives, though with the loss of the electorate and half his lands.[36] Few Protestant rulers were of this calibre, but neither should they all be tarred with the same brush as ruthless landgrabbers with an eye to the political main chance. This applies especially to the handful of princes who became Calvinist after the Peace of Augsburg had excluded that faith from parity with the other two. Foremost among them were the electors palatine. Frederick III (1559–76) as heir to a Lutheran principality needed no further justification to seize church lands, but contrary to his political interests chose the Reformed faith after consulting his theologians and lawyers. For the rest of the century the electors switched between Lutheranism and Calvinism according to their consciences and the balance among their councillors divided between the two faiths.[37]

Not only the introduction of the Reformation, but the timing and manner of secularisation had to take account of the political circumstances of individual rulers, the opinions of other princes, and the restrictions of imperial law. Whereas Philip of Hesse considered the decisions of the Diet of Speyer in 1526 sufficient legal justification to seize church property, Elector John of Saxony was more cautious. He quietly took over the administration of many houses, but did not proceed to a formal sequestration until the Saxon diet of 1531, when negotiations at the imperial level on this matter had broken down.[38] Sequestrations, falling short of outright seizure, were a legal device to deflect some of the criticism by Catholic rulers as well as to give the Estates part responsibility for the new order. The interest that the Estates had in providing for members of their families and ensuring that some of the monastic revenues were devoted to reducing the burden of state debts led them to seek a share in the administration of church lands. Although this was conceded in Hesse in 1527 it was never implemented, and in Ernestine Saxony it lasted only twelve years, until the elector was emboldened to incorporate the church lands into his demesne.[39] One of the main purposes in forming the League of Schmalkalden was to defend secularisations already undertaken against their condemnation in recent imperial diets and by the imperial courts. The protection of the League gave more rulers courage to follow their inclinations.[40]

At the same time the growing costs of introducing the Reformation and defending it militarily increased the economic pressures towards outright seizure. Even so Duke Ulrich of Württemberg was a maverick among Protestants when he flew in the face of the Treaty of Kaaden (1534) which had sealed the recovery of his duchy from the Habsburgs but guaranteed the ecclesiastical foundations their revenues. His defence of complete secularisation claimed polemically that the monks and heads of houses had abandoned their rights on taking pensions, that as their patron and founder he was entitled to aid if in financial need, and that anyway his ancestors had received certain taxes and labour services from the monasteries. His insistence that the majority of the confiscated lands were used for pious purposes did not ring true.[41] Catholic attacks on him as a landgrabber were reinforced by the anxieties of the south German theologians at his actions.

In consequence other Protestant rulers became more concerned than before to stress that church property was being used for religious and educational purposes in accordance with the intentions of their original endowments, as Georg von Carlowitz, chief minister to Maurice of Saxony, explained to the emperor in 1543 and 1546.[42] Philip of Hesse wrote in 1533 that he had established the university of Marburg, scholarships for students, two hospitals, and two secularised convents to provide dowries for poor noblewomen, and used the remainder to protect the Gospel, so that his subjects were taxed the less. Some endowments had been returned to the families of noble founders who could prove title, while certain estates went to those who served him or the principality for the benefit of the Gospel. By 1540 he was claiming that after meeting these obligations and now also supplementing the salaries of ministers, very little was left, over and above what the monasteries had formerly rendered in services, taxes and loans.[43] This self-justification need not be taken entirely at face value, but it may be conceded that expenditure on arming to defend the Reformation, and on attending imperial diets and religious discussions, the meetings of the Schmalkaldic League, and hearings of the Imperial Cameral Court in religious matters all arose out of the adoption of Protestantism. Since this was not an argument that could be used to persuade Catholic rulers, Saxony and Hesse took pains to complete their educational and charitable endowments in order to rebuff these critics, as well as to satisfy the demands of their theologians and the needs of the country. The wealthy abbey at Haina was probably deliberately chosen as the site for one of Hesse's hospitals so as to block the attempt by the émigré abbot to secure restitution with imperial assistance.[44] The formal grants to hospitals, schools and universities were rarely matched by equal speed in handing over the promised financial support, which often followed only several years later.

The problem remains of establishing the proportions of church property used for religious and similar purposes and for the various responsibilities of the state. Despite the imperfect nature of the surviving records, especially for the crucial early decades of the

Reformation, recent research strongly suggests that princes gained far more than used to be thought. For Hesse, a widely accepted estimate that 59 per cent of monastic property was devoted to religion, education and charity[45] is misleading because based on financial accounts of the 1580s which omit those parts of the country where monasteries were dissolved in the second half of the century, after most of the new endowments had been made, and because it ignores previous expropriations of monastic property by the landgraves. Moreover, like rulers in Bavaria, Lüneburg and elsewhere, from the early 1520s Philip of Hesse imposed heavy taxes and forced loans on the monasteries before they were dissolved. The Swabian League encouraged its members to seize monastic silver to pay for suppressing the Peasants' War. Between 1527 and 1540 a further 75,000 Gulden were raised in Hesse from monastic income and from selling seven monastic houses to meet military expenses. The hospital at Haina only received for its endowment one-fifth of the great wealth of this abbey. The delay of five or more years in completing the new endowments coincided with the period of heaviest payments to the ex-religious whose houses had been dissolved by 1528. Although the pensions of some three hundred monks and sixty lay brothers in twenty monasteries and 450 nuns and lay sisters in seventeen convents were not ungenerous, it has been estimated that the total paid to them in the end amounted to about 50,000 Gulden, or half the capital value of Haina.[46] As in most other principalities, the salaries of ministers, superintendents and school-teachers were paid mainly from the revenues of the former parish benefices, lesser benefices declared redundant by the Reformers, mass endowments and minor foundations gathered in new local common chests; only later were supplements added from the monastic revenues or the landgrave's own income after salary payments had been centralised on Marburg in 1539.[47] Ecclesiastical property strengthened state finances not least because it brought agricultural revenues in both cash and kind which kept pace with sixteenth-century inflation. The gross revenues of 16,500 Gulden from monastic lands in 1532 amounted to 16 per cent of revenues in the local districts (*Ämter*) or 14 per cent of total net revenues. As payments to the ex-religious declined, the share of church lands in the surpluses of the *Ämter* grew from 20 per cent in 1532 to 30 per cent in 1565, when at 25,000 Gulden they still represented one-seventh of the state's ordinary revenues.[48] Overall the lion's share of church lands probably passed through Philip of Hesse's hands, even though some of them no longer belonged to the state in the 1580s.

A similar verdict is appropriate for the two Saxonies. The sequestration accounts for the Ernestine electorate between 1533 and 1543 show that even in this period some lands were sold for the benefit of Elector John Frederick or put directly under his financial administration, but more were leased to nobles and officials on favourable terms, which was a major reason for ending the joint administration with the Estates in 1543 and recalling these leases.[49] Meanwhile a larger proportion of the monies received from the sequestrators, just over 100,000 Gulden, had been used to pay off the elector's debts than to support pensioned ex-religious, the new clergy, schools, the university of Wittenberg, and the poor.[50] Yet even if rulers received the major benefit from church property, it represented only a small proportion of their burgeoning expenses. In the same decade 430,000 Gulden were raised by means of an excise on beer and wine. Inflation was especially severe for the escalating diplomatic and military costs which the Reformation brought in its train. On the eve of the Schmalkaldic War John Frederick's coffers were bare. Extensive sales of ecclesiastical property were necessary in the 1540s. Nevertheless, the largest and most profitable rural monasteries were not alienated; five of them became new separate *Ämter* while others were incorporated into existing ones, increasing the demesne lands greatly.[51] The larger houses were similarly absorbed into Albertine Saxony, even though Maurice of Saxony had sold lands for nearly 200,000 Gulden, and then often below their true value, to his nobles and officials and to Leipzig and other cities.[52] The enormous expansion of Albertine Saxony in the second half of the century was the result less of the monastic confiscations than of war, inheritance and purchase. The dukes acquired ten noble lordships between 1559 and 1585, all three Saxon bishoprics, and from their Ernestine cousins half their lands, the electoral title, and the bulk of the Saxon mining revenues. Where necessary these acquisitions were financed with loans that were serviced by taxes voted by the Estates. Intervention in the politics of the Reformation era had paid off in territories, but it may well be that Maurice of Saxony had been encouraged to embark on his ambitious policies by the acquisition of monastic lands in the 1540s and by the creditworthiness which they brought him.[53]

The most extensive seizure anywhere of all forms of church property occurred initially in Württemberg. On the eve of the Reformation the monastic houses and secular clergy within the duchy enjoyed incomes, totalling 205,000 Gulden or one-third of the landed wealth of the country, which were double those of the duke himself. Half of this clerical wealth was in the hands of fourteen large monasteries whose prelates sat in the upper house of the diet.[54] Within two years of reconquering his duchy in 1534, Duke Ulrich confiscated all monastic property and at least half of the 1200 secular benefices. He regarded all forms of ecclesiastical property as fair game. Large quantities of church silver were transported to Stuttgart and melted down; the stones of several monasteries were incorporated into his extensive fortifications; his interest payments on debts to ecclesiastical institutions ceased; and their revenues in kind were often delivered directly to the kitchens of the ducal court. In 1538 he even ordered the gold paint to be scraped off altar paintings. Numerous houses of the clergy in the towns were sold between 1537 and 1541 for the benefit of Ulrich or his officials, without considering the interests of the urban communities which in other principalities were usually left most church property within their walls. Ulrich had acquired about three-quarters of all clerical property; after he had dissolved many benefices, the rest were shared by the surviving secular clergy with the local communities.[55] All forms of ecclesiastical revenue were administered by the duke's lay officials. The annual surpluses averaged 42,000 Gulden between 1534 and 1550. From 1541 these surpluses, after the deduction of not very large expenses, passed straight into the secular treasury, 346,000 Gulden alone between 1545 and 1550. Ulrich did more openly and on a grander scale what other Protestant rulers often practised while claiming greater disinterestedness.[56]

Ulrich's son Christopher (1550–68), conscious of the criticisms which Protestant as well as Catholic theologians had deployed against his father, made a clean start by deliberately adopting the policy that south German Reformers had advocated of keeping church funds separate. Indeed there were two distinct funds. The Common Church Fund (*Gemeiner Kirchenkasten*) collected the revenues of 1000 benefices, 100 canonries, twenty-two small monasteries, twenty rural chapters, and fifty houses of beguines and similar orders that amounted to 110,000 Gulden in 1560/1. It was now administered by an ecclesiastical council, not the treasury, and paid fixed salaries to the clergy throughout Württemberg. The Church Order of 1559 and, on the insistence of the Estates, Christopher's will of 1566 reserved the income of the *Kirchenkasten* for the church, with the rider that any surplus after its needs had been met might be used to redeem state debts or for other emergencies. Already in his reign 100,000 Gulden had been used in this way, in addition to an equal sum taken before monies reached the fund. A separate *Depositum* received the even greater revenues of the fourteen large monasteries, the surpluses from which were used to service an increasingly large share, up to 45 per cent, of the duke's growing debts, for which the Estates repeatedly took responsibility. After Christopher's death, the bulk of the *Kirchenkasten* continued to finance the church and a large part of the *Depositum* to reduce debts, but later dukes followed Christopher's example in drawing directly on both funds, especially during and after the Thirty Years War.[57]

In Württemberg, the confiscated church property had been put into separate funds on the initiative of the ruler and was thereafter devoted in good measure to its proper purposes through the continuing pressure of the Estates. In the Calvinist Palatinate, which had no Estates, Frederick III in 1576 put the monastic lands under an administration (*Verwaltung*) separate from the treasury, with only the surplus left after religious, educational and charitable expenditure going to meet the country's needs. These resources were kept intact, so that even after some monastic lands were assigned to the elector's hunting grounds and others to schools, hospitals, an orphanage, a residential college for the university of Heidelberg, and three new settlements for thousands of Netherlands refugees at Frankenthal, Schönau and Otterberg, substantial revenues in money, wine and grain remained in the early seventeenth century. The major part of this fund survived at least two centuries longer.[58] So too did similar funds established by the Guelph rulers during the Reformation in two of the three Brunswick duchies. The Estates had merely assented to decisions taken in 1545 by Duchess Elisabeth of Brunswick–Calenberg and in 1568 by Duke Julius II of Brunswick–Wolfenbüttel on the advice of their theologians to keep separate church funds. Despite these good intentions the monastic revenues were heavily used to satisfy noble and other creditors and were closely integrated into the administration of the state.[59] It was equally on the initiative of the rulers in Brunswick-Lüneburg,[60] Mecklenburg[61] and Pomerania[62] that by far the greater part of the monastic lands was incorporated into their demesnes. Where no Estates existed, or not supremely powerful ones, the major immediate financial benefit came to rulers, unless they chose of their own volition to set aside a separate church fund.

Circumstances in Brandenburg were different, because on the eve of the Reformation the nobles there already held some 60 per cent of the cultivated land, the church 24 per cent, the ruler only 13 per cent and the towns 3 per cent. During the Reformation the wealthier noble families exploited the elector's financial plight to obtain extensive properties of the church as pawnings. Yet even here church property was not divided as unequally as appears at first sight. During the second half of the sixteenth century Elector Joachim II and his successors by skilful financial management recovered most of the church property which had been pledged. The net result was that of sixty-six monasteries, fifty-two became part of the elector's demesne.[63] Recent work on a few areas within the Kurmark allows even more precise examination of the shift in landowning. In the lordship of Ruppin the church had owned 26 per cent of cultivated lands in 1500; by 1620 the ruler had nearly doubled his share from 21 to 39 per cent, whereas the nobles only increased theirs from 52.5 to 60 per cent. In Havelland the elector could increase his share over fivefold, from 3.25 to 18 per cent, the nobles by only 1 per cent to 72 per cent, although the secularised noble chapter of Havelberg retained a further 6 per cent out of the 26 per cent which had belonged to the clergy. Electoral holdings increased from 1 to 7.5 per cent in the Prignitz, noble ones from 73.5 to 77 per cent, in addition to which just over half of the 25 per cent of church lands remained with the Havelberg chapter and a secularised nunnery.[64] Already in 1500 the nobility had held the majority of landed estates. Secularisation if anything helped in the long term to redress the balance in favour of the ruler. In the principality of Küstrin, reunited with the electorate after the death of Margrave John (1535–71), that energetic autocrat had seized nearly all monastic lands for his demesne without consulting the Estates or having to pledge lands to the nobles.[65] In Brandenburg as a whole the nobles remained the largest landowners and dominant over the electors through the power of the purse exercised in the Estates.[66]

In Brandenburg as in many other states of northern Germany – Saxony, Pomerania, Schleswig–Holstein and Prussia – a greater addition to princely territories and finances than from monastic lands came from the dozen or so bishoprics acquired as secundogenitures or absorbed into the demesne, or both. This was a lengthy process usually completed only after 1555 but one in which the Estates had little or no say. Pomerania gained the bishopric of Cammin which occupied one-sixth of its area.[67] In Brandenburg west of the River Havel between a quarter and a third of the land had belonged to the sees of Havelberg and Brandenburg or their vassals and now came to the electors. The one opportunity available here for the nobles was to retain some of the cathedral chapters and collegiate churches already halfway towards secularisation before the Reformation. In 1520 Luther exempted these bodies from his strictures against mass endowments on the grounds that 'they were without doubt founded so that, since not every child of the nobility can be a landowner and ruler, they might be provided for in these foundations as is the custom in the German nation'.[68] It was widely believed in Europe that charity was intended not only nor even mainly for the very poor, but for the disadvantaged of each social group, the genteel poor. Acceptance of this principle may have helped the nobility in their struggle, usually conducted in the Estates, to secure the survival of many of the chapters as semi-autonomous bodies. The secularised chapters continued to control their own considerable property, albeit deprived of numerous formerly incorporated parishes, rights of patronage, and shares in fines from ecclesiastical jurisdiction. A similar combination of noble pressure and charitable instincts saved the handful of convents reserved for noblewomen in most states, though not in Württemberg, the Palatinate or Saxony. These usually modest endowments survived either as residences for unmarried noblewomen or, as in Hesse, as economic units yielding dowries.[69] Relatively few noblemen were abbots or monks in monasteries, other than in those houses immediately subject to the empire that were most likely to remain Catholic. Therefore no similar pressures favoured noble monks in the principalities as were exercised on behalf of noble nuns. Nobles had chosen rather to enter the houses scattered throughout Germany of the St John's and Teutonic military orders claiming immediacy of the empire. Both orders were harassed by many Protestant and some Catholic rulers in an extended struggle throughout the sixteenth century. In Protestant principalities they became subjects of the ruler and lost their patronage to benefices and their tax exemptions, but as Protestant institutions retained most of their lands, a compromise that suited their already half-secularised status.[70]

Except in the few principalities where subsequent financial difficulties forced rulers into sales and pawnings, the nobles received only a modest share of church lands at the Reformation, except those which they already effectively held. Although princes retained a greater proportion than is sometimes credited, it was never more than a small contribution towards their growing expenses. Further considerable resources were devoted – though more in topping-up exercises than fresh endowments – to charities and education, as well as the new churches. It must be emphasised that these endowments served not only the general welfare of society, that commonweal much spoken of in the early Reformation, but the interests of state power as well. It would be a false dichotomy to set them in the balance against the gains made by rulers. Orphanages, hospitals and urban common chests used for poor relief served to ameliorate escalating social problems that would only have undermined good order if left unchecked. Welfare and educational policies were initiated by princes whose Estates encouraged them, for the sake of objectives they all shared, to adhere to their original worthy intentions when faced in mid-century with other pressing financial demands.

Under the influence of the Reformers most Protestant states developed a coherent educational programme (*Bildungspolitik*) for all levels from elementary schools to universities. During the course of his reign Philip of Hesse fulfilled most of the programme he had outlined in 1526. Johannes Ferrarius (Eisenmann), first rector at Philip's new university of Marburg, in his *Von dem Gemeinen nutze* (1533) developed a political theory of the state in which the common weal formed the centrepiece; because education served the common weal in training preachers, lawyers, physicians, teachers, scribes and others who served the community, the ruler had as much responsibility for education as for keeping the peace, public morality or the economy.[71] The fullest educational scheme was presented by Duke Christopher of Württemberg in his church order of 1559 and was largely copied in the Saxon church order of 1580.[72] The Württemberg plans contained most of the elements found elsewhere: elementary schools, so-called particular schools (*Partikularschulen*) for the lowest secondary forms, colleges (*Pädagogien*) for the later forms preparing for university, monastic schools (unique to Württemberg) which used the former rural monasteries to train future theology students, a college for nobles (not founded until 1594), and scholarships at the university. These institutions had both religious and secular functions to serve government in both church and state. Luther's *Sermon on Keeping Children in School* (1530) not only calculated for the reader how many clerics, church servants and schoolmasters Saxony would need but devoted a long section to the learned professions of councillors, lawyers, secretaries and scribes whom the secular ruler would have to recruit from poor backgrounds and with the aid of scholarships to help in the task of turning his subjects 'from wild animals into human beings'.[73]

Gerald Strauss has shown, it is true, that elementary schooling was hardly established properly anywhere in the sixteenth century, and that the clergy failed adequately to inculcate the tenets of the new faith, or any faith, in the countryside.[74] His gloomy picture of Protestant educational underachievement overlooks, however, the secular purposes more adequately fulfilled by the higher stages in the system. Frequently benefices dissolved at the Reformation were used to support students and professors much as they had done previously, though control by the central government eventually replaced any local initiative. The four newly created and eight reformed Protestant universities in the empire often received the former monastic buildings (as in Heidelberg, Marburg and Leipzig), additional endowments from the monastic lands, or from rulers who themselves kept the lands, a common table and residential college for poor students, scholarships, and occasionally monastic libraries and the founding of a *Pädagogium* or *Gymnasium* in the same town to provide adequately trained entrants for the university.[75] The purposes of this generosity were revealed in the promises to Leipzig university graduates and to holders of scholarships at Marburg and Wittenberg of preferential treatment from the rulers when applying for posts as clergy, schoolmasters and local and state officials.[76] Having no university in his lands, the margrave of Brandenburg–Ansbach in 1565 founded forty theology scholarships at Wittenberg for his subjects, but made it a condition that on graduating they should serve in the margraviate or else repay their grants.[77] The bureaucrats of Hesse and Württemberg were increasingly educated at the local universities of Marburg[78] and Tübingen, a trend which also helped to assure their essential reliability in faith for states which adhered each to its own version of Protestantism. In Württemberg it was not only the sons of existing officials, but ordinary children from market towns and villages whose rise through the new educational pyramid broke the previous virtual monopoly among ducal councillors of patricians from the imperial cities.[79] The usefulness of the new bureaucracy hardly needs demonstration. Dr Craco, chancellor to the elector of Saxony, told the town of Freiberg in 1573 that its ancient privileges would no longer be confirmed, since many towns had gross and unreasonable legal customs that had been granted by former princes in stupidity and ignorance when they had not had as many learned men in their service as presently.[80] Professors of law at the universities were appointed part-time in the recently established supreme courts, theologians to the new ecclesiastical councils and visitations. Marburg university was founded as soon as the Hesse government was transferred to that town from Kassel.[81] The regimentation of universities by princes may have had its origins in the territorial universities before the sixteenth century, but it went up several notches when confessional strife subsequently intensified, a sure sign of how closely princely interests were served by universities.[82]

The influence of church property on the institutions of government cannot be measured only by a balance sheet of revenues gained. As important as any increase in resources to finance the domestic and foreign policies of the princes was the fact that their officials now administered the church lands, whether in a separate fund or as part of the demesne. Lower jurisdiction and other aspects of monastic rule were in either case integrated into the state. Even where church lands were supposedly under a separate administration, as in the Palatinate, it might be in the hands of those who simultaneously held posts in the ruler's demesne administration.[83] When monastic lands became *Ämter*, centralisation allowed streamlining, exchanges of outlying holdings with nearby *Ämter*, leases, sales of awkward parcels of land, and other forms of good estate management to increase yields. Such measures were even undertaken between 1571 and 1584 for the lands of the fourteen prelates in Württemberg despite the objections of the Estates, until the duke's administrators had taken effective control from every prelate and begun the process by which the original thirteen monastic schools were by 1595 reduced to a mere four.[84] In Albertine Saxony the whole nature of the *Ämter* changed in mid-century. Their main function was no longer the supervision of essentially judicial tasks by noble provincial governors, but administration of the much augmented demesne by non-noble financial officials.[85] Hesse's inventories of church lands, among the earliest of those compiled in many Protestant territories, gave considerable impetus to the later renewal of rental surveys and cartographic mapping of the principality in the process of modernising the administration.[86] The state had also come to control resources and expenditures previously beyond its orbit, like those on schools and hospitals.

The acquisition of church property and the strengthened administration which it encouraged were bound up with many less tangible advantages gained by means of the Reformation. Functions that had once been dispersed among several authorities became concentrated in the state. Officialdom penetrated more pervasively than before in towns, villages and families. Ecclesiastical jurisdiction was swept away to be replaced by state marriage courts, consistory courts, and the beginnings of Protestant church law, with ultimate control over the weapon of excommunication reserved to the prince, even in the

Calvinist Palatinate.[87] State patronage to parish benefices increased enormously, doubling in Hesse to reach 40 per cent of the total, and now exceeding half of all benefices in electoral Saxony and Württemberg. Moreover, noble patrons could only appoint ministers whose beliefs had been tested and approved by the state church.[88] Ministers, their superintendents – and university professors – were sworn state officials no longer enjoying tenured possession of benefices. Ecclesiastical councils (*Kirchenräte*), with their mixed lay and clerical membership on the Württemberg model, ranked alongside treasuries, supreme courts and privy councils among the leading central institutions of the early modern state. The Palatinate ecclesiastical council, unlike its secular counterparts in having no noble members and being bound by no existing traditions, probed more deeply into the affairs of local communities than any other central body; through its supervision of all higher education it vetted nearly the whole future ruling elite.[89]

The main instrument of ecclesiastical control in the *Ämter* was the visitation, 'the true expression of the early modern bureaucratic state', as Strauss has called it.[90] The first visitations were concerned mainly with all forms of church property and with the faith and discipline of clergy and laity, but already in 1525 Luther had called for visitation of secular government as well.[91] A similar mixture of ecclesiastical and political purposes was served by Duke Christopher's visitations in Württemberg. The need to monitor implementation of the duchy's voluminous ecclesiastical ordinances expanded into a General Visitation (1562–4) of the whole bureaucracy and of the effectiveness of secular legislation.[92] Everywhere the secular and ecclesiastical functions of the state similarly reinforced one another in the close co-operation of both sets of officials at all levels. The boundaries of the new superintendencies were usually drawn in conformity with the *Ämter*, not the old diocesan divisions.[93] The overlap between church orders and police ordinances was considerable, especially in their sumptuary provisions. Already in July 1524 the Hesse police ordinance had required priests to serve the territory by teaching the pure gospel, love of God and one's neighbours, obedience to authority and avoidance of unrest.[94] After 1525 rulers interpreted the Peasants' War as a consequence of misleading Protestant preaching – for Catholic rulers, any Protestant preaching – and took pains to ensure that gospel teachings on secular authority upheld the stability of the state. To this end the Prussian church order as late as 1558 expounded Luther's doctrine of the two regiments, emphasising that Christian freedom did not teach rebellion as claimed by the peasants in 1525 and by the Anabaptists.[95] Peter Blickle has suggested that rulers were inspired by a perceived necessity to control the Reformation from above in order to prevent an alternative Reformation from below by the communities, which would have spread such notions to the political sphere.[96] The discipline and order (*Zucht und Ordnung*), which in particular Calvinist church ordinances of the later sixteenth century sought to impose, matched the search for social discipline in the secular sphere.[97] Ideological commitment to the religious ethos of the state was required from all officials of church, state and university. Extensive purges were the order of the day when rulers of a different Protestant denomination came to power in Saxony and the Palatinate in the 1570s and 1580s. When princes like Frederick IV of the Palatinate declared their control and financial support of churches, schools and universities to be 'the foremost aspect of our ... government'[98] they were not merely paying lip service to the priority of matters concerning the faith.

Most German Protestant rulers, by contrast with English monarchs, successfully excluded the Estates from any significant part in introducing the Reformation, promulgating ecclesiastical ordinances, or governing the newly established churches, with the exception of some financial aspects of administering church property.[99] The rulers retained the upper hand as long as they remained of the same faith as the majority of their subjects and Estates, as was the case in most of the larger principalities during the sixteenth century. As heads of their churches their role differed in kind as well as degree from that in the pre-Reformation church. Formerly their main preoccupation had been rivalry with the bishops, now it was uniformity in confession coupled with social discipline. Secularisation added a whole new dimension to the territorial churches, but even visitations and control of the lower clergy were different in character and legal title from the period before the Reformation.[100]

Largely in response to the Reformation, a few Catholic rulers, notably the dukes of Bavaria, acquired the same objectives as their Protestant counterparts and employed similar means to achieve them: taxation of the clergy (ostensibly to finance defence of the faith against heretics and Turks), control of monastic property, visitation commissions and ecclesiastical councils of mixed lay and clerical membership, reform and discipline of the clergy without regard for the bishops, the censorship of seditious preaching, the promulgation of religious edicts, control of schools and universities, and more besides. The hardening of confessional divisions and the drive towards internal religious unity and uniformity within each state was a process in which Protestant and Catholic rulers reacted against one another.[101] Yet Protestant princes acquired considerable additional advantages. They controlled all church property and jurisdiction, enforced doctrines and church ceremonies of their own choosing, and did not have to make concordats with bishops or respect papal authority. Modelling themselves on Old Testament kings they could, if they wished, go as far as Duke Julius II of Brunswick–Wolfenbüttel, who for the first seven years of his reign acted personally as head of the church, as if he were its supreme superintendent. Although the electors of Brandenburg did not claim the title of *summus episcopus* until the mid-seventeenth century, in many respects they acted during the previous eighty years as if they already held it.[102] Only Protestant princes could advance the complementary nature of government in state and church to its limits. Significantly, the new genre of princely political testaments giving advice to their successors on the principles of government in both church and state was a Protestant invention widely disseminated but with few Catholic imitators. Lawyers deployed much ingenuity in devising arguments to justify Protestant supremacy over the church and so helped to introduce modern ideas of sovereignty into German political thought at the turn of the seventeenth century.[103]

By no means all rulers were able to take full advantage of the opportunities presented by the Reformation. The imperial cities, restrained by their own immediacy of the empire, their inferior rights of Reformation under the Religious Peace of 1555, and the considerable property held within their walls by independent foreign religious institutions, were more likely than princes to use confiscated church property for education, charity and the church, and thus to derive little direct material benefit for themselves.[104] Larger states were initially better placed than smaller ones to impose on their weaker neighbours of a different faith by expanding religious dominance in disputed or jointly ruled frontier areas. In small territories with weak instruments of government and in those severely divided by religion already soon after the Reformation, like Lippe, state power may even at first have declined. The Reformation could have one of two sets of contrasting consequences, according to circumstances, either promoting unity between subjects and ruler, and strengthening the latter's supremacy and the stability of the state, or undermining unity when a conflict over religion could mesh in with existing political, social and economic antagonisms.[105] Larger principalities either overcame such conflicts, as in the Palatinate, or did not experience them until the seventeenth century, when their rulers entered the fray already enjoying the substantial material advantages gained during the Reformation.

Notes

1. K. Körber, *Kirchengüterfrage und Schmalkaldischer Bund* (Leipzig, 1913), p. 33.
2. J. Janssen, *Geschichte des deutschen Volkes seit dem Ausgang des Mittelalters* (8 vols, Freiburg im Breisgau, 1887–94), vol. I, pp. 720–4.
3. *The Complaynt of Roderyck Mors*, ed. J. M. Cowper (Early English Text Society, E.S. XXII, London, 1874), p. 48; cf. J. J. Scarisbrick, *Henry VIII* (London, 1968), p. 524.
4. J. Hashagen, *Staat und Kirche vor der Reformation* (Essen, 1931), p. 302; idem, 'Die vorreformatorische Bedeutung des spätmittelalterlichen landesherrlichen Kirchenregiments', *Zeitschrift für Kirchengeschichte*, XLI (1922), pp. 63–5, 67, 69, 75; W. Dersch, 'Territorium, Stadt und Kirche im ausgehenden Mittelalter', *Korrespondenzblatt der deutschen Geschichts- und Altertumsvereine*, LXXX (1932), pp. 37–39; I. Höss, 'Die Problematik des spätmittelalterlichen Landeskirchentums am Beispiel Sachsens', *Geschichte in Wissenschaft und Unterricht*, X (1959), p. 359.
5. H. J. Cohn, *The Government of the Rhine Palatinate in the Fifteenth Century* (Oxford, 1965), pp. 141–3; L. G. Duggan, *Bishop and Chapter: The Governance of the Bishopric of Speyer to 1552* (New Brunswick, 1978), pp. 123, 148, 152–5.
6. W. Goerlitz, *Staat und Stände unter den Herzögen Albrecht und Georg 1485–1539* (Leipzig, 1928), pp. 232, 235, 248–57, 268; Höss, pp. 354–8.
7. P.-M. Hahn, 'Kirchenschutz und Landesherrschaft in der Mark Brandenburg im späten 15. und frühen 16. Jahrhundert', *Jahrbuch für die Geschichte Mittel- und Ostdeutschlands*, XXVIII (1979), pp. 188–203, 209–10, 215–20.
8. Goerlitz, pp. 261, 276; H.-M. Kühn, *Die Einziehung des geistlichen Gutes im albertinischen Sachsen 1539–1553* (Cologne, 1966), pp. 92–3; J. V. Pollet, *Julius Pflug et l'Allemagne du XVIe siècle* (Julius Pflug, *Correspondance*, vol. V, 2, Leiden, 1982), pp. 420–2.
9. K. Bosl, *Die Geschichte der Repräsentation in Bayern* (Munich, 1974), pp. 103–5; H. Heyden, *Kirchengeschichte Pommerns*, 2 vols, 2nd edn (Cologne, 1957), vol. I, pp. 185–6; P. Kirn, *Friedrich der Weise und die Kirche* (Leipzig, 1926), pp. 92–3.
10. M. Schaab, 'Pfälzische Klöster vor und nach der Reformation', *Blätter für deutsche Landesgeschichte*, CIX (1973), p. 254; Cohn, p. 147.
11. A. Brenneke, *Vor- und nachreformatorische Klosterherrschaft und die*

Geschichte der Kirchenreformation im Fürstentum Calenberg-Göttingen (2 vols, Hanover, 1928–29), vol. I, pp. 158–60; Heyden, vol. I, pp. 185–6.

12. H. Rankl, *Das vorreformatorische landesherrliche Kirchenregiment in Bayern (1378–1526)* (Munich, 1971), pp. 224, 272; Brenneke, vol. I, p. 168.

13. Körber, p. 17; Cohn, p. 146.

14. Rankl, pp. 257–9; H. Neumaier, 'Territorium und *ius circa sacra*. Die spätmittelalterlichen Priestereide in der Grafschaft Hohenlohe', *Blätter für württembergische Kirchengeschichte*, LXXXII (1982), pp. 7–10, 24, 26–8.

15. Cohn, pp. 148–9.

16. Kirn, pp. 36–50, 65; similarly in Brandenburg, B. Hennig, *Die Kirchenpolitik der älteren Hohenzollern in der Mark Brandenburg und die päpstlichen Privilegien des Jahres 1447* (Leipzig, 1906), pp. 188–9.

17. W. Heinemeyer, 'Territorium und Kirche in Hessen vor der Reformation', *Hessisches Jahrbuch für Landesgeschichte*, VI (1956), pp. 144, 148–50; G. Franz (ed.), *Urkundliche Quellen zur hessischen Reformationsgeschichte* (Marburg, 1954–55), vol. II (1954), pp. 69–70.

18. '*zusammenhängendes Stückwerk*', Hashagen, 'vorreformatorische Bedeutung', pp. 79–80; cf. J. W. Stieber, *Pope Eugenius IV, the Council of Basel and the Secular and Ecclesiastical Authorities in the Empire* (Leiden, 1978), pp. 343–6.

19. Höss, pp. 360–1. However, rulers issued detailed regulations for services in Austria and elsewhere also at times other than during schisms, H. von Srbik, *Die Beziehungen von Staat und Kirche in Oesterreich während des Mittelalters* (Innsbruck, 1904), pp. 221–3; Dersch, pp. 41–42.

20. J. Hansen, *Westfalen und Rheinland im 15. Jahrhundert* (2 vols, Leipzig, 1888–90), vol. I: *Die Soester Fehde* (Leipzig, 1888), pp. 65*–8*, 138*–41*.

21. G. Koller, *Princeps in ecclesia. Untersuchungen zur Kirchenpolitik Herzog Albrechts V. in Oesterreich* (Vienna, 1964), pp. 45, 147, 178; Hashagen, *Staat und Kirche*, pp. 550–5.

22. H. Reller, *Vorreformatorische und reformatorische Kirchenverfassung im Fürstentum Braunschweig-Wolfenbüttel* (Göttingen, 1959), pp. 48–60.

23. J. B. Sägmüller, 'Die Idee von der Säkularisation des Kircheguts im ausgehenden Mittelalter – auch eine der Ursachen der Reformation', *Theologische Quartalschrift*, IC (1917), pp. 279, 283–7, 299, 302; P. Mikat, 'Bemerkungen zum Verhältnis von Kirchengut und Staatsgewalt am Vorabend der Reformation', *Zeitschrift der Savigny-Stiftung für Rechtsgeschichte, Kanonistische Abteilung*, XCVIII (1981), p. 300.

24. C. G. Buder, *Nützliche Sammlung verschiedener meistens ungedruckter Schriften* (Frankfurt/Leipzig, 1735), pp. 31–7; L. von Ranke, *History of the Reformation in Germany* (London/New York, 1905), pp. 366–7.

25. *D. Martin Luthers Werke. Kritische Gesamtausgabe* (cit. *WA*) (55 vols, Weimar, 1883–1983), vol. XIII (1889), pp. 12–14.

26. 31 October 1525, *D. Martin Luthers Werke. Briefwechsel* (cit. *WA, Br*)

(18 vols, Weimar, 1930–84), vol. III (1933), pp. 594–6; Körber, pp. 44–52.

27.   22 November 1526, *WA Br*, vol. IV (1933), pp. 133–4; H.-W. Krumwiede, *Zur Entstehung des landesherrlichen Kirchenregiments in Kursachsen und Braunschweig-Wolfenbüttel* (Göttingen, 1967), pp. 67–8.

28.   Luther's opinions for Elector John, early January 1531 and August 1532, *WA Br*, vol. V (1935), pp. 3–7, 9; cf. H. Lehnert, *Kirchengut und Reformation* (Erlangen, 1935), pp. 127–30; K. Trüdinger, *Luthers Briefe und Gutachten an weltliche Obrigkeiten zur Durchführung der Reformation* (Münster, 1975), pp. 64, 87; Kühn, pp. 42–3.

29.   *Ein außführlich Bedenken wie es umb die Kirchen Güter geschaffen*, F. Hortleder, *Von den Ursachen des Teutschen Kriegs Kaiser Carls des Fünfften* (Frankfurt am Main, 1617), pp. 1111–20; F. Roth, 'Zur Kirchengüterfrage in der Zeit von 1538 bis 1540', *Archiv für Reformationsgeschichte*, I (1904), pp. 303–7, 310; Körber, pp. 167–9, 174.

30.   *Briefwechsel Landgraf Philipp's des Grossmüthigen von Hessen mit Bucer*, M. Lenz (ed.) (3 vols, Leipzig, 1880–91), vol. I, p. 48; vol. II (1887), pp. 40–1, 297–8.

31.   H. Liermann, *Handbuch des Stiftungsrechts*, vol. I: *Geschichte des Stiftungsrechts* (Tübingen, 1963), pp. 150–1.

32.   W. Borth, *Die Luthersache (causa Lutheri) 1517–1524* (Lübeck/Hamburg, 1970), pp. 88–91.

33.   H. Bornkamm, *Luther in Mid-career, 1521–30* (London, 1983), pp. 321–3, 333–6; W. Hubatsch, *Geschichte der evangelischen Kirche Ostpreußens* (3 vols, Göttingen, 1968), vol. I, pp. 10–14, 18–21.

34.   W. Maurer, *Die Kirche und ihr Recht* (Tübingen, 1976), pp. 137–8; G. E. Krodel, 'State and Church in Brandenburg–Ansbach–Kulmbach, 1524–1526', *Studies in Medieval and Renaissance History*, V (1968), pp. 157–63.

35.   D. B. Miller, 'The Dissolution of the Religious Houses of Hesse during the Reformation' (Yale University dissertation, 1971), pp. 122–3; B. Jaspers, 'Reformation und Mönchtum in Hessen', *Jahrbuch der Hessischen Kirchengeschichtlichen Vereinigung*, XXVIII (1977), pp. 58–62; J. C. Stalnaker, 'The Emergence of the Protestant Clergy in Central Germany: the Case of Hesse' (Berkeley dissertation, 1970), pp. 137–9; H. J. Hillerbrand, 'Religion and Politics in the German Reformation: the Case of Philipp of Hesse', *Journal of Medieval and Renaissance Studies*, III (1973), pp. 14–15.

36.   J. Mentz, *Johann Friedrich der Grossmütige 1503–54* (3 vols, Jena, 1903–08), vol. III, pp. 278–85, 312; R. Herrmann, *Thüringische Kirchengeschichte* (2 vols, Jena/Weimar, 1937–47), vol. II, pp. 55–57.

37.   V. Press, *Calvinismus und Territorialstaat* (Stuttgart, 1970), pp. 226–30; H. J. Cohn, 'The Territorial Princes in Germany's Second Reformation, 1559–1622', in M. Prestwich (ed.), *International Calvinism 1541–1715* (Oxford, 1985), pp. 146–9.

38.   Körber, p. 70; A. Hilpert, 'Die Sequestration der geistlichen Güter in den kursächsischen Landkreisen Meißen, Vogtland und Sachsen 1531 bis 1543', *Mitteilungen des Altertumsvereins zu Plauen im Vogtland*, XXII (1912), pp. 4–6.

39. W. Sohm, *Territorium und Reformation in der hessischen Geschichte 1526–55* (Marburg, 1915), pp. 32–4, 41; Hilpert, p. 38.

40. Körber, pp. 83–4, 90–1.

41. V. Ernst, 'Die Entstehung des württembergischen Kirchenguts', *Württembergische Jahrbücher für Statistik und Landeskunde*, 1911, vol. II, p. 396; Körber, pp. 164–5.

42. H. Helbig, *Die Reformation der Universität Leipzig im 16. Jahrhundert* (Gütersloh, 1953), pp. 75–6, 100.

43. Franz, *Urkundliche Quellen*, vol. II, pp. 175–6, 345.

44. J. B. Rady, *Geschichte der katholischen Kirche in Hessen 722–1566*; J. M. Raich (ed.) (Mainz, 1904), pp. 721–3.

45. W. D. Wolff, *Die Säkularisierung und Verwendung der Stifts- und Klöstergüter in Hessen-Kassel unter Philipp dem Großmütigen und Wilhelm IV.* (Gotha, 1913), pp. 13, 368–84; F. L. Carsten, *Princes and Parliaments in Germany* (Oxford, 1959), p. 160; H. C. E. Midelfort, 'Protestant Monastery? A Reformation Hospital in Hesse', in P. N. Brooks (ed.), *Reformation Principle and Practice* (London, 1980), p. 75.

46. E. G. Franz. 'Die hessischen Klöster und ihre Konvente in der Reformation', *Hessisches Jahrbuch für Landesgeschichte*, XI (1969), pp. 151–2, 158–61, 163–8.

47. Sohm, pp. 56–63, 108–9, 112–14.

48. K. Krüger, *Finanzstaat Hessen 1500–1567* (Marburg, 1981), pp. 136–7.

49. Hilpert, pp. 27, 34, 37, 67–9, 72–81, 111.

50. Ibid., pp. 127–33.

51. I. Höss and T. Klein, *Das Zeitalter des Humanismus und der Reformation* (*Geschichte Thüringens*, H. Patze and W. Schlesinger (eds), vol. III (Cologne, 1967), pp. 94, 165; Herrmann, vol. II, pp. 100–2.

52. Kühn, 89–90, 99–104; E. A. O. Brandenburg, *Moritz von Sachsen*, vol. I (Leipzig, 1898), pp. 298–9. For Carsten, p. 211, 'the bulk of the monastic spoils did not pass into Maurice's hands'.

53. Höss/Klein, pp. 242–4; Carsten, pp. 212–13; K. Blaschke, *Sachsen im Zeitalter der Reformation* (Gütersloh, 1970), pp. 17–18.

54. Ernst, pp. 383–5; E. Schneider, *Württembergische Reformations-Geschichte* (Stuttgart, 1887), p. 28.

55. Ibid., pp. 20–6; Ernst, pp. 386–90; R. Bütterlin, 'Der württembergische Staatshaushalt in der Zeit zwischen 1483 und 1648' (University of Tübingen dissertation, 1977), p. 50.

56. Ernst, pp. 391–3; W.-U. Deetjen, *Studien zur württembergischen Kirchenordnung Herzog Ulrichs 1534–1550* (Stuttgart, 1981), pp. 233–6. Duke Christopher later claimed to the Estates that his father had had 100,000 Gulden annually from church revenues, but this was probably an exaggeration, Carsten, p. 24; H. Hermelink, 'Geschichte des allgemeinen Kirchenguts in Württemberg', *Württembergische Jahrbücher für Statistik und Landeskunde*, 1903, vol. I, p. 91.

57. Ernst, pp. 399–413; Hermelink, vol. II, pp. 3–7; Carsten, pp. 34–9; Bütterlin, pp. 53, 78.

58. *Die evangelischen Kirchenordnungen des 16. Jahrhunderts*, E. Sehling (ed.) (15 vols, Leipzig/Tübingen, 1902–77), vol. XIV: *Kurpfalz*, J. F. G.

Goeters (ed.) (Tübingen, 1969), pp. 59, 489; Press, pp. 138–9; Schaab, 'Pfälzische Klöster', pp. 256–8.

59. P. M. Tschackert, *Herzogin Elisabeth von Münden* (Berlin/Leipzig, 1899), p. 30; Brenneke, *Calenberg-Göttingen*, vol. II, pp. 167–8, 179–80, 411–15, 459–65, 472–5; Reller, pp. 115–16, 123; A. Brenneke and A. Brauch, *Die calenbergischen Klöster unter Wölfenbütteler Herrschaft, 1584–1634* (Göttingen, 1956), pp. 3, 7, 39–42, 45–50, 73, 155–7, 165–83, 203, 213–20, 225; G. Schnath, 'Das Schicksal des Klosterguts in den früheren Welfenlanden', *Blätter für deutsche Landesgeschichte*, CIX (1973), pp. 265–6.

60. Körber, pp. 74–7.

61. The dukes incorporated at least 220 whole villages into their *Ämter*, but considerable debts had then to be serviced from the revenues, K. Schmaltz, *Kirchengeschichte Mecklenburgs* (3 vols, Schwerin, 1935–52), vol. II (1936), pp. 88–92; Lehnert, p. 105.

62. Despite protests by the nobles from the Diet of Treptow (1534) onwards, the majority of the forty-five ecclesiastical institutions that owned one-sixth of the country became part of the princely lands; urban church wealth was largely conceded to the cities, but the nobles and the new church received little, L. B. von Medem, *Geschichte der Einführung der evangelischen Lehre im Herzogthum Pommern* (Greifswald, 1837), pp. 34–6, 47–8, 59, 162–5, 202–3, 206–21; M. Spahn, *Verfassungs- und Wirtschaftsgeschichte des Herzogtums Pommern von 1478 bis 1625* (Leipzig, 1896), p. 111; Heyden, vol. I, pp. 229–30, 238–9; vol. II, pp. 9–15; Körber, p. 161; *Grosser Historischer Weltatlas*, vol. III: *Neuzeit*, 4th edn, J. Engel and E. W. Zeeden (eds) (Munich, 1981), map 10b, 'Kloster- und Stiftssäkularisation im Hzm. Pommern 1525–1544'.

63. G. Heinrich, *Besitzstand und Säkularisation in Brandenburg um die Mitte des 16. Jahrhunderts* (*Historischer Atlas von Brandenburg und Berlin*, Lieferung XXXIII, Berlin, 1971); H. Rössler (ed.), *Deutscher Adel 1555–1740* (Darmstadt, 1965), pp. 98, 266–7, 273.

64. P.-M. Hahn, *Struktur und Funktion des brandenburgischen Adels im 16. Jahrhundert* (Berlin, 1979), pp. 37–40, 44.

65. L. Mollwo, *Markgraf Hans von Küstrin* (Hildesheim/Leipzig, 1926), pp. 109–12, 464.

66. F. L. Carsten, *The Origins of Prussia* (Oxford, 1964), p. 166.

67. Heyden, vol. I, p. 193. Mecklenburg seized the sees of Schwerin and Ratzeburg, which were however poor and heavily indebted, Schmaltz, vol. II, pp. 82, 110.

68. *WA*, vol. VI (1888), p. 452; J. Heckel, *Die evangelischen Dom- und Kollegiatstifter Preußens* (Stuttgart, 1924), pp. 84–7, 202–20; Lehnert, pp. 62–6.

69. Ibid., pp. 74–82.

70. Mollwo, pp. 115–26, 491; Schmaltz, vol. II, pp. 15–16; A. Huyskens, 'Philipp der Großmütige und die Deutschordensballei Hessen', *Zeitschrift des Vereins für Hessische Geschichte, Neue Folge*, XXVIII (1904), pp. 131, 133, 180; H. H. Hofmann, *Der Staat des Deutschmeisters* (Munich, 1964), pp. 204–12.

71. W. Heinemeyer, 'Die Bildungspolitik Landgraf Philipps des Groß-mütigen von Hessen'. *Hessisches Jahrbuch für Geschichte*, XXI (1971), p. 101; B. Eckert, 'Der Gedanke des Gemeinen Nutzen in der Staatslehre des Johannes Ferrarius', *Jahrbuch der Hessischen Kirchengeschichtlichen Vereinigung*, XXVII (1976), pp. 187, 200–1; B. Unckel, 'Die Entwicklung des Schulwesens der Stadt Marburg seit der Reformation', in E. Dettmering and R. Grenz (eds), *Marburger Geschichte* (Marburg, 1980), pp. 240–1.

72. H. Ehmer, 'Bildungsideale des 16. Jahrhunderts und die Bildungspolitik von Herzog Christoph von Württemberg', *Blätter für württembergische Kirchengeschichte*, LXXVII (1977), pp. 18–23; Patze/Schlesinger, *Geschichte Thüringens*, vol. IV (Cologne, 1972), p. 66.

73. *WA*, vol. XXX, 2 (1909), pp. 526–88.

74. G. Strauss, *Luther's House of Learning* (Baltimore, Md, 1979), pp. 17–18, 249, 307.

75. K.-H. Wegner, 'Studium und Stipendium in Hessen vor der Reformation', in W. Heinemeyer (ed.), *Studium und Stipendium* (Marburg, 1977), pp. 3–6, 71–2; Helbig, pp. 65–74, 77–81.

76. Ibid., p. 96; W. Heinemeyer, '*pro studiosis pauperibus*. Die Anfänge des reformatorischen Stipendiatenwesens in Hessen', in *Studium und Stipendium*, pp. 93–4; Lehnert, pp. 116–17.

77. H. Jordan and C. Bürckstümmer, *Reformation und gelehrte Bildung in der Markgrafschaft Ansbach-Bayreuth* (2 vols, Leipzig, 1917–22), vol. II, pp. 16–17.

78. K. E. Demandt, 'Amt und Familie; eine soziologisch-genealogische Studie zur hessischen Veraltungsgeschichte', *Hessisches Jahrbuch für Landesgeschichte*, II (1952), pp. 130–1.

79. I. Lange-Kothe, 'Zur Sozialgeschichte des fürstlichen Rates in Württemberg im 15. und 16. Jahrhundert', *Vierteljahrsschrift für Sozial- und Wirtschaftsgeschichte*, XXXIV (1941), pp. 219–52; W. Bernhardt, *Die Zentralbehörden des Herzogtums Württemberg und ihre Beamten 1520–1629* (2 vols, Stuttgart, 1973), vol. I, pp. 77–9.

80. Blaschke, p. 94.

81. W. Heinemeyer, 'Zur Gründung des "*universale studium Marpurgense*"', in idem *et al.* (eds), *Academia Marburgensis* (Marburg, 1977), pp. 70, 84–6.

82. Helbig, pp. 125–33; G. A. Benrath, 'Die Universität der Reformationszeit', *Archiv für Reformationsgeschichte*, LVII (1966), pp. 32–3, 48; P. Baumgart, 'Die deutsche Universität des 16. Jahrhunderts. Das Beispiel Marburg', *Hessisches Jahrbuch für Landesgeschichte*, XXVIII (1978), pp. 72–4.

83. T. Karst, 'Pfälzische Klöster im Zeitalter der Reformation', *Mitteilungen des Historischen Vereins der Pfalz*, LXII (1964), pp. 52–5.

84. H. Hermelink, 'Die Änderung der Klosterverfassung unter Herzog Ludwig', *Württembergische Vierteljahrshefte für Landesgeschichte*, XII (1903), pp. 285–7, 297–9, 305, 317–23; cf. Herrmann, vol. II, p. 101; M. Schaab, *Die Zisterzienserabtei Schönau im Odenwald* (Heidelberg, 1963), p. 126.

85. K. Blaschke, 'Die Ausbreitung des Staates in Sachsen und der Ausbau

seiner räumlichen Verwaltungsbezirke', *Blätter für deutsche Landes-geschichte*, XCI (1954), pp. 82–4.

86.   It should be said that the great statistical surveys of the later sixteenth century with which Hesse set the pattern for other German states owed more to the problems generated by the partition of the country in 1567 and to the mathematical interests of Landgrave William IV. L. Zimmermann, *Der ökonomische Staat Landgraf Wilhelms IV.* (2 vols, Marburg, 1933–4), vol. I, pp. 64, 123–34, 143–9.

87.   O. Hintze, 'Die Epochen des evangelischen Kirchenregimentes in Preußen', in idem, *Regierung und Verwaltung*, 2nd edn, G. Oestreich (ed.) (*Gesammelte Abhandlungen*, vol. III (Göttingen, 1967)), pp. 67–9; *Evangelische Kirchenordnungen*, vol. XIV, pp. 53–6; Reller, pp. 73–7; Stalnaker, pp. 358–60.

88.   Hesse, calculated from W. Classen, *Die kirchliche Organisation Althessens im Mittelater* (Marburg, 1929), pp. 68–275, 339–40; G. Arndt, *Das Kirchenpatronat in Thüringen* (*Zeitschrift für thüringische Geschichte und Altertumskunde*, Beiheft X, 1927), pp. 16, 18; W. Becker, *Reformation und Revolution*, 2nd edn (Münster, 1983), pp. 68–9. The Brandenburg nobility were probably exceptional in the success with which they defied state control over the clergy whom they presented to benefices, Hahn, pp. 14–16.

89.   Bernhardt, vol. I, pp. 54–60; Reller, p. 87; Press, pp. 121–2, 127–8, 130; Cohn, 'Second Reformation', p. 159.

90.   Strauss, p. 258.

91.   Luther to Elector John, 31 October 1525, *WA Br*, vol. III, p. 595; Bornkamm, p. 488.

92.   H.-M. Maurer, 'Herzog Christoph als Landesherr', *Blätter für württembergische Kirchengeschichte*, LXVIII/LXIX (1968/9), pp. 122–31.

93.   *Evangelische Kirchenordnungen*, vol. XIV, p. 28; Reller, pp. 76, 146, 152; Blaschke, 'Ausbreitung des Staates', pp. 92–3; Hubatsch, vol. I, p. 48.

94.   Heinemeyer, '"*universale studium Marpurgense*"', pp. 55–6; Zimmermann, pp. 22–3.

95.   Hubatsch, vol. III (*Dokumente*), pp. 86–7.

96.   P. Blickle, *The Revolution of 1525* (Baltimore, Md/London, 1981), pp. 183–5. Whatever may be said against this thesis, which the author has elaborated in subsequent publications, it is hardly tenable to claim that the new territorial churches were not the antithesis to the communities' vision of a reformed church as expressed in the Peasants' War, but its implementation by other means, as does G. Zimmermann, 'Die Einführung des landesherrlichen Kirchenregiments', *Archiv für Reformationsgeschichte*, LXXVI (1985), pp. 146–68.

97.   P. Münch, *Zucht und Ordnung* (Stuttgart, 1978), p. 183.

98.   Press, p. 128.

99.   This topic requires fuller consideration than can be given here; for contrasting views see Carsten, *Princes and Parliaments*, pp. 431, 437, 440; V. Press, 'Formen des Ständewesens in den deutschen Territorialstaaten des 16. und 17. Jahrhunderts', in *Ständetum und Staatsbildung*

in Brandenburg-Preußen, P. Baumgart (ed.) (Berlin/New York, 1983), pp. 290–1.

100. Bornkamm, pp. 483–4; Becker, p. 64.
101. M. Spindler (ed.), *Handbuch der bayerischen Geschichte*, 4 vols, 2nd edn (Munich, 1977–81), vol. II (1977), pp. 310–12, 626–31, 640, 648; Bosl, pp. 142, 150, 165–70; E. Metzger, *Leonhard von Eck (1480–1550)* (Munich, 1980), pp. 240, 316–21; E. W. Zeeden, *Die Entstehung der Konfessionen* (Munich, 1965), pp. 95–8.
102. Reller, p. 135; Hintze, pp. 65–6, 69, 72–3, 77; J. Heckel, 'Die Entstehung des brandenburgisch-preußischen Summepiskopats', in idem, *Das blinde, undeutliche Wort 'Kirche'* (Cologne, 1964), pp. 375–84.
103. F. Hartung, 'Der deutsche Territorialstaat des 16. und 17. Jahrhunderts nach den fürstlichen Testamenten', *Deutsche Geschichtsblätter*, XIII (1912), pp. 268–72, 280; M. Heckel, *Staat und Kirche nach den Lehren der evangelischen Juristen Deutschlands in der ersten Hälfte des 17. Jahrhunderts* (Munich, 1968), pp. 77–8, 117–19.
104. A. Schindling, 'Die Reformation in den Reichsstädten und die Kirchengüter: Straßburg, Nürnberg und Frankfurt im Vergleich', in *Bürgerschaft und Kirche*, J. Sydow (ed.) (Sigmaringen, 1980), pp. 81–5; D. Heuschen, *Reformation, Schmalkaldischer Bund und Österreich in ihrer Bedeutung für die Finanzen der Stadt Konstanz* (Tübingen, 1969), pp. 58–9, 105–8; E. Trostel, *Das Kirchengut im Ulmer Territorium* (Stuttgart, 1975), pp. 181–4.
105. H. Schilling, *Konfessionspolitik und Staatsbildung* (Gütersloh, 1981), pp. 35–6.

9 The Problem of 'Failure' in the Swiss Reformation: Some Preliminary Reflections

Hans R. Guggisberg

The Zürich historian, Hans Conrad Peyer, has reminded students of the Swiss Reformation more than once that they should investigate not only its successes, but also its failures. He has pointed to a general deficiency of modern historical research on the Reformation period. Understandably historians have concentrated their questions concerning the religious renewal in diverse areas of Europe on where it happened, why it happened, and who made it happen. After all, the Reformation as an historical phenomenon can hardly be studied where it was barely attempted or did not occur at all. However, to explore failure and the reasons for it also remains an important task which the historian must not avoid. It has been neglected and repressed for far too long.[1]

This article will concentrate on some failures experienced by the Reformation movement in Switzerland. Of course this subject cannot be exhausted here; we have to content ourselves with pointing out some more accessible problems and formulating a few general observations in the hope that this may stimulate further discussion. Research on the rather scanty source material is under way, but has not yet been completed. Therefore anything said here can only be provisionally valid.[2]

Four questions will be considered. First, what is meant when we speak in general terms about the 'failure of the Reformation' or the 'failed Reformation' will be explained. Secondly, we shall try to discover in what parts of Switzerland the Reformation failed. Thirdly, we shall look at the reasons for this failure, and lastly we shall have to relate this to our title and ask how and why the Swiss confederation was able to survive the disruptions caused by the Reformation.

188

The Swiss Confederation, c. 1515

Legend:

- Cantons and City States (*Orte*) to 1515
- Mandated Territories
- Associate members
- *Freie Aemter*

Labels on map:

Rottweil

Mulhouse

Basel

Schaffhausen

Lake Constance

Constance

Appenzell

St Gallen

Toggenburg

Wildhaus

Rapperswil

Zürich

Baden

Kappel

Glarus

League of Ten Jurisdictions

Engadin

GRAUBÜNDEN

Rhine

League of God's House

Upper League

Lake Como

Lake Maggiore

Lucerne

Aare

Solothurn

Berne

Rhône

Fribourg

VALAIS

Neuchâtel

Lake Neuchâtel

Lake Geneva

I

Failure of reforming renewal presupposes attempts to make it succeed. In this context the reforming sermon has to be mentioned first, then also the circulation of books and pamphlets, the publication of these for learned disputation, and possibly also demands and suggestions for change coming from lay people critical of the tradition. The Reformation fails when such attempts at renewal do not succeed, i.e. when they do not produce an evangelical congregation or when such a congregation disappears after some time and unity in the old faith is re-established. If an unofficial balance between new and old confessions is achieved (which may later on be legalised) the modern historian does not talk of a failure of the Reformation although especially in this respect contemporary opinion may have disagreed.

How the Reformation failed in its beginnings and then disappeared entirely after a certain time can be observed very accurately in the case of some German cities during the first half of the sixteenth century. In recent years historians such as Martin Brecht, Robert Scribner and Hans-Christoph Rublack have studied a number of such cases.[3] Rublack especially has done some important pioneering work. It was with his studies on Würzburg, Bamberg and other ecclesiastical residences that he established the concept of a 'failed Reformation' in historical debate. We shall use it in our discussion here and follow Rublack's definition. However, it has to be emphasised that the failure of the Reformation in certain Swiss cities resulted from different preconditions than those prevailing in the cities of southern and western Germany studied by these scholars.

II

Obviously the question about the *localities* of the failed Reformation in the Swiss confederation has to be dealt with on two levels, that of the confederation as a whole and that of its individual member states. To put it more simply: the problem has to be considered with regard to the confederation and to the cantons.

It cannot be denied that the Reformation ended in compromise for the confederation as a whole. The thirteen cantons consisted of three groups: the Protestant group comprising the city republics of Zürich, Berne, Basel and Schaffhausen; the Catholic group with the rural cantons of Uri, Schwyz and Unterwalden as well as the cities of Lucerne, Zug, Fribourg and Solothurn and their territories. In Glarus and Appenzell, both rural cantons, special regulations for parity were introduced. Shifts in the confessional balance were to take place even after 1531 in the present region of western Switzerland. But despite their strong impact they were not to alter the proportion of religious parties and forces among the thirteen cantons of the Swiss confederation.[4]

It is commonly known that as regards the confederation the Second Peace of Kappel was very largely based on the principle of parity. This is not the place for a detailed analysis of that treaty. The crucial point was undoubtedly the agreement allowing both parties to retain their confession. Measures such as the re-Catholicisation of the *Freie Ämter* in the Aargau and the lordships of Rapperswil, Gaster and Weesen as well as the restitution of the convent of St Gallen and of the abbot's seigneurial rights deviated from the principle of parity. They represented local and regional setbacks for the Reformation, but from our viewpoint today the mutual recognition of the 'other' faith was much more significant. The principle of parity had already been offered in the First Peace of Kappel (1529) by the Protestant cantons. Now the Catholic cantons, too, agreed with it, and it was also kept up in the subsequent treaties with Berne, Basel and Schaffhausen. It is conceivable that the entire development might have been different if the Catholic cantons had tried to utilise the victory and enforce the re-Catholicisation of the whole confederation. As is well known, the imperial court felt that the Catholic cantons should have done precisely this and have thus eradicated all heresy.[5] But they did not, for they knew that their forces would have been insufficient for the total subjugation of Zürich and the other Protestant cantons. For similar reasons the Protestants also had shown moderation in the First Peace of Kappel. This First Treaty was to remain the basis for the whole future development of joint inter-confessional life in the old confederation.[6] It was, in the words of the legal historian Fritz Fleiner, 'a work of politicians, not of theologians'.[7] For Zwingli the treaty of 1529 was, of course, a great disappointment for the Swiss reformer had envisaged the Protestantisation of the entire confederation.[8]

Attempts to exploit fully the victories of 1529 and 1531 most probably would have led to the collapse of the confederation or, as Hans Conrad Peyer has so convincingly suggested, the confederate network (*Bundesgeflecht*). No one wanted to take such a risk, however, either in 1529 or in 1531. If the First Treaty still had left some possibilities of changing the religious pattern of the confederation as a whole as Zwingli intended it, these were blocked off completely after the Second Peace of Kappel. Any official influence by the whole confederation or even by a majority of its cantons on the religion of the other cantons had been rendered impossible. The confessional position of individual cantons continued to be determined by their authorities. Thus in effect the principal rule applied everywhere, which from the early seventeenth century was to be defined generally as *cuius regio eius religio*.

It is true after the Second Peace of Kappel in the Mandated Territories (*Gemeine Herrschaften*) there still existed some limited freedom for individual communities to choose their confession. It was possible to return to the old faith but impossible to introduce the Reformation where it had not taken place before. For this reason some Mandated Territories came entirely under the influence of the Catholic cantons. The communal majority in religious matters provided for in the Second Treaty was restricted to the Catholics. Where adherents of the new faith were in the majority both confessions were granted equal status. Gradually the idea of majority decision faded away and the principle of parity spread down to the smallest political units. This was basically confirmed in the Third Peace Treaty of 1656. The Fourth Treaty of 1712 enforced it fully in the Mandated Territories as well. But within the thirteen cantons strict confessional unity was maintained until the end of the *ancien régime*.[9]

The Second Peace of Kappel was certainly not an ideal solution. Many contemporaries did not think it was, and even with the historical detachment of four centuries it still appears problematical in many ways. But – and this is the crucial point – it saved the existence of the confederation.

All areas of the confederation which ultimately rejected the Reformation and remained Catholic showed certain 'beginnings' of reforming propaganda and activity in the 1520s. Clergymen and humanist school teachers as well as lay people voiced their criticisms of church tradition. In some places criticism of this kind had led to suggestions for changing the relationship between church and state, and also the jurisdiction of the church.

From 1522 the religious question was debated by the confederate diet. On 15 December of that year it recommended to all cantons that they should ban the preaching of the 'new doctrine'. Basel and Zürich were asked to prevent the printing of 'such new booklets'.[10] In the course of the debates leading to these decisions the terms 'old faith' and 'new faith' (*alter Glaube, neuer Glaube*) became generally accepted. They obviously originated from adherents of the 'old faith' since they did not in any way coincide with the reformers' view of themselves. At first Zürich stood isolated on the Protestant side and experienced increasing pressure from those who were clearly opposed to the Reformation. By 1524 the dividing lines had already become quite evident. In the so-called 'Beckenried missive' the cantons of Lucerne, Uri, Schwyz, Unterwalden and Zug asked the powerful city republic of Berne to stay with them and not to take sides with Zürich. They informed Berne of their decision 'to remain with the Christian church order as in the past, and with the old, true and correct Christian faith, also to eradicate, prevent, punish and suppress this wrong and erroneous doctrine of Luther, Zwingli and Hus in all our territories as far as we can'.[11]

From that time until the founding of the Swiss Confederacy (1848) the 'five inner cantons' formed the nucleus of the Catholic confederation. Later on, with the addition of Fribourg and Solothurn, they became the 'seven inner cantons'. Among the Associate Members (*Zugewandte Orte*) mainly Valais was on their side. During 1524 they continued to court Berne (which proved unsuccessful) and dissociated themselves more and more clearly from Zürich. The attack on the Carthusian priory of Ittingen by the peasants of Stammheim fatally widened the gulf. In their 'religious concordat' (*Glaubenskonkordat*) of 1525 the five inner cantons and Fribourg showed that reforming thinking certainly prevailed in their leadership. They agreed to discipline the clergy and to act jointly against abuses in the church. They also alleviated the tax burden of the rural population and the conditions of bondage. But in religious matters they were unequivocally committed to retaining the Catholic tradition.[12]

Since I share the view that in the beginning the Reformation was an 'urban event'[13] I am particularly interested in the relevant developments of 'beginnings' in the four Swiss cities which ultimately remained Catholic.

Lucerne

The city republic of Lucerne was the leader of the confederate cantons opposed to the Reformation in the 1520s. Increasingly it became the predominant canton (*Vorort*) within the Catholic confederation. There was a very close connection between its leading families and mercenary service, and this explains the identity of interests between them and central Switzerland.[14] The beginnings of reforming activity always have to be seen against this political backdrop. They can be recognised in a small group of humanist clergymen and laymen. Its most prominent members included Oswald Myconius, a Latin schoolmaster (who in 1531 succeeded Oecolampadius as leader of the Basel church), the canon Johann Xilotectus, a friend of Vadianus and Beatus Rhenanus, and the priest Jodocus Kilchmeyer who started as a village preacher and also became a canon in 1519. Myconius and Xilotectus were criticised as 'Lutherans' early on; the schoolmaster who was indeed one of Zwingli's closer friends was officially ordered by the council in 1521 not to speak to his pupils about Luther. Early in 1522 the *Sodalitas Lucernensis evangelica* was greatly strengthened when Dr Sebastian Hofmeister became reading master with the Franciscans. On 29 March 1522 at the traditional Musegg procession Konrad Schmid, commander of the Order of St John at Küssnacht on Lake Zürich (a prominent follower of Zwingli) for the first time gave a sermon in German, conveying the central message of the Reformation. Catholic resistance grew stronger; it was led by the stipendiary priest Johannes Bodler and clearly supported by the city council. By July Hofmeister was made to leave the city; Myconius lost his teaching position in August, and a few months later he moved away too.[15]

In July 1522 Zwingli and some of his followers asked the bishop of Constance in a petition to permit free (i.e. evangelical) worship and to abolish celibacy. Jodocus Kilchmeyer, among others, had signed the letter.[16] As he also supported marriage of priests from the pulpit the Lucerne council accused him of seducing weak clergymen to disregard church laws. Kilchmeyer and also Xilotectus were married secretly. Their situation became increasingly precarious as anti-Reformation propaganda grew more intense. By the end of 1524 both canons gave up their prebends and left the city.[17] Thus the crucial personalities who might have been able to carry the Reformation through had disappeared from Lucerne. It is very difficult to estimate the extent to which the ideas of the Reformation spread beyond their small group. After 1523/24 the authorities repeatedly acted against activities relating to the 'new faith' in the city and the country, but the picture remains fragmentary and without inner coherence: a city craftsman is banished for spreading reforming pamphlets, two peasants are arrested for taking part in Reformed services in Bernese and Zürich territory. A chaplain loses his post for criticising the worship of saints and for calling the blessing of the weather superstitious; another clergyman takes part in the Berne colloquy (1528) and then leaves his home city Lucerne voluntarily. The Anabaptists too are severely persecuted.[18]

In two known cases a larger number of people clashed with the Lucerne authorities because of their Reformed convictions: in 1528 fourteen men, mostly peasants and craftsmen, were fined, deprived of their civic rights and banished because they had met in the village of Adligenswil to read the Bible using a New Testament in Luther's translation.[19] In the summer of 1531 when tensions in the confederation neared their peak the council discovered that a pamphlet from Zürich was circulating in Lucerne, defending, among other matters, the food embargo against the five inner cantons. Again there was a wave of arrests; the ten prisoners were accused of having contributed to the food embargo. They were interrogated and tortured but then given only light fines and released. It had not been possible to prove them guilty of high treason.[20] There were further, similar occurrences. These always appear to be isolated incidents without visible connections.[21] An integrated Reformation movement did not exist in Lucerne at any time.

Zug

The first information about events relating to the Reformation date from the first half of 1522. Here too the authorities appear to have taken a clear anti-Reformation stance from the start.[22] A court document from Zürich speaks of 'those from Zug who wish to stay with their old customs' and adds, they had 'spoken to their priests to stay quiet and preach as in the past'.[23] Thus, for instance, chaplain Bartholomäus Stocker had to vow on taking office that he would not introduce any 'innovation' and drop any contacts with Lutheranism.[24]

As in Lucerne there were a number of clergymen also in the small city republic of Zug who were positively inclined towards church renewal. The best known among them was Werner Steiner, a Master of the University of Paris, former field chaplain to the Swiss troops in Italy and pilgrim to Jerusalem. Decorated with the honorary title of a papal protonotary and freed from material worries though a canon's prebend from the convent of Beromünster, he lived as a private scholar in his home city from 1520. From Zwingli's first appearance he had personal contact with him. He married in 1522. But he did not declare himself unreservedly for the Reformation before 1529, i.e. when he fled to Zürich.[25] Some of his friends had been forced to leave Zug before. Nothing is known about the number of those who were not part of the clergy and favourably inclined towards the Reformation, but it probably was very small. Contemporary sources stress again and again that the people (*Volk*) of Zug were opposed to the religious renewal. Stocker confirms this in a letter to Zwingli (15 July 1522) when he says that it is almost impossible to give his 'incorrigible' (*unbelehrbar*) fellow citizens an understanding of the new faith. Also when together with Steiner Stocker advocated marriage for priests he had to 'suffer much derision, trouble and defiance because of it'.[26]

All the same the council felt from time to time that it had to take steps against reforming trends and tendencies. Thus it even opposed participation in the first Zürich colloquy. During the second Zürich colloquy adherents of the new faith were persecuted in Zug, but nothing is known about the initiators or the extent of these incidents. They may have been connected with the reforming propaganda coming from the nearby convent of Kappel, especially from its abbot Wolfgang Joner and the young Heinrich Bullinger. The atmosphere at the diet which met in Zug in the summer of 1524 was marked by a great deal of agitation. Zwingli and his followers were violently attacked. The attack on the priory of Ittingen further inflamed the population, and the council barely managed to stop a troop of soldiers leaving the city who wanted to take revenge by attacking the convent of Kappel. Early in 1526 the council undertook a survey on religious matters in the four Zug parishes, and this showed that almost everybody wanted to stay with the faith of their forebears and not to separate from the Forest Cantons. Subsequently Werner Steiner and his friends met growing difficulties. When he left the city the 'beginnings' of the Reformation in Zug had virtually disappeared.[27] However, after a while cautious toleration of the adherents of the Reformation did reappear: in 1537 Werner Steiner could risk visiting his home city again, and he was even received with honorary wine.[28]

More interestingly, there is proof of a group of adherents of the new faith again existing in Zug in the 1550s. But it is not known what status it had, who belonged to it, and for how long it survived. The following can be gleaned from an anonymous 'thorough report' (*Gründtlicher Bericht*) of 2 February 1556. At that time there was some interest in Zug in evangelical exegesis of the Bible and there were – very much in contrast to the Forest Cantons – many people who owned a bible (in the Zürich translation) and read it. The city priest, Max Seiler, preached several times against the doctrine of good works. When he was interrogated, he dissociated himself from Luther but declared that his preaching was solely based on the Scriptures. Among those who read the Bible were also members of the political elite, e.g. the city's standard bearer. But they had to be careful. Loyal Catholics would not listen to them in a conversation: they acted like 'deaf dogs'. The priest was suspected of opposing mercenary pensions. After a period of toleration the authorities reverted to measures of compulsion. They had the bibles collected, taken to the city hall and publicly burnt by the hangman of Lucerne on 28 January 1556. The author of the report writes as a Protestant who took part in the religious discussions and who talks about his personal experience. When he refers to the emigration of Reformed families from Locarno (1555) he shows that he anticipates a similar fate for his group.[29]

The 'thorough report' proves that the minority which inclined towards Protestantism was tolerated until the winter of 1555/56. A glance at the official correspondence of that time shows that the other Catholic cantons knew about the situation in Zug. There was evidently general and widespread suspicion, which went so far that the Zug council had to defend itself. As early as 26 November 1555 it had declared officially that it had no wish to separate from the Catholic cantons and that it recognised the dangers threatening the Catholic faith on its own territory.[30] At a conference of the five inner cantons in Lucerne in March 1556 the representative of Zug justified his position: the 'Zwinglian priest' was dismissed, the Bible and other 'Zwinglian books' were confiscated and burnt. Their sale was severely punished in Zug territory. In spite of all this the representatives of the Forest Cantons and Lucerne reminded Zug not to isolate itself from them.[31]

Fribourg

The city founded by the dukes of Zähringen in the Uechtland offers a picture of the 'beginnings' of the Reformation which resembles that of Lucerne and Zug, although here the humanist background is more tangible. Since the thirteenth century crafts and manufactures had been developing in Fribourg. As a result of the economic advance a privileged upper class emerged which at the start of the sixteenth century had become a political oligarchy. The cultural and educational aspirations of the Fribourg patricians were based on the general humanist philosophy of the period. As elsewhere they were also shared by foreigners. The creator, promoter and central figure of the humanist movement in Fribourg at the start of the sixteenth century was Peter Falck, a versatile patrician who had held many public offices. He alone had everything that was required to make his home city a centre, albeit a provincial one, for *studia humanitatis*: wealth, contacts with international scholars and an inclination and talent for patronage. He seems to have systematically built around himself the Fribourg group of humanists. In 1519 he died of the plague on his second journey to Jerusalem, i.e. at a time when the Reformation had hardly begun to spread in Switzerland. Falck was more patron than scholar. His personality reflects the character typical of Fribourg humanism which was not active and productive but receptive and therefore fragile (the printing industry only became established in Fribourg towards the end of the sixteenth century). Falck's death severely weakened Fribourg humanism, or at least initiated its demise: this was not a favourable precondition for disseminating the ideas of the Reformation.[32]

As with Lucerne and Zug they first appeared in Fribourg in the early 1520s. The defensive reaction of the authorities was very vehement from the outset. On 22 April 1522 the ensigns told the council of two hundred that Luther's 'evil, damned and devilish sect' should not be tolerated in Fribourg under any circumstances and that those who were revealed to be Lutherans should be severely punished.[33] After a search of all private libraries books and pamphlets of the Reformation were publicly burnt in 1523. The council ruling of December 1523 also told inn-keepers to sound out their guests and report any heretical remarks immediately to the authorities.[34] In the following years repression continued unabated. Although the sources on the whole are scanty, the numerous repressive measures taken by the authorities reflect the presence of a lively reforming opposition. They show that the authorities were worried and also frightened by the protagonists. We have the names of a few of these but otherwise little is known about them. They too were mainly clergymen, partly from Falck's group, but also some who had come to Fribourg later. In most cases they did not stay long but up until 1530 newcomers continued to arrive.[35] In 1522 some council members who tended towards the new faith tried to appoint Oswald Myconius, suspended from his teaching post in Lucerne, as schoolmaster in Fribourg. This attempt failed because of the Catholic majority in the council, but it does illustrate that the friends of the Reformation felt quite powerful. The year 1523 probably was the peak of their optimistic self-confidence; it also brought the acute danger of a decisive religious change closer on several occasions. But from 1524 the adherents of the new faith seem to have been pushed increasingly on to the defensive.[36]

In its religious policies the Fribourg government did not receive much backing from the church authorities. The bishop of Lausanne gave encouragement only in writing. The council therefore called two clergymen to Fribourg who were to become the pillars of 'Catholic resistance'. In 1523 the Alsatian Hieronymus Mylen assumed his office as a preacher at St Niklaus, and in 1525 the provincial of the Rhenish-Swabian province of the Order of St Augustine, Konrad Treger, returned to his home city in order to continue his struggle for the old faith from there. Mylen and Treger both acted as defenders of orthodoxy in close co-operation with the government.[37] But the religious policies of Fribourg did not simply aim to eradicate the Reformation. Very soon their main objective became the preservation of the traditions of the old faith, i.e. they sought to serve Catholic reform.[38]

Solothurn

In Lucerne, Zug and Fribourg the beginning of the Reformation and its suppression basically took a similar course, even if their struggles differed in intensity. Solothurn offers a different, independent and, above all, more complex picture.[39] Here the religious renewal came closest to a breakthrough, closer even than in Fribourg. The events were very much part of the development in the confederation as a whole, and so they have to be considered in that context.

During the growth of the Reformation Solothurn's position within the confederation was very problematic. Since the thirteenth century the city had been an ally of Berne, which had capital jurisdiction in the Solothurn territories of Kriegstetten and Bucheggberg and also possessed the advowson of Bucheggberg. But Solothurn was also the residence of the French ambassadors. Its relations with Basel in the late 1520s were strained because of border disputes. In any event confessionally the political elite of the city was more inclined towards the side of the five inner cantons.

At the Baden Colloquy (1526) Solothurn had still been clearly in the Catholic camp, but after the breakthrough of the Reformation in Berne (1528) it became a mediator between the religious factions in Switzerland. The Aare city kept its distance from the 'Christian Civic Union' of Protestant Swiss cities (*Christliches Burgrecht*) and the 'Christian Alliance' of the Catholic inner cantons (*Christliche Vereinigung*). It remained neutral in the first Kappel war, and reluctantly joined Berne's side in the second. Even before the peace it participated in mediation. But for a long time the five inner cantons refused to acknowledge the city's neutrality.

The Reformation began relatively late in Solothurn. There was no particularly noticeable propagation of humanist ideas. The Reformation in Zürich did not cause any sparks to ignite spontaneously. There were a few chaplains in the spring of 1522 who preached at the collegiate church of St Ursus along the lines of the new faith. The council issued a ban, and through skilful manoeuvring peace in town and country could be preserved for the time being.[40] The adherents of church renewal only became really active towards the end of the 1520s.

As long as Berne was still Catholic its religious mandates applied also in parts of the Solothurn territory. In 1528 the council with its Catholic majority permitted freedom of choice in confessional matters, and this of course noticeably helped the new faith to spread. The Protestants were further strengthened by the outcome of the first Kappel war and also by the mandate of 26 September 1529 which confirmed the freedom of religious choice.[41]

The most radical advocates of church renewal at that time, however, were not clergymen and scholars but members of the boatsmen's guild, i.e. representatives of the urban middle class. Despite a council ban they removed the pictures from their altar in the Franciscan church on 23 November 1529.[42] This resulted in dramatic confrontations and the threat of imminent civil war. Yet surprisingly the authorities were still prepared to compromise, and they made further concessions to the adherents of the new faith: henceforth two preachers were to hold evangelical services in the city, and the Protestants were to have the use of the Franciscan church on weekdays and of the church of St Ursus on Sundays.[43] Two polls conducted in all parishes showed that the majority of the rural population adhered to the old faith, but also that there were groups of adherents of the new faith everywhere and that these were growing rather than declining. During 1530 and 1531 this development, which was supported by Berne, continued without interruption. Neither did the appearance of the Anabaptists markedly interfere with it. In the rural areas the Protestants even gradually gained the majority.[44] Thus Solothurn for a long time stood on the edge of religious change. If the evangelical cantons had won the second Kappel war it would undoubtedly have taken place. But understandably the victory of the Catholic party in the confederation as a whole started the reversal in Solothurn. By and by the Protestants lost everything they had gained in 1528/29. The process of systematic re-Catholicisation, led by the authorities, began in the city and finally also affected the rural parishes. The Protestant uprisings of 1533, which again were started by members of the boatsmen's guild, could not alter this movement, which did not bring Solothurn back to the edge of religious change but to that of civil war. When that danger had been settled with confederate mediation the city republic completed its return to the camp of Catholic cantons. Only in the villages of the Bucheggberg did Reformed worship continue to be permitted.[45]

III

We now turn to the *causes* for the failure of the Reformation in the areas of the confederation which remained Catholic, and here again we have to progress from the general to some individual problems. First we will look at the reasons for rejection which all five or rather seven Catholic cantons had in common, and then we shall concentrate again on the four cities already studied.

A particularly vivid summary of the most important and generally valid arguments against accepting the Reformation is expressed in the above-mentioned 'Beckenried missive' of the five inner cantons (1524). Here the danger of confessional division is seen not only in the destruction of church traditions, the secularisation of life and the contempt of God, the Virgin and all saints, but above all in the 'disruption of ecclesiastical and secular authorities' (*Zerrüttung geistlicher und weltlicher Obrigkeiten*), i.e. in the dissolution of the religious, political and social foundations of the confederate network.[46]

Without doubt the historian Hans Dommann had this in mind when he said the reasons for the five inner cantons' rejecting the Reformation were 'in their entirety and strength not easily comprehensible' and were in no way based on material considerations alone but also determined by ideas and mentalities.[47] Contemporary observers too saw it in this way. A letter of 3 June 1529, addressed by the council of Berne to Zürich, states that the people of the inner cantons wanted to remain with the old faith 'from real piety' (*uss rechter fromkeit*).[48]

It has never been doubted that there were also material reasons against an acceptance of the Reformation. They are well-known and need no further comment. The most important ones include the dependence on revenue from mercenary service abroad, the fear of being overrun by Zürich and the dynamics of its policies, and the concern about maintaining control over the Mandated Territories. As Dommann observed correctly, the members of the political elite in the five inner cantons saw themselves as 'bearers and keepers of the traditions of the confederate state in its basic units, the rural and urban communities, which were to preserve equality within the system of alliances'.[49] To them, centralist aspirations such as those emanating from Zürich seemed sinister, dangerous and ungodly, a new form of the threat which previously the Habsburg claim to power had presented. They certainly did not treat the church with subservience. On the contrary, the state authority possessed and maintained the power to interfere in religious and church affairs also in the Catholic cantons. The politicians were sufficiently confident to enforce the reform of the clergy (where this was deemed necessary) on behalf of the state and without parting from traditional popular feeling or from the church.

Moreover, just as for Zwingli, a separation between the religious and the state spheres was unthinkable to the statesmen of the Catholic cantons. Zwingli sought to re-establish religious unity by subjecting the Catholic cantons to *his* doctrine; equally the Catholic cantons fought for religious unity in *their* faith, first for the entire confederation and, when this proved impossible, for their own territories.[50]

This brings us back to the cities which remained Catholic. The above-mentioned general arguments against the Reformation prevailed there, as they did in the rural cantons. In Fribourg and especially in Solothurn this concurrence may at times not have been quite as clear, but after 1531 uniformity had largely been restored.

Knowing that the sources are fragmentary and that the picture may well be changed through further research we turn first to the reasons for the failure of the Reformation common to all four cities. Hans-Christoph Rublack's studies on urban history which were mentioned before and which have appeared as a collection under the title *Gescheiterte Reformation* are based exclusively on residences of the ecclesiastical princes, i.e. on centres of church power.[51] The four cities,

Lucerne, Zug, Fribourg and Solothurn, were not princely residences but free, though in part very small, republics. In their resistance to the Reformation they received very little visible help from their bishops who resided elsewhere. Therefore it would be wrong to suggest that the Reformation did not get a chance there because they were centres of church power where the church was defending itself. Indeed the resistance against reforming activities in all four cities clearly originated from the secular authorities.

The same phenomenon – conservative councils versus progressive advocates of religious and church renewal – can of course also be observed in cities where the Reformation finally succeeded.[52]

The rejection of the Reformation by Catholic authorities corresponds to the generally hostile attitude shown by Protestant authorities towards Anabaptists and other exponents of a 'radical Reformation': everywhere the propagators of change threatened not just the religious but also the political unity of communities. They appeared to be harbingers of social revolution as well, not only disturbing traditional law and order but also endangering trade, commerce and economic prosperity. The city authorities, however, wished to protect and strengthen all these.

Therefore the anti-Reformation attitude of the Lucerne, Zug, Fribourg and Solothurn governments, despite its significance for the failure of renewal, does not appear to be extraordinary, let alone unique. Besides, the resistance varied in its intensity. Whereas the Fribourg council probably displayed the greatest intransigence, the Solothurn government acted with much more lenience and only became staunchly anti-Protestant after 1531.

Other reasons for the failure of the Reformation which can be seen everywhere are:

1. In all four cities the governments were opposed to the Reformation not only on principle, but they also all had a firm grip on the municipal church institutions. They could use these to repel reforming propaganda, and they also had the authority to carry out internal church reforms once the Protestant opposition had been suppressed.
2. The adherents of the new faith were in a minority everywhere. The only exception was the rural parishes of Solothurn where the Protestants gained the majority in 1530/31. But the reversal set in immediately after the Second Peace of Kappel.[53]
3. None of the four city republics produced a charismatic leader

who might have been able to integrate the reforming attempts and bring about lasting success.

4. Zwingli's Reformation in Zürich frightened rather than inspired the smaller city republics and their political elites. Lucerne especially may well have felt a very real danger of being 'taken over' by its neighbour Zürich after the breakthrough of the new teaching there. Fribourg regarded mighty Berne with similar suspicion.[54]

5. Between the adherents of the old faith and those who were committed followers of the new faith there must have existed a considerable group of people who were undecided and who therefore weakened the impetus of the Reformation. This can be proved for Solothurn especially but it probably also occurred elsewhere.[55]

6. Very little can be said in general terms about the social background of the followers of the Reformation in the four cities. Certainly they mainly belonged to the middle-classes of craftsmen and peasant burghers, but they also included some members of the local elites. The holders of crucial political power were always on the side of the old faith. Nowhere, except in Solothurn, was there a cohesive picture of the Reformation firmly rooted in the middle-classes. But even in Solothurn it is only the boatsmen's guild which, as a collective body, assisted in propagating the Reformation.[56]

7. The centres of political (and military) power were of course the cities, and the most important political leaders came from the cities. The authorities, therefore, were able to enforce their rejection of the Reformation on the rural communities even if these originally or at some time had inclined towards the new teaching. Again, the example of Solothurn illustrates this very clearly.[57]

Two more reasons for the failure of the Reformation should be mentioned which played a particular part in individual local cases:

1. In Lucerne and Zug opposition to the Reformation must also have been consolidated greatly by the many personal contacts and by the identity of interests between mercenaries and those who controlled the Gotthard pass.[58]

2. In Solothurn, the establishment of the French embassy in 1530 certainly helped the Catholic party.[59]

It is commonly known that in the early phases of the urban Reformation humanist critics always played an important and sometimes a crucial role, but this in itself has nothing to do with the local success or failure of religious renewal. In a provincially modest way this can also be seen in our four cities, most clearly in Lucerne and Zug. In Fribourg humanist interests and activities were already past their peak and on the decline when reforming propaganda set in. It therefore started from a more difficult position *vis-à-vis* the orthodox forces than elsewhere. Conversely, in Solothurn humanist interests had hardly spread in the city when the first stirrings of the Reformation could be felt. The reforming activities remained relatively weak for a long time and only grew stronger (with the assistance of Berne) in the late 1520s. The *studia humanitatis*, however, only blossomed there after the systematic re-Catholicisation of the city republic had begun.[60]

IV

We have seen that the Swiss Reformation ended in a compromise for the confederation as a whole, and that it failed in many cases in the cantons themselves. We have looked at the course of events that led to this failure in several places, and we have tried to show some reasons for this, especially with regard to the cities which remained Catholic.

Zwingli did not succeed in his aim of a Protestant confederation. But the Catholic cantons were not capable either of ridding Switzerland of the new faith. The Reformation presented the confederation with the confessional divide and all its long-term problems. It shook the confederate network but it did not ultimately destroy it. Switzerland was spared the decades of religious strife which the empire, France and the Netherlands had to endure. In the late sixteenth and during the seventeenth century the confederation went through a period of religious hardening and increasing cultural drought. But as a state it had survived the crisis of the Reformation more or less intact.

The question why this was possible has often been put and answered. The integrating effect of the French mercenary alliances has been referred to repeatedly in this context, and the common interest shared by all cantons in maintaining their authority over the Mandated Territories has been particularly stressed.[61] Peter Stadler recently treated the whole problem very thoroughly; he pointed out how important the early completion of territorialisation was as the foundation of federalist traditions.[62] In the present context I would add the following thesis to his findings: Switzerland survived the crisis of the Reformation because the Reformation did not achieve its aim, that is, because it succeeded only partially and partially it also failed.

Notes

1.   H. C. Peyer, reviews of B. Moeller (ed.), *Stadt und Kirche im 16. Jahrhundert* (Gütersloh, 1978) and W. J. Mommsen (ed.), *Stadtbürgertum und Adel in der Reformation* (Stuttgart, 1979), *Zwingliana*, XV (1979/82), pp. 163, 317.
2.   I dealt with the subject of the 'failure of the Reformation' in Switzerland in a recent seminar at the University of Basel. I am grateful to the following students who worked on the documents referred to in this article, and who made many useful suggestions: Marianne Brändli, Philipp Egger, Christoph Maier, Barbara Pauk, André Stocker, Christoph Windler.
3.   M. Brecht, 'Die gescheiterte Reformation in Rottweil', *Blätter für württembergische Kirchengeschichte*, LXXV (1975), pp. 5–22; R. Scribner, 'Why was there no Reformation in Cologne?', *Bulletin of the Institute of Historical Research*, XLIX (1976), pp. 217–41; H.-Chr. Rublack, 'Reformatorische Bewegungen in Würzburg und Bamberg', in Moeller, *Stadt und Kirche*, pp. 109–24; H.-Chr. Rublack, *Gescheiterte Reformation: Frühreformatorische und protestantische Bewegungen in süd- und westdeutschen geistlichen Residenzen* (Stuttgart, 1978).
4.   Because of limited space the Associate Members (*Zugewandte Orte*) and their confessionalisation will not be examined.
5.   H. Meyer, *Der Zweite Kappeler Krieg* (Zürich, 1976), p. 219.
6.   H. R. Guggisberg, 'Parität, Neutralität und Toleranz', *Zwingliana*, XV (1979/82), pp. 632–49, esp. 633f. The two peace treaties are printed in *Eidgenössische Abschiede* (hereafter abbreviated *EA*), vol. IV, 1b, 1478–83 and 1567–71; the Second Peace of Kappel also in E. Walder (ed.), *Religionsvergleiche des 16. Jahrhunderts*, vol. I (Quellen zur neueren Geschichte, VII), 2nd edn (Berne, 1960), pp. 5–14.
7.   F. Fleiner, 'Die Entwicklung der Parität in der Schweiz', in idem, *Ausgewählte Schriften und Reden* (Zürich, 1941), p. 82.
8.   G. R. Potter, *Zwingli* (Cambridge, 1976), p. 369. Cf. also G. W. Locher, *Die Zwinglische Reformation im Rahmen der europäischen Kirchengeschichte* (Göttingen/Zürich, 1979), pp. 168f, 505; U. Gäbler, *Huldrych Zwingli: Eine Einführung in sein Leben und Werk* (Munich, 1983), pp. 111, 133.
9.   H. C. Peyer, *Verfassungsgeschichte der alten Schweiz* (Zürich, 1978), p. 92; Guggisberg, 'Parität', p. 634f.
10. L. von Muralt, 'Renaissance und Reformation', in *Handbuch der Schweizer Geschichte*, vol. I (Zürich, 1972), pp. 389–570, esp. 467; *EA*, vol. IV, 1a, p. 255, n.

11. Ibid., p. 410 (8 April 1524).
12. Ibid., pp. 572–8.
13. A. G. Dickens, *The German Nation and Martin Luther* (London, 1974), p. 182.
14. J. Dierauer, *Geschichte der Schweizerischen Eidgenossenschaft*, vol. III (Gotha, 1907), p. 59; P. Stadler, 'Eidgenossenschaft und Reformation', in H. Angermeier (ed.), *Säkulare Aspekte der Reformationszeit* (Schriften des Historischen Kollegs, V) (Munich, 1983), pp. 91–9, esp. 94; K. Messmer and P. Hoppe, *Luzerner Patriziat: Sozial- und wirtschaftsgeschichtliche Studien zur Entstehung und Entwicklung im 16. und 17. Jahrhundert* (Lucerne/Munich, 1976), pp. 77–93; S. Grüter, *Geschichte des Kantons Luzern im 16. und 17. Jahrhundert* (Lucerne, 1945), pp. 50–108.
15. W. Brändly, *Geschichte des Protestantismus in Stadt und Land Luzern* (Lucerne, 1956), pp. 4–47.
16. *Huldreich Zwinglis Sämtliche Werke*, E. Egli, G. Finsler *et al.* (eds), vol. I (Leipzig, 1905), pp. 189–209; Brändly, *Geschichte des Protestantismus*, p. 45.
17. Ibid., p. 65.
18. Ibid., pp. 61ff, 84, 85.
19. Ibid., pp. 81ff.
20. Ibid., pp. 97ff.
21. The events are described in great detail ibid., esp. pp. 55–108.
22. E. Gruber, *Geschichte des Kantons Zug* (Berne, 1968), pp. 72–6; W. Köhler, 'Aus der Reformationsgeschichte des Kantons Zug', in R. Doggweiler (ed.), *Geschichte der protestantischen Kirchgemeinde des Kantons Zug* (Zug, 1939), pp. 83–7.
23. W. Meyer, 'Der Chronist Werner Steiner', *Der Geschichtsfreund*, LXV (1910), pp. 57–215, esp. 95; cf. E. Egli (ed.), *Actensammlung zur Geschichte der Zürcher Reformation* (Zürich, 1879), p 89 (no. 257)
24. J. Zürcher, 'Die katholische Restauration im Stande Zug', *Zuger Neujahrsblatt*, 1941, pp. 27–75, esp. 28, n. 12.
25. In Zürich Steiner wrote a number of historiographical works, cf. R. Feller and E. Bonjour, *Geschichtsschreibung der Schweiz*, vol. I, 2nd edn (Basel/Stuttgart, 1979), pp. 142–4.
26. Meyer, 'Der Chronist Steiner', p. 101.
27. Gruber, *Geschichte des Kantons Zug*, p. 74f; Köhler, 'Reformationsgeschichte', p. 85.
28. Meyer, 'Der Chronist Steiner', p. 155.
29. The document is printed in K. Müller, 'Drei Aktenstücke zur Kirchengeschichte des Kantons Zug im 16. Jahrhundert', *Zuger Neujahrsblatt*, 1905, pp. 3–10, esp. 3–6.
30. Ibid., p. 8.
31. *EA*, vol. IV, 2, p. 3.
32. On humanism in Fribourg around Peter Falck cf. R. Ruffieux (ed.), *Geschichte des Kantons Freiburg*, vol. I (Fribourg, 1981), pp. 302–11; A. Wagner, *Peter Falcks Bibliothek und humanistische Bildung* (Berne, 1926).
33. Staatsarchiv Fribourg, Projektbuch, fo. 74v. The formal council decree

was issued on 26 August, cf. J. Strickler (ed.), *Actensammlung zur Schweizerischen Reformationsgeschichte*, vol. I (Zürich, 1878), p. 173 (no. 473); L. Waeber, 'La réaction du gouvernement de Fribourg au début de la réforme', *Zeitschrift für Schweizerische Kirchengeschichte*, LIII (1959), pp. 105–24, 213–32, 290–318, esp. 107.

34.   This document is printed in A. Büchi, 'Peter Girod und der Ausbruch der Reformbewegung in Freiburg', *Zeitschrift für Schweizerische Kirchengeschichte*, XVIII (1924), pp. 1–41, 305–23; cf. 322f. The original is in Staatsarchiv Fribourg, Missiven 8, fo. 148v.

35.   Heinrich Cornelius Agrippa von Nettesheim also stayed in Fribourg in 1523/24. He worked as a doctor and for some time held the post of city physician. During that year he also worked on his main work *De occulta philosophia*. He does not appear to have had a visible influence on the reforming activities.

36.   Büchi, 'Peter Girod', p. 16f.

37.   Ruffieux, *Geschichte des Kantons Freiburg*, p. 325ff; cf. L. Waeber, 'Le prédicateur de Fribourg (H. Mylen) et son conflict avec Berne au moment de la Réformation', *Zeitschrift für Schweizerische Kirchengeschichte*, XLV (1951), pp. 1–12, 115–45, and H. Wicki, 'Der Augustinerkonvent Freiburg im Uechtland im 16. Jahrhundert', *Freiburger Geschichtsblätter*, XXXIX (1946), pp. 3–49 (about K. Treger, pp. 8–25).

38.   Waeber, 'La réaction', pp. 213ff.

39.   B. Amiet and H. Sigrist, *Solothurnische Geschichte*, vol. II (Solothurn, 1976), pp. 7–45; L. R. Schmidlin, *Solothurns Glaubenskampf und Reformation* (Solothurn, 1904); H. Haefliger, 'Solothurn in der Reformation, 1519–1534', *Jahrbuch für solothurnische Geschichte*, XVI/XVII (1943/44), pp. 1–120; Markus Angst, 'Warum Solothurn nicht reformiert wurde', *Jahrbuch für solothurnische Geschichte*, LVI (1983), pp. 5–29; Barbara Pauk, 'Gescheiterte Reformation in Solothurn? Studien zur solothurnischen Kirchen- und Religionsgeschichte in der ersten Hälfte des 16. Jahrhunderts' (Lizentiatsarbeit, University of Basel, 1984).

40.   Berne and the five inner cantons began their campaigns to win Solothurn over in 1523. Staatsarchiv Solothurn, Reformationsakten 1523–1533.

41.   Amiet/Sigrist, *Solothurnische Geschichte*, vol. II, pp. 16, 19.

42.   On the boatsmen's guild as the agent of reforming propaganda and on the background to their action cf. Pauk, 'Gescheiterte Reformation in Solothurn?', pp. 37ff.

43.   Amiet/Sigrist, *Solothurnische Geschichte*, vol. II, p. 20.

44.   Ibid., p. 28. During the month of January 1530 the Berne reformer Berchtold Haller preached in Solothurn every day.

45.   Ibid., pp. 38–45.

46.   *EA*, vol. IV, 1a, pp. 410–11.

47.   H. Dommann, 'Das Gemeinschaftsbewußtsein der V Orte in der Alten Eidgenossenschaft', *Der Geschichtsfreund*, XCVI (1943), pp. 115–229, esp. 145.

48. *EA*, vol. IV, 1b, p. 212; O. Vasella, 'Der Glaubenskampf in der Eidgenossenschaft', *Schweizer Schule*, VII, 1.8.1950.
49. Dommann, 'Gemeinschaftsbewußtsein', p. 147.
50. Ibid., p. 151.
51. Cf. above n. 3.
52. Basel is a very good example.
53. Cf. above p. 192.
54. This was continually nourished by the joint administration of Murten, Orbe-Echallens and the territories of Grandson. Gradually in all these areas the Reformation won through: in 1530 in Murten, and in 1554 in Orbe-Echallens and Grandson. Cf. Ruffieux, *Geschichte des Kantons Fribourg*, pp. 330—5, and Waeber, 'Le prédicateur de Fribourg', pp. 123ff.
55. Angst, 'Warum Solothurn nicht reformiert wurde', pp. 15–18.
56. Cf. above, p. 200f.
57. Angst, 'Warum Solothurn nicht reformiert wurde', p. 15.
58. Cf. Dommann, 'Gemeinschaftsbewußtsein', p. 146.
59. Angst, 'Warum Solothurn nicht reformiert wurde', p. 25.
60. Amiet/Sigrist, *Solothurnische Geschichte*, vol. II, pp. 193ff.
61. Cf. Guggisberg, 'Parität, Neutralität und Toleranz'.
62. Stadler, 'Eidgenossenschaft und Reformation', p. 94f.

10 Economic Conflict and Co-operation on the Upper Rhine, 1450–1600

Tom Scott

In the vast array of studies concerned with the transition from feudalism to capitalism in early modern Europe two divergent and conflicting strands of interpretation have traditionally dominated research: the one which locates the mainsprings of economic development in towns as centres of mercantile enterprise, the other which regards the rural economy as the cradle of agrarian capitalism and proto-manufacturing from which a fully-fledged industrial revolution finally emerged.*

The inadequacy of both approaches, as historical geographers have recently emphasised, lies in their mutual isolation and exclusivity.[1] Town and country are neither self-contained nor self-explanatory categories; rather, their economic and social evolution is only comprehensible within the framework of a regional analysis which attributes the dynamic of expansion to the dialectical relationship between urban centres and their hinterlands. Theoretical underpinning for a regional analysis can readily be derived from the methodology of central-place systems pioneered by Walter Christaller[2] and latterly revised by Gilbert Rozman in his studies of urban networks in Asia, Russia and western Europe.[3]

A serious drawback to much of central-place theory, however, lies in the unspoken assumption that the multiplication of central places or the intensification of urban networks occurred essentially without conflict or competition. Historians tracing the development of a commercial system in fifteenth- and sixteenth-century Germany have observed the large metropolitan cities of the south and west or the Hanseatic cities in the north progressively dominating and exploiting the resources of their hinterlands, but for the mass of middling craft towns the truth was often very different. The latter came to face stiff economic competition from the surrounding countryside, particularly in those areas which were already agriculturally diversified and resilient. To understand the transformation of the early modern German economy, therefore, it is essential to examine in detail the relations between town and country within a given economic region.

I

In the late Middle Ages, particularly in areas of rapid economic transition such as the Upper Rhine, those relations were coming under severe legal, political, social and above all economic strain, which manifested itself most obviously in a blurring of the traditional separation of function between town and country. The symbiosis between urban market centre and rural hinterland was fundamentally disturbed by the consequences of the late medieval agrarian crisis, but in the long run this crisis struck much more lethally at the mass of middling craft towns than at the countryside. For that reason it is better to speak not of an agrarian crisis, but of a general structural crisis of the economy as a whole.[4] The consequences of the Black Death, from which the Upper Rhine was not spared, had socioeconomic as well as legal repercussions for the rural population. As a result of the decline in peasant numbers feudal lords were often compelled to concede greater legal rights to their villeins in order to keep them under their seigneurial jurisdiction. Landflight was common until, in the course of the fifteenth century, lords throughout south-west Germany began to reintroduce serfdom in an altered form as a means of achieving the geographical consolidation and political exclusivity of their frequently scattered territories.[5] Simultaneously with a legal amelioration in the fourteenth century went improved economic prospects for those who survived the repeated outbreaks of plague. The slump in population meant that many holdings went uncultivated, and these could therefore be taken over for often much reduced prices, though it would be unwise to exaggerate the extent of this phenomenon in the fertile and thickly populated Rhine valley itself: deserted farms and villages are more a feature of the marginal and inaccessible uplands of the Black Forest, which had only been brought into full cultivation in the thirteenth century. The peasant who held a small tenement which barely provided himself and his family with a livelihood had a unique opportunity of acquiring a larger holding, or at least of consolidating and rationalising his scattered strips.

Together with these changes went a considerable diversification and specialisation of the rural economy. That was evident on the one hand in the spread of stock-rearing, a livelihood which was intrinsically more profitable and more immune from crisis than cereal agriculture: it was labour-extensive, provided the basis for added value in production through the working of hides and the use of tallow in addition to the baseline value of meat and dairy produce, and was less affected by the vagaries of weather. On the other hand, a (proto-)manufacturing economy began to develop in the countryside, characterised by the greater cultivation of so-called industrial crops – hemp, saffron, woad, madder – and fully-fledged manufactures themselves, particularly woollen-, fustian- and linen-weaving. These developments were even more pronounced in those areas which were characterised even before the Black Death as centres of specialised production and monocultures, and where the laws of succession actively encouraged the subdivision of holdings and recourse to subsidiary earnings, namely the areas of partible inheritance. That was especially true of the wine-growing regions of the Middle and Upper Rhine which by definition created secondary employment for coopers, smiths, wine-dealers and middlemen. The flexibility created by the growing diversification and specialisation of the rural economy contributed significantly to the long-term recovery of the agrarian sector after the Black Death and provided the rural population with a more secure and resilient basis of existence beyond the primary agricultural sector alone.

The consequences of the wave of plague outbreaks for the towns were by contrast catastrophic. It is true that the few emerging long-distance trading cities which formed the cradle of early capitalism had sufficient economic and political weight not only to weather the storm but even to turn the situation to their advantage by exploiting their less fortunate brethren and their various hinterlands, but these cities made up no more than a fraction of late medieval German communes. The middling craft towns, which formed the bulk of urban centres, experienced a severe economic decline, precisely because their largely artisan or workshop production prevented them from exploiting the late medieval boom in long-distance trade and capital-intensive investment in mining, and to a lesser extent textiles. In contrast to the countryside the economic structure of such towns was exposed as particularly inflexible. Craft production was bound by fixed, regulated and labour-intensive ordinances; it yielded profits too small to permit much expansion of employment through the reinvestment of accumulated capital. Population decline in the middling towns led, moreover, to a crisis of municipal finances. Too few taxpayers survived to shoulder the burden of recurrent and relatively fixed public expenditure. The volume of civic debt grew; the annual payment, or redemption, of *rente* charges devoured an ever-increasing proportion of the municipal budget, until in the course of the fifteenth century several cities were forced into insolvency, one consequence of which was a spate of gild revolts.[6]

The issue of economic survival was compounded for the towns by a contracting market for their craft goods in the countryside as well as among their own citizens. The sale of agricultural produce by contrast remained relatively stable despite the slump in cereal prices, or even because of it, since the poorer consumers, who had previously gone hungry now found themselves able to buy more foodstuffs for the same amount of money and thereby adequately to meet their subsistence needs. After a relatively sluggish start, caused by fresh outbreaks of plague in the late fourteenth century, the population of the Upper Rhine began to recover, and by 1460/70 was expanding at a tempo which, by the turn of the century, was threatening to create renewed rural overpopulation. This recovery contributed to and intensified the incipient price rise which continued throughout the sixteenth century, the first great age of European inflation. Unlike earlier centuries, however, the rural population seems not at first to have immigrated into the craft towns in significant numbers. This suggests that peasants were for the first time in a position to turn their backs upon urban employment, and thereby to reduce the dependence of the countryside upon the urban craft economy and market system. How could that be so?

II

The main source of information on these developments is the series of urban gravamina which are first voiced in the mid-fifteenth century and which continue unabated though with growing intensity throughout the sixteenth. The towns list, *inter alia*, four heads of grievance:

1. Crafts are increasing in the countryside.
2. The rural population no longer brings its produce in sufficient quantity to the urban markets, but sells instead in villages to travelling merchants or pedlars; worse, if it visits urban markets at all, it brings craft goods which compete directly with artisan production.

3. The urban markets are declining in the face of new market foundations in the surrounding countryside.
4. Territorial rulers prevent their subjects from visiting the long-established urban markets and force them instead to use new territorial markets. For the most part these are:
   a) new foundations of the 15th/16th century;
   b) primarily village markets beyond the control of urban council or guild jurisdictions.

These grievances prompt in turn the following historical questions:

1. Is the rise of country crafts attributable to the emigration of urban masters from the towns, or is it an endogenous consequence of changes in the structure of the rural economy?
2. Why does the rural population prefer either to avoid the urban markets, or else to supply them with competitive goods?
3. How can we explain the timing and extent of these new market foundations? Are they a consequence of a changed rural economic structure which creates the preconditions for the viability of such markets, or are they rather themselves the stimuli for a transformation of the rural economy?
4. To what extent should these new market foundations be interpreted as political acts, i.e. were they created as a deliberate instrument of princely policy, designed to promote territorial autarky?

Village crafts

It is extremely doubtful whether urban craftsmen emigrated to the countryside in appreciable numbers. It is well known that the national–liberal school of economists in the late nineteenth century blamed increasing guild protectionism in the middling craft towns – the so-called closed urban economy (*geschlossene Stadtwirtschaft*) – for the emigration of ambitious and entrepreneurially-minded craftsmen and thus for the economic decline of such towns. Since we now know, however, that protectionism was in most cases the understandable and predictable reaction to an already far gone population decline and concomitant economic slump rather than its cause, this explanation falls to the ground. The issue is much more whether the towns in their gravamina were not in fact trying to draw attention to another deleterious circumstance, namely that craft production was being carried out in the countryside with greater success than in the towns themselves.

What are the origins of these country crafts, and in what form were they practised? That the countryside had always had its quota of local craftsmen is no novelty, though the prevailing view suggests that these were located in marginal areas where low returns from poor agricultural land forced the peasantry into taking up a supplementary occupation, or else in areas of impartible inheritance where the excluded siblings were forced into rural crafts to compensate for their landless or cottar status.[7] Yet it is possible to demonstrate that in the Upper Rhine, a highly fertile area characterised by partible inheritance, such craftsmen were very common, not least because the intensive practice of monocultures, above all viticulture, necessitated a constant supply of tools and casks from the workshops of coopers, smiths and carpenters. But may not the relatively meagre archival records conceal the existence of village craftsmen in the fourteenth century? Or, to put it another way, only when records become more continuous, do we begin to hear more frequently of country crafts? This objection cannot be sustained. Since the complaints over village craftsmen are essentially contained in urban gravamina, we would expect to find them in the surviving grievances of the guilds in the many urban revolts in southern Germany during the fourteenth century. But those grievances are concerned exclusively with inner-urban conflicts. It is only in the second wave of guild revolts at the end of the fifteenth and the beginning of the sixteenth century that such complaints make their appearance.

There is, however, another objection in principle. Are these craftsmen not in fact peasants who are eking out an existence through subsidiary craft production? The continuing depressed market for agrarian produce after the Black Death might be thought to offer at best a very precarious existence for the agriculturalist. When the population began to recover from the mid-fifteenth century, country crafts were an obvious alternative for peasants deprived of an inheritance by the subdivision of holdings. If such had generally been the case, it would have meant that country craftsmen would have been the poorest and least powerful of the village community. How they could then have constituted a serious economic threat to the established and privileged urban craftsmen would remain a mystery.

The sources for the Upper Rhine reveal that the phenomenon of village craftsmen cannot be explained away by these devices. For one thing, it stands beyond reasonable doubt that many village craftsmen carried out their trades full-time; for another, some can be shown to be craftmasters who must have qualified in their profession and who therefore can be discounted as mere casual craftsmen. In any case, such craftsmen cannot be assigned to the poor and the powerless in their village communities. In this connection it is worth asking how so many village craftsmen could have emerged as agitators and leaders in the German Peasants' War of 1524–26 if they had really belonged to the lower ranks of village society which were excluded from the village community and therewith from a say in village affairs.

Marxist historians have sought the origins of an inchoate craft economy in the countryside in the impact of an expanding early capitalist mode of production. Urban merchants and craftsmen with surplus capital to invest, which the regulations on competition imposed by guild protectionism prevented them from deploying profitably within the towns, sought instead to employ the rural population which lay outside municipal control as wage-labourers who would supply the additional capacity in outwork, using the raw materials and tools supplied by the urban contractor, in order to evade gild limits on production and quality. This so-called putting-out system is indeed an unmistakable feature of early capitalism; there were many village craftsmen engaged in the proto-industrial production of mass goods, particularly textiles, who should be regarded as the forerunners of a later industrial proletariat. But these early capitalist wage-workers constitute only a part of village crafts. From the spread of uneven and disparate sources we can detect four distinct categories of village trades on the Upper Rhine in this period:

1. Those craftsmen who were an integral part of village life or whose trade required them to work in the country: inn-keepers, smiths, millers, fishers, charcoal-burners, bathhouse-keepers.
2. Those craftsmen who were 'put out' (*verlegt*) by urban capitalists: woollen-, linen-, fustian-weavers, hemp-bleachers.
3. A mass of genuine craftsmen, some of whom were masters, many of whom were full-time tradesmen, some of whom had apprentices or journeymen working under them: coopers, cartwrights, butchers, cobblers, carpenters, tailors, bakers, furriers, masons, tilers, potters, coppersmiths, pewterers, saddlers and fullers (though the last may have been *verlegt*).
4. Village middlemen and dealers: oil-dealers, wine-dealers,

mercers, haberdashers, clothiers and drapers, as well as itinerant pedlars.

The inadequacy of the sources makes it impossible to quantify these craftsmen, but several instances of craft concentration within one village can be adduced on the right bank of the Rhine, both in the fertile plain and in the Black Forest uplands. From the accidental listing of witnesses in court proceedings there existed in the village of Eschbach in the Breisgau in 1586, for instance: two smiths, one smith's apprentice, one cartwright, one carpenter, one cooper and one weaver.[8] At the beginning of the century a similar list from the lordship of Triberg in the Black Forest records: four tailors, six carpenters, two butchers, one draper, two weavers, one cartwright.[9] Again, in 1562 the Austrian town of Villingen in the eastern Black Forest listed amongst the profitable crafts that were burgeoning in the countryside millers, bakers, cartwrights, cobblers, clothmakers, as well as voicing its grievance at the establishment of salt-chests in the villages which detracted from its municipal revenue.[10]

When all allowances are made for existing craftsmen, 'by-employments' and 'put-out' wage-labourers, there remains an indisputable concentration of 'genuine' village craftsmen working in the countryside beyond gild control who were encroaching upon the urban craftsmen's livelihood. Moreover, such craftsmen, if they were masters, must have occupied a senior rank within the village community, rather than being lumped together with the landless and labourers. In this context it is worth pointing out that among the rural outburghers of Freiburg im Breisgau who enjoyed greater rights and privileges than their fellow villagers and who should accordingly be counted as part of the village notability (*Ehrbarkeit*) many craftsmen can be found.[11]

The growth of these craftsmen is, in my view, a direct consequence of the transformation of the rural economy in the wake of the late medieval crisis. Diversification and specialisation in the countryside made it possible for sections of the rural population to withdraw completely from the primary sector and concentrate instead on the secondary (manufacturing or craft) sector or even tertiary (services) sector of production. That such craftsmen did not emigrate to the towns, as had occurred before, where conditions of production were certainly better, i.e. less primitive, can be explained by the continuing financial and economic predicament of the gild-ruled lesser towns of the fifteenth century, of which Freiburg im Breisgau is itself a prime example. As long as such towns could not offer attractive employment and sought by means of protectionism to limit and restrict productive capacity, village craftsmen had little incentive to set up shop in the towns where they immediately faced high taxation and interference in their freedom of production.

The problem of village craftsmen, however, was only part of a much wider complex of economic transformation which threatened the traditional gild towns. The complaints of towns throughout Outer Austria especially in the Breisgau, at territorial diets in 1483,[12] 1517/ 18,[13] 1524[14] and 1557[15] paint a vivid picture of a flourishing rural petty-capitalist economy. They list especially:

1. The establishment of salt-chests (i.e. salt staples) in the villages, whereas salt trading and revenues had always formed a major component of urban income.
2. Trading in iron goods supplied directly to the many rural crafts which required them.
3. Trading in cloth, presumably as a result of the putting-out system, though the complaint was also directed at sales to consumers in the villages which bypassed urban markets.
4. Trade in comestibles brought from outside the region (e.g. dried fish, herrings).

Alongside these activities there arose a series of early industrial enterprises in the countryside, mostly on the initiative of the territorial ruler, one suspects. It might be wondered why the towns were unable either to draw these villagers into the web of restrictions and controls imposed by the urban gilds or else to suppress competition within their market franchise (*Bannmeile*). But such efforts, though common in relatively unitary, sizeable territories not victim to political fragmentation, were hardly effective in the Breisgau, since many craftsmen resided in the margravial villages beyond the political control of the Outer Austrian towns. Only in the Austrian territories on the left bank of the Rhine, in Alsace and the Sundgau, which displayed greater geographical cohesion and administrative integration between town and country, were such attempts successful, notably in Belfort, where in the late fifteenth century one-quarter of leatherworkers and nearly half the butchers in the guilds were in fact villagers.[16]

Market evasion

One of the principal reasons for villagers evading urban markets lay in the series of prohibitions by territorial lords against their subjects' patronising markets under foreign jurisdiction, a common source of conflict both in the Breisgau and in the eastern Black Forest lands of the counts of Fürstenberg. It is likely, in addition, that the diversification of rural production and the resulting creation of a group of non-peasants in the villages created a demand for the supply of foodstuffs directly to the countryside. In areas of monoculture this certainly happened. One of the most striking remarks to emerge from the protracted quarrel between the margrave of Baden–Durlach and the Outer Austrian towns over the former's revival of a market at Malterdingen in 1573 was that Austrian peasants from the Black Forest valleys round Waldkirch, Elzach and Triberg brought butter, cheese and tallow to market there in return for buying the produce of the Rhine valley itself, corn and wine.[17] There was, in other words, a lively exchange in agricultural products themselves between different areas of specialisation within the Upper Rhine as a region. At the same time, though, the Emmendingen and Malterdingen markets were also accused of trading in wool, linen, leather, shoes and other craft goods brought to market by both margravial and Austrian subjects, some of which products, it emerged, had in fact been bought up earlier by forestallers at the Villingen market who transported their wares across the Black Forest to margravial markets on the Upper Rhine where they fetched higher prices and paid lesser or no tolls.[18]

That the towns complained of villagers bringing manufactured goods instead of agrarian produce to urban markets is not in itself surprising, since in most cases higher prices could be obtained there. But the sources do not reveal this to be a very common practice: the peasants, after all, also had to pay the higher tolls and stallage charges demanded by the towns, and they would find it more convenient to patronise the series of new local markets. There are, however, repeated urban ordinances against middlemen who bought up goods in the countryside (in itself an indication that craft goods were manufactured there) by forestalling or regrating, and then, having cornered a particular market, unloaded their consignments at the urban markets in the face of diminished competition. Apart from the repeated grievances of the Outer Austrian towns, we find complaints

at such market evasion by Baden–Baden in 1563,[19] Pforzheim
(Baden–Durlach) in 1588, where the gilds protested at foreign traders
at village marriages and church-ales,[20] and a general complaint by
Baden–Durlach butchers in 1556 that foreigners were buying up and
driving away cattle outside regular market hours.[21] One consequence
of this market evasion was that urban guildsmen, in order to dispose
of their wares at all, were forced to go into the countryside to visit
local fairs, church-ales and informal markets and to compete with
village craftsmen there. The margrave of Baden–Durlach in 1549 in
reply to an Austrian complaint at market competition pointed out
that urban craftsmen in both his lordships *and* in the Outer Austrian
Breisgau were selling wares outside village churches on Sundays and
holidays, a charge which is borne out by the available evidence.[22] The
decline in urban markets, it is true, may have been compensated by
guildsmen hawking in the villages, but while that might help urban
craftsmen to survive it contributed nothing whatever to the recovery
of the middling towns' finances, which depended in large measure on
toll and market revenues and on consumption taxes.

New market foundations

The analysis so far has tacitly assumed that village craftsmen were
indeed able to visit a series of country markets rather than remain in
dependence on the towns. And it is a signal feature of the fifteenth and
sixteenth centuries how many new markets were established – both
weekly markets and annual fairs – in just one area, the Breisgau on
the right bank of the Rhine (see map and tables). Whereas up to 1400
the only official markets had been located exclusively in the Austrian
towns, the margraves in succeeding years made strenuous efforts to
found and patronise their own territorial markets: several in 1418,
some further attempts throughout the fifteenth century, specific
endeavours to revive Malterdingen in the early sixteenth century, and
then a series of refoundations (Sulzburg, Emmendingen, possibly
Malterdingen again) between 1550 and 1573.

  That these markets were designed to serve territorial-political as
well as merely financial-autarkic interests does not need to be stressed.
But it is hard to explain the spate of foundations merely as a political
act. These markets would have declined and petered out (as some of
the margravial markets indeed did)[23] unless the economic infrastruc-
ture had reached a degree of development and diversification which

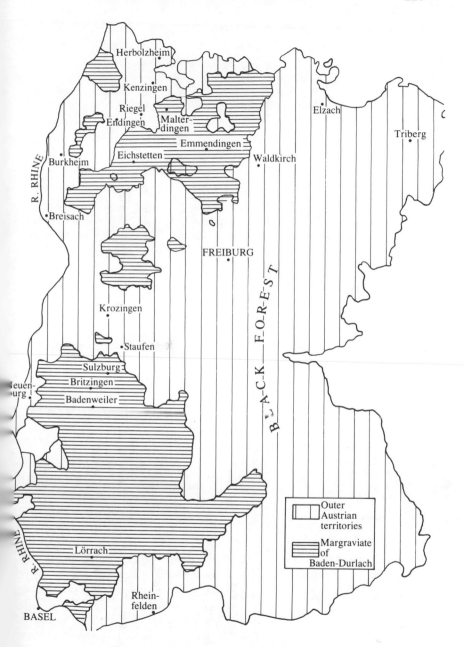

South-west Germany in the sixteenth century

Markets in the Breisgau, 1400–1600

Austria

	Year	Place	Day of weekly market	Fair
	Before 1400			
E		Freiburg	daily	2
E		Breisach	Tuesday + ?	1
E		Waldkirch	Saturday	1
E		Endingen	?	1
E		Kenzingen	?	2
E		Neuenburg	Saturday	?
F	1418	Neuenburg		2
F	1472	Burkheim	Wednesday	2
F	1473	Burkheim	Saturday	+1 = 3
F	1481	Triberg		
F	1493	Breisach	Saturday	+1 = 2
F	1498	Riegel		+1 = 2
F	1521	Breisach		+1 = 3
F	1523	Neuenburg		+1 = 3
E	1563	Ehrenstetten		1
E	c.1570	Freiburg	Thurs + Sat	6
		Breisach	Tuesday	5
		Staufen	Wednesday	4
		Heitersheim		1
		Offnadingen		1
F	1573	Elzach	Tuesday	
E	1576	Krozingen	?	
F	158?	Herbolzheim	Thursday	3

Baden

	Year	Place	Day of weekly market	Fair
F	1403	Lörrach	Wednesday	1
F	1418	Badenweiler	Tuesday	1
		(1498 transferred to Britzingen)		
F	1418	Emmendingen	Wednesday	1
F	1418	Eichstetten	Saturday	1
		(16th c. transferred to Malterdingen)		
F	1442	Sulzburg	(Monday)	2
F	1498	Britzingen	Tuesday	1
		(transferred from Badenweiler)		
E	1510	Malterdingen	Saturday	1
		(1528 ordered to change to another day)		
?RF/E	(1550)	Malterdingen	Saturday	1
E	c.1570	Ballrechten		1
		Kandern		1
		Schopfheim		3
RF	1571	Sulzburg	Saturday	1
		(1573 transferred to: Monday)		
RF	1573	Emmendingen	Friday	(1)

made such markets at least *seem* viable. I would argue that it was both the increasing division of labour and the new range of rural craft products which made such markets necessary and viable. For one thing, the towns can hardly have had any great interest in increasing their own capacity in craft production unless their population recovered greatly, nor indeed were they interested in greater market turnover, despite the prospect of higher revenues, if all that meant was that the market was going to be flooded with cheaper competing goods from the countryside. The market foundations of the fifteenth and sixteenth centuries must be seen, therefore, as the consequence, not the cause, of a revived and diversified rural economy, though that they in turn helped the rural economy to expand further is more than likely.

How far these village markets represented a real threat to the long-standing urban markets is a much debated question. A village market held once a week, let alone the occasional country fair, could hardly jeopardise a large urban market held twice-weekly or even daily. But that is not the point: it was the accumulation of many small village markets in the radius of the towns' immediate hinterland which constituted the danger, especially if as so often the territorial lords deliberately established their village markets on the same day as existing town markets. In this context the lament of the Austrian towns Endingen, Kenzingen and Waldkirch at the height of hostilities in 1574 is revealing: the margravial markets were taking off so rapidly, they said, that one margravial village (market) was better and more patronised than three Outer Austrian towns put together.[24]

Indeed, the table of market foundations contains a bias which understates their true impact:

1. Informal markets – i.e. without charter – took place on Sundays, holidays, church-ales, and at weddings.
2. Village markets usually raised little or no tolls or stallage.
3. Village markets often used lesser weights and measures.
4. Village market days frequently were set to clash with urban markets.
5. The introduction of new territorial tolls and taxes, e.g. in Outer Austria in 1556, put up the cost of visiting the established town markets.

The classic conflicts between the towns and the new market foundations occurred, not surprisingly, between Outer Austria and the margraviate of Baden–Durlach, for their territories intersected and overlapped, while the latter was in any case unusually under-developed in urban centres until well into the fifteenth century.[25] A glance at the map will show just how far the geographical location of Sulzburg, Emmendingen and Malterdingen impinged upon or cut across Austrian market areas, trade routes and towns: Neuenburg and Staufen; Kenzingen, Endingen and Burkheim; Waldkirch and Freiburg im Breisgau, the regional centre itself.

Similar conflicts, however, arose along the length of the Upper Rhine, especially between the twin margraviates of Baden–Durlach and Baden–Baden, and among many lesser or intermediate territorial lordships, as the prospect of increased revenues from commerce and exchange encouraged many lords in an age of gathering inflation to found local markets. There were even occasional conflicts within a given territory between the established towns and village upstarts. In the Austrian Breisgau the foundation of a local market in the village of Krozingen in 1576 provoked the wrath of its neighbours Staufen, Neuenburg and Breisach, all with recognised urban markets.[26] Nor was the problem confined to the Upper Rhine valley; in the Black Forest, the Austrian territory of Villingen was faced in the 1560s and 1570s with persistent market evasion stemming from rival markets promoted by the lords of the surrounding territory, the counts of Fürstenberg;[27] and Villingen became entangled in a similar dispute with its other neighbour, the duchy of Württemberg.[28]

Territorial politics

The increasing economic competition between town and country must be set in the context of the early modern territorial principality. In an area of advanced political fragmentation such as the Upper Rhine the efforts of independent princes to consolidate their scattered possessions were particularly evident. But a unitary territory with uniform jurisdiction and dependence of the subject could only be fully realised if it was accompanied by some regulation of economic life, especially the establishment of economic and commercial exclusivity. This goal was promoted not simply through the foundation of indigenous markets but by the adoption of autarkic policies:

1. Prohibitions upon subjects' visiting foreign markets outside the territory.

2. Restrictions on foreigners, whether peasants, craftsmen or middlemen, having access to territorial markets or domestic guilds.
3. Prohibitions on the export of vital commodities, above all foodstuffs.

Within the territory, moreover, the logic of the would-be unitary state required that its economic policies apply across the board without discrimination. Most of the craft ordinances promulgated by the margraves of Baden during the sixteenth century embraced rural and urban craftsmen without distinction; few accorded the latter any priority over the former. The consequence of such policies, therefore, was further to diminish the autonomy and authority of the urban craft economy whilst elevating the position of its rural competitors whose existence was explicitly recognised and accepted.

The interests of princely autarky, however, did not necessarily rule out co-operation across territorial boundaries when overriding issues of economic and financial regulation were at stake. Not only were common craft constitutions for neighbouring territories with long-standing links, such as the twin margraviates of Baden, regularly drawn up, but also regional ordinances which applied to politically heterogeneous areas such as the Upper Rhine in general point to a growing awareness that certain fundamental problems in an age of economic transformation could only be tackled satisfactorily by co-operation not conflict.

III

Throughout Europe the sixteenth century was the great age of what is known in German as *Polizei* – economic regulation and social welfare legislation; governments began for the first time to intervene in the economy on a large scale for purposes other than the merely fiscal. At imperial and provincial level in Germany the authorities began to tackle issues such as monopolies, price-rigging and forestalling, as well as concerning themselves with regulating and securing supplies of essential commodities.[29] What gave such policies their singular character on the Upper Rhine was, on the one hand, the need to co-operate across territorial, geographical, linguistic and, by the sixteenth century, confessional divisions, and, on the other, the dominating influence which the towns rather than government agencies exerted over *Polizei*, since the Habsburgs were content to let Outer

Austria subsist in benign administrative neglect: the chancery in the small Alsatian commune of Ensisheim was understaffed, whilst a treasury was not formally established until 1570.[30] On the Upper Rhine, therefore, it is possible to observe how the interests of primary economic agents – the towns – were directly reflected in regional economic legislation without being filtered or distorted by the wider political considerations which informed Outer Austrian governmental policy.

On the Upper Rhine there already existed a venerable tradition of co-operation over minting and coinage, which by the late fourteenth century had become institutionalised in the form of the Raven Coinage League.[31] From the outset the League was an inter-territorial association, whose four mainstays comprised two imperial free cities, Basel and Colmar, and two Austrian territorial towns, Freiburg im Breisgau and Thann in Alsace, the major Outer Austrian minting centre. In the sixteenth century the complexity of allegiance increased, as Basel first joined the Swiss Confederation and then in 1529 went Protestant, as did Colmar much later in 1575. Even though two of its leading members were politically independent of the Habsburgs as territorial princes, the business of the Raven Coinage League continued to be dealt with at regional diets under the auspices of the Outer Austrian government. Within the framework of the League the growing welter of *Polizei* legislation did not, however, correspond to the circulation area of the Raven coinage itself, or to the geographical location of its members. To take the best documented example, even though the frequent assemblies called throughout the sixteenth century to regulate cattle trading, meat prices and forestalling were regarded by the Outer Austrian authorities as representing the four territories under their jurisdiction, namely (Upper) Alsace, the Sundgau, Breisgau and Black Forest,[32] both Villingen and Waldshut lying on the eastern fringes of the 'outer lands' refused to participate despite their subjection to Austria since, as they claimed, they did not belong to the Raven Coinage League but to the coinage area of the city of Constance.[33] Conversely, invitations to attend the diets were sent regularly to, and on occasion accepted by, geographical neighbours on the Upper Rhine who were not League members. Local lords on the south-western borders of the ecclesiastical principality of Basel in the Doubs and towards Burgundy,[34] and particularly the dukes of Württemberg who owned the county of Montbéliard,[35] were drawn into consultation, though not always participation.

This suggests that the participants – meaning essentially the towns – were developing an inchoate awareness of the Upper Rhine as a self-defined and independently identifiable economic region which transcended the formal category of a coinage association. By what attributes, then, were the towns on the Upper Rhine slowly recognising the emergence of an economic region? The area of economic co-operation expressed by diet attendance did not stretch northwards throughout the whole of the Upper Rhine: it usually excluded Strasbourg, almost certainly a conscious decision by the other towns to avoid being swamped by the economic power of that commercial metropolis.[36] But it did extend southwards beyond the Upper Rhine basin itself over the foothills of the Jura to include the territory of the bishop of Basel in the Ajoie/Elsgau, and also well beyond the Belfort Gap into the fringes of Burgundy. Given the degree of territorial fragmentation on the Upper Rhine the region of economic co-operation can ultimately be defined only in its own terms, that is to say, by the common economic and especially commercial interests of those whom it embraced. That becomes evident when one examines the southern and south-western borders of the region. The lands past the Belfort Gap, above all the county of Montbéliard, lay on the main cattle route from Burgundy to the Upper Rhine and its major cattle market and entrepot at Cernay in Alsace. For its part, the bishop of Basel's territory in the Ajoie was one of the principal suppliers of grain to the Upper Rhine; indeed, it was an indispensable corn basket for the southern Upper Rhine whose economy had diversified so heavily into non cereal agriculture.

The economic and commercial interests which lay behind regional co-operation emerge with telling clarity from the warrants of summons to the diets concerned with *Polizei*. The Outer Austrian government in Ensisheim as the formal patron and organiser of the diets was inclined, not surprisingly, to restrict attendance to Austrian subjects or long-standing members of the Raven Coinage League alone.[37] But both the Austrian towns and the free cities who already shared a tradition of co-operation at local level[38] insisted on extending invitations to further specified towns and lordships outside Austria or the League on the grounds that their economic interests were directly affected by the business of the diets. Only against this background is the invitation to Sélestat intelligible, for it lay north of the *Landgraben*, the traditional frontier between Upper and Lower Alsace and the dioceses of Basel and Strasbourg, and was a member of the Strasbourg coinage area. From 1503 onwards Colmar, Sélestat, Kaysersberg and Ammerschwihr as four adjacent imperial cities of the

Alsatian Decapolis had co-operated on meat policy and pricing,[39] and it was Colmar in the late 1520s which pressed to have its neighbour invited to the Outer Austrian meetings,[40] despite the government in Ensisheim's opposition, on the grounds that its economy depended upon free access to Upper Alsatian markets.[41] In succeeding decades Sélestat appears regularly to have attended the assemblies and to have adopted their resolutions.[42] By contrast, the bishop of Strasbourg was invited to send representatives on behalf of his one territory which lay in Upper Alsace, the Upper Mundat around Rouffach, but was debarred from sending delegates from any of his other territories, all of which lay north of the *Landgraben* around the city of Strasbourg itself.[43]

The emergence of an economic region based upon co-operation over essential supplies and resources and the control of market access should not be taken to imply that such a region cannot be subsumed within or integrated into other and larger economic regions whose frontiers are defined by supra-regional rather than inner-regional concerns. A hierarchy of interlocking and overlapping economic regions can doubtless be constructed,[44] in which at one level Strasbourg may be seen to function as the capital of a vast commercial area spanning the whole of the Upper Rhine.[45] But the conclusions from current research point in a somewhat different direction. In the first place, economic co-operation over *Polizei* on the Upper Rhine reflects the intensification of inner-regional, rather than transregional, commercial activity. It may well be correct to suggest, therefore, that the key to economic recovery in the sixteenth century lies as much in the faster circulation of goods and services within a region as in the revival of international commerce along certain clearly visible lines of trade. It may also be the case that the traditional picture of an economic region defined and indeed dominated by the radius of influence of its leading city at the apex of a central-place system is too static and unilinear. For the region under review was not dominated by one city; on the contrary, it rested upon a tripod of three cities, Basel, Colmar and Freiburg, whose level of economic activity by the middle of the sixteenth century was roughly similar.

The economic region of the Upper Rhine whose origins can so clearly be discerned in the sixteenth century has even managed to survive the baleful influence of the nation state. The *Regio*, the international economic planning association based in Basel, keeps alive the spirit of regional co-operation and identity among the Alemannic communities in France, West Germany and Switzerland, whose interests transcend the political and national frontiers of which they so often have been the victim.

Notes

*   This study presents the preliminary findings of a large-scale research project on economic transformation on the Upper Rhine, 1450–1600. For that reason references have been kept to a minimum. Archives and libraries are cited by the following abbreviations:

AAEB	Archives de l'Ancien Evêché de Bâle, Porrentruy
ADHR	Archives Départementales du Haut-Rhin, Colmar
AN	Archives Nationales, Paris
AVC	Archives de la Ville de Colmar
AVKy	Archives de la Ville de Kaysersberg
AVRf	Archives de la Ville de Rouffach
AVTh	Archives de la Ville de Thann
BNUS	Bibliothèque Nationale et Universitaire de Strasbourg
HSA	Württembergisches Hauptstaatsarchiv, Stuttgart
GAEm	Gemeindearchiv Emmendingen
GLA	Badisches Generallandesarchiv, Karlsruhe
SABs	Staatsarchiv des Kantons Basel-Stadt
StAFr	Stadtarchiv Freiburg im Breisgau
StAVl	Stadtarchiv Villingen
TLA	Tiroler Landesarchiv, Innsbruck.

1.   John Langton and Göran Hoppe, *Town and Country in the Development of Early Modern Western Europe* (Historical Geography Research Series, XI) (Norwich, 1983); cf. also the introduction to Tom Scott, *Freiburg and the Breisgau: Town-Country Relations in the Age of Reformation and Peasants' War* (Oxford, 1986).
2.   Walter Christaller, *Central Places in Southern Germany* (Englewood Cliffs, NJ, 1966).
3.   Gilbert Rozman, 'Urban Networks and Historical Stages', *Journal of Interdisciplinary History*, IX (1978), pp. 65–91.
4.   For the older view cf. the classic formulation by Wilhelm Abel, *Agrarkrisen und Agrarkonjunktur. Eine Geschichte der Land- und Ernährungswirtschaft Mitteleuropas seit dem hohen Mittelalter*, 2nd edn (Hamburg/Berlin, 1966), p. 59f. Cf. also idem, *Strukturen und Krisen der spätmittelalterlichen Wirtschaft* (Quellen und Forschungen zur Agrargeschichte, XXXII) (Stuttgart/New York, 1980), pp. 10ff.
5.   Cf. Peter Blickle, 'Leibherrschaft als Instrument der Territorialpolitik im Allgäu', in Heinz Haushofer and W. A. Boelcke (eds), *Wege und Forschungen der Agrargeschichte. Festschrift zum 65. Geburtstag von Günther Franz* (Frankfurt am Main, 1967), pp. 51–66.
6.   Erich Maschke, 'Deutsche Städte am Ausgang des Mittelalters', in Wilhelm Rausch (ed.), *Die Stadt am Ausgang des Mittelalters* (Beiträge

zur Geschichte der Städte Mitteleuropas, III) (Linz, 1974), pp. 1f, 20f; Scott, *Freiburg*, p. 130.

7. Cf. Peter Kriedte, Hans Medick, and Jürgen Schlumbohm, *Industrialization before Industrialization. Rural Industry in the Genesis of Capitalism* (Cambridge/Paris, 1981), pp. 14f, 24.
8. GLA 81/10, 47.
9. StAFr, C 1 Fremde Orte 23a (Triberg), (1505).
10. StAVl, W 2 [1974].
11. StAFr, E 1 A II a 4.
12. TLA, Kanzleibücher, ältere Reihe, Lit. D Embieten.
13. StAFr, C 1 Landstände 1; 3.
14. GLA 79/1657; BNUS, MS. 845, fo. 10.
15. StAFr, B 5 IXa, vol. I, fo. 287v ff; HSA B 17 4*, fo. 66f.
16. Cf. Bruno de Villele, 'Belfort à la fin du Moyen Age' (PhD dissertation, University of Besançon, 1971).
17. GLA 229/64261 (3 Sept. 1573); 229/64263 (30 April 1575).
18. The Austrian Breisgau towns were further hamstrung by an increase in territorial toll rates in 1560 which led to their markets losing custom to their margravial neighbours. StAFr, B 5 IXa, vol. I, fo. 437v ff; B 5 XI, vol. XIX, fo. 55ff; TLA, Kanzleibücher, Gemeine Missiven 1560, fo. 989ff.
19. GLA 74/6368.
20. GLA 74/10502.
21. GLA 74/3395.
22. GLA 74/9619.
23. The weekly market at Emmendingen had languished for much of the sixteenth century, until it was formally revived in 1572. GLA 198/203. Cf. Hansjörg Englert, 'Das Emmendinger Stadtrecht von 1590' (PhD dissertation, University of Freiburg, 1973), pp. 47–9.
24. GAEm, Akten V, 2 166, no. 1 (1573 [= May 1574]).
25. Meinrad Schaab, 'Städtlein, Burg-, Amts- und Marktflecken Südwestdeutschlands in Spätmittelalter und früher Neuzeit', in Emil Meynen (ed.), *Zentralität als Problem der mittelalterlichen Stadtgeschichtsforschung* (Städteforschung. Veröffentlichungen des Instituts für Vergleichende Städtegeschichte in Münster, Reihe A VIII) (Cologne/Vienna, 1979), p. 232.
26. GLA 229/56506.
27. GLA 184/478; 479; HSA B 17 5*, fo. 150ff; StAVl, E 18 [1516].
28. GLA 81/10, 47; HSA B 175*, fo. 195ff.
29. Cf. Fritz Blaich, *Die Reichsmonopolgesetzgebung im Zeitalter Karls V. Ihre ordnungspolitische Problematik* (Schriften zum Vergleich von Wirtschaftsordnungen, VIII) (Stuttgart, 1967).
30. Cf. Georges Bischoff, *Gouvernés et gouvernants en Haute Alsace à l'époque autrichienne. Les états des Pays Antérieurs des origines au milieu du XVIe siècle* (Publications de la Société Savante d'Alsace et des Régions de l'Est, grandes publications XX) (Strasbourg, 1982), p. 157.
31. Julius Cahn, *Der Rappenmünzbund. Eine Studie zur Münz- und Geldgeschichte des oberen Rheinthales* (Heidelberg, 1901).

32. Cf. ADHR, E dépot 4 (Ammerschwihr), AA 25 (1575); SABs, Fleisch K 2 (1575).
33. GLA 81/54 (1545); 81/55; 56 (1559).
34. GLA 81/53 (lordship of Montot, Haut-Marne, 1527); StAFr, A 1 VI e (29), 13 March 1527–11 September 1528 (counts of Worb in the Trybelberg).
35. AAEB, B 209/6 (1555); AN, K 2208/I. It seems, however, that Württemberg representatives attended meetings only on behalf of its lordships of Horbourg and Riquewihr in the north of Upper Alsace, rather than for Montbéliard itself.
36. Only in 1555 does Strasbourg appear to have been invited. SABs, Fleisch K 2.
37. Cf. GLA 79/1644 (1515).
38. Cf. for instance local meat agreements between Kaysersberg, Riquewihr, Kientzheim and Ammerschwihr in 1516 and 1518. AVKy, BB 9, fo. 166f; BB 10, fo. 5.
39. AVTh, HH 4; Bischoff, *Gouvernés*, p. 209.
40. AVC, HH 59/30; 59/87 (1528).
41. AVC, HH 59/30 (1528); 59/32 (1529); 59/89 (1533). The Outer Austrian government had sought to deny Sélestat access. ADHR, C 179/4 (1529).
42. SABs, Fleisch K 2 (1555); ADHR, C 181/1 (1559); 181/3 (1560).
43. AVRf, BB 3, fo. 256f (1544); AAEB, B 209/6 (1555).
44. Participation in the Outer Austrian meetings which dealt with corn prices and forestalling, for instance, was not identical with that for meat assemblies since the supply areas differed.
45. Cf. J. C. Russell, *Medieval Regions and their Cities* (Studies in Historical Geography) (Newton Abbot, 1972), p. 91f.

Part III

11 Luther in Europe: His Works in Translation 1517–46

Bernd Moeller

In a lecture held in the anniversary year 1983[1] Geoffrey Elton stirred up historians, as he loves to do occasionally, with an emphatic declaration against the thesis that Luther was the father of the Reformation. Elton is not questioning the fact that the Wittenberg Professor was '*Reformator der deutschen Lande*' – '*das ist wohl Ehre genug*'. Rather, he is registering his doubt that Luther was '*für ganz Europa der Ursprung der Reformation*'.

As proof of his theory Elton turns to the example of England. The latest research into the early sixteenth century has shown how virulent the pre-Reformation heretical movement, Lollardy, was. This movement was a very specific precondition for the acceptance of European Reformation impulses. In this way, says Elton, the English Reformation was not '*rein deutsch*'. He challenges Reformation historians in other European countries to look for factors in their areas which could have caused an independent preparation for the radical change of the Reformation.

I hope that it will not be taken amiss if I respectfully point out that Elton's thesis is not altogether new. I hope all the more that in delivering further proof of this thesis I can cast the facts in a somewhat brighter, and partly different, light.[2]

The published non-German translations of Luther's works are naturally fundamental to an estimate, and understanding, of his influence outside Germany. Research into these translations has advanced greatly over the last ten years. Detailed studies are now available for the most important language areas. The Supplement to Josef Benzing's *Luther-Bibliographie* prepared by Helmut Claus and Michael Pegg[3] reflects the latest research and equips us better to tackle this question. Even the bibliographical amateur can now command an insight into the whole material. It seems to me, therefore, that the time has come to transfer the subject out of the realm of the bibliographer into that of the historian, in order to try to present a complete picture and form an opinion.

I

According to the latest research, 682 publications (singly and as collections) of Luther's works appeared in a total of 3897 editions during his lifetime. These and the following figures represent minimum values. Many editions, especially translations, have survived in unique copies, strongly suggesting that others have been lost or forgotten totally.[4] Furthermore, determination of the various editions and even the establishment of authorship can be problematic. It is not always easy to distinguish excerpts and adaptations of Luther's works from his own authorised editions. Finally, the whole complex of works centring around the bible translation has not been included in these figures.

Of the 3897 extant editions of Luther's works published in his lifetime approximately three-quarters (2946 to be exact) were printed in the High German dialect and 164, or 4.2 per cent, in Low German. Together, these German editions make up almost 80 per cent of the entire corpus. Six hundred and twenty-eight editions, or about 16 per cent, are printed in Latin. We are left with a total of 155 translated editions of Luther's works, or 4 per cent of the whole, spread over ten contemporary European languages. These editions will be our main focus of attention.

The Dutch translations, with a total of fifty-eight editions and fifty-one separate titles are by far the most numerous.[5] The Danish translations come next with twenty-eight editions and nineteen titles,[6] followed by those in French with twenty-two editions and fifteen titles,[7] those in Czech with nineteen editions and nineteen titles,[8] and those in English with fourteen editions and twelve titles.[9] There are eight documented Italian translations from Luther's lifetime,[10] three in Polish,[11] and one each in Spanish,[12] Swedish[13] and Finnish.[14]

In addition to being the largest group of extant Luther translations, the Dutch editions were among the earliest to appear. Translations printed before the end of the year 1520, that is, before the turning point in Luther's life marked by his excommunication, have been attested in only two languages – Dutch and Czech. The oldest known edition not in German or Latin is a Czech translation of *The Blessed Sacrament of the Holy and True Body of Christ*, dated 8 May 1520.[15]

Another Czech and four Dutch editions were published in the same year.[16]

Printed translations of Luther's works in the other European languages cannot be attested until much later, the earliest being one Italian[17] and two French[18] editions, recently found, that date from 1525. The oldest known Danish translation appeared in Rostock in 1526,[19] and the earliest editions actually printed in Denmark appeared in Viborg as late as 1529.[20] The oldest surviving English translations, both printed in Antwerp, date from this year as well.[21] The only work of Luther to be printed in Swedish during his lifetime appeared in 1528[22] and the only surviving contemporary translation of Luther into Spanish was published in 1540.[23]

Which of Luther's works, then, came to be translated? An investigation of the entire corpus of foreign editions reveals surprising congruencies. The majority of these editions comprise translations of works dealing with questions of faith, such as how individuals should care for their souls or simply what people should believe. In 1930, on the basis of preliminary bibliographical research on Luther's early German works, the historian Heinrich Dannenbauer advanced the thesis that Luther above all became well-known as *ein religiöser Volksschriftsteller* (a writer of popular religious works).[24] We are now in a position to confirm the truth of this thesis for the non-German-speaking parts of Europe as well.

Best represented in the corpus of translations are the catechism texts, headed by *The Short Form of the Ten Commandments*, written in 1520 with thirteen editions in four languages.[25] This is followed by *The Small Catechism* of 1529 with nine editions in four languages[26] (the world-wide dissemination of this book did not begin until after Luther's death). The *Personal Prayer Book* of 1522 comes next with seven copies,[27] followed by more catechism texts[28] and several early spiritual works.[29] One of Luther's most famous works also has its place in this select group of translations, *The Freedom of a Christian*, with five editions in five languages.[30] Yet one cannot help noticing that the great Reformation works of Luther appear rather seldom on the list, and that two categories of texts are all but unrepresented: the theological works (that is, theological in the strict sense of the word)[31] and those polemical works critical of the Church.[32] As far as I know the *Address to the Christian Nobility of the German Nation* and *On the Babylonish Captivity of the Church*, both written in 1520, were each translated only once.[33] The pamphlet *On the Papacy in Rome Against the Most Celebrated Romanist in Leipzig* is missing altogether, as is the earlier *Ninety-Five Theses*, and from a later period *The Bondage of the Will*.

Despite the divergent historical circumstances in each country and linguistic region, the production conditions of the non-German editions of Luther's works appear to have been similar everywhere; the vast majority of these works is traceable to individual translators, printers and places of publication. This is most clearly evident in the case of the Netherlands, the country in which the greatest number of translations were published: all of the nineteen Dutch and twenty Latin editions on the market by the end of the year 1522 were printed in Antwerp, Leiden or Zwolle. Thirty-two of these thirty-nine works appeared in one of four printing offices (de Grave and Hoochstraten in Antwerp, Seversz. in Leiden, Corver in Zwolle). Moreover, several of these printers clearly specialised in particular types of works, Seversz., for instance, more in theological works,[34] de Grave in works on piety. This concentration of editions around individual translators, printers and places of publication may be partially a factor of the close contact Luther maintained with his Dutch brothers in the Augustinian monastic order (especially those in Antwerp). Several facts support the idea that it was Jakob Propst, Luther's friend and former student at Wittenberg, who brought about the publication of not less than six Dutch translations through the printing office of de Grave from 20 September 1520 until 13 March 1521 – a genuine publicity offensive.[35]

Much the same was true for the other group of early translations, the group of editions published in Czech. Here it was above all the printer and translator Velensky and the Prague lawyer and Wittenberg graduate Sobek who played a leading role.[36] The latter introduced his translation of *The Freedom of a Christian* with the effusive remark: 'This little book deserves to be printed in gold instead of ink.'[37] In France the great Parisian printing office of Pierre Vidoue, recently credited with printing ten of Luther's Latin editions in 1520 and 1521, has proved to be another early centre of Luther's publication outside Germany.[38] Another French printer, Simon Du Bois, was active in Paris and Alençon and published a whole series of Luther's works in French after 1525.[39] Whereas Vidoue showed a preference for polemical works, Du Bois concentrated on works of a spiritual nature. Similarly, English translators such as Tyndale, William Roye and John Frith (Tyndale and Roye had been students in Wittenberg too)[40] deserve to be mentioned, as well as the enterprising Willem

Vorsterman in Antwerp, who in 1531 published six Danish translations.[41]

Antwerp was in every respect a centre of the multilingual dissemination of Luther's works in Europe. Editions were published there in
Latin, Dutch, Danish, English, and even French[42] and Spanish.[43] In
the first half of the sixteenth century nearly 100 printing offices were
in operation and over 2000 books were printed in Antwerp.[44] The
publication of books in foreign languages, especially French, flou-
rished in Strasbourg as well,[45] becoming an independent branch of the
city's printing industry after 1525. An early French translation of
Luther from that year also happens to be the earliest known French
book to be printed in Strasbourg.[46]

II

An attempt to evaluate these observations calls first of all for several
summarising statements.[47]

First, in comparison with the voluminous publication of Luther's
works in Germany, publication in the other European languages was
extremely modest. For every twenty of Luther's writings in German,
not even one was translated during his lifetime. Even considering all
of these translations together, they represent only a small fragment of
Luther's complete works. In no language but German could one gain
even a partially rounded picture of Luther's thought.

Secondly, all things considered, the translations came late. Disregarding the special circumstances surrounding the Dutch and Czech
translations,[48] Luther's works first appeared in Europe in translated
form at a time when he was already excommunicated and scorned,
branded as an outsider and enemy of the established order. Consequently, a large portion of his translated works appeared, at least in
the 1520s, not under the name Luther[49] but rather in manifold
disguises; either anonymously, under pseudonyms,[50] or under other
persons' names, such as Erasmus,[51] or even some pious Cardinal.[52]

Thirdly, translations were not the only books through which
Luther exerted an influence outside Germany. We must recall that
linguistic boundaries were not clearly delineated. German editions of
Luther's works often crossed the borders of the Holy Roman Empire,
reaching German-speaking communities and, not seldom, cities with
German-speaking majorities. Luther's works could be disseminated
in non-German-speaking areas from these cities[53] just as easily as by
German students and merchants abroad.[54] We can also count on the

existence of multilingual readerships in some places.[55] Furthermore, Luther's Latin works and those of his works translated into Latin were at all times and places accessible to a large group of non-German readers. According to my calculations, these Latin originals and translations make up 214 of 682 titles, or almost a third of Luther's complete works[56] (though, as I said earlier, only about 16 per cent of the total number of editions). For those who read Latin, the need for translations into the various national languages was thus partially eliminated.

Luther can be considered the first German to exert a significant intellectual influence outside Germany and also as the first German whose influence was determined by Germany's unique geographical situation, at the centre of Europe, surrounded by non-German-speaking areas and nations. Luther ultimately changed not only the course of German history but that of the whole of Europe.

However, our observations concerning the history of Luther publications tend to support Elton's view that the preconditions for receptiveness to this intellectual stimulus inside and outside the German language area were very different. This was not only due to different religious, social, political or educational conditions in each single nation but is true in a general way. Basically, Germany on the one hand and all the neighbouring countries on the other were separated by a chasm in this matter. As far as transmission was concerned the chasm consisted of the fact that Luther's great accessibility in Germany had no parallel on the other side of the border. The mechanisms of multiplication, and the degree of understanding and support which we can observe in Germany, at least in the towns,[57] were therefore also lacking.

The factors which created this disparity most likely arose in the early period of Luther's public appearance. Modern scholars estimate that by the time Luther was declared a heretic at the turn of the year 1520, 600,000 copies of his works were already on the market, perhaps as many copies as there were readers in Germany.[58] As we have shown, translations were scarcely in existence at this time, and that meant that in non-German-speaking areas Luther was only accessible to the person who could read Latin and only in so far as Latin editions of his works were available.

The reasons for this development are obvious. It was only natural that Luther should become known more slowly outside Germany and German-speaking areas. Writers have always had difficulty overcoming language barriers, and this problem was especially acute in an age still inexperienced in the business of translation. However, this delay in the appearance of translations had special consequences for Luther: it enforced a social selection process in his foreign readership which was essentially the same as the selection process fostered by the humanist movement. Before 1520 Luther was read all over Europe by humanists, the 'friends of Latin', and received wide attention and sympathy from them,[59] whereas he scarcely had an opportunity to make himself or his ideas known to those who only understood their mother tongue. After 1520, when translating had begun and the dissemination of translations became a possibility, the publication of Luther's works had become an illegal, subversive activity.[60]

The situation could be expressed in this way: Luther first became popular abroad as a heretic, not as a reforming theologian. Accordingly, one could only respond to him as a supporter or as an enemy.[61] Furthermore, he was mainly known from hearsay, through slogans, or as a symbolic figure, scarcely on account of his works. Even when there was an opportunity to read these works in one's own language, it was most often not Luther under whose name they appeared. To translate, print and sell his books abroad was more a risk than a business. In Germany a man could get rich in this way; elsewhere he risked his head. Thus the papal curia achieved in most of Europe what it could not achieve in Germany: it silenced Luther,[62] if not the Reformation. Luther the heretic, not unlike Jan Hus a century before, became nationally isolated.

The hiatus separating Germany from its neighbouring countries in the question of Luther's reception is an old problem for historiography; it has occupied many minds and inspired numerous interpretations, both trite and profound. Great pronouncements on Luther and his historical significance come to mind. Thomas Mann called him a 'giant incarnation of the German character'[63] and Luther has at times figured in the theory of Germany's unique path in the modern era. The state of affairs, however, which I have been describing, the special circumstances surrounding the history of the transmission of Luther's works, has hardly been perceived or reflected upon.

In no way do I mean to claim that this explanation of the problem is the only valid one. It simply represents one factor among others. I am also aware that the problem of transmission itself depends on a variety of extraneous circumstances. To offer but one example: the restrictions to which Luther's publication outside Germany were subject may seem striking in comparison with the relative absence of such restrictions in Germany, but seen from another perspective the developments we are talking about were sensational enough. Until Luther, scarcely a single German book had been translated, much less translated into more or less every neighbouring language.[64] More phenomenal, perhaps, was the publication of these translations at a time when the experience, tradition and institutions favourable to such an enterprise were still entirely absent.

The only remotely comparable case I am aware of is Sebastian Brant's *The Ship of Fools* which was translated into French, English and Dutch between 1497 and 1509.[65] Upon closer examination, however, the circumstances under which the translations were made were clearly different. *The Ship of Fools* is a single literary work and the point of its translation was not so much the transmission of intellectual and religious impulses as of literary values. In the case of Luther, a well-known and recognisably German author, it was the content which was acknowledged, and that was something completely new.

Until Luther, a European was hardly accustomed to receiving intellectual impulses from Germany; a general mistrust of, and sometimes an aversion to, things German was prevalent in several countries. This was most palpable in the Romance region,[66] especially in Italy,[67] where throughout the late Middle Ages a feeling of national superiority over the peoples on the other side of the Alps existed, particularly with regard to intellectual and cultural traits. This feeling took on an aggressive quality when it came to Germans, who had first appeared in Italy as conquerors and foreign rulers. It was a literary commonplace and a factor of Italy's national identity in the Renaissance that Germans were seen as barbarians, disfigured by drunkenness, gluttony, greed, coarseness, ignorance and an atrocious language.[68] This attitude was partially obviated in the area of religion: Italians sometimes viewed German piety as exemplary.[69] Luther's appearance, however, could have the effect of confirming the negative stereotype precisely in this area. The papal curia and Italian public opinion largely came to agree with one another in their opinion of Luther. '*Il tedesco infidel*' marked from that time on the typical German.[70] 'What does the pope care about Germany?', Luther is said to have been asked by Cardinal Cajetan at his interrogation in Augsburg in October 1518.[71]

There were national-cultural confrontations of a similar nature in other areas, too, where nationalities and languages were in a minority or simply intermingled, namely, in the north-east, east and south-east of Germany.[72] Another tone was audible, however, in the early Czech translations of Luther. Let me conclude with a quotation from the preface of a Czech edition published in 1520:

God, who has led the Czechs from darkness into light through Hus' preaching, has now shown this same mercy to the German people through D. Martinus, whose gifts one can only compare with those of the Apostle Paul. For six hundred years no one has understood his epistles and their message of man's salvation as Luther has. Miraculously, God has opened his heart to this proud and blinded people, who had previously persecuted the Czechs. Let us rejoice over them, as over a lost sheep that has been found again.[73]

Notes

1. Given at a conference of the *Sonderforschungsbereich* 'Spätmittelalter und Reformation' at Tübingen in September 1983. Through Professor Volker Press and with Professor Elton's consent a copy of the article was made available to me before publication.
2. The following paper was first delivered in German in October 1983 as a lecture at the Luther Congress organised by the *Akademie der Wissenschaften der DDR* in Halle a. d. Saale, and subsequently in other places. Thanks are due to Marion Salzmann and John W. Tanke for translating the article.
3. J. Benzing, *Lutherbibliographie* (Baden–Baden, 1966) (cit. B); H. Claus and M. Pegg, *Ergänzungen zur Bibliographie der zeitgenössischen Lutherdrucke* (Gotha/Baden–Baden, 1982) (cit. CP). Four further editions have just been discovered by G. Quarg, 'Seltene Lutherdrucke der Universitäts- und Stadtbibliothek Köln', *Gutenberg-Jahrbuch*, 1985, pp. 155–61, bringing the known total of editions published in Luther's lifetime to 3897.
4. It is difficult to judge how great the loss is. Where it is possible – as in francophone areas – to make a comparison with the contemporary censorship lists (cf. F. M. Higman, *Censorship and the Sorbonne. A Bibliographical Study of Books in French censured by the Faculty of Theology of the University of Paris, 1520–1551* (Geneva, 1979)), the result suggests the need for caution. Almost all the titles in these lists can also be found in modern bibliographies.
5. W. Nijhoff and M. E. Kronenberg, *Nederlandsche Bibliographie van 1500 tot 1540* (3 vols in 6, The Hague, 1923–61); C. Ch. G. Visser, *Luther's geschriften in de Nederlanden tot 1546* (Assen, 1969).
6. L. Nielsen, *Dansk Bibliografi 1482–1550* (Copenhagen/Christiania, 1919).
7. W. G. Moore, *La Réforme allemande et la littérature française* (Strasbourg, 1930); R. Peter, 'Les premiers ouvrages français imprimés à

Strasbourg', *Annuaire des Amis du Vieux-Strasbourg*, IV (1974), pp.
73–108; ibid., VIII (1978), pp. 11–75; ibid., X (1980), pp. 35–46; idem,
'La réception de Luther en France au XVIe siècle', *Revue d'Histoire et
de Philosophie Religieuses*, LXIII (1983), pp. 67–89; F. M. Higman,
'Les traductions françaises de Luther, 1524–1550', in J.-F. Gilmont
(ed.), *Palaestra bibliographica* (Aubel, 1984), pp. 11–56. We have not
taken into account the earliest French publication of Luther's hymns,
as dealt with by E. Müller, 'Les cantiques de Luther dans les recueils de
langue française', *Bulletin de la Société de l'Histoire du Protestantisme
français*, CXXIX (1983), pp. 47–72, nor is the interesting collection of
ecclesiastical texts from the Middle Ages and the Reformation considered, as described by F. M. Higman, 'Luther et la piété de l'Église
Gallicane: le Livre de vraye et parfaicte oraison', *Revue d'Histoire et de
Philosophie Religieuses*, LXIII (1983), pp. 91–111. The latter was
published fourteen times between 1528 and 1545; there are a number of
extracts from Luther's works in it, varying according to the edition.

8.　　*Knihopis českých a slovenských tisků od doby nejstarší až do konce
XVIII. století*, vol. II, 4 (Prague, 1948), nos. 5110–22, 5125, 5127 f; R.
Říčan, 'Tschechische Übersetzungen von Luthers Schriften bis zum
Schmalkaldischen Krieg', in *Vierhundertfünfzig Jahre lutherische
Reformation 1517–1967. Festschrift für Franz Lau zum 60. Geburtstag*
(Göttingen, 1967), pp. 282–301; M. Bohatcova, 'Erasmus, Luther,
Melanchthon und Calvin in gedruckten tschechischen Übersetzungen
aus dem 16. und 17. Jahrhundert', *Gutenberg-Jahrbuch*, 1974, pp. 158–
65. The bibliographical details in CP are now precise.

9.　　A. W. Pollard and G. R. Redgrave, *A Short-Title Catalogue of Books
printed in England, Scotland, and Ireland and of English Books printed
abroad 1475–1640*, vol. II, 2nd edn (London, 1976); W. A. Clebsch,
'The Earliest Translations of Luther into English', *Harvard Theological
Review*, LVI (1963), pp. 75–86; idem, *England's Earliest Protestants
1520–1535* (New Haven/London, 1964). Concerning Luther's hymns
translated into English, printed in 1536 or 1535, see R. A. Leaver, 'Die
Datierung von Coverdale's "Goostly Psalms"', *Musik und Kirche*, LI
(1981), pp. 165–71; idem, 'A Newly Discovered Fragment of Coverdale's Goostly Psalms', *Jahrbuch für Liturgik und Hymnologie*, XXVI
(1982), pp. 136–50. Unhelpful for our problem is B. Cottret, 'Traducteurs et divulgateurs clandestins de la Réforme dans l'Angleterre
henricienne, 1520–1535', *Revue d'Histoire Moderne et Contemporaine*,
XXVIII (1981), pp. 464–80.

10.　　S. Seidel Menchi, 'Le traduzioni italiane di Lutero nella prima metà del
Cinquecento', *Rinascimento*, XVII (1977), pp. 31–108. See below, n. 17.

11.　　Research into the Polish translations seems at the moment to be open
to question. Cf. K. Estreicher, *Bibliografia polska*, vol. XXII (Cracow,
1907–8); F. W. Neumann, *Studien zum polnischen frühreformatorischen
Schrifttum*, vol. I (Leipzig, 1941); Wl. Chojnacki, *Bibliografia polskich
druków ewangelickich . . . 1530–1939* (Warsaw, 1966), p. 114.

12.　　Nijhoff/Kronenberg (as n. 5), no. 4221. As early as 1531 a Luther
publication in Spanish is mentioned, which no longer exists: A.
Redondo, 'Luther et l'Espagne de 1520 à 1536', *Mélanges de la Casa de
Velázquez*, I (1965), pp. 109–65, esp. 154 n. 3. Cf. below, n. 43.

13. I. Collijn, *Sveriges bibliografi intill år 1600*, vol. I (Uppsala, 1934–38), pp. 351–4; A. Andersson, 'Die erste Original-Ausgabe des Sommertheiles von Luthers Kirchenpostille', *Zentralblatt für Bibliothekswesen*, X (1893), pp. 486–9.

14. Collijn (as n. 13), vol. II (Uppsala, 1927), p. 34ff; S. Heininen *Die finnischen Studenten in Wittenberg 1531–1552* (Helsinki, 1980), p. 50. I am doubtful whether there were Estonian translations of Luther's works in a barrel of Protestant books which was confiscated in Lübeck in 1525: P. Johansen, 'Gedruckte deutsche und undeutsche Messen für Riga 1525', *Zeitschrift für Ostforschung*, VIII (1959), pp. 523–32; C. A. Holtbecker, '450 Jahre estnische Buchgeschichte', *Archiv für die Geschichte des Buchwesens*, XV (1975/76), pp. 1297–302.

15. B 514; Řičan (as n. 8), pp. 282–3; A. J. Lamping, *Ulrichus Velenus . . . and his Treatise against the Papacy* (Leiden, 1975), pp. 60–1.

16. B 204; 202; 83; 10; 11; Řičan (as n. 8), p. 283; Visser (as n. 5), pp. 31 ff. A further ten publications of Luther in Latin can be proved for the Netherlands up to the end of 1520: B 257; 459; 618; 619; 628; 757; 758; CP 818d; 818e.

17. A collection of texts printed in Venice containing the *Kurze Form der Zehn Gebote des Glaubens und des Vaterunsers*, of which there were consequently at least seven editions: Seidel Menchi (as n. 10), pp. 40ff; CP 18a; 18b; 19; 19a; 19b. A further edition from 1532 has recently been discovered by S. Seidel Menchi in the University Library in Ghent.

18. A Strasbourg edition of *Von der Freiheit eines Christenmenschen*: Peter, 'Ouvrages' (as n. 7), *Annuaire des Amis du Vieux-Strasbourg*, X (1980), pp. 36–7; CP 766a; a Paris edition of the *Preface to Romans*: Higman, 'Traductions' (as n. 7), p. 22; not in CP. Older Luther translations into French are proved by court case files (cf. Moore, as n. 7, 102ff) and manuscripts: R. Marichal, 'Antoine d'Oraison, premier traducteur français de Luther', *Bibliothèque d'Humanisme et Renaissance*, IX (1947), pp. 78–108. A collective volume which appeared in Basel in 1523 contained extracts from *Von weltlicher Obrigkeit* in French: Moore (as n. 7), pp. 106–7.

19. The *Decem praecepta* (1518): Nielsen (as n. 6), no. 163; CP 201a.

20. *Auslegung deutsch des Vaterunsers* (1519) and *Vom Abendmahl Christi* (1528): Nielsen (as n. 6), no. 144; CP 279a; 2514a.

21. A part of *Responsio ad librum Catharini* (1521) and *Das 7. Kapitel zu den Corinthern* (1523): *Short-Title Catalogue* (as n. 9), no. 11394; Nijhoff/Kronenberg (as n. 5), no. 2982; B 888; 1680; Clebsch, 'Translations' (as n. 9), pp. 76ff. Two publications preceded this. One, the translation of Luther's 1522 sermon on the parable of the wicked mammon, occupied roughly one-sixth of Tyndale's book *The Parable of the Wicked Mammon*, 1528: J. F. Mozley, *William Tyndale* (London, 1937), p. 127. The other, a letter from Luther to Henry VIII of 1st Sept. 1525, together with the king's answer, was printed twice in English (London, *c.* 1528): B 2401a; 2401b; cf. *D. Martin Luthers Werke. Kritische Gesamtausgabe* (cit. *WA*), *Briefwechsel*, vol. XII (Weimar, 1967), pp. 73–4. The *Introduccion . . . vn to the pistle off Paul to the Romayns* in the 1526 edn of Tyndale's English New Testament (*Short-Title Catalogue* (as n. 9), no. 2824; separate, ibid., no. 24438) is a

'periphrastic translation' of Luther's introduction in the *Septembertes-tament* of 1522: Clebsch, *England's Earliest Protestants* (as n. 9), p. 145.

22. The first 7 sermons of the *Sommerteil* of Luther's *Kirchenpostille*. Cf. above n. 13.

23. *De libertate Christiana* (1520), translated by Francisco de Enzinas, published in Antwerp: cf. above n. 12. It has recently been proved that the Spanish Catechism, which appeared in 1529 in Alcalá de Henares (M. Bataillon, *Erasme et l'Espagne* (Paris, 1937), p. 373ff), contains long extracts from Luther's *Decem praecepta* and his *Auslegung deutsch des Vaterunsers*: C. Gilly, 'Juan de Valdés: Übersetzer und Bearbeiter von Luthers Schriften . . .', *Archiv für Reformationsgeschichte*, LXXIV (1983), pp. 257–305.

24. H. Dannenbauer, *Luther als religiöser Volksschriftsteller* (Tübingen, 1930) described Luther in this way in regard to his publications in Germany up to 1520.

25. B 812–15; 605; CP 18a; 18b; 19; 19a; 19b; cf. above n. 17.

26. B 2661–6; CP 2666a–c; J. M. Reu (ed.), *Quellen zur Geschichte des kirchlichen Unterrichts in der evangelischen Kirche Deutschlands zwischen 1530 und 1600*, vol. I, 3, 1, 1 (Gütersloh, 1927), pp. 45* ff.

27. B 1307–13; 1317–18. For further Danish translations connected with the *Betbüchlein* not mentioned by B see K. Gierow, 'Den evangeliska bönelitteraturen i Danmark 1526–1575' (Dissertation theol., University of Lund, 1948), p. 15ff, esp. 25ff; extracts from the *Betbüchlein* can also be found in the French collection (cf. above, n. 7); the subject matter of the earliest Finnish translations (cf. above, n. 14) is also prayer.

28. *Decem praecepta*: B 202–4; CP 201a; cf. above n. 23. *Auslegung deutsch des Vaterunsers*: B 278–9; CP 279a; cf. above, ns 17, 23.

29. The most successful, each with four publications, were *Sermon von der Betrachtung des hl. Leidens Christi* (1519): B 337; 338a; 339–40; *Tessaradecas consolatoria* (1520): B 605–8.

30. B 766–9; CP 766a.

31. Cf. Visser (as n. 5), pp. 178ff.

32. Polemical emphases in the originals were indeed diluted in the Italian translations: Seidel Menchi (as n. 10), p. 98.

33. B 698; 717.

34. His special interest was in the early disputations: CP 85; 818e; cf. 818d. About the printer, who was also a bookseller, cf. J. D. Bangs, 'Reconsidering Lutheran Book Trade: The So-Called "Winkelkaesboek" of Pieter Claesz. van Balen', *Quaerendo*, IX (1979), pp. 227–60, esp. 246–7.

35. Visser (as n. 5), pp. 31ff, 152ff; A. Duke, 'The Face of Popular Religious Dissent in the Low Countries, 1520–1530', *Journal of Ecclesiastical History*, XXVI (1975), pp. 41–67, esp. p. 42. Since all these (B 202; 83; 10; 11; 608; 179) are each preserved in only one copy we can assume loss of further publications. On the printer, see A. Rouzet, *Dictionnaire des imprimeurs, libraires et éditeurs des XVe et XVIe siècles dans les limites géographiques de la Belgique actuelle* (Nieuwkoop, 1975), pp. 80–1. Visser comments that after the closure of the Antwerp

Augustinian monastery on 6 October 1522 no more of Luther's writings were edited by de Grave. Visser (as n. 5), p. 156. About Propst's publicity 'offensive' cf. O. Rudloff, *Bonae Litterae et Lutherus. Texte und Untersuchungen zu den Anfängen der Theologie des Bremer Reformators Jakob Propst* (Bremen, 1985), pp. 126ff.

36. Řičan (as n. 8) gives CP 514 and 889 to Velensky; CP 918; 799; 682; 769; 1697 to Sobek. The publisher Velensky placed Luther alongside humanist authors such as Ficino, Pico and Erasmus. Cf. Lamping (as n. 15).

37. Řičan (as n. 8), p. 285.

38. Ph. Renouard, *Imprimeurs Parisiens, libraires, fondeurs de caractères et correcteurs d'imprimerie* (Paris, 1898), pp. 366–7. The proof for this group of publications is a by-product of Claus and Pegg's bibliography. The following titles are concerned: B 86; 211; CP 652a; 706a; 710a; 727a; 783a; 797a; B 853; CP 912.

39. A. Tricard, 'La propagande evangélique en France. L'imprimeur Simon Du Bois (1525–1534)', in G. Berthoud *et al.* (eds), *Aspects de la Propagande religieuse* (Geneva, 1957), pp. 1–37; Moore (as n. 7), p. 127ff; E. Droz, *Chemins de l'hérésie*, vol. I (Geneva, 1970), pp. 52ff, 333ff; Higman, 'Luther et la piété' (as n. 7).

40. Clebsch, 'Translations' and *England's Earliest Protestants* (as n. 9).

41. B 337; 377; 1312; 1313; 1477; 1886. As early as 1529, Vorsterman had published Christiern Pedersen's Danish translation of the New Testament. He obviously had a close connection with Pedersen who was in Antwerp from 1529 to 1531: M. E. Kronenberg, 'De drukker van de deensche boeken te Antwerpen (1529–1531) is Willem Vorsterman', *Het boek*, VIII (1919), pp. 1–8; Rouzet (as n. 35), pp. 239–40.

42. Moore (as n. 7), pp. 83ff.

43. According to a (doubtful) report by Aleander (Th. Brieger (ed.), *Aleander und Luther 1521* (Gotha, 1884), p. 81; Gilly (as n. 23), p. 297ff), Luther's works had been published in Spanish at Antwerp as early as spring 1521. At any rate we often later hear of Luther's works being imported to Spain from Flanders: Redondo (as n. 12), p. 131; Bataillon (as n. 23), p. 204. And the Spanish edition of 1540 comes from Antwerp, see above n. 12.

44. A. Dermul and H. F. Bouchery, *Bibliographie betreffende de Antwerpsche drukkers* (Antwerp, 1938), pp. 11–12. Visser (as n. 5), p. 27, and F. C. Avis, 'England's Use of Antwerp Printers', *Gutenberg-Jahrbuch*, 1973, pp. 234–40, esp. p. 234, estimate the book production to be even greater. It was Antwerp which to a large extent supplied the English bookmarket. Cf. idem and E. Armstrong, 'English Purchases of Printed Books from the Continent 1465–1526', *English Historical Review*, XCIV (1979), pp. 268–90, esp. p. 288.

45. An Italian translation of *An den christlichen Adel* also appeared in Strasbourg in 1533: B 698; Seidel Menchi (as n. 10), p. 64; idem, 'Humanismus und Reformation im Spiegel der italienischen Inquisitionsakten', in A. Buck (ed.), *Renaissance – Reformation. Gegensätze und Gemeinsamkeiten* (Wiesbaden, 1984), pp. 47–64, esp. p. 51.

46. Peter, 'Réception' (as n. 7), p. 79. Some of the Strasbourg publishers, in

particular Johann Herwagen, also seem to have concentrated on Latin translations of Luther's works; such an undertaking aimed at an international market too. M. U. Chrisman, *Lay Culture – Learned Culture. Books and Social Change in Strasbourg, 1480–1599* (New Haven/London, 1982) does not consider this phenomenon. Martin Bucer, in the foreword to his Latin translation of Luther's sermons on the epistles of Peter and Jude, wrote on 4 July 1524:

> *Iohannes Heruagius chalcographus pius ... nuper ubi accepisset, quae in duas d. Petri Epistolas et unam Iudae uir sanctus* [Luther] *populo suo lingua uernacula disseruit, contendit a me argumentis minime uulgaribus, ut ea latina redderem, quando illa fratribus Gallis, apud quos felicibus admodum initijs gloria gliscit euangelij, usui futura, nullus possim inficiari.*

J. Rott (ed.), *Correspondance de Martin Bucer*, vol. I (Leiden, 1979), p. 261, 1. 8–14. Similar quotations in M. de Kroon, *Studien zu Martin Bucers Obrigkeitsverständnis* (Gütersloh, 1984), p. 65 n. 124.

47. In the following I am thankful for inspiration to H. J. Hillerbrand, 'The Spread of the Protestant Reformation of the Sixteenth Century: A Historical Case Study in the Transfer of Ideas', *South Atlantic Quarterly*, LXVII (1968), pp. 265–86; idem, *Men and Ideas in the Sixteenth Century* (Chicago, 1969), pp. 38ff.

48. Cf. p. 236f.

49. This holds true, according to Seidel Menchi (as n. 10), p. 32, for all known Italian translations.

50. In the 1527 French translation of Luther's *Die Epistel des Propheten Jesaia* (B 2266) the author is described as '*docteur de Cleremont*', which, according to Peter, '*Réception*' (as n. 7), p. 78 n. 34, could be an allusion to Luther (*lauter = clair*).

51. One tradition of the early Italian collection (CP 18b; 19b; Seidel Menchi (as n. 10), p. 61) appeared in this manner, as did the recently discovered edition, see above, n. 17. In 1538 Luther heard of an Italian monk who was locked up in Bologna because he owned such books. *WA Tischreden*, vol. IV (Weimar, 1916), no. 3907. In the 1529 English translation by Roye (B 1680) the actual Luther text is placed before a short text by Erasmus whose name, however, appears on the front page as author of the whole publication: Clebsch, 'Translations' (as n. 9), p. 78ff. In Spain, too, Luther's works appeared disguised by Erasmus' name: J. C. Nieto, 'Luther's Ghost and Erasmus' Masks in Spain', *Bibliothèque d'Humanisme et Renaissance*, XXXIX (1977), pp. 33–49.

52. CP 1814a; Seidel Menchi (as n. 10), p. 88.

53. Cf. for instance the Baltic: R. Wittram, 'Die Reformation in Livland', in W. Hubatsch (ed.), *Wirkungen der deutschen Reformation bis 1555* (Darmstadt, 1967), pp. 411–43, esp. pp. 426ff.

54. A clear example: H. Ammann, 'Oberdeutsche Kaufleute und die Anfänge der Reformation in Genf', *Zeitschrift für württembergische Landesgeschichte*, XIII (1954), pp. 150–93. We even have evidence that in 1522 a German merchant passed on knowledge of Luther in India: H. Kämmerling-Fitzler, 'Der Nürnberger Kaufmann Georg Pock ...

in Portugiesisch-Indien und im Edelsteinland Vijayanagara', *Mitteilungen des Vereins für Geschichte der Stadt Nürnberg*, LV (1967–68), pp. 137–84, esp. p. 181.

55. Of the no less than 3849 books Canon Jan van der Haer of Gorkum possessed in 1531, seventy-one were by Luther; of these, forty-seven were in Latin, thirteen in Dutch, two in Low German, and nine in High German: Visser (as n. 5), p. 23.

56. One hundred and sixty-two titles appeared originally in Latin; fifty-two were translated into Latin from German originals.

57. B. Moeller, 'Was wurde in der Frühzeit der Reformation in den deutschen Städten gepredigt?', *Archiv für Reformationsgeschichte*, LXXV (1984), pp. 176–93.

58. Idem, *Deutschland im Zeitalter der Reformation*, 2nd edn (Göttingen, 1981), p. 62; idem, 'Luther und die Städte' in *Aus der Lutherforschung. Drei Vorträge* (Opladen, 1983), pp. 9–26, esp. p. 18.

59. Proofs of this are too numerous to be listed here. There is a famous letter from Froben to Luther of 14 February 1519, in which he reports that his Latin edition of Luther has been sent to '*Gallia, Hispania, Italia, Brabantia, Anglia*'. *WA Briefwechsel*, vol. I (Weimar, 1930), no. 146. This can be confirmed by national witnesses in each case; cf. e.g. R. J. Knecht, 'The Early Reformation in England and France: A Comparison', *History*, LVII (1972), pp. 1–16. Non-German readers who had a knowledge of Latin naturally concentrated on the Latin works which perforce caused a certain degree of one-sidedness in their knowledge of Luther. It is similarly significant that the 1521 Sorbonne judgement against Luther was based on all his Latin works which appeared before the end of 1520, but did not consider any of his German writings: F. T. Bos, 'Luther in het oordeel van de Sorbonne' (Dissertation theol., University of Amsterdam, 1974), pp. 53ff.

60. Even in the earliest Luther translations in the Netherlands which appeared in 1520 (see above n. 16), the printer de Grave felt himself induced to legitimise Luther by descriptions such as '*hochgelehrter Doktor in der Gottheit*': Visser (as n. 5), p. 173.

61. Effusive claims of loyalty to Luther are especially to be found in Czech editions. As Říčan (as n. 8) has shown, this is probably the result of an effort to use the German reformer in the debate within the Hussite movement.

62. Censorship mandates in the style of the Edict of Worms and the burning of Luther's works are found throughout Europe.

63. Th. Mann, *Deutschland und die Deutschen* (Berlin, 1947), p. 13: '*Martin Luther, eine riesenhafte Inkarnation deutschen Wesens*'.

64. Erasmus, who wrote in Latin and was admittedly not a German, was translated into many European languages roughly at the same time as Luther. The number of Erasmus translations is probably much higher, but in his case we are not yet considering forbidden and subversive, heretical literature. See above, n. 51.

65. F. Zarncke (ed.), *Sebastian Brants Narrenschiff* (Leipzig, 1854); D. O'Connor, 'Sebastien Brant en France au XVIe siècle', *Revue de Littérature Comparée*, 1928, pp. 309–17; B. Quillet, 'Le Narrenschiff de

Sebastian Brant, ses traducteurs et ses traductions aux XVe et XVIe siècles', in J. L. Alonso Hernandez *et al.* (eds), *Culture et marginalités au XVIe siècle* (Paris, 1973), pp. 111–24; E. Dubruck, 'On Pierre Riviere, French "Translator" of Brant's *Narrenschiff*, *Bibliothèque d'Humanisme et Renaissance*, XLI (1979), p. 109f; P. Aquilon, 'La réception de l'Humanisme allemand à Paris à travers la production imprimée, 1480–1540', in *L'Humanisme allemand (1480–1540): XVIIIe Colloque de Tours* (Munich/Paris, 1979), pp. 45–79, esp. p. 46.

66. France: K. L. Zimmermann, 'Die Beurteilung der Deutschen in der französischen Literatur des Mittelalters . . .', *Romanische Forschungen*, XXIX (1911), pp. 222–316 (refers above all to the twelfth and thirteenth centuries); F. Kern, 'Der mittelalterliche Deutsche in französischer Ansicht', *Historische Zeitschrift*, CVIII (1912), pp. 237–54. According to W. Radczun, *Das englische Urteil über die Deutschen bis zur Mitte des 17. Jahrhunderts* (Berlin, 1933) the English attitude towards the Germans was similar to that of the French.

67. Literature on this topic is abundant. See for example P. Amelung, *Das Bild des Deutschen in der Literatur der italienischen Renaissance (1400–1559)* (Munich, 1964); K. Voigt, *Italienische Berichte aus dem spätmittelalterlichen Deutschland* (Stuttgart, 1973); H. Liebmann, *Deutsches Land und Volk nach italienischen Berichterstattern der Reformationszeit* (Berlin, 1910); B. McClung Hallman, 'Italian "National Superiority" and the Lutheran Question, 1517–1546', *Archiv für Reformationsgeschichte*, LXXI (1980), pp. 134–48; E. Grigorich Gleason, 'Sixteenth Century Italian Interpretations of Luther', ibid., LX (1969), pp. 160–73.

68. This conflict also sheds light on the militant feeling of superiority to the '*Welschen*' shown by German humanists such as Celtis and Hutten and even to be glimpsed in Luther. Cf. from the abundant literature: F. H. Schubert, 'Riccardo Bartolini', *Zeitschrift für bayerische Landesgeschichte*, XIX (1956), pp. 95–127; F. L. Borchardt, *German Antiquity in Renaissance Myth* (Baltimore, Md/London, 1971).

69. A travel report from 1517 is especially well known for showing this: J. R. Hale (ed.), *The Travel Journal of Antonio de Beatis: Germany, Switzerland, the Low Countries, France and Italy, 1517–1518* (London, 1979). K. Voigt, 'Die Briefe Antonio de' Costabilis und Cesare Mauros von der Gesandtschaft Ferraras zu König Maximilian I. (1507/08)', *Römische Historische Mitteilungen*, XIII (1971), pp. 81–136 has collected (pp. 123ff, n. 166) other favourable comments on German piety.

70. Amelung (as n. 67), p. 128.

71. *WA Tischreden*, vol. III (Weimar, 1914), no. 3857. McClung Hallman stresses again that this attitude towards the Germans also strongly influenced papal politics concerning the Reformation; indeed, even a knowledge of the German language was lacking in the Curia.

72. For detailed considerations see M. Bucsay, *Der Protestantismus in Ungarn 1521–1978,* 2 vols (Vienna, 1977–79), vol. I, pp. 44ff; G. Schramm, 'Danzig, Elbing und Thorn als Beispiele städtischer Reformation (1517–1558)', in Hans Fenske, Wolfgang Reinhard, and Ernst

Schulin (eds), *Historia Integra. Festschrift für Erich Hassinger zum 70. Geburtstag* (Berlin, 1977), pp. 125–54, esp. pp. 132ff.

73. Řičan (as n. 8), p. 283. Cf. ibid., pp. 287, 291. This sounds almost like an echo of Luther's earlier renunciation of the '*bickarden auß Böhem*' to be found in his 1518 exegesis of Psalm 109. *WA*, vol. I (Weimar, 1883), p. 697, 12–21.

12 Europe as Seen Through the Correspondence of Theodore Beza

Bernard Vogler

Among Reformation figures leaving a substantial correspondence is Theodore Beza, Calvin's successor. From 1960, a team of Genevans under the late Henri Meylan and Alain Dufour has been publishing this correspondence which so far runs to eleven volumes, covering the period to 1570.[1] The 814 pieces up to 1570 (in reality, 856 in all including enclosures referring to a sole correspondent) permit an initial outline of his historical contribution to the spread of the Reformation, especially in relation to geographical distribution, network of correspondents, and content to be made.[2]

I. THE CORRESPONDENTS

The body of correspondence increases from 1553, accelerates in 1557 (thirty-eight pieces) and almost disappears from August 1558, between 13 August and the end of the year. In 1561, the Colloquy of Poissy created a great flood of forty-six letters between August and December. From 1564, the annual average is maintained at between seventy and ninety, or six to eight per month, not including lost correspondence.[3] As for the network of correspondents, a significant expansion only occurs from 1565, which, taken with 1566, marks the peak. Much of this refers to French correspondents and Morely's heterodoxy, though there is some Polish correspondence.

Three correspondents in the period up to 1563 stand out, with no more than four appearing more than twenty times up to 1570. The most frequent correspondent is Bullinger, with 305 letters, 37 per cent of the total body of preserved correspondence. If from 1551 Zwingli's successor seems to be the favourite correspondent, except in 1556 and 1558, a year which shows a clear cooling of relations provoked by

252

concessions made the year before by Beza during the negotiations with German Lutherans, and from May 1562 to May the following year, due to the troubles in France, then there is a resurgence of contact in 1563. After this the number varies between twenty and forty per year, or between one-third and one-half of the total: 61 per cent of these are in the hand of Beza himself. This interest is mutual. Bullinger became the patriarch of the Reformed Churches in the German-speaking countries as well as in Eastern Europe,[4] mainly as a result of a more abundant correspondence than that of Beza, with more than 12,000 letters preserved.[5] Nevertheless, Beza experienced a rapid rise to fame in French-speaking communities between 1549 and 1561.[6] Their letters are in fact personal journals containing information gathered by their authors and intended for use by their correspondents: theological, ecclesiastical, military, diplomatic, and political matters are covered.

Contacts with Calvin become closer from 1556 solely in order to recruit pastors for the rapidly-growing 'dissident' churches in France. Only later do we see evidence of a more egalitarian relationship. After the Colloquy of Poissy and his long sojourn in France between 1561 and 1562, Beza writes more frequently to keep Calvin and the Genevan Church informed of events. This explains why more than three-quarters of the letters originate with Beza. On the other hand, contact with Farel stops when Beza settles in Geneva at the end of 1558. Of the twenty letters we have, nineteen are written by Beza, evidently worried by the fate of his French co-religionists. The fourth correspondent, Haller, head of the Bernese Church, has twenty-five out of thirty letters written by Beza: two-thirds of these deal with the years 1564 – where Beza tries to convince his correspondent to accept the renewal of the French alliance for Berne in return for the royal agreement to respect the Pact of Amboise – and 1566, where Beza is taken up with the problems created by the Elector Palatine's involvement with the unity of the Reformed Church, then threatened with exclusion from the Peace of Augsburg.

Among the others, only two appear more than ten times. These are Bullinger's son-in-law, Gwalther (seventeen pieces), with whom contact, however infrequent, beginning in 1553 continues, except for the year 1570, where Beza, anxious to maintain mutual goodwill with Zürich (although each takes a contrary stance in the disciplinary conflict dividing the theologians of the Palatinate), tries to keep up good relations with the latter through his intermediary.[7] The other correspondent is a politician, Zurkinden, Chancellor of Berne (four-

Beza's correspondents by geographical distribution

	1550	1551	1552	1553	1554	1555	1556	1557	1558	1559	1560	1561	1562	1563	1564	1565	1566	1567	1568	1569	1570
Total letters	3	6	7	12	16	15	20	38	21	8	9	67	35	46	73	77	90	65	74	79	93
New correspondents	3	3	1	2	6	4	3	8	4	4	–	12	5	8	10	28	27	14	16	7	17
Switzerland	2	5	7	11	14	14	14	32	17	7	6	51	24	34	62	33	35	31	46	51	51
Bullinger	1	2	4	8	6	4	3	10	4	2	3	6	4	21	41	23	22	26	37	48	30
Calvin	1	1	–	1	3	3	5	10	7	1	2	33	18	4	–	–	–	–	–	–	–
Farel	–	2	2	–	3	3	5	5	2	–	–	–	–	1	–	–	–	–	–	–	–
Zürich	1	3	4	10	7	7	3	14	6	3	3	12	5	23	44	25	23	26	38	48	34
Berne	–	1	–	–	–	1	1	2	–	–	–	–	–	1	15	7	7	4	3	2	4
Basel	–	–	–	–	–	–	–	1	2	1	1	2	–	1	–	–	–	2	2	–	2
Other Germanophone regions	–	–	–	–	1	–	–	–	–	–	2	–	3	3	1	–	–	2	–	1	4
Geneva	–	1	1	1	4	4	5	10	7	2	2	35	19	4	–	–	1	–	–	1	2
Neuchâtel	–	–	2	–	2	3	5	5	2	–	–	–	–	1	–	–	4	–	–	–	–
Other Francophone regions	–	–	–	–	–	–	–	–	1	–	–	–	1	1	–	1	1	1	–	–	5
France	1	1	–	–	–	–	–	–	2	–	–	9	8	6	9	23	39	24	5	5	1
Nobles	–	–	–	–	–	–	–	–	–	–	–	3	2	6	6	8	11	7	2	5	1
Pastors	–	–	–	–	–	–	–	–	–	–	–	1	–	1	–	7	20	13	3	1	–
Institutions	–	–	–	–	–	–	–	–	–	–	–	4	3	–	1	4	4	2	–	–	–
Empire	–	–	–	–	1	1	4	5	–	3	4	4	3	1	1	6	6	4	6	15	21
Low Countries	–	–	–	–	–	–	–	–	–	–	–	–	–	1	1	3	4	–	1	1	3
England	–	–	–	–	–	–	–	–	–	–	–	–	–	1	1	3	2	1	2	2	2
Scotland	–	–	–	–	–	–	–	–	–	–	–	–	–	–	–	–	2	–	–	–	–
Poland	–	–	–	–	–	2	–	–	–	–	–	1	–	1	–	7	2	4	7	1	9
Hungary	–	–	–	–	–	–	–	–	–	–	–	–	–	–	–	–	–	5	5	2	6
Spanish, Italian and Vaudois refugees	–	–	–	–	–	1	–	–	–	–	3	–	1	–	–	2	3	1	1	1	–

teen pieces). Through him Beza hoped to influence Bernese politics towards France and Savoy during the restoration of the bailiwicks lost in 1536, and which currently isolated Geneva and its ally, Berne. It is unfortunate that in this case Beza's letters have not been preserved. Zurkinden, however, complains that Beza overvalues his power, considering himself no more than a mere secretary.

The rest of the 180 correspondents identified appear infrequently, suggesting the necessity of a geographical study. The thirteen Cantons and their allies represent the lion's share with 63 per cent. Indeed, Zürich stands well above these, with 61 per cent, thanks to Bullinger and Gwalther, who are considered as near-exclusive correspondents, with the exception of the congregation of Zürich (eight pieces spread out between 1551 and 1563). For Geneva, the 100 pieces include ninety directed to Calvin. It is hardly surprising that after his death and Beza's refusal to travel after 1563, the presence of Geneva fades somewhat, likewise for Berne, where the exchange is virtually limited to Haller and Zurkinden (forty-four out of forty-seven). It only begins in 1563 with the opening of negotiations between Berne and France for the re-establishment of treaties, and between Berne and Savoy, which primarily involved Geneva. The latter provoke a flurry in 1564, with fifteen pieces. Afterwards, these contacts are pursued at a more leisurely pace, in the region of about 5–10 per cent of the annual total. Contacts with Basel (twelve letters) remain limited: it is true that its church president Sulzer shows a certain inclination towards the Lutherans in the 1560s, that Castellio is suspect, and that the Genevans needed neither the university nor the publishing industry of Basel. Strangely, the main correspondent is Sulzer; the exchanges are usually due to specific needs: rendering mutual services, appeals to help refugees in Geneva, and the like.[8] Beza also ignores the rest of German-speaking Switzerland. There are occasional exchanges for specific reasons with individual theologians such as Ambrosius Blaurer, now living in seclusion in Biel, and in 1570 with Ulmer, the church president of Schaffhausen, who wrote to make a recommendation in favour of a grant-aided scholar of the town magistrate.[9]

French-speaking Switzerland plays a minor role (twenty pieces), with the exception of Farel with thirteen pieces, of which four, in 1570, relate to a call for help on behalf of Genevan refugees. Beza seems to have neglected Neuchâtel completely after Farel's death, and Lausanne after his departure in 1558.

In fact, Beza's attention is directed towards his compatriots, to whom he becomes the undisputed counsellor after 1560, with 136 pieces, or 16 per cent of his output. In this correspondence we can distinguish four periods: insignificant production up to 1560 (five pieces), about ten letters per year from 1561 to 1564, then a sudden increase from 1565 to 1567, due in particular to the Morely affair and the various disputes within the churches, among them Orléans and Lyons, and finally, a clear decline with a single letter in 1570.[10] His correspondents may be divided into three groups. First, the nobility: twelve personages with forty-six pieces, involving the leaders of the Huguenot party, such as the Prince de Condé (five), Coligny (eight), and the Queen of Navarre with eight letters, of which three concern the Morely affair (1567) and the methods needed to introduce the Reformation into Béarn.[11] To these, we may add Renée de France, Duchess of Ferrara, from 1566 to 1568, to whom he sends pastoral letters[12] in which he urges her to be more resolute, entreating her to set aside family affection, as had Margaret of Savoy. The latter had taken the initiative in soliciting Beza's aid in furthering the negotiations then under way between the Duchy of Savoy and the city of Geneva. Other rare appearances are made, once or twice, by Anthony of Navarre, the Prince de Porcien, Madame de Soubise, and the Baron des Adrets.

A second group is made up of pastors, twenty-one *in toto*, with forty-six pieces, mainly from Lyons, Orléans and Paris, who were facing internal difficulties. Among them we may note des Gallars of Orléans, with nine letters addressed to Beza between 12 August 1566 and 21 January 1567, dealing with the Morely affair (which affected him directly), to Morely on discipline, and finally the pastor Jean Taffin of Metz (three pieces), criticised by Beza for handing over a Bucerian profession of faith to brothers in the Low Countries.[13] Finally, Beza took the liberty of addressing directly a number of 'dissident' churches, nine in all,[14] and the Consistory of Toulouse,[15] and three times, every such church in France,[16] all of which took place between 1561 and 1567. Beside these three groups there are a very few isolated cases, such as the Hebrew scholar Mercier, the Collège de France (in 1563 and 1565), an advocate from Troyes, Pithou, from 1565 to 1569, a monk Picherel, who was a biblical commentator and who held Beza in high esteem despite the religious divide between them,[17] and the legal expert Hotman (four pieces).

With even the francophone Low Countries there was only limited contact, despite the religious unity and the events which took place in 1566: thirteen pieces in all, of which ten appeared in the years 1565, 1566, and 1570, and none before 1564. It would appear that losses were more numerous in this period and that links were more regular with Zürich than with Geneva. The thirteen pieces are distributed between eight correspondents, namely three theologians, two of them refugees, one of them in the Palatinate, Dathenus, and the other a pastor from the Dutch congregation of Cologne, Van Ceule. The pastors from the province of Holland wrote to Beza twice in 1565 to plead with him to refute their opponent Coornhert.[18] The other correspondents are political figures, Marnix de Sainte-Aldegonde, collaborator of William of Orange and former pupil of Beza, who sought advice in 1566 to counteract pantheist tendencies,[19] then a magistrate of Ghent, Utenhove, and Crespin, author of the martyrology, and finally a poet from Tournai, des Masures. It should be noted that during the iconoclastic crisis, Beza maintained his distance in respect of the 'violence and confusion whose outcome could not be but disastrous'.[20]

Contact with England begins late (1563) and is extremely limited: just fourteen pieces. It is clear that the Anglican Church is far from responding to Genevan aspirations, and that the queen objected strongly to interference in English affairs. Moreover, Beza cannot accept the position of a woman as head of the Anglican hierarchy. For this reason, only one letter is addressed to her, in the form of an official introduction to the New Testament, in 1564.[21] Relations remained difficult, and in 1566 Beza complains that 'everything Genevan is suspect over there'.[22] Correspondents appear infrequently: they are mainly politicians, such as the queen's Secretary of State Cecil (1563 and 1565), Sir Walter Mildmay, Chancellor of the Exchequer (1570), and the returned Genevan exile Sir Anthony Cooke (1565). The sole church dignitary to appear is Edmund Grindal, Bishop of London and latterly Archbishop of Canterbury, with three letters.[23] The French Church in London, as with many other refugee congregations,[24] experienced difficulties which obliged Beza to intervene with the Church and its pastor Jean Cousin in 1569.[25]

If the contact with England is surprisingly weak, the almost non-existence of Scottish correspondence (three pieces) is puzzling, and indicates a possible major loss of letters. Despite good personal relations between Beza and Knox, and their solidarity in religious matters, only one letter from Beza (1569), in which he clarifies the reason for his not writing for three years – postal difficulties and the troubles[26] – was received. The other two consist of a letter from the professors and pastors of Scotland, which illustrates their loyalty to the later Swiss confession,[27] and one from a military officer, the Scot Robert Stuart.[28]

In contrast, contact with the Holy Roman Empire increases (eighty-three pieces), namely 9 per cent: a first radical increase in 1556–57, connected with Beza's travels in search of broad agreement with the Lutherans, then a plateau from 1558 to 1568, with a strange gap after the publication of the Heidelberg Catechism (1563), and finally, a strong increase between 1569 and 1570, where these letters constitute 19 per cent and 22 per cent of the total, because of the disciplinarian debate in the Palatinate, and the progress of Reformation beliefs in Saxony and at Nuremberg.

From the geographical point of view, there are four main centres. The first is Strasbourg (twelve pieces), thanks to correspondence with theologians sympathetic to the Reformation: Zanchi who had to leave Strasbourg at the request of the church president Marbach (1563), and the Rector Jean Sturm. Second is Nuremberg (eight pieces), due to Dr Camerari in the main and to the pastor Durnhoffer. These two correspondents do not appear, however, until the end of the period, when Melanchthonian ideas predominated in the imperial city. Although we have no letters from Melanchthon himself, Wittenberg, where Lutheran orthodoxy was not to be established before 1575, is represented by his son-in-law Caspar Peucer (nine pieces), and by a university master, Rüdinger. Paradoxically, the exchange of letters with Heidelberg (twelve) is limited: it includes the Elector Frederick III, the lawyer Erastus at the time when the latter was one of the principal figures there and the theologians Olevian and Strigel. Outside these four centres there was isolated correspondence with students, pastors such as Pincier, writing to Welter in Nassau, and Toussain, head of the Church in Montbéliard, two landgraves of Hesse, the group of Reformed pastors from Emden in East Friesland, and the philologist Camerarius of Leipzig.

In reality, nearly half the letters deal with theologians (thirty-seven pieces), academics, church leaders or simple pastors. Other academics (thirty letters) are represented by a few names such as Joachim Camerarius (eleven pieces), Jean Sturm, Peucer, and Simonius. These are followed by politicans (sixteen pieces): three princes, the Elector Palatine Frederick III (four pieces) and the Landgraves Philip and William of Hesse, and influential men such as Erastus (four pieces), the diplomat Languet, a Frenchman in the service of electoral Saxony (three pieces), and Herdesianus, a noble and consul of Nuremberg.

Contacts with Eastern Europe were established late. With Poland (thirty-three pieces) they begin properly in 1565. From then on, Beza is much in demand, mainly on the matter of anti-trinitarianism. His main correspondents include the two theologians Thretius (ten letters) and à Lasco (eight letters). Among others figure two noblemen, a master, a humanist, and Prince Nicolas Radziwiłł, patron of the adherents of Reform in Lithuania. Beza, anxious about the advances made by the anti-trinitarians, is concerned to provide arguments for his followers, notably in a preface (15 August 1570) addressed to the nobility, pastors, and faithful of Poland.[29]

With Hungary, contact maintained by Bullinger and Zürich began in 1568, producing thirteen pieces, of which three-quarters (nine pieces) concern Dudith, former Bishop of Pécs who after his wedding (1567) settled in Poland, where he was in sympathy with the anti-trinitarians, from whose cause Beza unsuccessfully tried to turn him in a long epistle.[30] On the same basis, contact with the Hungarian reformers, which was then expanding, was limited: two letters to Melius,[31] the leader of the Hungarian Reformed Church (1579), one to a Hungarian student of theology in 1568 and, finally, a long letter from the Fathers of the Upper Hungarian Church in the same year.[32]

If Scandinavia is totally lacking because of its Lutheranism, the Mediterranean countries are represented only by a pastor from the Vaud, Lentulus, who in 1561 describes the troubles of his countrymen,[33] and by Italian and Spanish refugees. These include unstable elements who sow dissension in their host communities, always excepting the Italian physician Grataroli, a refugee in Basel, who writes to Beza four times between 1557 and 1563. Equally, there is the Spanish refugee, Cassiodoro de Reina, who was in charge for a while of the refugee communities in London and Strasbourg, but whose ideas were hardly orthodox (four pieces). There was also a Spanish monk who caused problems in the London community in 1568 and 1569, and two Italians who were accused in 1566 of sowing dissension in the Church in Lyons: one of them is referred to as a 'Church troublemaker'.[34]

II. CONTENT

Beza's correspondence, from his settling in Lausanne, then Geneva, over a period of about twenty years, allows an insight into his preoccupations. The position of his co-religionists in France remains at the centre of his worries, and he made periodic efforts to support their cause. In 1552, he proposed an agreement between France, England, and the Swiss Cantons to oppose both pope and emperor.[35] In 1554, he closely followed the plan to receive in Geneva those Vaudois[36] who had been persecuted in Merindol and Cabrières in Provence.[37] Before the Colloquy of Poissy, he nurtured the illusion that the Reformation would be established throughout the kingdom either by royal prerogative, or by intervention by princes of the blood royal or even by the Estates-General. In 1557, he made two journeys through the Swiss Protestant cantons and through the Lutheran principalities of the south-western empire. His intention was to raise and send a delegation to Henry II. In the spring it was to plead in favour of the persecuted Vaudois in Piedmont, and in the autumn in favour of several Protestants who faced the death penalty. But the diplomatic intention of creating closer relations was transformed into a Profession on the Last Supper which provoked Bullinger's wrath. We see this in the sheer brevity of the phraseology and the curtness of the style.[38] Occasionally, he is most precise and persistent: on 22 September 1557, he addressed a hand-written request to the councils of Zürich, Basel and Schaffhausen for a second embassy, supported by an educational project.[39]

From 1559 to 1561, the correspondence is a remarkable source of information on the state of France before the Wars of Religion. Beza is then at his peak: the indispensable counsellor of Protestant princes and of French Churches, and a diplomatic intermediary. Nevertheless, he is anxious to maintain his control over the churches in France, and to keep them in patient submission to royal authority.

In spite of this hectic activity, he managed somehow to follow closely the changes occurring in the Palatinate, in which the elector was moving slowly towards Calvinism. In addition, he oversaw the theological conflicts of the Polish Reformation which together with Calvin he supported against anti-trinitarianism.

In 1562, with the outbreak of the Wars of Religion, Beza became a leader of the Huguenot Party. The party engaged in an intensive correspondence with all the churches of France, and with pastors, witness appeals to the churches of the kingdom (20 March and 5 April 1562)[40] to demand money and troops, and to Swiss and German co-religionists to raise troops and to seek to block those of the adversary. After the defeat at Dreux, he even attempted to cause the Swiss, Germans and English to intervene.

From 1563 Beza ceased travelling. Henceforward, his correspondence became the major instrument of influencing events. France remained at the centre of his activities. In 1564, he tried to get agreement with his Swiss friends Bullinger and Haller over inclusion in the treaty of Lausanne of a clause which might guarantee observation of the edict of pacification. In 1565 he addressed the Reformed nobility of France, asking them to maintain discipline in church matters and to sustain doctrinal purity.[41] His letters include valuable information on the internal struggles of the Huguenot Party, on the schism in several major churches such as Lyons and Orléans, on the semi-clandestine caucuses during the second and third Wars of Religion, on internal stresses, intrigues, factional disputes, and the like. From time to time, he deplores '*impietas*', '*avaritia*', and the capriciousness and taste for luxury of the French Churches.[42] In an unpublished letter to Coligny, Beza defines the links between civil and ecclesiastical authority, and strongly defends the disciplinary authority of the consistories. In addition, he assigns to ministers the role of the counsellor-prophet, and to the princes that of foster fathers of the Church.[43] In 1568, he conveys confidential messages from certain Swiss protestant military chiefs to the Huguenots. In general terms, from 1567 to 1570, military and political problems predominate to the point that information about the pastors and the communities becomes scarce.

In spite of its political range and interest, that part of the correspondence which relates to French affairs shows up the limitations of Beza's understanding of the French situation. As a man of the north, Burgundy, he underestimated the distinction between northern France, where the Protestants remained a small minority, and southern France, where they constituted a majority in many towns. Furthermore, with the exception of Margaret of Navarre, most of his correspondents are from the north. Despite a long stay at Nérac, albeit at a princely court, he seems not to understand the Midi and its urban environment.

More seriously, however, Beza made two major miscalculations. Influenced by the course of the Reformation in the Protestant territories of the empire and in the Swiss confederation, he overestimated the role of the elites in imposing the Reformation from above. As only part of the nobility and the urban classes subscribed to the Reformation, they were unlikely to be able to use their authority to impose it upon the population at large.

Furthermore, the iconoclastic movement which emerged during the first War of Religion in 1562 deeply shocked a large section of the population, especially among the lesser folk, the peasantry, and the urban artisans who clove to traditional religion and images. From then on, the Protestants were regarded by these groups as outsiders and heretics. This process intensified over the following years and totally passed Beza by.

The focuses of interest are more clearly defined; for Switzerland, the main concern is to oppose the raising of troops on behalf of the French king and the Catholics; in 1566, Beza is most concerned with the elaboration of the Swiss Confession, then in 1569–70 by the hand-over of the bailiwicks given up by the Treaty of Lausanne (1564) to Savoy, which isolated Geneva from the rest of the confederation. In fact, in the case of the Swiss cantons, Beza's interest was confined to relations with France and matters of purely Genevan concern. Beza, like Geneva itself, was kept at arm's length from the diets of the Reformed cantons.

Inside the empire, Beza undertook several missions between 1557 and 1559, in which he attempted to revive the idea of a symposium between Lutheran and Swiss theologians, which by settling once and for all the question of the Last Supper, would lead to union among the Protestants to the benefit of their French co-religionists. This approach opened up opportunities for him in Germany, particularly at Wittenberg. Afterwards, he viewed with sympathy the progress made by Calvinism in the Palatinate; then he was anxious about the polemic between the Reformed Protestants and the Lutherans concerning the Heidelberg catechism. His strict attitude here – 'May the Lord protect us from the heaven of the Brentists as much as from the hell of the Papists'[44] – allows for a certain uncharacteristic moderation in the polemic itself. In 1566 he was much involved in negotiations to protect the Elector Palatine from conviction by the Diet of Augsburg. It is for this reason that he was one of the leading figures and supporters of the Later Swiss Confession of 1566; he also intervened with the English and Scottish pastors to seek their signature to it, as well as that of certain German princes. He was convinced that a conviction would seriously weaken the position of the Reformed Protestants in France and the Low Countries. Later on, Germany played but a small part: moderation in the polemics between Lutherans and Reformed Protestants, worries about image worship, and a hesitancy in replying to some of his opponents such as Andreae of Tübingen are his major preoccupations. During the dispute on discipline – either the Genevan or Zürich model – Beza tried not to aggravate the quarrel and to preserve brotherly contacts with Zürich.

In fact, after his failure of 1557, he only occasionally intervened on behalf of the reformers or theologians on the fringes of the reforming movement, just as he did in the rest of Protestant Europe. His reticence on the question of the Low Countries which after all played a major part in European politics from 1566 onwards is truly astonishing. In fact, Beza and Bullinger divided up the task of spreading the reforming message between them: Beza concentrated on the kingdom of France whereas Bullinger turned his attention more towards the Low Countries, the empire, and Central Europe.

Readers will be aware that the published correspondence is confined to preserved pieces which, according to Alain Dufour, may represent only a quarter or a third of the total. Some have disappeared by accident or by inadvertency. For example, only two out of five letters written between 19 December 1562 and 31 January 1563 have survived.[45] Only one letter out of twenty written by Beza on 7 June 1565 has been found.[46] Others were intercepted by opponents, a frequent concern for the author: in 1565, he had wanted to avoid letters to Ambrosius Blaurer falling into the hands of others.[47] Moreover, he himself destroyed some letters out of sheer caution: in 1565, he incinerated a large number of letters he had received every month.[48]

As regards the historical value of his correspondence, Beza has at his disposal a complete system of distribution; just as the English diplomat resident in Strasbourg in 1566, Dr Christopher Mundt, was closely in touch with the Palatinate and the church president of Zürich[49] and with correspondents in such towns as Schaffhausen, Nuremberg, Heidelberg and Augsburg, so too the correspondence between Beza and Bullinger seems to be primarily an exchange of information. Some letters are proper information sheets for the pastors and the civil authorities of Zürich and Berne.[50] Beza's letter of 12 April 1562 exists in three copies in Neuchâtel, Berne and Zürich.[51] Bullinger, for his part, conveys information received to Blaurer, his informant on German affairs, and to the pastors of Grisons with their connections with Italy.

But in spite of the quality and accuracy of the news obtained – about the alliance between the pope and the Five Catholic Cantons in 1565, for example – the correspondence is not infallible: the coronation of Charles IX took place in Reims, not in Saint-Denis.[52] Sometimes Beza lacks judgement and is carried away by extremes of optimism: he contemplates the possibility in 1561 and 1563 of the conversion of the young Charles IX.[53] Furthermore, during the war years, news is sporadic: Beza complains of this in 1567.[54] Despite its limitations and losses, this correspondence makes an essential contribution to the Reformation forum in the period 1550–70: the ascendancy of Bullinger and the Swiss towns as major correspondents, the pride of place of France as far as content is concerned, interest in the empire, Poland and Hungary, and in political, diplomatic, military, theological and cultural matters. Although living in Geneva from 1563, Beza, together with Bullinger, is the most active theologian in European Protestantism.

Notes

1. *Correspondance de Théodore Bèze*, ed. H. Aubert, F. Aubert, H. Meylan, A. Dufour, C. Chimelli, and B. Nicollier (Geneva, 1960ff).
2. Among the reviews note esp. that on the first 3 vols. by E. Trocmé, 'L'ascension de Théodore de Bèze (1549–1561), au miroir de sa correspondance', *Journal des Savants*, 1965, pp. 607–24.
3. Cf. below n. 48.
4. On Bullinger see the recent summary with a good bibliography by F. Busser in *Theologische Realenzyklopädie*, vol. VII (Berlin, 1981), pp. 375–87.
5. This correspondence is in the course of being published by F. Busser (ed.), *Heinrich Bullinger. Briefwechsel*, vol. I: *Briefe der Jahre 1524–1531* (Zürich, 1973).
6. On this development cf. Trocmé, 'L'ascension'.
7. On this conflict cf. *Correspondance de Théodore Bèze*, vol. XI (Geneva, 1983), nos. 775, 778, 798, 801.
8. Cf. ibid., vol. IX (Geneva, 1978), nos. 592, 624.
9. Cf. ibid., vol. XI, nos. 773, 777.
10. On the philosopher Peter Ramus cf. ibid., no. 810.
11. Ibid., vol. VIII (Geneva, 1976), nos. 527 A and B, 540.
12. Ibid., vol. VII (Geneva, 1973), nos. 468, 523; ibid., vol. VIII, no. 567.
13. The letter of 24 August 1565 is in ibid., vol. VI (Geneva, 1970), no. 412.
14. The churches were those in Paris (three letters), Lyons (three letters), the Dauphiné, Alençon, Nîmes, La Ferté, Besançon, La Rochelle and Orléans.
15. Letter of 28 October 1564 in *Correspondance de Théodore Bèze*, vol. V (Geneva, 1968), no. 363.
16. Letters of 20 March and 5 April 1562, appendices III and V, and that of March 1566, appendix IV, in ibid., vol. IV (Geneva, 1965), pp. 254, 259, and ibid., vol. VII, p. 331. In 1562 after Vassy a rallying-cry to the Protestant party engaged in the war was at stake, while in 1566 Beza was seeking to re-invoke the 1559 Confession of Faith.
17. Ibid., vol. VIII, no. 570.
18. Ibid., vol. VI, appendices IV and VIII.
19. Ibid., vol. VII, nos. 445, 455.
20. Ibid., no. 489, p. 198.

21. Ibid., vol. V, no. 371.
22. Ibid., vol. VII, no. 476, p. 143.
23. The two other English correspondents are the Puritan leader Coverdale (1566) and the Dean of Oxford Sampson (1567).
24. Ph. Denis, *Les églises d'étrangers en pays rhénans (1538–1564)* (Paris, 1984).
25. *Correspondance de Théodore Bèze*, vol. X (Geneva, 1980), no. 659.
26. Ibid., no. 677, which refers to another letter of 1566, now lost.
27. Ibid., vol. VII, appendix IX.
28. Ibid., no. 507.
29. Ibid., vol. XI, appendix IV.
30. Ibid., no. 780 of 18 June 1570.
31. Ibid., nos. 750, 781. On Melius see the recent article by L. Makkai, 'Peter Melius, the Hungarian Reformer', *Études historiques hongroises*, 1985, pp. 1–18.
32. *Correspondance de Théodore Bèze*, vol. IX, appendix IVb.
33. Ibid., vol. VI, pp. 309–10.
34. Ibid., vol. VII, nos. 471, 475.
35. Ibid., vol. I (Geneva, 1960), no. 22, p. 77.
36. On the Vaudois in Provence cf. G. Audisio, *Les Vaudois du Lubéron. Une minorité en Provence (1460–1560)* (*sine loc.*, 1984).
37. *Correspondance de Théodore Bèze*, vol. I, no. 44, p. 128. The project in the end came to nought.
38. Cf. ibid., vol. II (Geneva, 1962), no. 98, p. 75.
39. Ibid., appendices XI and XII.
40. Ibid., vol. IV (Geneva, 1965), appendices III and IV, pp. 254, 259.
41. Ibid., vol. VI, appendix II.
42. Ibid., vol. VIII, pp. 69, 94.
43. Ibid., appendix VII.
44. Ibid., vol. V, p. 37.
45. Ibid., vol. IV, p. 125, no. 1.
46. Ibid., vol. VI, p. 106, no. 14. All the letters sent the same year to Thretius have likewise been lost.
47. Ibid., p. 168.
48. Ibid., p. 179.
49. Ibid., vol. VII, p. 176, n. 16.
50. Ibid., vol. IV, no. 249.
51. Ibid., p. 84.
52. Ibid., vol. III (Geneva, 1963), p. 115.
53. Ibid., p. 226, letter of 25 November 1561; ibid., vol. IV, p. 146, letter of 12 May 1563.
54. Ibid., vol. VIII, p. 186.

13 Bodin's Universe and its Paradoxes: Some Problems in the Intellectual Biography of Jean Bodin

P. L. Rose

I

Positivistic biographies of Bodin (the only ones there are) have not been much interested in the peculiar quiddity of Bodin's thought but rather sought to place Bodin within various traditions of European thought, seeing him variously as one of the inventors of 'sovereignty', the predecessor of Montesquieu's climatic determinism, a contributor to the bullion theory of inflation, an influence on seventeenth-century English political thought, or one of the founders of the liberal theory of religious toleration. Such approaches have emphasised the positivistic character of Bodin's thought to the neglect of its religious, or, as his biographers reprovingly say, its mystic, element.[1]

There is surely room for a different kind of biography of Bodin which will integrate those aspects of his mind rooted in his own curious religious sensibility and those ideas of his which appeal so much to Whiggish historians of political theory. The focus of a biography of this kind would be on the fabric of Bodin's thought, on his unique combination of opinions, on the connections between various aspects of his thought, and on the interplay of his thought and personality, of his religion and political action. Such a biography would seek to reconstruct Bodin's ideas as he himself understood them, not as his contemporaries received them. Granted this approach would be almost solipsistic but it might uncover things undreamed of in the more conventional universe of Bodin's less idiosyncratic contemporaries.

Taking Bodin whole seems a reasonable alternative to an unfortunately general tendency to detach selected ideas of interest from their original context in Bodin's thought and personality. Most studies of

Bodin have concentrated on two of his works and tended to separate his politico-historical books and his religious writings into rigid compartments.[2] The result of this brutal dissociation and rending of the fabric has been the manufacture of numerous apocryphal difficulties and false paradoxes in Bodin's life and his thought. One might instance the often cited paradox whereby a Bodin of *politique* convictions was quick to embrace the Catholic League in 1589.[3] Sometimes the paradoxes take the form of internal contradictions in Bodin's thought which have the effect of turning Bodin into a muddled chaotic thinker and a hopeless mixer of categories who occasionally caught a glimpse of the pure sun of truth (e.g. of 'sovereignty') through a miasma of congenital stupidity.

One finds a frequent inclination among modern commentators to polarise Bodin's thought by labelling approved elements of that thought as rational or modern and its more disreputable or quaint features as superstitious or medieval. In defence of this practice Bodin's own practice of distinguishing between the 'natural' and 'divine' subjects of his books is often cited (though he is also castigated for his blithe disregard of his own distinction in introducing angels and demons and God into naturalistic discussions of political sovereignty).[4] Here perhaps lie the roots of a great deal of misconception about Bodin for when he uses this opposition of categories he should not be taken to be opposing naturalistic to religious explanations as is usually assumed. In Bodin's universe the natural does not mean the secular and the non-religious but rather is a part of his religious vision. The natural, for Bodin, of course designates the world of nature and is applied to those explanations arising out of that world such as his climatic theory of history. But this admittedly naturalistic content does not pre-empt or exclude the presence of additional – and often fundamental – elements of religious explanation in these theories. As will be seen, Bodin's theories of history and politics are natural and religious at the same time; it is only to a modern mind accustomed to oppose secular or naturalistic ideas of politics to divine and religious ones that Bodin appears to be a paradoxical thinker.

All Bodin's ideas are religious, even such apparently purely naturalistic ones such as sovereignty; for Bodin's conception of sovereignty depends on two principles of an essentially religious character. One of these is the principle that the preserving or governing power of God inhibits the tendency of all things natural and human to degeneration and decay; the other principle is that God preserves by the action of his will in giving laws which maintain the universe. From these archetypal religious principles, which dominate all of Bodin's thought from 1566 or even earlier, flows the political theory of sovereignty as the power to make laws which will preserve the state from its inherent tendency to degenerate into disorder. This religious and moral foundation, built into Bodin's theory of sovereignty from its birth, renders sterile any attempt to understand Bodinian sovereignty in purely political, juristic or naturalistic terms.

In Bodin's universe there are certainly subject divisions of convenience between politics and witchcraft, between natural philosophy and ethics, between economics and theology and so on, but the entire vision which holds this universe together and makes sense of each of its constituent parts is religion. To extrude religion from the study of Bodin's politics means distorting the meaning of the *République*.

To demonstrate these claims fully in the space of an article is impossible and a full biography of Bodin, phrased in his own categories and drawing out the religious essence of each of Bodin's works, would demand a book. Perhaps, however, the present paper may serve as the critical framework for such a portrait of Bodin.

Much of what follows is negative in that it attempts to demolish a clutch of misconceptions and false paradoxes concerning Bodin in a very short space. But some reconstructions of particular aspects of Bodin's thought are ventured and if they seem fragile when considered individually, nevertheless taken collectively they seem to me to acquire a certain cumulative and corroborative power which lends each one plausibility. To construct a coherent picture in which all the departments of Bodin's universe are reasonably well related to one another is all that it is intended here.

II

The best known, or rather the most notorious, paradox in Bodin has been the fact that the man who wrote the 'enlightened and rationalistic' *Heptaplomeres* defending religious freedom of belief could at the same time be capable of perpetrating the 'superstitious and intolerant' *Démonomanie* which demanded the prompt burning of all witches. For Voltaire, the *Démonomanie* damned Bodin irredeemably as the 'proctor-general of Beelzebub' but most rationalistic commentators have coped with this paradox by quickly dismissing the work as an inexplicable aberration. Let us try to do better.

It goes without saying that belief in witches was widespread among

French intellectuals in the sixteenth century and far from treated as superstition. Bodin's biographers implicitly accept this when they excuse the *Démonomanie* as an 'uncharacteristic' lapse into the superstition of his own time. But was this belief so uncharacteristic of Bodin's *own* thought? Far from being an aberration it can be easily demonstrated that the *Démonomanie* forms an integral part of Bodin's mental universe. Indeed the *Heptaplomeres* and the *Démonomanie* both depend on the same core of religious and philosophical doctrines.[5] In both we find the central belief in a universe of spirits – angelic and demonic – and this in turn depends on Bodin's fundamental belief in a great divine creator intervening in human affairs and using his angels and demons to establish cosmic justice. If we destroy this spiritual universe, we also destroy justice and with it the moral and intellectual aspects of human life.

Does this kind of Providential intervention through angels and demons destroy man's free will? Here is one of the recurrent paradoxes of Western thought but Bodin, both in the *Démonomanie* and his later religious writings, devoted all his efforts to showing that it was *une question mal posée*. For Bodin the entire problem of grace and free will arose out of Christian misconceptions of God and man. Instead Bodin sought an alternative religious understanding drawing heavily on Jewish ideas and sources such as Philo and Maimonides. This is a question to which we shall return but it is mentioned here because the concept of will and free will is central to all of Bodin's thought and dominates both the benighted *Démonomanie* and its alleged antithesis, the enlightened *Heptaplomeres*.[6]

We can now appreciate why a chance judicial encounter with witches in 1578 was enough to trigger the violent outburst of the *Démonomanie*. Placed in a highly receptive frame of mind thanks to his religious opinions Bodin could easily be shocked into an instant and intense recognition of witches. With the whole religious structure of his mind being already attuned to these beliefs, the actual details of the demonology could be elaborated quickly enough. In the first place Bodin's belief in a moral universe governed by Providence was bound up with the idea of a universe inhabited by angels and demons in direct contact with man. The contact sometimes takes the good form of prophecy as mediated by angels to man, sometimes the evil form of sorcery as between demons and men. This belief in spiritual conversation was absolutely central to Bodin's religion. Secondly, man's free will enabled him to choose either to obey or violate the commandments of God. In disobeying God man exposed himself to the demons who were there either to punish him for disobedience or to incite him to graver disobedience still. The witches' pact with the devil was simply the most explicit acknowledgement of disallegiance to God. Witches destroyed cosmic justice and harmony and called forth the retribution of both God and man. Hence it is not as surprising as some think to find that Bodin's theory of religious toleration did not apply to witches and atheists. The basis of that theory was Bodin's conviction that all religions shared to a greater or lesser degree an understanding of a divine being and should, on that precise account, be tolerated. Atheism and witchcraft dishonoured and disregarded God – in a word, they were not religions; consequently they fell outside the scope of Bodin's concept of religious toleration, a concept which was scarcely that of the Enlightenment. Seen thus Bodin's seemingly lunatic ideas about witches appear perfectly logical and consistent with his general religious thinking.

What has been said so far should not only be a warning against treating the *Démonomanie* as a 'superstitious' work but also have cautioned us about seeing the *Heptaplomeres* in the excessively rationalistic light in which it is often regarded. The *Heptaplomeres* is in fact based on a religious vision of cosmic peace and harmony rather than upon an eighteenth-century sort of philosophical belief in natural religion as is often thought. Bodin was careful to point this out in the text in his refutations of Toralba (the advocate of natural religion) and this stance again is perfectly consistent with all his other published writings. Bodin preaches a religion formed both of nature *and* revelation, *but* – the revelation is not Christian. God reveals his purpose to man through a series of prophets whom he has inspired and of whom the greatest are Moses and Christ (Christ, it should be noted, is never described by Bodin as the divine redeemer or saviour).[7] This intensely prophetic theism depends so heavily on the Old Testament that it resembles Judaism without ritual (if there is such a thing). At any rate it earned Bodin the reputation of being a secret Jew or of Jewish descent.[8]

There is, consequently, considerable reason to doubt whether the theory of toleration for which the *Heptaplomeres* is famous can be placed in the naturalistic or philosophical tradition as is so often done. Bodin's theory is certainly far closer to Castellio in being based on a religious vision of harmony though unlike Castellio's Bodin's vision is not at all Christian.

III

Those commentators who have written on the *Heptaplomeres* and the *Démonomanie* have steered clear of the *République* and the *Method*. But awareness of the religious problem in Bodin is critical for an understanding of the apparent paradoxes in these two more 'secular' works.

The *Method* is of course known to everyone as one of the great documents of critical historiography for its refutation of the Four Monarchies theory which had seen in the historical succession of the world empires a prophetic unfolding of the divine will. Its status as a modern and secular work has been further consolidated by its seemingly naturalistic explanations of historical causes. By means of the cyclical theory, for instance, the rise and fall of empires are seen as a phenomenon rooted in nature rather than being the result of divine grace or displeasure. Bodin's modernistic predilection for the natural over the divine may further be seen, it is said, in his theories of geographical and climatic determinism which were resumed in part by Montesquieu. So much for the modern aspects of the *Method*. Now for the contradictions.

The first of these is quite well known; it is that Bodin does introduce a *supernatural* and *superstitious* factor into his historiography by his adoption of astrology and number mysticism. But more important than this is the fact that Bodin invokes divine providence and intervention in a manner which seems to contradict his own emphasis on naturalistic explanation. So too does he introduce such demonic personages as the 'prince of fluid matter' and other assorted spirits. Finally, does not Bodin's insistence in this work on human free will contradict his determinist views of historical causation? These paradoxes, having been conjured up, can just as swiftly be dispelled.

Astrology and numerology, of course, were not universally regarded as superstitious in the sixteenth century, but neither were they entirely seen as supernatural. In so far as they connected phenomena in the natural universe with human history they were indeed naturalistic explanations, though ultimately of course, like everything in the created universe, they were supernatural in that they were ordained by God's will.[9] ('When I speak of natural causes', says Bodin in the *République*, 'I do not mean immediate (efficient) causes, but rather celestial and more remote causes.')[10] The puzzlement which some writers experience on encountering superstitious and supernatural astrology in Bodin reflects their own, not Bodin's, categories.

The remaining more substantial 'paradoxes' may be resolved if four aspects of Bodin's religion are kept in mind. First, one should note that in the *Method* Bodin is careful to avoid ascribing omnipotence to natural causes. This permits him to accept the existence, as it were, of habitual laws of nature and at the same time retain a belief in miracles which contravene those laws (rather like the nominalistic distinction between the *potentia absoluta* of God represented by his intervention to produce miracles and his *potentia ordinata* reflected in the habitual working of the universe).[11] Secondly, for Bodin God and nature are not mutually exclusive for God acts through and in nature at all times. Thirdly, the fact that human free will and natural causation shape history does not preclude the operation of Providence. Fourthly, the division in Bodin's religious thought between 'supernatural' and 'natural' is predicated upon his distinction between the incorporeal God on the one hand and all his creation on the other. Such spiritual entities as demons and angels belong, 'paradoxically', among the corporeal creatures and though they share a certain universal *pneuma* or *spirit* (which emanates from what might be called the *Logos* or the *Shekinah*) their corporeal *pneuma* is quite different from that of the transcendent God himself. The demons are part of the *natural* world although they belong to its department of *extraordinary* or *violent*, rather than *ordinary*, beings and forces. (This appears clearly in Bodin's *Theatrum*, a religious account of the natural universe, where he distinguishes for instance between 'ordinary' winds arising out of natural causes and 'violent or extraordinary' tempests raised by demons.) Bearing these points in mind it comes then as no surprise to find the 'prince of fluid matter' in the *Method* acting as the *natural* spirit which on God's command breaks down the order and justice of both the natural universe and human society and accelerates the natural process of decay inherent in both nature and society, a process restrained only by divine or human will.[12] This very demon symbolises the connection between Bodin's naturalistic and his religious ideas of history. The prince is there as a *natural* cause; he is not merely a diabolically *religious* interloper in the rationalistic historical *Method*. In thinking that Bodin, by rejecting the Four Monarchies theory and advocating natural causation and largely secularised history, most of his critics have mistaken Bodin's insistence on positive truth as far as it may be rationally ascertained for the abolition of the religious element in history. Just as with the *Démonomanie* and the *Heptaplomeres* so too is Bodin's vision of a God ordaining justice in the natural and human universe central to the *Method*.

IV

Bodin's *Theatrum* expounds a religious vision of nature in a dialogue where the physicist is guided by the mystagogue to an understanding of nature which will transform him into a priest.[13] The whole natural universe including all mobile, mutable and corporeal beings constitutes the realm of physics and 'it is the duty of a physicist to treat of angels and demons which are such beings ... metaphysics pertains only to that incorporeal substance which is God himself'. Metaphysics *is* theology. This view of the universe is a curious one, neither wholly materialist nor spiritual. Although it tends to reduce much of what is commonly considered spirit to *nature*, nevertheless spirit is not seen as *material* and there is too a higher realm of spirit which governs the universe. The purpose of physics 'is to grasp a shadow of the Creator through his works'. God himself remains incomprehensible but the understanding of angels and demons, stones and metals, plants and animals, strengthens man's intellectual recognition of God.

Bodin was perhaps the first modern writer to use the term *laws of nature* in physics.[14] He did so out of a religious belief in divine will which he saw imposing law by command on nature. This recognition of laws of nature might seem to be at odds with Bodin's free admission of miracles in nature. But he regarded both miracles and natural law as effects of divine will. The same hand that imposed the laws of nature might also suspend them, usually through the agency of demons. Laws of nature, like demons, are therefore part of the picture of divine justice and one should not be too surprised by the co-existence of such an apparently 'scientific' notion with a 'superstitious' religious one.

It might seem too that Bodin's panpsychic idea that every being in the universe from rocks to men has its own tutelary angel would predispose him to the cause of natural magic. But paradoxically Bodin was one of the most vehement critics of Paracelsus and the magicians. Bodin blamed Paracelsus for separating the demons from their role as executors of divine justice, for giving them an independent, natural existence and for trying to use demons for purely human and usually vicious ends.

Bodin understood the divine laws of nature as intended to prevent the natural degeneration of the universe by imposing a fixed pattern or government upon it. When the pattern breaks down as the result of demonic action, then matter becomes fluid and formless. One stage in this degeneration is the production of monsters which occurs when God allows the demons to relax the fixity of the laws of nature. Such a suspension of order is usually a punishment for human disobedience of divine law as may be seen in Bodin's denunciation of the breeders of botanical and animal hybrids. For Bodin this flagrant disregard of the Deuteronomic prohibitions is punished by the emergence of monstrous and infertile specimens.

The same religious attitude underlies Bodin's attacks on those alchemists who seek to make mercury a seventh chemical metal in order to establish correspondences with the planets. 'This is to insult the divine law' whose imposition of order forbids the mixing of heavenly and earthly hierarchies in this disorderly way. Again we see Bodin's constant fear that the fixed order of nature may break down into fluid matter because of divine displeasure with human vice.

This is the context of Bodin's notorious criticism of Copernicus. For Bodin Copernicus' theory rendered the universe chaotic and hastened its degeneration by postulating four natural notions of the earth – rotation, revolution, trepidation and the pull towards the central sun. 'If this is granted', says Bodin, 'the very foundations of physics fall into ruins, for all agree that a body may have only one natural motion, the others being violent or voluntary. Yet nothing violent in nature can endure continuously.' Hence Copernicus' theory in Bodin's eyes effectively denies the existence of the laws of nature since the additional motions are not ordinary ones but rather extraordinary. Moreover, the diminishing power of these violent motions could only accentuate the natural degeneration of the universe.

Bodin recognised well enough that not all of nature may be fitted into rigid categories and he was aware that the classification of comets was a difficult problem. Here one sees clearly how it was possible for Bodin to be at once credulous and sceptical. In discussing recent comets he admits that the comet of 1573 had no parallax and seemed to be one of the fixed stars. But this opinion, he says, should be rejected since the doctrine of parallax is uncertain and anyway the star disappeared. On the other hand, Bodin is equally doubtful whether comets are terrestrial exhalations; vapours cannot rise that high from the earth. The fact that such ordinary, physical explanations of comets appeared too inconclusive to the sceptical Bodin persuaded him to resort to the (for him) far more certain theological explanation that they were manifestations of divine will portending great events.

We have then in the *Theatrum* a magical universe whose fixed order is fragile and susceptible to degeneration through both human evil and natural decay. Only the law of God preserves the laws of nature and with them the universe.

V

Famous books acquire mythologies of their own, a process promoted greatly by the practice of considering them in isolation from the rest of their author's *oeuvre*. One cannot hope here to dissolve much of the mythological incrustation of the *République* but at least reviewing it in the light of his other writings might expose its accumulation.

The main 'paradoxes' of the *République* may be summed up roughly as follows.

1. The first charge is that the *République*'s weird combination of positive command law and natural law testifies to the hopeless conceptual confusion of its author. As a leading authority has remarked, 'Bodin's doctrine of sovereignty appears to undermine the very possibility of natural law thinking ... It is not possible to conceive a law of nature if command is the essence of law.'[15] Now this is true enough if 'natural law' is understood in the seventeenth-century usage of the phrase. But the point is that Bodin never uses such terms as natural and civil law in their usual seventeenth-century senses, a peculiarity that has been mistaken for stupidity. In fact Bodin is most exact about his terms and meanings. 'There is certainly a difference between *droit* and *loy*. The former means nothing more than equity while *loy* signifies command. For *loy* is nothing other than the command of the sovereign, using his power.'[16] *Droit* he restricts to meaning a reasonable and conventional norm associated with equity. From this it follows that Bodin could scarcely have meant *droit naturel* in the seventeenth-century sense of natural law. *Loi*, on the other hand, always refers to the command of the sovereign, whether of the king of France or of God himself. Bodin speaks often of the *lois* made by the king, and those of nature and God, consistently using the same word. Not only a king's command, but also the commands of natural and divine law constitute Bodin's concept of 'positive command law' or as he usually calls it sovereignty. To oppose Bodin's theory of sovereignty and command law to his ideas of natural law is therefore to construct a false paradox and signifies a fundamental misunderstanding.

2. Bodin's running together of divine and natural law has also been taken as proof of his intellectual confusion. Bodin understood, it seems, by 'natural law' both the natural moral law and the physical laws of nature, seeing both of these as instituted by the command of God. For Bodin natural law is essentially religious, emanating as it does from the will of a creating God.[17] Interestingly enough, Bodin was the first modern author to apply the legal metaphor to physics and indeed even anticipates Descartes' use of the phrase 'the great legislator of nature'.[18] As to the moral law Bodin seems to derive his notions not from the Stoics but – as in the case of the physical law – from Philo who had pointed to the Noachite laws as natural laws. For both Philo and Bodin these natural laws were superseded by the Mosaic law. Moreover, for both Philo and Bodin the Ten Commandments were the embodiment *par excellence* of all law, natural, civil and divine.[19] The major distinction between natural and the divine law, with which it is so closely identified in Bodin, seems to be that the natural Noachite laws were unwritten whereas the Mosaic law was enacted. But the two are nearly congruent as is seen by the fact that Moses himself had written in Genesis an account of God's earlier institution of natural law.[20]

We encounter, therefore, in Bodin an essentially religious vision of law which insisted on law as command and emphasised the correlation of natural and divine law. This religious conception of law forms the skeleton of Bodin's juristic theory of kingship which is really more an advanced species of theocracy than of secular absolutism. The voluntaristic notions of D'Ailly and other medieval writers had prepared the way, but it took Bodin's unique combination of interests in Hebraic religion and legal philosophy and his massive exposition of sovereignty in the *République* to bring this final transformation of theocracy to the centre of the stage.[21] Here it seems to me lies Bodin's true significance in the history of political thought.

As a corollary to the idea of command and natural law and its theocratic underpinning it may be suggested that when Bodin compares the law-giving powers of the king with those of God he is not drawing *analogies* but rather stating the participation of God and king in the same dual functions of law-giving and of preserving, whether in the limited world of the state or in the entire universe. Making Bodin a mere analogiser of God and king is as bad as construing him a precursor of Hobbes or a

simple 'law and order' philosopher.[22] The relationship between
God and king is not just one of analogy but of collaboration; for
Bodin, it is not metaphor but reality. If we go on to the next
'paradox' we can see some of the implications of this relationship.

3. Bodin mixes aspects of divine right theory with a pragmatic
   theory of sovereignty and also advocates absolute but limited
   monarchy: here as usual the root of the trouble lies in the labels.
   Franklin has managed to reconstruct convincingly Bodin's
   understanding of absolutism and shown how different it was
   from how seventeenth-century theorists perceived it.[23] Bodin
   actually built quite definite 'constitutional' limits into the doctrine of royal absolutism while insisting that absolute sovereignty was not constitutional. Thus, he restricted the king's right
   to levy excessive taxes without consent and to force his subjects'
   religion. More generally, he disallowed the king's right, though
   not his ability, to violate natural and divine law. The content of
   Bodin's concept of resistance, as opposed to constitutional
   limitation, is more problematic, but he himself was notorious for
   leading what might cautiously be called the 'constitutional'
   resistance to Henry III's levying of taxes at the Estates of 1576.
   The rationale for this opposition was that the king's actions
   would effectively destroy the ability of the French monarchy to
   preserve the French state. It was philosophically absurd that a
   king whose law-giving (or governing) power had the purpose of
   preserving the state should use that same governing power to
   destroy the state. As in his religious and physical thought,
   Bodin's political thinking is dominated by the notion that
   voluntaristic intervention is necessary to prevent the natural
   degenerative tendency of all created things.

4. There is, it is often said, a disturbing co-existence between practical political thinking in Books I–V and the 'fanciful' numerology of the sixth book of the *République*. If, however, one
   remembers the fundamentally religious outlook of Bodin and
   treats the *République* as an attempt to understand human
   politics within the framework of divine cosmic justice, then
   Book VI ceases to be an irrelevant ramble and becomes instead
   the crowning argument of the work. Again, while the subject
   matter of politics demands attention to concrete political observation and study of human character – just as in the *Method*
   human history had required a sometimes positivistic attitude to

historical facts – nevertheless divine and natural law must always be the boundary of human action.[24] The numerology of Book VI is in fact the interface of human and divine politics; it is a real and natural, not a supernatural or metaphysical, expression of divine justice. Book VI is the crux of the *République* and to dismiss it lightly as being of a quaintly marginal relevance to the 'hard' core of political argument is fatal to comprehending the essentially religious nature of that argument.

5. Most critics have also written off as 'cloudy mysticism' the 'soft' material on virtue in chapter I of Book I. The affinity of the *République* with the later moral and religious writings of Bodin is marked, both in words and ideas, and it is impossible to understand the *République* divorced from Bodin's theory of virtue. In the first chapter of the book Bodin proclaims the individual good and the good of the republic to be the same; the object of the state is not 'order' but the promotion of the citizens' contemplation and enjoyment of the highest sovereign good – *ce grand Prince de nature*, God himself. Despite the objections of many, says Bodin, the good and happiness of a citizen are identical with those of an individual man and so in contributing to individual contemplative virtue the republic also consolidates its own security. 'If a man is judged virtuously wise and happy, so too the republic will be happy, and a republic having many such citizens will be fortunate even if it is not powerful or wealthy.' 'The principal end of the well-ordered republic is contemplative virtue ... political actions are the necessary road to the achievement of contemplation ... as they approach this principal end the nearer, so are well-ordered republics the happier.' The true essence of politics and the state is virtue – not mere order as sometimes argued – and the true essence of virtue is *vera religio*.

VI

In a rather recondite juristic section of the *République* is to be found the germ of a major biographical paradox which bears on our general understanding of the twenty years of Bodin's life between the publication of the *République* and his death in 1596 and affects our whole understanding of Bodin's personality.[25] Here the problems of personality and thought intersect in the most dramatic way. According to recent commentators, Bodin in the edition of 1583 advocated his support for Henry of Navarre in the contest for the succession to the French throne and made his views even plainer in the Latin version published in 1586. Then, in 1589–90, Bodin suddenly reversed, deserting Henry IV for the Catholic League's candidate, the cardinal Charles de Bourbon. Beyond question Bodin supported the League's man in 1589–90 but his critics have gone far beyond this 'fact' to infer that Bodin committed himself to the League's whole programme and betrayed himself up and down, abandoning his earlier belief in religious toleration, his earlier juristic theory of the crown law of succession, his personal loyalties to Navarre, his *politique* ideas of politics and monarchy and his prohibition of religious war.

In rebuttal, the first point to make is that Bodin never was a committed member of Navarre's party. As to the alleged changes in successive versions of the *République* there has been incredible confusion over what Bodin actually said, let alone what he changed. Despite what his current critics allege, Bodin never directly supported Navarre in the 1583 edition; these critics have also failed to notice that in the 1586 edition Bodin actually came out with a firm juridical argument against Navarre. Moreover, I think it can be shown that it was juridical principle, not coercion or opportunism, which was behind this elucidation in the edition of 1586. There are obvious signs in the 1583 version that Bodin was deeply troubled by the extent to which his succession theory relied on Roman law; in preparing his Latin translation of 1586 he put these doubts to rest by changing his whole theory so as to conform more to French custom. This had the effect of eliminating Navarre as the prime claimant to the throne although it made him second in line as we shall see. These remarks are intended to suggest that Bodin's betrayal of Navarre under the threats of the League in 1589–90 is nothing more than a myth concocted by modern historians.[26]

Yet apart from this editorial muddle there still remains the 'fact' that Bodin, paradoxically for a *politique*, supported the League in 1589–90. The only way to dispel this 'paradox' is to look at it through Bodin's own eyes and interpret it again in the light of his religious sensibility. From his earliest to his final writings a recurrent theme is that of divine retribution awarded as part of divine cosmic justice. Under the catastrophic impact of the civil war which followed Henry III's assassination of the Guise in 1589 the theme of divine chastisement through war came to dominate Bodin's letters and writings – and not only his, but those of many other well-known *politiques* such as Guillaume du Vair. Given the fact that from 1586 Bodin believed in the juristic right of the cardinal to succeed to the throne, given that many *politiques* who were royal officials collaborated like Bodin with the League in the hope of being able, as du Vair put it, to 'slacken the violence cunningly', given too that a main theme of Bodin's moral and political thought in the *République* and later was the absolute duty of all citizens to take sides in a civil war, given the League's control of his residence of Laon, given that Bodin always maintained that order and authority were preferable to anarchy and frequently cited the maxim *Salus populi suprema lex esto*, and most of all given his conviction that the conflict was all part of God's vengeance on a sinful France which had polluted religion and justice – all this makes it easily understandable how the *politique* Bodin could accept the war with a certain feeling of gratification and at the same time declare himself publicly and privately for the League. If Bodin's earlier political thought in the *République* was intrinsically religious, just so too his support for the Catholic League and resort to a religious language of politics in 1590 was not at all uncharacteristic. The accidental outbreak of the civil war and prevailing external circumstances forced Bodin to behave in a certain conventional fashion but his behaviour was deeply in tune with that religious sensibility which had long formed part of his character. As he abruptly remarked in his *Lettre* to a *politique* correspondent: '[I hear] that you were staggered to learn that I was a *Ligueur*; in answer I tell you that I am pleased to know you are well.' Bodin knew his own religious mind well enough not to be surprised at his actions.[27]

But to revert to his support of the League. This is not a simple fact; rather it conceals a cluster of facts and problems. What does 'support' mean? Precisely which policies of the League did he support? How did his views evolve during the five years of protracted war after 1589? These are questions rarely posed but it can be said that there is no trace in Bodin's League letters of any support for the League's revolutionary third fundamental law of the crown – Catholicity. Certainly Bodin urged Henry IV to convert, but so did those of Bodin's *politique* friends who were closely tied to Navarre's party. And Navarre himself in 1593 took their advice. Finally, even Bodin's illicitly published League *Lettre* implicitly acknowledged the right of Navarre to succeed his uncle the cardinal, a right the League repudiated. The biographical 'paradox' here stems ultimately from a crude use of labels like *politique* and *ligueur* without appreciating the variety of political complexions which either party comprised.

VII

Before leaving Bodin and the League one further 'paradox' might spring to the critically alert mind. How could Bodin have supported the League and acquiesced in religious war at the very same time he was composing the eirenic *Heptaplomeres* preaching a harmonious peace among all religions? The obvious answer is that the *Heptaplomeres* was an escape from the horrors of war and typical of a widespread movement among French writers of the time. Bodin himself said in 1591 that he had been forced by experience of massacres and disaster to devote himself to subjects of moral and religious philosophy. It would be wrong to take this as an escapist statement. Rather it seems that Bodin turned to those moral subjects in an effort to explain why such disasters were occurring. We should further note the surprising fact that the concept of religious war was not excluded from the peaceful *Heptaplomeres* though Bodin's idea of religious war was certainly not that of the Catholic League. For Bodin, as we have seen, it was sometimes a chastisement by God, sometimes a war against atheists and sectarian traducers of true religion; not as the League would have it the pursuit of a narrow confessional and political programme.[28] If we agree that Bodin's understanding of religious war and religious peace was indeed profoundly rooted in his vision of God, then both the League *Lettre*'s theme of divine vengeance and the embracing of peace and harmony in the *Heptaplomeres* may be seen as related facets of Bodin's prophetic religion. For him, Isaiah, the prophet of universal peace, represented the loving aspect of God; Jeremiah's prophecies of war and destruction were the grimmer countenance of the Creator. War and peace were both constituents of divine cosmic justice. As Bodin said in his last work on moral philosophy – a religious interpretation of ethics – fear of the Creator is inseparable from love of him.[29] There was no paradox here, simply two complementary sides of true religion.

True religion supplies another dimension to Bodin's perception of religious war. Since all religions shared the essentials of *vera religio* and since external confessional details were for Bodin a matter of indifference, no single church could claim to fight for true religion. On the other hand, Bodin boldly affirms in the *Method* that 'he who would not die for *vera religio* is impious'. The meaning here is that men of all religions must fight against the anti-religions of the atheists and witches, and the hypocrites of all churches. In advocating war *pro vera religione* Bodin was not urging war by Catholics on Huguenots or *vice versa*. Nor, it should be stressed as a corollary, did he oppose civil religious wars between Catholics and Huguenots for merely rationalistic and prudential or *politique* reasons. He opposed conventional religious warfare of the sixteenth century for the very same reason that he demanded war against the witches – namely, the principle of *vera religio*. (One suspects too that many other *politiques* besides Bodin were far more affected by religious feeling than is usually thought.)

Vera religio emerges then as the central vision holding the key to all of Bodin's thought. But what exactly did he mean by true religion? First, belief in a providential God transmitting his intentions to man through the agency of angels and prophets, spirits and men. In Bodin's later works Moses figures as the greatest of prophets, the Decalogue as the divine law of nature and the duty of man is defined again and again in the command of Deuteronomy 'to choose life and love God wholeheartedly'. *Vera religio* is, in Bodin's succinct definition, 'the turning of a pure heart towards God'. Such a religious sensibility is more Hebraic than Christian and the influence, often acknowledged by Bodin, of the two greatest Jewish philosophers, the Alexandrian Philo and the medieval Maimonides, is readily apparent here. From them came much of Bodin's sense of prophecy as well the substance of his critique of the determinist views of Aristotle. A devoted Aristotelian, Maimonides had nevertheless parted company with his master over the eternity of the universe and also rejected the idea of a universe governed strictly by necessity which could not be overridden even by the remote God who was the 'first cause' of it. Such a non-intervening, non-providential God was as unacceptable to Maimonides as to Bodin. To Maimonides also Bodin was indebted for his non-Christian view of virtue. Bodin rejected the Christian division of the virtues into moral, intellectual and theological. Instead he conceived all virtue as intellectual since love of God, which subsumed faith, hope and charity, depends on knowledge of God although ultimately intellectual virtue itself depended on a choice made by free will. But if the higher virtues were no longer theological they were still religious, just as indeed were the rest of the virtues. One should beware of thinking that Bodin's abolition of the theological virtues meant a secularising of virtue as natural. Even free will which might naturally incline to virtue over vice had been granted to man for a religious end. Moreover, virtue was for Bodin 'divinely implanted' into man. Such a position may seem reminiscent of Stoic theories of natural virtue springing from the seeds of divine light placed in man, or contrarily it may recall Aquinas' notion that divine grace perfects nature and natural virtue. But it would be very dangerous to view Bodin through Stoic or Thomist spectacles because these lenses produce deterministic distortions which Bodin sought at all costs to escape. Rather one should look once more to Jewish sources – and there are sound contextual reasons for doing so.

It was Jewish sources with their stress on both divine and human will and the Deuteronomic command to choose willingly life which provided Bodin with an alternative path to that which leads through the deterministic minefields of Christian theology. The defence of free will against determinism, whether of the religious or philosophical kind, whether Aristotelian necessity or Christian grace, was a constant preoccupation of Bodin's. But he also found free will wholly compatible with an intervening God of providence. God's will and man's free will were both aspects of Bodin's voluntaristic conception of the universe and they are the underpinning of all of Bodin's writings. The particular guise that the voluntarism took depended on the precise subject matter of the book – political command in the *République*, pacts with the devil in the *Démonomanie*, willing love of God in the *Heptaplomeres*.

VIII

This paper has insisted on the synthetic unity of Bodin's thought and the need to interpret his work as a whole. But an evolutionary approach is needed at the same time if we are not to distort his thought. The role of biographical accidents in stimulating Bodin to cast his general philosophy in particular guises such as the *Démonomanie* or the League writings has already been mentioned but there are other areas where biographical attention is indispensable. The most important of these is the evolution of Bodin's religious thought itself, a subject full of uncertainties and paradoxes.[30] We now know that Bodin was a Carmelite in his youth but left the order about 1548, perhaps after being placed on trial for heresy. (Carmelite spirituality with its emphasis on prophecy and mystic love may have helped shape Bodin's religious sensibility.) It has been argued that he then went to Geneva and became a Calvinist minister but the evidence for this seems very dubious. In 1562 he took a parliamentary oath of Catholicism although a celebrated letter of the 1560s shows an aversion to Catholic ritual bordering on blasphemy. In 1569 he was arrested with many Huguenots and, refusing to commit himself to the Catholic faith, was kept in prison for a year and a half. In 1572, it seems, he narrowly escaped being murdered in the St Bartholomew Massacre by allowing himself to be vouched for as a Catholic. Thereafter he seems to have remained for the rest of his life officially a member of the Catholic church although his private opinions consisted of the group of beliefs he called *vera religio*. In looking at Bodin's particular works, therefore, one must always bear in mind which phase of his religious biography they represent. This is especially important with the *Method* composed during the confused decade of the 1560s which was perhaps the critical period for the emergence of Bodin's mature religious sensibility. It was, it seems, in 1567–68 that Bodin underwent a spiritual conversion which left him convinced God had sent him a guardian spirit for the rest of his life to counsel against evil. So was achieved Bodin's elevation to the status of a prophet of the first (lowest) degree. This religious turmoil may have directly impinged on Bodin's political views if as Franklin has argued there was an apparent shift in Bodin's politics from 'constitutionalism' to 'absolutism' between the 1566 edition of the *Method* and the appearance of the *République* in 1576.[31] But to demonstrate this shift fully two things still appear necessary. One is a proper collation of the variants of three editions of the *Method* of 1566, 1572 and 1576, which might document the change rather more precisely than has been done. Secondly, and more importantly, a deeper study of Bodin's general development between 1566 and 1576 is required. Much more attention needs to be paid to the shift from the optimistic enthusiasm, almost a belief in 'progress', of 1566 to the more pragmatic and restrained outlook of 1576, a change perhaps best registered in the modulations of Bodin's religious thought in this period. I suspect, however, that one may find, as with the history of Bodin's view of the Bourbon succession, that the *République* represents more a clarification of previously blurred ideas than a real shift or reversal of opinion.

Yet despite the need to understand Bodin's thought in an evolutionary way it can be said that much of his intellectual stance was settled from fairly early on. In fact, a close examination of the early *Oratio* of 1559 shows that he had even then arrived at many of his mature views though in a rough and sometimes inchoate form. Above all he had arrived by 1559 at a vision of the Great God of Nature which would fuse together the divine and the natural in a synthesis typical of his mature thought. In his subsequent writings, the music (and his favourite metaphors are musical – the harmony of the universe, the great choir of creation) remained the same, though in each opus the libretto changed to suit the subject.

Bodin's addiction to such universalising metaphors has tended to attract the description 'Platonic' to his thought. There are indeed many Platonic elements to be found in Bodin but it seems to me that Philo was a far more powerful communicator of this kind of thinking to Bodin. In the 1550s Philo was attaining popularity in France. In 1552, Turnèbe (with whom Bodin later exchanged charges of plagiary) brought out the Greek edition of Philo and two years later the Latin translation followed going into several editions. In Philo were to be found many of the sources of Bodin's religion – the principles of order and hierarchy of being, the equivalence of natural and divine law, the peculiar non-Stoic and non-Christian idea of the *pneuma* and its application to both the human soul and the angelic and demonic spirits, the Hebraic idea of prophecy and its links with virtue, the idea of a revealing Great God of Nature. There too may be the seeds of Bodin's political concepts of law and sovereignty and the emphasis on the twin functions of law giving and preserving. It seems that it was Bodin's first reading of Philo in the 1550s which inspired him to conceive of a universal, non-confessional religion, predominantly naturalistic in character though leaving some small allowance for revelation. This marks the first stage of Bodin's conversion to *vera religio*. A second stage was attained by 1566 with Bodin's embracing a Judaised *vera religio* which revolved around the two poles of purification and prophecy and exalted the role of prophetic revelation. It was a re-reading of Philo in 1567–68 that precipitated the third stage where Bodin received the marks of prophecy including the acquisition of a guardian angel. Through these conversions Bodin arrived at the greatest of paradoxes, a natural religion which was at the same time revealed, with a God who was both transcendent and immanent.

Looking back over the various topics discussed it should be fairly clear that the main polarity of this collection of bogus 'paradoxes' is between what might be called the natural and the divine. The solution to all these 'paradoxes' as well as to the real problems depends really on looking at Bodin on his own terms and when this is done it soon becomes clear that what seems to us to be a constant tension between God and nature never appeared as such to Bodin. This fundamental paradox of the divine and the natural has troubled most Christian thinkers who have generally tried to reconcile the rift between a transcendent Creator and Creation by a vision of Christ as the great restorer of the broken bond. But we should remember that Bodin for most of his life was not a Christian. For him the two apparently opposed qualities of God and creation were reconciled in his unifying formula of the Great God of Nature, the great Legislator of Nature, the immanent yet transcendent God. Every single area of Bodin's encyclopaedic concern – history, ethics, politics, law, natural philosophy – is suffused with this religious spirit. To try to extract and isolate any of these interests from their original religious matrix, to remove the Great God from Nature, is the surest way of producing 'paradoxes' in Bodin's universe. Fifty years ago J. W. Allen remarked that Bodin was essentially a religious thinker. This paper should have illustrated that bald, but accurate, judgement.

Notes

1. H. Baudrillart, *Jean Bodin et son temps* (Paris, 1853) and R. Chauviré, *Jean Bodin, auteur de la République* (Paris, 1914) are the only two full-length biographies to be published.
   The main works of Bodin discussed in this paper are *Methodus ad facilem historiarum cognitionem* (Paris, 1566); *Six livres de la République* (1st edn, Paris, 1576; referenced to the enlarged 2nd edition, Paris, 1583); *Démonomanie des Sorciers* (Paris, 1580); *Lettre de M. Bodin* (on the League) (Paris, 1590); *Paradoxon ... virtutis* (Paris, 1596); *Theatrum universae naturae* (Lyons, 1596); *Heptaplomeres* (manuscript, c. 1588–96). The French version of the *Paradoxe* and the *Lettre* of 1590 have been reprinted in my edition of Jean Bodin, *Selected Writings on Philosophy, Religion and Politics* (Geneva, 1980).
2. For bibliography see *Jean Bodin. Verhandlungen der internationalen Bodin-Tagung*, ed. H. Denzer (Munich, 1973). Also the *Actes du Colloque international 'Jean Bodin'* (Angers, 1985).
3. Discussed below, section VI.
4. For Bodin's distinctions of natural, human and divine see, e.g. *Method for the Easy Comprehension of History*, trans. B. Reynolds (New York, 1969, re-issue), p. 15ff.
5. Good treatments integrating the *Démonomanie* with Bodin's other religious writings are G. Roellenbleck, *Offenbarung, Natur und jüdische Überlieferung bei Jean Bodin* (Gütersloh, 1964). U. Lange, *Untersuchungen zu Bodins Démonomanie* (Frankfurt, 1970). C. R. Baxter, 'Jean Bodin's Daemon and his Conversion to Judaism', in *Verhandlungen*, ed. Denzer, pp. 1–21. C. R. Baxter, 'Jean Bodin's *De la Démonomanie des Sorciers*. The Logic of Persecution', in *The Damned Art*, S. Anglo (ed.), (London, 1977), pp. 76–105.
6. A full account of Bodin's Judaising strategy will be found in my *Bodin and the Great God of Nature* (Geneva, 1980).

7. One of the first to point this out was P. Mesnard, 'La pensée religieuse de Bodin', *Revue du Seizième Siècle*, XVI (1929), pp. 77–121. In later years Mesnard's own attachment to Christianity apparently led him to neglect his earlier findings and to insist on Bodin's Catholicism. This produces great difficulties for the interpretation of Bodin's religious biography and may have effectively blocked Mesnard from writing the general biography he no doubt planned. Many of Mesnard's later articles, however, are indispensable for an understanding of particular works of Bodin.

8. My *Bodin and the Great God of Nature* explains why it is better to refer to Bodin's religion as 'Judaised religion' rather than Judaism. As far as can be established Bodin was not of Jewish descent. See J. Levron, *Jean Bodin et sa famille* (Angers, 1950).

9. Bodin seems to be following Philo and Augustine here. See R. M. Grant, *Miracle and Natural Law in Graeco-Roman and Early Christian Thought* (Amsterdam, 1952), pp. 23ff, 218ff.

10. Bodin, *République* (Paris, 1583), p. 542. Cf. P. Mesnard, 'Jean Bodin à la recherche des secrets de la nature', in *Umanesimo e esoterismo*, ed. E. Castelli (Padua, 1960), pp. 221–34.

11. Bodin's position is very close to that of Philo with whose works he was well acquainted. Cf. Grant, *Miracle*, p. 23ff.

12. *Method*, p. 17.

13. For excellent accounts of the *Theatrum* (though minimising the Judaised character of this work) see P. Mesnard, 'The Psychology and Pneumatology of Jean Bodin', *International Philosophical Quarterly*, II (1962), pp. 244–64. Idem, 'A fisica de Jean Bodin segundo o *Anfiteatro da Natureza*', *Revista Portuguesa de Filosofia*, XVII (1961), pp. 164–200.

14. *Theatrum*, p. 191f.

15. A. P. d'Entrèves, *Natural Law*, 2nd edn (London, 1970), p. 67.

16. *République*, p. 155. Cf. M. Bazzoli, 'Il diritto naturale nella *République* di J. Bodin', *Critica Storica*, VII (1968), 586–93. M. Isnardi-Parente, 'La volontarisme de Jean Bodin: Maimonide ou Duns Scot?', in *Verhandlungen*, ed. Denzer, pp. 39–51.

17. For the background see M. B. Foster, 'Christian Theology and Modern Science of Nature', *Mind*, XLIII (1935), pp. 439–66; XLIV (1936), pp. 1–27.

18. See, for instance, *Theatrum naturae*, p. 191f, for Bodin's idea of physical laws of nature. The phrase '*ce grand législateur de nature*' occurs (albeit it in a moral setting) in the French version of Bodin's *Paradoxon* (*Paradoxe*, Paris, 1598, p. 33). The reference eluded E. Zilsel's survey 'The Genesis of the Concept of Physical Law', *Philosophical Review*, LI (1942), pp. 245–79.

19. For example, in the *Heptaplomeres*. See the translation by M. L. D. Kuntz, *Colloquium of the Seven* (Princeton, NJ, 1975), p. 249. For difficulties in the interpretation of this and other passages, see my *Bodin and the Great God of Nature*.

20. Much of this sort of thinking is to be found in Philo, including an intriguing statement (*De legatione*, p. 68) that *arche* (sovereignty, rule)

is indivisible and cannot be shared. The remark is actually put into the mouth of Caligula and refers to the division of sovereignty *between persons* rather than to the division of sovereignty itself. (The Latin text of Philo was well known to Bodin. The relevant quotation runs: '*quod naturae leges societatem non ferant imperii*'. See Philo, *Lucubrationes omnes* (Lyons, 1555), p. 626.)

21.   F. Oakley, *The Political Thought of Pierre d'Ailly. The Voluntarist Tradition* (New Haven, 1964), ch. 6. Isnardi-Parente, 'Volontarisme', sees Bodin as a Scotist rather than a Maimonidean, but the Jewish influence seems to me to be more important. Bodin's strategy was to use convenient Scotist citations as specious support for opinions which were intrinsically anti-Christian. (Note also that Bodin's theory of toleration has an element of religious voluntarism in that it advises the sovereign not to force the conscience of willing belief of the subject but rather to let *vera religio* rule. Even the prudential theory of toleration in the *République* is religious for prudence consists in recognising the natural and divine law.)

22.   It is misleading to depict Bodin largely in terms of a believer in hierarchies and order. The significant thing about Bodin's hierarchism is the he combines hierarchies with a powerful voluntarism which lends dynamism to an otherwise static form of political theory.

23.   J. H. Franklin, *Jean Bodin and the Rise of Absolutist Theory* (Cambridge, 1973).

24.   *République*, IV, ch. 2, argues that divine causes are a higher form of political explanation than are natural causes, but does not deny the need to understand natural causes.

25.   P. L. Rose, 'The *Politique* and the Prophet. Bodin and the Catholic League 1589–94', *Historical Journal*, XXI (1978), pp. 783–808.

26.   P. L. Rose, 'Bodin and the Bourbon Succession to the French Throne 1583–94', *Sixteenth Century Journal*, IX (1978), pp. 75–98. Much of the blame for the myth of Bodin's betrayal might be laid on poor old Richard Knolles whose 1606 English translation of the *République* now circulates widely in a facsimile edition edited by K. D. McRae (Cambridge, Mass., 1962). Though largely following the Latin *Republica* of 1586 Knolles conflated the variant editions and, in the present case of the succession law, he incorporated a sentence from the French text of 1583 which Bodin expressly struck out from the Latin version of 1586. As it stands that sentence renders the whole English passage self-contradictory and introduces a confusion which is absent from Bodin's own writing. In commenting on the *République* one needs always to consult at least the French editions of 1576 and 1583 as well as the Latin translation of 1586.

27.   *Lettre de M. Bodin* (Paris, 1590), p. 3.

28.   *Paradoxon*, preface (lacking in the French version). Cf. the French version, *Paradoxe*, p. 98, for the explanation of war as divine retribution for moral and religious evil.

29.   *Paradoxe*, p. 96f.

30.   A reconstruction of Bodin's religious development is attempted in Rose, *Bodin and the Great God of Nature*.

31.   Franklin, *Bodin*, ch. 3.

14 'History of Crime' or 'History of Sin'? – Some Reflections on the Social History of Early Modern Church Discipline

Heinz Schilling

I

The German reader is used to the existence of academic schools of thought who, whether young or old, at conferences or with the publication of collections of essays are mainly concerned with purity of theory rather than plurality of scholarly opinion. For that reason the book *Crime in England 1550–1800* is particularly impressive,[1] for here the procedure is the complete opposite. The editor, Professor Cockburn, and his ten co-authors invited a historian of great integrity to write the introduction to their publication; they could be certain that he would carefully examine the methodological and theoretical approach of the 'Social History of Criminality', then still in its infancy, and scrutinise its first substantial results with regard to their general historical soundness. And Geoffrey Elton – for it was he who had been asked to write the introduction – was prepared to check and critically comment on the evidence, argumentation and conclusions of a line of research which is altogether contrary to his own understanding of the historian's task and method.[2] The contributors and the editor in his introduction obviously agreed on the maxim that 'it is by isolating and correcting error that progress comes, and in the very difficult region of historical inquiry ... the practitioner need not object to having traps and pitfalls pointed out to him'.[3]

Elton expressly warns of one such trap, the unreflected and in his opinion historically and anthropologically nonsensical inclusion of church jurisdiction in the history of criminality. Instead he pleads for a strict factual and methodological separation between the 'history of crime' and the 'history of sin'. In accordance with the subject of the collection of essays Elton refers to the early modern society of England. However, given the interlocking relationship between state and church, religion and society which was a constituent of the early modern world,[4] this presents a methodological problem relevant to the history of old Europe and its transatlantic off-shoot societies in general. But this problem manifests itself in specific ways, according to the concrete political, confessional and, above all, legal conditions of state and church. Elton's arguments against confusing state and church jurisdiction are primarily aimed at the situation in early modern England which was determined by the constitution of the Anglican church as the established state church. This becomes particularly clear from his observations on the attitudes of state and church communities towards the royal and episcopal courts – 'respect for the King's courts and contempt for those of the Church'.[5]

Does this statement and the resulting postulate of a qualitative difference between ecclesiastical and state jurisdiction also apply to the other European countries? For instance, to the countries of Tridentine Catholicism, whose episcopal courts resembled the English church courts in their organisation and institution but differed from them in terms of ecclesiastical law and in their religious-theological foundation? And what happened in areas where the Reformation had been wholly completed, clerical jurisdiction abolished and new Protestant forms of 'jurisdiction over sin' by the church introduced? Within Protestantism one should expect obvious differences between countries with a mixed form of state–church jurisdiction within the framework of the Lutheran consistory constitution, i.e. especially in the German territorial states and the Scandinavian monarchies on the one hand, and in countries with Reformed church discipline on the other. And the practice of Reformed church discipline in Zürich and the Zwinglian and Erastian churches differed greatly from that in Geneva and the presbyterian congregations of France, the Netherlands, Scotland, eastern Europe and the few Calvinist areas of the empire on even the states of New England. Finally, there is also the very different system of church discipline which prevailed in congregations outside the church traditions of their respective states, for instance with the Anabaptists, notably the Mennonites, and the Hutterites, but also with Lutheran and Calvinist dissenters in Catholic countries and territories or in Anglican England. The complexity of these conditions can perhaps be illustrated by the fact that with the Protestant underground congregations, the so-called 'Churches of the

Holy Cross' (*Kreuzkirchen*) in the Catholic territories on the Lower Rhine both the Lutherans and the Calvinists had presbyterian constitutions and therefore a congregational system of church discipline. Similarly, even in a Lutheran territorial church such as that in the duchy of Württemberg congregational church discipline was established under the influence of pietism in the mid-seventeenth century;[6] this was based, besides the example of neighbouring Switzerland, on autochthonous Lutheran ideas as well, not least on the early utterances of the Wittenberg reformer himself.

It is conceptually questionable whether all these forms can properly be called 'jurisdiction' as it was understood by Anglican and Catholic bishops. But apart from this there is another problem: with respect to politics, society, and above all consciousness – a factor rightly stressed by Geoffrey Elton with regard to the English – the concrete implications and consequences for the individual and for society differed greatly from case to case.

My own particular field of study is Calvinist–presbyterian church discipline in certain German and Dutch cities. Taking this area I wish to enlarge upon some facts and arguments which may, I hope, help to develop further the methodological and factual questions raised by Elton. But before I do so my brief outline of the western European controversy over the historical classification of church discipline needs to be complemented by a critical glance at the way German historiography has treated this subject. On account of its very different scholarly traditions German research into early modern history at present hardly recognises an alternative between the 'history of crime' and the 'history of sin'. All the same, the general historical classification of ecclesiastical jurisdiction in general, and of Protestant church discipline in particular, provides some comparable problems of method and of substance.

The 'social history of criminality' which has been studied intensively for some time in France, the Netherlands and the Anglo-Saxon countries, has not succeeded in gaining similar influence upon German research on early modern history.[7] The explanation for this lies partly in the specific German tradition of legal and constitutional history and in the priority accorded to the formation of the early modern state. But even more important has probably been the fact that German research on early modern history possesses a wider paradigm for the interpretation of historical developments which could easily subsume the 'social history of criminality', namely 'social and fundamental discipline' developed by Gerhard Oestreich in the

1960s,[8] which since the 1970s has had a strong influence on the younger generation of German and, to a considerable extent, of international early modern historians. In the history of scholarship the paradigm of 'social discipline' offers a productive link between the older tradition of constitutional history and Max Weber's thinking on historical development. Oestreich, however, distances himself explicitly from Weber's concept of rationality when he introduces 'disciplining' as a new category of interpretation.[9] Referring back to the social and state philosophy of Justus Lipsius, he reasserts social discipline as a social process preceding rationality. But because he sees disciplining as a universal development during the transition from old to modern Europe Oestreich, in historiographical terms, is an early example of the eminently fertile Weber reception among post-war West German historians.

Mainly concerned with the early modern state and its achievements in establishing political order, German historians began to reflect on 'social discipline' on state lines. Social processes which occurred independently of the process of state formation were hardly considered, or else they were understood as being subordinate to the process of disciplining and education controlled by the state. Thus in his introduction to the study of the early modern state and its administration Hans Maier described this phenomenon within the framework of *Polizei* and general law and order enforcement by the early modern territorial state and its civil service.[10] And Oestreich too regarded social discipline as a central feature of absolutist states in particular; his pertinent definition has always been cited in the subsequent discussion: 'We see fundamental disciplining as a general process which was consciously promoted or independently led by *monarchical absolutism* and took place in the most diverse areas.' Owing to the dissolution of older forms of public power during the sixteenth and seventeenth centuries 'the hour of order by the early modern absolutist state had arrived'; this state regimented in detail private and public life in order to enforce its own monopoly of power and to pacify the potential conflict between the Estates and the confessions.[11] According to Oestreich, two spiritual forces or ethical systems lent themselves to this development: neo-stoicism, which addressed itself mainly to the political, military and intellectual elite, and a catalogue of Christian virtues specifically assembled for this purpose, which was intended mainly for the subjects. Oestreich believes the philosophical system which operated independently of early modern confessional boundaries to have been the earlier and most effective force for a long period,[12] whereas the Christian virtues played a more derivative role and were used as instruments under the influence of stoic philosophy within the states irrespective of their confession. A doctoral thesis suggested by Oestreich is currently trying to trace this with regard to the newly accentuated Christian work ethic which was used to discipline the poor and vagrants, in other words to integrate social fringe groups who in the sixteenth century were greatly on the increase and presented the early modern state with considerable problems of law and order.[13]

In accordance with these governmental concerns the 'disciplining' activity of the churches – and this means at first almost exclusively the Protestant churches – appeared within the general framework of the state's efforts to maintain law and order.[14] Oestreich especially emphasises the partnership between church and secular institutions and the functional equivalence of church and state discipline.[15] Apart from late medieval and early modern changes in society, economy and the state he locates the necessity and dynamics of social regulation by the state above all in the failure of ecclesiastical jurisdiction in the medieval church, 'so questions of discipline and morality which had originally been settled by the church became part of secular discipline'.[16]

A main task to which Gerhard Oestreich devoted the last years of his life very clearly aimed at widening the state-oriented concept of 'fundamental disciplining' in order to formulate a broad social historical paradigm.[17] For the churches this would certainly have resulted in greater emphasis on their independence over against government, as chronology itself shows, for in Protestant areas, at least, the renewal of religiously motivated church discipline after the failure of ecclesiastical jurisdiction by the late medieval church was certainly not a secondary consequence brought about through state discipline. The reformers, Luther as much as Zwingli and Calvin, as well as Bucer, Brenz and à Lasco,[18] rather regarded the reform of ecclesiastical jurisdiction, that is, its adjustment to the new Protestant theology, as a central part of their reforming task. For this reason all Protestant churches from the very beginning seriously attempted to regulate the ban and proper Christian discipline. The Calvinists with their presbyterian church discipline were able to produce the most visible success, since it was underpinned by the institutions of church and state.

The intrusion of secular authorities into church discipline described by Oestreich also signalled the imposition of Christian and religious duties on the state; but that 'secularisation' of discipline was only one escape from the spiritual and moral crisis of old church jurisdiction towards the end of the Middle Ages. The other, offered by Reformation theology, brought a turning-in upon itself to the lost or forgotten religious and pastoral centre of ecclesiastical jurisdiction. Except for Zwingli, the reformers were not satisfied with the secular state solution, but developed their own model on a religious-theological foundation – a Protestant church discipline which replaced the externalised and badly discredited ecclesiastical court of the late medieval church. Protestant church discipline was a creative, indigenous church reaction to the failure of medieval church jurisdiction, which Oestreich rightly saw as the reason for the encroachment of the state upon tasks originally belonging to the church. On the one hand, this turning point of the Reformation affected church jurisdiction through a new sense of responsibility on the part of the congregation which the old church had long since lost. On the other hand, this new approach fitted into the process of differentiation in early modern society postulated by Niklas Luhmann and other social scientists, in so far as the mix of religious-spiritual discipline and purely secular jurisdiction which had formed a constitutent part of the medieval ecclesiastical courts had been abolished in principle within the Protestant countries of the early modern period. The Protestant authorities also used renewed church discipline for their own interests, with the result that only too often a 'criminalisation of sin' occurred. Historical reality therefore contains various forms of mix and transition between the two extremes of church discipline, autonomous congregational discipline and discipline controlled by the state. But the awareness of qualitative differences between church and secular punishment, between 'sin discipline' and 'crime discipline', continued and because of that the relationship between the two principles also remained tense within the different forms of church discipline under state regulation.

For the historian this leads to a methodological duty to distinguish at the outset of his inquiry between 'disciplining of sin' and 'punitive discipline'. It is only thereafter that we can concentrate on functional equivalences or describe how the church was made to serve the state. An appropriate historical evaluation of church discipline, however, must regard this second step as important as the first in the context of what, with Oestreich, I regard as modern 'fundamental disciplining'. Moreover, it becomes clear that behind the process apparently only controlled by the state there also stood the independently active forces of church and society.

Two further observations which can only roughly be sketched here underline this point: ban and church discipline were exercised by the Lutheran pastor or the assembly of Reformed church elders. But this was carried out on behalf of the congregation assembled under the word of God. Therefore church discipline was not merely exercised by the church or its leadership downwards. Secular fundamental disciplining provides a similar picture since it was influenced not merely by the controlling forces of the state but also by the co-operative forces of the community. The second remark concerns the temporal precedence and qualitative preponderance of princely and aristocratic ideals: the 'disciplining effect of *prudentia civilis*', Oestreich wrote, was transmitted to 'the civil service of state and city and the military' at first by the 'Estate of princes'; only by a further step was it transferred from the kings and princes to the commoners.[19] However, the independent importance of church discipline, especially in its presbyterian form, also makes this supposition relative, for the disciplining measures we have studied were taken by thoroughly 'bourgeois' presbyteries;[20] they aimed at the same time, with and independently of these princely ideals, towards a concentration and disciplining of life in the Christian civic sense. This can be seen especially in the early modern pioneering society of the northern Netherlands where, together with Justus Lipsius and Maurice of Orange, the leading lights of the neo-stoicist doctrine of princes, 'bourgeois' regents and churchmen were at work with their anti-princely views.

II

We may now turn to specific historical examples – the Calvinist–presbyterian church discipline in Germany and the Netherlands, or rather the history of this church discipline in the cities of Emden, Groningen and Leiden. I am currently examining these within a wider research project which hopes to produce historical, social and occupational profiles of the Reformed presbyteries in these cities.[21]

In all three cities the Reformed presbyteries were relatively independent of the power of the state and the city council. This has to be kept in mind with regard to my later arguments, since the legal and political historical framework is very important when dealing with the question of convergence or divergence of church discipline and criminal jurisdiction. The congregation in Emden, whose church ordinances were used by Groningen as a direct, and by Leiden as an indirect, example, even showed strong signs of a voluntary church in the mid-sixteenth century. This tradition influenced the life of the congregation later on as well, although in 1595 Calvinism became the official confession of the entire city. In the Dutch cities the Reformed congregations had the status of an established church. This resulted in a special relationship with the authorities of city and province and closely entwined personal ties between the presbytery and the political elite.[22] But irrespective of this connection with the political powers the presbyteries did not lose their formal autonomy in Emden or in Groningen and Leiden. In contrast to the Anglicans in England and the Zwinglians in Zürich the Reformed congregations in these cities were not state churches. Indeed, even the legally prescribed delegation of members of the magistracy to the church council, which Calvin had had to accept in Geneva, was unknown in the north-west. The actual scope for action enjoyed by the Reformed presbyteries in these cities was also much greater than that of their sister congregations in the Reformed parts of the empire with a territorial church constitution which had to submit to strict regulation and control by the territorial authority.

Both theology and church constitutional law as well as the actual implementation of church discipline support this view. The former can be obtained from the theological writings of Calvin and – for the emergence of church discipline in north-western Europe equally important – those of the Polish reformer John à Lasco,[23] as well as from the ordinances of the churches and church councils in individual congregations.[24] The latter are documented in a long series of church council reports which begin in Emden in 1557, in Leiden in 1584, and in Groningen in 1595, and which, except for some minor gaps, have survived until the present day. The proposed study examines these reports quantitatively for every half century in five-year sections, starting with the five-year survey period from 1527 to 1532 in Emden and ending with the years 1821 to 1825. In this way the range of activities of the three presbyteries may be described comprehensively and analysed by the focal points within each of the periods under investigation and by secular change. Not only will church discipline be considered, but the entire spectrum of presbyterian activity – besides moral discipline doctrinal discipline with its aim of dogmatic purity, the pastoral care of the individual and of the congregation as a whole, the governance and administration of the church at local and synod level, and lastly social welfare and care for the poor which the elders carry out together with the deacons.

Therefore the church discipline which we are trying to define is not treated here in isolation but is from the outset related to the other activities of the elders. This approach corresponds with Geoffrey Elton's demands for the theoretical, methodological and factual distinction between church discipline and other forms of early modern disciplining, since it follows the basic assumption that the historical relevance of church discipline cannot adequately be determined if moral discipline is artificially separated from the complete spectrum of the church's activities and aspirations. Rather, it explicitly aims to consider its theological foundations and implications in the widest sense as well.

The foundations of church discipline in church constitutional law provide the first two arguments for a factual and methodological distinction between 'history of sin' and 'history of crime': in Emden, Groningen and Leiden the church congregation was not only the object, but equally the subject, of church discipline. The aim of this discipline was not the earthly perfection of the individual or his punishment, be it understood as penance or as deterrence, but the sacral-transcendental unity of the eucharistic community. There is nothing that corresponds to this in criminal jurisdiction or in discipline by the state authority's police, at least not in its princely absolutist form dominant in Europe, which is in the forefront of the paradigm of social discipline. On the contrary, in the latter case the lines running from the top downwards, from the authorities to their subjects, became increasingly stronger and clearer at the expense of communal and co-operative self-regulation which in the Middle Ages was still strong even in this sphere. Criminal jurisdiction and police laws in early modern times were more and more stringently embodied in sovereign state power; they became sovereign acts, enforced from above. In the different regions of Europe varying forms of such communal and co-operative bodies still remained active in criminal justice and *Polizei*, but these tasks were delegated to them by the state and were no longer founded on the community.

By comparison the legal foundation of church discipline was much more complex. It was understood as the Lord's commandment to his congregation. It was put in the hands of the presbytery, a body separate from the congregation; but the presbytery exercised church discipline on behalf and by authority of the congregation. That found expression first of all in the choice of elders. Direct election by the congregation was very rare, but the congregation played a central symbolic part in their inauguration. Moreover, the congregation's participation in church discipline is evident from the fact that they had the power to pass judgement on the actions and conduct of pastor and elders: the presbyteries exercised self-discipline at regular intervals, *censura morum* as it is called in the sources. At least in the early phase the date of such self-discipline was announced in advance to the congregation from the pulpit, and the congregation was asked to come forward to the presbytery with complaints and accusations against the ministers *and elders*. These and other complaints from their own midst were then discussed at a regular meeting by the church council.[25] In the course of time the elders tried again and again to escape from this control by the congregation, but that did not alter the essential understanding of discipline. This emerges most clearly in the ritual implementation of church discipline, since here the congregation's responsibility was symbolised, even renewed, in each individual case: with all major offences the church council's sentence had to be carried out publicly in front of the congregation because it represented the origin of discipline and the power of reconciliation. This becomes particularly striking in those cases where for reasons of discretion only the offence, but not the name of the sinner, is mentioned. The elders could conclude only the more trivial cases on their own with simple admonitions, but the congregation was present even then as the focal point of the act of discipline – in Emden this was reflected even in the use of language since the presbytery in such cases was often referred to as 'the congregation'.[26]

Even more than in its reliance on the congregation the essence of church discipline is revealed in its orientation towards the eucharistic community. I can see no parallel with this in any form of secular state discipline, not even in the sense of a functional equivalent. The central position which church discipline in the sixteenth and seventeenth centuries held in the activities of the presbyteries and generally in the life of the congregations was not based on the wish to perfect mankind but aimed to purify the Christian community of saints. The community of saints did not constitute itself as an utopian ideal freed from sin and evil but as the eucharistic congregation under the commandment of its Lord, oriented towards Christ and aware of earthly imperfection. Herein lies the theological-religious essence of Reformed church discipline which excludes any *a priori* equation with the multitude of secular disciplining measures. This does not imply, to reiterate the point, that such church discipline with its orientation towards the sinner and his reconciliation with the eucharistic community did not also have political and social consequences. Rather it is argued that these consequences can only be correctly determined and comprehensively acknowledged if the religious-theological essence of discipline is considered. That is in the first place a methodological and epistemological statement; only concrete individual case studies can show what this means for our picture of the historical reality of church discipline.

At the same time the orientation towards the eucharistic community brought with it the decisive supersession of the externalised ecclesiastical jurisdiction of the late Middle Ages which had lost almost all connection with church and congregation. The Reformed eucharistic discipline, by returning to the central religious essence of communal Christian and church life, remedied that defect in the spirit of the Reformation, and thus it denied the necessity which Oestreich postulated for state-controlled disciplining and the enforcement of public order in questions of discipline and morality originally regulated by the church.

The evaluation of the Emden church council reports, which has been virtually completed, shows that even the end of early modern church discipline was not only determined from outside, i.e. by changes in the social and intellectual climate as, for instance, the advance of a new view of man in the course of the Enlightenment. Rather the renunciation of individual church discipline which won through in Emden during the first half of the eighteenth century, having reached a quantitative and qualitative climax in the last decade of the seventeenth century,[27] was very closely connected with changes in the understanding of church and congregation. This is obvious enough, since church discipline was indispensable as long as the purity of the eucharistic community was seen as a constituent part of the Christian congregation. At all events, the Emden theologians tried to establish a new foundation for this congregation during the same period when church discipline was coming to an end. Their aim was evidently to preserve the original concept of the Reformed congregation at Emden, based as it was on an explicit supposition and not on institutional membership, into an era which no longer regarded church discipline as a suitable guarantee for constituting and securing such affiliation to the congregation.[28]

A further argument against the historiographical equation of church discipline and criminal justice follows from the qualitative difference in the objectives of each procedure. The main aims of the state in punishing crime at the beginning of the early modern period were penance, sanction and deterrence, and the early modern state's procedures dissociated themselves consciously from other criminal justice, whether it represented older forms based on locality, clientele or kinship, or was non-punitive.[29] Whether and how the delinquents took or accepted their sentence was not of much concern to the judges and assessors.

Church discipline in this respect was totally different, even in cases where it dealt substantially with offences which could also be the object of criminal justice; the main purpose was not to punish, but to save the sinner and the purity of the congregation which his crime had violated from eternal damnation. Even if church discipline did contain an aspect of punishment[30] it was, contrary to criminal justice in the early modern state, not predominantly punitive but always pastoral in character, and this applied to the individual as much as to the congregation as a whole. Church sentences – as long as they were not mixed with secular sentences as described above – were of a different quality compared to state sentences, for with them acceptance and inner conversion were decisive. The delinquent was a sinner whose inner attitude towards his offence and his church sentence was essential for the result of the disciplining procedure by the church – a connection which was outside the secular interests of state courts. The church procedure in its objective went beyond punishment, striving for insight and the wish to change, even if this was only partial and temporary. Church discipline, therefore, was essentially not just punishment and expiation, it was *penitential discipline*.

In principle – and this matters for a systematic distinction – a disciplinary procedure by the church was only concluded when a confession of guilt had been made and the sentence passed had also been accepted at heart as a church penitence. The Emden church council records contain many cases where the elders at the beginning denied the sinner participation in holy communion despite his formal confession of guilt and compliance with the sentence because they were not sufficiently satisfied about the genuineness of his repentance. This has to be seen in the first place as a pastoral measure which concerned not only the delinquent who was to be allowed an opportunity for proper conversion, but for the congregation as a whole, especially the eucharistic community which had to be protected from being harmed by an unrepentant and, moreover, hypocritical sinner. The ban from communion which was almost regularly enforced for graver offences was always more than punishment. To criticise the decisions of the presbyteries for such exclusion from communion, therefore, is to miss the essence of this early modern church discipline, even if it seems justified from the viewpoint of modern pastoral theology.[31] The fact that the denial of communion could result in social stigmatisation and therefore, in terms of social history, must appear as a particularly severe 'sentence' does not contradict what has been said. Rather it illustrates and emphasises once again the complexity of the early modern world where the individual and society had both sacral *and* secular existence.

Only towards the end of the early modern period can intentions and reflections in secular legal thought be observed which are comparable to the objective of Calvinist–presbyterian church discipline as I have described it. Especially as a result of the spread of Enlightenment notions of law, secular criminal justice in the late eighteenth century sought not only to punish but, increasingly, to reform the delinquent.[32] This clearly shows a functional similarity to church discipline. But by this time the latter had long ceased to be practised, at least in the congregations studied here. From this chronology the question arises whether such a development in the secular sphere had in any way been influenced by the older church discipline and its concentration on the conversion of the sinner. Our material does not provide an answer to that.

The distinction between 'penitential church discipline' and 'punitive secular discipline' emerges with particular clarity in cases of adultery: in the Lutheran areas with a territorial church constitution they were, as is well known, brought before the newly created consistories. Therefore, in contrast to the Middle Ages and to the early modern Catholic and Anglican states, matrimonial jurisdiction was removed from the church. But since the consistories comprised representatives of state and church the unity of church and secular discipline remained, and with it the mixture of penitential and punitive discipline. This, however, was not the case with the Calvinist–presbyterian solution which is our subject here. Adultery cases were brought before two separate institutions: before the presbytery they were the object of penitential church discipline, and before the matrimonial court of the city or the state that of punitive secular discipline.

Thus in Emden, for example, matrimonial criminal jurisdiction was the responsibility of a matrimonial court residing in the city; this consisted of two commissioners of the count, two Emden city councillors and one Emden preacher, and it sat in judgement formally on behalf of the territorial prince.[33] Conversely, the presbytery of the Reformed congregation, which did not have any officials of the city or the territorial prince as assessors, had no power of jurisdiction in matrimonial and divorce matters. As the analysed reports show, the church council always abided by this restriction of its competence and almost never dealt with matrimonial and divorce matters in terms of criminal jurisdiction. When it dealt with matrimonial or sexual offences, as it did with relative frequency up to the early eighteenth century,[34] this always happened in terms of the penitential discipline described above. Its active concern lay beyond the sphere of secular justice. It was exercising discipline of sins, not jurisdiction over matrimony.

The practice of Calvinist–presbyterian church discipline as it appears in the church council reports of the three congregations offers a number of further arguments against confusing the 'history of sin' and the 'history of crime'. For instance, the formal course of church disciplinary proceedings was ultimately based on voluntariness and, except in some special cases, did not involve an attendance enforced by the public beadle. In this respect church discipline was also pastoral educational work by the preachers and elders who had to persuade the member of their congregation suspected or convicted of an offence to face their discipline. Especially in the Dutch cities the 'defendant' found it relatively easy to opt for the alternative and escape from an impending church disciplinary procedure by formally 'leaving' the established church. And conversely the disciplinary efforts of the church had to come to an end when the elders became convinced that the sinner was incurably impenitent and any further measures would be in vain. In such cases the member was 'cut off' from the congregation and left on his own – such a conclusion to a case would be unthinkable in secular criminal jurisdiction. Finally, the special personal or fraternal commitment may be mentioned which was shown by the elders and preachers in many individual cases in order to make church discipline become the turning point in the religious, moral and social life of their 'brother' or 'sister'. The Emden reports in particular allow insight into church disciplinary procedures where the presbytery or individual members of it indeed wrestled with the offender over months if not years to lead him back onto the right path. In one matrimonial case the writer emphasised that it 'lasted for a good three consecutive hours' ('wol 3 stunden nah einander duirde', Kirchenratsprotokolle Emden, 8.4.1566). Especially in matrimonial and family disputes, in offences which were caused by extremity, in young people and 'those weak in the flesh', the elders spent much time trying to change the living conditions and the personal attitude of the offenders, over and above judging and punishing them through the church disciplinary procedure, in order to create the preconditions for a Christian way of life in the congregation and in society. None of these elements are found in criminal proceedings and other forms of secular punitive discipline at all, at least not with such intensity.

III

The arguments derived from our specific case studies strengthen Geoffrey Elton's demand for a methodological and factual distinction between 'sin' and 'crime', between the history of church discipline and the history of criminal justice. However, in order to clarify the scope and thrust of this historical argument two additional points must be made. The first refers to the question of how widespread was the type of autonomous congregational church discipline which we have described. The second concerns my own historical purpose in making such a distinction.

1. What has been said about the character of church discipline and about its relationship to criminal jurisdiction and state police discipline applies first of all only to cases where autonomous church discipline existed. Besides the examples studied here this applies also notably to Protestant established *free and minority* churches, e.g. the 'Churches of the Holy Cross' (*Kreuzkirchen*) in the Lower Rhine area, whether Calvinist or Lutheran. Where the secular power had a direct influence on the composition and activity of the Calvinist presbyteries, the preconditions necessary for such autonomous congregational church discipline did not exist. This was the case in the Reformed territorial churches of the empire or – under differing circumstances – in Scotland.[35] In these cases we are dealing with a form of church discipline that has deviated from its pastoral-theological origins and has gone some way to meet the civil moral discipline of the state. Since the independence of the presbyteries was considerably restricted and the elders could be bound summarily by the norms and objectives of the concepts of secular state discipline, the systematic distinction between church and state discipline became blurred.

These legal circumstances within an established church then gave rise to what Bruce Lenman and Geoffrey Parker have aptly called the 'criminalisation of sin',[36] i.e. the application of church discipline to other than the religious purposes which had formed its core. With that the basis of church discipline as described above had been departed from – either because the state or local civil law courts had united church discipline with their own punitive discipline, or because the congregation itself had lost sight of its original religious-theological preconditions. Such degeneration of church discipline was not rare in the early modern period. Indeed it can be said that it constituted the rule and that the consistent implementation of 'pure' church discipline was the exception which was facilitated by special circumstances created, for instance, by persecution or the existence of a religious minority.

The frequent 'criminalisation of sin' was caused by the structural interlocking of religion and society in early modern times. On the one hand this awakened the desire of the developing early modern state, in most instances hiding behind the ethos of protection, to use church and religion for its own purposes, to make them instruments of policy. On the other hand it meant that especially those churchmen working for reform advanced far into the secular state sphere in order to Christianise it, i.e. to submit it to the religious and moral norms which they found in the Bible. Moreover, they were only too willing to call for the assistance of the state when they encountered internal church opposition. Unmistakable signs of church discipline having degenerated were fines and prison sentences.[37] In this way conversion and repentence were substituted by punishment in the sense of secular punitive jurisdiction or rather by a compensatory deal as had been typical of medieval criminal justice. Sin had been 'criminalised'.

This betrayal of the theological principles of church discipline was not at all connected with any particular confession. Rather the decisive factor again consisted in the general conditions governing the law of the established churches. The use of church discipline by the civil state authority occurred primarily in confessional churches with a national or territorial constitution where state and church communities were largely identical – in Calvinist Scotland just as in Lutheran Sweden or in the Lutheran territorial states of the empire. And even Calvin, or should one say especially Calvin, the most determined advocate of autonomous congregational church discipline, did not infrequently (to put it cautiously) fail to observe it in practice in Geneva.[38] But because its theological justification of church discipline was slightly different and because of the particular historical conditions of its dissemination, Calvinism on the whole possessed a greater potential to resist such a degeneration of church discipline than Lutheranism.

The criminalisation of church discipline in Scotland, or comparable phenomena cited by German historians in the case of Reformed territorial churches within the empire,[39] cannot be regarded as evidence of an essential identity of state and church discipline in principle. On the contrary, it is precisely in the face of a confused historical reality that the need for methodological differentiation becomes crucial and obliges the historian all the more to distinguish in his systematic analysis between crime and sin, punitive state discipline and penitential church discipline.

2. To insist on the distinction between 'history of sin' and 'history of crime' is not intended to idealise the efforts towards moral church discipline but to submit them to an adequate historical assessment. Within early modern society church discipline was of eminent social historical importance especially as an ecclesiastical phenomenon in itself. This means on the one hand that the moral and doctrinal discipline of the various confessions has to be defined within the context of ecclesiastical and theological history, but on the other hand that the general and social consequences have to be examined as well. This, however, can only properly be done if we take religious structures and impulses seriously. Treated as the 'history of sin', the study of church discipline can tell us more about the cohesive forces that kept the world of the *ancien régime* together than a 'history of crime', which blurs 'sin' into 'crime' and allows church discipline to be absorbed by criminal justice.

Church discipline of the kind we have described was also undoubtedly 'social disciplining'. For it presented the person concerned with direct social consequences and in some circumstances with the most unpleasant one of all, the ban on participation in communion, which came closest to the religious core of the discipline. But above all church discipline was also bound up with longer-term social-historical developments which pointed in directions very similar to those of the state's disciplinary efforts. Its original disciplinary intentions, however, had a very different theoretical basis from the social discipline of the early modern state, especially in its most rigorous form – criminal justice. Early modern 'social disciplining' was, as Gerhard Oestreich repeatedly pointed out, an extremely complex phenomenon. We can only hope to comprehend it with sufficient exactness if we consider the dual polarity of church and state discipline, for this accounts for the scope and complexity of social disciplining in old Europe. To reduce it to one pole only must lead to the obliteration of precisely that dynamism inherent in the confessional-Christian impulses of early modern Europe which led to the transformation of the old European order into the modern world. That applies to Protestantism as much as to Tridentine Catholicism. The submission of sin under crime implies a foreshortening of the vast process of secularisation in terms of governmental interests alone. It is much the same in terms of 'everyday' history (*Alltagsgeschichte*), because it is often incapable of distinguishing crucial facts or epochs since it is only interested in early modern fundamental disciplining as a process that takes place from above, as a punishment which cannot be differentiated any further and which breaks in upon the everyday world of the individual person.

The best chance of achieving a historically satisfactory definition of the effects of church discipline on the one hand and state discipline on the other rests in the analysis of specific historical examples with methodologically appropriate and conceptually sharp definitions. The distinction which Geoffrey Elton demands between sin and crime, between the history of church discipline and the history of criminal jurisdiction is an important step in this direction.

Notes

1.   J. S. Cockburn (ed.), *Crime in England, 1550–1800* (London, 1977). I am limiting the notes to a few remarks since I am planning to examine in detail the problems outlined in this essay, in a study on the composition and activity of Calvinist presbyteries.

2.   Elton has repeatedly commented on historiographical trends in England and Europe, putting forward a middle path between the fashionable overestimation and cautiously traditional negation of structural and social history. Cf. esp. G. R. Elton, 'Historians Against History', *The Cambridge Review*, 18 November 1983, pp. 203–5; also idem, 'The History of England' (Inaugural Lecture as Regius Professor of History, held 26 January 1984), p. 24f, and *passim*.

3.   Elton in Cockburn, *Crime in England*, p. 14.

4.   A point which gives rise to several general theoretical, methodological and factual conclusions relevant to the early modern period; cf. the reflections by H. Schilling, *Konfessionskonflikt und Staatsbildung* (Gütersloh, 1981), pp. 15–39; idem, 'Konfessionalisierung als gesellschaftlicher Umbruch', in S. Quandt (ed.), *Luther, die Reformation und die Deutschen* (Paderborn, 1982); H. Schilling, 'The Reformation and the Rise of the Early Modern State' to be published in 1986 in a supplementary volume of the *Sixteenth Century Journal*, ed. James Tracy.

5.   Elton in Cockburn, *Crime in England*, p. 3. The case study by R. W. Wunderli, *London Church Courts and Society on the Eve of the*

Reformation (Cambridge, Mass., 1981) shows that by the late fifteenth century the ecclesiastical courts in England had also lost their procedural superiority over secular courts and were therefore hardly ever asked to decide legal disputes.

6. M. Brecht, *Kirchenordnung und Kirchenzucht in Württemberg vom 16. bis zum 18. Jahrhundert* (Calw, 1967).

7. Cf. H. Reif (ed.), *Räuber, Volk und Obrigkeit – Studien zur Geschichte der Kriminalität in Deutschland seit dem 18. Jahrhundert* (Frankfurt, 1984), with essays on the late early modern period and on the nineteenth and twentieth centuries. The important study by D. Blasius, *Bürgerliche Gesellschaft und Kriminalität* (Göttingen, 1976) deals with the period before the 1848 revolution.

8. Cf. Brigitta Oestreich in the introduction to G. Oestreich, *Strukturprobleme der Neuzeit* (Berlin, 1980), p. 9, with reference to idem, *Geist und Gestalt des frühmodernen Staates* (Berlin, 1969), pp. 187, 236.

9. Fundamental and pioneering in this respect are Gerhard Oestreich's many studies, collected in *Geist und Gestalt* and *Strukturprobleme der Neuzeit*, published posthumously by Brigitta Oestreich.

10. H. Maier, *Die ältere deutsche Staats- und Verwaltungslehre*, 2nd edn (Munich, 1980).

11. Oestreich, *Geist und Gestalt*, p. 195; cf. also pp. 187, 192.

12. Oestreich, *Strukturprobleme*, pp. 367–79, esp. 374ff.

13. R. Jütte, 'Poor Relief and Social Discipline in 16th-Century Europe', *European Studies Review*, XI (1981), pp. 25–52; idem, *Obrigkeitliche Armenfürsorge in deutschen Reichsstädten der frühen Neuzeit. Städtisches Armenwesen in Frankfurt a.M. und Köln* (Cologne/Vienna, 1984). Cf. also K. Wiedemann, *Arbeit und Bürgertum. Die Entwicklung des Arbeitsbegriffs in der Literatur Deutschlands an der Wende zur Neuzeit* (Heidelberg, 1979). But Wiedemann does not agree that the Reformation brought a radical qualitative change.

14. Detailed and instructive on the public order tasks of the early modern state and on the use of the churches Maier, *Staats- und Verwaltungslehre*, pp. 70–3; 127, 147ff. In line with his subject Maier deals mainly with the German territorial state and therefore with territorial church constitutions. He does not explicitly examine church discipline and its relationship with police discipline; he only says in passing, p. 127, 'such a transfer of the rights of censorship to the institutions of the state [as the Strasbourg councillor and university rector Obrecht proposed – H. Schilling] had up to then not taken place outside Calvinist city states and their polity which united spiritual and secular rule'. Our analysis of church discipline in the city republics of Emden, Groningen and Leiden proves that, on the contrary, the separation between spiritual church and secular discipline characterised the autonomous congregational church discipline of north-western continental European Calvinism. Typical of the moral state discipline represented by Obrecht are the fines which Maier rightly remarks on, e.g. for sexual offences; they are completely unknown in the type of church discipline studied here.

15. Cf. esp. Oestreich, *Geist und Gestalt*, p. 192.

16. Idem, *Strukturprobleme*, p. 368.

17.   Ibid., introduction by Brigitta Oestreich, pp. 7–9.
18.   Since this is to be examined in detail in a separate study the evidence is not advanced here.
19.   Ibid., p. 375f.
20.   H. Schilling. 'Calvinistische Presbyterien in Städten der Frühneuzeit', in W. Ehbrecht (ed.), *Städtische Führungsgruppen und Gemeinde in der werdenden Neuzeit* (Cologne/Vienna, 1980), pp. 385–444; H. Schilling, 'Das calvinistiche Presbyterium in der Stadt Groningen während der Frühneuzeit und im ersten Viertel des 19. Jahrhunderts – Verfassung und Sozialprofil', in idem and H. Diederiks (eds), *Bürgerliche Eliten in den Niederlanden und in Nordwestdeutschland. Wandlungs- und Differenzierungsvorgänge vom 15. bis zum 20. Jahrhundert* (Cologne/Vienna, 1985), pp. 1–32.
21.   Its aims are described in H. Schilling, 'Reformierte Kirchenzucht als Sozialdisziplinierung? – Die Tätigkeit des Emder Presbyteriums in den Jahren 1557–1562', in W. Ehbrecht and H. Schilling (eds), *Niederlande und Nordwestdeutschland* (Cologne/Vienna, 1983), pp. 261–327.
22.   Cf. n. 20; on the Dutch type of established church constitution (*Öffentlichkeitskirche*) cf. H. Schilling, 'Religion und Gesellschaft in der calvinistischen Republik der Vereinigten Niederlande', in F. Petri (ed.), *Kirche und gesellschaftlicher Wandel in deutschen und niederländischen Städten* (Cologne/Vienna, 1980), pp. 197–250.
23.   Latest biography with detailed bibliography, M. Smid, 'Laski, Johannes', in *Neue Deutsche Biographie*, vol. XIII (Berlin, 1982), cols. 658–9.
24.   For Emden published in E. Sehling (ed.), *Die evangelischen Kirchenordnungen des 16. Jahrhunderts*, vol. VII, 2, 1: *Niedersachsen; Außerwelfische Lande* (Tübingen, 1963), pp. 307–724, here esp. vol. VII, 3, 9, pp. 542, 554: *Ordnunge der versamlinge der predicanten und olderlingen* (between 1564 and 1573). For Groningen: *Kerkenordre der Stadt Groningen*, published in H. H. Brucherus, *Geschiedenis van de opkomst der Kerkhervorming in Groningen* (Groningen, 1821), pp. 425–70.
25.   Cf. Archiv der Reformierten Gemeinde Emden, Kirchenratsprotokolle 17 April, 1 May and 30 October 1559.
26.   Cf. ibid., 13 December 1557; cf. also J. Weerda, 'Der Emder Kirchenrat und seine Gemeinde', part II (Dissertation habil., University of Münster 1948), pp. 156–9.
27.   Assuming 100 per cent for the total agenda of the presbytery (administration, politics, discipline, etc.) church discipline in Emden during the five-year survey periods accounted for the following percentages, 1558–62: 45 per cent; 1596–1600: 51 per cent; 1645–49: 49 per cent; 1695–99: 51 per cent; 1741–45: 27 per cent; 1791–95: 12 per cent; 1821–25: 9 per cent. These figures reflect the present state of research. Small changes may still result from individual corrections in the second stage of statistical work. But this does not affect the trend in the development. Apart from that the changes require detailed interpretation which cannot be given in this context.
28.   This, too, is to be described in greater detail in the proposed study.
29.   The rapidly swollen flood of literature on the history of criminality

makes bibliographical completeness impossible. Beside the collection
of essays by Cockburn cited in n. 1 the following publications have
been especially important for my own study of these problems: M. R.
Weissner, *Crime and Punishment in Early Modern Europe* (London,
1979); V. A. C. Gatrell, B. Lenman, and G. Parker (eds), *Crime and the
Law. Society and History of Crime in Western Europe since 1500*
(London, 1980); A. Soman, 'Deviance and Criminal Justice in Western
Europe, 1300–1800', *Criminal Justice History*, I (1980), pp. 3–28; O. H.
Hufton, 'Crime in Pre-Industrial Europe', *Newsletter of the Internatio-
nal Association for the History of Crime and Criminal Justice*
(*IAHCCJ*), IV (1981), pp. 8–35; G. Parker, 'Crime and the early
modern Historian. A review article', *Tijdschrift voor Geschiedenis*,
XCIV (1981), pp. 595–601. B. Lescaze, 'Crimes et criminels à Genève
en 1572', in *Pour une histoire qualitative. Études offertes à Sven Stelling
Michaud* (Geneva, 1975), pp. 45–71; J. A. Sharpe, 'Crime in Pre-
Industrial Europe', *IAHCCJ*, IV (July 1981), pp. 9–35; idem, *Crime in
Seventeenth-Century England. A County Study* (Cambridge, 1983).

30. On this in detail R. Ley, *Kirchenzucht bei Zwingli* (Zürich, 1948), p.
     126f, cf. also n. 1.
31. Ley, *Kirchenzucht*, p. 129.
32. The development in the history of criminality cannot be traced here in
     detail and is, in any case, controversial among historians of crime. Cf.
     M. Foucault, *Surveiller et punir. La naissance de la prison* (Paris, 1975),
     and the thoughtful and wide-ranging sketch by B. Lenman and G.
     Parker, 'The State, the Community and the Criminal Law in Early
     Modern Europe', in Gatrell/Lenman/Parker, *Crime and Law*, pp. 11–
     48.
33. Agreement in the Osterhus Accord of 1611, after matrimonial jurisdic-
     tion in the sixteenth century had been a matter of controversy between
     city and state authorities. Published in H. Wiemann, *Die Grundlagen
     der landständischen Verfassung Ostfrieslands. Die Verträge von 1595 bis
     1611* (Aurich, 1974), pp. 214–61, here 243.
34. Assuming 100 per cent for the share of church discipline in the total
     activity of the presbytery as quoted in n. 27, the following percentages
     applied in the five-year survey periods for cases in the fields of marriage
     and family, and sexuality: 7 per cent and 8 per cent (1557–62); 12 per
     cent and 9 per cent (1596–1600); 17 per cent and 11.5 per cent (1645–
     49); 31 per cent and 19 per cent (1695–99); 21 per cent and 35 per cent
     (1741–45, but the absolute figures then were very low!). These figures
     require careful interpretation (cf. above, n. 27).
35. Cf. H. Jedin, K. Latourette, and J. Martin (eds), *Atlas zur Kirchen-
     geschichte* (Freiburg im Breisgau, 1970), p. 75: *Organisations- und
     Verfassungsskizzen 'Reformierte Kirchenverfassung der Kurpfalz um
     1600'* (types of German territorial churches), and *Reformierte Kirchen-
     verfassung Frankreich 1559* (autonomous congregational organisation
     corresponding to that found in Emden and the Netherlands).
36. Lenman/Parker (see n. 32), 'State and Community', p. 37f. They are
     here primarily concerned with Scotland besides Geneva. Scottish
     church discipline differs in a few yet significant points from church

discipline in Emden and the Netherlands. This was one of the main results of the comparative conference on 'Social Control on Local Level in Early Modern and Modern Europe', organised by Jan Sundin in Stockholm in 1983. The contributions have so far only been hectographically reproduced.

37.   The state used matrimonial and sexual offences in particular for welcome additional revenue; one can go so far as to talk of a 'tax on sin'. This applies to the matrimonial courts of territorial states and churches as it does to state police discipline in general. Cf. the suggestions made by Georg Obrecht, reported in Maier, *Staats- und Verwaltungslehre*, p. 127.

38.   W. Köhler. *Zürcher Ehegericht und Genfer Konsistorium* (2 vols, Leipzig, 1932–42); in greater detail J. Plomp, *De Kerkelijke Tucht bij Calvijn* (Kampen, 1969), esp. p. 341ff.

39.   P. Münch, *Zucht und Ordnung, Reformierte Kirchenverfassungen im 16. und 17. Jahrhundert* [Nassau-Dillenburg, Palatinate, Hessen-Kassel] (Stuttgart, 1978); idem, 'Kirchenzucht und Nachbarschaft. Zur sozialen Problematik des calvinistischen Seniorats um 1600', in E. W. Zeeden and T. Lang (eds), *Kirche und Visitation* (Stuttgart, 1984), pp. 216–48, esp. n. 24. If the general conditions governing the law of the established churches and the systematic distinction outlined in the text above are considered, the contradiction between Münch's and my assessment is removed.

15 What is a 'Religious War'?

Konrad Repgen

I

For many people today the word *Religionskrieg* is an emotive one. Occasional news items about bloody battles in the Near East between Moslem sects leave us baffled, and the civil war between Christians in Northern Ireland seems painfully embarrassing. Many people evince a similar reaction to the European confessional wars of the early modern period. The mere historical fact of the *Konfessionskrieg* in the sixteenth century strikes large sections of the present-day world as a scandal.

It was not always so. The moral duty to show confessional solidarity and to impose religious-political viewpoints by (if necessary) warlike means was one of the stereotype lines of argument of the sixteenth century.[1] There were always, it is true, individuals and relatively small groups who thought otherwise, since religious truths cannot be asserted through violence. But the dominant postulate in the sixteenth century was and remained the opposing view based on the passage in St Luke 14, 23 'compel them to come in' ('*compelle intrare*'). This had been used since the time of St Augustine to legitimise the use of coercion against heterodoxy. In the thirteenth century the states had formulated a complementary secular law. This was founded on scholasticism's concept of truth[2] which had been developed since the twelfth century, and a view of man associated with it.

This old European principle of the politically and juridically binding consequences of theological positions and ecclesiastical decisions was only rendered suspect by the Enlightenment,[3] but as we know the latter never prevailed completely. Voices affirming religious war as something at least self-evident, or even as a good thing, are still to be heard in the nineteenth and twentieth centuries.[4]

Alongside this positively or negatively charged meaning of *Religionskrieg*, our term – whose synonyms are *Glaubenskrieg* and *Konfessionskrieg* or (when referring to France 1562–98) *konfessioneller Bürgerkrieg* – makes its appearance as a value-free, descriptive con-

311

cept in the language of historically educated people and is universally understood. Hence, without further discussion, it was possible to use it in the title of a recent reference work on the political history of ideas.[5] Similarly, without any reference to negative connotations, the term *Religionskrieg* is employed in the encyclopaedias,[6] in standard works on general and ecclesiastical history,[7] and in the academic literature.[8]

In contrast to this empirical finding there is a total lack of relevant literature on the term *Religionskrieg* as used in secular and ecclesiastical history. If one wishes to explain what a *Religionskrieg* was to a non-historian, it is necessary to indulge in wide-ranging and involved accounts whose aim is not to convey conceptual clarity but to put across the historical view. In this way it is certainly possible to demonstrate how it came about that religious and political matters were so indissolubly linked and the consequences this had. But it would not explain to modern man why the label of 'religion' is employed as the sole catchword in this description, whereas in actual fact it was indisputably a case of the *interlinking* of religion *and* politics.

This procedure seems all the more problematic in that the actual reasons for war, even in the confessional age, can hardly ever be exclusively or even predominantly attributed to the complex 'religion'. The Schmalkaldic War of 1546–47 was certainly waged by Charles V with the object of making the Protestant German Estates attend the Council of Trent and ultimately bow to its decisions, so as to overcome the split in the church. But the catchword 'religious war' would not be an adequate description of the reasons which led the emperor or the pope to go to war; nor would it apply to Philip of Hesse, and definitely not to Maurice of Saxony.[9]

In addition, there is a second problem: not all the military conflicts of the age of confessional wars can be assigned to the type *Religionskrieg*.[10] However one defines religious wars, they constitute no more than a proportion of such conflicts – whether it is the greater part depends on which perspective one considers important.

Summarising all this, one might ask whether it would not be better to avoid altogether terms so fraught and open to misunderstanding as *Konfessionskrieg, Glaubenskrieg* and *Religionskrieg*. For several reasons which cannot be discussed here I would disagree, but argue instead that the term *Religionskrieg* offers a most useful conceptual label[11] for a dozen and a half to two dozen European wars and rebellions between 1529 and 1689. However, a precondition for its continued use should be that we identify more exactly what the term

Religionskrieg can and should denote – and what it cannot and should not. My thesis is as follows: the term *Religionskrieg* is a typological concept, which can be used as a legitimation type (though not as a motivation type) for a number of early modern wars, particularly those of the sixteenth century. This thesis might seem somewhat complicated at first glance. It conceals, however, a state of affairs that is relatively simple yet of fundamental importance to political history as a science, as G. R. Elton has taught us.[12]

In order to understand the facts we must first bear in mind that the designation 'war' is always a term that is arrived at by consensus. It does not proceed from any kind of pre-existing logical system but comes into everyday use through dissemination in contemporary propaganda and then, generally by way of contemporary accounts and chronicles, passes into historical tradition. This endures as long as the will to remember it persists. The designation 'war' cannot therefore be systematically derived but can only be explained historically.[13]

Similarly, it is historically explicable that not all major military conflicts are termed 'wars' either in their day or subsequently.[14] Thus it is possible in German to speak of the *Geldrischer Erbfolgestreit* – the struggle for the Guelders Succession[15] – when referring to the military conflict over the succession in Guelders and Zutphen 1539–43, which was fought out between the Duke of Cleves and the emperor as the ruler of Burgundy. By including the term 'succession' in the designation of the war one is simultaneously mentioning two different things by name. One is the aim of the two adversaries to succeed Charles of Egmont, who died in 1538; the other, the legal grounds on which both legitimised the use of military force. 'Succession' thus stands both for the motivation – the objective and for the legitimation, the public justification of war.

My thesis therefore implies that wars should only be termed *Religionskriege*, in so far as at least one of the belligerents lays claim to 'religion', a religious law, in order to justify his warfare and to substantiate publicly why his use of military force against a political authority should be a *bellum iustum*. This proposal represents a step with far-reaching implications. To explain it, we must take our inquiry further afield and argue methodologically.

II

To allow the use of the term *Religionskrieg* only in respect of the legitimation, but not of the motivation, of a war in the sixteenth (and seventeenth) centuries[16] may be justified by the fact that all the many European wars between the thirteenth and the nineteenth centuries can be assigned to one of a clearly defined number of legitimation types.[17] This method of classification permits us to impose some kind of order on a chaos which it has not been possible to bring under control until now by the traditional methods of political history. To devise war types of this kind and make them the starting point of historical reflection means, however, deviating from half a millennium of historiographical tradition by ceasing to inquire chiefly and from the outset into the motives of the protagonists concerned, and proceeding instead from the concrete legitimation in each case.

This procedure offers considerable advantages for understanding the history of international relations. We know that in early modern Europe it was not peace but war that was the norm: the years without war in the sixteenth century can easily be counted on the fingers of both hands. From the late fifteenth century to the end of the eighteenth century there were approximately 250 wars in Europe.[18]

Well over 500 belligerents took part in these wars; for in many military conflicts there were more than two powers involved. With the historian's usual methods, however, the overall history of the sum of the political decisions which preceded each concrete resolve to wage war remains inaccessible. For what can the historian say on the subject?

Those of a *narrative* persuasion seek answers in terms of causality, a concern which has been at the centre of historiography ever since the age of Renaissance humanism. They seek to argue in terms of 'because – therefore', uncovering actual facts or hypotheses about them, that is to say, probabilities. They therefore have to rely on convincing sources for the motives behind the statesmen's actions and decisions. In this quest they reach the limits of what can be presented with a fair degree of certainty as fact, or at least as a likely probability, much more often and much sooner than we would like. One of the most recent standard works on German history 1547–48 states, 'The question of the motives which prompted Paul III [to take part in the Schmalkaldic War] can hardly be answered with absolute certainty on the basis of the available sources.'[19]

The same applies to many, in fact to most cases: certainty is seldom attainable, for the simple reason that the sources necessary for this never existed or have been lost. But even if we did possess these sources our problem would not be capable of solution. For – and this is my second point – it would quite exceed the capacity of any historian, even the most gifted and diligent, if he were expected to determine the motivation in well over 500 political opinion-forming and decision-making processes which each culminated in a 'yes' to an actual war: he would need not one, but many lifetimes for the task. Thirdly, dividing the work up would not be very helpful in this case; for as the history of historiography based on the division of labour demonstrates, the solution of the problem which one is searching for would either have to be known in advance or would have to be derived from meta-historical presuppositions. In the first case one would be faced with a circular argument; in the second, one would be shifting the question from history on to another discipline, dispensing with a historically verifiable and hence profitable answer. Fourthly, for methodological reasons which cannot be explained here, motives and motivations can only be perceived with the aid of hermeneutic methods. Hermeneutics aims at perception of the particular, the specific, the individual. But this can only be compared with something else which is particular, specific and individual by reference to a third, universal property that is contained within it. It is scarcely possible to come up with a framework that can be employed comparatively by treading the path of purely hermeneutic historiography.

Yet little headway can be made using *analytical* methods either. Since no individual action can be adequately derived from the sum total of its preconditions and circumstances, and hence truly explained, each of these procedures leads at best in the right direction but never gets to the heart of the problem. Thus the use of quantifying techniques on the theme of 'the European wars' has a long tradition.[20] The results that can be achieved in this way are, however, of doubtful value; the gain in knowledge is hardly commensurate with the labour invested. The use of sociological models and categories has not proved very profitable.[21] Insight and overview are less accessible in this way than with traditional research into motives and causality.

So must we capitulate, adopting epistemological pessimism and minimalism as our motto and declaring the bankruptcy of our discipline with regard to a general framework for the history of the relations between states? In my view, no. It is possible to impose on the confusing wealth of detail an interpretation of the whole as a precondition for a historical understanding of each particular by distinguishing between wars on the basis of the legitimation types employed in them, the modes of argumentation publicly advanced to justify concretely each of the 250 wars by each participant in them.

The formation of such war legitimation types is therefore not merely a classificatory game of the kind which we encounter so often in modern political science, but a sensible reduction of complexity.

This procedure is not concerned with the formation of war concepts but with the conceptual ordering of war types, which is something else. Type formation is, of course, a widespread practice in the science of history because it is of great practical utility. Its chief aim is to order multifarious individual phenomena in such a way as to yield a characteristic of relative universality common to all of them.[22] Since 'each individual thing [also] contains a universal element', as Ranke observed,[23] classification on the basis of this universal element is the genuine precondition of any real comparison. The purpose of type formation is not to supplant the narrative or analytical explanation; rather, it is to facilitate a certain approximation, to convey a certain initial lucidity and thereby to set the comparison in motion. The specific nature of the particular, its individuality, is rendered visible with the aid of the type concept. Therefore, anyone who wishes to make historical comparisons must use types. In our case we are not dealing with ideal-typical abstractions, as have become fashionable since Max Weber, but with facts which can be ordered in terms of real types.

For if we ask what was the historically, concretely tangible element and at the same time the actual common element in all European wars since the High Middle Ages, it turns out that, beside a few trivial facts (as, for instance, that war meant the use of physical violence to the point of death), from the twelfth century on there was *one* theoretically undisputed norm that applied: war should only be waged by Christians as a just war. The theoretical conditions which had to be fulfilled for a military conflict to be morally legitimised were subsequently discussed in an increasingly extensive and detailed literature – first by jurists (Gratian), then theologians (Aquinas) and finally also by philosophers (Hobbes). All these Christian theoreticians who elaborated the norm of the *jus ad bellum* proceeded from two preconditions: first, that there was a legitimate right to wage war in definable circumstances; secondly, that war was a legal process which could (not must) ensue when there was no arbiter empowered to impose and implement a right in law which had been infringed or was due to one of the parties. Every power engaging in war therefore had to prove publicly, not only for political, psychological and moral reasons but also on legal grounds, that its particular concrete recourse to war was sufficiently justified, and that its war was a *bellum iustum*.

For this reason we find that war legitimations are roughly equal in number to the belligerents.

This proof was adduced by the states in their formal declarations of war and in the war manifestos which partly replaced them, partly supplemented and accompanied them.[24] After the invention of printing they were almost regularly published, but unfortunately nowhere systematically collected or listed. It is therefore a laborious but worthwhile business to record them. True, they say nothing directly, it should be emphasised once again, about motives and causality, that is, about the matters in which we have been interested since Machiavelli and Guicciardini, and especially since Niebuhr and Ranke. The European war manifestos do not state *why* A waged war against B or C, or D and E against F and G. But they do state *what* A–G publicly presented to their own followers, to non-aligned third parties and to their adversaries as the justificatory grounds, and how they justified that this particular war was a *bellum iustum*. Naturally it cannot be inferred from these texts *whether* war X or Y was just or unjust for B or A. Declarations of war and war manifestos are legal documents similar to a suit in a court of law: they do not offer causes but grounds, they are documents with a specific purpose, they are, quite plainly, propaganda. But not everything in this war propaganda is falsified. And even if it were, this would not detract from its importance as an historical source. For all the European war manifestos nearly without exception follow *a relatively small and manageable number of patterns of argumentation*. To the best of my knowledge we are dealing with approximately twelve main concepts, twelve types of legitimation.[25] In them we have a framework, an instrument enabling us to assign each concrete war to a specific legitimation type. It turns out, and it will not come as a surprise, that several types of legitimation are often interlinked in order to justify a military conflict that is imminent or has already begun.

The value of this procedure, the practical use of this legitimation framework, lies in the access which it affords to the substance of the issue through a preliminary orientation independent of hermeneutic considerations. It is not that by assigning a particular war manifesto to one or other of the legitimation types one has said everything there is to say about matters on which the historian is able to comment; nor is it by any means the case that research into causality and motivation is about to be thrown on the scrap heap. But these war legitimation types do provide the history of international relations with an initial stage that makes it possible to classify the individual and specific in

terms of the universal – the real task of the historian[26] – more efficiently than in any other way. The formation of war legitimation
types is a cumbersome phrase, but it denotes something highly useful
and essentially straightforward (since it derives from perceptions
immanent within the texts themselves) from which the history of the
early modern period and not least the history of the confessional age
may profit.

   Let us thus return to our question of what a religious war is,
illustrating this with the example of the Schmalkaldic War of 1546–
47, which is almost universally designated or described as a 'religious
war'.

III

To begin with, let me emphasise something which cannot be proved
here, that the legitimation *Religionskrieg* was something new to the
sixteenth century. Prior to that, war was not justified with the
argument of 'religion'; for the Crusade was, as will become apparent
below, something different.[27] Neither the Albigensian Wars nor the
Hussite Wars were waged as *Religionskriege*, whereas the Schmalkaldic War was, at least on the part of the pope, the Elector of Saxony
and the Landgrave of Hesse.[28]

   I think I am correct in saying that the coupling phrase 'religious
war' (*Religionskrieg*) was not yet accepted usage in 1546–47. It is
possible that it first arose in French in the 1560s (*guerre de religion*),[29]
whence it was adopted by German (and other languages). Later, the
phrase was well known throughout Europe. In 1632 Urban VIII
rejected a petition under ecclesiastical law against Richelieu's Protestant alliances precisely because it did not involve a *guerre di
religione*, as the Spanish and Austrian Habsburgs claimed.[30] At the
same time there appeared in Germany pamphlets in which the events
of the war were discussed in the light of its character as a *Religionskrieg* – for and against.[31] But from the time of the *Reichsabschied* of
1530 at the latest the matter was the subject of a political discussion,
even though the catchword *Religionskrieg* was not used and various
circumlocutions were preferred. Thus the emperor reserved the right
in the famous, indeed notorious, Regensburg Treaty with Philip of
Hesse of 13 June 1541, to embark on military intervention against the
landgrave too, in the eventuality that 'war was waged against all
Protestants in general on account of religion' ('*von wegen der religion
wider alle protestantes in gemain krieg bewegt wurd*').[32] Now, the

Schmalkaldic War of 1546–47 was, of course, not a war waged by the emperor against *all* Protestants. It was not only the pope who was allied with Charles V, but also Maurice of Saxony. For this reason the emperor had ensured in 1545 that the war alliance with Paul III finally signed on 16 June 1546 in Rome[33] was not geared to a 'war on the Protestants' but to military coercion to force the Schmalkaldic League to send representatives to the Council of Trent. None of those involved were in any doubt that such a war, if the emperor should get his way (which was by no means certain), would affect not only the allies of Schmalkalden but all Protestants – though to what extent and with what consequences was another story.

In the treaty between the two Habsburg brothers and Bavaria of 7 June 1546, which secured for the emperor (to use the modern term) the logistics of the Danubian Campaign of 1546, there is consistently no mention of the Schmalkaldic League, but of those '*qui ab unione catholicae ecclesiae deviarunt*'; the emperor undertakes '*quam citissime ... adversus eos, qui ab religione ... deviarunt, bellum movere adque inchoare*'.[34] No less clear, and tending even more pointedly in the direction of *Religionskrieg* on account of their rhetorical style, were the papal breves of 3–11 July 1546.[35] In these the pope informed Catholic Europe – and, moreover (to the understandable anger of the emperor) the confessionally mixed Swiss confederation, which immediately passed the text on to the League of Schmalkalden – of the alliance, the '*foedus*', whose goal was the '*exstirpatio*' of heresy in Germany. This would take place if necessary, after all other methods had failed, '*ferro atque armis*', in other words with military force.

In view of the overwhelming abundance of such evidence, is there any disputing the fact that for the emperor, too, in 1546 the Schmalkaldic War was about religion, so that 'religion' in this case was not only the legitimation but also the motivation? Did he not write to his sister Mary on 9 June 1546, after the final decision to attack had been taken (in the commonly cited translation by Iserloh,[36] which reproduces almost word for word the earlier version by Bizer[37]):

> If we failed to intervene now, all the Estates of Germany would be in danger of breaking with the faith ... After considering this and considering it again, I decided to embark on war against Hesse and Saxony as transgressors of the peace against the Duke of Brunswick and his territory. And although this pretext will not long disguise the fact that it is a matter of religion, yet it serves for the present to divide the renegades.

This translation is in point of fact very loose in the crucial final sentence. Strictly speaking it should read: 'And thus, as this pretence and pretext for the war will not entirely cause the said renegades from Catholicism to believe themselves that it is a matter of religion . . .'[38] So the emperor does not expressly concede, even in the innermost circle of political decision-making, that his public justification of the Schmalkaldic War is only a pretence and a pretext. Rather, he is talking about the political opportuneness of one legitimation or the other for the impending war.

As far as we know, Charles V only once made an official, public statement on his *ius ad bellum* against the Schmalkaldic League.[39] It is the imperial declaration of outlawry on the Elector of Saxony and the Landgrave of Hesse, dated 20 July 1546 but not published until early August.[40] This document, which his legal advisers must naturally have spent a long time honing, emphasises only those crimes which could be considered a 'breach of public peace' (*Landfriedensbruch*). There is no mention here of offences against the imperial religious law. The *bellum contra deviatores ecclesiae* is given its legal justification in the *crimen laesae majestatis*[41] – it is the same legal argumentation with which the emperors in the Thirty Years War legitimised in 1618, 1619, 1625 and 1631 their military intervention against the Bohemians, the Palatinate, the Lower Saxon Circle along with its new colonel, the King of the Danes, and finally the Leipzig Covenant, in fact virtually the whole of Protestant Germany,[42] the same legal grounds, too, which Philip II cited in 1567 when sending the Duke of Alba to Belgium to take action against the revolt in the Netherlands.[43] From the emperor's point of view, the Schmalkaldic War was a *Reichsexekutionskrieg* (a war to maintain the integrity of the empire), if one takes not the motivation but the legitimation as the criterion for classifying it as a war type. The emperor is putting down a revolution, as befits his office, nothing else. This argument gave Charles V a psychological and propagandistic lead which the Schmalkaldic League was unable to pull back, no matter how assiduously they, too, used the channels of publicity, which indeed they dominated.[44]

The Schmalkaldic declaration of war on 11 August 1546, the *Verwahrungsschrift* in the legal terminology of the day,[45] makes of its argumentation much harder going. Of course it stresses that the emperor had imposed outlawry without bringing any legal action against those outlawed, which was in breach of the electoral capitulation's terms of 1519.[46] But this citation failed to dismiss the counter argument familiar to any jurist schooled in Roman and ecclesiastical law, that in notorious cases there was no need of a formal legal action.[47]

In terms of imperial constitutional law the Schmalkaldic position was problematic. The argument could not, despite all their words, be dismissed. Their legal entitlement to conquer the lands of Brunswick was a poor one. For this reason the core of their reasoning is not constitutional and procedural law, but the appeal to 'this our true Christian religion, which the pope calls heresy' ('*Diese vnsere wahre christliche religion, welche der Papst ketzerei nennet*'). The elector and the landgrave argued that the 'pure doctrine of the Gospel, of our true Christian religion and the Augsburg Confession' ('*der reinen lehre des evangelii, vnserer wahren christlich religion vnd Augsburgischen Confession*') were faced with the danger of immediate suppression and eradication. Consequently, military resistance was permitted and commanded, both by divine law and by natural law. Thus, to summarise all this in a single phrase, they are declaring a *preventive religious war*. True, they were hard put to substantiate the right to '*praevenire*' with facts about imperial policy. Their comments on Charles V's alleged intentions and motives were a construct, an assertion, not proof. Their strongest argument in this respect was provided by the aforementioned breve of Paul III of early July 1546 to the Swiss,[48] whose text had been available to the allies since the end of July. In their manifesto they quoted some passages from it in German translation.[49]

We now come to the third of the participants in this war, the pope. He, too, publicly justified his part in the war in the summer of 1546 – probably less from pressure to give his legitimation than from his desire to drag the emperor to the altar of Farnese politics. Then as now, a publicly declared political position signified a commitment to political goals.

It appears that an independent papal war manifesto was never published. The legitimation of military intervention was effected differently, in two ways: first, indirectly, semi-publicly, through the formulation and despatch of the aforementioned breves; for their text could scarcely be expected to remain secret for long. The second commitment was the public ceremony whereby the pope's two grandsons had the responsibility for leading the Schmalkaldic War conferred on them on 4 July 1546 in Rome: the first, the cardinal, as legate, the second, Ottavio, the layman, as commander of the strong papal army, who was handed an imperial sceptre, '*donatum ad bellum in Lutheranos gerendum*'.[50] It was thereby demonstrated to the Christian public at large that the pope was waging war on the Protestants. For him, too, just as for the Schmalkaldic League, it was a *Religionskrieg*, albeit the other way round. A papal bull of indulgence of 25 July suggested the same theme.[51] In it the faithful were urged to accompany the war on the German Protestants with prayers and charitable works. This bull, which went on to play a certain part in Schmalkaldic war propaganda,[52] leads us to our final point, which can be quickly elucidated.

IV

We have demonstrated (with no claim to novelty) that the emperor on the one hand, and the Schmalkaldic League and the pope on the other, legitimised the war with differing legal arguments: the emperor was combating rebellion and a breach of the public peace; the pope and the Schmalkaldic League were waging a religious war. This has been designated by Heinrich Lutz, quite in accordance with the sources, a *Ketzerkrieg* (war on heretics);[53] similarly, with regard to the later sixteenth century, J. R. Hale speaks of religious war as a 'crusade'.[54] I consider both terms less appropriate than *Religionskrieg*; for instead of focusing attention on what was historically new about the events of the sixteenth century, they tend to distort our view of it.

The West had already experienced war on heretics. Innocent III in his day had conducted the struggle against the Albigensians as a crusade against Christians;[55] as late as the fifteenth century the campaigns against the Hussites[56] and against the Utraquist King of Bohemia Podiebrad[57] had been waged as a real 'crusade' in the traditional forms, with crusading bulls and so on. A 'war on heretics' was thus war in the legal form of the crusade, if one examines the traditions prior to the sixteenth century. And the memory of it had by no means been extinguished. When the pope received the emperor's offer of alliance against the Schmalkaldic League,[58] he immediately asked his legates at the Council of Trent for an expert comment. This came on 7 June 1546.[59] The document, at least the section which interests us, was presumably formulated by Del Monte, the experienced canonist, who five years later himself became pope (Julius III, 1550–55).

According to Del Monte there were three ways to deal with heresy in Germany: first, through a tolerable agreement ('*qualche accordo tollerabile*'); secondly, by inducing it to bow to the Council; thirdly, by force. True, this last way was harsh ('*par rigido*'), but, especially when the first two possibilities had failed, it was religiously correct: 'it is possible to proclaim a crusade against the heretics with the same indulgences and privileges that are granted for the recovery of the Holy Land' (*'che si possa bandire la cruciata contra gl'heretici con le medesime indulgentie et privilegii, che si concedano per recuperationen de Terra Santa'*). This would really have been *Ketzerkrieg*, with all its consequences, something quite different from the bull of indulgence of 15 July 1546, which was concerned with the receiving of the sacraments, prayer and good works.

As far as I can see, no project such as that envisaged by Del Monte was considered in the further discussions and plans which preceded the Schmalkaldic War on the part of the pope or on the part of the emperor. The reason for this has been formulated succinctly and clearly by Jedin: 'Canonically it was plausible: politically it was impracticable.'[60] This sentence could, however, be extended so as to constitute a general statement about the types of war legitimation of the sixteenth century: the time for crusades against Christians was past.[61] *Konfessions-, Glaubens-* or *Religionskrieg* was something new – both with regard to legitimation and with regard to the form that resulted from it.

This fact should be borne in mind if one wishes to make use of the term *Religionskrieg*, a conceptual designation so important for a proper understanding of the sixteenth century. War and the use of military force against heterodoxy was a right assumed by all four of the great churches. War, however, was no longer waged and justified as a crusade but as *Religionskrieg*, as the military solution to conflicts arising from the protection of confessional possessions or from confessional conquest. For *ancien régime* Europe that was something new.

Notes

1. H. G. Koenigsberger, 'The Organisation of Revolutionary Parties in France and the Netherlands during the Sixteenth Century', *Journal of Modern History*, XXVII (1955), pp. 335–51.
2. Important for this topic is J. Fried, 'Wille, Freiwilligkeit und Geständnis. Zur Beurteilung des letzten Templergroßmeisters Jacques de Molay', *Historisches Jahrbuch*, CV (1985), pp. 388–425, esp. p. 419ff.
3. A very early example, though not yet anti-ecclesiastical in tone, of hostility to this principle is contained in the anti-French pamphlet of 1689: *Discours Von den Religions-Kriegen ins gemein/Und in specie, Ob auch der jetzige einer seye Oder nicht?* (Freystadt, 1689).

4.   Otto von Bismarck, *Erinnerung und Gedanke* (Berlin, 1932), pp. 351, 15ff: '*Es ist daher erklärlich, daß aus kirchlichen Meinungsverschiedenheiten Religionskriege entstehen.*'

5.   Iring Fetscher and Herfried Münkler (eds), *Von den Konfessionskriegen bis zur Aufklärung* (*Handbuch der politischen Ideen*, vol. III) (Munich/ Zürich, 1985).

6.   Cf. the article '*Religionskrieg*' in *Der Große Herder*, vol. IX, 4th edn (1934); *Der Große Duden*, vol. III (1935); *Meyers Enzyklopädisches Lexikon*, vol. XIX (1977): *Meyers Großes Universal Lexikon*, vol. XI (1984); *Brockhaus Enzyklopädie*, vol. XV (1972).

7.   Cf. H. Lapeyre, *Les monarchies européennes du XVIe siècle. Les relations internationales* (Paris, 1967), pp. 167–83: '*Les guerres de religion en France*'; A. Bourde and E. Temine, 'Frankreich . . . (1453–1660)', in J. Engel (ed.), *Die Entstehung des neuzeitlichen Europa* (*Handbuch der europäischen Geschichte*, vol. III) (Stuttgart, 1971), pp. 772–80: '*Die Religionskriege*'; K. D. Schmidt, 'Die katholische Reform und die Gegenreformation', in *Die Kirche in ihrer Geschichte*, ed. M. Jacobs, vol. III, fasc. L/1 (Göttingen, 1975), p. 44; Hubert Jedin, 'Katholische Reform und Gegenreformation', in idem (ed.), *Handbuch der Kirchengeschichte*, vol. IV (Freiburg im Breisgau, 1967), pp. 533f, 670, 682. Cf. R. S. Dunn, *The Age of the Religious Wars 1559–1689* (*Norton History of Modern Europe*, vol. II) (London, 1971); E. W. Zeeden, *Hegemonialkriege und Glaubenskämpfe 1556–1648* (*Propyläen Geschichte Europas*, vol. II) (Frankfurt am Main, 1977), p. 11f.

8.   Sections 275–312 of Dahlmann-Waitz, 10th edn (1985–) are headed: '*Reformation und Konfessionskriege*'. Among the specialised studies cf. R. Schnur, *Die französischen Juristen im konfessionellen Bürgerkrieg des 16. Jahrhunderts* (Berlin, 1962); H. Dreitzel, 'Hermann Conring und die politische Wissenschaft seiner Zeit', in M. Stolleis (ed.), *Hermann Conring (1606–1681). Beiträge zum Leben und Werk* (Berlin/ Munich, 1983), pp. 135–72, at p. 142: '*Die Überwindung des konfessionellen Bürgerkriegs*' (i.e. the Thirty Years War).

9.   Horst Rabe, *Reichsbund und Interim. Die Verfassungs- und Religionspolitik Karls V. und der Reichstag von Augsburg 1547/1548* (Cologne/ Vienna, 1971).

10.   Not, for example, the conflict over the Spanish and Portuguese succession between 1580 and 1583, the Danish War of Kalmar against Sweden, 1613–15, both Savoyard wars against Mantua, Spanish Milan and Tuscany, 1613–17, or the Italian Wars as a whole.

11.   On conceptual typology see Theodor Schieder, 'Der Typus in der Geschichtswissenschaft', in idem, *Staat und Gesellschaft im Wandel der Zeit* (Munich, 1958), pp. 172–87; K.-G. Faber, *Theorien der Geschichtswissenschaft*, 4th edn (Munich, 1978), pp. 89–100.

12.   G. R. Elton, *The Practice of History* (Sydney, 1967); idem, *Political History* (London, 1970); idem and R. W. Fogel, *Which Road to the Past? Two Views of History* (New Haven/London, 1983). Cf. Konrad Repgen, 'Ende der angelsächsischen Theoriedebatte?', *Historisches Jahrbuch*, CVI (1986).

13. H. Lübbe, 'Was heißt "Das kann man nur historisch erklären"?', in idem, *Geschichtsbegriff und Geschichtsinteresse. Analytik und Pragmatik der Historie* (Basel/Stuttgart, 1977), pp. 35–47.

14. Some provisional reflections in Konrad Repgen, 'Über die Geschichtsschreibung des Dreißighährigen Kriegs. Begriff und Konzeption', in idem and E. Müller-Luckner (eds), *Krieg und Politik 1618–1648. Europäische Probleme und Perspektiven* (Munich, 1986).

15. Cf. Karl Schottenloher (ed.), *Bibliographie der deutschen Geschichte im Zeitalter der Glaubensspaltung 1517–1585*, vol. IV (Leipzig, 1938), nos. 37190, 37197: '*Krieg*'; 37191: '*Streit*'; 37194, 37201: '*Fehde*'. In contemporary usage also '*coniuratio*', ibid., 37187.

16. The seventeenth century is here disregarded, though my arguments apply fully to it as well.

17. Konrad Repgen, 'Kriegslegitimationen in Alteuropa. Entwurf einer historischen Typologie', *Historische Zeitschrift*, CCXLI (1985), pp. 27–49.

18. An extensive listing of the wars, though in need of revision, is given by Q. Wright, *A Study of War*, 2nd edn (Chicago/London, 1965), Tables 31–42 (for 1480–1918), and by G. von Alten (ed.), *Kriege vom Altertum bis zur Gegenwart* (*Handbuch für Heer und Flotte. Enzyklopädie der Kriegswissenschaften und verwandter Gebiete*, Sonderband IX) (Berlin, 1912), pp. xvii–xxiv.

19. Rabe, *Reichsbund und Interim*, p. 56.

20. Cf. G. Bodart (ed.), *Militär-historisches Kriegs-Lexikon (1618–1905)* (Vienna/Leipzig, 1908); idem, *Losses of Life in Modern Wars: Austria-Hungary, France* (Oxford, 1916).

21. The most recent attempt at a survey is by W. H. McNeill, *The Pursuit of Power. Technology, Armed Force and Society from A.D. 1000* (Oxford, 1982).

22. Schieder, 'Typus'.

23. Leopold von Ranke, 'Die Großen Mächte', in idem (ed.), *Historisch-politische Zeitschrift*, II (1833–36), pp. 1–51, here at p. 2.

24. See the diplomatic notes exchanged before the commencement of hostilities or analogous dramatic gestures such as Charles V's allocution before the pope and his curia on 17 April 1536.

25. Repgen, 'Kriegslegitimationen', p. 43:
    Diese lauten – in alphabetischer Reihenfolge, also: unabhängig von der Zeit, in der sie zuerst begegnen; unabhängig von der Häufigkeit, mit der sie auftreten; und unabhängig von den Staaten, die sie verwenden – folgendermaßen: Abwehr einer Universalmonarchie – Bekämpfung von Rebellion – Erbrecht – Gleichgewicht – Handelsinteressen – Kreuzzug bzw. Türkenkrieg – präventive Abwehr drohender Gefahren – Religionsrecht – Verteidigung der eigenen Untertanen gegen einen kriegerischen Überfall – Verteidigung ständischer Freiheiten – Vertragsverpflichtungen – Wiedergutmachung erlittenen Unrechts.

26. In the debate over historical theory in the 1960s and 1970s it was often overlooked that Ranke regarded this as a crucial postulate.

27. See below, p. 322f.

28. Since Catholics legitimated these wars as crusades, it would be interesting to enquire whether the Albigensians and Hussites also legitimated their wars as *Religionskriege*, but in fact they argued differently.

29. The Edict of Amboise (19 March 1563) referred to '*troubles, seditions et tumultes ... suscités de la diversité des opinions pour le faict de la religion*' and also talked of '*ceste guerre*'. Cf. E. and E. Haag, *La France protestante*, vol. X (Paris, 1858), p. 61f.

30. Details in A. Leman, *Urbain VIII et la rivalité de la France et de la maison d'Autriche de 1631 à 1635* (Lille/Paris, 1920).

31. Cf. D. Böttcher, 'Propaganda und öffentliche Meinung im protestantischen Deutschland 1628–1636', *Archiv für Reformationsgeschichte*, XLIV (1953), pp. 181–203; XLV (1954), pp. 83–98.

32. M. Lenz (ed.), *Briefwechsel Landgrafen Philipp's des Großmüthigen von Hessen mit Bucer*, vol. III (Leipzig, 1891), pp. 91–6, here at p. 96.

33. *Nuntiaturberichte aus Deutschland* (cit. *NB*), sect. 1, vol. IX: *1546–1547* (Gotha, 1899), pp. 575–8.

34. K. Lanz (ed.), *Correspondenz des Kaisers Karl V.*, vol. II: *1532–1549* (Leipzig, 1845), pp. 648–52, here at p. 649.

35. *Annales Ecclesiastici*, ed. O. Raynaldus, *ad annum 1546*, nos. 58–60 (to the 13 Cantons); no. 96 (to the king of France); no. 98 (to the king of Poland); no. 101 (to Venice); bo. 102 (to the Elector of Mainz).

36. Erwin Iserloh, 'Die protestantische Reformation', in Hubert Jedin (ed.), *Handbuch der Kirchengeschichte*, vol. IV (Freiburg im Breisgau, 1967), p. 299. Iserloh's translation follows Karl Brandi, *Karl V. Werden und Schicksal einer Persönlichkeit und eines Weltreiches* (Munich, 1937), p. 470f.

37. Ernst Bizer, 'Reformationsgeschichte 1532 bis 1555', in K. D. Schmidt and E. Wolf (eds), *Die Kirche in ihrer Geschichte*, vol. III (Göttingen, 1964), p. 142.

38. '*Et combien que ceste couverte et pretexte de guerre ne pourra du tout encourir que lesdits desvoyez ne pensent bien, que ce soit pour la cause de la religion, toutes fois sera ce occasion de les séparer ...*' Brandi, *Karl V.*, vol. II: *Quellen und Erörterungen* (Munich, 1941), p. 370.

39. For a different view see Heinrich Lutz, 'Friedensidee und Friedensprobleme der Frühen Neuzeit', in *Wiener Beiträge zur Geschichte der Neuzeit*, vol. XI (Vienna, 1984), pp. 28–54, here at p. 42 with n. 21, though the reference does not contain the citation.

40. Text in F. Hortleder, *Der Römischen ... Maiesteten ... Handlungen und Außschreiben ...*, vol. II: *Von der Rechtmäßigkeit ... deß Teutschen Kriegs ...*, 2nd edn (Gotha, 1645), pp. 312–18.

41. R. Liebenwirth, 'Crimen laesae majestatis', in *Handwörterbuch zur deutschen Rechtsgeschichte*, vol. I (Berlin, 1971), cols. 648–51.

42. Cf. the patents of Emperor Matthias (18/30 June 1618) and Ferdinand II (11 December 1619), the edictal annulment (29 January 1620), the monitorial mandates (30 April 1620, 29 December 1625), and the advocatory mandates (3 April 1626, 14 May 1631).

43. Geoffrey Parker, *The Dutch Revolt* (Harmondsworth, 1979 edn), p. 89.

44. O. Waldeck, 'Die Publizistik des Schmalkaldischen Krieges', *Archiv für Reformationsgeschichte*, VII (1909), pp. 1–55; VIII (1910/11), pp. 44–133.

45. Grimm's *Wörterbuch*, vol. XXV (Leipzig, 1956), col. 2091. Hortleder, *Handlungen*, observes:
    Verwahrungsschrifft: idiomate nostro eleganter dicitur, epistola, qua adversario inimicitias bellumque ingenue denuntiare solemus adeoque honori et existimationi nostrae cavere, ne eum dolose ac proditorie agressi esse videamur, quod Aurea Bulla vetat tit. 17. sub poena infamiae.
    For the text of the Schmalkaldic declaration of war cf. ibid., pp. 410–13.

46. Karl Zeumer (ed.), *Quellensammlung zur Geschichte der Deutschen Reichsverfassung in Mittelalter und Neuzeit*, 2nd edn (Tübingen, 1913), pp. 309–13, here p. 311f (§ 22).

47. This view was extensively discussed in the political treatises which defended the ban upon the Elector Palatine of 22 January 1621.

48. See above, n. 35 and Waldeck, 'Publizistik', part I, p. 22f.

49. In Hortleder, *Handlungen*, p. 412, ¶ 9.

50. *NB*, sect. 1, vol. IX, pp. 98, 24.

51. Cf. Waldeck, 'Publizistik', part I, no. 10 and Hortleder, *Handlungen*, pp. 268–72, 272–9 (German translation with polemical glosses by Nikolaus von Amsdorf).

52. Waldeck, 'Publizistik', part I, p. 23.

53. Heinrich Lutz, *Das Ringen um die deutsche Einheit und kirchliche Erneuerung* (*Propyläen Geschichte Deutschlands*, vol. IV) (Berlin, 1983), p. 276.

54. J. R. Hale, 'Armies, Navies and the Art of War', in *New Cambridge Modern History*, vol. III, ed. R. B. Wernham (Cambridge, 1968), pp. 171–208, here at p. 207: 'Moreover, there was no war now that could not be represented as a crusade' (on the Dutch Revolt).

55. The starting point was Canon XXIII of Gartian's Decretals. Cf. M. Villoy, 'L'idée de la croisade chez les juristes du moyen-âge', in *Comitato Internazionale di Scienze Storiche. X Congresso Internazionale di Scienze Storiche, Roma 4–11 Settembre 1955. Relazioni III: Storia del Medioevo* (Florence, 1955), pp. 565–94, here pp. 574–7. A precise basis in law was offered by Canon XXVII of the 3rd Lateran Council. Text in *Conciliorum Oecumenicorum Decreta*, 2nd edn (Basel, 1962), p. 200f. On this issue cf. H. Wolter, 'Das Hochmittelalter', in Hubert Jedin (ed.), *Handbuch der Kirchengeschichte*, vol. III, 2 (Freiburg im Breisgau, 1968), pp. 187–205; Jonathan Riley-Smith, *What were the Crusades?* (London, 1977).

56. Cf. for example Martin V's Bull of 1 March 1420. Text in F. Palacky (ed.), *Urkundliche Beiträge zur Geschichte des Hussitenkrieges vom Jahre 1419 an*, vol. I: *1419–1428* (reprinted Osnabrück, 1966), pp. 17–20.

57. For Podiebrad's deposition by Paul II on 23 December 1466 cf. Ludwig Pastor, *Geschichte der Päpste*, vol. II (Freiburg im Breisgau, 1923), pp. 404–7. On the Wrocław attempts to persuade the pope to launch a crusade against the king of Bohemia cf. E. Laslowski, *Beiträge zur Geschichte des spätmittelalterlichen Ablaßwesens* (Breslauer Studien zur historischen Theologie, XI) (Wrocław, 1929), pp. 42–74.

58. *NB*, sect. 1, vol. VIII: *1545–1546* (Gotha, 1898), pp. 53f, 512f.

59. *Concilium Tridentinum*, ed. Goerresiana, vol. X (Freiburg im Breisgau, 1916), pp. 114–16, n. 78.

60. Hubert Jedin, *Geschichte des Konzils von Trient*, vol. I, 2nd edn (Freiburg im Breisgau, 1951), p. 418.

61. On the basis of the papal breves of 13 May 1580, 14 April 1600 and 20 January 1601 concerning the Irish rebels P. Rousset, 'L'idéologie de croisade dans les guerres de religion au XVIe siècle', *Schweizerische Zeitschrift für Geschichte*, XXXI (1981), pp. 174–84, here at p. 175, argues that these enterprises were crusades. There is a kernel of truth in that, but his definition of 'crusade' is too imprecise. In applying the term to Cromwell Rousset admits as much, 'La "croisade" puritaine de Cromwell', ibid., XXVIII (1978), pp. 15–28.

16 Cardinal Reginald Pole and the Path to Anglo-Papal Mediation at the Peace Conference of Marcq, 1553–55

†Heinrich Lutz

From the 1530s onwards, England occupied a key position in the conflict between the papacy and the European Reformation movements, as it also did in the struggle for European supremacy waged for decades between Charles V and France. From the summer of 1553, both sets of interests and conflicts intersected in a new and direct manner. After the death of her Protestant brother, Edward VI, the accession of Mary Tudor to the English throne meant that European politics – in which England was the decisive factor in the struggle between Valois and Habsburg – were inextricably linked to the religious situation, in which the long-term success or failure of the Catholic restoration in England was the pivot of the struggle between Rome and the Reformation. Consequently, analysis of the efforts, from 1553, to achieve a papal *and* English mediation in the European struggle for hegemony is of great interest for both the political and religious development of Europe at that time.

The history of these efforts, which reached their high point in the Anglo-papal mediation between Valois and Habsburg at the peace conference of Marcq (near Calais) in May/June 1555, and which carried on until the conclusion of the Truce of Vaucelles (5 February 1556) can only be understood with close reference to the internal and external history of England under Queen Mary. It is no less closely bound to the fortunes of the papacy under Julius III, Marcellus II and Paul IV. Among the figures who played an active role, the most important was the English cardinal, Reginald Pole. As papal legate since 1553 he had not only been entrusted with the return of England to the Roman Catholic Church, but also with the task of mediating between King Henry II of France and the Emperor Charles V. The theological, ecclesiastical and political dimensions of the activities of this firm advocate of Catholic reform are broad and complex. Historical research today is still far from reaching a consensus in its assessment of his personality and his achievements. The divergences and doubts in the evaluation of the personal element still have a distorting effect on objective judgements of the peace efforts and their importance.

The sources for French and English diplomatic activity between 1553 and 1556 are still only incompletely available in old editions. The situation is better for the Habsburg documents. While there is no publication in the original, there is nevertheless one edition carefully translated into English by Royall Tyler.[1] In addition, there are now the papal diplomatic documents, which I have edited in three volumes for the years 1552–56.[2] Attention should be drawn, in particular, to volume XV of the *Nuntiaturberichte aus Deutschland* (*Nunciatory Reports from Germany*) published in 1981. At the suggestion of Hubert Jedin, the volume goes beyond the thematic limits of the series and contains the correspondence of Reginald Pole as peace legate from 1553 to 1556, as far as it is known to contemporary research.[3] (It is possible that the archive of the Congregation of the Faith in Rome, which remains inaccessible, contains further additions to this political correspondence. It is beyond doubt that it contains theological manuscripts by Pole.)

It will be the task of the following short sketch to present some material from the newly collected and edited sources, which will make possible a more accurate analysis of the developments leading up to the Peace Conference of Marcq, with particular reference to the English and papal perspective. In view of the current state of discussion, such an orientation to the sources seems worthwhile, in order to provide a better basis both for possible interpretations of the peace efforts, and of the role and personality of Reginald Pole. I have explained elsewhere my own particular interpretation, which understands Pole's ideas and policies on peace in terms of a radicalised Erasmianism.[4] This is not the issue here, rather the concern is with pragmatic – and also methodological – suggestions for situating these forces, aims and decision-making processes in the wider course of European history.

I

The starting point must be the longer-term constellation of interests and political goals of France, England, the Habsburgs and the papacy.[5] The resumption of the European war in autumn 1551, after settlement had apparently been reached in 1544, was based on the old tensions, but opened a new round of intensified confrontation. With the help of the German Protestants, the Turks and his Italian allies, King Henry II sought to destroy Habsburg hegemony. However, the French offensive and the initial success of the 'great coalition' did not at all dispose Charles V to conclude a new compromise peace. On the contrary, the emperor's resolve finally to crush France and exclude it from the European system of states as an independent factor, whatever the cost, hardened during 1552/53. The war – as the emperor explained with reference to Pope Julius III's attempts to mediate, which got under way in 1552 – could only come to an end if France once and for all lost the possibility of 'doing evil'. The dramatic change in England, with the accession of Queen Mary in July 1553, brought forth two different plans, one after the other, from the Habsburg side. Above all, it was Charles V's aim to draw England into the Habsburg sphere through the marriage of his son Philip to Mary (thereby winning decisive superiority over France). However, following the success of the marriage project and the arrival of Philip in England, the constellation was altered. The firm English position, which was a refusal to be drawn into the continental conflict, had been expressed from the start by the queen and the majority of her advisors and had also already led to English attempts at mediation. Now the political calculations of Philip and some of his advisors began to take the same direction. Against strong resistance from Charles V the English royal couple finally succeeded in setting up the Anglo-papal double mediation at the Conference of Marcq.

For Pope Julius III, the question of peace had a threefold significance. He saw in the conflict between the two monarchs the 'ruin of Christendom', that is, the prevention of defence against the Turks, and the encouragement of Protestantism. Since the rebellion of Siena (July 1552), which had been supported by the French, he had been confronted by the spread of the war to central Italy, in the closest proximity of the papal states and Rome. And following the accession of Mary, he wished to improve the chances of Catholic restoration in England by a settlement of the European conflict. However, many months passed before these plans could be effectively linked to the dominant tendency on the Habsburg side, and to the interests of the 'peace party' at the French court.

On 6 August 1553, the pope designated Cardinal Reginald Pole, who was at that time staying at Lake Garda, as Legate '*pro restauranda fide in regno Angliae*'; on 19 September, he added to this task that of '*Legatio pro pace*': the cardinal-legate was to set out immediately to meet both Charles V and Henry II.[6] The Roman sources clearly show that this second mission also had a strong tactical component: in the face of sharp criticism by the imperial court of the appointment of the legate for the English restoration, the peace mission was undoubtedly intended to ensure an immediate journey northwards. In the peace question Pole was to continue the task with which the two cardinal-legates, Capodiferro and Dandino, who had been sent to France and Brussels, had been entrusted since spring 1553.[7] Pole, who had previously been considered pro-Habsburg, and had been the emperor's candidate in the conclave of 1549, was now suspected in Brussels either of wanting to marry the English queen himself or of encouraging her marriage to his nephew Courtenay, as was advocated by France and by a national, anti-Spanish group in London. The full extent of the Brussels criticisms of Pole's mission was still not known in Rome when the pope, on 20 September 1553, elucidated the relationship between the two issues as follows:

> In order to do everything possible on our side and in order to support this enterprise [restoration in England] as much as we possibly can, we yesterday, in the same consistory – after the two peace legates had been ordered back – added the peace legation to your mission . . .
>
> May God (should the sins of Christendom be already partly expiated and these two monarchs turn their gaze towards peace) soften their hearts and let them find out what great guilt by omission and commission they will have to account for on the day of the Last Judgement; and may God allow them to win honour from one and the other of the legations! We, however, – to state our opinion openly – have little hope that these monarchs will grant this wish a hearing, because although they maintain that they are Catholic and godly, and have God and justice in view, we nevertheless surely know that selfishness darkens their sight, so that they do not see the misfortune and the ruin of poor Christendom and of our faith and our religion . . .
>
> *Summa summarum*: whatever the justification that enables you to begin and continue your journey – it will be of the greatest satisfaction to us – and that also because the passive waiting on events

harms our reputation and our cause and benefits the prestige of the heretics and schismatics, and that not only in England, but in all other parts of Christendom.[8]

Unlike Julius III, however, Pole immediately emphasised the equal status of his two missions. He saw matters in terms of a grand political-theological plan, in which reunion and church reform (in England and the whole of Europe) were closely linked to the peace question. Only through a lasting European peace settlement – over and above the pressing issue of the English reunion – can the reform and unity of the church be attained and secured.[9] He rejected the imperial court's view that he had only been appointed to the second mission *'per un colore'*. He immediately had his secretary, Fiordibello, explain to the Bishop of Arras, the emperor's leading minister, 'that one would labour in vain to bring a kingdom to union with the Catholic Church, if one did not wait and persevere in concluding and establishing a good and true peace between these two princes.'[10] However, the transferral of the peace legation only increased the distrust of Pole and papal policies at the imperial court. It was seen as a manoeuvre to benefit France: if the legate first journeyed, as announced, to Charles V, and only then went on to Henry II, the public blame for the continuing failure to establish peace would be placed on the former. So Charles V insisted to Rome that the legate could not continue his journey northwards. From October to December 1553, Pole remained at Dillingen, the residence of the Bishop of Augsburg, Cardinal Otto Truchseß von Waldburg. Not until 1 January 1554, when the marriage treaty between Mary and Philip had been completely settled, was the legate allowed to journey on to the imperial court.

On the French side, interest in Pole's peace mission had from the beginning been closely connected with the attempt to win the legate to an anti-Habsburg policy in relation to England. On the other hand, since mid-August, 1553, negotiations had been going on between France and England on the possibility of an English peace mediation.[11] In the correspondence of Pole's secretary, Fiordibello, who had been despatched to Brussels, the suggestion of also drawing the English queen into the mediation first occurs in the middle of October.[12] Simultaneously, the Bishop of Arras also mentioned (to the legate Dandino, departing for Rome) the readiness of the French king to recognise the English queen as *'mezana della pace'*.[13] The idea of an English peace initiative was in this case, however, linked to the imperial minister's serious doubts of the chances of papal mediation. In England itself, the advantages of a peace agreement between Charles V and France for a stabilisation of the situation established by the marriage treaty were extensively discussed at the end of 1553. Simon Renard, the imperial ambassador in London, while observing Pole's activity with untiring suspicion, emphatically recommended an agreement with France, both in the Habsburg interest and with reference to the situation in England.[14] It was clearly necessary for Pole and papal policy to link both perspectives, and combine the papal initiative with action from the English side. This was attempted once the legate was finally able to negotiate with Charles V in January 1554.

II

On 21 December 1553, the imperial commissioners left Brussels for London with the definitive text of the Mary–Philip marriage contract, and on the following day Charles V gave Pole permission to end his enforced residency at Dillingen and come to the imperial court.[15] The queen had not only pressed the emperor to allow the legate to continue his journey; she had, among other things, expressed the desire to be married by Pole. The cardinal also received information that the English queen was favourably disposed towards mediation, and immediately passed this on to Rome.[16] In view of the evident difficulties facing a speedy completion of the restoration in England and of continuing his journey there, the cardinal and Pope Julius III were agreed that Pole should place the peace initiative in the foreground during the following months.[17]

Meanwhile, Pole and Julius III had also reached agreement on the question of the marriage between Mary and Philip. Originally, the legate had been of the opinion that in view of her age the queen should not marry at all.[18] The project of a marriage to Philip appeared inopportune to him, first of all on political grounds – an unwillingness to allow 'that my country should pass into the hands of a stranger'[19] – and still more in relation to the Catholic restoration. He feared that the reunion mission ('not very acceptable to that population') would be handicapped by the queen's marriage to a foreigner, against which the English population had a stronger aversion than against the reunion.[20]

After the pope's unequivocal endorsement of the Spanish marriage, and after the conclusion of the marriage contract, things looked different. Disregarding the continuing French attempts to play Pole off against the Spanish marriage and its advocates in England, the legate adjusted to the new situation. He endeavoured, first of all, to win Philip's support for the reunion, and then, also, for the peace initiative. It is true that the biblical comparison of Charles V and Philip with David and Solomon, which Pole set forth to the English king's father confessor,[21] referred in the first instance to the success of the now imminent reunion of England with the papal church. But this comparison could also be understood as a reference to the different positions of father and son on the peace question which subsequently became evident. On the one side David, whom God had forbidden the building of the temple because his hands were stained by so many wars, even if they had been just and legitimate; on the other side his son Solomon, whose hands were untainted, who would successfully carry out the construction and rule in peace. This vision of Philip as prince of peace deserves consideration for Pole's further activity.

However, this is only true of the period after autumn 1554. The first round of negotiations, between January and April 1554, which led the legate first to Brussels and then to the court of Henry II in Fontaine-bleau, brought great problems and no visible successes. Keeping the subsequent realisation of the Anglo-papal mediation in mind, these negotiations can only be touched on briefly here. Attention should be drawn to a number of viewpoints and factors. First of all, Pole's own experiences, and his ideas about war and peace should be noted. His earlier missions, as Paul III's peace legate to Charles V and Francis I in 1537 and 1539, are of considerable importance in this respect. These missions which were dominated by the English question, and whose aim was Franco-Habsburg solidarity against Henry VIII, are still not adequately researched.[22] Furthermore, the new developments in Rome must be borne in mind. Pole's Catholic reform friend, Cardinal Morone, probably the best curial diplomat of the sixteenth century, had been placed in charge of the Roman end of the English mission and the peace legation.[23] Subsequently, the correspondence between Pole and Morone paralleled and took precedence over the official exchanges between the legate and the Roman state secretariat. The involvement of Morone also demonstrated the effort the pope was making, through the display of greater flexibility and by granting extensive authority to Pole, to overcome the deadlock which had been reached in the peace question in the summer and autumn of 1553 with the ending of the Dandino–Capodiferro legations.

The existing state of the peace question, from which Pole now had to work, can be read from a statement which Charles V had handed to cardinal-legate Dandino on 1 September 1553, and which summed up his conditions.[24] It is clear from this and from the reply that Henry II presented to Pole in April 1554 that not only was a restoration of the Peace Treaty of Crépy, 1544, at issue, but ultimately the sum of European disputes which had arisen since the beginning of the war in 1521, indeed since the beginning of the great Franco–Burgundian and Franco–Aragonese conflicts. The imperial document placed all the blame for the resumption of the war in 1551 on the French. It demanded the restitution of the parts of the empire occupied by Henry II (i.e. of Metz, Toul and Verdun; whether this also included previously asserted claims over Provence, Dauphiné, *Regnum Arelatense*, was not stated); restitution of Lorraine, evacuation of Siena, restitution of Savoy and Piedmont; return of all places in Luxemburg and other hereditary lands of the emperor which had been occupied since 1544; restitution of all places occupied by the French and Turkish fleets; reparation for all losses which the emperor and his subjects had suffered, including those due to the Turkish fleet; confirmation of previous peace treaties, 'since if these are not valid it cannot be seen on what grounds it is still worth entering into negotiation with France'. Henry II's counter-demands, which were handed over to Cardinal Pole at the beginning of April 1554, went, if anything, even further as a maximum programme: return of Milan and Asti, return of the three kingdoms of Naples, Sicily and Aragon, restitution of sovereignty over Flanders, etc., but above all, compensation for the fact that the Duke of Orléans had not been invested with Milan after 1544.[25]

Pole had a two-pronged response to this reciprocal escalation of demands. Pragmatically, he emphasised the distinction between those provisions of the earlier peace conferences which had actually been carried out and those which had not been carried out. The questions of Milan, Savoy and Piedmont therefore took precedence, and the emperor's long list was consequently differentiated. On the other hand, in a theological-political memorandum presented to both monarchs he emphasised peace as a Christian duty of conscience, and called on them in Christian love to subordinate their quarrels, if need be, to the highest ecclesiastical authority (the Council).[26] In this text, which was soon disseminated in printed editions, the two rulers were summoned before God's judgement seat:

If the emperor or the king declare themselves ready for peace, but assert that the other side is not worthy of trust, I would reply: God cannot be mistaken, for he sees into every heart. Whoever therefore has the just desire [for peace] will truly be certain of God's help and will thereby avoid the anger of God in this and the other world ... Their majesties have more cause to think of God's judgement than of anything else ... If, in matters of war, which lie within the decision of princes, one takes up arms out of pride or of covetousness, then here all the lying pretexts of the general welfare or of just defence, with which he would like to deceive people, will not help him.

The seriousness and depth of this theological-political exhortation was one thing; quite another meanwhile was the fruitless course of the negotiations Pole was conducting, now in Brussels, then in France, then again in Brussels. In Brussels, the accusation was levelled at Pole that by returning from France with empty hands, the emperor would once again receive the sole blame for the failure to establish peace. Since the imperial court also objected to Pole's direct intervention in the reunion and to an eventual journey on to England, the legate was forced to retire from Brussels to the nearby Benedictine abbey of Dilighem. This further compulsory residence lasted until October 1554, when Pole was summoned to London by the English royal couple for the conclusion of the reunion negotiations. Meanwhile, despite all the difficulties, he continued his efforts in the peace question. Even if the new initiative which actually led to the Conference of Marcq only succeeded after his arrival, the preparations which led up to it can be followed through the preceding months of waiting.

Soon after his arrival in Brussels in January 1554, Pole began to influence the English ambassadors there in favour of mediation by the queen between the emperor and Henry II. He explained to them how honourable and advantageous this would be for England 'that now more needs peace than all other kingdoms more affected by the war'.[27] This clear reference to the internal conditions in England as a motive for the interest in peace was contained in a note of 28 January 1554, from Pole to Morone. Only a week later, the legate reported the outbreak of Wyatt's rebellion which confirmed his fears. In May, the legate forcefully encouraged the queen, both by letter and through his secretary, Henry Penning, who had been sent to London, to take the initiative in the question.[28] Mary promised to attempt to persuade the emperor to allow the legate to continue his negotiations with France by letter and and by messenger. So the idea of an Anglo-papal double mediation can be traced from May 1554 onwards. As far as procedure is concerned, Pole had already suggested to the emperor in February a delegate conference on neutral (English) soil.[29] In June, he intensified his efforts, presumably also in view of Philip's imminent arrival in England.

Worth noting also is the way the queen discussed Pole's proposals with Charles' ambassador, Simon Renard.[30] She expressly made her reply to Pole dependent on the emperor's attitude – '*si elle pouroit satisfaire au désir dudict cardinal, sans desplaire à votre Majesté*'. Pole meanwhile made use of the influence of Mason, the English ambassador, on the imperial court, while Simon Renard and the Bishop of Arras remained sceptical of the suggestion of a peace conference under English (and papal) direction, and negotiations on a peace initiative continued between France and England. Renard went so far in his opposition to Pole's initiative and the English support for it as to suggest the secret surveillance of Mason's correspondence, with the aim of his recall as ambassador.[31] When the legate despatched Michael Throckmorton to England in order to greet and congratulate Philip on English soil, he emphasised the great importance of a peace initiative, to which the king's personal interest as well as his concern for the general welfare should lead him.[32] Furthermore, he had Throckmorton give the queen a draft of a letter on the peace issue, which Mary was to address to the emperor.[33] Mary immediately showed the draft letter, in which the queen mentioned French consent, explicitly proposed herself to Charles V as mediator, and solicited the emperor's agreement, to Renard and discussed the matter with him.[34] The ambassador's counter-arguments persuaded the queen to ask Charles V before sending the letter, which in the event was never written.

In July, the legate once more undertook an attempt to win the queen and Chancellor Gardiner over to mediation, and simultaneously to influence the French to the same effect through England.[35] However, Pole's letters to the queen and to the French High Constable, Anne de Montmorency, quickly fell into the hands of the imperial ambassadors in England. They informed Charles V that they were confident of persuading the queen not to pass Pole's letter on to Montmorency and to dissuade her from supporting the legate's latest initiative.

The extent to which these counter-measures by the imperial court combined political and military motives – for example, hopes of decisive military success during the summer – with concern for the very complex reunion negotiations, on account of which Pole was not yet allowed to leave for England, cannot be followed here. Neither is it possible to pay attention to the different attitudes of the political forces in England and France to the peace question. Gardiner, at any rate, already seems to have been one of the advocates of mediation. The tone of Philip's reply to Pole's peace exhortation had also been positive.[36] The further exploratory peace discussions which took place during August and September in London and Brussels (by way of Antoine de Noailles and between Ferrante Gonzaga and Montmorency) pointed in the same direction. At the same time, there were new initiatives from Rome for a peaceful settlement of the Siena question, which directly affected the emperor.[37] However, it was only after Pole had arrived in London in November 1554, and had concluded the negotiations on the reunification of the English church with Rome, that he could effectively take the peace question in hand and, with the support of the English royal couple, prepare the planned peace conference.

III

The legate himself, now Archbishop of Canterbury and primate of England and carried along by the tide of the reunion success, found himself in a much stronger position, personally and politically, to achieve success in the peace mission. He could directly influence England's leading figures, and above all the royal couple, and present his arguments for the necessity of peace to England. The English queen's readiness to link her interest to peace with Pole's papal mediation went without saying. However, a new strong factor of support was King Philip. He also had other and more far-reaching motives than either considerations directly related to England's internal and external political situation or Pole's theological-political scheme. Philip was increasingly concerned about the future of his continental European inheritance following the absence of decisive successes against France in the campaigns of 1552, 1553 and 1554, and in the face of the catastrophic development of state finances in Spain and the Netherlands. The situation in Italy was especially worrying, since, despite the imperial victory over the French allies, the Republic of Siena and the Florentine '*Fuorisciti*' at Marciano (2 August 1554) Habsburg supremacy was far from secure.[38] In Upper Italy, the problems of Savoy and Piedmont were completely unsolved. From the winter of 1553/54 the whole, already precarious, military and political balance of forces in Italy was largely threatened by the French Constable Montmorency's support for the radical offensive plans of the Italian '*Fuorisciti*'. Accordingly, various initiatives to negotiate a settlement for Italy and for the whole war got under way in Brussels in autumn 1554. Besides the papal efforts to end the Sienese war, there were a Ferrarese peace action and an exploratory sounding from Lorraine which also took in Savoy.

The more actively Philip concerned himself with the emperor's abdication plans in the winter of 1554/55, and particularly with the succession problems in Italy, the greater was his interest in negotiations with France. By July 1554, Charles V had signed a first general abdication instrument in favour of Philip; this was followed on 20 October 1554 by Philip's investiture with the kingdom of Naples (which was a papal fief).[39] Philip committed the relative independence from his father, which he had for the first time in London, to the realisation of the peace conference with increasing vigour. While Pole was strengthened in his hopes of Philip as 'prince of peace', the French ambassador in London also found the king properly described as a '*grand amateur du repoz*', who was anxious to see peace established between his father and Henry II.

Furthermore, since his arrival in England, Pole could negotiate directly with the French. The French ambassador in London, Antoine de Noailles, and soon also his brother, the protonotary François de Noailles, who had been sent to the English court from France on special mission, became constant discussion partners of Pole and his staff. So, as early as the beginning of January 1555, the legate had managed to secure the French king's agreement in principle to a congress of ambassadors on neutral English mainland territory (at Calais).[40] From Rome, too, there was active support and encouragement for the new initiative in the peace question. The success of the Catholic restoration in England was confidently interpreted as a step on the way to the Peace of Christendom. Morone wrote to Pole from Rome on behalf of the pope: may it please God 'after this miracle of spiritual peace in England, to let us see the other miracle of a worldly peace between Christian princes'.[41]

Meanwhile, in London, the further steps to prepare the peace conference were not without disturbances and difficulties. Certainly Philip's declaration that he would approach the emperor to secure a positive response to the plan for a peace conference followed very quickly after the securing of French agreement.[42] However, the attempts the legate now made to ensure the success of the coming conference through substantial preliminary negotiations in London immediately met fundamental resistance from the French diplomats,[43] quite apart from the persistent and comprehensive suspicions on the imperial side. In addition there were difficulties between Pole and Gardiner, which were apparently not only due to the chancellor's personal jealousy of the legate, but also involved complicated substantial and procedural questions of the planned mediation. Pole had no intention of being pushed from the forefront; it seemed to him politically necessary in view of the increasingly pro-Habsburg colouring of English policies to underline, through his person and position, the absolute impartiality of the mediation.

The delay in the emperor's consent to the ambassadors' conference caused problems, and had considerable consequences. Week after week passed while Pole and the English court waited with increasing impatience for the reply from Brussels. On 19 January 1555, the legate despatched Abbot Parpaglia to the emperor with an urgent letter: 'I beg God to open the way for a good thing that is so great and necessary for the whole of Christendom.'[44] Parpaglia had to wait in Brussels for the whole of February without any response being forthcoming. It is understandable that during this time conjecture grew ever stronger that the emperor's attitude was negative. On the other hand, for the moment the agreement was not in question from the French side. Henry II expressed the motive to Antoine de Noailles: 'The main thing is to keep the English gently in their present position.'[45] Finally, Philip decided to win the emperor's agreement to the peace conference by sending his personal representative, Ruy Gomez, to Brussels. Parpaglia later confidentially reported to the French high constable what great pressure Philip had to bring to bear on his father. The king had gone so far as to let his father know 'that if the emperor rejects peace negotiations, he would act without him'.[46]

Ruy Gomez was not able to return to England with the emperor's agreement until the middle of March; a little later Parpaglia delivered a corresponding declaration of readiness by the emperor to the legate.[47] On 14 March, on the basis of consultation with Philip, Pole was already able to outline the personal and organisational framework of the conference to the nuncio in France. If the Cardinal of Lorraine and the Constable represented France, the Duke of Alba and the Bishop of Arras could participate on the imperial side, and, in addition, Pole on behalf of the pope and Chancellor Gardiner for the English queen. Ardres was proposed for the French quarters, Gravelines for the imperial side, and Guines for the legate and Gardiner.[48]

Pole and the queen were now quickly able to make firm arrangements with France for the conference. It was hoped that it could be opened on 20 or 25 April on English territory near Calais. Both the legate and the English wanted to get proceedings under way soon, in order to forestall the larger military operations which, dependent on the seasons, usually began in May. But more time was lost. It was, finally, unforeseeable that the opening of the congress would coincide with the election of a new pro-French pope – Paul IV was elected on 23 May; it contributed considerably, however, to the negative outcome of this attempt at a settlement.

A further delay occurred when the emperor was supposed to name his delegates officially. Presumably, this second delay in Brussels was linked to the death of Pope Julius III on 23 March. It seems that Charles V immediately feared the election of a pro-French pope, and a consequent shift of the European constellation of forces against the Habsburgs.[49] In fact, the conclave ended on 9–10 April with the election of Marcellus II, who desired the strictest neutrality in order to speed up the task of conciliation and, as a result, the reform of the church. The new pope, a friend of Pole's for many years, immediately renewed the legate's peace mission in the most emphatic manner. When news of the election reached England, it produced deep satisfaction at the royal court and in Pole's circle. The cardinal had earlier rejected the emperor's call for him to proceed to the conclave in Rome. (Whether the suspicion, expressed at court, that the emperor wanted to keep Pole away from the management of the peace conference was justified, must be left open.)[50] Pole did what he could to ensure that the vacancy at the Holy See did not bring the conference preparations to a standstill. On 28 April he informed the queen from Richmond of the news of the election of Marcellus II. At the time, the birth of an heir to the throne was expected any day (it soon turned out to be a mistake). In his symbol-laden mode of expression, Pole linked both temporal and ecclesiastical hopes: 'Just as God has heard the prayers of his church in this election, which was tantamount to an act of birth of the church ... so may he hear us too with regard to the other two imminent births, by giving your majesty a son as our prince and Christendom that peace which it longs for.'[51]

However, not only did knowledge of Mary's false pregnancy soon weaken Habsburg political positions, but the peace and reform pope, Marcellus II, was unable to fulfil any of the high expectations placed in him; he died during the night of 31 April. The next conclave began on 15 May. Many contemporaries, including some in the cardinal's own entourage, believed that it was probable that Pole would now be elected pope. There are indications that Pole himself took seriously the possibility that he might shortly be able to work for peace and reform from the throne of St Peter. But things turned out quite differently. It is true that the great respect for Pole's reforming views and work for peace was reflected in the fact that in the conclave many of the cardinals of the French group, led by Farnese, supported the Englishman. That was quite exceptional; Farnese had thereby brushed aside the clear instructions of Henry II, who had insisted on the candidature of Cardinal Ippolito d'Este, a prince of the church who was both worldly and pro-French and untouched by the reform movement. But Pole's opponents, Caraffa above all, raised strong objections *'per conto d'heresia'*. The imperial party was split, and the Englishman's chances were gone.[52] The election, on 23 May, of the uncompromisingly anti-Habsburg and pro-French cardinal, Gian Pietro Caraffa, was not only a political defeat for Charles V and Philip. The new pope, who considered Pole to be a concealed heretic, and therefore all the more dangerous, represented a serious handicap both for Pole's personal fate and his work for the English church and European peace.

IV

However, this is to run ahead. The months from March until May 1555 were filled with intensive organisational preparations for the conference.[53] Pole and the English succeeded in overcoming French suspicions on account of the new delay on the imperial side. In May, agreement was reached on delegations, whose composition corresponded to the importance of the proceedings. The Duke of Medinaceli (who, in terms of protocol, had the highest rank), the Bishop of Arras, Bugnicourt, Lalaing and Viglius van Zwichem represented the imperial side, and the Cardinal of Lorraine, the High Constable, Anne de Montmorency, Charles de Marillac, Jean de Morvilliers and Claude de l'Aubespine represented France. Apart from Chancellor Gardiner, the Earl of Arundel and Lord Paget belonged to the English delegation.

The building preparations and facilities planned by Pole, with the English, were significant pointers to the conception of the conference.[54] The English had erected five spacious houses in a circular arrangement in open country near the hamlet of (La) Marcq, close to Calais. These served the delegations, coming variously from Ardres (French), Gravelines (Imperials) and Calais (Pole and the English), for meetings. The legate and the English delegation had two separate houses, which were situated opposite one another and between the houses of the Imperials and the French. This gave spatial expression to the double character of the Anglo-papal mediation and to the independence of the legate, on which Pole continued to place the greatest importance. In the centre was the hall for joint discussions, with the legate's chair at the head of the conference table. Next to him, but set back a little were the places intended for the English delegation. This demonstrated the precedence of the 'spiritual power' within the framework of the double initiative. A carefully planned system of entrances and exits allowed movement at any time between the mediators and each of the opposing parties which was not subject to observation by the other. French and Imperials, on the other hand, could only meet each other in the middle hall, together with the mediators.

This ingeniously designed construction and negotiating system, in which the mediators could have their intentions expressed undisturbed, could have made a Thomas More happy. Unfortunately, the preparatory discussion of issues was far less advanced than the procedural preparations. It has already been seen that Pole's efforts since January to establish a substantial preliminary understanding on the negotiating framework and, where possible, on important points of conflict had been rejected by the French. On the imperial side, where there had been such damaging delays, first of all in agreeing to the conference at all, and then again on the nomination of delegates, the possibilities of preliminary understanding were even less. It is not possible here to look more closely at the continuous English attempts to establish preliminary clarification, and what consequences this had for the course of negotiations. Only one question, which was however of central importance, shall be referred to briefly.

Since the beginning of his conciliation efforts the legate had paid great attention in the sphere of territorial disputes to the Savoy–Piedmont–Milan complex of problems. While the emperor for some time completely refused to talk about these questions, which had, after all, been settled by earlier treaties, Pole insisted, realistically, that the *non-execution* of their provisions made new negotiations necessary:

> It seemed to me, that the disputed questions dealt with before are of two kinds. Some are repeatedly raised and each time resolved in almost the same way. Although they were dealt with and resolved in

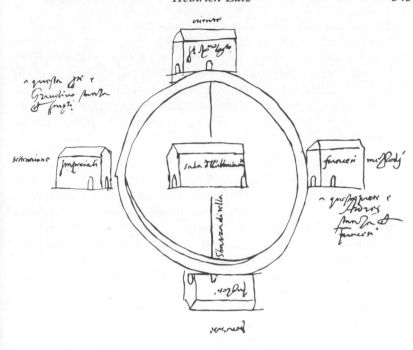

Plan of the 'wooden lodgings' at the Peace Conference of Marcq (1555)

the previous treaty [Crépy, 1544], these decisions, however, remained unexecuted. These cases must be dealt with again and settled. This is the case, for example, with Savoy, Piedmont and Milan etc.[55]

Milan above all. Here the pragmatic question of non-execution was tied up with a political-ethical question. Had it been the emperor's duty, following the death in 1545 of the Duke of Orléans, who had been due to become Duke of Milan and marry a Habsburg princess, to make an equivalent concession to France in order to ensure European peace? Pole seems to have taken a clear position on this issue. A memorandum on the disputed territories, which was written in the legate's circle in February/March 1554, and filed in his correspondence, states:

The emperor must now not make greater difficulties because of the hand-over of the Duchy of Milan than he did in 1544 ... for the reason, above all, which at that time moved him to hand it over, can have been none other than the emperor's desire for peace and the welfare of Christendom. This reason is more valid than ever today, as the war among Christians has won an even greater extent. Therefore today peace is even more necessary and useful for Christendom.[56]

As with all the other outstanding questions there was no preliminary agreement on the Milan question. But what kind of understanding was there between Pole and his English co-mediators? What position did Philip, did the various pro-Habsburg or 'neutralist' groups in England have on the question of Habsburg concessions, and in particular on the Milan question? It appears that at this point Gardiner was closest to the position of Pole, who, given his sense of peace as a Christian duty, believed that concessions were necessary and possible on both sides.

The English ambassador in Brussels expressed his opinion quite explicitly during the preparatory stage of the conference. On 11 May Mason wrote to Petre, the Secretary of the Council, 'The giving up of Milan would help all.'[57] This recommendation of a single exemplary concession should probably be seen in the context of the French preparations for the conference. During the formulation of the negotiating programme it was agreed to give Milan central importance: all the efforts of the French peace legation were to be concentrated on it. The emperor could be offered the restitution of all other war losses against Milan: 'put forward only the matter of Milan, where our right is incontestable.'[58] What Philip thought about the conditions of a settlement with France and to what extent his ideas had any influence on the negotiating programme of the English mediators and of the emperor is unknown. It is certain, however, that in general he desired the settlement and influenced the emperor to this end. Charles V was willing to consider certain concessions over Milan, if they were linked to the definitive settlement of all other points of conflict.

These brief references, using the Milan question as an example, show that although the lack of preliminary understanding was a problem, the expectations with which the legate and the English mediators approached the conference cannot be criticised as altogether unrealistic. The coincidence at this moment of the theological-political concept of peace, of which Pole was the spokesman and exponent, with the direct interests of England and with internal Habsburg and French developments, is clear.

This was the state of affairs on 23 May, when the legate opened the conference with a greeting in Italian. He referred to England's reunion with the rest of the church. In his characteristic manner he emphasised the relationship and obligation of spiritual and temporal responsibility. He introduced himself and the English delegates: the grace of God had made use of them in reconciling England with the Lord and his church; now that this work had succeeded the same men were turning their efforts to conciliation between the monarchs. The apostle's greeting, '*pax huic domui*', had particular force for the meeting, 'since on the peace negotiated in this house depends the peace in all other parts of Europe'.[59] At the close of the opening session the English offered wine and sweetmeats, and the legate toasted the health of all those present. But the difficulties which were to become increasingly dominant during the course of the conference were brought into the open as early as the debate on order of business, chaired by Gardiner, which followed Pole's address.

V

Neither the course of the peace conference, nor the reasons for its breakdown, nor the continuation of peace negotiations by Pole after the conference, which then became part of the background to the Armistice of Vaucelles, can be dealt with here. In conclusion only *one* further aspect will be mentioned to complete and round matters off. The common programme of Pole, his English co-mediators and Popes Julius III and Marcellus II was European peace and unity of the church. But the policies of the new pope, and also his theological and political programme, soon led in quite another direction. Paul IV saw the emperor and Philip as the real disturbers and impediments to European peace and the unity and reform of the church, as he understood them.[60] He went so far as to pursue, through a military alliance with France, the overthrow of Habsburg domination in Italy and, if possible, in the whole of Europe. The curia's double-bottomed policy during 1555/56, the work, above all, of the cardinal and favourite, Carlo Caraffa, which paired an ostensible commitment to peace with preparation for war, can be followed in detail on the basis of the documents published in volumes XIV and XV of the *Nuntiaturberichte aus Deutschland*. The equation of a policy of Christian peace with the unity and reform of the Church, as advocated by Pole, was therefore called in question by the papacy under Paul IV.

The total collapse of this anachronistic and unrealistic policy with disastrous consequences for all the goals hoped for by Rome was one thing. Quite another was how the Protestants saw and experienced the relation of peace and true Christendom. For however much Reginald Pole can be counted part of the peaceful wing of Catholic reform, which was open to some of the reformers' concerns, no retrospective study can overlook how strongly his peace programme, otherwise reminiscent of Erasmus, was anchored in the aim of united action against the '*mal fideli*' by the pacified Christian princes.

It was taken for granted that the peace which he aimed for as legate was a '*pax catholica*', in the same way as Cateau-Cambrésis, 1559, was to be, though much more directly motivated by the persistent idea of the elimination of Protestantism in England. There was a similar view of things in the French and imperial camps. In France, concern over the spread of Protestantism was an increasingly strong motive for ending the war. To the emperor and to King Ferdinand it was clear that determined action '*pro concordia ecclesiae*', that is, against the Protestants, would only be possible after a peace treaty.

Many representatives of European Protestantism were well aware of this. And that explains the fierce polemics against the linking of the peace idea and the suppression of Protestantism which followed the resumption of the European war in 1551/52. Every peace initiative emanating from Rome inevitably appeared like a conspiracy to repress all tendencies deviating from Rome. This fear explains the vehemence of Pier Paolo Vergerio's attacks on Pole's peace legation as well.[61] Calvin was strongly influenced by the failure of the Franco-Protestant military alliance of 1552, the reversal in England 1553/54, and the readiness of the German Protestant princes to conclude a religious peace with the 'papists'. This path, without weapons and of peace, seemed to him one that harmed the true gospel and led the Protestants to ruin.[62] Calvin feared the religious peace in Germany, and feared even more the establishment of a European peace, which he equated with the beginning of a war of extermination against the Protestants. So it was precisely from this side that the traditional unity of worldly peace and religious-ecclesiastical values, for which Pole stood, was fundamentally put in doubt. These far-reaching perspectives and transformations must also be taken into account in any serious attempt to assess, on the basis of new sources, the significance of Pole's peace mission and of the English peace policies at this time, and to situate them in the course of European history.

Notes

1. *Calendar of Letters, Despatches and State Papers, relating to the negotiations between England and Spain,* vols X–XIII (London, 1914–54) (cit. Tyler). The comprehensive account by R. Tyler, *The Emperor Charles the Fifth* (London, 1956) remains stimulating, but leaves something to be desired in its elucidation of the rich source materials which the author himself had prepared.
2. *Nuntiaturberichte aus Deutschland,* Erste Abteilung 1533–1559, vol. XIII: *Nuntiaturen des Pietro Camaiani und Achille de Grassi, Legation des Girolamo Dandino (1552–1553)* (Tübingen, 1959); vol. XIV: *Nuntiaturen des Girolamo Muzzarelli, Sendung des Antonio Agustin, Legation des Scipione Rebiba (1554–56)* (Tübingen, 1971); vol. XV: *Friedenslegation des Reginald Pole zu Kaiser Karl V. und König Heinrich II. (1553–1556)* (Tübingen, 1981). Referred to below as *NB*, vols XIII, XIV, XV.
3. Hubert Jedin's comment during a conference at the German Historical Institute in 1955 led to the decision to devote a whole volume of the *Nuntiaturberichte aus Deutschland* to Pole's peace mission. The importance of the matter – the European dimension of the mediation – as of the person meant that it seemed worth providing more extensive documentation of the French and English side of things. Since Pole was entrusted with the mission for the return of England in August 1553 and with the peace mission in September 1553, it was necessary to choose a principle of selection which did justice to the interplay of the two tasks in the legate's correspondence without including all the correspondence concerned with the English mission. For the period from August 1553 until Pole crossed over to England in November 1554, all traceable correspondence was included, for the subsequent period only those pieces which were of relevance to the peace legation. For the relationship of this new edition to the older ones of Quirini, Rawdon Brown, Ancel, etc., see the introduction to *NB*, vol. XV.
4. H. Lutz, *Christianitas afflicta. Europa, das Reich und die päpstliche Politik im Niedergang der Hegemonie Kaiser Karls V. (1552–1556)* (Göttingen, 1964), p. 276ff; idem, *Ragione di Stato und christliche Staatsethik im 16. Jahrhundert,* with a documentary appendix: *Die Machiavelli-Kapitel aus Kardinal Reginald Poles 'Apologia ad Carolum Quintum Caeserem',* 2nd edn (Münster, 1976); idem, 'Friedensideen und Friedensprobleme in der frühen Neuzeit', in G. Heiss and H. Lutz (eds), *Friedensbewegungen: Bedingungen und Wirkungen* (Vienna, 1984), pp. 26ff.
5. Overview in E. Fueter, *Geschichte des europäischen Staatensystems von 1492 bis 1559* (Munich/Berlin, 1919); E. R. Harbison, *Rival Ambassa-*

dors at the Court of Queen Mary (Princeton, NJ, 1940). Also the opening chapters of Lutz, *Christianitas*, and the contributions in idem (ed.), *Das römisch-deutsche Reich im politischen System Karls V.* (Munich/Vienna, 1982). For England see most recently D. M. Loades, *The Reign of Mary Tudor. Politics, Government and Religion in England, 1553–1558* (London, 1979). Loades has not used the new volumes of the nunciatory reports (1959 and 1971) with their important sources for Anglo-imperial relations.

6.   *NB*, vol. XV, pp. 1f, 50ff.

7.   For these missions, see the documents in *NB*, vol. XIV and in *Acta Nuntiaturae Gallicae*, vol. IX: *Correspondance du Nonce en France, Prospero Santacroce (1552–1554)*, ed. J. Lestocquoy (Rome, 1972); also Lutz, *Christianitas*, pp. 246ff.

8.   *NB*, vol. XV, p. 52f.

9.   On the question of Pole's theology and 'orthodoxy', see the bibliographical references in the introduction to *NB*, vol. XV; important: D. Fenlon, *Heresy and Obedience in Tridentine Italy. Cardinal Pole and the Counter-Reformation* (Cambridge, 1972); P. Simoncelli, *Il caso Reginald Pole. Eresia e santità nelle polemiche religiose del Cinquecento* (Rome, 1977); J. I. Tellechea Idigoras, *Fray Bartolomé Carranza y el Cardenal Pole. Un Navarro en el restauración católica de Inglaterra (1554–1558)* (Pamplona, 1977). Also, now, the valuable information in the annotated edition of the Inquisition's trial of Cardinal Morone: M. Firpo and D. Marcato, *Il processo inquisitoriale del Cardinale Giovanni Morone*, Edizione critica (3 vols, Rome, 1981–85).

10.   *NB*, vol. XV, p. 67f.

11.   See W. B. Turnbull (ed.), *Calendar of State Papers, Foreign Series, of the Reign of Mary* (London, 1861), pp. 5, 7, 11. For the earlier peace soundings by the Duke of Northumberland 1552/53, cf. W. K. Jordan, *Edward VI: The Threshold of Power* (London, 1970), pp. 170ff; a more extensive analysis drawing on the imperial documents is to be desired.

12.   *NB*, vol. XV, p. 65.

13.   *NB*, vol. XIII, p. 388 n. 1.

14.   Tyler, vol. XI, pp. 471ff.

15.   In his letter to Pole of 22 December, Charles V referred to the intervention of Pedro de Soto, who had travelled to Brussels from Dillingen on the legate's behalf; *NB*, vol. XV, p. 104 n. 1.

16.   See ibid., p. 108.

17.   Ibid., p. 109; Morone to Pole, 8 January 1554: '*Che non essendo maturo il tempo di passare in Inghilterra, V. S. Rev^ma deve pigliar il negozio della pace per negozio principale.*'

18.   '*e lasciar le cose della successione del regno avere il suo ordinario corso.*' Ibid., p. 118.

19.   Ibid., p. 78.

20.   Ibid., p. 118.

21.   Pole to Bernardo Afresneda, 6 October 1554; printed in A. M. Qurini (Querini), *Epistolarum Reginaldi Poli S. R. E. Cardinalis et aliorum ad ipsum collectio*, vol. IV (Brescia, 1752), pp. 168ff.

22.   See the references in *NB*, vol. XV, p. xxvi n. 34.

23. Ibid., p. xxx f.
24. *NB*, vol. XIII, p. 436f.
25. *NB*, vol. XV, pp. 347ff.
26. Pole's *Discorso di pace* was disseminated in contemporary editions and translations as a programmatic text on the Christian concept of peace. See the reprint ibid., pp. 381ff; for the reference quoted above p. 399.
27. Ibid., p. 120.
28. *NB*, vol. XIV, p. 67 and vol. XV, p. 195.
29. Ibid., p. 130: Plea to the emperor that he authorise Pole to say to the French king in the emperor's name, '*di aver impetrato da lei che ella si contentasse di mandare qualche personaggio in alcun luogo neutrale per cominciare a trattare la pace*'.
30. See Renard's report of 8 June, Tyler, vol. XII, p. 272; the French text which is quoted above is in Ch. Weiss, *Papiers d'État du Cardinal de Granvelle*, vol. IV (Paris, 1843), p. 275f, and the further references in *NB*, vol. XV, pp. 195ff.
31. Tyler, vol. XII, p. 281.
32. Pole and Philip, *NB*, vol. XV, p. 202f.
33. Ibid., p. 204 n. 1: In his draft-letter Pole first of all lets the queen summarise the state of Anglo-French negotiations:

> *Onde, avendo io per il mio ambasciatore in Francia cercato d'intendere bene l'animo del re circa la nostra amicizia in tanta vicinità della guerra, et essendomi stato risposto ch'esso non solo non intende di romper meco l'amicizia, ma più presto di confirmarla et accrescerla ogni di più, con soggiogere che, quando il tempo portasse di trattar pace, mi avria sempre per buon mezzo, mi sono mossa a scrivere a V. M^{ta} con pregarla e supplicarla, con ogni maggior affetto che io posso, che, avendomi fatti tanti altri grandi onori, massimamente di darmi suo figliuolo eredezdi tanti regni per marito e consorte, voglio anche farmi questo di aprirmi la via che io possa essere buon mezzo a trattar questa pace, assicurando V. M^{ta} che, per quiete e salute della Cristianità così lungamente travagliata e tanto afflitta per queste guerre e per la tema che si può avere di molto peggio continuandosi in esse, io mi riputaria di essere più onorata, quando Dio mi dasse grazia di essere mediatrice in accordare e reconciliare così due gran principi, che di ogni onore che è piacciuto alla bontà divina sopra ogni mio merito farmi. E la maggior dote che V. M^{ta} potria darmi, insieme col re suo figliuolo, saria questa.*

When Pole wrote to Montmorency he expressly mentioned the promised readiness of the queen, in accordance with an enclosed copy, to request the emperor's agreement to mediation. She had then omitted to do so in view of the contrary opinions expressed by Montmorency to her ambassador; now Pole was going to personally entreat his support for the English mediation (ibid., p. 209f). Presumably this refers to Pole's draft letter for the queen of 21 June.

34. Tyler, vol. XII, p. 307f; cf. *NB*, vol. XV, p. 208 n. 2.
35. See ibid., pp. 208ff: Pole's letter to Montmorency and the references in the notes.
36. Ibid., p. 212f.

37. *NB*, vol. XIV, pp. 135ff; also Lutz, *Christianitas*, pp. 308ff.
38. Ibid., pp. 306ff, 317ff.
39. Ibid., p. 320f.
40. See *NB*, vol. XV, pp. 231ff, 235ff. For characterisation of the brothers and their diplomatic activity, see Harbison, *Rival Ambassadors*.
41. *NB*, vol. XV, p. 234.
42. See Pole's letters to the nuncios in France and Brussels (Gualterio and Muzzarelli) of 11 January, ibid., pp. 236f and 237 n. 3.
43. See the reports of Ambassador Noailles and of his brother in R. A. Vertot, *Ambassades de Messieurs de Noailles en Angleterre* (Leiden, 1763), vol. IV, pp. 116–20ff, and the ambassador's reprinted report of 20 January with extensive presentation of Pole's arguments and suggestions. The legate insisted that, '*qu'il estoit besoing devant que aulcunement s'assembler, de sçavoir sur quoy l'on debvoit traicter, et mesme que l'on fust d'accord*'. In contrast, Noailles described the legate's task as, '*que cela me sembloit debvoir venir de luy, qui estoit arbitre neutre, estant assez instruict des differends d'entre vous sire* [Henry II] *et led. empereur*'. Finally, the ambassador recognised the principle of preliminary agreement on the negotiating programme, but yet again left the initiative to Pole.
44. *NB*, vol. XV, p. 239 n. 3.
45. Vertot, *Ambassades*, p. 180.
46. Bibliothèque Nationale, Paris, F. fr. 5210 folio 37^{r-v} (Marillac's report of the Conference of Marcq); cf. Harbison, *Rival Ambassadors*, p. 240f; Lutz, *Christianitas*, p. 384f.
47. *NB*, vol. XV, p. 244f.
48. Ibid., pp. 241ff.
49. Cf. Lutz, *Christianitas*, pp. 374ff.
50. Ibid., p. 385 and n. 213.
51. *NB*, vol. XV, p. 256 n. 2.
52. For both conclaves in spring 1555, see the source and literature references in Lutz, *Christianitas*, p. 376 n. 191 and p. 379 n. 198.
53. For details of the conference preparations see in *NB*, vol. XV nos. 86, 87, 88, 89, 96, 97, 98, 100, 101 and *7a, *9a, *9b, *9c as well as the references in vol. XIV, pp. 217ff.
54. See the reproductions of contemporary plans and sketches in Brown's edition, vol. VI, 1, p. 80 and in Lutz, *Christianitas*, p. 387.
55. *NB*, vol. XV, p. 135: Pole to Julius III, 12 February 1554.
56. Printed in ibid., pp. 343ff, here p. 345.
57. Turnbull (as n. 11), p. 166f.
58. See Lutz, *Christianitas*, p. 388.
59. Ibid., p. 391.
60. For the policies and an assessment of Paul IV see Lutz, *Christianitas*, p. 380ff, also the introduction and documents in *NB*, vol. XV, pp. 265ff.
61. See most recently Simoncelli, *Il caso Reginald Pole*, p. 77ff; also *NB*, vol. XV, p. xxiv, 183, 202.
62. See Calvin to Vermigli (18 January 1555) and the further correspondence between Calvin and Bullinger; *Corpus Reformatorum*, vol. XLIII, col. 389 and vol. 44, cols. 392, 451, 563f.

17 Orange, Granvelle and Philip II*

H. G. Koenigsberger

I

On 23 July 1561 Orange and Egmont wrote their famous first letter to Philip II, denouncing the political role of Cardinal Granvelle and complaining that they were excluded from all important decision making in the government of the Netherlands.[1] The overt opposition of the Netherlands high nobility to the leading minister of the regency government, a government of which they were themselves members, has traditionally been seen as a milestone in, or even the beginning of, the *voorspel*, the events leading up to the revolt of the Netherlands. Now this is rather curious. There was nothing remarkable about aristocratic factionalism or about complaints about a royal minister, either in the Netherlands or anywhere else in early modern Europe. Complaints against Granvelle himself were not new.[2] Has it not simply been hindsight which has endowed the intrigues against the cardinal with more than incidental importance? Were not the real forces causing the revolt much more fundamental than the ambitions of a handful of near-bankrupt noblemen, most of whom eventually took no part in the revolt? Were not the causes of the revolt rather the social upheavals due to the industrialisation of the Flemish countryside, the distress caused in the big cities by disruption of trade, unemployment and high food prices, the spread of Protestant teaching together with the dislike of religious repression even by those who had every intention of remaining good Catholics, the defence of Netherlands liberties against monarchical autocracy, or simply the assertion of Netherlands nationalism against Spanish imperialism? Or again, if one prefers to use the terminology of the modern social sciences, was it not the dysfunction and final breakdown of a society, rather than the actions of a few individuals, which caused such a massive upheaval as the revolt? These questions, which are really arguments and formulations of causes, do indeed have much validity and the answer to them should be at least a qualified yes. Here I shall only argue that historical instinct and the need for an orderly and

353

dramatic presentation, which are the immediate reasons for our historiographical tradition about the actions of Orange and Egmont, may still be justified by the historical evidence.[3]

The government of Philip II in the Netherlands, like all early modern governments, depended ultimately on the co-operation of the local elites. At the same time, no popular movement was successful for more than a short time unless it had the support and leadership of this elite. At a time when both criticism of the king's policy and fear of popular revolt were growing,[4] a prolonged breakdown in co-operation between the monarchy and the Netherlands elite was a serious matter. It was so regarded at the time,[5] and it is therefore a legitimate subject for continued historical study.

Historians have given different reasons for the breach between Orange and Granvelle. Was it a basic clash between two opposed political philosophies? Or were there more specific reasons, such as the appointment of Margaret of Parma, rather than Christina of Lorraine, as governor-general? Was it the publication of the plan for the new bishoprics or Orange's unapproved marriage with the Lutheran daughter of the hated Maurice of Saxony? Or was it, as the German historian Ernst Marx maintained in a famous controversy with Orange's biographer, Felix Rachfahl, that the prince, Egmont and Glajon only became fully aware of Granvelle's domination of the government when they returned to Brussels from their provincial governments in the spring of 1561 and began to attend meetings of the council of state regularly?[6] Was Orange piqued by the regent's renewal of the Antwerp magistrate in the spring of 1561 without consulting him? For as burgrave of Antwerp Orange claimed the right to be consulted and had indeed been so by the king himself in 1558.[7] Perhaps all these events played their part cumulatively. It is certainly difficult to assign them any clear order of importance. Here I propose rather to try to look more closely at the terms in which the struggle between Orange and Granvelle was fought, at Philip II's reaction to it and at its historical implications for the Netherlands and for the Spanish empire.

In the Middle Ages the internal politics of the states of western Europe were largely determined by the relations between the kings and their most powerful feudal vassals. By the sixteenth century the feudal nobility had finally given up its earlier ambitions to become as independent of the monarchy as possible (as the German princes had done very successfully) and had thrown in their lot with the monarchies. It could be a very profitable alliance. In France and in the

Netherlands the rulers used the great nobles as provincial governors.[8] In this position they were held to represent both the king's authority in the province and also the interests of the community of the province at the king's court.[9] Naturally, only members of the greatest families were usually appointed to these posts; for the provincial nobility would not have obeyed someone below their own rank. The governors fulfilled essential functions for the monarchies. Not only did they organise the defence and public security of their provinces, but they acted as the king's all-purpose administrative agents, immediately subject to his commands. They would enforce royal legislation and ordinances without being hampered by all the legal precedents, traditions and *esprit de corps* of the lawyers in the parlements and provincial courts. Since they were appointed for life they were, in their turn, most favourably placed to advance their own and their families' influence by building up clienteles of lesser nobles and of local royal officials. This they did directly through their command of the companies of *gens d'armes*, in France, and of the *bandes d'ordonnance*, in the Netherlands, and indirectly by channelling royal patronage to their followers. They came from a small group of families which were closely linked by intermarriage with each other and, through their younger sons, with the noble families just below their own exalted level. These latter families, in their turn and in the same way, were linked with other lesser noble families. At the top of this social grouping family connections often extended beyond the frontiers of the state, from the Netherlands especially to France but also to Germany.

In the first half of the sixteenth century the system of provincial governorships had worked well for the monarchies. Charles V, Francis I and Henry II had enjoyed loyal and effective service from their great seigneurs, even when some of their families such as the Egmont and the Montmorency were split in their allegiance in the wars between these rulers. For these wars were straightforward dynastic power struggles in which, according to the ethos of the time, a nobleman's honour was fully preserved by loyal service to his own sovereign. Just as importantly, the system worked well because for the monarchies it was an age of expansion: territorial expansion, such as the incorporation of Groningen, Utrecht and Guelders in the Netherlands, which provided provincial governorships and a host of lesser positions; and economic expansion, both for the countries as a whole and more particularly for the governments. Increased tax revenues and greatly expanded credit facilities were used to extend government activities, especially warfare, and this meant more rewards for government service.

It was in the nature of these conditions that they could not last. In the 1550s this fact became unhappily apparent. Economic expansion gave way to economic crisis or, at best, to shifts in the patterns of trade with deeply disturbing social results. Government expenditure, optimistically overstretched for decades by continual warfare, finally out-ran taxable resources and available credit. Peace when it was finally concluded did not end the international rivalries between the great powers and was not expected to last. It did, however, cut off the prospect of new military commands for the high nobility and of expanding territorial patronage for the monarchies. The simultaneous injection of religious emotions into politics shattered the simple ethos of loyalty between monarch and ruling elite. These new conditions made the personality of the ruler more important than ever. Where, for whatever immediate cause, confidence in his person collapsed, the whole system of consensus politics between prince and high nobility was also likely to collapse. Different sections of the elite and especially its more ambitious individual members were driven to safeguard their positions and prospects. They could do this by one or both of two methods: by systematically expanding their own local power base far beyond anything they would have deemed necessary previously and by attempting to capture control of the central government. Neither line of policy was, at least initially, regarded as anti-monarchical or as inherently treasonous; both hinged crucially on the control of patronage.

The economic and financial crisis struck the whole of western Europe. Collapse of confidence in the person of the ruler occurred in France, Scotland and in the Netherlands. The phenomenon of such a collapse was not entirely fortuitous. It was always very likely to occur at the moment of a disputed succession or of the succession of a child or a woman and of the setting up of a regency, especially if it was the regency of a woman. There was statistically at least a fifty per cent chance of this happening at the end of any reign,[10] and this was precisely what happened in these three countries. It was these three countries, too, which slid into civil war and again in all three of them the immediate cause of the civil wars lay in the behaviour of the high nobility.

II

It looks as if Granvelle was the first person fully to appreciate the nature of the crisis precipitated by Philip II's appointment of Margaret of Parma as regent for the Netherlands. It had been an appointment made very much *faute de mieux*, designed to keep out Christina of Lorraine with her French connections and, even more, Philip's detested and feared cousin, Maximilian of Bohemia. To Granvelle it therefore seemed necessary, above all, to maintain royal authority by himself directly controlling government patronage and, indirectly, by extending his own reputation and influence. Was it Granvelle who suggested to the king the setting up of the famous secret *consulta*, the inner advisory committee for the regent, consisting of himself, Viglius and Berlaymont, which was designed to by-pass the council of state? It seems at least likely; but while this move was necessarily secret, another was deliberately public. Probably in 1559 and possibly before the setting up of the *consulta*, Granvelle wrote to Philip:

> Not for anything in the world would I be deemed importunate by Your Majesty, but no less would I wish that my relatives and friends should tax me with undue carelessness in my own case . . . for it is so many years now that I have received any favour [*merced*] . . . Now, forced by necessity and to avoid the opposition of my family and of everybody else who are expectantly waiting to see how Your Majesty will treat me.

He hoped that the king would now show him his favour publicly.[11]

Granvelle's arguments were entirely conventional and must have seemed perfectly reasonable to the king. In any case, he arranged for Granvelle's elevation to the cardinalate and to the archbishopric of Malines. Granvelle was pleased to be a cardinal and he accepted the archbishopric although he had doubts about the whole policy of the new bishoprics and although both he himself and his friends in Spain thought he had been rather hard done by to have been made to give up the much richer bishopric of Arras. If he wanted to play a prominent political role in the Netherlands and preserve royal authority, there was no way in which he could have turned down this expensive honour. For the whole scheme, together with the incorporation of the Brabantine abbeys in the new bishoprics, was designed not only to fight the growing threat of heresy but to increase government influence in the Estates of Brabant.[12] At the same time it signalled to everyone that Granvelle was a man of influence with, and trusted by, the king. Having earned the king's patronage, he could therefore be relied upon to dispense patronage in turn to his own clients. As it turned out, the policy worked rather too well. It gave the impression that Granvelle had more influence with the king than he actually did.

Orange was just as concerned about his clientele as Granvelle. For a while, and because they had been friends, they could arrange to split royal patronage by making deals, 'log rolling'. As late as January 1561 Orange wrote to Granvelle, signifying his pleasure at the king's appointment of the Seigneur de Chasteauroulleau to the position of *chevalier de la cour de parlement* of Dôle. He went on to agree to give the captaincy of Arguel, which Chasteauroulleau had held, to Granvelle's cousin, the Seigneur Pancras Bonvalot.[13] But by the summer of 1561, whatever degree of trust had been left between the prince and the cardinal had evaporated in hard competition. In their letter to the king of 23 June Orange and Egmont referred three times to the damage to their *honneur et réputation* and another time to their *honneur et estimation*.[14] Now, in the sixteenth century, *honneur* and *estimation* referred to the image others had of a man's ability to dispense patronage. Orange and Egmont, just as Granvelle, claimed that 'everyone' was watching and, in their case, mocking. For Egmont was a successful military leader in the king's service, second only to the Duke of Alba – and Alba had held the post of viceroy of Naples, and was currently serving as one of the principal shapers of royal policy in the king's own Council of State in Spain. Orange was an independent prince in his own right, like the Duke of Savoy, the previous governor-general. His marriage to a princess of the electoral house of Saxony showed his own view of his social-political status and was meant to show it to the world. With the king in Spain and the government of the Netherlands entrusted to an inexperienced and not very intelligent woman – a great change, this, from the formidably intelligent and forceful Mary of Hungary – Orange would expect, and would be expected, to play the leading political role in the country. In modern language neither Egmont nor Orange could afford to play second fiddle to a jumped-up civil servant from Franche-Comté.

Over the next two years both sides built up their clienteles. Orange's precise political objectives in this period are notoriously difficult to penetrate;[15] but it looks as if he and his friends were aiming at a position in the Netherlands similar to that enjoyed by the Guise in France during the reign of Francis II. This meant obtaining the decisive voice in decision making in the government and control of both central and local patronage in order to build up irresistible support in the country. In this strategy the provincial governorships were crucial. Mansfeld in Luxemburg was the most blatant in exploiting his position. It was reported that he 'tyrannises the provincial council, signs any requests by his secretary, appropriates fines and browbeats the attorney-general in his chambers'.[16] He sold positions in the town councils for ten gold florins, let off a murderer for 100 *écus* and, horror of horrors, received the Jews in his province.[17] In Hainault Berghes' behaviour was almost equally autocratic. In March 1560 Margaret of Parma had recommended his appointment to the king precisely because he had local influence and could therefore counter-balance the excessive authority of the Estates and of the bishop of Cambrai.[18] The appointment turned out to be a great disappointment for the regent. Berghes exercised quasi-dictatorial powers over the clergy yet failed to take effective action against heresy in a province which, because it bordered on France, was particularly exposed to the infiltration of Calvinist preachers.[19]

Orange, as one would expect, acted more subtly and, at the same time, with a surer aim for the acquisition of power. He tried to obtain the nomination as 'First Grandee' of Zeeland, a position which would have made him the sole representative of the nobility in the assembly of a province of which he was the governor.[20] More sinister still, he tried to be appointed *ruward*, or *surintendent*, of Brabant. This position, as Granvelle wrote in alarm to the king, would have made him supreme in a province which the ruler had always taken care to administer without the intervention of a provincial governor.[21]

There is no doubt that Orange and his friends were highly successful in attaching large numbers of the nobility and of government officials to themselves. But inevitably their policy aroused jealousy and opposition. They failed to win over Berlaymont, although they tried to tempt him with the promise of support for his son's election to the bishopric of Liège[22] – a promise which was in itself a measure of their growing influence in the region. More serious still than their failure with Berlaymont was the resistance to their overtures by the Duke of Aerschot and with him the resistance of the whole huge clan of the Croy and its widespread connections in the Walloon provinces. Margaret and Granvelle gleefully reported to Philip a quarrel which had arisen during a wedding party attended by all the great seigneurs. Aerschot had declared to Egmont that he was not willing to join the league against Granvelle, that they should not lay down the law for him and that, if they did not wish him for a friend as an equal, he did not care, 'for he had as much following of nobles and friends as any of them'.[23]

There is equally no doubt that Granvelle was building up his own party. In the spring of 1562 he wrote to Philip that the seigneurs no longer accepted his invitations for dinner but that he did not really mind and that he invited 'gentlemen, councillors and even burghers to gain their goodwill in case these [i.e. the seigneurs] should push matters further'.[24] A year later he was still using the same tactics. Many now had their eyes opened to the true nature of the seigneurs' policy, he informed the king, and many of the nobility had excused themselves to him that they could not do what they wished for fear of offending the seigneurs; but he, Granvelle, was entertaining them and keeping his friendship with them. This was the more necessary as Orange did not even bother any more about being *surintendent* of the Estates of Brabant because in effect he exercised a great part of the powers of this office anyway and he did this with the help of van Straelen, the Antwerp banker and superintendent of the taxes of the novennial *aide* of 1558.[25] He himself, Granvelle added virtuously, had asked the regent to excuse him from attending the *consultas*, so as to prevent further jealousy. But it was an empty gesture, and his enemies knew it; for he had arranged that Margaret should continue to consult him privately.[26] It was also well known that Viglius, the president of the privy council through which all patronage business was handled, was a faithful 'cardinalist'.[27]

By the spring of 1563 Granvelle was unequivocally presenting the struggle for the control of patronage and, hence, for power in the Netherlands, as the principal issue between himself and the seigneurs.[28] Soon afterwards he knew of the ultimatum Orange, Egmont and Hoorn had sent to Philip on 11 March, threatening to resign from the council of state – not, significantly, from their provincial governorships – unless the cardinal went. At almost exactly the same time the Edict of Amboise (19 March 1563) granted the French Huguenots at least a limited degree of toleration and, no doubt ominously from Granvelle's point of view, specially favoured the Huguenot nobility. He feared, as yet without giving any evidence, that one of the seigneurs in the Netherlands would make himself leader of the heretics, presumably just as had happened in France.[29] In July he wrote to Philip that the *superintendencia* which Orange was claiming in Brabant would allow him to appoint the margraves of the four principal cities. The margraves were the representatives of the central government for criminal jurisdiction in these cities. If Orange controlled them, Granvelle argued, he would be more powerful than the duke of Brabant (i.e. Philip II or his regent). It was the cardinal's opposition to this aim which was the main reason for the quarrel between them.[30]

In the next letter, on 25 July, Granvelle voiced his fears of the seigneurs' plots with German troops but added, perhaps sincerely, that not all of them knew of the ultimate plans.[31] On 20 August, in a long, confused and almost hysterical letter to the king, Granvelle concentrated on the demands for the summoning of the States General. What he feared was not the traditional assembly of the Estates of the different provinces who would listen together to the king's proposals and then deliberate and answer separately, but a joint meeting where all discussed and resolved on the proposals together. This was that they had done in 1558, when the States General had hammered out the conditions of the huge nine-year *aide* together with the then regent, the Duke of Savoy. Granvelle had opposed the joint sessions at that time but had been overridden by Savoy. He was particularly angry about the loss of royal authority which, he claimed, had been involved in allowing the States General to administer the nine-year *aide*. Straelen, the commissioner for this tax, had become his special *bête noir*.[32] Now Granvelle returned to the charge. Joint meetings would encourage the Estates to put forward demands they would not dare to make singly. By this he meant particularly the question of the new bishoprics and the placards against heresy. If the Estates controlled taxation, the government would lose its credit on the money market and would no longer be able to raise loans on its own authority. The States General, even if they showed good will, would be so slow raising money on credit that, if there was a rebellion or an invasion, the enemy would have captured half the country before the government could raise any troops and, within a short time, both the country and the Catholic religion would be lost. Orange and Berghes were in league with Straelen and even with some of the associates of Schetz, the king's financial agent in the Netherlands. They wanted to change the constitution so that they could command the state, and the regent, or even the king himself if he came, would have no further say.[33]

But in spite of all these dire predictions Granvelle still raised doubts about the success of Orange's and Berghes' policy with the Estates. Would the Estates really want to pay for the garrisons and service the king's enormous debts, just because the great lords called the tune?[34]

Much of the fault lay with the prelates and their refusal to consent to the *aides* because of the plans to incorporate their abbeys in the new bishoprics. This had made the clergy hated and had exasperated the king, although it was really the fault of others. The abbots had 'allowed themselves to be led like buffalos without thought of the disastrous results this might have for them'.[35]

In December 1563 the States General met in Brussels. It was a traditional meeting in which the provinces discussed the government proposals separately and not in joint session as in 1558. Granvelle thought it best to stay away, for fear the seigneurs would not come at all if he was there. As it was, he admitted that they were trying hard to get the *aides* accepted; but they were doing this by trying to build up their own following. Orange entertained the deputies of Flanders and Artois, of which Egmont was governor. Egmont entertained those of Orange's provinces of Holland, Zeeland and Utrecht. They gave dinner parties for seventy or eighty persons. The marquis of Berghes claimed that the States General would pay the seven million florins the king owed the troops, if only they were allowed to negotiate together. 'The Estates of Brabant want to be the head', Granvelle commented sourly, and 'the marquis wants to be the cock.' Aerschot had got tired of the festivities and had left. Granvelle thought that the Estates and the cities, too, were getting tired of the behaviour of the great lords.[36]

III

The pattern then was this: both Granvelle and the great seigneurs were trying to build up networks of clients among the lower nobility, government officials and town councils so as to have the greatest possible political influence in the Netherlands without, however, formally derogating the powers of the king. Neither side could pursue their policy quite openly. The cardinal could not afford to appear to be building up a private following or even to oppose the seigneurs outright. They were still the king's councillors and, in the Eboli party and especially in the secretary Eraso, they had powerful friends at court. Eraso, moreover, had a kind of secret service in the Netherlands in the persons of two officials in the administrations of the Spanish troops in the Netherlands, Alonso del Canto and Cristóbal de Castellanos, and in the Augustinian friar, Lorenzo de Villavicencio. These three ran a campaign against the cardinal's alleged softness towards heretics, and they had the ear of the king. Later, after

Granvelle had left the Netherlands and after Eraso had fallen from favour in Madrid, Villavicencio effortlessly transferred his allegiance to the Alba party and switched his campaign against the seigneurs.[37] These circumstances go far to explain the repulsive tone of Granvelle's letters to the king, his constant disclaimers of his own interests in the control of patronage and his assurances in his own implicit belief in the uprightness of Orange and his friends, followed by innuendos about their personal loyalty and trustworthiness in religious matters. The trick was similar to that used by Shakespeare's Mark Anthony: 'For Brutus is an honourable man' – and it was just as effective.[38]

Orange, for his part, had to be equally guarded.[39] Not only must the king not suspect him of claiming loyalties which properly belonged to the ruler, but neither must his own aristocratic allies. While all the provincial governors were trying to build up their clienteles, it looks as if only Orange and Berghes really thought in terms of a Guise-like takeover of the whole government machinery. The constant demand for the summoning of the States General was a part of this policy. Perhaps some of the seigneurs really believed that this body could restore consensus in religion. Certainly they wanted to use it in their political game and thought they could control it. This was what Granvelle and, eventually, Philip II also thought. Hence their attempts to split the league of seigneurs, especially by detaching Egmont from it and their refusal to summon the States General. Certainly, Granvelle's interpretation of Orange's policy in the early and mid-1560s is supported by what we know, much more unambiguously, about the prince's later policy. The constitutional arrangements which he made for the Archduke Matthias in 1577 left effective power with himself and with the States General.[40] In order to dominate the States General Orange consistently built up a party of his own followers in the towns. He did so in Holland after 1572, for instance by his appointment of Pieter Adriansz. van der Werff as burgomaster of Leiden, even though van der Werff did not belong to a patrician family in that city.[41] Once the civil war with Don John of Austria broke out, both sides systematically deposed opposing magistrates and had their own followers elected or they simply appointed them.[42]

Orange and Granvelle, then, had a very clear view of the nature of power in the Netherlands and their respective policies were entirely logical. But how successful were they in their attempts to control the towns? Evidently, much work remains to be done on this topic; but such evidence as there is suggests that neither the prince nor the cardinal were very successful. Thanks to the forthcoming book by Dr Guy Wells we know most about Antwerp.

Every spring, half of the city council of eighteen, the *schepenen*, were replaced. They were chosen by the regent in her *consulta* with Viglius, Berlaymont and/or Noircarmes, the margrave of Antwerp and the chancellor of Brabant. The *consulta* chose from a list of nine candidates proposed by the city council and from another nine proposed by the *wijkmeesters* and *hooftmannen van de porterije*. These were the very respectable, propertied persons who made up the 'third member' of the *breede raad* of Antwerp. On no occasion did the regent impose a candidate from outside this group. Not even the Duke of Alba did that. The council could make doubly sure of controlling its own renewal by putting forward unsuitable candidates, unknown and obviously unqualified men, or close relatives of actual councillors. This practice would further restrict the choice of the regent and her *consulta*.[43] Granvelle and Orange would each therefore be able to attract allies in the Antwerp magistracy. Jan van Schoonhoven, burgomaster in 1564–65, was a cardinalist and so was Hendrik van Berchem, a persecutor of heretics in districts under his private jurisdiction outside Antwerp. The banker van Straelen and the pensionary Wesenbeke, as is well known, were or came to be Orangists. But neither Granvelle nor Orange could hope to pack the Antwerp council with a majority of his own clients or even organise a solid and reliable voting block. Some of the patrician families deliberately kept contact with both sides. Much the same happened in the French civil wars, and it happened probably in most early modern politics, because preservation of the family and its property was regarded as more important than the views or even the personal fate of the family's individual members. The Antwerp council as a whole was most anxious to avoid committing itself to either side. Its aim was to preserve the city's privileges and independence, especially its independent jurisdiction which assured foreign merchants their personal safety in the city, and to escape too close a scrutiny of their religious convictions. Such a policy was not the same as that of the cardinal who wanted a much clearer stand on the placards and the prosecution of heretics and who tried to get the city to accept the establishment of the new bishopric of Antwerp, as well as supporting the government over the *aides* demanded from the Estates of Brabant. The prince of Orange was therefore seen as a useful ally in the blocking of policies which threatened the basis of Antwerp's trade and prosperity. But he was also a dangerous ally; for the Antwerp magistracy could not afford to antagonise the Brussels government and the king because it relied on them to uphold its privileges and trade treaties with foreign powers. Even the maintenance of law and order in the city and the position of the city oligarchy depended in the last resort on the support of the government. Fairly minor disturbances, such as those of 1554, demonstrated the helplessness of the council in the face of a popular movement and its need to rely on the government's soldiers as a sanction of last resort.[44]

Other towns of the Netherlands may not have been as independent as Antwerp. The methods of renewal of their magistrates varied, and so did the influence which either the Brussels government or the provincial governors could exert. In Hainault the governor and *grand bailli* was held to control the renewal of the magistrates of the Hainault towns.[45] The appointment of Berghes as governor therefore turned out to be particularly unfortunate for the government.[46] In Flanders, Egmont, as governor, shared the annual renewal with several other noble commissioners and, no doubt, had the decisive voice.[47] The governor of Holland was required to consult with the *schout* in each town.[48] Orange, however, became notorious for his high-handed interference in the renewal of the magistrates.[49]

But for all their efforts, it does not look as if the seigneurs were very successful in making the city councils into their clients. When Granvelle had left the Netherlands, the seigneurs who now dominated the council of state found, just as Granvelle had foreseen, that they could still not persuade the cities to grant the *aides* which were essential to maintain the country's defence. As far as we can tell at present, the town councils remained remarkably impervious to the party-building efforts of either the Brussels government or the provincial governors, at any rate until the outbreak of open civil war.[50] They pursued their own interests, including their religious preferences, which one could characterise for most of them as a non-persecuting Catholicism, and they did not allow themselves to be integrated into the parties in the way this was happening in France.

This does not mean that the towns were not aware that the game was being played for very high stakes. This became apparent as early as 1562 over the question of the Biervleet tolls. Ghent had built a canal to the lower Scheldt estuary and petitioned the government for exemption from the tolls at Biervleet. It was a serious challenge to the commercial supremacy of Antwerp and Granvelle tried to use it deliberately to put pressure on the city to give up its opposition to the establishment of its bishopric. By brilliant diplomacy and great determination, especially on the part of Wesenbeke, Antwerp was able to block this challenge without surrendering in its opposition to the bishopric.[51] But in his dying weeks as Margaret's principal minister Granvelle returned to the charge. The occasion was the embargo on English imports, in November and December of 1563, when he advised the regent to pursue a hard line in order to bring pressure both on the English government and on Antwerp. The city lost its English trade to Emden, but also to Flanders, for the Flemish cloth industry received English semi-manufactured cloths via France, or even more simply from extensive smuggling.[52]

After the embargo was lifted, the rivalry between Antwerp and Flanders persisted and now came to involve the great nobles. Egmont supported an attempt by Bruges to have the staple of the Merchants Adventurers moved to Bruges instead of back to Antwerp. The Antwerp council turned to Orange. Somewhat tardily, the prince gave his support. The city won this bout, for the regent was not willing to antagonise Antwerp even more. The city was still much too important for the economy of the Netherlands and the finances of Philip's government. But the victory was not due to the prince's intervention, and the city knew it.[53]

Once the common enmity to Granvelle had disappeared, the league of seigneurs was showing evident signs of strain.[54] While they now dominated the council of state, they were not able to win control over government patronage. Apparently to everyone's surprise in Brussels, this control passed to Margaret's Spanish secretary, Armenteros. By the early summer of 1564, Viglius was complaining about it to Granvelle.[55] At the same time the provincial governors were still extending their powers in their provinces. 'Armenteros governs everything now', Viglius wrote to the cardinal in October. In Flanders, especially in Bruges, he continued, there was great opposition to the inquisitor Titelmans. The magistrates of the cities were still ready to maintain the law, but they could no longer be relied upon because 'the authority of the governors, with the connivance of Her Highness (i.e. Margaret), increases so much that everyone seeks to please them or at least not to displease them'.[56]

In these circumstances it was quite logical that the seigneurs' next move was try to subordinate the council of finance and the privy council to the council of state. If they could achieve this, they would have outflanked both Armenteros and Viglius with the other friends of Granvelle who still remained in the government of the Netherlands.

In this move Orange, Egmont and Berghes were united, although we simply do not know whether their ultimate political aims were identical. But more crucial even than this question is another: would their political victory have been enough, or rather, would it have produced a reasonably stable situation?

IV

The struggle between Orange and Granvelle and their respective allies had been a struggle for power within a given political context. Neither side had had any intention of breaking this context or of breaking out of it. The ultimate sovereignty of the king (however this ambiguous term might have been interpreted at the time) had not been called into question, nor had the maintenance of the Catholic religion. Unlike Condé and Coligny, none of the great lords of the Netherlands had proclaimed himself a leader of a Calvinist movement. Their opposition to the new bishoprics and the inquisition was political and emotional but not religious. The Brabantine abbots and the city councils all over the Netherlands who were in the forefront of this opposition were defining their property, their legal rights and their political autonomy. On the other side, Granvelle was certainly worried about the spread of heresy. But he saw the fight against it in terms of political power – and that, precisely, was his quarrel with Orange. 'It is laughable', he wrote to Gonzalo Pérez in 1563, 'to send us depositions made before the inquisitors in Spain so that we should look for heretics here: as if there were not thousands professing heresy to whom we dare not say anything.'[57]

Yet while the contestants accepted the context of the struggle, this context was not stable. Forces which neither Granvelle nor Orange could control broke in on the struggle, swept the contestants aside and radically altered its terms. Both Orange and, much later, Granvelle, managed eventually to return to the struggle, but only after they had accepted the new terms. The forces over which in the mid-1560s they had no control were of course the spread of the Protestant movement and Philip II's reaction to this movement. The history of Protestantism in the Netherlands, the formation of the Compromise, the hedge preaching, the conventicles, the image breaking, the alliance between Calvinist nobles and burghers and the formation of the *gueux* as a fighting force – all these are well known, and I will not rehearse them here. The king's policy, however, requires a brief account. Inevitably, this account owes a great debt to the still unpublished work of David Lagomarsino and María José Rodríguez-Salgado who, between them and without always agreeing with each other, provide the most detailed and best-documented analysis of the politics of the Spanish court.

The key to an understanding of Philip II's policy is his view of the nature of his empire and of his own position as its ruler. Charles V had failed to have Philip succeed him as emperor; yet Philip thought of his dominions essentially in imperial terms, just as his father had done. He was the ruler of each of them, reigning over them not as king of Spain but as their own prince and by virtue of their own laws of succession. He had sworn to uphold their rights and privileges. If at times he chose to overrule certain of these rights and privileges, it was only in order to defend even greater rights of his subjects: to live under his, Philip's, rule, to which God had entrusted them, and to live within the true Catholic faith, without being led astray from their salvation. Of both these rights he himself, and no one else, was the judge.[58] When he was still in the Netherlands, after the emperor's abdication, he ruthlessly exploited the financial resources of Castile to carry on the war with France from the Netherlands. The emperor himself, both from Brussels and, later, from Yuste, fully supported and even increased the pressure on Spain.[59] There is every reason to take seriously Philip's *cri de coeur* to Emmanuel Philibert, his regent of the Netherlands, in 1557:

> Although I have ordered that my cities in Spain be sold for the defence of the Netherlands (and although I understand very well that they do not believe this), there is nobody in Spain who has got the money to buy these cities, for the whole kingdom is so poor, much poorer than the Netherlands ... I for my part am doing what I can and will risk my person for them and join the army which is to defend these states and I will give them all the money I have ... And for all this they thank me here by saying or thinking that I care nothing for them and that I prefer an inch of Spanish earth to a hundred leagues here. All this I cannot but feel strongly and grieve much over it, for it is so much without cause.[60]

Yet this hostility, which Philip recognised, was unavoidable. The supranational policy which the king pursued by force of his inheritance was never likely to be acceptable to subjects who had to pay for it, especially when the king was not among them to distribute royal patronage and personally supervise the administration of their country. England, Scotland and France all experienced deadly faction fights for control of patronage and power during royal minorities and regency governments. All of Philip's dominions, except the one in which he himself resided, were permanently in the position of needing regency governments. In 1559, when Philip had been absent from Spain for six years, that country, too, was on the brink of rebellion. The one point on which nearly everyone agreed during the 1560s was the need for the king's return to the Netherlands to solve its problems. The question was how this could be done. Spain was beset by mortal enemies in the Mediterranean, enemies who could, or so it was believed, count on the support of a 'fifth column', the Moriscos in southern and eastern Spain. In the event, Spain was plunged into civil war, the revolt of the Moriscos, before the most serious stages of the civil war in the Netherlands had even begun. Moreover, the regent whom Philip would have had to leave in Spain, the Infante Don Carlos, was showing progressively more alarming signs of mental instability. Yet there was no obviously acceptable alternative to Carlos.

Perhaps a much greater integration of the different parts of Philip's empire would have resolved at least some of his problems. Granvelle, at least, seems to have thought so. Quite consistently with his view of the nature of politics he urged the king to internationalise his patronage and give *encomiendas* of the Spanish orders of knighthood to the Netherlands; for then they would have to support the country from which they were deriving their income, and their relatives and clients would be won over with them. Even if only two or three Brabanters were honoured in this way, the cardinal assured the king, 25,000 would support him the more willingly in hope of similar advancement. In Italy, too, some high positions in government or in the military or naval establishment should be given to some of the principal Netherlands seigneurs who had shown their prowess in these fields. Orange himself, of course, 'would not serve badly [as viceroy] in Sicily, for he would then be far from Germany and perhaps live with greater contentment'.[61]

It was an astonishing proposal, coming as it did in March 1563, at the very height of the cardinal's quarrel with the prince. Granvelle was certainly quite serious about his idea, for he came back to it in a later letter,[62] and I do not think he proposed it only to get his most dangerous opponent out of the Netherlands. Philip also took the suggestion seriously, but could not see it in the same way. As to the *encomiendas*, he replied, they were given only to persons who took the habit (i.e. religious vows) and many did this only to get an *enco-*

mienda. Besides, there were so many people in Spain who served him and whom he could not reward except with money, which he needed for other purposes, or with *encomiendas*; and those who did not get one became disgruntled. Still, he was considering one for Gosuin de Varick, governor of Diest, who may have been connected with Orange. As to positions in Italy, there were very few, mainly vice-royalties. For these, because of the importance of religion, it was necessary to find someone about whom one could feel absolutely safe, not only about his own religious beliefs but about the way he handled such beliefs. With the prince of Orange one just could not know whether it would work out in the way Granvelle suggested.[63]

Here indeed was the heart of the matter. It was the unreliability of the civil authorities, both of the cities and of the provincial governors, in dealing with heresy which, as Dr Rodríguez-Salgado has convincingly argued, made the maintenance of the inquisition and the enforcement of the placards in the Netherlands a matter on which Philip would never give way. In Naples and Milan, and even in Galicia in Spain, the civil authorities could be relied upon to the extent that the introduction of the inquisition could be given up in the face of local opposition, or at least postponed indefinitely.[64]

The exchange between Philip and Granvelle showed the central ambiguity at the core of Philip's empire: here was a king who could speak only Spanish fluently, who lived in Spain, who surrounded himself with Spanish advisers and who, for seemingly good reasons, was reluctant to extend his imperial patronage to all his subjects. It did not matter that all his dominions, just as all countries of Europe in the sixteenth century, bitterly resented having non-natives appointed to 'their' offices and that hardly anyone really wanted to have a truly imperial, international administration. The provinces of the Netherlands were notorious sticklers on this point, even against each other. It did not matter that, in fact, very few Spaniards were appointed in the Netherlands and not many more in Italy. It did not matter that Philip's imperial policies, and not least his policies in the Netherlands, often ran counter to the interests of his Spanish subjects. The overwhelming impression which Philip gave to his contemporaries was that he was a Spanish king, ruling a Spanish empire in the interests of the Spaniards.

Nowhere was this clearer than in Philip's policy towards France. When the first civil war broke out, in the early summer of 1562, Philip wanted to support the Catholics. The Netherlands, however, refused to co-operate in a policy of intervention. Granvelle and Margaret of

Parma counselled against it. The Order of the Golden Fleece voted unanimously against any military action in France.[65] Philip felt this attitude to be both humiliating towards himself and desperately dangerous for the Netherlands. The reports from Chantonnay, Granvelle's brother and Philip's ambassador in France, became more and more alarming. Thus in January 1563 Chantonnay wrote of talk among members of the French royal council, of how, now that heresy had gained a foothold in France, the Netherlands were ripe to fall. They were disenchanted with the Spaniards and would choose either the king of Bohemia as their ruler or, because Maximilian might not be strong enough to defend them, the king of France himself. Philip would be quite unable to mount a diversionary attack from Italy or from Spain. Once the Netherlands had fallen and its warships had joined with those of France, England could not be held and then Spanish commerce with the Indies could no longer be protected. The duke of Savoy would then no longer be able to deny passage to French troops into Italy and the Milanese would be pleased to throw off the burden of Spanish rule. In all this the French would undoubtedly get help from the Turkish fleet and from the Moors.[66]

No doubt, the French councillors, 'important persons but not principal ones', as Chantonnay characterised them,[67] were whistling in the dark to keep up their courage in the middle of a civil war, or perhaps they were just trying to frighten Philip's ambassador. If so, they were more successful than they could have hoped. Chantonnay reported their views in the classic form of a domino theory where one future disaster inexorably leads to another. But, for all the usual implausibilities of this theory, there were sufficient reasons for Madrid not to take the threat lightly. Philip had distrusted Maximilian ever since his cousin had edged him out of the succession to the Holy Roman Empire. Maximilian was known to have ambitions in the Netherlands and, when one thinks of the later venture by his son, the Archduke Matthias, such ambitions were far from impossible. Moreover Alba, to whom Chantonnay addressed his letter, had himself in earlier years argued that the Netherlands were strategically very difficult to defend, especially without the presence of their prince. Philip knew all about this argument. He had himself summarised it for his father in 1544 when Charles V was wondering whether to give the Netherlands or Milan as a dowry for a Habsburg princess marrying the second son of Francis I.[68] Finally, both Charles V's earlier experience and the ineffectiveness of the mismanaged Spanish intervention from Milan in the French civil war underlined the point made by the French councillors about the invulnerability of France from attacks mounted from Italy or from Spain. Without troops in the Netherlands that were under his complete control, which the *bandes d'ordonnance* clearly were not, Philip could neither pursue a credible great power policy in north-western Europe nor even assure the safety of a dominion for which he regarded himself just as much responsible as for Spain. There was no alternative to co-operation with the Netherlands nobility.[69]

The first implication of the full realisation of this fact was the necessity of throwing Granvelle to the wolves. It is quite likely, as Professor Lagomarsino has argued with a convincing wealth of documentation, that the cardinal's enemies at court, Secretary Eraso and the Eboli party, egged on by the personal enmity of Simon Renard and the fanaticism of Fray Villavicencio, would in any case have won this round against Granvelle's supporters, Alba and Gonzalo Pérez. They certainly organised the political mechanics of Granvelle's recall from the Netherlands.[70] Yet Philip's action in this case was very much part of a pattern of political behaviour which he followed consistently whenever one of his ministers, viceroys or governors ran up against local opposition that seemed for the moment insuperable. So it was with Margaret of Parma and, later, with her son, Alexander Farnese, with the Marquis of Mondéjar in Andalucia, with Antonio Pérez and with the Duke of Alba himself. With the viceroys of Sicily the practice became a regular system. Machiavelli had recommended making a show of sacrificing unpopular ministers.[71] In fact it was difficult to avoid doing this where an early modern ruler had to rely on the co-operation of a local elite. The almost universal contemporary lament of the fickleness of princes had much justification, for such fickleness was built into the system of early modern government.

Granvelle had faithfully carried out Philip's policy in the Netherlands. In the process he had become unacceptable to a large section of the local elite. As a result, the country was left virtually undefended against both military and religious attack. There was no way – and here I am again following Dr Rodríguez-Salgado's argument – in which Philip could have continued Granvelle in office. Failing his own return to the Netherlands, he had to come to some sort of terms with those who commanded the local defence forces, the *bandes d'ordonnance*. Since Orange and his friends had always proclaimed their loyalty, both to the king and to the Catholic religion, Philip had to hope that this alliance would still maintain his ultimate authority, and that the struggle against heresy would, at least, not be further weakened.

It was a forlorn hope. Psychologically and politically the aims of the players in this game were too contradictory to make genuine co-operation possible. The tragi-comedy of mutual misunderstanding during Egmont's visit to Madrid shows that this fact was not immediately clear to most of the participants but that, on the contrary, there was quite a lot of mutual good will. One may well suspect, however, that Orange at least saw the situation more clearly and was not very surprised by the outcome. The immediate result was stasis, a seizing up of the political process and a virtual standstill of the administrative machine. Again, this was an inbuilt hazard of early modern régimes, and Philip II's empire, with its geographically separate entities and its ethnic and religious tensions, was particularly prone to it. In Sicily, for instance, stasis was practically a permanent condition; for in the island the viceroy and the civil courts, on the one side, and on the other the Spanish inquisition, allied with the proto-Mafia of disgruntled nobles and bandits, held each other in an immovable balance. Philip reacted by changing the viceroys every three or six years and otherwise making soothing noises to both sides. Neither party, nor anyone else in Sicily, threatened his sovereign authority or the Catholic religion.[72]

In Spain and in the Netherlands, however, such masterly inactivity was in the long run not possible. In Andalucia stasis developed from the conflicting claims and manoeuvres of the inquisition, the *audiencia*, i.e. the supreme civil court of the province, the archbishop of Granada, his hostile cathedral chapter and the governor of the province, the Marquis of Mondéjar. All this manoeuvring took place at the expense of the Morisco population and against the background of Moorish raids across the Straits from North Africa. Philip, anxious both over defence and over the apparent resurgence of Islam among the nominally Christian Moriscos, backed the hard-line religious policy of Cardinal Espinoza against Mondéjar, the *de facto* protector of the Moriscos. To satisfy local interest groups, as well as his personal enemies at court, the king relieved Mondéjar of his responsibilities for the Moriscos and for internal security. The result was an explosion, the rising of the Moriscos against the paralysed civil and military authorities,[73] followed by more than two years of civil war, then the dispersal and, finally, in the early seventeenth century, the expulsion of the Moriscos.

In the Netherlands stasis overtook the regime when, year after year, the Estates of Brabant refused to pay the *aide* for defence which the government had asked for in 1558; when the provincial governors and the city councils blocked the government's religious policy; and when the noble members of the council of state boycotted that body. Then, just as in Andalucia, the dismissal of the principal minister did not succeed in setting the government machinery in motion again. Here, too, the king's initiative in religious policy then triggered the reaction of forces outside the parties of the political and administrative elites, forces which the stasis had allowed to gather strength. They came into the open in the Compromise, the image breaking and the military actions of the armed *gueux*. This was the tragedy of Philip II's empire. For William of Orange it was an opportunity which he had helped to create but which he had not intended and whose nature became clear to him only with time. If for him the story in the end also turned to tragedy, it was at least a tragedy followed by catharsis: the foundation of a new, independent state, the United Provinces of the Netherlands.

Notes

* This paper has also appeared in *Bijdragen en Mededelingen betreffende de Geschiedenis der Nederlanden*, IC (1984), and is included in my collection of essays *Politicians and Virtuosi* (London, 1986).

1. N. Japikse, *Corrispondentie van Willem den Eerste Prins van Oranje* (The Hague, 1934), pp. 311–15. Antoine Perrenot did not become Cardinal Granvelle until 1561; but for the sake of convenience I shall refer to him by this title throughout.
2. M. van Durme, *Antoon Perrenot* (Brussels, 1953), pp. 158–60. K. J. W. Verhofstad, *De regering der Nederlanden in de jaren 1555–1559* (Nijmegen, 1937), pp. 45–7.
3. In doing this I have had the advantage of using three important but as yet unpublished studies: David Lagomarsino, *Philip II and the Netherlands 1559–1573*; María José Rodríguez-Salgado, *From Spanish Regent to European Ruler: Philip II and the Creation of an Empire*; and Guy E. Wells, *Antwerp and the Government of Philip II 1555–1567*. I would like to thank all three authors for making their typescripts available to me.
4. There were riots in Antwerp as early as 1554. Wells, *Antwerp and the Government of Philip II*, pp. 49–57. Philip II to duke of Savoy, 2 May 1557, writes of the danger of being caught by a revolt without soldiers or money to put it down. Emmanuele Filiberto duca di Savoia, *I Diarii delle campagne di Fiandra*, ed. E. Brunelli (Biblioteca della società storica subalpina, CXII, N.S. 21) (Turin, 1928), pp. 182–3.

5. Marcantonio Mula, 'Relazione di Filipp II re di Spanga, 23 settembre 1559', in E. Albèri, *Le relazione degli ambasciatori veneti al Senato*, ser. 1, vol. III (Florence, 1853), p. 401: '*e già se ne* (i.e. "*manifesta sollevazione de popoli*") *son visti qualche segni nelli Paesi Bassi.*'

6. E. Marx, *Studien zur Geschichte des niederländischen Aufstandes* (Leipzig, 1902), pp. 167ff.

7. Ibid., pp. 174–5.

8. Robert E. Harding, *Anatomy of a Power Elite: The Provincial Governors of Early Modern France* (New Haven/London, 1978). Paul Rosenfeld, *The Provincial Governors from the Minority of Charles V to the Revolt* (Standen en Landen, XVII) (Louvain/Paris, 1959). There was no exactly similar position in England or Spain. The powers of the lords-lieutenant of the English counties were not nearly as extensive, while Spanish viceroys and governors-general, although having even greater powers, were not appointed for life.

9. See for instance the typically dual role played by the count of Hoochstraten, governor of Holland, in the 1530s. H. G. Koenigsberger, 'Patronage and Bribery during the Reign of Charles V', in idem, *Estates and Revolutions* (Ithaca, NY/London, 1971), pp. 166–75.

10. Idem and George L. Mosse, *Europe in the Sixteenth Century* (London, 1968), p. 249.

11. Ch. Weiss, *Papiers d'État du Cardinal de Granvelle*, vol. V (Paris, 1844), pp. 657–9.

12. Geoffrey Parker, *The Dutch Revolt* (London, 1977), p. 48 n. 24. I wish to thank Professor Parker for letting me have a photocopy of Granvelle's letter of 12 May 1576 where he specifically makes this point.

13. L. P. Gachard (ed.), *Correspondance de Guillaume le Taciturne*, vol. II (Brussels, 1850), pp. 4–6.

14. See above, n. 1.

15. Cf. K. W. Swart, 'Willem van Oranje en de Vestiging van de Macht van de Nederlands Statenvergadering', p. 2. I wish to thank Professor Swart for letting me have a copy of the typescript of his article, a shortened version of which appeared as 'The Foundation of the Dutch Republic', *History Today*, XXXIV (1984), pp. 41–4.

16. Rosenfeld, *Provincial Governors*, p. 52.

17. Morillon to Granvelle, 9 December 1564. Weiss, *Papiers d'État*, vol. VII (Paris, 1849), p. 533.

18. Margaret to Philip II, 17 March 1561. L. P. Gachard (ed.), *Correspondance de Marguerite d'Autriche, Duchesse de Parme, avec Philippe II*, vol. I (Brussels, 1867), p. 148.

19. Rosenfeld, *Provincial Governors*, p. 51.

20. Ibid., p. 53.

21. L. P. Gachard, 'La chute du cardinal de Granvelle en 1564', in idem, *Études et notices historiques concernant l'histoire des Pays-Bas* (Brussels, 1890), p. 110.

22. Margaret to Philip, 6 February 1563. Weiss, *Papiers d'État*, vol. VII, pp. 5–6.

23. Ibid.

24. Granvelle to Philip, 13 May 1562. Ibid., vol. VI (Paris, 1846), pp. 557–

60. '*cavalleros, y consejeros y aun burgeses por ganarles la voluntad para en caso que quisiessen estos* [i.e. the league of seigneurs] *rebolver mas las cosas.*'

25.   Granvelle to Philip, 10 March 1563. Ibid., vol. VII, pp. 19, 38.
26.   Ibid., p. 21.
27.   Van Durme, *Antoon Perrenot*, p. 177.
28.   Granvelle to Philip, 10 March 1563. Weiss, *Papiers d'État*, vol. VII, p. 21.

> *Y porque veo que se ofenden mucho de que no entren en la consulta, y en renovar el magistrado de las villas, en lo qual no conviene en ninguna manera que tengan parte, porque seria la ruina de la authoridad de* V.M., *por quitarles el sentimiento que muestran tener de que entrevenga yo en ello, he suplicado á Madama* [i.e. the regent, Margaret of Parma] *lo que ántes muchas vezes, que consienta que yo me abstenga de las consultas, y que de lo que de mí quisiere ser informada lo haré aparte* [my underlining].

29.   Granvelle to Philip, 9 May 1563. Ibid., pp. 74–5.
30.   Ibid., pp. 135–8.
31.   Ibid., p. 165.
32.   F. Rachfahl, *Wilhelm von Oranien und der niederländische Aufstand*, vol. I (Halle/The Hague, 1906), pp. 553–68. Verhofstad, *De regering*, pp. 116–49. Wells, *Antwerp*, ch. 3, section C, pp. 168–92; ch. 4, section D, pp. 236, 243.
33.   Archivo General de Simancas, MS Estado 524, fo. 23–29. I would like to thank Dr Rodríguez-Salgado for making a photocopy of this MS available to me. Weiss, *Papiers d'État*, vol. VII, pp. 181–7, leaves out some of the most interesting passages of this letter.
34.   Archivo General de Simancas, MS Estado 524, fo. 24.
35.   Granvelle to Philip, 8 September 1563. Weiss, *Papiers d'État*, vol. VII, p. 206.
36.   Granvelle to Philip, 10 December 1563. Ibid., pp. 259–65.
37.   For a detailed description of the careers and activities of these three persons see Lagomarsino, *Philip II and the Netherlands*, part II.
38.   Among many examples see Granvelle to Philip, 12 March 1562. Weiss, *Papiers d'État*, vol. VI, p. 534, and 22 May 1563. Ibid., vol. VII, p. 79.
39.   Rosenfeld, *Provincial Governors*, p. 54, esp. n. 255.
40.   H. G. Koenigsberger, 'Why did the States General of the Netherlands become revolutionary in the Sixteenth Century?', *Parliaments, Estates and Representation*, II (1982), p. 109. Both for the above article and for the present paper I wish to thank Professor Swart for drawing my attention to some of the documentation supporting this point.
41.   J. C. H. de Pater, *Jan van Hout (1542–1609)* (The Hague, 1946), p. 34. See also C. Hibben, *Gouda in Revolt* (Utrecht, 1983), ch. 3.
42.   C. H. Th. Bussemaker, *De Afscheiding der Waalsche Gewesten van de Generale Unie*, vol. I (Haarlem, 1895), pp. 240–1. L. P. Gachard (ed.), *Extrait des Registres des Consaux de Tournay, 1472–1490, 1559–1572, 1580–81* (Brussels, 1846), pp. 114–16.
43.   Wells, *Antwerp*, pp. 89–94. Strictly speaking, the whole council was

changed, but half of the new one had to be selected from the membership of the old.
44. Ibid., pp. 233–6, 239–41 and passim.
45. Rosenfeld, *Provincial Governors*, p. 23.
46. Cf. above, p. 359.
47. Archives Générales du Royaume, Brussels. Papiers d'État et de L'Audience MS 809[3], folders for 1561–66. No folio numbers. Rosenfeld, *Provincial Governors*, p. 23.
48. Ibid., p. 24.
49. Ibid., pp. 54–5.
50. Cf. Wells, *Antwerp*, p. 237.
51. Ibid., pp. 259–65.
52. Ibid., pp. 275–85.
53. Ibid., pp. 299–303.
54. E.g. Morillon to Granvelle, 1 April 1564. Weiss, *Papiers d'État*, vol. VII, p. 452.

Le conte d'Egmont et le prince d'Orenges se caressent, touttefois l'on s'apperceoit que c'est simulation . . . Les femmes ne se cèdent en rien, et se tiegnent par le bras, incedentes pari passu; et si l'on rencontre une porte estroicte, l'on se serre également ensemble, afin qu'il n'y ayt du devant ou derrière.

This characteristic comic opera aspect of Netherlands politics before the storm – there are similar scenes in Mozart's *Le nozze di Figaro* and in Verdi's *Falstaff* – had already flowered luxuriously in the grotesque manoeuvres of the courts of Madrid and Brussels to arrange the resignation-dismissal of Granvelle. See Van Durme, *Antoon Perrenot*, pp. 207–18.
55. Viglius to Granvelle, 12 June 1564. G. Groen van Prinsterer (ed.), *Archives ou Correspondance Inedite de la Maison d'Orange-Nassau*, ser. 1, vol. I, 2nd edn (Leiden, 1841), pp. 263–5.
56. Ibid., pp. 317–19.
57. 17 June 1563. Weiss, *Papiers d'État*, vol. VII, p. 106.
58. See for instance Philip's reply to a petition of the Estates of Brabant, in 1562, against the incorporation of the abbeys in the new bishoprics. The king maintained that, in case of a doubtful interpretation of the *joyeuse entrée*, the decision could not rest with the Estates. They should 'plustost considérer et interpréter qu'il n'y ait privilège, quelque fort qu'il soit, qui ne deut cesser pour tel bien que le présent, *cum summa sit ratio quae pro religione facit et salus populi suprema lex est*'. Gachard, *Correspondance de Marguerite d'Autriche*, vol. II, p. 143.
59. Rodríguez-Salgado, *Spanish Regent to European Ruler*, ch. 5.
60. Philip to Savoy, London, 27 May 1557. Archives Générales du Royaume, *Les Archives et les Bibliothèques d'Italie*, vol. I, *Manuscrits divers 1172*, fos. 225–27.

Y aunque he mandado que, para defender esos Estados, porque los tengo en mucho (aunque entiendo muy bien que no lo creen así) me vendan las ciudades que tengo en España, no se halla nadie que tenga

*dinero, porque todo el Reyno está pobre y harto mas qu'esos Estados
... yo, de mi parte, lo que puedo hago, qu'es poner con ellos my
persona y juntar el exercito, y traer para defension d'esos Estados un
todo quanto dinero tengo ... y esto agrandezánmelo ay de manera que
dirán ó pensarán que no los tengo en nada y que quiero mas un palmo
de tierra en España que ay cien leguas. Todo esto no puedo dejar de
sentirlo mucho y dolerme mucho dello, siendo tan sin causa.*

Garchard's copy of the original in Turin. Partly quoted in Verhofstad,
De regering, p. 113 n. 90.

61. Granvelle to Philip, 10 March 1563, Weiss, *Papiers d'État*, vol. VII, pp.
    53–5.
62. Granvelle to Philip, 13 June 1563. Ibid., pp. 156–7.
63. Philip to Granvelle, 13 June 1563. Ibid., pp. 85–9.
64. Rodríguez-Salgado, *Spanish Regent to European Ruler,* pp. 481ff.
65. Viglius, *Mémoires*, ed. A. Wauters (Brussels, 1862), pp. 46–7. Gachard,
    'La chute', p. 109.
66. Chantonnay to Alba, Paris, 16 January 1563. *Archivo Documental
    Español*, publ. R. Academia de la Historia, vol. V, *Negociaciones con
    Francia (1563)* (Madrid, 1952), pp. 33–6.
67. '*Personas principales, no de los mayores que de los que entran en
    consejo . . .*' Ibid., p. 33.
68. Philip to Charles V, Valladolid, 13 January 1544. M. Fernández
    Alvarez (ed.), *Corpus Documental de Carlos V*, vol II (Salamanca,
    1975), pp. 306–9. F. Chabod, '¿Milan o Los Paises Bajos? Las Discu-
    siones en España sobre la "alternativa" de 1544', in *Carlos V (1500–
    1558). Homenaje de la Universidad de Granada* (Granada, 1958), pp.
    367–70.
69. Here I am following Dr Rodríguez-Salgado's interpretation, *From
    Spanish Regent to European Ruler,* pp. 449ff and *passim.*
70. Lagomarsino, *Philip II and the Netherlands*, part II.
71. N. Machiavelli, *Il principe*, ch. VII.

    *E perchè conosceva le rigorosità passate avergli generato qualque odio,
    per purgare gli animi di quelli popoli, e guadagnarseli in tutto, volle
    mostrare che se crudeltà alcuna era seguita, non era nata da lui* [i.e.
    Cesare Borgia], *ma dall'acerba natura del ministro* [i.e. Ramiro
    d'Orco]. *E preso sopra questo occasione, lo fece una mattina mettere a
    Cesena in duo pezzi in su la piazza con un pezzo di legno e un coltello
    sanguinoso a canto. La ferocità del quale spettacolo fece quelli popoli
    in un tempo rimanere soddisfatti e stupidi.*

    With Philip II's ministers the cutting in pieces usually applied to
    their careers rather than their bodies, although Juan de Escobedo
    might not have thought so if his assassins had left him any time to
    reflect on his fate.

72. H. G. Koenigsberger, *The Practice of Empire* (Ithaca, NY, 1969), pp.
    161–70.
73. Cf. K. Garrad, 'The Causes of the Second Rebellion of the Alpujarras
    (1568–71)' (PhD Dissertation, University of Cambridge, 1956).

18 The Shape of Anti-clericalism and the English Reformation

A. G. Dickens

Anti-clericalism has become an unduly capacious word. It can contain intellectual manifestos based upon theology, philosophy and history: the erastian treatises of Marsiglio, of Wycliffe, of numerous sixteenth-century champions of the state. At the other extreme it can be used to describe a squalid feud between a vicar and his parishioners: for example, the story so attractively disentangled and presented by Geoffrey Elton in his essay 'Tithe and Trouble, an Anticlerical Story'.[1] Again anti-clericals did not need to be laymen, for many of the fiercest attackers were themselves priests. During the period with which we shall be mainly concerned – the later fourteenth to the mid-sixteenth century – an unprivileged clerical proletariat harboured some justifiable grudges against its prelates and its monastic rivals. Yet the churchmen had also to face more 'respectable' critics. Many bishops and senior clergy proclaimed the need to impose discipline upon the numerous misfits in the profession: some did not hesitate to castigate the whole system of recruitment and training.

These assorted sources and types of criticism have usually been regarded as contributing in varying degrees to the Protestant Reformation; but in a challenging article of 1983[2] Christopher Haigh began by pronouncing anti-clericalism a 'fiction' invented by modern historians, whom he reproved for accepting this 'explanatory tool' in order to fuse together some 'disparate phenomena'. His arguments, advanced with considerable forensic skill, should sober all of us who have so glibly cited anti-clericalism as a factor in this situation, and should compel us to re-examine the complicated phenomena and their impact upon the early stages of the Reformation in England. Yet having done so to the best of his ability, the present writer still finds himself unable to follow Dr Haigh very far along his venturesome path. After all, disparate factors do often fuse together to attain a common historical result, and in analysing episodes as many-sided as the English Reformation we are by no means compelled to shrink from theories of multiple yet interrelated causation. Moreover, in order to grasp the Tudor heritage of anti-clericalism we cannot afford to start with Richard Hunne in 1512. Rather must we return to the fourteenth century and link its concepts with those of the sixteenth, in this instance a task in considerable part already accomplished by Professor Helen C. White forty years ago.[3]

Doubtless we should beware of according excessive weight to public and private anti-clericalism within a Reformation which contained other ponderous factors. At its heart the Reformation was an international struggle between ecclesiastical traditions and biblical sources. Yet the manifest inadequacies of monothematic explanations compel us to question the apparent tendency of able and reputable scholars such as Professor Scarisbrick and Dr Haigh[4] to belittle the whole theme of Protestant conversion and to revive the old concept of the early English Reformation as consisting of opportunist acts of state, devoid of long-term social or mental causes and almost unaccompanied by religious phenomena. At all events I cannot help supposing that such a theory must be based upon an unduly selective use of the evidence and a disposition to undervalue the rational appeal of a Christianity based upon the authentic sources of the New Testament. Consequentially it would involve a failure to assess the vigour Protestantism had attained by 1553 in such areas as Kent, Essex, London, the Thames Valley, East Anglia, East Sussex and Gloucestershire.

It seems far from difficult to demonstrate that English anti-clericalism, however defined, underwent a long and massive expansion from the later fourteenth century. Whatever the case, pre-Tudor criticism of the clergy was emphatically not initiated by early Protestants or parliamentary lawyers: such attitudes had become widespread in Catholic English society at least a century before the troubles surrounding the case of Richard Hunne. The position of a priesthood corporately rich, buttressed by ecclesiastical law, socially and psychologically powerful through the confessional, had attracted hostile reactions since the days of Walter Map. Yet two centuries later these reactions multiplied, when the papacy itself was traversing a period of discredit and when the effects of the Black Death contributed to the estrangement of the peasant classes from ecclesiastical and lay landlords alike. Readers of G. R. Owst's works will need no reminder that English fourteenth- and early fifteenth-century preachers were no mere formal moralists. They constantly upbraided the arrogance and vices of the clergy in passionate, bitter and concrete terms. Some anticipated or followed Langland in preaching a quasi-socialist gospel, aspiring to lift the institutional church and the rest of the feudal system off the backs of the poor. There was no chasm between homily and anti-clerical satire.[5] At this stage there arrived three of our greatest writers to observe and to exacerbate the situation. Langland, Wycliffe and Chaucer not only raised the criticism of churchmen to new and striking forms: they eventually transmitted their attitudes to the early Tudor age, when printing swiftly magnified the impact of all three.

Langland in particular came from the heart of the aspirant nation. In his *Vision of Piers Plowman* he approached social and ecclesiastical issues from the angle of the common people, maintaining a fanciful yet earnest radicalism which spared the spiritual functions and the underlying holiness of the church. Around the sturdy figure of Piers Plowman, whose labours kept the community alive, the author propounded a body of home truths which was to become equally applicable to mid-Tudor England. He anticipated the Protestants of the future by steadily basing authentic Christian standards on the recorded sayings of Christ.[6] He displayed scant respect for the covetous and soft-living clergy of his own time, seeing them as even guiltier than laymen for the corruption of a society wherein everything was done for money. The bishops he denounced as less charitable than the Jews. Like Chaucer he found too many secular priests eager to leave their flocks and seek lucrative chantries in London. The friars, having corrupted the other religious orders, had abandoned their original mission among the poor in order to build expensive churches and hobnob with rich ladies. Pardons, privileges, even scholastic learning seemed to Langland ineffective aids towards salvation. The honest ploughman, who fed all these drones, stood nearer to Christ than did any smart schoolman or friar. Amid the tensions between school and state, Langland found himself aligned with king and commons against papacy and priesthood.[7] With striking prescience he announced that a king would arise to purge the clerics, whom the nobles would thrash until they blew away like chaff.[8] Hence instead there arose a tenacious popular tradition, coupling the social gospel with hostile criticism of the hierarchy.

This tradition achieved a delayed but maximum force through the printing houses. Indeed within the area of literature embracing Langland, Wycliffe and Chaucer the fourteenth century invaded the sixteenth in great force, most especially during the relaxation of controls in the reign of Edward VI, when it inspired and harmonised with the socio-religious gospelling then prevalent. This large group of neo- and pseudo-Plowman writings displays some highly varied relationships with the original work by Langland. Explained in detail by Helen White in 1944,[9] the sequence has since been further investigated by John N. King, and from the angle of Wycliffism by Anne Hudson.[10] Since this process is crucial to my present argument, I must supply some specific examples. Among the earliest Tudor contributions is the poem *God spede the Plough*,[11] which already gave an economic twist to the presentation. In 1531 *The praier and complaynte of the ploweman unto Christe* (*Short Title Catalogue* [*STC*], 20036, allegedly printed in Antwerp) made an assault upon the friars along what seemed to be Lollard lines. About 1550 *A godly dyalogue between Pyers Plowman, and a popish preest* (*STC*, 19903) attacked transubstantiation. *I playne Piers which cannot flatter* (*STC*, 19903a), and *Pyors Plowman's exhortation, unto the lordes, knightes and burgoysses* [sic] *of the parlyamenthouse* (*STC*, 19905) both probably date from the same year 1550, the latter modernising the medieval Ploughman as a radical spokesman against enclosures and the misuse of monastic lands. As for the *Plowman's Tale*, an eloquent assault on the whole church system, it appears to be a medieval poem rewritten in would-be Middle English spelling by a sixteenth-century Protestant. In 1542 it gained illicit entry into the Chaucer canon by its inclusion in the second comprehensive edition of Chaucer's works (*STC*, 5069). This item puzzled the worthy John Leland, who not only confused it with the original *Vision of Piers Plowman*, but imagined Chaucer to have been a disciple of Wycliffe, since he so 'vigorously inveighed against the bad morals of the priests'.[12] Another hybrid, the poem *Pierce the Ploughman's Crede*, probably written near the end of the fourteenth century, printed in 1553 and 1561 (*STC*, 19904, 08), stated the case in Wycliffite terms and with special animus against the friars.[13] Rival heroes such as *Jack up Lande*, who in 1540 was also made to attack the friars (*STC*, 5098), merely aspired to reincarnate Langland's staunch and devout character. The climax arrived in the year 1550 with the publication by Robert Crowley[14] of the original *Vision of Piers Plowman*, substantially Langland's text, yet with some meaningful modifications. It went through four quarto editions within one year (*STC*, 19906–7–7a–8) and was to be reprinted as late as 1561 by Owen Rogers. By modern standards Crowley must in this instance be judged a tendentious editor. Altering archaic diction, misreading certain words, he also modified points of substance wherever he found Langland's religious doctrine wholly unacceptable to Protestant readers.[15] His marginal glosses are numerous and intrusive, being intended to display the *Vision* as an apocalyptic prophecy of the English Reformation, and to identify the mission of Piers Plowman with the crowd of reformist tracts appearing in the Edwardian years. For good measure and in that same *annus mirabilis* 1550, Crowley also published, as by Wycliffe, *The true copye of a prolog wrytten in an olde English Bible* (*STC*, 25588). Wycliffite texts were also going into print under Protestant guidance, such as the long-notorious *Wycklyffe's Wycket*, which appeared under other auspices in 1546 and in two further editions in 1548 (*STC*, 25590-91-91a).

With even more significance Wycliffe had founded that wide scatter of Lollard groups which survived many persecutions well into the mid-sixteenth century. Increasingly proletarian in membership, it permeated and coloured the incoming stream of Continental Protestantism. These Lollards proved the most obdurately anti-clerical of all sectarians, and modern research continues to enlarge their contribution at the grass roots of the English Reformation.[16]

Though the sociable, non-apocalyptic Chaucer cannot compare with his two outstanding contemporaries as a serious scourge of the priesthood, his ever-expanding readership, following the various editions of the *Canterbury Tales* in 1478, 1484, 1492, 1498 and 1526,[17] communicated a memorable irreverence in an idiom more modish and comic, more intelligible to Tudor readers than those of Langland and Wycliffe. Such readers can hardly have failed to observe that of the five clerics and clerical officials in the *Prologue to the Canterbury Tales*, four were rogues and hypocrites, while the fifth, the virtuous country parson, is deliberately framed within the unworthiness of his mercenary colleagues. For good measure he is also given a brother, none other than the Ploughman, endued with the same practical goodwill and directly drawn from the Langland tradition.

This censorious and satirical outlook persisted alongside a heartfelt if theologically vulnerable fund of piety. Likewise the employment of chaplains as servants and agents – as with James Gloys of the Pastons – is criticised (as will appear) by Sir Thomas More, yet should be put alongside a widespread respect for the priestly office still inculcated by the doctrines of transubstantiation and the sacrificial mass.

Yet at any moment that respect could become bitterly critical, directing its force not only against mercenary priests and minor officials of the church, but also against lordly prelates and well-fed monks, sometimes even against the socially influential friars. So far from dying out, these anti-clerical forces, hitherto substantially Catholic, remained very much alive in the earlier years of Henry VIII, and highly capable of active alliance with the invasion of Lutheran theology.

While fifteenth-century squires used their chaplains as secular servants, the common people were far from displaying a uniform respect for clerical status. Cases of assaults on clergymen occur in the *Paston Letters* and elsewhere,[18] while Thomas Gascoigne in his near-contemporary *Liber Veritatum* presents the tumults of the disastrous year 1450 as a popular assault upon several unpopular bishops, two of whom had in fact been killed by mobs.[19] According to this upright figure of the clerical establishment – Gascoigne was chancellor of the University of Oxford[20] – the people hated the hierarchy not just as politicians and courtiers, but on account of their manifest professional shortcomings:

> Nearly everyone was heard crying out 'woe unto the bishops', who grow rich, who wish to be called lords, to be served on bended knee, who ride about with so many and such fine horses, and will do nothing by way of preaching to save men's souls, for the bishops either do not know how to preach or cannot, being burdened by worldly business or bodily pleasures, or else cannot indeed preach any but those ill practices of which the bishops themselves are guilty ... This was common talk about the bishops among clergy and laity, and day after day there was more stir among the people and they slew the Bishop of Chichester, Adam Moleyns, and the Bishop of Salisbury, William Ayscough, and persecuted the Bishop of Chester [i.e. Lichfield], one Booth, and the Bishop of Norwich, Walter Lyhart, and many rectors and vicars in Kent, and despoiled them at Salisbury and Hungerford.[21]

Against the clergy in general Gascoigne presents the case in his *Sermon on the Seven Streams of Babylon.*[22] His seven streams of evil signify the following: unworthily ordained clerics, absent parish priests, pluralists, the appropriation of churches and tithes to men who did not have the immediate cure of the parishioners, the abuses of absolution, indulgences, dispensations and licences. He does not hesitate to tell lurid stories about papal provisions, gross absenteeism and parish priests who kept concubines. He even relates how a bishop of St David's refused to allow conscience-stricken priests to discard their illicit partners, explaining frankly that he himself would then lose four hundred marks annually, which they had hitherto paid him for their quasi-marital privileges.[23]

Here we must recall that in citing such authorities our present purpose is far less concerned with the accuracy or typicality of such information than with the critical attitudes of the day, deserved or undeserved. With equal vividness one could cite the heavily Pauline and censorious views of John Colet, Dean of St Paul's, together with the scriptural humanism of his friend Dr William Melton, chancellor of York. The latter, formerly the Cambridge tutor of John Fisher, possessed copies of Valla, Pico, Erasmus and More: he wrote humanist Latin and entertained constructive views on clerical rehabilitation.[24] In his *Sermo Exhortatorius*, published about 1510, Melton demands that the church should deliver itself from the host of *rudium et stolidorum clericorum* by insisting upon a linguistic and scriptural education devised to enable the lower clergy to study and expound the Bible. When ordinands lack a fluent reading knowledge of Latin, they also lack the basis of self-education. Without this orientation rural clergy in particular tend to merge into their secular backgrounds by hunting, dicing, wenching, tavern-haunting and making money by unclerical occupations. More pointed still was Colet's notoriously frank convocation sermon, delivered on 6 February 1512. The members of this assembly, called especially to deal with heretics, were doubtless shocked to hear that they themselves were largely to blame for heresy. Parish priests, thundered Colet, 'seke none other thynge in the people than foule lucre, wherof cometh occasion of evyl heresies and yll christendome in the people'. Nor was the preacher content to leave his audience of distinguished clerics with the illusion that the faults lay only with ignorant country parsons. He referred also to the 'gredynes and appetite of honour and dignitie', the 'heaping of benefices upon benefices', which marked the careerist senior clergy. Learning itself, and especially scholastic learning, would not solve the problems: a pure life and an education in the scriptures would alone enable the priesthood to reform itself, and consequently the people. A century ago Colet's admirable biographer, J. H. Lupton, remarked how closely his thought and expression foreshadow those of Latimer's *Sermon of the Plough*.[25]

The contribution of medieval erastian policies and theories to the revolutionary changes of the sixteenth century admits of widely ranging interpretations. It was of a different order from the heritage of popular anti-clericalism and proceeded with a different tempo. The ecclesiastical relations of the Lancastrian and Yorkist rulers, together with those of Henry VII, have been somewhat idealised by Baumer and other modern historians working within this field. The Statutes of Provisors (1351–89) and Praemunire (1353–93) had a real purpose, even though their strength was never fully exerted until 1531, when Henry VIII used these reserves of power to intimidate and fine the convocations of the English clergy. Meanwhile the fifteenth-century kings had experienced occasional problems with popes and bishops and had usually solved them without delay, owing to these and other modes of pressure. English jurists and officials never forgot that English benefices and ecclesiastical corporations owed their endowments to royal and noble benefactors, while the kings never forgot their claim to be lords of all the land in England. Even if a diocesan bishop did not serve as a royal minister, he always belonged to the pyramid of secular government, sharing as a magnate in its administrative functions and its feudal obligations.

Even under the 'orthodox' Henry IV there was no lack – and little repression – of lay acrimony against the opulent church. In 1404 and again in 1410, the parliamentary knights in brutal terms urged the king to seize the temporalities of the English Church, which according to their assurances would enable him to maintain a strong army and still retain a vast sum for general purposes. Contemporaneously (1402) one of the few English clergy of that day to spend a prolonged period in Rome, the chronicler Adam of Usk, denounced the corruption and venality of the Curia in terms hardly excelled by any sixteenth-century Protestant.[26] At the other end of the century the oft-vaunted 'cordial' relations between Henry VII and the church had some distinct limitations. In this sphere Henry seemed to have all the powers a medieval king could require, yet he aspired to gain even more. No pope ventured to dispute his nominations to benefices, the most lucrative of which he packed at will with his civil servants. His courts continued to maintain jurisdiction over the real estate of the English Church, including advowsons. However firmly the first Tudor monarch maintained doctrinal discipline throughout the realm, the English bishops can hardly have regarded his reign as a honeymoon between church and state. His policy involved heavy financial exactions, notably the recognisances taken of the bishops in his later years, which left them owing enormous debts to the Crown.

Seen in terms of erastian political philosophy, the late medieval situation displays a similar patchwork of conservative quiescence and potential menace. Fourteenth-century Europe gave birth to a spectacular series of revolutionary erastian theorists: John of Paris, Dubois, Occam, Marsiglio of Padua and Wycliffe. Especially were the last two destined to major revivals in sixteenth-century England, and in a manner not altogether dissimilar to the mid-Tudor recrudescence of Langland and the social gospellers. True, in most of the English thinkers of the fifteenth century, the imagined prohibitions inspired by natural law curbed any tendency to seek solutions in an absolutist monarchy. Yet again, Baumer's otherwise perceptive survey may overstate the restraints upon royal intervention, for example when he takes seriously Bishop Pecock's assumption that the king had no authority over the *sacerdotium* and its servants, being master only of the temporal sphere.[27] In terms of actual policies this Gelasian fairyland had not existed, even in early medieval England. The fifteenth century is distinguished by the apotheosis of the common law and the rise of a powerful *esprit de corps* among its practitioners, rather than by any material pressures put upon the church. Though Sir John Fortescue, Chief Justice of the King's Bench,[28] became so influential among the legal profession, his *De Laudibus Legum Angliae* (1468–71; printed 1546) did not disturb his innate reverence for the church. His *Governance of England* (1471–76), unprinted until 1714 but available in numerous manuscripts, did seek to deliver the monarchy from oppression by over-mighty subjects and saw as indispensable the endowment of the Crown with a large, non-parliamentary revenue. With the example of Thomas Cromwell before us, we might well ask how this could ever have been done save by a huge contribution from the landed wealth of the English Church. Yet there is no evidence that Fortescue so much as considered this seemingly obvious solution. Even the next generation of common lawyers, as represented by anti-clericals like Edmund Dudley and Christopher St German, moved rather slowly toward the legal control of the church and even more slowly toward a confiscation of its wealth.

In this realm of erastian political theory the foreign texts which certainly influenced educated opinion in England were two in number: the *Defensor Pacis* of Marsiglio and the *Disputacio inter clericum et militem* often attributed to Occam but more likely written by Pierre Dubois in support of King Philip the Fair. The effects of the former are well known. This radical masterpiece, intended to demonstrate that the secular state could supply all the demands of human life, and to recommend that the clergy should be confined to the purely spiritual sphere, was to be translated in 1533–34 by William Marshall,[29] financed by his patron Thomas Cromwell. Its arguments were to be almost slavishly followed by the episcopal backers of the Henrician Revolution, Edward Fox and Stephen Gardiner.[30] The *Disputacio*, a far shorter and more superficial work, sees the clerical disputant dealt a poor hand by the author and doomed to a heavy drubbing at the hands of his lay opponent. The Latin text, printed at Cologne in 1473, went into many editions. Soon afterwards it became available in English, though at first in the antiquated translation by John de Trevisa († 1412), who had originally used it as a preface to Higden's *Polychronicon*. It sold well and was still in 1540 being read and republished, perhaps also following Cromwell's wishes.[31]

Meanwhile under both literary and pragmatic influences English lawyers and officials saw the spirituality and the temporality as basically divided interests. Siding wholly with the latter, they developed a partisanship which would have shocked Fortescue. Among the earliest of such works is *The Tree of Commonwealth*, written in 1509–10 by that unduly maligned minister of Henry VII Edmund Dudley, used in manuscript by various later scholars and perhaps by politicians, which remained unprinted until 1859.[32] Here, well before the emergence of Luther's godly princes, Dudley argued that church reform at the hands of the Crown had become a task of great urgency. For this unintellectual pragmatist the king was by right not merely the protector but the active overseer of the church, whose responsibility for appointing the bishops extended also to training their consciences and causing them to correct wrongdoers. Moreover, the king should foster concord within the realm by acting as judge in disputes between clergy and laity. 'And no man', concludes Dudley, 'can do it but the Prince.'

Though born about two years earlier than Dudley, Christopher St German (1460–1540) survived that unfortunate minister by thirty years.[33] The son of a Warwickshire knight, educated at Oxford and the Inner Temple, he practised successfully in the London courts for several decades before achieving, at an advanced age, national prominence as an author. This occurred around 1530–32, when his Latin textbook for law students (1523, 1528) went into English, and under the title *Doctor and Student* ruled the market until the advent of Blackstone's *Commentaries*. St German was not a theologian but a jurist. Knowing how eager the churchmen were to silence him by a prosecution for heresy, he astutely avoided any sign of Protestantism,

while waging a sharp controversy with Sir Thomas More and supporting step by step the Henrician changes of the 1530s. More than
any writer of that day, he formidably personified the common law of
England, which he almost equated with the law of reason itself. A
disciple of both Sir John Fortescue and Marsiglio of Padua, he
exalted the King-in-Parliament as the organ of an almost omnipotent
nation state, legally entitled to tax at will and to redistribute the
temporal goods of its subjects, whether laymen or ecclesiastics.
Frequently accusing the English Church of transgressing its statutory
and customary limits, he published in 1532 *A treatyse concernyng the
division betwene the spirytualtie and temporaltie* (*STC*, 21586), a clear
recognition of the reality of anti-clericalism and one eventually to be
repeated in Parliament both by Cromwell and by the king himself.
Thus during the four decades which separated the statutes restricting
sanctuary (1497) and claims to clerical privilege (1489, 1497) from the
infinitely more decisive changes by the Reformation Parliament, both
anti-clerical sentiment and erastian theory developed apace and
contributed not a little to the acceptance of those changes by the
majority of the English people. As an episode illustrating this process,
I should plead for more emphatic recognition than that accorded by
Christopher Haigh to the crisis of 1515, especially to that angry
dispute before the king between the claims of church and state in
regard to benefit of clergy. It involved not merely bishops *versus*
judges, but also two bold royalist chaplains on their way to bishoprics: Drs Standish and Veysey: not to mention Wolsey, who naturally
sought to fudge the issue, being employed by both sides. While this
scene scarcely formed a prelude to the Henrician Reformation, it
should not be regarded as a mere sequel to the Hunne case. It
constituted a public line-up and a roll-call, having some instructive
functions, not least for the young king himself.[34] As for the confisca-
tory Reformation, this could only begin when the king wanted it to
begin.

By this stage of our discussion we have provided much evidence
concerning the development of these forces, though not yet moving
from the thinkers who remained basically Catholic across to the
Protestant propagandists, whose contribution to, and relationship
with, national opinion Christopher Haigh also appears to minimise.
Even now we are far from having exhausted the theme of early Tudor
anti-clericalism which continued to arise from non-Protestant critics.
Yet another of these was Alexander Barclay, who in 1503 adapted to
English conditions Sebastian Brant's satire *The Ship of Fools*.[35] Here,

while he also subjects evil secular officials to attack, he is even more severe against greedy ecclesiastics, whether haughty bishops, artful friars or unworthy parish priests. With still more passion, Barclay's rival John Skelton wrote his satire *Colyn Clout* about 1519, producing in this figure an updated relative of Piers Plowman.[36] Skelton accepts that English society has gone sadly astray and that the clergy, especially the prelates, are to blame. At the supposed dawn of a new age he continues to pursue old enemies: ignorant priests, apostate monks, hypocritical friars and above all absentee bishops, striving for worldly honours. These last live in magnificent palaces while the poor starve: they ordain disorderly drunkards to the priesthood, and though themselves upstarts, aspire to rule the kingdom. Yet Skelton's choice of targets remains wide and it is quite incorrect to regard him as a mere enemy of Wolsey,[37] though he attacked the cardinal by implication in 1519, and more openly in his later works, such as *Why come yet nat to court?* At bottom Skelton is less a rebel than a champion of order and authority, no proto-Protestant, but a strong devotee of the Virgin Mary, a doctrinal conservative who detested Lutherans and their young Cambridge imitators of the 1520s.[38]

The weighty heritage of late medieval anti-clericalism was broadened by humanism, then refocused on Pauline religion by the Lutherans. To the humanist influences we have already seen in Melton, Colet and Skelton we need to add the ruthless but amusing ridicule directed by Erasmus upon warlike popes, stupid monks and superstitious pilgrims. Though translations into English of the relevant satirical works were negligible until 1549 – a factor which delayed his direct impact – educated men and trendsetters had long enjoyed this aspect of Erasmus, the most devastating anti-clerical of them all. Meanwhile the rising intellectual and moral standards demanded by the Christian humanists continued to inspire Thomas More, even after he had become the chief defender of the clergy against Tyndale and St German. More was a hard controversialist, and would scarcely have made concessions to those opponents had not the accepted verdicts obliged him so to do in order to maintain his credibility with the English public. What did this great Catholic think about the parish clergy of his day? He complained, and with justice, that people made far more fuss over a scandalous cleric than over a scandalous layman. But he had no doubt whatever that anti-clericalism existed as 'allmoste an universal dyvysyon and grudge of the whole corps of the temporaltye, agaynste the whole body of the spyrytualtye', which he blamed squarely upon the 'apostate' clergy and not on the persecution of heretics.[39]

Without question he believed and proclaimed that there existed many bad and ignorant clergyman, and he attributed their presence to the inadequate selection procedures maintained by the bishops, and to demeaning patronage by lay people:

> I wote well there bee therein many very lewde and naught [wicked]. And surely where so ever there is a multitude it is not without miracle wel possible to bee other wyse. But nowe yf the bishops would once take unto priesthed better ley men & fewer (for of us be they made) all the matter were more than half amended ... But for the noumber, I would surely see such a way therin, that we should not have such a rabell, that every meane man must have a priest in his house to wait upon his wife, whiche no man almost lacketh now, to the contempe of priesthood in as vile office as his horse keper.[40]

This passage is no mere opinion of More's Erasmian early manhood: it comes in *The Dialogue concerning Tyndale*, published in 1528–29. True, modern research has tended to qualify the harshest verdicts – at all events those of the gutter-press represented by Simon Fish and John Bale – which grossly exaggerated the sexual prowess and deviance of the supposedly celibate caste. Cheered by the humane moderation of such scholars as Margaret Bowker[41] and Peter Heath,[42] Christopher Haigh seeks to knock all the props from under allegations of anti-clericalism by arguing that the actual shortcomings of the clergy were so slight as to leave little reason for such critical sentiments on the part of Tudor popular opinion.[43] Here in my view he surpasses by an appreciable margin not merely the original sources but the verdicts of these same modern scholars upon whom we chiefly depend. Dr Bowker, Mr Heath, Dr Houlbrooke and a number of others not only admit the existence of anti-clerical opinion but provide not a little documented information on the misdeeds, sexual and otherwise, of some fifteenth- and sixteenth-century English clergymen.[44] Agreed, in all our opinions the old black and dark-grey colours have paled a good deal, yet Dr Haigh's independent alternation of pure-white and off-white tones would seem to spring from an over-ardent revisionism.

Be that as it may, the minority of errant and really ignorant clergy, together with some inevitable maladjustments between them and the laity, should not encourage us to oppose Professor Scarisbrick's recent but by no means altogether novel picture of the genuine piety in pre-Reformation parish life: the people to whom the ministry of the late medieval church still brought hope and consolation amid the pains and bereavements which beset Tudor society. Alongside the tensions and the misfits there remained ample room in England for those attractive holy clubs of the day, the parish guilds, with their true love of the saints, their desire to erect and adorn buildings worthy of the company of heaven, their touching solicitude for deceased relatives in purgatory, their trust in redemption through a judicious amalgam of works and faith.[45]

So far we have scarcely mentioned the phase of a specifically Protestant anti-clericalism demanded by Luther's assertion of the priesthood of all believers and his rejection of the ordained priesthood as a separate order of men. Certainly among the mid-Tudor writers the anti-clericals and erastians enjoy a preponderance far greater than Dr Haigh's dismissive treatment[46] of a tiny sample would suggest. Can we reasonably dismiss the full list as quite unrepresentative of public opinion throughout much of England? When originally drafting this present essay I put down the more obvious critics I could recall off-hand. This partial list does at least constitute a most varied company: William Tyndale, Edward Hall, William Turner, John Frith, Sir Francis Bigod,[47] Wilfrid Holme,[48] Sir Richard Morison, John Bale, Henry Brinklow,[49] Jerome Barlow, Robert Crowley, John Knox, Peter Moone,[50] John Ramsey,[51] Thomas Lever, John Foxe and, of course, the anonymous authors of numerous surviving printed works listed in the *Short Title Catalogue*. At this point I had the good fortune to encounter the recent substantial book by John N. King, *English Reformation Literature. The Tudor Origins of the Protestant Tradition*,[52] which adds to my list many pamphleteers, satirists and playwrights hitherto mere names to myself, such as William Baldwin, Luke Shepherd, William Samuel, Francis Seager, Walter Lynne, William Punt, Randall Hurlestone, William Kethe, most or all of whom qualify for our list of those who before 1558 attacked the old priesthood and the Catholic concept of ecclesiastical authority. These men were not remote intellectuals but writers aiming at the common people. This must apply especially to those who worked to serve the little companies of players, which – even when hunted by the Marian government – preached the 'new' doctrines in tavern yards and out-buildings.[53] Dr Haigh was wholly justified when he asked how far Tudor writers should be taken to represent popular opinion, yet it would surely be an extreme answer to imagine so large a number –

indeed the majority of serious English writers in this field – as inhabiting a separate cultural world, neither influencing, nor being influenced by, lay opinions, even those of tradesmen, craftsmen or husbandmen. We have more than enough evidence to indicate that contemporary religious problems were often discussed in the public house. More significantly still, by far the largest group of those who acquired convictions strong enough to make them martyrs were craftsmen, members of a more or less literate element within the working class.

Towards the end of his article Christopher Haigh reveals that he does not literally take anti-clericalism to be a modern fiction; indeed he shows that it was manifested and manipulated by lawyers, merchants and parliamentarians to secure the passage of anti-clerical legislation through the Reformation Parliament.[54] Though there is evidence for waves of unpopularity against ecclesiastical jurisdiction in 1529 and 1532, Dr Haigh rightly urges that it must have been appreciably stimulated and contrived by such interest groups. So long as they kept to the City of London, where the evidence for a widespread hatred of church courts, tithes and other ecclesiastical exactions is so massive,[55] such anti-clericals would meet little opposition. An impressive campaign could easily be staged and made to seem like a national uproar. Yet I presume that this manipulation is hardly a discovery: I do not recall any historian writing about the Tudor period who has been so foolish as to claim that the English Reformation had no urban pressure-groups, but was conducted – or for that matter should have been conducted – on the basis of opinion among the peasantry! Cromwell's part in the Commons' Petition of 1532 has been common knowledge for over a century,[56] while nobody appears ever to have alleged that this viewpoint was shared by the whole, or even by the majority of Englishmen in the mid-1530s. Those among us who have worked for many decades on the Pilgrimage of Grace and other popular rebellions of the period are the least likely to overlook the conservative areas and aspects of Henrician society, while Geoffrey Elton's more recent *Policy and Police*[57] should have prevented later observers from underestimating the geographically widespread dissent from the Henrician changes. All the same, do we not find here yet another situation which should forbid us to make simple and sweeping generalisations about Tudor public opinion? Not for a moment does the conservative dissent of the 1530s destroy the virtual certainty that within twenty years Protestantism had become a strong and seemingly ineradicable force in the south-east, and had already gained a foothold in many other areas of England. Instances of anti-clericalism had occurred even amid the Pilgrimage of Grace.

The most constructive and stimulating aspect of Christopher Haigh's article lies in his keen aspiration to penetrate to the grass roots of Tudor parish history and to understand through direct evidence the norms of church life amid husbandmen, tradesmen and craftsmen. Yet this aim still remains very ambitious, thanks not only to marked regional and even local differences, but also to the notorious gaps and irregularities among our main sources, the diocesan archives. In addition, a high proportion of these surviving archives has not yet been explored with such aims in view. At first sight the known evidence looks profuse enough: indeed it seems all too prone to foster the illusion that we already know almost everything about tensions between clerics and laymen, or about the social history of early Protestantism and other related fields. When this illusion begins to build on negative evidence, however, it should be resisted. To cite an ultimate *reductio ad absurdum*, I recall a beginner taking up Dr Fines' *Dictionary of Early English Protestants*[58] and confidently 'deducing' that there were not so many more than 3000 Protestants in England during the period 1525–58, such being the approximate number of actual names which this laborious inspection of the extant sources had yielded. In fact at least five major factors must forbid such a fallacy: that no surveys of religious opinion were ever compiled before 1558; that during most of these years an agonising death threatened people who evinced Protestant beliefs; that a great deal of the original documentation has been lost;[59] that incontrovertible evidence shows a large element of the population as consisting of so-called 'neuters', who could not meaningfully be labelled either Catholics or Protestants. Finally, the imprecise yet massive and trend-revealing evidence nowadays being drawn from the religious phraseology of wills shows that in some areas, towards the end of Edward VI's reign, the number of wills indicating Protestant sympathies was already tending to rival or even surpass the number of those representing the attitudes of conventional Catholic testators.[60]

The foregoing fallacy is indeed only a somewhat absurd example of a type of risk we all run: that of forcing negative evidence to sustain quasi-statistics far beyond its real power. In other cases the dangers are more concealed, yet for that reason more insidious. For example, in questioning the evidence for anti-clericalism, Dr Haigh produces figures from a few dioceses which purport to show that incumbents rarely sued parishioners for unpaid tithes.[61] These figures, however, are dependent on the bold assumption that in each diocese the extant archives preserve all, or nearly all, the cases which actually occurred. Moreover, other dioceses unmentioned in this passage – for example York, Norwich and Peterborough – do show far more numerous records of tithe-causes.[62] Whereas we still need more provincial research on such causes, recent research on Tudor London continues to stress their importance as a prime factor in the divisions between laity and clergy. 'Quarrels over tithes', writes Dr Susan Brigden, 'provide the background against which all the hostility between Londoners and their parish priests must be seen.' She proves the point in great detail and has since been supported by Dr Wunderli.[63] That the situation was totally different elsewhere has still got to be proved. Similar considerations apply to the discussion concerning popular attitudes toward the church courts. I decidedly agree with Christopher Haigh in doubting whether public hostility toward these courts corresponded with the propaganda set forth by the secular politicians in 1532, yet before we enunciate broad conclusions we still need to search for more evidence and perhaps in the end to make subtler distinctions.

In the case of the dioceses of Norwich and Winchester the scholarly research of Dr Houlbrooke revealed signs that some litigants may have had recourse to the church courts in preference to the secular courts, because of their lower costs and shorter delays.[64] Yet Dr Haigh may well be treading uncertain ground when he deduces from this case a general access of prestige for ecclesiastical jurisdiction. Elsewhere Dr Houlbrooke does not fail to stress those darker features of ecclesiastical jurisdiction which attracted unpopularity, while amid the rich documentation of the London courts and of the consistory court of Canterbury, scholars have recently pointed towards a reverse of decline in church court litigation after 1500.[65] Moreover if some litigants approved the church's handling of suits between party and party, a more ambivalent situation obtained in the archdeacons' courts, which meted out punishments for the sexual offences of poor people. As Dr Haigh himself suggests,[66] the supporters of this institution, 'the bawdy court', were probably the richer people, anxious to discipline their inferiors and doubtless to avoid contributing to the upkeep of illegitimate children. On balance, this side of the church's jurisdiction can scarcely have added to the 'grudging respect', claimed by him as generally accorded until the Reformation, after which he unkindly suggests that 'contempt' set in. On all these problems the future will doubtless bring forth further inquiries regarding lay attitudes to ecclesiastical jurisdiction. Such inquiries might do worse than begin with Chaucer's rascally Summoner!

Can we progress into Henrician parish society and generalise effectively on the theme of discord and harmony between incumbent and parishioners? Were many of the parishes really hotbeds of rancour, or may we join Dr Haigh in envisaging rather simple and bucolic villagers, satisfied with their parson, unable to estimate his intellectual competence, turning a blind eye to a few moral foibles, and still reverencing priests on account of their role in the super-natural transaction of the mass? Pending a vastly more complete examination of the difficult evidence than any yet attempted, I continue to suppose that the norms most probably lie somewhere between these two contrasting models. As a very humble contribution to the future task, I propose to draw attention to a sample-packet of information I recently collected from a manuscript act book in the Northamptonshire Record Office.[67] It refers to the record of a visitation, spasmodically conducted by the vicar-general of the diocese of Peterborough, most of it between the summer of 1546 and that of 1548, but dragging on in an attenuated form almost to the end of the reign of Edward VI. Many offences and shortcomings emerged: they are seldom dated, but should be recent. The area itself, comprising Northamptonshire and Rutland, already contained some Protestant groups as at Northampton, Oakham, Oundle, Lowick, Geddington and other places, yet this changing doctrinal scene makes less impact than the old problems of social discipline and the maintenance of church fabrics. The data relevant to our present inquiry must here be summarised briefly. The vicar of St Giles, Northampton, a former monk and a strong religious conservative, was charged with assaulting his sexton and polluting the church with the latter's blood. At Wardley a layman called Alyn Batt had 'violently, shamfully and cowardly stryken his curate, the parson of the same towne, one the heid with an hatchett, without any occasion showyd or given by the said parson unto the said Alyn Batt'. Two men blasphemed in the church at Rothwell and used the curate 'uncharitably'. Numerous incumbents were accused by their church wardens with illegally refusing to repair the chancels of their churches, to subscribe to the cost of installing bibles, or with failure to show hospitality or give alms. At Great Billing the parson had an annual income of £21 (well above average) but gave nothing away. The curate at Sulgrave had offended people by wearing modish lay costume. At Kislingbury the priest is said to be 'a common haunter of alehouses, givinge him selfe to drynkyng, ryotinge and playinge at unlawful games'. These accusations he denied but was further accused of being 'a brawler and slanderer, a chider and a scolder'. At Culworth four parishioners testified 'that we have an unquyet vicar, and that he will not folowe the Kinges injunctions by the wrytinge of the boke of regester'.

Earlier in the reign a few Northamptonshire clergy had shown themselves as by no means natural celibates. A middle-aged rector of Great Addington, no unlettered yokel but a bachelor of law, had two children by his cook, a married woman who had duly done a spell in the village stocks. In 1526 this rector had become so unpopular that he discarded priestly attire and intimidated his critics by perambulating the village clad in chain mail. In our visitation of 1546 there are very few cases of this type, the most notable being the complaint of the Pilton wardens that they had on 3 March 1545 at 11 pm taken their parson 'starke naked' in the house of a parishioner, along with the latter's wife. The four witnesses were not alone but *cum multis aliis*, having apparently organised a mass-spectatorship appropriate to this rare event in the ecclesiastical history of Pilton. It is nevertheless noteworthy that the victim remained rector there until his death in 1558!

The rest of the complaints against the clergy also illustrate the atmosphere, but in themselves amount to little. A chantry priest retained and refused to deliver money left by a lady to found an obit. Moreover, this same lowly denizen of the hierarchy did not possess a surplice but sat in the choir without one, 'more lyke a servynge man than a prest, to evell ensample of other'. The Protestant legislation of 1547 naturally proved distasteful to conservative clerics, for example to the master of the almshouse or hospital at Oakham. He was presented in November 1548 because he had never preached since the Royal Visitation, but had haunted taverns and unlawful games. Furthermore, he had enticed people from the parish church to his private Latin services and had distributed holy bread and holy water, 'forsakynge the herynge of Goddes worde and followynge his [? own] traditions'. Yet in general most charges are rather trivial, suggesting poor relationships and lack of co-operation between parsons and wardens, rather than serious offences on either side. Doubtless some untoward events were hushed up, yet it should not be overlooked that in theory about 300 parishes were due to be visited during these years. The untidy record suggests that a large (though now uncertain) number were in fact gradually examined before Edward's death, and so far as the record goes they displayed no conspicuous faults, a likelihood which puts the above evidence in due perspective. All in all, in so far as the area may have typified much of England, it suggests that the relations between laity and parish clergy were better than the rancorous hotbed, though falling distinctly short of the idyll. This mediocre situation accords more or less with the standard recent works on the English parish life of that period, and it broadly harmonises with my own impressions of Henrician Yorkshire and other areas. For example, the act book (Greater London Record Office, DL/C/330) of the vicars-general of the diocese of London covering the years 1520/1 to 1538/9 affords similar impressions of London, Middlesex and Essex. It adds somewhat to the already considerable evidence for the unpopularity of apparitors and other ecclesiastical officials. More strikingly it contains some ninety cases alleging clerical indiscipline, including illiteracy, plus a further thirty-four allegations of sexual misconduct by clerics. This may be compared with sixty-four sexual cases against lay people, alongside fifty-two matrimonial cases, many involving bigamy. Yet considering the length of the period and the clerical standards of that day, these figures should be taken to imply mediocrity, not infamy.

Our attitudes to this complex subject should begin and end with a clear realisation that the sources will never allow us to assess the prevalence of medieval or Tudor anti-clericalism with any sense of finality or exactitude. During these periods, problems of mass psychology are seldom amenable to quantification. As yet neither church nor state made surveys of public opinion: we remain largely dependent on common sense and can seldom expect to achieve more than strong probabilities. Nevertheless, the surviving evidence for an extensive fund of anti-clericalism in English society is impressive both in total bulk and in the variety of its sources, its origins and its forms. It ranged from universalist theories to parochial tensions; its obsession with the shortcomings of bishops and priests yielded place to a vision of the secular ruler as the fount of discipline; and in countries where papal authority was rejected, the ruler became *summus episcopus* with authority even to issue doctrinal codes. Meanwhile the Christian-egalitarian dream of the poor underdogs, anti-clerical as well as anti-feudal, normally remained somewhat obscure save in times of popular rebellion. These visionary aspirations, best characterised in England by the Piers Plowman tradition, were dragged to the literary surface in printed form during the sixteenth century. Even so, they failed again to establish firm influence upon governmental or ecclesiastical policies. As Wycliffe and his successors had understood, the reduction of the clergy to spiritual functions and the restoration of the laity could only be achieved in alliance with the state. Yet in the event the state itself was forced to retain a modified 'magisterial' Church and a modified 'impracticable' ideal of a society based on Christian brotherhood, an ideal still forced to take refuge within the persecuted sects. A similar process, attended by more lurid disasters but eventually ending likewise in the liberation of these sects, occurred through much of central Europe. If we must generalise about England, it should also be against some such broad European background, and extended across a long period, embracing the later Middle Ages at one extremity and the Industrial Revolution at the other. Neither the old context of ecclesiastical history nor the present fashionable context of social anthropology can provide an appropriate analysis, since neither covers enough of this huge spectrum.

Within the international context and advancing in the late fourteenth century, English anti-clericalism developed into a highly articulate and self-conscious movement of opinion and propaganda. Not without a distinctly democratic, egalitarian, anti-hierarchical complexion, it descended in both popular and erastian mainstreams into the Tudor period, when it received a new access of vitality from printing and was eventually taken over by Protestant doctrine. The Protestants did not simply concern themselves with the faults of the clergy. They developed a religious motive based on what they took to be an overdue recovery of authentic, documented Christianity and a consequent rejection of the imaginative but sub-Christian elements hitherto so powerful in popular church life. This doctrinal development became a dominant force in English anti-clericalism, dividing the clergy themselves and strengthening the attack upon that large part of their membership which still sought a conservative reaction.

Taking full advantage of this situation, the Protestant activists appropriated and expanded the old anti-clericalism. Appealing by arguments fair and foul to the lay public, they loudly rebuked and often exaggerated clerical faults in order to show that something beyond human frailty was involved. Guided by Luther, they said explicitly what Catholic anti-clericalism had hesitated to say. They claimed that a defective priesthood had inevitably developed out of a defective theology. The latter had taken the form of a pharisaic code of physical observances, a misplaced confidence in 'good works' as titles to salvation, an exaltation of coenobitic and ritualist ideals which Christ had never enjoined. Thus in their view anti-clericalism had developed a creative function. It no longer demanded a mere disciplining of clergymen: it demanded a reduced concept of priesthood, a revision of devotional attitudes, an institutional restructuring of the medieval church.

That the Protestants, once in power, made errors of their own in regard to the definition and the presentation of the gospel message, few modern scholars would doubt. Yet Christopher Haigh completes his article by making the specific claim that the post-Reformation clergy were so unpopular as to raise a new anti-clericalism far more intense than that of previous periods:

> The minister who stressed Bible-reading to a largely illiterate congregation, who denigrated the cycle of fast and feast linked to the harvest year, who replaced active ritual with tedious sermons to pew-bound parishioners, and who refused to supply protective magic for this world and the next, was naturally less popular than his priestly predecessor. Hence, as Keith Thomas has noted, the rise of the cunning men and wizards, whose prevalence is a demonstration of the shortcomings, from the parishioners' point of view, of the reformed clergy . . . Anticlericalism, in short, was not a cause of the Reformation; it was, however, a result.[68]

This eloquent phraseology does not conceal some distinctly selective tactics. Can we possibly dismiss the abundant evidence that a vast number of Tudor and Stuart people found the English bible fresh and revealing, whether they could read or merely listen to others? Again, in point of fact, the Anglican Prayer Book was (and still is) just as closely anchored as its medieval parent to the cycle of fast, feast and harvest year. Who exactly 'denigrated' the seasons and major feasts? And what of those two stereotyped characters, so oddly reminiscent of G. K. Chesterton's jolly Catholic inn-keeper and his opposite number, the evil-hearted Calvinist grocer? Keith Thomas, it is true, suggests an analogy, even a kinship, between the pre-Reformation priest and the 'cunning man', both having been dispensers of mental comfort to the uneducated.[69] But Keith Thomas then goes on to attribute a high efficacy to the Protestant alternative, a firm belief in divine Providence, in a universe where nothing happened by magic or chance.[70]

From several viewpoints we should suspect any simplistic identification of the old regime with comfort, and the new with mental confusion and clerical tyranny. On the contrary, after a close study of devotional writings, Professor Steven Ozment concluded that around

1500 the 'tyranny' of the confessional and priestly control by penance antagonised the people of the German and Swiss cities, driving them to the easier yoke of Protestantism.[71] Even purgatory, ostensibly a ray of hope, was then commonly depicted in such appalling terms as to alarm and depress, rather than to hearten the struggling believer. There are also some obvious risks in equating white magic – the curing of disease and bad harvests by pagan rituals – with the so-called magic of the mass. The Roman Church never accepted any sort of secular magic as a valid component of Christianity and like the Protestant churches, the Counter-Reformation made vigorous efforts to cleanse society of magic in all its forms,[72] a crusade not understood by the addicted populace.[73] Whatever their interactions (which are obscure) the one was an integral feature of historic Christianity, the other a superstition doomed to decline with the advance of human knowledge.

So much for the image of the old-time popular priest, dispensing official and unofficial 'comfort' in alternate doses. How common in England was that alternative stereotype: the over-educated anglo-puritan, with his boring bible stories and his endless, erudite sermons? Certainly he does not sound much like George Herbert, or Robert Herrick, or Robert Burton, or indeed like most of the scores of Jacobean and Caroline divines we know intimately. Indeed, if we weigh the odds, and allow applicants from among Patrick Collinson's 'godly people', we should find few of these so negatively repellent.

Certainly amid the increasing freedom of that later century we should expect to find some middle-class liberals making their protest, together with a larger number of muted objectors who, according to the moralists and ecclesiastical visitors, spent the times of divine service in the ale-houses. On the other hand we need to allow for attitudes toward sermonising very different from our own. In the fifteenth century and much later, ordinary people did not despise preachers: they despised non-preaching clerics. Most Tudor and Stuart parishioners, the descendants of Piers Plowman, were still vitally interested in their own eternal salvation, as well as in curing their material problems by magic formulae. Lacking newspapers and other modern anodynes against the boredom of weekday life and labour, many of them positively enjoyed sermons. On both sides of this coin, our evidence seems likely to remain inconclusive, because most of it comes from the middle ranks of society and from townsmen.

Yet despite those stereotypes and the doubts they are bound to engender, it may well be that Christopher Haigh's antithesis contains elements of truth: he has in his favour at least one distinct Continental parallel. Not long ago Professor Gerald Strauss analysed numerous visitation reports from different regions of Germany. These established that the Lutheran clergy of the late sixteenth and seventeenth centuries aroused the resentment of their flocks by excessive zeal, in particular by making heavy demands on their meagre leisure-time in order to instruct them in the catechism.[74] Professor Strauss also showed that the new-style, educated Catholic priests of the Counter-Reformation exercised similarly unpopular pressures.[75] I do not doubt that research will reveal some roughly parallel resistances against the more rigorist and devoted English puritans, the teachers who naively thought that a Christian society could be created by sheer system and will-power. At the same time these examples, unless they prove very numerous and widespread, can hardly be accepted as a universal spiritual despotism, in its turn productive of a deeply anti-clerical society. A note at the end of his controversial essay on anti-clericalism suggests that Dr Haigh might for this purpose draw upon his own admittedly impressive article of 1977, 'Puritan Evangelism in the reign of Elizabeth I',[76] which I remember reading with deep appreciation in typescript. Here in justifiably gloomy colours he depicts the grim struggle waged by 'godly' but unpopular Elizabethans to break the heroically entrenched Catholicism of Lancashire, upon which even by 1600 they had made relatively little impression. Indeed, throughout considerable areas of that county Protestantism never wholly predominated. Yet in its religious history Lancashire proved the least typical area of England, and for very good religious, geographical, social and economic reasons, which Christopher Haigh has fully explained in his weighty and authoritative book.[77] True, there were other slow-moving districts in the North and the West, but none to match this. 'The county fought the Reformation more vigorously and with greater success than did any other part of England.'[78] There must be one certain outcome: that the case of Lancashire cannot possibly be elevated into a nationwide picture of England, least of all in regard to Elizabethan anti-clericalism. If such a thesis is to carry any conviction, the evidence must not only be massive but must be drawn from a number of areas far more typical of England as a whole.

On the basis of the foregoing arguments my provisional deductions are as follows:

1. Anti-clericalism, a natural reaction against the wealth and powers of the medieval church, should not be dismissed as an invention on the part of modern historians. A strong body of evidence suggests that it was already widespread a century and a half before the Reformation. This major heritage from the Middle Ages was ultimately bequeathed to Protestant dissent, partly by Lollardy and other channels of popular transmission, but also by the voluminous printing of its major writers and their subsequent imitators. If we continue to begin the story in the days of Richard Hunne and Cardinal Wolsey, we truncate its patterns and minimise the weight of this phenomenon.

2. The erastian claims of fourteenth-century philosophers became a major component of anti-clericalism. These ideas also underwent a sixteenth-century revival in print, being eventually used both to demand and to justify the secularisation of church property in favour of the state.

3. The various forms of anti-clerical thought and action developed alongside the survival of a substantial measure of traditional Catholicism, which remained strong at least until 1530, and in certain areas of England survived to meet Counter-Reformation missionaries in the mid-Elizabethan decades. Historians upset the balance of the whole period if they dwell too exclusively either upon anti-clericalism or upon traditional piety. The one does not exclude the other, and both could contend within the same individual mind.

4. Many of the harsh censures upon the lower clergy came from disciplinary reformers who retained all the essentials of Catholic doctrine, as well as from radical dissenters and 'heretics', clerical or lay. While the early English Protestants inherited critical attitudes toward the clergy, in their case such attitudes were strengthened by Luther's teaching on 'the priesthood of all believers', as opposed to the Catholic concept of the clergy as a separate order of men with indelible spiritual characteristics.

5. The alleged evidence of clerical depravity and ignorance adduced by the more rabid Protestant critics has been greatly modified by modern research. All the same, serious charges – both general and individual – are by no means rare, whether in court records or in the testimony of 'respectable' critics, Catholic and Protestant. The recruitment and training of the late medieval parish clergy left much to be desired: inevitably some of them provided enough

fuel to maintain a smouldering antagonism among the laity. Yet our present information on this aspect of public opinion does not enable us to generalise freely, for example to pronounce the laity either 'satisfied' or 'dissatisfied' with their clergy.

6. Before and during the Henrician and Edwardian Reformations, parish feuds and lawsuits could arise anywhere, owing to personal factors; yet the highest tides of criticism arose in London and other parts of southern England, as opposed to most areas in the mainly conservative West and North. This geographical pattern corresponds broadly with the diverse regional developments of both Lollardy and early Protestantism.

7. Most modern authorities rightly regard the pressures of the ecclesiastical courts and of the system of tithes as in some degree contributory causes of popular anti-clericalism. Nevertheless the surviving evidence, which tends to be diffuse and inharmonious, scarcely warrants a prime emphasis on these two factors. Both were very prominent in London, whence at present a high proportion of the evidence comes, but London cannot be assumed to typify the kingdom as a whole.

8. As already suggested, the traditional complaints against wealthy and secularist bishops, grasping priests, roving monks and hypocritical friars, acquired a more revolutionary character when they linked up with Protestant doctrinal criticism. Most fundamentally, the Reformation demanded a reference back to the Christianity taught by Christ and the Apostles, and documented in the New Testament. This biblicism, scorning the numerous unscriptural accretions and innovations of the ages, had unpleasant consequences for the conservative clergy of the sixteenth century. Their moral and intellectual shortcomings, real and invented, could be exhibited by Protestant propaganda as the inevitable result of false doctrine, the 'bad fruit' which proved the defective character of the tree itself.

9. The stimulation and manipulation of anti-clerical opinion, in order to encourage reform and confiscation by the state, necessarily occurred as a result of deliberate activities by the political classes: common lawyers, merchants, parliamentarians, royal officials, pamphleteers. Yet the fact should not be permitted to obscure the all-important role eventually played by working-class activists and martyrs in the advancement of the Protestant cause. So far as concerns the very numerous anti-clerical writers, it

would seem quite unrealistic to dismiss them as little related to public opinion, including the opinion of manual workers.

10. The suggested affinities between Catholic priests and the 'wise' men and women who practised the white magic of spells and potions should be treated with caution. Again, an antithesis between 'comforting' old-style priests and irritating Puritan preachers seems too simplistic and selective to fit the complexities of religious life and thought during the Tudor period. As yet there appear no convincing indications that anti-clerical feeling became a stronger force throughout Elizabethan England than it had been prior to the Reformation. We should neither exaggerate the unpopularity of Puritan divines nor underestimate late medieval anti-clericalism. Any such attempt to compare two unquantifiable forces seems unlikely to command widespread acceptance.

Notes

1. G. R. Elton, *Star Chamber Stories* (London, 1958), ch. 6, 'Tithe and Trouble'.
2. C. Haigh, 'Anticlericalisam and the English Reformation', *History*, LXVIII (1983), pp. 391–407.
3. Helen C. White, *Social Criticism in Popular Religious Literature of the Sixteenth Century* (New York, 1944).
4. J. J. Scarisbrick, *The Reformation and the English People* (Oxford, 1984); C. Haigh, 'The Recent Historiography of the English Reformation', *Historical Journal*, XXV (1982), pp. 995–1007.
5. M. R. James (ed.), *Walter Map. De Nugis Curialium* (Oxford, 1983), pp. xliii–xliv. G. R. Owst, *Literature and Pulpit in Medieval England* (Oxford, 1961), pp. 224–6, 272–86 *passim*, 305–6, 366. On the violent anti-clericalism of the risings of 1381 and 1450, see ibid., p. 290.
6. For the points which follow, see J. F. Goodridge (trans.), *Langland, Piers the Plowman* (Harmondsworth, 1966), pp. 63, 91, 101, 107, 114ff, 121, 126, 130–5, 149, 181–8.
7. Ibid., pp. 59, 263–4, citing J. J. Jusserand, *Piers Plowman* (London, 1894), pp. 71, 112, 128–36. Compare Jusserand in *Modern Philology*, VII (1909), p. 272ff.
8. Goodridge, *Langland*, p. 121.
9. White, *Social Criticism*, pp. 1–40.
10. J. N. King, 'Robert Crowley's Editions of *Piers Plowman*: a Tudor Apocalypse', *Modern Philology*, LXXIII (1976), pp. 342–52; Anne Hudson, *Lollards and their Books* (London, 1985), pp. 227–48.
11. *EETS*, Orig. Ser., XXX (1867), pp. 69–72.
12. King, 'Editions', p. 343, n. 5.

13.   *EETS* (as n. 11), Preface, p. xi and Text, pp. 1–32.
14.   J. W. Martin, 'The Publishing Career of Robert Crowley', *Publishing History*, XIV (1983), pp. 85–98.
15.   King, 'Editions', pp. 345–51.
16.   Cf. A. G. Dickens, 'Heresy and the Origins of English Protestantism', in idem, *Reformation Studies* (London, 1982), pp. 363–82; idem, *Lollards and Protestants in the Diocese of York* (London, 1959, 1982); J. F. Davis, *Heresy and Reformation in the South-East of England* (Royal Historical Society Studies in History, XXXIV) (London, 1983). For the publication of Wycliffite works by Protestant Reformers, see Margaret Aston, *Lollards and Reformers* (London, 1984), ch. 7 and on Wycliffe's high reputation among Tudor Reformers, ibid., ch. 8.
17.   *STC*, 5083–4–5–6.
18.   See e.g. Gascoigne's examples below and those cited by E. F. Jacob, *The Fifteenth Century* (Oxford, 1961), pp. 288–9.
19.   *DNB*, s.v. Moleyns, Adam; Ayscough, William and n. 21 below.
20.   On Gascoigne's career and work, see Winifred A. Pronger, 'Thomas Gascoigne', *English Historical Review*, LIII (1938), pp. 606–26 and LIV (1939), pp. 20–37; A. B. Emden, *Biographical Register of the University of Oxford* (3 vols, Oxford, 1957–9), vol. II, pp. 745–8.
21.   J. E. T. Rogers (ed.), *Loci e Libro Veritatum* (Oxford, 1881), pp. 41–2.
22.   Ibid., pp. 53–99.
23.   Ibid., pp. 35–6.
24.   References in A. G. Dickens, 'The Writers of Tudor Yorkshire', in idem, *Reformation Studies*, pp. 221–2; the *Sermo Exhortatorius* is *STC*, 17806.
25.   Colet's Latin Text (1511–12) is *Oratio habita ad clerum in convocatione*, *STC*, 5545; the English version (1530) is *The sermon of Doctor Colete*, *STC*, 5550, reprinted in J. H. Lupton, *A Life of John Colet* (London, 1887), pp. 293–304. For the comparison with Latimer see ibid., p. 185. On the broad issues see P. I. Kaufman, 'John Colet's *Opus de sacramentis* and Clerical Anticlericalism', *Journal of British Studies*, XXII (1982), pp. 1–22.
26.   References in B. Wilkinson, *Constitutional History of England in the Fifteenth Century* (London, 1964), pp. 378–9, 386–90, 393.
27.   F. L. Van Baumer, *The Early Tudor Theory of Kingship* (New Haven, 1940), p. 17.
28.   On Fortescue see C. Plummer (ed.), *The Governance of England* (Oxford, 1885) and S. B. Chrimes (ed.), *Sir John Fortescue, De Laudibus Legum Angliae* (Cambridge, 1942).
29.   *DNB*, s.v. Marshall, William; *STC*, 10498, 15986, 17817 [Marsiglio], 24238, 25127, 26119.
30.   Edward Fox, *De vera differentia* (1534, 1538; *STC*, 11218–9) and the English translation by Henry, Lord Stafford (1548; *STC*, 11220); Stephen Gardiner, *De vera obedientia*, 1535 (*STC*, 11584), and the English editions maliciously published by his enemies in 1553 (*STC*, 11585–6–7).
31.   *EETS*, Orig. Ser., CLXVII (1924) ed. A. J. Perry, who describes the MSS; *STC*, 12510–11–11a; *DNB*, s.v. Trevisa.
32.   D. M. Brodie (ed.), *The Tree of Commonwealth* (Cambridge, 1948),

points out, pp. 12–13, that it was used by Stow and by Sir Simonds D'Ewes. It was possibly known by the author's son John Dudley, Duke of Northumberland.

33. On St German see Van Baumer, *Theory of Kingship*, ch. 3 *passim*; J. B. Trapp (ed.), *The Yale Edition of the Complete Works of St. Thomas More*, vol. IX, *The Apology*, pp. xli–liv and Appendix A. For St German's works: *STC*, 21559–21588. A close analysis of *Doctor and Student* is in R. E. Rodes, *Lay Authority and Reformation in the English Church* (Notre Dame, Ind., 1982), pp. 69–77.

34. A. G. Dickens, *The English Reformation* (London, 1964 *et seq.*), pp. 97–8.

35. *Cambridge History of English Literature*, vol. III (Cambridge, 1909), pp. 56–67; *STC*, 3545–6; for the translation of Brant by H. Watson, *STC*, 3547 (1509), 3547a (1517).

36. *Cambridge History of English Literature*, vol. III, pp. 67–79; M. Pollet, *John Skelton. Poet of Tudor England*, trans. J. Warrington (London, 1971).

37. *Cambridge History of English Literature*, vol. III, pp. 74–5 on the wide scope of *Colyn Clout*, directed as it is against lordly bishops, ignorant priests, cheating friars, roving monks and nuns.

38. Pollet, *John Skelton*, ch. 9, 'The Last Years and the Struggle against the Lutherans'; *STC*, 22609, *A replycacion agaynst certayne yong scolers* (*c.* 1528).

39. Trapp, *The Apology* (as n. 33), p. 129.

40. W. E. Campbell and A. W. Reed (eds), *The Dialogue concerning Tyndale by Sir Thomas More* (London, 1927), pp. 225, 228. More then discusses celibacy, making the point that the church does not compel men to become priests.

41. Margaret Bowker, *The Secular Clergy in the Diocese of Lincoln 1495–1520* (Cambridge, 1969), idem, *The Henrician Reformation: the Diocese of Lincoln under John Langland 1521–1547* (Cambridge, 1981).

42. P. Heath, *The English Parish Clergy on the Eve of the Reformation* (London, 1969).

43. Haigh, 'Anticlericalism', p. 392ff.

44. Heath, *English Parish Clergy*, ch. 7 and pp. 192–6; Bowker, *Secular Clergy*, pp. 118–24, 151–4, 172–8. A balanced summary on celibacy and sexual morality is in R. A. Houlbrooke, *Church Courts and the People during the English Reformation 1520–1570* (Oxford, 1979), pp. 177–83. On the London church courts and sex-offences see R. M. Wunderli, *London Church Courts and Society on the Eve of the Reformation* (Cambridge, Mass., 1981), ch. 4. Clerical incontinence – most leniently corrected – was a serious problem at Chichester: S. Lander, 'Church Courts and the Reformation in the Diocese of Chichester 1500–1558', in R. O'Day and F. Heal (eds), *Continuity and Change. Personnel and Administration of the Church of England 1500–1642* (Leicester, 1976), p. 218.

45. Scarisbrick, *Reformation*, ch. 2. Sylvia Thrupp, *The Merchant Class of Medieval London* (Ann Arbor, Mich., 1962), pp. 174–90 displays the ambivalent relations of this class with the church.

46. Haigh, 'Anticlericalism', pp. 393–4.

47. Bigod's *Treatise concerning Impropriations, Yorkshire Archaeological Society Record Series*, CXXV (1959), pp. 41–58 attacks idle, gluttonous and immoral monks with a violence approaching that of Bale.

48. On Wilfred Holme's *Fall and Success of Rebellion*, see Dickens, *Lollards and Protestants*, pp. 114–31. This tract makes another intensive attack on the religious orders.

49. Brinklow's *Complaynt of Roderyck Mors* (*EETS*, Extra Ser., XXII (1874, 1904) is yet another late derivative from Langland in its championship of the poor and its violent attacks on oppressive authority, both lay and clerical. It is harshly anti-papal, anti-episcopal and anti-pluralist: cf. chs. 13, 14, 19, 20, 22, 23, 24.

50. E. G. Duff, *The English Provincial Printers ... to 1557* (Cambridge, 1912), p. 110; *STC*, 18055–6; *Notes and Queries*, CXIX (December 1954), pp. 513–14; J. N. King, *English Reformation Literature. The Tudor Origins of the Protestant Tradition* (Princeton, NJ, 1982), p. 498.

51. On Ramsey see references in n. 50 above; *STC*, 20661–2–3; King, *English Reformation Literature*, p. 500.

52. See above, n. 50.

53. On the early Protestant theatre see E. K. Chambers, *The Medieval Stage* (Oxford, 1903), vol. II, pp. 216–26; Ian Lancashire, *Dramatic Texts and Records of Britain* (Cambridge, 1984), especially nos. 320–29, 1087–1110; H. Gee and W. J. Hardy (eds), *Documents of English Church History* (London, 1896, 1910), p. 375. *Acts of the Privy Council*, ed. J. R. Dasent (32 vols, London, 1890–1907), vol. IV, pp. 73, 426; vol. V, pp. 234, 237–8; vol. VI, pp. 102, 110, 118–19, 148–9, 168–9; John Christopherson, the Catholic playwright, cited in Lancashire, *Dramatic Texts*, no. 322; the two biographies of John Bale, respectively by Honor McCusker (Bryn Mawr, Pa., 1942) and J. W. Harris (Urbana, Ill., 1949).

54. Haigh, 'Anticlericalism', p. 394ff.

55. Cf. e.g. the articles cited in n. 63 below.

56. 'That the petition of the Commons against the spirituality really emanated from the Court is placed beyond a doubt by the fact that four corrected drafts of it exist in the Record Office, the corrections generally being in Cromwell's hand', J. Gairdner, *Introduction* (1880) to *Letters and Papers of Henry VIII*, vol. V, p. xix.

57. G. R. Elton, *Policy and Police. The Enforcement of the Reformation in the Age of Thomas Cromwell* (Cambridge, 1972); especially ch. 3, 'In Every Part of the Realm'.

58. J. Fines, *A Biographical Register of Early English Protestants 1525–1558*: at the time of writing vol. I alone was printed (Sutton Courtenay, 1981), but a full and revised edition will shortly appear. I am grateful to Dr Fines for the prolonged loan of his typescript.

59. Even in the impressive archives of the diocese of Lincoln, the gaps from 1547 onwards are grievous: see Bowker, *Henrician Reformation*, p. 181.

60. E.g. P. Clark, *English Provincial Society ... Religion, Politics and Society in Kent* (Hassocks, 1977), pp. 41–2, 58–9, 76; Elaine Sheppard, 'The Reformation and the Citizens of Norwich', *Norfolk Archaeology*, XXXVIII (1983) pp. 44–58; W. J. Sheils, *The Puritans in the Diocese of*

Peterborough (Northamptonshire Record Society, XXX) (Northampton, 1979), pp. 15–17; G. J. Mayhew, 'The Progress of the Reformation in East Sussex 1530–1559: the Evidence from Wills', *Southern History*, V (1983), pp. 35–67; Dickens, *Lollards and Protestants*, pp. 171–2, 215–18, 220–1; D. M. Palliser, *The Reformation in York, 1534–53* (Borthwick Institute, York, 1971), p. 32; Claire Cross, 'Parochial Structure and the Dissemination of Protestantism in Sixteenth-Century England: a Tale of Two Cities', in D. Baker (ed.), *Studies in Church History*, XVI (1979); Claire Cross, 'The Development of Protestantism in Leeds and Hull, 1520–1640', *Northern History*, XVIII (1982), pp. 230–8.

61. Haigh, 'Anticlericalism', p. 402.

62. Contrast the small figures in the dioceses selected by Dr Haigh with e.g. the much larger figures given for York by Canon J. S. Purvis, *Tudor Parish Documents of the Diocese of York* (Cambridge, 1948), p. 180. At York there survive in manuscript, from the fourteenth century to 1560, some 1385 causes, of which 311 concern tithe. Of these 311 about 121 are between incumbents and parishioners. In addition, between 1540 and 1560, no less than 135 tithes causes are between lay tithe-farmers and parishioners. On the considerable numbers of tithe-causes extant at Norwich (1519–69) and at Winchester (1527–66) see Houlbrooke, *Church Courts*, pp. 273–4.

63. Susan Brigden, 'Tithe Controversy in Reformation London', *Journal of Ecclesiastical History*, XXXII (1981), pp. 285–301; Wunderli, *London Church Courts*, pp. 108–13. Cf. on London tithes Helen Miller, 'London and Parliament in the Reign of Henry VIII', *Bulletin of the Institute of Historical Research*, XXXV (1962), pp. 128–49, and J. A. F. Thomson, 'Tithe Disputes in Later Medieval London', *English Historical Review*, LXXVIII (1963), pp. 1–17.

64. Houlbrooke, *Church Courts*, pp. 271–2.

65. B. Woodcock, *Medieval Ecclesiastical Courts in the Diocese of Canterbury* (London, 1952), pp. 109–10, 125; Wunderli, *London Church Courts*, pp. 136–8; Lander, 'Church Courts' (as n. 44), p. 228.

66. Haigh, 'Anticlericalism', p. 401; Houlbrooke, *Church Courts*, pp. 49, 86, 271.

67. The following evidence is presented in more detail in A. G. Dickens, 'Early Protestantism and the Church in Northamptonshire', *Northamptonshire Past and Present*, VIII (1983–4), pp. 30–3.

68. Haigh, 'Anticlericalism', pp. 406–7.

69. K. Thomas, *Religion and the Decline of Magic* (Harmondsworth, 1973), pp. 32–57 *passim*.

70. Ibid., p. 95.

71. S. E. Ozment, *The Reformation in the Cities* (New Haven/London, 1975), pp. 8–9, 28, 49–53. Cf. T. N. Tentler, *Sin and Confession on the Eve of the Reformation* (Princeton, NJ, 1977), *passim*.

72. Thomas, *Religion and the Decline of Magic*, pp. 308–14, 483–4.

73. Ibid., p. 316.

74. G. Strauss, *Luther's House of Learning* (Baltimore, Md/London, 1978), chs. 12–14.

75. Ibid., pp. 288–91.

76. *English Historical Review*, XCII (1977), pp. 30–58.
77. C. Haigh, *Reformation and Resistance in Tudor Lancashire* (Cambridge, 1975), chs. 6–15.
78. Ibid., p. 86.

19 For True Faith or National Interest? Queen Elizabeth I and the Protestant Powers

E. I. Kouri

Both possibilities mentioned in the title imply that Queen Elizabeth had a foreign policy. But even this may be doubted. For we may ask how far her decisions to cope with new situations were consistent and prompted by traditionally accepted notions and how far by short-term reactions to events. Historical research today is still far from reaching a consensus in this matter. Using a rough oversimplification, we can state that there are two main conflicting strands of interpretation. One of them assumes that she was in her policy making more or less rational and constant. In its clearest form this interpretation has been maintained by the doyen among historians of Elizabethan foreign policy, R. B. Wernham.[1] In contrast, Charles Wilson, especially in his controversial study on Queen Elizabeth's Dutch policy, has little to say to her credit in this respect: he sees her policy as both inconsistent and incompetent, and her reign as a story not so much of policy as of its absence.[2] Less extreme than Wernham, but still seeing consistency in her policy, are Conyers Read and A. L. Rowse. Recent studies by Wallace T. MacCaffrey and George Ramsay have tended to dwell on the *ad hoc* nature of the queen's policies, though not so exclusively as Wilson.[3]

In Counter-Reformation Europe as a whole, *les deux protectorats* were widely recognised, that of England over the continental Protestants and that of Spain over the Catholics. Queen Elizabeth's policy towards the Protestant powers was accordingly characterised by Protestant ideology and religious terminology. But in her political calculations the significance of these states was inevitably determined to a large extent by matters nearer England's shores. Further, any policy – confessional or otherwise – that she may have been trying to follow was necessarily shaped by the constraints of the time; by the various pressure groups representing conflicting strategic, ideological

411

or commercial interests and by her limited finances. If indeed a policy with the Protestant powers is discernible, we may ask to what extent it was guided by 'True Faith', i.e. the idealistic defence of Protestantism as such, and to what extent by 'National Interest', or England's supposed political advantage.

In this paper the queen's relations with the German states, and to a lesser extent with the Scandinavian powers, are treated as the main point of interest. For the German Protestant principalities and the northern Lutheran monarchies were traditionally the senior representatives of the New Religion, whereas the Protestants in France, Holland and Scotland were, for most of the time discussed here, rebels fighting the lawful authority and the political role of those in Switzerland and Eastern Europe was still relatively small in international affairs. Moreover, research in the archives of sixteen countries suggests that Germany and Scandinavia were not, as has so often been assumed, of negligible significance in the story of Elizabethan foreign affairs.

I

At the European settlement of Cateau-Cambrésis of 1559 England lost Calais, her last continental possession. This alteration in the country's strategic situation forced her to abandon, albeit reluctantly, her former continentalist policy and move towards an insular defensive policy based upon sea power. But she could never entirely keep to the passive policy of maintaining a balance among the continental powers and trying to exploit the Habsburg–Valois struggle for hegemony. Thus near the beginning of Elizabeth's reign English foreign policy made the radical change from traditional rivalry with France to hostility against Spain and a nervous stance towards the Catholic powers in general. From now on the long-term Spanish threat dominated English foreign policy; moves in other sections of the international front usually produced a change in England's short-term aims only. In the queen's diplomacy there were two main rhythms: one dictated by the wars in France, and the other by the events in the Low Countries. She tried to hold Spain back from the domination of western Europe until the recovery of the French monarchy could provide an effective continental counterweight to Spanish power. The queen's dealings with her co-religionists form part of the complex changes in European politics that led to the formation of large-scale Protestant and Catholic alliances, and finally to the Thirty Years War. At that time, however, England was no longer the champion of the Protestant cause.[4]

In any assessment of Elizabethan foreign policy, we must ask to what extent the queen could control and did control the necessary day-to-day decisions. Yet it is a commonplace that it was she who played the decisive part in shaping policy. Usually she discussed its outlines with a few of her most influential ministers, but she made up her mind alone. On most issues of domestic policy there was a consensus at the centre of the policy-making scene; the earlier factional concept of Elizabethan politics can be dismissed, at least as far as the middle years of her reign are concerned. The faction struggle in her early reign, mainly between Cecil and Leicester, gave way after the crisis of the late 1560s to relative stability; and not until the bitter factionalism of the 1590s was the uneasy balance at council and court gravely disturbed by the rivalry between Essex and Cecil and their respective followers.[5]

The Elizabethan régime was Protestant from the very outset, but in confessional aspects of foreign policy the councillors did not always agree. The interventionist party led by Leicester and Walsingham, and later by Essex, was supported by a number of the queen's other councillors and diplomats of a Puritan outlook. They thought that England should not remain indifferent to the conflict of Catholic and Protestant powers reaching from Scandinavia to the shores of the Mediterranean. According to them, the best solution was the identification of English interest with the Protestant interest and the pursuit of a firm Protestant alliance policy, to which the German states and Scandinavian powers were the key. Other strands of this policy involved the provision of sufficient aid to those fighting the Catholic monarchs in the Netherlands and France, keeping power in Scotland in Protestant hands and the attempt to convert and reduce all Ireland to obedience.[6] The wisdom of this straightforward commitment to a common cause of Protestantism was questioned by the anti-interventionists – even those, like Burghley, who in principle were sympathetic to Protestant policies. The queen, in contrast to many of her councillors and advisors, clearly followed a cautious non-involvement strategy. Her reluctance to subsidise her co-religionists in Scotland or on the continent, however, sometimes arose from lack of money, and not just stinginess, as is sometimes maintained. She often thought it unwise to commit herself whole-heartedly to the defence of continental Protantism, although it fitted well with her strategic plans in general, since it would have hindered her attaining her political objectives elsewhere. Her dealings with her fellow-Protestants show something of the nature of her policy making in general. Asked to give his opinion on it, Sir Walter Raleigh said: 'her Majesty did all by halves.'[7] For her policy towards the Protestant powers, this criticism seems to be fair enough. Undoubtedly, however, the same criticism could be levelled against Philip II of Spain, Frederick II of Denmark, many of the German princes, or even against the Sultans. All of them were careful not to put everything on one card.

Although traditional dynastic rivalries had lost much of their former importance, after Cateau-Cambrésis there was to be no slackening of international tension. Religious differences cut across frontiers and disrupted national communities to such an extent that the political character of Europe was soon permanently changed by the polarisation of religious allegiances. Militant Calvinism started to take the lead in Protestant politics and to score successes in France, the Netherlands, Scotland, Germany, Switzerland, Poland and Hungary. This inevitably led to confrontation with Tridentine Catholicism. Statesmen often had to ask at this time whether foreign policy should be guided by consideration of national interest or religious allegiance. The question was most pressing in France, where the country remained under a Catholic monarch, but there was a breakdown of order as the Huguenots were trying to establish a right to their religion. Later, however, the French Crown had to decide whether to support the Huguenots in their anti-Spanish policy or to make common cause with France's traditional rival, Spain, against the heretics. In England the Catholics found themselves trapped in a conflict of loyalties: whether to take part in the various plots supported by Spain and the pope against the heretic queen or to maintain their loyalty to her as their sovereign.[8]

Among the Huguenots and the Dutch rebels, as Professor Koenigsberger has pointed out, religion was the binding force that held together the divergent interests of the different classes and provided them with an organisation and propaganda machine that created the first parties, in the modern sense, in European history.[9] Even some ruling princes thought it right and sometimes meritorious that political leagues should be joined, or arms taken up, with religion as *ultima ratio*. There were a few among Elizabeth's internationalist councillors who were ready to go to war for Protestantism, though the queen herself was far more cautious. There is little doubt that both Philip II of Spain or Elector Frederick of the Palatinate pursued ideologically motivated foreign policies. Needless to say, they seldom forgot their temporal ambitions.[10]

Since the days of Cateau-Cambrésis and the Council of Trent there had been ever stronger rumours about a Catholic League, headed by the pope and leading Catholic monarchs, to extirpate the New Religion and its adherents. The Franco-Spanish meeting in Bayonne in 1565 was seen among the Protestants as a confirmation of their fears. During the pontificate of the new Medici pope, Pius IV (1560–65), the Counter-Reformation was successfully launched to regain lost territories.[11]

The stepping up of Catholic activities, both ecclesiastical and temporal, gave the Protestant powers reason to believe that the Catholics had already concluded a secret alliance. A strong Protestant league would therefore not only be necessary in case of war but also effective in forestalling it. 'ein schwert das andere in der schede behielte' was the policy in Calvinist Heidelberg. This figure of speech about preventing war was echoed by minor Lutheran princes.[12] Although Queen Elizabeth, at least in the early days of her reign, was not so sure about the existence of such a league as some of her interventionist ministers, she wholly understood from the very beginning its propaganda value. Later the threatening developments, especially in France and the Netherlands, made her speak much more seriously about the Tridentine plan to annihilate the heretics and about the necessity of a powerful Protestant counter-league.[13] In fact there was no offensive Catholic league, as numerous Protestants were inclined to think, and the attempts at a united Protestant front were counter-productive, causing increased papal and Spanish diplomatic activity. The energetic Cardinal Alessandrino, for example, did his best to persuade the Catholic states to give generous aid to the French Crown against the Huguenots. The argument used by him was strikingly similar to that used by the foremost champions of the Protestant League: if one of the fellow believers is attacked because of his religious beliefs, the others should hurry to help the one in real trouble instead of worrying about their own defence; should his house fall, it must per *ragione di stato* sooner or later bury the others beneath its ruins.[14]

One of the factors spreading disunity among the German Protestants was that the Peace of Augsburg of 1555 had included only those who subscribed to the creed of the *Confessio Augustana*. Only they were granted a civil and political status equal to that of the Catholics; but the Calvinists, Zwinglians and Anabaptists were not included in the settlement. When Elector Frederick of the Palatinate, surnamed the Pious, as the first prince in the empire adopted Calvinism in 1563, there was a sudden polarisation of political and religious opinion. The Calvinist Palatinate soon distinguished itself by a militant anti-Catholic and anti-Habsburg policy. Frederick favoured a pan-Protestant alliance and thus soon became England's most important ally in the empire.[15] The Palatine statesmen were well aware that, ever since the principality embraced Calvinism, the German Lutherans had been suspicious not only of their theological but also increasingly of their political views: '*last baldt auf P[falz] gelegt werden möcht, als wen sie eine neue conspiration suchen wolt, dan was P[falz] tut ist übel getan*', remarked Elector Frederick sourly.[16] They also knew that despite the abundant use of religious phraseology, there was a prevailing suspicion among the Lutherans that Queen Elizabeth was eager to ally with her fellow-Protestants only as a means of obtaining support against the great Catholic powers. In the Palatine propaganda for her this was promptly rebutted: militarily strong, geographically and politically secure, England would be able to solve her own problems without any help from outside. It would also be much easier for her than for the Germans to follow a policy of insular isolation. Elizabeth's proposals for a common Protestant front must therefore come from idealistic motives. The Lutherans should observe that the hostile measures adopted by the Catholics were ultimately directed *contra omnes ultramontanes*. The Spaniards, for example, were not only intent on making the Netherlands a *colonia Hispaniorum*, but were also forcing Westphalia and the duchy of Jülich to live under the same kind of constant fear as was the lot of the principalities facing the Turks, the arch-enemies of the empire.[17]

Despite the obvious difficulties Queen Elizabeth treated the German Protestants as a single group. Even in the latter part of her reign, English diplomacy was practised on the assumption that foreign policy could be conducted in isolation from recent doctrinal developments. Although she had closest links with the Calvinist Palatinate, she also tried to get a foothold in the Lutheran territories. But there were political quarrels and doctrinal differences between the various groupings among the Lutherans themselves. So it is no surprise that the English had no success here. In fact, such was the *furor theologicus* and the intolerance of the principalities, that even the political position of the Protestant Estates was weakened.[18]

Most of the conservative, compromising and peace-loving Lutheran princes could not see Queen Elizabeth's proposals as a desirable alternative to the policy of the Austrian Habsburgs. Although the establishment of militant Calvinism in the Palatinate and of Tridentine Catholicism in Bavaria might mean that confessional conflicts would not only spread through the rest of Germany but also draw in foreign powers, the German Lutherans evidently did not regard the situation as serious enough to warrant a commitment to anything that might be construed as a violation of the Peace of Augsburg or as a challenge to the emperor and the Catholic Estates. Of course, the permanency of this federative and inter-confessional policy depended on the parity of the two religious groups and on the emperor's capacity to keep the peace between them.[19]

During the emergence of the nation states cynical power politics aimed at new territories and wealth often overshadowed more idealistic aims. Protestant and Catholic ideologies, with their religious terminologies and concepts, were used by both camps for political ends. In the history of German Protestantism there are plenty of examples that show how little weight the confession sometimes had beside political consideration. In 1551 the members of the Schmalkaldic League formed an alliance with Henry II of France, the persecutor of the French Protestants. In the following year, in return for generous subsidies for use against the emperor, they handed over to the king the bishoprics of Metz, Toul and Verdun.[20] There had been many other occasions when Lutheran princes, pursuing ruthless foreign policies to increase their individual power, had placed political expediency before confession. A good example was Maurice of Saxony, who subordinated his confession to his political advantage by his alliance in 1546 with Charles V against his fellow Protestants, receiving as a reward the electoral dignity and the electoral lands confiscated from his relative John Frederick of Saxony–Weimar. Only a few years later, Maurice sought the alliance of other German states rebelling against the emperor and defeated him.[21] As another example one may also quote the prolonged negotiations between the French Crown and a number of Protestant princes in 1567.[22] But negotiating with, and seeking ties with, powers across the religious line was only one side of the matter. There was intense rivalry, sometimes open warfare, between states of the same religion.

II

Traditionally, England and the Catholic powers, especially France, had looked upon the strength of the German Protestant states and cities, and to a lesser extent the Scandinavian powers, as an essential factor in European diplomacy. The French had seen them as a counterweight to the Austrian and Spanish Habsburgs, the English as an insurance against isolation. Queen Elizabeth and her government recognised the necessity of being on good terms with the German Protestants as a prophylactic measure against Spain, France and even the emperor. When she thought the balance of power in Europe might change radically against the interests of her country, she mounted intensive diplomatic campaigns in Germany and in Scandinavia to gain allies.

Queen Elizabeth conducted prolonged negotiations with a number of suitors, some of them major political figures and some of them German princelings who had little to offer but themselves. These negotiations were not only matrimonial but political in nature. One of the suitors of royal blood was Eric XIV of Sweden, who, for his part, was desperately seeking an ally outside the Baltic area. The queen's dealings with Eric form a striking example of the fluctuation of the religious tone in her Protestant diplomacy. Early in the correspondence she wrote that he '*propter religionis erga Deum rectissimum cultum . . . merito nobis carissimus esse debeat*', but in her game to buy England a major European ally he was nothing but a plaything '*donec Deus mentem nostram alio converterit.*'[23] Although the Privy Council, fearing a triangular alliance between Denmark, France and Scotland, had urged the queen to accept the Swedish matrimonial proposal, her mind was never changed and the ardent Nordic suitor was forgotten.

Soon, however, the queen would be stressing more seriously the common 'True Faith' with this remote and obscure kingdom. The closing of the Antwerp market to the English in the 1560s drastically changed the pattern of the country's overseas trade: from now on it had to shift the bulk of its trade to the German and Baltic area. Here Sweden, thanks to its expansionist policy, especially in the areas which had earlier belonged to the Teutonic Order, exercised considerable control over the profitable Russian trade.[24] The pro-Catholic policies of Eric's successor, John III, well suited the plans of the Roman Church, which in trying to win back the *heretici oltramontani* paid special attention to North Europe.[25] John (whom Queen Elizabeth knew personally) was not only busy courting the pope, but was also making sympathetic gestures towards Philip II of Spain.[26] Had the Catholic powers, and Spain in particular, gained enough influence in Scandinavia, there would have been a serious threat to English trade in the Baltic area.

The growing importance of the *Balticum* in the commercial calculations at the same time increased the political activity of the major powers in the region. In the course of the sixteenth century the northern kingdoms, particularly Denmark, began to feature in European affairs. The French had even maintained a resident ambassador at the Danish court since the early 1540s.[27] The English, for their part, had a resident agent in Germany, but only unofficial sources of information in Denmark and Sweden.[28] The possibility of co-operation between France and Denmark, and of French and Spanish expansion into the Baltic area were the greatest problems in English security policy in northern Europe. The increased English diplomatic activity was a precautionary measure adopted in case the Catholics decided to take advantage of the weakening of the Protestant front or even attempted to use the northern powers to threaten England's political and commercial interests. A strong and friendly Baltic was vital for the queen's foreign policy.

For England the relatively strong Lutheran states in Scandinavia – with their close political, economic, dynastic and religious ties with the Protestant ruling houses of Germany – were potential allies, but the English were outwitted there by the French with their superior understanding of the area. Sweden as well as Denmark sometimes followed a policy of *rapprochement* towards France and against the Habsburgs, as it had done earlier, even in the form of a political treaty.[29] Now Denmark controlled the Sound and the Great and Little Belts; and although the English discovered in 1553 the northern route through the White Sea to Russia, the great bulk of their trade went through the Sound. The queen was well aware that her finances were largely dependent on the trade in the North Sea and the Baltic conducted by English companies. These played an interesting part in mercantile diplomacy as well as in her policy of financing German mercenary armies fighting for 'True Faith' in the Netherlands and France.[30]

Essential to Elizabeth's plans for the Baltic had been the prevention of Catholic expansion to the East and securing her own access to the markets there. The English penetration of the area was greeted by increasing suspicion from the great Catholic powers and engendered a sour reaction besides from the Hanseatic League. The maritime cities gradually came to fear English commerce almost as much as Spanish political aggression; and such powers as the duchies of Prussia, Pomerania and even Mecklenburg regarded English intentions with uneasiness. To avoid increasing hostility, Elizabeth hesitated for a long time before interfering, for example, with the flourishing Hansa trade of war-material with Spain and Portugal. When she at last acted, she tried to play down the ill feelings of her fellow-Protestants by referring to the same principles and assumptions of the *ius gentium* in naval warfare that the German arms suppliers had cited in protest. At this time these principles were common to all the main powers.[31] But despite all precautions the English confiscation policy was seen almost as piracy by both Germans and Scandinavians.[32] Here too, therefore, Elizabeth's real prospects of advancing her commercial and other secular ambitions under the pretext of common religion were less hopeful than she appears to have thought. The prolonged battle over the privileges of the Merchants Adventurers and the Eastland Company on the Continent, which were held in exchange for corresponding Hansa privileges in England, was a good example of the nagging disputes which weakened the solidarity of the Protestant camp. At the same time these commercial conflicts between the powers of the same religion illustrate the limits which temporal interests imposed upon religion as a guide in international affairs.

There was continual diplomatic communication between Queen Elizabeth and the representatives of the other Protestant powers. The treatment accorded to foreign diplomats varied with the gravity of the international situation, and perhaps with the queen's moods. In the accounts of Danish and Swedish envoys there are complaints about her treating them high-handedly. On several occasions she did not hesitate to show her contempt for Dutch emissaries (who were not of high enough rank for her liking), though she saw even more clearly than they did all the strategic advantages that helping the Dutch and French would bring – such as preserving the continental coast of the English Channel from domination by her enemies. Occasionally she was sharp, and even rude, to the Huguenots, and to a lesser extent with the representatives of various German princes, who by using biblical language tried to remind her of her responsibilities as a patron of the oppressed brethren in faith. Johann Wolf from Zweibrücken, for example, was warned by her that the Germans would be gravely mistaken if they thought of her as a simple and foolish woman who gave money so that Elector Frederick and John Casimir could conduct a war in France as they pleased. As the diplomat tried to defend his pious countrymen, who were fighting for the Huguenots and spending a considerable amount of their yearly income for this purpose, she rounded on the unfortunate man and accused the Germans of being selfish, fickle, evasive and tight-fisted. She requested that these observations be passed on to the German princes. Finally she denounced the French Protestants who acted as changeably as an illogical woman (her words). The audience lasted an hour and a half.[33]

III

Early in Elizabeth's reign, when her country's place in international affairs was still somewhat uncertain and she badly needed allies, not least because of the growing French influence in Scotland, she stressed theology and confessional unity in her dealings with her fellow-Protestants, and especially with those of Germany, much more than she did in her last years: *'pura illa Christi religio, quae in scriptis propheticis, apostolicis et symbolis tradita est, in omnibus nostri regni ecclesiis reponatur'*, she wrote in July 1559 to Augustus of Saxony, the political leader of the German Lutherans.[34]

Even when the queen's religious words appear most sincere, they often had as background the hard politics of national survival. It must be remembered that the use of certain stereotyped religious formulae in the diplomatic correspondence was part of the *commune bonum* of the time; and Elizabeth followed this practice. The letters of condolence, for example, were usually packed with them. Sometimes, perhaps, the sentiments were genuine, as in the case when Elizabeth wrote, on 8 June 1588, to the Danish government because of the sudden death of Frederick II, stating that his death was not only a sad bereavement to her but also a grave loss for Christianity, which the king had protected and furthered during his lifetime. The *'respublica Christiana vera'* could not mourn enough for the *'religionis munitissimum columen'*.[35] The Scandinavian powers had usually tried to stay neutral in the various European wars of the time, but Frederick II, anxious to offer his mediation, had during the last years of his life played an important part in Anglo-Spanish peace negotiations. Two days after the queen signed the letter, her fleet was driven back to Plymouth after struggling in vain against adverse winds at the mouth of the Channel – she had sent it to destroy the Armada at the Spanish coast. There was also no doubt that there would be a decisive battle in which also the fate of the 'True Faith' would be at stake. Frederick's death was a blow not only for the English but also for the West European Protestants fighting the Spanish *tercios*.[36] The fact that the Danish King was accepted as a honest broker by His Most Catholic King as well as by Queen Elizabeth reflects the growing friendliness between Copenhagen and Madrid, which persuaded her to take new political initiatives in order to ensure at least the benevolent neutrality of the Baltic states.

Again, when the queen was informed of an assembly to be held at Magdeburg in 1577 to discuss the ideological differences between the Protestants as a whole and the *rabies theologorum* among the German Lutherans in particular, she forthwith sent the German-born Daniel Rogers as *ad hoc* envoy via Heidelberg to the meeting. The main reason for Rogers' mission, however, was to negotiate in the Palatinate the terms for a loan to a mercenary army and to induce the Count Palatine John Casimir, who was usually willing to oblige if suitably rewarded for his pains, to fight the Spaniards in the Netherlands.[37] This ambitious adventurer, a wild and hard-drinking Calvinist *condottiere*, was on several occasions persuaded by the queen to fight for 'the cause of common faith', especially when there was the prospect of Spanish or Guise warships in the English Channel. When the threat seemed to be imminent, she even promptly paid the promised subsidies to him and his *Reiter* and *Landsknechte*. Maintaining her credibility by such means, she was able, should the need arise, to raise a mercenary army in Germany – thus avoiding the loss of English lives. Although John Casimir's expedition into the Netherlands ended in disaster – as had happened before and would happen again – the queen did not let her protégé down. When he visited England in 1578, he was given a hero's welcome and was invested with the Order of the Garter.[38]

In her diplomatic dealings with her co-religionists Queen Elizabeth posed as a sincere Protestant, but she was usually averse to spending money, not to mention sending regular troops, for the common cause. So, for example, when in the summer of 1583 Navarre had sent Jacques de Ségur-Pardaillan, who had served as a Huguenot envoy in several missions to England, to the queen to ask for help, she refused to give any. In order to get rid of him as soon as possible, she recommended him warmly to a number of European Protestant potentates, including Frederick II of Denmark, and the leading German princes.[39] Although she was well aware that the main purpose of the Huguenot mission was to organise a pan-Protestant political alliance, including England and the German states (which were supposed to provide most of the necessary finance) as well as Navarre and Denmark, in her letter she mentioned only the theological bait of the Huguenot missions: she spoke of a common synod of the Protestants in order to achieve unity in doctrinal matters, particularly those concerning the Eucharist.[40]

Queen Elizabeth's 'theological' arguments were always of a homely sort. It is difficult to find covenant theology, for example, mentioned *expressis verbis* as a proper justification for Protestant alliances. We may note in passing that the Palatine statesmen were less scrupulous in using such terminology to advance their secular aims.[41] In her propaganda in Germany Elizabeth referred frequently to the long-term Catholic programme for destroying the Protestant religion, but she was not astute enough to appeal to German pride of independence by suggesting that a close Protestant co-operation would defend the *fürstliche Libertät* or even the *Freiheit der deutschen Nation*. This argument was freely used by the Palatinate.[42]

Needless to say, the majority of the Lutheran princes suspected the real motives of Elizabeth's diplomacy, despite its conspicuous use of Protestant ideology and religious phraseology, to be primarily secular, i.e. political and national. The English policy of confiscation and narrow pursuit of trading interests had increased antipathy towards England, especially in the Baltic area, and when the queen, frightened by the serious Anglo-Spanish crisis in the late 1560s, started a propaganda campaign in Germany to achieve a wide-based Protestant defensive alliance, the majority of the Lutheran princes thought simply that '*die Königin wollte durch dieses verbundnuss Ihre eigene prophan sache mit Frankreich und Hispanien ausrichten*'.[43]

The English envoys sent to the Lutheran states of Germany and Scandinavia were often instructed to tell their hosts that Queen Elizabeth accepted the doctrines formulated in the *Confessio Augustana* – but usually without convincing them. So the minor princes like Brunswick-Wolfenbüttel or Mecklenburg-Güstrow said on one occasion that they did not know what her religious beliefs were – Calvinist, Zwinglian or even Catholic – but they assumed they were not Lutheran and were anyway a cover for cynical nationalism. They accused her of having involved herself in the French Civil War under the pretence of religious motives, but in reality to advance her own political aims abroad.[44] Even the two Lutheran Electors attacked her religious stance: Augustus of Saxony gave notice that he would enter into an alliance with the queen only if she were willing to adopt religious beliefs which conformed to the *Confessio Augustana*.[45]

Joachim of Brandenburg, for his part, would never ally with Calvinists and Zwinglians. If the Germans were willing to enter into some special agreement with the extremist English, he maintained, they ought to make a still closer alliance with Lutheran Denmark and Sweden. The apparently dominant role of religion in politics among the Germans, in contrast to the English, is well illustrated by the treatment of a French king, desirous to become a member of the Schmalkaldic League: '*wenn er auch zu irer religion trete, so wollten sie in einnemen.*'[46]

Elizabeth's religious beliefs were time and again cited by the Germans as the obstacle to co-operation. But were doctrinal matters really at the centre of German rejection of the queen's proposals? Certainly there were principalities which dismissed them mainly because of theological objections. The strict Gnesio-Lutherans (who thought themselves to be the only genuine Lutherans), especially those of Saxony–Weimar, condemned the English as Zwinglians, and as such little better than Calvinists or Huguenots, whom they thought worse than even the Catholics.[47]

In the course of time confessional-ideological conflicts developed among the Protestants as a whole, theological differences being endemic among the German Lutherans. All this weakened their position as a political group, while the Catholics were gathering strength. A good example of the diminishing solidarity is to be seen as early as during the Second War of Religion in France. The influential Duke Christopher of Württemberg, who knew his way around both at the imperial court and in diplomacy with France, and who had played in the mid-1560s an important role as a mediator in the Anglo-Austrian match, wrote that Prince Condé's cause was '*mer ein privat affect aus hass vnd neid so er zu ettlichen hatt dann ein iusta causa belli*' and that the Palatinate tried to help the Huguenots '*zur erhaltung des Zwinglianismi vnd Calvinismi welches aber gegen gott noch sonsten pollicite nit verthediget kan werden*'.[48] In doing so he no doubt expressed the feelings of the majority of his fellow princes, who considered the wars in France not so much wars of religion as the struggle of ambitious noblemen.

Because of the traditionally close relations between the Netherlands and the empire the German Lutherans were more favourable towards the Dutch rebels than towards the Huguenots. But even there Augustus of Saxony, citing biblical passages, forthrightly condemned, at least in writing to the Duke of Alba, the political doctrine justifying active resistance against lawful authority.[49] This disapproval of re-

bellion against a legitimate ruler was even more strongly expressed by
Queen Elizabeth, who also deeply distrusted the religious enthusiasm
of the French and Dutch Calvinists.

Generally speaking, the Lutheran rulers of Germany, with the
exception of princes like Adolph of Holstein or Joachim of Brandenburg, paid more attention to religion in their policy making than did
Queen Elizabeth. In the Cologne War 1583–85/89 the point at issue,
at least in her eyes, was not so much the *reine Lehre*, as many of the
Germans preferred to see it, but the strategically situated lands of the
Cologne Electorate.[50] The Lutherans, however, had little in common
with their fellow princes (like those of the Electoral Palatinate or
Nassau-Dillenburg) who, mainly for confessional reasons, saw it as
their duty to help other Protestants within their boundaries of the
empire or elsewhere even if that meant violating the valid constitutional laws.

Of course, the Lutheran princes themselves sometimes used religious talk as a cover for political manoeuverings. When it suited
them, they reacted favourably to Queen Elizabeth's policy for *defensio
religionis* against the papal, Spanish and French intrigues, particularly when they thought they would soon be needing her help against a
possible spreading of an international conflict into the empire.[51] On
the other hand, Augustus of Saxony answered the Huguenot diplomats' desperate plea for help for their cause in France with hypocritical words of comfort: the church built upon the true Gospel would
gain victory at the end in spite of temporary reverses.[52] During the
Second War of Religion his total help for the Count Palatine John
Casimir's army sent to France to fight the Catholics had been one
horse! John Casimir's Gnesio-Lutheran brother-in-law, the restless
Duke John William of Saxony-Weimar, a pensioner of the French
Crown, had at the same time led an army into France to fight the
Huguenots.[53] John William – who had earlier made efforts to meddle
in European affairs, even at one stage proposing to Queen Eliza-
beth[54] – and John Casimir both used religious arguments to justify
their actions.

Other Protestant rulers also exploited their co-religionists by the
political use of theological arguments. For example, Henry, King of
Navarre, knowing that without England's firm political, financial and
possibly military support the Huguenot cause would soon be lost,
went on reminding the queen of her responsibilities as the leading
champion of Protestantism to defend the New Religion and its
adherents. Although such requests for overt military help were

consistently backed by the internationalists and interventionists at the English policy-making centre, Elizabeth, especially after the unlucky intervention of the early 1560s, preferred to pursue a policy of officially correct neutrality. Not until the end of her reign did she send English regular troops.[55]

Elizabeth was well aware of the dangers to her continental strategy that might be caused by those princes among her co-religionists who (like herself) were often guided by national interest and not by confessional considerations. A good example was Adolph of Holstein, one of her former suitors and member of the Order of the Garter. Not only was his prosperous duchy situated strategically between the North Sea and the Baltic, but he also shared with her a general hostility towards the Hansa. Yet this Lutheran *condottiere* was a Spanish pensioner as well and did not have any qualms about putting his well-trained mercenaries at the disposal of the Spaniards in the Netherlands.[56] Special attention was paid to him in English instructions; and even in the technical documents, such as codes and ciphers, his name was mentioned after the electors.[57] At one time the Danish king was persuaded to restrain his uncle from fighting the Dutch (and the English).[58]

It has been suggested recently that Queen Elizabeth was not unmoved by religious considerations in the making of her policy. According to this interpretation, she sincerely supported freedom from religious persecution and liberty of conscience. On the other hand, because of her attitudes towards inherited sovereignty, she was reluctant to support Protestant rebellions in Scotland, France and the Netherlands.[59] But we may ask which oppressed Protestants in all Europe she was willing to help. Within the Catholic territories of the empire there was a growing tendency to persecute all Protestants; and within the Lutheran territories not only were Catholics and Anabaptists harassed, but also Calvinists, Zwinglians and even Lutherans of a different doctrinal persuasion from that of the current ruler. There was little the queen could do for any of them. Even worse was the situation in the Spanish mainland or in Italy. Those who needed help most desperately were the Huguenots and the Dutch Protestants, who were both rebels and inflexible Calvinists, for whom the queen had little sympathy. Of the world's oppressed Protestants perhaps the Scots received some help from idealistic motives.

One should not, however, conclude that she was personally not religious. Compared with some of the German princes, such as William of Hesse and Frederick of the Palatinate, or northern monarchs, such as John III of Sweden, she was certainly less familiar with the finesses of doctrinal questions and more impatient with the *rabies theologorum* in general. No doubt she accepted the basic doctrines of the Protestant faith and as a relatively liberal and tolerant ruler was conspicuously uneasy with the demands of her more rigorously Puritan subjects, not to mention the numerous exhortations made by her foreign co-religionists.[60]

IV

The provocative question asked in the title of this paper *For True Faith or National Interest?* implies the existence of an either-or situation. The task of measuring the impact of ideology on the day-to-day policy making of a ruler is not simple. It is in principle hard to tell if Elizabeth's diplomacy was motivated by 'True Faith', i.e. from idealistic defence of Protestantism, or from secular motives, which might be characterised as in the 'National Interest'. For England, like many other Protestant states, was threatened by the Catholic powers, whose aggression was partly occasioned by confessional zeal: a Protestant state in the latter half of the sixteenth century could not keep national security and the maintenance of Protestantism completely apart. Needless to say, national security merges into military and commercial strength; and for the English to lose an important market to the Catholics, for example, would appear to all parties as a weakening of Protestantism. In Counter-Reformation Europe not only would an idealist and a practitioner of *Realpolitik* make the same decisions, but they would often give the same reasons for them, even if they interpreted their reasons differently.

It must not be forgotten that many of the decision makers, even the queen, had money invested in the commercial enterprises of the day, and thereby had an interest in the policies that supported them. If we keep in mind this personal interest and also some of the pressures she had to take cognisance of at council and court, and if we remember her vagueness about doctrine and impatience with nice theological distinctions, we may conclude that she would identify as her political ideals national interest and the national confessional allegiance. If the pragmatically-minded queen had been asked if her policy was motivated by 'True Faith' or 'National Interest', she might well have answered 'yes'.

In this Queen Elizabeth would thus be ranged with a number of other rulers of her time. But it will be admitted that she was successful. If she had no policy, but just drifted with events, this lack of policy was what was required to achieve the aims she might have had. Perhaps she was guided by Higher Powers – as her Advanced Protestant subjects and some earlier historians thought. While she was alive, the Catholic threat was contained, Protestantism as a whole was maintained and her country not only found the strength to meet various internal crises, but had parried the external threats as well. England rose from being a second-rate power in Europe to being one of the main influences in international affairs, in short: 'a new and greater England emerged from the day-to-day turmoil of life.'[61]

Notes

Archives and libraries are cited by the following abbreviations:

AE	Archives des Affaires Étrangères, Paris
AGR	Archives Générales du Royaume, Brussels
AGS	Archivo General de Simancas, Simancas
ASV	Archivio Segreto Vaticano, The Vatican
BL	British Library, London
BN	Bibliothèque Nationale, Paris
CUL	Cambridge University Library, Cambridge
DZA	Deutsches Zentralarchiv, Merseburg
GHA	Geheimes Hausarchiv, Munich
GLA	Badisches Generallandesarchiv, Karlsruhe
GStA	Geheimes Staatsarchiv, Munich
HaStA	Württembergisches Hauptstaatsarchiv, Stuttgart
HHStA	Haus-, Hof- und Staatsarchiv, Vienna
HStA	Hessisches Staatsarchiv, Marburg
KA	Kammararkivet, Stockholm
MLHA	Mecklenburgishes Landeshauptarchiv, Schwerin
RA	Rigsarkivet, Copenhagen
SAL	Staatliches Archivlager, Berlin
SLHA	Sächsisches Landeshauptarchiv, Dresden
SRA	Riksarkivet, Stockholm
StA	Staatsarchiv
StaA	Stadtarchiv
TLHA	Thüringisches Landeshauptarchiv, Weimar
WAPS	Wojewódzkie Archivum Państwowe w Szczecinie, Stettin

Manuscripts cited without location are from the Public Record Office, London.

1. R. B. Wernham, 'English Policy and the Revolt in the Netherlands', in *Britain and the Netherlands*, vol. I (London, 1959), pp. 29–40; idem,

'Elizabethan War Aims and Strategy', in *Elizabethan Government and Society: Essays Presented to Sir John Neale* (London, 1961), pp. 340–68; idem, *Before the Armada: The Growth of English Foreign Policy, 1485–1588* (London, 1966); idem, *The Making of Elizabethan Foreign Policy, 1558–1603* (London, 1980); idem, *After the Armada: Elizabethan England and the Struggle for Western Europe, 1588–1595* (Oxford, 1984).

2. Charles Wilson, *Queen Elizabeth and the Revolt of the Netherlands* (London, 1970).

3. For the earlier interpretation see Conyers Read, *Mr Secretary Walsingham and the Policy of Queen Elizabeth* (3 vols, Oxford, 1925); idem, *Mr Secretary Cecil and Queen Elizabeth* (London, 1955); idem, *Lord Burghley and Queen Elizabeth* (London, 1960); A. L. Rowse, *The England of Elizabeth* (London, 1950). For the newer interpretation see Wallace T. MacCaffrey, *The Shaping of the Elizabethan Regime: Elizabethan Politics, 1558–72* (London, 1969); idem, *Queen Elizabeth and the Making of Policy, 1572–1588* (Princeton, NJ, 1981); G. D. Ramsay, *The City of London in International Politics at the Accession of Elizabeth Tudor* (Manchester, 1975); idem, 'The Foreign Policy of Elizabeth I', in C. Haigh (ed.), *The Reign of Elizabeth I* (London, 1984), pp. 147–68.

4. E. I. Kouri, *England and the Attempts to Form a Protestant Alliance in the late 1560s: A Case Study in European Diplomacy* (Annales Academiae Scientiarum Fennicae, Ser. B, CCX) (Helsinki, 1981), pp. 193, 197.

5. See esp. MacCaffrey, *Queen Elizabeth*; and Simon Adams, 'Eliza Enthroned? The Court and Its Politics', in Haigh, *Reign of Elizabeth*, pp. 55–77.

6. Kouri, pp. 14–15.

7. Edward Edwards, *The Life of Sir Walter Raleigh . . . together with His Letters* (2 vols, London, 1868), vol. I, p. 245. Sir Francis Walsingham said of England's policy towards the Dutch: 'So our half-doing doth breed dishonour', Wilson, p. 105.

8. Arnold Pritchard, *Catholic Loyalism in Elizabethan England* (London, 1979). See also Adrian Morey, *The Catholic Subjects of Elizabeth I* (London, 1978).

9. H. G. Koenigsberger, 'The Organisation of Revolutionary Parties in France and in the Netherlands during the Sixteenth Century', *Journal of Modern History*, XXVII (1955), p. 350.

10. For confessional policy see esp. Ernst Walter Zeeden, *Die Entstehung der Konfessionen. Grundlagen und Formen der Konfessionsbildung im Zeitalter der Glaubenskämpfe* (Münster, 1965), pp. 40, 123; idem, *Das Zeitalter der Gegenreformation* (Freiburg im Breisgau, 1967), pp. 106–7, 112–15, 189–91, 210–16, 265–7; idem, 'Grundlagen und Wege der Konfessionsbildung in Deutschland im Zeitalter der Glaubenskämpfe', in *Gegenreformation* (Wege der Forschung, CCCXI) (Darmstadt, 1973), pp. 96–101; idem, *Hegemonialkriege und Glaubenskämpfe 1556–1648* (*Propyläen Geschichte Europas*, vol. II) (Frankfurt am Main/Berlin/Vienna, 1977), pp. 11–12, 16, 81–2, 151–3, 160, 225; idem, *Konfessionsbildung. Studien zur Reformation, Gegenreformation und katholischen Reform* (Spätmittelalter und Frühe Neuzeit. Tübinger Beiträge zur Geschichtsforschung, XV) (Stuttgart, 1985), pp. 278–83.

11.   Hubert Jedin, *Geschichte des Konzils von Trient*, vol. IV (Freiburg im Breisgau, 1975). For the treaty of Cateau-Cambrésis see still: Alphonse de Ruble, *Le traité de Cateau-Cambrésis* (Paris, 1889).

12.   See, for example, the Palatine memorial, *s. d.* (late April 1569), SLHA, Geh. Arch., Loc. 7278, Copy; GStA, Ks 16682, Draft. Frederick of the Palatinate to Christoph Ehem, 6 June 1569, GHA, Korrespondenzakten 982/II, Copy. Report of the Brandenburg–Ansbach delegation, 10 September 1569, StA Nuremberg, Ansb. Rel. Akt. 31, Orig.

13.   See, for example, Elizabeth I's instructions to Sir Thomas Bodley of 27 April 1585, SP 81/3, Copy; and Bodley to Sir Francis Walsingham, 31 May 1585, BL, Cotton MS. Galba, D IX, fo. 47r, Orig. See also the letters Queen Elizabeth sent on 27 April 1585 *mutatis mutandis* to Frederick II of Denmark, RA, TKUA, England A I 1, Orig.; William of Hesse-Kassel, HStA Marburg, 4f Frankreich 620, Orig.; Augustus of Saxony, SLHA, Geh. Arch., Loc. 7280, fos. 18r–19r, Orig.; and John George of Brandenburg, ibid., fos. 2r–4r, Copy; Louis of Württemberg, HaStA Stuttgart, Rep. A 63, Bü 64, Orig. Copies of Elizabeth's letters to the electors of Saxony and Brandenburg, dukes of Brunswick-Lüneburg, Holstein and Württemberg, landgrave of Hesse-Kassel, Count Palatine John Casimir and Thomas Bodley (mostly in the form of extracts) in SAL, StA Schwerin, Aw 103, fos. 296r–299r, 304v–305r; and in CUL, Dd. 3.20, fos. 224r–230r. Elizabeth's letters to Württemberg and Holstein, printed in E. I. Kouri (ed.), *Elizabethan England and Europe* (*Bulletin of the Institute of Historical Research*, Special Supplement, XII) (London 1982), pp. 45–9. The letter to Hesse is printed in E. I. Kouri (ed.), 'Six Unprinted Letters from Elizabeth of England to German and Scandinavian Princes', *Archiv für Reformationsgeschichte*, LXXIII (1982), pp. 246–8.

14.   Michele Bonelli to Giovanni Antonio Fachinetti, 9 February 1569, ASV, Segr. di Stato, Nunz. Ven. 8, Copy, The extract printed in *C[alendar of] S[tate] P[apers] R[ome] 1558–71*, p. 298, is taken from fo. 84, not fo. 80.

15.   For a short introduction to Palatine history see Claus-Peter Clasen, *The Palatinate in European History 1555–1618* (Oxford, 1966); and for the Upper Palatinate Volker Press, 'Die Grundlagen der Kurpfälzischen Herrschaft in der Oberpfalz 1499–1621', *Verhandlungen des Historischen Vereins für Oberpfalz und Regensburg*, CXVII (1977), esp. pp. 43–61; idem, *Calvinismus und Territorialstaat: Regierung und Zentralbehörden der Kurpfalz 1559–1619* (Kieler Historische Studien, VII) (Stuttgart, 1970).

16.   The minutes of the Palatine Council meeting, 14 July 1568, GStA, Kb 89/3a, Draft.

17.   The Palatine memorial, *s. d.* (May 1569), SLHA, Geh. Arch., Loc. 7278, Copy; GStA, Ks 16682, Draft. Among the English MSS. there is an undated Latin summary of the Palatinate embassy to Saxony (May 1569), BL, Lansd. MS. 100/23.

18.   Ernst Koch, 'Striving for the union of Lutheran churches: the church-historical background of the work done on the Formula of Concord at Magdeburg', *Sixteenth Century Journal*, VIII (1977), pp. 108–15; and Gerhard Müller, 'Alliance and confession: the theological-historical

development and ecclesiastical significance of Reformation confessions', ibid., pp. 136–40. See also Bernhard Lohse, 'Das Konkordienwerk von 1580', in *Kirche und Bekenntnis. Historische und theologische Aspekte zur Frage der lutherischen und der katholischen Kirche auf der Grundlage der Confessio Augustana* (Wiesbaden, 1980), pp. 106–22; Jörg Baur, 'Abendmahlslehre und Christologie der Konkordienformel als Bekenntnis zum menschlichen Gott', in *Bekenntnis und Einheit der Kirche. Studien zum Konkordienbuch im Auftrag der Sektion Kirchengeschichte der Wissenschaftlichen Gesellschaft für Theologie* (Stuttgart, 1980), pp. 195–218; and Gottfried Adam, 'Erwählung im Horizont der Christologie', ibid., pp. 219–33.

19. *Der Augsburger Religionsfriede vom 25. September 1555. Kritische Ausgabe des Textes mit den Entwürfen und der Königlichen Deklaration*, ed. Karl Brandi, 2nd edn (Göttingen, 1927). See also Fritz Dickmann, 'Das Problem der Gleichberechtigung der Konfessionen im Reich im 16. und 17. Jahrundert', in *Zur Geschichte der Toleranz und Religionsfreiheit* (Darmstadt, 1977), pp. 203–51; Otto Dann, *Gleichheit und Gleichberechtigung. Das Gleichheitspostulat in der alteuropäischen Tradition und Deutschland bis zum ausgehenden 19. Jahrhundert* (Historische Forschungen, XVI) (Berlin, 1980), pp. 114–16; Heinz Duchhardt, *Protestantisches Kaisertum und Altes Reich. Die Diskussion über die Konfession des Kaisers in Politik, Publizistik und Staatsrecht* (Veröffentlichungen des Instituts für Europäische Geschichte Mainz, LXXXVII) (Wiesbaden, 1977); Martin Heckel, *Deutschland im konfessionellen Zeitalter* (*Deutsche Geschichte*, vol. V) (Göttingen, 1983), pp. 33–66.

20. Gaston Zeller, *La réunion de la Metz à la France 1552–1648* (Publications de la faculté des lettres de l'université de Strasbourg, XXXV) (Paris, 1926).

21. S. Issleib, 'Moritz von Sachsen und die Ernestiner 1547–1553', *Neues Archiv für sächsische Geschichte und Altertumskunde*, XXIV (1903), pp. 248–306. For the German territorial princes and their policies in general see Ernst Walter Zeeden, 'Das Zeitalter der Glaubenskämpfe (1555–1648)', *Handbuch der deutschen Geschichte*, vol. II, 9th edn (Stuttgart, 1970), pp. 192–5. In English there are two studies by F. L. Carsten, *The Origins of Prussia* (Oxford, 1954) and *Princes and Parliaments in Germany from the Fifteenth to the Eighteenth Century* (Oxford, 1959). The last chapter of the latter is published also in German: idem, 'Die deutschen Landstände und der Aufstieg der Fürsten', *Die Welt als Geschichte. Zeitschrift für Universalgeschichtliche Forschung*, XX (1960), pp. 16–29. See also Henry J. Cohn, *The Government of the Rhine Palatinate in the Fifteenth Century* (Oxford, 1965).

22. See esp. The Resolution of the Maulbronn convention, 17 July 1567, GStA, Ks, 16680, Orig.

23. Elizabeth I to Eric XIV, 22 June 1561, SRA, Anglica 514, Orig. In my forthcoming *Politics, Commerce and Religion in the Elizabethan Period* a number of documents related to the Anglo-Swedish match will be printed *in extenso*.

24. For a comprehensive survey on Swedish foreign policy on the period

see Wilhelm Tham, *Den svenska utrikespolitikens historia* (2 vols, Stockholm, 1960). See also Henryk Zins, *England and the Baltic in the Elizabethan Period* (Manchester, 1972); Artur Attman, *The Struggle for Baltic Markets: Powers in Conflict, 1558–1618* (Acta Regiae Societatis Scientiarum et Litterarum Gothoburgensis, Ser. Humaniora, XIV) (Gothenburg, 1979).

25.   Oscar Garstein, *Rome and the Counter-Reformation in Scandinavia until the Establishment of the S. Congregatio de Propaganda Fide in 1622* (2 vols, Oslo, 1963–80); Vello Helk, *Laurentius Nicolai Norvegus* (Kirkehistoriske studier, II, 2) (Copenhagen, 1966).

26.   See esp. the numerous documents preserved in AGS, Secr. de Estado, 687.

27.   Gaston Zeller, *Les temps modernes. Histoire de relations internationales* (2 vols, Paris, 1953), vol. I, pp. 82–4. Concerning French diplomacy in the Baltic see H. F. Rördam, 'Résidents français près de la cour de Danemark', *Bulletin de l'Académie royale des sciences et des lettres de Danemark*, XIII (1898), pp. 619–69; Alfred Richard, *Charles Danzay, ambassadeur de France en Danemark* (Poitiers, 1910), pp. 10–78; and G. Baguenault de Puchesse, 'Un ambassadeur de France en Danemark au seizième siècle', *Revue d'histoire diplomatique*, XXV (1911), pp. 185–94. Since the mid-sixteenth century the northern powers had used mainly native diplomats. For Sweden see KA, Kammaren före 1630, Diplomaträkenskaper, 1542–1719, 3–6.

28.   For Sir Francis Walsingham's sources of intelligence, *c.* 1580–90, see SP 12/232, fo. 12. For Robert Cecil's intelligence service in 1598, see SP 12/265, fo. 133.

29.   For Swedish foreign policy in the mid-sixteenth century, see esp. the balanced and well-documented study by Sven Lundkvist, *Gustav Vasa och Europa. Svensk handels- och utrikespolitik 1534–1557* (Studia historica Upsaliensia, II) (Uppsala, 1960).

30.   So, for example, of the £20,000 paid to the Huguenots in the summer of 1569 £7469 was delivered at Hamburg through the Merchants Adventurers and the remaining £12,531 in London: The instructions to Sir Thomas Gresham, 28 July 1569, BL, Lansd. MS. 102, Draft. Payment of the loans started on 30 July 1569; see E 351/31. The loan was advanced against the security of jewels sent to England by the Huguenots: see Coligny to Cecil, 6 June 1569, and the inventory of the jewels sent to England, 12 June 1569, BL, Cotton MS. Caligula, E VI, Orig.; Copy in BN, Moreau 718.

31.   In early 1589, after accusing the Hansa of having supported the Spaniards, some 60 Hanseatic vessels in Lisbon were seized on the order of the Privy Council: *A[cts of the] P[rivy] C[ouncil], 1588–89*, p. 192; see the declaration of the Privy Council on 27 July 1589, *Kölner Inventar*, ed. K. Höhlbaum and H. Keussen (*Inventare hansischer Archive des sechzehnten Jahrhunderts*, I/II) (2 vols, Leipzig, 1896–1903), pp. 937–9. See also *A declaration of the causes which moved the chief commander to take and arrest in the mouth of the river of Lisbon certain ships* (1589). It was written by Robert Beale: BL, Add. MS. 48023, fos. 220–29, Draft. Elizabeth I to John Frederick of Pomerania-

Stettin, 15 December 1597, WAPS, Rep. 4, P I Tit. 14, Nr. 8, Orig.
Printed in Kouri, *Elizabethan England*, pp. 66–71. For international
practices see Antonio Maria Salviati to Ptolemaio Galli, 2 October
1577, ASV, Segr. di Stato, Nunz. Francia 10, Orig.; Rudolph II to
Elizabeth I, 12 August 1582, HHStA, SAAS England, Hofkorrespon-
denz 2, Copy; Frederick II of Denmark to the Hansa Towns, 15
December 1585, BL, Add. MS. 48009, fos. 757–60, 763–64, Copies.

32.   According to Camden, the Germans' attitude amounted to 'hatred':
William Camden, *The historie of the most renowned and virtuous
Princesse Elizabeth* (London, 1630), p. 413. Even when the ships of
neutral or friendly states were victims of the English confiscation
policy, the queen usually refused all the claims for restitution or
redress: see, for example, Elizabeth I to Christian IV of Denmark,
7.6.1592 and 30.11.1594, RA, TKUA, England A I 1, Orig. Elizabeth I
to George Frederick of Brandenburg, 20.7.1594 and 12.5.1595, SAL,
StA Königsberg, HBA, G 747 and G 748, Orig. See also Albert
Frederick of Prussia to Elizabeth, 25 September 1569, SAL, StA
Königsberg, HBA, Konzepte G, 1263, Draft. The German princes tried
also to obtain safe-conducts from the queen for their ships: John Albert
of Mecklenburg-Schwerin to Elizabeth, 8 April 1569, BL, Cotton MS.
Galba, B XI, Orig.

33.   Johann Wolf's account, October 1569, HStA Marburg, 4f Pfalz 798,
Copy. In June 1568 the Huguenots owed 50,000 livres and 27,000
Gulden to the Palatinate: see John Casimir to Frederick of the
Palatinate, 3 June 1568, GStA, Ks 16681. I have found no evidence that
the Huguenots paid the money back at all. In 1577 the Palatinate's
ordinary revenue was given as 122,940 Gulden: GLA 77/6135 [1
Gulden = 3*s*. 9*d*; 1 livre (sol-denier) = 2*s*.].

34.   Elizabeth I to Augustus of Saxony, 3 December 1559, SLHA, Geh.
Arch. Loc. 8019, Orig.

35.   *Nec vero nobis solum hoc tam acerbo casu incredibile detrimentum
accidit, sed religioni etiam Christianae (cuius dum vixit unicus fautor
erat quamque studiose sempre auxerat) grave vulnus inflictum est. Non
satis igitur dolenter nec sui clementissimum et optimum principem nec nos
fidissimum fratrem et amicum coniunctissimum nec respublica Christiana
vera religionis munitissimum columem deflere possumus.* Elizabeth I to
the Danish Chancellor and Councillors, 8 June 1588, RA, TKUA,
England A I 1, Orig.

36.   In the summer of 1586 a Danish ambassador negotiated with Queen
Elizabeth: *C[alendar of] S[tate] P[apers] S[panish] 1580–86*, pp.
584–5; and in the following spring Frederick II sent an ambassador to
Philip II: *CSPS 1587–1603*, p. 235. Later, Frederick II proposed to
despatch commissioners to Emden in August and asked the English
and the Spanish to do the same: Walsingham to Buckhurst, 13 June
1587, SP 84/15; Burghley and Sir James Croft to Andrea de Loo, 14
June 1587, SP 77/1. In August 1587 the queen suggested to Frederick II
that the Anglo-Spanish peace negotiations should be held in late
September at Bergen-op-Zoom: Elizabeth I to Frederick II, 23 August
1587, RA, TKUA, England A I 1, Orig. In September she decided to

send Daniel Rogers to Denmark: Burghley to Walsingham, 11 September 1587, SP 12/203; Instructions for Rogers, 20 September 1587, SP 75/1.

37. Kervyn Lettenhove (ed.), *Relations politiques des Pays-Bas et l'Angleterre sous le regne de Philippe II (Chroniques belges inédites*, X) (11 vols, Brussels, 1882–1900), p. 281. See also Elizabeth I to Louis VI of the Palatinate, 21 August 1577, SLHA, Geh. Arch., Loc 7278, fo. 232r, Copy. Copies in HaStA Stuttgart, A 114, Bü 9, Nr. 2; DZA, Hist. Abt. II, Rep. 13, Nr. 15cd, Fasc. 4, fo. 19r–v; SP 104/163, fo. 29v; BL, Add. MS. 48128, fo. 151r. Printed in Kouri, *Elizabethan England and Europe*, pp. 32–3. There are numerous documents relating to the convention of Magdeburg in BL, Add. MS. 480485.

38. In Friedrich von Bezold (ed.), *Briefe des Pfalzgrafen Johann Casimir mit verwandten Schriftstücken* (3 vols, Munich, 1882–1903) appear a number of Queen Elizabeth's letters which throw light on Anglo-Palatine dealings on behalf of the Dutch rebels and the Huguenots.

39. Instructions to Jacques de Ségur-Pardaillan, 15 July 1583, AE, Correspondance Politique, Allemagne 2, Copy. Copies also in SP 78/10, fo. 2; BL, Add. MS. 48126; DZA, Hist. Abt. II, Rep. 11 Nr. 82, Fasc. 5, and Nr. 89, Fasc. 3; GStA, Ks 16693; StaA Frankfurt am Main, Reichssachen III, Mb A 1. On 6 October 1583 Queen Elizabeth sent *mutatis mutandis* letters to Frederick II of Denmark, RA, TKUA, England A I 1, Orig.; Augustus of Saxony, SLHA, Geh. Arch., Loc. 9304, fo. 73r; John George of Brandenburg, DZA, Hist. Abt. II, Rep. 11, Nr. 89, Fasc. 3, fo. 13r–v, and SLHA, Geh. Arch., Loc. 9304, fo. 20r–v, Copies. Copies of the queen's letters to Augustus of Saxony, John George of Brandenburg, Jacques de Ségur-Pardaillan, Julius of Brunswick-Wolfenbüttel, Louis of Württemberg, John Casimir and Louis of the Palatinate as well as William of Hesse-Kassel in CUL, Dd. 3.20, fos. 198v–203r.

40. The internal theological development in Germany in the early 1580s was determined first by the questions about the doctrines of the Lord's Supper and Christology, and secondly by the arguments concerning original sin and justification by faith. In the East German archives, particularly, there is still a great amount of material – little used or unseen – relating to the various meetings held by the quarrelling theologians: see esp. DZA, Hist. Abt. II, Rep. 13:6/3–6, 9; 7–8a; 13a; 14cd/1–2; 14c(2); 14ef; 15ab/1–12; 15e; 15g–o; 15s–u; 16/1, 5; 17/2–9; Rep. 14: 7/1–5; 8b/1–4; 8c/2–7; 9a/4. SLHA, Geh. Arch., Loc. 9310, 10303, 10306, 10309–10, 10316–17, 10321–26.

41. The Palatine memorial, *s. d.* (May 1569), SLHA, Gen. Arch., Loc. 7278, Copy; GStA, Ks 16682, Draft. See also the minutes of a secret session of the Palatine *Oberrat* at Heidelberg, 7 December 1569, GStA, Ks 16683, Copy. For the role of covenant theology in policy making in general see Gerhard Oestreich, 'Die Idee des religiösen Bundes und die Lehre vom Staatsvertrag', in *Zur Geschichte und Problematik der Demokratie: Festgabe für Hans Herzfeld* (Berlin, 1958), esp. pp. 19–20.

42. John Casimir of the Palatinate to John of Brandenburg-Küstrin, 25 July 1569, DZA, Hist. Abt. II, Rep. 14, Nr. 8a Fasc. 1, Orig.; idem to

Julius of Brunswick-Wolfenbüttel, 25 July and 6 August 1569, GStA, Ks 16682, Copies.

43. Report of the Mecklenburg delegation at the Convention of Erfurt, 10 September 1569, MLHA, Reichstagsakten, III 037, Draft.

44. Report of the Brandenburg–Küstrin delegation, 10 September 1569, DZA, Hist. Abt. II, Rep. 14, Nr. 8a, Fasc. 1, Orig.; Report of the Mecklenburg delegation, 10 September 1569, MLHA, Reichstagsakten, III 037, Draft.

45. Christoph Ehem's report, 19 September 1569, GStA, Ks 16682, Copy.

46. Report of the Saxony–Weimar delegation, 10 September 1569, TLHA, Ernestinisches Gesamtarchiv, Reg. 344, Orig.; Report of the Mecklenburg delegation, 10 September 1569, MLHA. Reichstagsakten, III 037, Draft; Report of the Brandenburg–Ansbach delegation, 10 September 1569, StA Nuremberg, Ansb. Rel. Akt. 31, Orig.

47. Nicolaus Schenk von Schmiedberg to John Casimir, 25 September 1569, GStA, Ks 16682, Draft.

48. Christopher of Württemberg's memorandum, s. d., HaStA Stuttgart, G 2–8 XLIX, Bü. 2/1a, Draft. For his part in trying to arrange a match between Queen Elizabeth and Archduke Charles of Austria see esp. HaStA Stuttgart, A 114 England 5, and HHStA, SAAS England, Dipl. Korr. 16.

49. Augustus of Saxony to the Duke of Alba, 6 December 1567, AGR, Secr. Allem. 175, Orig.

50. Gebhard's most active ally at the time, the Count Palatine John Casimir, was supported by English and Dutch money, while Spanish and Bavarian troops reinforced his rival, Ernest von Wittelsbach. For the Cologne War see Max Lossen, *Der Kölnische Krieg* (2 vols, Munich/Leipzig, 1882–97); Günther von Lojewski, *Bayerns Weg nach Köln. Geschichte der bayerischen Bistumspolitik in der zweiten Hälfte des 16. Jahrhunderts* (Bonner Historische Forschungen, XXI) (Bonn, 1962); Franziska Jäger-von Hoesslin (ed.), *Die Korrespondenzen der Kurfürsten von Köln aus dem Hause Wittelsbach (1583–1761) mit ihren bayerischen Verwandten* (Publikationen der Gesellschaft für Rheinische Geschichtskunde, LXI) (Düsseldorf, 1978).

51 Augustus of Saxony to George Frederick of Brandenburg (and *mutatis mutandis*) Ulrich of Mecklenburg-Güstrow, Joachim Ernest and Bernard of Anhalt, 26 June 1569, SLHA, Geh. Arch. Loc. 7278, Drafts. There are three copies of this letter at GStA, Ks 16682, fos. 341–2, 370–71, and Ks 16683, fos. 52–53; and idem to Frederick II of Denmark, 24 June and 17 July 1569, RA, TKUA, Sachsen A I 8, Orig. Joachim of Brandenburg to Christoph Ehem, 28 May 1569, DZA, Hist. Abt. II, Rep. 11, Nr. 1, Fasc. 1, Copy, and Rep. 14, Nr. 1 Fasc. 4, Draft; idem to John of Brandenburg–Küstrin, 13 June 1569, DZA, Hist. Abt. II, Rep. 14, Nr. 8a Fasc. 1, Orig.

52. Augustus of Saxony to de Vézines, 4 August 1569, SLHA, Geh. Arch., Loc. 7278; GStA, Ks 16682; HStA Marburg, 4f England 1, 4f England 4, Copies. See also Vézines to Augustus of Saxony, 3 August 1569, SLHA, Geh. Arch., Loc. 7278, Orig.

53. In a list of the German pensioners of the French Crown about 1565, John William's pension is 23,160 livres and that of John Frederick, John William's brother, 15,000 livres. The total sum paid to the German pensioners was 117,340 livres: BN, 500 Colbert 397, Copy.

54. At the TLHA there are numerous documents relating to the Anglo-Saxon match: Ernestinisches Gesamtarchiv, Reg. D 371 and 420; see also Reg. J 190 and Reg. K 1.

55. See esp. H. A. Lloyd, *The Rouen Campaign 1590–1592* (Oxford, 1973); and Wernham, *After the Armada.*

56. Duke Adolph drew yearly 6000 florins from Spain, the highest sum it paid to a German prince: Charles Weiss (ed.), *Papiers d'État du Cardinal de Granvelle, d'après les manuscrits de la bibliothèque de Besançon* (*Collection de documents inédits sur l'histoire de France*), 9 vols (Paris, 1841–52), vol. VIII, p. 183.

57. See, for example, code and cipher for Henry Killigrew's mission, 28 January 1569, SP 106/1, Copy. Warrant for Killigrew's mission, 26 January 1569, PRO 2/15, Orig. Instructions for Killigrew's mission, 26 January 1569, BL, Cotton MS. Galba, B XI, Draft; Cotton MS. Julius, F VI and Add. MS. 48018, Copies.

58. Elizabeth I to Frederick II of Denmark, 27 April 1586. RA, TKUA, England A I 1, Orig.

59. Simon Adams, 'The Queen Embattled', in *Queen Elizabeth I: Most Politick Princess* (London, 1984), p. 41.

60. For the numerous studies on Elizabethan Protestantism see esp. Patrick Collinson, *The Elizabethan Puritan Movement* (London, 1967); idem, *Archbishop Grindal 1519–1583. The Struggle for a Reformed Church* (London, 1980); idem, *The Religion of Protestants. The Church in English Society 1559–1625* (Oxford, 1982); idem, *Godly People. Essays on English Protestantism and Puritanism* (London, 1983). See also P. G. Lake, *Moderate Puritans and the Elizabethan Church* (Cambridge, 1982).

61. G. R. Elton, *England under the Tudors*, 2nd edn (London, 1974), p. 475.

20 Queen Elizabeth I, the Emperor Rudolph II, and Archduke Ernest, 1593–94

R. B. Wernham

The conversion of Henry IV to Catholicism in 1593 gave Queen Elizabeth I and her ministers serious cause to review their continental policies. Many of its effects were certainly much to England's advantage. The collapse of Spain's ally, the Catholic League, in France within the next twelve or eighteen months, if it did not entirely restore the balance between Spain and the French monarchy, at least removed their conflict from the heart of France to its frontier. The distraction of Spain's resources from 1589 to intervention in France also allowed the Dutch, by the summer of 1594, to clear the north-eastern Netherlands right up to the German border and so make their conflict with Spain now likewise a war fought mainly on their southern frontier along or south of the Rhine and Maas. All this made it possible for England by the end of 1593 to withdraw her troops from Normandy and by the end of 1594 from Brittany as well and to begin suggesting to the Dutch that the time had come for them to carry out their treaty obligation to reimburse Elizabeth's expenses on their behalf since 1585.[1]

But for England Henry IV's conversion did bring anxieties as well as relief. It is true he was quick to sign a reciprocal 'bond of amity', promising never to make a separate peace with Spain.[2] But like his grandson Charles II of England, Henry IV had too often already shown himself: 'a King Whose word no man relies on'. And the rumours inspired by the curious secretive mission of his servant La Varenne to Madrid in the summer of 1593[3] did little to encourage trust. Anyway, the reconciliation that Henry was seeking with the pope hardly seemed likely to strengthen his friendship with the excommunicated Elizabeth.[4] Even though he might not be prepared to join a Catholic crusade against her, he might well be persuaded to make his peace with the Most Catholic King of Spain and so to leave

England, with only the Dutch to help her and with Ireland breaking into open rebellion, to face the full might of Spain, and of a Spain whose Atlantic naval forces were fast recovering from the disaster of 1588. Nor was this all. At just about the time of Henry IV's conversion, the endemic border squabbles in Hungary and Croatia flared up into full-scale war between the Emperor Rudolph II and the Turks. And even before that happened, Catholic propagandists were publishing at Prague and throughout Germany plausible libels, with doctored documents, accusing Elizabeth of encouraging Turkish attacks on Christendom. Moreover, the Hanseatic Towns of northern Germany, together with Danzig and the Scandinavian countries, Lutheran though they were, were becoming increasingly aggrieved over English interference with their trade in corn, timber, metals, and naval stores to Spain and Portugal. In retaliation the Hansa cities were seeking to persuade the emperor and the imperial diet to ban the English Merchants Adventurers from Stade, and indeed from all Germany, on the ground that as a monopolist company they infringed the laws of the empire. It seemed possible, therefore, that unless new policy initiatives were taken England might find herself faced by the more or less open hostility of almost the whole of Europe.

Now, although Henry IV's conversion did not actually take place until 12 July 1593, already by the early spring it had become highly probable and Elizabeth and her ministers were growing palpably anxious about the possible consequences for England. It was partly on account of this anxiety that on 14 April Burghley drafted a letter from the queen and instructions for Dr Christopher Parkins for a mission to the emperor.[5] After protesting about the libels that accused the queen of stirring up the Turks, Parkins was to offer the services of the English ambassador at Constantinople, Edward Barton, to mediate a peace between the emperor and the Turk as he had done between the Turk and the Poles three years earlier. Parkins was then to point out that

> as by the war that is to proceed from the Turk all the parts of Germany and the east parts of Christendom and some great part of Italy shall feel the burden of the same ... so on the other part of Christendom westward it is lamentably seen how all France, the Low Countries, our realms of England and Ireland, and now of late the kingdom of Scotland is already threatened from Spain and provoked to rebellion ... [and] ... all these wars attempted by the

King of Spain against so many kingdoms and countries are only to conquer the same without any colour of title.

The queen therefore hoped that as she would move the Turk to peace with the emperor in the east, so the emperor would 'admonish the Pope and advise the King of Spain to alter their violent course' in the west. For, once Christendom was united and at peace with itself, the Turks would hardly dare to attack it.

Parkins was at Stade before the end of May and reached Prague early in June. At private audiences on 16 June and 4 July he presented to the emperor the matters contained in his instructions, with the assurance that 'Her Majesty for the public good of Christendom will be as ready to hearken [to peace], if it be soundly and sincerely handled, as the King of Spain'. Also 'for that Her Majesty by her own speech willed me to make some insinuation in good sort of the Garter, I made mention that this kind of honour, as a singular outward bond of friendship, had been granted and gratefully accepted of many emperors'. In discussions with the emperor's ministers he also justified the queen's treatment of the Hansards and protested against their efforts to get a ban imposed upon the Merchants Adventurers.

On all these matters Parkins received encouragingly friendly answers. The emperor promptly ordered the suppression of the libels against the queen and readily accepted her denial of encouraging the Turks. He promised that he would deliberate 'how far he might use Her Majesty's friendly offer' of mediation, though 'his state was such that it behoved him not to fear the power of any adversary'. On 10 July Curtius, the vice-chancellor, further told Parkins that 'the Emperor had this day sent a messenger into Spain with special letters to the King and to his own ambassador there resident, to the effect of peace, exhorting the King that he should not use in this treaty any men that gained by wars, or rash wits'. Finally, while disclaiming knowledge of any mandate against the Merchants Adventurers, the councillors wished that some messenger from the queen might argue the English case against the Hansa before the imperial diet as Parkins had stated it to them. The emperor had also spoken about his brother, Archduke Ernest, going to take up the government of the Spanish Netherlands and 'it seemeth that the good disposition of these princes, fitly handled, may be used to some good effects'.[6]

The good effects, however, were slow to appear. A number of copies of the libels against the queen were seized and destroyed. But the emperor's ministers did not forward to Constantinople the letters for Barton[7] that Parkins had left with them nor did they communicate with him themselves. Barton, therefore, who had long been pressing the Turks to send their navy against the Habsburg King of Spain, found it difficult to persuade the sultan, and even more difficult to persuade the bellicose grand vizier Sinan Pasha, to call off their attack on the King of Spain's Habsburg cousin, the emperor.[8] Meanwhile there seemed no sign of the emperor's efforts moderating Spanish aggressiveness, at least not against France or England. The revival of Spain's Atlantic naval forces was gathering pace and in Brittany the advance of the League and Spanish forces towards Brest threatened to provide them with the forward base that the 1588 Armada had lacked.[9]

So, when late in January 1594 Archduke Ernest at last arrived in Brussels, some of Elizabeth's ministers – particularly, it seems, Burghley and his son Sir Robert Cecil – felt that the time had come to remind him of his brother's promises. They drew up a paper of 'Divers reasons to move Her Majesty to send some special gent. to the Archduke Ernestus being lately come into the Low Countries'.[10] The envoy should, they suggested, mention Barton's dealings with the sultan, with Sinan Pasha, and through the sultana to get the Turks to call off their warlike preparations.[11] But he should also complain that the emperor had failed to inform the queen whether he wanted those dealings to be continued or was able, and preferred, to deal with the Turks by force of arms; nor had the emperor made any report about the success of his urging the King of Spain to peace. The queen could not think that Archduke Ernest had left the hereditary Habsburg lands, so threatened by the Turks, unless it were to procure a general peace that would allow him to take back to Austria and Hungary the Spanish forces prepared for wars in France and the Low Countries. Yet the King of Spain was making new and increased preparations for war, especially against Brittany and France and at sea against her realms. To procure a general peace in Christendom

> we think the only means, and the best, to be to withdraw these foreign forces which the King of Spain maintaineth apparently in his opinion to conquer France and consequently to subdue the Low Countries to a servitude and thereby to have commodity to invade ours as hath been determined of long time by the councillors of Spain. But if these forces may be totally removed and sent into Hungary against the common enemy, then there may be a most certain general peace obtained in Christendom.

For neither Elizabeth nor the French king nor the people of the Low Countries wanted anything more than 'to possess their own rights with peace and quietness'.

These were, of course, the same terms that Elizabeth had consistently and repeatedly been urging upon Spain ever since the first negotiations with the Duke of Alba in 1567–68 – the withdrawal of foreign troops and the restoration of the Netherlands to the rights and liberties that they had enjoyed under Charles V and his predecessors,[12] so that neither 'the French possess nor the Spaniards tyrannise in the Low Countries'.[13]

But before the queen had time to make up her mind (assuming that the paper was in fact put before her) to send such an envoy to the archduke, something occurred that very considerably lessened any hope that the Spaniards might listen to peace upon such conditions. The Earl of Essex claimed to have uncovered a plot to poison the queen by Dr Ruy Lopez, her Portuguese physician. Was this perhaps a neatly timed countermining of the Cecils' readiness to explore pacific alternatives to continued war against Spain? The plot, Essex claimed, was the work, if not of the king of Spain himself, certainly of the Count of Fuentes and Esteban de Ibarra, his principal ministers in Brussels, and of Cristóbal Moro, one of his secretaries of state in Spain. The queen and the Cecils were at first sceptical about the earl's claims and historians have generally remained very doubtful about Lopez's guilt.[14] But by further frenetic questioning and threats of torture Essex was able to extract confessions from the doctor and two other Portuguese involved with him, Manuel Luis Tinoco and Estevão Ferreira de Gama. These finally convinced most of the councillors and, more or less, the queen herself.

This, of course, put quite a different complexion upon any mission to the archduke. There appeared now very little foundation for the hope expressed in the Cecils' paper that Philip II, beset by age and infirmity, might 'in his preparation to death' be conscience-stricken at the heavy effusion of Christian blood in his wars.[15] And Fuentes and Ibarra were now Ernest's leading and most influential councillors. The first reaction, therefore, of the Cecils (assuming it was indeed they who had drafted the original paper) was to add an extra instruction for the proposed envoy to the archduke.[16] He should now begin by saying that the archduke, as a prince born in appearance to be a sovereign lord of countries, would answer the queen more honourably than previous governors of the Low Countries, men of inferior rank. She could 'make good manifest proofs of a great multitude of persons, whereof sundry have been *openly and* justly condemned, that have many times since the difference betwixt us and the King of Spain attempted to put us in danger of our life by many wicked *and strange* ways, who have been hired thereto both by governors, councillors, and other ministers of the King of Spain'. Even since the archduke was named as governor, some who had come to the Netherlands from Spain with authority from the king, had furthered attempts upon her life; attempts to burn her ships with fireworks, 'whereof some were devised to have poisoned all persons in the ships'; and a vain attempt by Sir William Stanley to get the new earl of Derby to head a rebellion. Fuentes and others had corrupted her physician and some of her own chamber to poison her. In proof of this there were letters ready to be shown from Fuentes, his secretary, and the king's principal councillors in Spain, as well as the confessions of some of the practisers. The queen was sure that the archduke would deal with these matters in honourable sort.

Clearly this additional instruction represented a change of tactics. It would have put the emphasis much less upon the search for peace with Spain and much more upon that policy which Burghley had advised back in 1583 when he suggested that one way, and not the worst, of dealing with the Netherlands problem 'might be to seek either the winning of the Prince of Parma from the King of Spain or at least to have the matter so handled as that the jealousy thereof may arise betwixt them'.[17] In Parma's time many attempts had been made to achieve such a separation: it was indeed almost an annual affair. In October 1586 an agent of Walsingham's (probably Thomas Barnes) had written that he had spoken with Parma and that 'about the offer which your honour did present him touching Holland and Zeeland, I find him marvellous well disposed'. A year later, in September 1587, Walsingham's secretary directed the same agent (?) to repeat the overture, adding that Her Majesty 'could far better endure (Parma) as Duke of Burgundy and her neighbour than the King of Spain'.[18] At just that time, too, Mendoza heard – the information was perhaps deliberately fed to him by Walsingham – that John Herbert would be going as one of the peace commissioners to Bourbourg with a secret mission to urge Parma to seize the Netherlands for himself, promising that if he did so Elizabeth and Henry III of France would aid him to the utmost of their power.[19]

The defeat of the 'invincible' Armada and the fact that many Spaniards blamed Parma for its failure naturally gave fresh encouragement to hopes that, as Lord Henry Seymour wrote in August 1588, 'the Duke of Parma ... now may easily be entreated to make a division of the Low Countries with Her Majesty'.[20] And indeed in September a Genoese, Giacomo Fiesco Morone, brought the duke an unsigned letter from Sir Horatio Palavicino with just such a proposal. Parma's angry public reaction – certainly politic but also quite possibly sincere[21] – by no means ended these attempts to drive wedges between him and his Spanish master. Early in 1589 Henry III of France tried it. Later in the year Du Plessis Mornay told Buzenval, Henry IV's ambassador in Holland, that if Parma would assume the sovereignty of the Netherlands, he might rely upon the aid of Henry and probably of Elizabeth too.[22] In August 1590 Burghley, to show Parma the malice of the Spaniards towards him, sent him through Carlo Lanfranchi, an Italian banker at Antwerp, the decipher of a letter from Juan Moreo, the Spanish agent with the League, to the secretary Juan d'Idiaquez at Madrid.[23] At about the same time Burghley, truthfully or politicly, instructed Robert Bowes, the English ambassador in Scotland, to deny the report of one John Bailey, sent by Parma's secretary to tell James VI that Elizabeth had 'moved and offered marriage betwixt the Duke of Parma and the Lady Arabella (Stuart)', a possible rival claimant to the King of Scots for the English succession. Burghley declared that neither the queen nor he himself had ever thought of such a thing.[24] In October 1591 Burghley once again sent Parma secretly a packet of intercepted letters and Sir Robert Sidney at Flushing noted that 'here are practices to stir the Duke of Parma against the King of Spain', though they seemed to take little hold with him.[25] In 1592 there were reports that Michael Moody, Sir Edward Stafford's old servant and now a double agent, was employed into the Low Countries to practise again a marriage between Parma's son and the Lady Arabella. The exiled Charles Paget was apparently also involved and he heard, though he hardly believed, that so was Thomas Barnes.[26] But the movers and motives behind this are obscure: it may well have more to do with the politics of the English exiles than with intrigues by the English government.

Upon Parma's death in late November 1592 Burghley at the queen's direction was very quick to urge the Dutch States General to send secret messengers to move the principal towns of Flanders and Brabant to seize the opportunity to throw off 'the government by Spaniards and Italians ... before any government can be stabilised'.[27] A year later Palavicino again sent an agent, Bernardo Moica *alias* Hippolito Carpino, over to the Spanish Netherlands, though Moica's commission seems to have been mainly intelligence gathering under cover of seeking to arrange the ransoming of another Italian, or several others, held prisoner in England.[28] Earlier, in the summer of 1593 some of the Charles Paget-Thomas Morgan faction among the English exiles had made peace overtures of some kind – in the queen's name they alleged – to Count Peter Ernst von Mansfeld, who was acting as governor-general during the interval between Parma's death and Ernest's arrival; but here again the ultimate movers and motives are uncertain.[29]

It was therefore natural enough that some of Elizabeth's ministers, Burghley in particular, should consider making yet another attempt to drive a wedge between the governments in Brussels and Madrid upon the coincidence of the discovery of the Lopez plot with the arrival in the Spanish Netherlands of a new governor-general who perhaps might not quite see eye to eye with his Spanish master. But if these counsels were in fact put before Elizabeth, it was to be another six or seven months before she took any action on the lines they suggested. The reasons for this delay can only be guessed at. The most likely seems to be that the queen still found it somewhat difficult to believe in the guilt of Dr Lopez. He was tried and condemned on 28 February and Tinoco and Ferreira a few days later. They were all due to be executed on 19 April, but on 18 April the queen stayed the warrant for the execution until further order[30] and in fact it was not until fully three months after his trial and conviction that Lopez was eventually executed at Tyburn on 7 June. Even then, apparently, Elizabeth 'by a rare exercise of her prerogative' allowed his widow Sara and her five children 'to retain much of the Doctor's property'.[31]

Now, if Elizabeth was not wholly convinced about the guilt of Dr Lopez, she could hardly be confident about the guilt of Philip II. And given her high respect for the kingly office, she would need to be confident indeed before she consented to a public denunciation of the King of Spain as a plotter of murder and a hirer of assassins. As recently as 1591, while approving warmly of most of a discourse by Burghley aimed at dissuading the Dutch from listening to peace overtures, she had not seen 'how it may be justified to charge the King of Spain with seeking or procuring directly her death, and therefore would have that allegation altered or someway mitigated or else left out'.[32] Her attitude, it seems, must have been the same now and this would virtually rule out the sending of an envoy to Archduke Ernest to inquire about the progress, or lack of progress, of the imperial moves towards a peace with Spain. For it would be clearly impossible for such an envoy to make no reference to the Lopez plot and the accusations against the Spanish ministers and their king.

Anyway, with the approach of the campaigning season all intelligences suggested that the Spanish government was in no mood to listen to peace upon any terms acceptable to Elizabeth. A considerable Spanish army was gathering in Milanese territory and Piedmont to reinforce the duke of Savoy and to attempt to recover Lyons for the League.[33] By the end of March the Spaniards in Brittany, considerably reinforced from Spain, were beginning to build on the Crozon peninsula the first of the two forts by which they hoped to close the entrance to Brest harbour.[34] In April Palavicino had intelligence from 'colui di Brusselle' (presumably Bernardo Moica *alias* Hippolito Carpino) not only of Spanish dealings with Catholic lords in Scotland but also of great preparations in the Spanish Netherlands to send forces to aid the League in northern France.[35] And indeed at the end of the month Count Karl von Mansfeld did lay siege to La Capelle. All this made the arrival of Dr Hartius and Comans at The Hague early in May with somewhat vague peace overtures from the archduke, look like nothing better than a device to trick the Dutch out of the war and so free the Spanish Netherlands army to concentrate upon the conquest of France.[36]

These dwindling hopes of peace, however, did nothing to weaken the queen's reluctance to denounce Philip II publicly for plotting her assassination. The trial and condemnation of Lopez and his alleged associates did, it is true, produce that spring a veritable barrage of such propaganda from her ministers and others. Lengthy abstracts of the evidence against the conspirators and reports on their trials and confessions were compiled. Burghley set William Waad to work to draw up a report and he got from the solicitor-general, Sir Edward Coke, additions to a draft report of his own.[37] He also drafted a speech to be made by the queen on the affair[38] – there is no evidence, however, that she ever delivered it! These various reports followed much the same lines, if generally more elaborately, as the additions that had been proposed to the instructions for an envoy to the archduke, which as we have seen probably originated with the Cecils. And perhaps as a counterblast to all this Cecilian activity, Francis Bacon also wrote a report on the conspiracies for Essex.[39]

Elizabeth, however, was as unwilling to allow any of this to be published as she was to remonstrate publicly with the archduke and it was not until September 1594 that she at length came round to the idea of sending an envoy to him. On 11 September she wrote asking for a passport and safe conduct for Sir Thomas Wilkes, whom she wished to send to him to communicate certain matters which closely concerned her and were also of very great importance to the King of Spain.[40] Yet even now, as Wilkes' instructions[41] made very clear, she was not sending him to make a public denunciation of Philip II. Elizabeth, a sovereign queen by birth, was sending Wilkes because she was persuaded that the archduke would give her remedy for her complaint, being himself of princely birth, the son of Emperor Maximilian II and brother of the present emperor, with both of whom she was on terms of amity.

Wilkes was therefore to deliver his message first in private, though he might, if the archduke thought good, afterwards communicate it to his council providing those of Low Country birth were present. But what he had to say was truly of a nature to be opened only to the King of Spain himself or to the archduke as the supreme governor of those countries. For it concerned the life of a queen and the honour of the King of Spain so deeply that, if what was alleged against him was true, 'all riches of his Indias would never recover him the honour that he should lose in the judgement of the princes and other potentates of the world that should hear thereof, besides the condemnation of him in the secret sight of God to the danger of his soul'. The archduke must have heard that three Portuguese – the queen's physician Dr Lopez, Estevão Ferreira de Gama, and Manuel Luis Tinoco – had been executed in June for conspiring her death. Although this conspiracy had originated with the Count of Fuentes and secretary Ibarra in Brussels and had been furthered by the king's secretary Cristóbal Moro at Madrid, the queen had not intended to inform the archduke of it. But within three months afterwards another attempt to kill her was devised at Brussels by a number of English exiles maintained there at the King of Spain's charge. Three of the would-be assassins – young Edmund Yorke, Richard Williams, and Henry Young – had been taken and had confessed. In view of this doubling of the conspiracy by some Spanish ministers residing there with the archduke, and because by the confessions of some of the offenders the King of Spain was 'himself said to have been a party thereto, as was affirmed by the Count of Fuentes in avouching the king's letters written to him for the matter', the queen felt that she must now inform the archduke.

Wilkes was thereupon to offer as proof copies of the assassins' confessions and to say that certain original letters proving those confessions might be inspected at Ostend. Further he was to demand that the archduke inform the King of Spain of the accusations against him; that Fuentes and Ibarra be ordered not to leave the Low Countries until the king took order about them; that seven of the leading English rebels – Sir William Stanley, Holt, Owen, Throckmorton, Paget, Dr Gifford, and Dr Worthington – be sent over to England for trial as traitors; and that other rebels, named in a list, be deprived of their Spanish pensions and banished from the Low Countries. Finally, Wilkes was to threaten that if the King of Spain failed to express his detestation of these conspiracies, 'we shall be forced to publish to all the world a just condemnation of him and shall not forbear to denounce open war which we have, contrary to the general desire of our subjects, hitherto forborne, using only defensive means to withstand his hostility'.

By her own account, then, it was the discovery of the second plot, of Yorke, Williams, and Young, following so close upon that of Lopez, Tinoco, and Ferreira, that had brought Elizabeth this far towards public denunciation of the King of Spain. And on top of these, although it was not mentioned in Wilkes' instructions, there was the arrest by the Dutch of the Namur priest Michel Renichon and his confession that he had been set on by the archduke and his ministers to assassinate Count Maurice of Nassau.[42] Moreover, a young Frenchman had been executed back in August 1593 for plotting to kill Henry IV and many more such plots were rumoured, while in December 1594 another conspirator was to get so far as to stab the king in the mouth and knock out one of his teeth.[43] Altogether it was a year so full of plots and rumours of plots that it is small wonder if Elizabeth came at last to suspect that where there was so much smoke there could well be some fire.[44]

There may also have been some other considerations that made the idea of an approach to the archduke attractive at this time. The rapid collapse of the Catholic League in France and Henry IV's developing interest in the possibility of joint Franco-Dutch assaults upon the Spanish Netherlands were arousing the old English fear of 'the French possessing' the Netherlands that was never far below the surface. In July, when Henry had invited the queen, through Edmondes, to join them and take her share in their conquests, Edmondes had answered that having once refused the sovereignty of the whole of the Low Countries, she was unlikely to accept a part. He also thought that she would neither desire that the French should settle a possession in those countries nor would she have them change their dependence upon her to dependence upon France.[45] It may well have been thought that neither of these things might happen if the archduke could be weaned away from Spain into neutrality or peace. Then indeed neither the French would possess nor the Spaniards tyrannise in the Netherlands.

In this connection it is significant that on 17 August, less than a month before the request to the archduke for a passport for Wilkes, the queen had written to the emperor. She did not, it seems, accept Dr Parkins' suggestion of 3 August[46] that she should ask to be informed of the effect of Rudolph's sending into Spain to exhort the king to a general pacification. But she did once again express her readiness to mediate with the Turk and she further informed the emperor that the sultan in open audience 'himself by his own mouth said in the hearing of your ambassador and all the company assembled that if he had followed the advice of us, naming us the Queen of England, and that Your Majesty's ambassador there detained had not by evil offices hindered it, this war had not proceeded'. Referring then to the sentence that the Hansa towns had obtained in their favour at the recent Regensburg diet, she also hoped that the emperor would not grant a mandate for its execution without hearing her answer as he had promised Parkins.[47] Clearly, efforts to continue and strengthen amity with the House of Austria were by no means being relaxed.

The attempt at dealings with Archduke Ernest in the Low Countries was, however, to prove very short-lived. Ernest did very promptly send the passport and safe conduct for Wilkes.[48] But Elizabeth found both the style and the substance of his covering letter very strange. She therefore 'disdained herself to write any more to the Duke', though Burghley had drafted a letter for her. Instead, she instructed certain of her privy councillors – Burghley, Essex, Buckhurst, Heneage and Cecil – to reply to Richardot, the archduke's councillor who had delivered the passport. The draft of their letter was again made by Burghley but 'this was corrected and reformed by Her Majesty's self as she gave me instructions'. The letter complained that the archduke in the style of his addressing her had failed to show the respect due to her as a sovereign princess, a respect that she had always received from kings and monarchs and even emperors. In its substance, too, his letter required that Wilkes should say nothing to the King of Spain's disservice. Not knowing what the archduke would interpret as to the king's disservice, the queen had changed her mind. She now felt that it would serve no purpose to send an envoy to him and, little though she liked touching the honour of the royal estate, she meant now to publish the matter to the world. The councillors asked Richardot so to inform the archduke and they returned the passport and safe conduct.[49]

This letter of 20 October ended the brief approach to the archduke. For some reason, presumably contrary winds, it was 10 November before it reached Ostend and was forwarded by the governor, Sir Edward Norris, to Brussels.[50] Richardot replied five days later, professing astonishment that the queen should be offended by the style used in the archduke's answer and should break off upon so feeble a ground. And, he said, the actions of his king and the archduke were so justified before God and the world that he scorned to speak of the queen's threat of publication.[51]

That threat, however, was now carried out. Burghley, with the assistance of Sir Robert Cecil and William Waad and possibly others, drafted yet another account of the plots of Lopez, Ferreira, and Tinoco and of Yorke, Williams, and Young, with their confessions implicating the King of Spain, his ministers, and the leading English Catholic exiles in their pay. In November 1594 the final agreed version of this was printed and published under the title of *A True Report of Sundry Horrible Conspiracies of late time detected to have by barbarous murders taken away the Life of the Queen's most excellent Majesty*. And on 28 November Burghley sent Edmondes a French translation fresh from the press for publication in France.[52]

So ended both the attempt at discussions with Archduke Ernest and Queen Elizabeth's rearguard action against publicly denouncing King Philip II as the instigator and paymaster of assassins. It had taken the better part of nine months to persuade her; but at last Burghley, Essex, and the rest of her councillors had got their way.

Notes

1.   Cf. R. B. Wernham, *After the Armada* (Oxford, 1984), pp. 514–21.
2.   S[tate] P[apers] France, vol. XXXII, fo. 58.
3.   Cf. J. L. Motley, *History of the United Netherlands* (4 vols, London, 1860–67), vol. III, pp. 306–9; Wernham, *After the Armada*, pp. 505–6.
4.   As Burghley feared: SP France, vol. XXXI, fo. 222.
5.   J. Strype, *Annals of the Reformation* . . . (4 vols in 7, Oxford, 1824), vol. IV, pp. 213–20.
6.   SP Germany, Empire, vol. I, fos. 144–53.
7.   SP Germany, States, vol. VII, fo. 144.
8.   SP Turkey, vol. II, fos. 202, 207, 215, 227.
9.   Wernham, *After the Armada*, pp. 521–3, 526–7.
10.   There are two copies of this paper, both with an initial marginal note

that they are in 'The form of an instruction from Her Majesty'. The first (SP Flanders, vol. V, fo. 108), endorsed as February 1593/[4], has corrections and additions by Burghley, who has changed the references to 'Her Majesty' and 'she' into 'we'; the second (ibid., fo. 117) has corrections in Sir Robert Cecil's hand.

11.   For these see SP Turkey, vol. II, fos. 221, 225, 281, 283, 303, 305.
12.   R. B. Wernham, 'English Policy and the Revolt of the Netherlands', in J. S. Bromley and E. H. Kossmann (eds), *Britain and the Netherlands*, vol. I (London, 1959), pp. 29–40.
13.   As the earl of Sussex had put it. *C[alendar of] S[tate] P[apers] F[oreign]*, vol. XIII, p. 120.
14.   At least since A. Dimock, 'The Conspiracy of Dr. Lopez', *English Historical Review*, IX (1894), pp. 440–72; e.g. M. A. S. Hume, *Treason and Plot. Struggles for Catholic Supremacy in the Last Years of Elizabeth I* (London, 1901); *Dictionary of National Biography*, s.v. Lopez, Dr Roderigo; L. Wolf, 'The Jews in Elizabethan England', *Transactions of the Jewish Historical Society of England*, XI (1928).
15.   SP Flanders, vol. V, fo. 110v. For rumours at this time of Philip II's ill health and impending retirement see for example SP France, vol. XXXIII, fo. 67; SP Italian States, vol. I, fo. 163.
16.   SP Flanders, vol. V, fo. 112, also fo. 121. Words printed in italics are added by Burghley in fo. 112.
17.   *Somers Tracts*, ed. W. Scott (13 vols, London, 1809–15), vol. I, p. 170.
18.   Conyers Read, *Mr. Secretary Walsingham and the Policy of Queen Elizabeth* (3 vols, Oxford, 1925), vol. III, pp. 265–6 and notes.
19.   *CSP Spanish*, vol. IV, p. 140.
20.   *State Papers relating to the Defeat of the Spanish Armada*, ed. J. K. Laughton (2 vols, London, 1894), vol. II, p. 198.
21.   Motley, *United Netherlands*, vol. II, pp. 539–40; *Correspondance de Philippe II sur les affaires des Pays Bas*, ed. J. Lefèvre (4 vols, Brussels, 1940–60), vol. III, pp. 361, 365; L. Stone, *An Elizabethan: Sir Horatio Palavicino* (Oxford, 1956), pp. 264–5.
22.   *Correspondance de Philippe II*, vol. II, p. 389; *Mémoires et correspondance de Du Plessis Mornay*, ed. A. D. de la Fontenelle de Vaudoré and P. R. Auguis (12 vols, Paris, 1824–25), vol. IV, p. 270.
23.   *L[ist and] A[nalysis of] S[tate] P[apers Foreign]*, vol. II, para. 613.
24.   *CSP Scotland and Mary Queen of Scots*, vol. X, pp. 360, 369.
25.   *LASP*, vol. III, para. 703.
26.   Ibid., paras. 72, 76, 79; *CSP D[omestic], 1591–94*, pp. 99, 117, 209, 244; *Douai Diaries*, intr. T. F. Knox (London, 1878), pp. 405, 408.
27.   T. Wright (ed.), *Queen Elizabeth and her Times* (2 vols, London, 1838), vol. II, p. 423.
28.   *LASP*, vol. IV, paras. 550–1, 554–5; H[istorical] M[anuscripts] C[ommission], *Salisbury MSS.*, vol. IV, pp. 500, 512; and cf. Stone, *Palavicino*, p. 254.
29.   *Correspondance de Philippe II*, vol. IV, pp. 197, 215; *Douai Diaries*, p. 408.
30.   HMC, *Salisbury MSS.*, vol. IV, pp. 512–13, 515.
31.   *CSPD, 1595–97*, p. 15: also *Dictionary of National Biography*, s.v.

Lopez, Dr Roderigo, citing Sara's petition of August 1594 and attached inventories of the property in HMC, *Salisbury MSS.*, vol. IV, p. 601.

32. Quoted in Conyers Read, *Lord Burghley and Queen Elizabeth* (London, 1960), p. 471, from BL. Harleian MS. 6995, fo. 32.

33. SP France, vol. XXXIII, fo. 305; SP Spain, vol. IV, fo. 230.

34. SP France, vol. XXX, fos. 68, 329.

35. HMC, *Salisbury MSS.*, vol. IV, pp. 500–1, 512, 529, and cf. ibid., vol. V, p. 28.

36. SP Holland, vol. XLVIII, fo. 191; SP Treaty Papers (Holland), vol. XXXV, fos. 145, 153; *Correspondance de Philippe II*, vol. IV, pp. 238–9, 245.

37. *CSPD, 1591–94*, pp. 411ff; HMC, *Salisbury MSS.*, vol. IV, p. 491; W. Murdin (ed.), *A Collection of State Papers relating to ... the reign of Elizabeth* (London, 1759), pp. 669–75.

38. *CSPD, 1591–94*, p. 462. Is this the 'address' that Dimock says 'the queen issued', 'Conspiracy', p. 468?

39. *The Works of Francis Bacon*, ed. J. Spedding *et al.* (14 vols, London, 1857–74), vol. VIII, pp. 274 ff.

40. SP Flanders, vol. V, fo. 129.

41. Ibid., fo. 132.

42. SP Holland, vol. XLVIII, fos. 104, 133, 220.

43. SP France, vol. XXXII, fo. 85; vol. XXXIV, fo. 291.

44. If she had seen Philip's letter of 25 October 1588 to Parma (*Correspondance de Philippe II*, vol. III, pp. 365–6) with its very warm praise of Balthasar Gérard, '*qui avec si grands valeur osta de ce monde*' William of Orange, an '*exploict si important à la Chrétienté*', she might perhaps have been a little less charitable and earlier suspicious.

45. HMC, *Salisbury MSS.*, vol. IV, p. 560.

46. Ibid., p. 576.

47. SP Germany, Empire, vol. I, fo. 161.

48. BL. Cotton MS. Vespasian C. viii, no. 54; SP Flanders, vol. V, fo. 152; *Correspondance de Philippe II*, vol. IV, p. 261. Ernest wrote to Philip II on 28 October N.S. that Wilkes' mission would only have dealt in deceit and trickery and that he really came as a spy. Ibid., p. 262.

49. SP Flanders, vol. V, fos. 155, 159, 160, 429; HMC, *Salisbury MSS.*, vol. V, pp. 12–16; *Correspondance de Philippe II*, vol. IV, p. 261.

50. SP Holland, vol. XLIX, fo. 214.

51. BL. Cotton MS. Vespasian C. viii, no. 53; SP Flanders, vol. V, fo. 429; *Correspondance de Philippe II*, vol. IV, p. 267.

52. *CSPD, 1591–94*, p. 558; HMC, *Salisbury MSS.*, vol. IV, p. 630; vol. V, p. 2; Murdin, *State Papers*, p. 680; BL. Lansdowne MS., vol. LXXVII, no. 67; Read, *Burghley*, pp. 478–9 and ns. 28–36 at p. 586.

21 The Settlement of the Merchants Adventurers at Stade, 1587–1611

G. D. Ramsay

Since at least the eleventh century there has been a town at the site of Stade on the lower reaches of the river Schwinge, just above its mouth in the estuary of the Elbe opposite Hamburg. After a century or so of prosperity and prominence as a member of the Hanseatic League, Stade entered into a period of slow decline in the later Middle Ages, and by the sixteenth century had sunk so far as to allow its active membership of the League to lapse.[1] An Englishman, *circa* 1595, described it as 'a poor town, about the bigness of Barking or Gravesend'.[2] With its sister towns nearby, Bremen and Buxtehude, it was subject to the archbishop of Bremen, who was entitled to certain dues from shipping in its harbour. These mattered less, however, than the pretensions of its ambitious neighbour Hamburg on the other side of the Elbe. Hamburg claimed to regulate and tax all shipping on the river, and in particular to enforce the carriage of all corn on its waters for sale at its own market.[3] The prosperity of Hamburg, and possibly its political pretensions, received some further stimulus in 1567 by the completion of an agreement with the Company of Merchants Adventurers of England, the gist of which was that the English company received extensive rights for its membership in the marketing of woollen cloths in the city. The Englishmen were expected to attract much other business to their cloth mart thus established by the Elbe; and their advent in fact laid the foundations for the subsequent rise of Hamburg to a place among the half-dozen most important seaports of northern Europe. But for nearly a quarter of a century the development of Hamburg was hindered and its position under threat because the English were driven to transfer their cloth mart to the modest haven of Stade nearby. How the interruption could have occurred is the subject of this essay, but first, a glance at the Merchants Adventurers and their mart towns is necessary.

The full significance of the privileges granted to the English at Hamburg was revealed in 1569, when the international market at

Antwerp was suddenly closed for political reasons and the bulk of
English industrial exports was diverted from the Scheldt to the Elbe.
There was an immediate and visible stimulus to business of all sorts at
Hamburg. But the Anglo-Hamburg agreement did not equally benefit
the other member cities of the Hanseatic League, whose jealousy was
aroused by the brash advent of prosperity to Hamburg. More
ominously, the concessions to the Merchants Adventurers at Hamburg were limited in time to ten years. When the expiry of the
agreement drew near in 1577 there were attempts, promoted particularly by Lübeck and Danzig, to persuade the burgomasters and
senators of Hamburg not to renew their concessions. The English,
who now lacked security for their recently re-opened traffic at
Antwerp, sought some prolongation from Hamburg. The burgomasters and senators, torn by an embarrassing conflict of interests,
were willing to grant this for one year only. The official English cloth
mart at Hamburg thus came to an end in 1578. The Merchants
Adventurers regretfully evacuated the premises in the Gröninger-
straße leased to them under the 1567 agreement and prepared to face
the hazards of unsettled business that now loomed ahead. New
options for trade were examined. Some cloth dealers, independently
as 'interlopers', took to escorting their textiles to Nuremberg and
elsewhere in the German interior for disposal; some moved their
activities to the Baltic; some tentatively ventured to the Mediterranean. The company itself transferred its headquarters back to Emden,
which it had already tried out in 1564.[4]

In addition to this market town in north-west Germany the
company maintained another settlement in the Netherlands, for
generations usually at Antwerp, but the security of trade normal there
before 1569 was never restored, so that in 1582 the company transferred its Netherlands mart to safety at Middelburg, as it was hoped.
Any hope of a happy return to Antwerp was ultimately to evaporate
when in 1585 the city fell to the Prince of Parma, the viceroy
appointed by his uncle Philip II of Spain. The company was weakened
by this 'often flitting from one place to another', and alarmed by the
increasing refusal of merchants in the early 1580s to accept its
discipline.[5] At the periphery of trade some, as already mentioned,
were pursuing new markets in the Atlantic, the Baltic or the Mediterranean beyond company jurisdiction. Others, still seeking to serve the
former consumers but sensitive to the drawbacks of using Middelburg, were trying out alternative ports nearby; and the company
resented the erosion of its authority and prosperity by some English

merchants' irregular shipments of cloth to Calais, Gravelines, Dunkirk and Nieuwpoort, thereby maintaining 'a continual traffic with those of Flanders and other places under the government of the Prince of Parma' – with whom the Queen of England was still precariously at peace.[6] Some even preferred the risks of taking their cloths to Hamburg rather than Emden, and thence carrying their wares into central Germany and beyond.[7] The centralised control exercised until 1569 by the Company of Merchants Adventurers from its headquarters in Antwerp thus seemed to be in process of disintegration. Somewhat belatedly, the lord treasurer Burghley tried to prop it up by a circular issued to customs officers in March 1586, directing them not to permit cloth shipment to Netherlands or German ports other than the official market towns, Middelburg and Emden, to which most exports were still in name at least being directed.[8]

The English cloth export trade inevitably ran into danger because it could not be insulated from the domestic troubles of the Netherlands, where the civil commotions of the 1570s, often accompanied by violence, grew into full-scale warfare in the 1580s. The Dutch rebels could hold out in the maritime provinces of Holland and Zeeland thanks to their command of the sea, but on land the Prince of Parma from 1579 onwards gradually but remorselessly was able to recover the others. Emden lay just outside the jurisdiction of Philip II and his representative, but could not escape the consequences of its situation on the Netherlands frontier. In 1580 the adjacent province of Groningen gave its adhesion to Parma, who installed garrisons at its capital town and at the port of Delftzijl on the estuary of the Ems just opposite Emden. A Dutch blockade of the Ems before long was instituted, and in 1583 was intensified by the rebels' seizure of the fishing village of Oterdum. Before long, the citizens of Emden were with good reason complaining of the lawlessness of the fighting men just outside their harbour. The frontier was not respected, violence reigned, and peaceful commerce was throttled.[9] The English were recognised as neutrals, but the Merchants Adventurers usually took the precaution of paying for an escort of warships. This did not prevent the seizure of fifty packs of English cloths in January 1585, with a market value of perhaps £2000, nor the subsequent erosion of security.[10] The prosperity of Emden, marked since 1578, rapidly ebbed, while its suzerain the Count of East Friesland had to endure Parma's alternate blandishments and threats as well as the enmity of his own subjects who considered him too favourable to the Spanish side.

While the state of affairs at Emden was thus going from bad to worse, the situation at Middelburg, the other mart town of the Merchants Adventurers, was only a little better. Middelburg lay on rebel territory, but at a much shorter sailing distance from London than Emden, and on an island, so that it seemed 'best assured from sudden peril and invasion'.[11] But danger loomed when in 1582 Bruges submitted to Parma, and Sluys and Bergen-op-Zoom lay under threat; Sluys fell in 1587 and Bergen had to endure a long siege. Had it too fallen, the waterways at Middelburg would have become so unsafe as to render its trade 'of no value'.[12] The struggle of the Dutch entered a new phase with the murder of the Prince of Orange in July 1584 and its sequel, the treaty of Nonsuch, just over a year later. This brought into existence a *de facto* alliance between the Queen of England and the rebel States General, and pointed to a state of war between Elizabeth and Philip II, though no formal declaration was ever made.

The cloth traffic eastwards was in addition seriously endangered by the war for the succession to the electorate of Cologne which began in 1583 when the archbishop Gebhard Truchseß von Waldburg sought to carry his principality over to the Lutheran camp. For some years Spanish troops were active in the Rhineland, assisting the Bavarian prince who was to be his supplanter. The security of trade was thus seriously at risk not merely at the English mart towns on the coast but in the interior of Germany as well. The Company of Merchants Adventurers, consulted at about this time by the Privy Council, urged that the queen should be asked to send an envoy to cultivate the friendship of the German princes and to encourage the Hamburgers to restore to the English the privileges they had enjoyed in the years 1567–78. Hamburg, in the opinion of the company, was 'a fit and convenient place for the trade of the said Merchants Adventurers and the vent of English commodities', if only it might be made available 'by a reasonable treaty'.[13] To this suggestion the English government did not now demur.

Meanwhile, the discouraging plight of the merchants at Middelburg and Emden was reflected in the dullness of the cloth market at Blackwell Hall in London. The crisis there was not one to be conjured away in a season or two, as on some previous occasions, since it was the outcome not just of a temporarily saturated market but of the chronic political insecurity of the ports where the Merchants Adventurers met their foreign customers. Nor was it merely that some merchants were avoiding the mart towns and seeking to sell cloths in other places; they were turning to other business and not dealing in cloths at all but, for example, financing privateers.[14] Country clothiers remembered 1584 as the first year when there was a shortage of buyers at Blackwell Hall, when cloths 'began to stand in the market'.[15] It was in May that year that the government, doubtless scenting trouble, took the Merchants Adventurers again into consultation with regard to the safety of their markets on the continent. In particular it sought to see how matters stood in the long-simmering controversy with the Hanseatic League.[16] The moment was a favourable one for Anglo-Hansa reconcilation, for in July 1584 the emperor signified his wish that the Hansa towns should settle their differences with the English by negotiation rather than action.[17] This imperial intervention offers a convenient point at which to pick up the thread of Anglo-Hansa politics.

At London the Hanseatic League had for centuries maintained its permanent *Kontor* or mercantile settlement, known to the English as the Steelyard. Its residents annually elected a president, known as the Alderman, to serve as representative of the inmates. In September 1584 he put forward some anodyne proposals designed broadly to remove the grievances of Hansa merchants in England and conversely to enable the Merchants Adventurers once more to establish their mart at Hamburg.[18] Both the English Privy Council and the Hansa Congress at Lübeck gave general approval, and ultimately a new Hansa delegation accordingly arrived in England in June 1585. Unfortunately, its three members were hopelessly at odds with each other and unable to overcome the disagreements that had hobbled earlier such missions. Like their predecessors of 1560, the envoys were instructed to seek restoration of the privileges that had been wrested from the English Crown in 1474; and the queen had not abated her refusal to consider this.[19] But she welcomed the envoys graciously; they laid their wishes before the Privy Council and had lengthy discussions with its secretary Robert Beale, as well as with lord treasurer Burghley, secretary Walsingham and other persons of consequence.[20] Progress proved slow, despite the anxiety of the Hamburg member of the delegation, senator Johann Schulte, a dealer in cloths, to rebuild all bridges.[21] He was in private touch with the merchant adventurer John Robinson, for which he was subsequently denounced as a traitor by his intransigent colleague Dr Georg Liseman.[22] The queen heard of the ill-harmonised discussions with dismay. She received the envoys more than once in audience, sometimes for them a disconcerting experience. She was as well or better versed than they in Latin, the language of negotiation. Perhaps to assuage the tedium, she laughed and scoffed at them, interrupting their flowery compliments on one occasion, and when a further hearing was sought she audibly exclaimed *Deus avertat* (God forbid). When finally it emerged that they lacked authority to conclude any agreement that would restore the Merchants Adventurers to Hamburg, she dismissed them, sending letters to their home towns sorrowfully pinning responsibility for the failure of the talks on their disunity.[23]

One good reason for Hansa obstinacy lay in the plight of the cloth export traffic and the slackness of the market at Blackwell Hall. The Hansards were in a strong position, and knew it: the longer trade remained in the doldrums, the more eager were the English to seek the re-establishment of their mart at Hamburg. At Emden conditions remained anything but secure. The trustworthiness of the Count of East Friesland was under suspicion, and the Ems continued to be blockaded by the rebel Dutch, in whose opinion the seaborne traffic at Emden benefited the Spanish enemy. They urged that the Merchants Adventurers might with advantage transfer their mart to Amsterdam, Delft or indeed any town in the province of Holland.[24] This was not an inducement that governor Milward of the company found attractive. He urged that the whole traffic of the cloth merchants should not be committed totally to market towns in the United Provinces. That would, as he saw it, put not only English exports but the foreign policy of the queen at the mercy of the Dutch rebels, who by threat of an embargo upon English cloths might veto any action of hers 'if the same be to their disliking'.[25] Despite the failure of the long drawn-out negotiations throughout 1585, the Merchants Adventurers continued in the next year to yearn for a return to Hamburg, English hopes being fed by messages from the burgomasters and senators and private assurances from Schulte that his city was seriously bent upon agreement and did not insist upon a return to the conditions laid down in the treaty of 1474.[26] The Privy Council in March 1586 actually yielded so far as to permit Italian and other foreign merchants at London to ship English textiles to Hamburg on condition that they did not break bulk in northern Germany, as if in anticipation of a renewal of the old links.[27]

The situation needed more than hopeful diplomatic gestures, however. Serious trouble was reported in May 1586 among the unemployed clothmakers at Bath, and the Privy Council could do no more than order the Somerset justices to see that the clothiers set the poor to work.[28] There was worse to come. In the autumn the harvest failed in the west country, where broadcloth making and agriculture were intimately connected. Before the end of the year the industrial workers there were in such straits that the council summoned representatives of the clothiers and the Merchants Adventurers to explain themselves before it, 'each against the other'. The merchants were warned that the London cloth market would be opened to their rivals, both English and foreign, if there was no improvement.[29] That failed to occur, so that in the spring of 1587 the situation appeared to brook no delay. The merchants had no faith in opening the cloth market to Staplers, Hansards and others as a remedy; but the famished weavers and spinners of Gloucester, Somerset and Wiltshire could not have been mollified by excuses based on distant marketing problems at Emden and Middelburg. Burghley was aware that distress among the textile workers was a by-product of the international struggle against Philip II, but he happened to be on a sick-bed, and the queen insisted upon immediate action.[30] So the threats which for months if not years had been hanging over the Merchants Adventurers were implemented on 23 May, when a startling announcement was made in the Council Chamber that the cloth trade at London was now to be thrown open. The solemnity of the occasion was heightened by the presence of the alderman and secretary of the Steelyard, as well as a couple of doubtless sceptical city aldermen, Sir Roland Hayward and Sir Edward Osborne.[31] To comfort the English merchants, the government agreed to accredit two envoys to Hamburg to seek the resettlement of the Merchants Adventurers there.

The envoys thus dispatched in an hour of something approaching panic were Governor Richard Saltonstall of the Merchants Adventurers and Dr Giles Fletcher, a civil lawyer of some diplomatic experience.[32] They were received with all due courtesy at Hamburg by the burgomasters and senate, and were no doubt encouraged to find that the friendly Schulte was among the five commissioners appointed to treat with them for the restoration of company privileges in their town. But before long they ruefully had to admit that when it came to actual bargaining the Hamburgers 'had the advantage upon us every way'. To begin with, there were present in the river half-a-dozen English ships laden with cloths from London; they had tactlessly been allowed by the company to sail from the Thames and were now at anchor in the Elbe awaiting, as if so many hostages to diplomacy, the conclusion of an agreement that would enable them to discharge their freight. Then there were other Englishmen at Hamburg, not members of the company; some of them were Staplers, some mere interlopers, who sought to explain how the recent opening of the cloth market at London to all and sundry had made an agreement with the company agents superfluous. The alderman of the Steelyard had sent a sly message to point out how the English offers were not made upon any goodwill borne to Hamburg but because the standstill of the English textile industry was forcing the queen to make concessions 'for fear of a rebellion'. The influence of the other Hansa towns was believed to be thoroughly hostile to any dealings with the English: 'they of Lübeck write most slanderous words against us.' Most decisive of all, Spanish diplomatic weight had now been flung into the scales with the aim of bringing to nought any Anglo-Hamburg *rapprochement*.[33]

The war into which the Queen of England and the King of Spain had now drifted was of vital concern to the Hamburgers. They had far-reaching interests in the dominions of both and were sensitive to pressure from either party. Burghley was correct in his view that the root of all English trade difficulties lay in the conflict with Philip II.[34] His viceroy the Prince of Parma from 1585 commanded military strongholds from Breda and Antwerp northwards to Groningen and Delftzijl that constituted a perpetual menace to the Merchants Adventurers' mart towns at Emden and Middelburg. But even more serious than this military threat, at least as far as the success of Anglo-Hamburg negotiations was concerned, was the Iberian commercial link with the Hansa towns. It was Hansa ships that carried to Spain and Portugal the necessities for prosecuting war with England – the timber and other shipbuilding materials available in the Baltic, and also the corn needed not only for conversion into mariners' biscuit but to feed the people of Spain itself, where corn was in chronically short supply. To secure the continuity of these deliveries Parma, no mean master of diplomatic arts, was deploying all his resources. In 1587 he sent Dr Georg Westendorp from Groningen on a round of his Hansa neighbours to check the activities of Dutch rebels in the Baltic, to discourage trade with rebel Dutch towns, and to hinder any resumption of the English settlement at Hamburg.[35] The English had long been aware that without Baltic products no Armada could be prepared or its crews and soldiers fed. But the merchants of Hamburg shared in the prosperity that this Baltic–peninsular commerce was bringing to their colleagues of Lübeck and Danzig; indeed, Hamburg held a certain primacy among them.[36] In its senate there sat men from a score or so of leading families who were too interested in the peninsular trade to be swayed by any English proposals.[37]

Before long, Saltonstall and Fletcher grasped that their mission was likely to fail; when the senate called a meeting of the citizenry it was evident that hostile views prevailed. It was at this point that the significance of the nearby riverside port of Stade suddenly sprang clear. For years its traders had been smarting from interference with their shipping on the Elbe by the Hamburgers. They had recently filed a protest with the imperial chamber court, the supreme law court of the empire, though with no practical result other than the issue of an imperial *privilegium* of 28 February 1586 which could not be enforced. They needed another and more effective protector to shield them from the Hamburgers, and when they learnt that Hamburg was at odds with the English it looked as if one might be at hand. The guiding spirit in their quest was Reiner Lange, humanist and schoolmaster, who in 1587 became the first headmaster of the town Athenaeum or grammar school. He subsequently rose to become first town clerk (*Syndikus*) and later burgomaster, and was to prove a shrewd mentor for his adopted town in the international negotiations into which it now ventured.[38] To the overtures from Stade the Merchants Adventurers had plenty of reasons for responding: only recently the English merchants trading to the Baltic in the Eastland company had foiled the Danzigers by moving their headquarters to the small port of Elbing not far distant. The pattern of events might be repeated.[39] As for the archbishop of Bremen, suzerain of Stade, no opposition need by expected from his quarter: the see was heavily invaded by Lutheranism and indeed on the road towards secularisation. A new archbishop had been duly elected in 1586 – a boy of twelve, son of the Duke of Holstein and thus a princelet of the Danish royal family, who was being brought up as a Lutheran.[40] During his minority the archbishopric was governed by a regency council, in effect the dean and chapter of the cathedral wearing different hats. Provided the customs dues were paid, they were unlikely to intervene.

At what point the Merchants Adventurers decided to look into the offer from Stade we do not know; there may have been competition from the King of Denmark, who in 1585 had put forward his port of Flensburg as a site for an English cloth market.[41] But Saltonstall and Fletcher were certainly in touch with the municipality of Stade soon after their arrival in Hamburg in June 1587, and lost little time in despatching three company members to open negotiations.[42] These went sufficiently smoothly for Saltsonstall and Fletcher to betake themselves in person to Stade in early August. They met the chief magistrates of the town, who gave satisfactory answers to all their queries.[43] On either side there were preliminary points to clear up: the

Englishmen had to consult their masters at London before coming to a final decision, while the Staders understandably insisted that before committing themselves to any settlement they must first be sure that the talks at Hamburg had been broken off.[44] News of these proceedings led to a momentary weakening on the part of the Hamburgers, who in their alarm went as far as to issue a decree that the English might freely traffic within their city until the following Easter.[45] But this temporary concession did not suffice to halt developments at Stade, where a full formal agreement between the town and the Company of Merchants Adventurers was quickly reached. It was embodied in a document of fifty-six articles, dated 28 September 1587, and in its terms was largely identical with the corresponding instrument drawn up twenty years earlier to establish the mart of the company at Hamburg. As on the previous occasion, the settlement was to last for ten years.[46]

The news of this smart piece of international diplomacy produced a tonic effect on the disposal of English cloths at London. The opening of the market by the proclamation of 23 May 1587 had failed to lift the depression. There was no sudden rush of entrepreneurs, whether English or foreign, to transport woollen goods to the war-ridden continent, though one or two traders, notably the climber Stephen Soame, sought to exploit the occasion to enter the Company of Merchants Adventurers cheaply by a side door, much to the resentment of its members who had duly served their apprenticeship.[47] Soame was on the threshold of a civic career that was to take him to the mayoral seat in less than ten years; his hand is in all likelihood to be discerned in the artless letter purporting to come from the country clothiers in October, thanking the lord treasurer for the opening of the market and the rise in the prices fetched by their products.[48] But the Merchants Adventurers with much greater verisimilitude were able to explain the revival of the market by their settlement at Stade, where the first cloth fleet, which sailed in the autumn, was met by 'great repair of merchants and merchandises', and business was satisfactorily brisk.[49] Not only did the merchants dispose of their cloths, but they also found 'very good wares' to bring home in exchange, predominantly German and Baltic products. These included linens and fustians in quantity; wires for virginals, awl-blades and other metalwares probably from Nuremberg; deal, clapboard and wainscot; and even a few silks and satins from the south.[50] Looking back, some merchants adventurers were of the opinion that their first market at Stade exceeded the best they had had for twenty years.[51] The long depression had been lifted.

But while the cloth market had thus been restored to life and the persistent economic malaise dispelled, some shadows remained. The Count of East Friesland lamented to the Queen of England how her merchants had ungratefully stolen away from his town of Emden without taking their leave, a charge they were at pains to deny.[52] The King of Denmark also wrote in grumbling tones to protest at the transfer of trade from his bank of the Elbe to the other side, and predicted trouble for the Englishmen from the Hamburgers; he would have preferred the company to settle its market on his territory.[53] The Hanseatic League in its anger took up the reception of the Merchants Adventurers at Stade with the emperor at Prague. After a long delay he sent a rescript to the dean and chapter of Bremen to command those of Stade to cease their dealings with the English; but as the revenues of the archbishopric were benefiting from the increase of toll receipts brought by the advent of the English to Stade the dean and chapter had sufficient reason to disregard the imperial order.[54] The Merchants Adventurers found Stade a more friendly location than Hamburg, its citizens less pro-Spanish and its ecclesiastical prejudices less in evidence.[55]

At Hamburg itself counsels were painfully divided. An exchange of messages continued between burgomasters and senate and the English government, with the alderman of the Steelyard sometimes also joining in. Hopes persisted that the Merchants Adventurers might yet be lured back, with all the business they would attract. The undaunted Schulte wrote to Burghley and Walsingham to urge that bygones should be bygones, while the municipal rulers explained how they collected dues from shipping in the Elbe simply to meet the costs of keeping the navigation channels clear of sand and the river free of pirates.[56] But the English were no longer desperate for a settlement at Hamburg, nor did the party of conciliation control the actions of the town. When the Hamburgers renewed their approaches to the queen, she replied to them with some asperity at the end of April 1588. The Hamburgers, her letter said, had only themselves to blame for driving the English merchants away by their lack of consistency in negotiation. She went on to reproach them for 'their great affection to the King of Spain, manifest in many ways', and for their compliance 'upon the solicitation of the Duke of Parma'. As for re-activating the 1567 treaty, now tardily offered by Hamburg, it must be upon novel and specific conditions: it must be with the consent of the town of Stade, and also with the assent of the other Hansa towns 'under the Seal of their Society', neither in fact likely to be granted.[57]

In the following month some hardening of attitudes was precipitated by events on the northern waterways. In May 1588 the moment of truth arrived. News came to Hamburg that the cloth fleet of the Merchants Adventurers, bound for Stade, had set sail from the Thames. The town thereupon posted some armed vessels at the mouth of the Schwinge to await the arrival of the English ships – whether to put a stop to the unlading of the valuable cargoes or merely to collect riverine tolls is not clear. But there had been some warning of this challenge, so that the thirty-six English merchantmen were escorted by three men-of-war that had been detached from the force recently organised to receive the Spanish Armada, now expected at any moment in northern waters.[58] In the face of this display of strength the Hamburgers prudently withdrew amid the jeers of the English mariners. Some neutral shipping seems to have been drawn into this perilous but decisive episode.[59] Neither Hamburg nor the Hanseatic towns in general possessed the naval strength to challenge the English, and it became clear that they did not wish to repeat the confrontation.[60] With the defeat of the Spanish Armada a few weeks later, the hard-liners at Hamburg suffered a set-back and the situation crystallised. The new mart town of the Merchants Adventurers was seen to be not only commercially tolerable but safe in the political sense.

But other issues remained to keep the English and the Hamburgers at loggerheads, and the English had demands to make of the Hansa towns in other fields of contact. These demands soon came to the fore and eclipsed for the time being the question of the cloth mart. The English had now been drawn into a *de facto* war with the King of Spain, whose Armada could not have been fitted out but for the shipbuilding materials that had systematically been transported from the Baltic lands where they originated, thanks to the Hansa merchants who organised the shipments. The English government had long cast a disapproving eye upon this traffic: how long might it be allowed to continue? In May 1588 the alderman of the Steelyard had a disagreeable interview with the Privy Council, in which he was reproached for the pro-Spanish activities of the Hamburgers and for their undue deference to the Prince of Parma, Westendorp being mentioned.[61] In August, with the certainty that the Armada had at last appeared and been scattered, English diplomatic activity became more intensive and peremptory. Thomas Bodley was sent with all speed to northern Germany and Denmark to make sure that no succour was given to any Spanish ships that might seek refuge in those parts; at Hamburg he was to 'use the best and most forcible reasons you may, to persuade those of Hamburg not to victual or any way to relieve the Spaniards'.[62] Late in October the alderman and secretary of the Steelyard were again summoned before the Privy Council to receive a stern dressing-down from the lord chancellor in the name of the queen, with a warning that Hansa shipments to Spain must cease.[63] That was to be the new focus of friction.

In 1584 the queen had hesitated to accede to a Dutch suggestion that Hansa trade with Spain should be forcibly halted on the grounds that by giving offence to the Danish and south German third parties any such intervention would give rise to more ill-feeling than it was worth.[64] But it remained true that the King of Spain could neither feed his mariners nor furnish his navy with ships without the regular consignments of corn, timber and other supplies from the Baltic. In the winter of 1584–85 the English ambassador at Paris passed on news of how purchases of Baltic commodities from Hamburg, Lübeck and other Hansa towns were being stepped up; then in the spring came information of extensive shipping movements.[65] With the deterioration of international relations in 1585 Elizabeth's scruples vanished. In the autumn she sent formal warning to the city of Hamburg that if war arose she would not permit the passage of corn or munitions of war to Spain and Portugal, though she had no wish to interrupt ordinary trade.[66] She also extracted some assurance from the King of Denmark that, if need be, he would stop the passage of grain and victuals through the Sound.[67] At the same time, there came ominous news that Hamburg ships on their voyages to Spain were taking the Atlantic route north of Scotland.[68] In 1587 her warning to the Hansa towns was again transmitted, both directly to Hamburg by letter as well as verbally through the alderman of the Steelyard.[69] Nevertheless, her ministers continued to receive intelligence of such shipments during the next year or so, right down to the sailing of the Armada.[70]

The simple fact that an Armada could have been built and sent forth in 1588 was proof of the English failure to prevent Hansa merchants from transporting Baltic products to Spain. The defeat of one Armada was not, however, enough to prevent the building of a second Spanish invasion fleet, for which plenty of evidence was reaching England during the winter of 1588–89.[71] In early April 1589 William Milward, sometime governor of the Merchants Adventurers, was reporting from Stade how at Hamburg and Lübeck there were many ships almost ready to sail, freighted with corn and all manner of munitions for the King of Spain.[72] A little later he was explaining how money was scarce at Hamburg because the merchants there had sunk all their cash in the Iberian trade.[73] But since the arts of navigation and naval administration were not sufficiently refined to make interception of the Hansa ships at sea a calculable possibility, it was only by striking at the shipping in Spanish harbours that an effective blow against offensive preparations could be delivered. That was what Norris and Drake were instructed to do when they led their expedition later in that same month of April.[74] No doubt they were well aware of the possibility of catching the Hansa fleet, though this was not specifically mentioned in their instructions; it must have been a topic generally discussed, and doubtless embellished by many a rumour. By mid-May it was known that the Hansa ships with their prohibited cargoes had sailed, and on 18 May a peremptory signal was sent in the name of the queen to Norris and Drake to intercept them.[75]

Whether this formal order from the queen reached the English fleet in time to affect the course of events is more than doubtful, but that does not in fact matter. The English force had already sailed to the mouth of the Tagus and had landed troops on the road to Lisbon. By an extraordinary piece of good luck, Norris and Drake were able to fulfil the order and hopes of their queen. The vast convoy of Hansa shipping, laden with contraband goods, simply sailed into the squadron of English and Dutch warships waiting in the roadstead off Cascaes. As one of Norris' colonels recorded, a total of three score Hansa ships from Danzig, Stettin, Rostock, Lübeck and Hamburg became the legitimate prize of the waiting English. Their principal lading, he noted, was corn, masts, cables, copper and wax, all prohibited long since; there were also some large ships with small cargoes, intended as he surmised as reinforcements for the navy of the King of Spain.[76] The sixty ships were seized and taken mostly to Portsmouth, where the contraband was removed and sold for the profit of the shareholders in the enterprise.

The expedition led by Norris and Drake has not gone down in the annals of naval history for its significant achievements. It raised small profit for its organisers; it failed to disrupt Spanish transatlantic traffic; it did not free the English from renewed fears of invasion; its immediate fruit was the appearance of unpaid and mutinous soldiers and sailors in the streets of London.[77] Indeed, it did not even put an end to the passage of forbidden Baltic products to Spain, so worthwhile were the profits of those who slipped past the English blockade. In October 1589 the queen issued a special commission to her admiralty to enable the disposal of the seized goods to be more speedily effected, taking credit herself for returning the ships and any non-contraband freight of which there was probably very little.[78] In February 1590 the alderman of the Steelyard was pleading for some compensation for the 'great loss' of the Hansa merchants, and for some assurance for the future.[79] Perhaps this was in the mind of Burghley when about this time he was busying himself with the definition of contraband and of the English regulations to be applied to Hansa shipping bound for Spain.[80] A clear and cool justification for the seizure by Norris and Drake was composed by Robert Beale and circulated on the continent in both English and Latin versions.[81] The queen also sent various agents to northern Germany to explain her actions, in particular Dr Christopher Parkins. He lingered throughout the summers of 1590 and 1591, scolding and exhorting the senators of the Hansa towns, and exacting due deference to his mistress.[82] The traveller Fynes Morison, visiting the same region in 1591, noted how Stade had begun 'lately to grow rich, not without the envy and impoverishment of the Hamburgers'; these he found to be 'unmeasurably ill-affected to the English', whom they vilified as 'robbers and pirates'.[83] In so hostile an environment any return of the Merchants Adventurers to Hamburg had become remote, and the immediate future of the mart at Stade was secure.

The 1590s were in fact to prove a decade of busy Hispano-Hansa commerce despite the ravages of English privateers in the Atlantic and Channel.[84] In the later years of the decade it even burgeoned into fuller political co-operation, which cannot here be explored. By an imperial mandate, engineered largely by Hispano-Hansa diplomacy, the Merchants Adventurers were banished from the soil of the empire from 1597 to 1601. The company survived this final onslaught upon its traffic in Germany, partly owing to the staunchness of the Staders in keeping faith with it, partly owing to the support of various Protestant princes of the empire.[85] What ultimately put an end to the cloth mart at Stade was the advent of international peace. James I patched up the English quarrel with both Spain and the Hansa in 1604. The natural advantages of Hamburg as a mart town for the Merchants Adventurers in communications, financial facilities, presence of customers made themselves felt; and in 1611 the company returned to Hamburg, where it maintained a settlement for nearly two centuries. Stade ceased to act as a major centre for international trade. It fell under Danish influence, suffered from hostile military incursions during the Thirty Years War, then from 1648 passed with the archbishopric of Bremen under Swedish control. By a curious quirk of politics, the former ecclesiastical territories of Bremen and

Verden were annexed by the peace of Utrecht in 1713 to the electorate of Hanover, whose ruler shortly afterwards became King of Great Britain, so that London and Stade thenceforth shared the same sovereign. But the momentary hopes that the English might return to the Schwinge were soon extinguished. The Merchants Adventurers had lost their privileges and English trade was flowing irrevocably in other channels.

The significance of the Merchants Adventurers' settlement at Stade is not to be measured by the shortness of its life. It was above all a successful wartime expedient, as important in preserving the access of English textiles to their continental consumers as the defeat of the Armada was in maintaining national independence in the face of the Spanish threat. Neither was complete without the other. The finances of the English Crown and the economic life of the kingdom to a great extent hung at that time on the free movement of woollen cloths shipped by the Merchants Adventurers to north-west Europe, as the queen and her chief ministers were well aware. It was a realistic perception of this dependence which had led the regent of the Netherlands in 1563 and her successor the Duke of Alba in 1568 to attempt to interrupt the cloth traffic. Schulte and his confederates still hoped to revive the bargain that had been struck with the Merchants Adventurers in 1567 which had brought in its wake much profit to the city. But political conditions had changed, and in 1587 the King of Spain and his able lieutenant Parma in the Netherlands were able to tip the balance against any resuscitation of the agreement with the Merchants Adventurers. In the emergency that now confronted the Englishmen they found a timely refuge in Stade which enabled their company to regroup and ultimately to survive the full-scale hostility of the Hanseatic League and its allies from 1597 onwards.

Notes

1. By not paying membership fees. Stade to Lübeck, 8 December 1584. *Kölner Inventar*, ed. K. Höhlbaum and H. Keussen (*Inventare hansischer Archive des sechzehnten Jahrhunderts*, I/II) (2 vols, Leipzig, 1896–1903), no. 2256.
2. Treatise possibly by Arthur Nedham, undated, *c.* 1595. BL. Cotton MS. Galba E I, no. 58.
3. For the history of Stade see H. Wohltmann, *Die Geschichte der Stadt Stade an der Niederelbe*, 3rd edn (Stade, 1956); also Heinz Leptien, 'Stade als Hansestadt', *Stader Archiv*, Neue Folge XXIII (1933), pp. 1–

197; E. Weise, 'Die Hanse, England und die Merchant Adventurers. Das Zusammenwirken von Köln und Danzig', *Jahrbuch des Kölnischen Geschichtsvereins*, XXXI/XXXII (1957), pp. 137–64; F. Willerding, 'Die englische Handelsgesellschaft in Stade', *Archiv des Vereins für Geschichte und Altertümer der Herzogtümer Bremen und Verden*, Neue Folge, 1919, pp. 16–41.

4. For the events mentioned above, see R. Ehrenberg, *Hamburg und England im Zeitalter der Königin Elisabeth* (Jena, 1896).

5. For the quotation, 'Reasons for the continuance . . .', 27 December 1587, *C[alendar of] S[tate] P[apers] F[oreign], 1586–8*, p. 457.

6. Merchants Adventurers to Privy Council, undated, *c.* 1583, S[tate] P[apers] 12/175/94, printed in *Tudor Economic Documents*, ed. R. H. Tawney and Eileen Power (London, 1924), vol. II, pp. 66–8.

7. Statement by Merchants Adventurers to Privy Council, undated, *c.* 1584, SP 12/175/93.

8. Burghley to customs officers, 4 March 1585/6. BL Lansdowne MS. 44/23.

9. B. Hagedorn, *Ostfrieslands Handel und Schiffahrt vom Ausgang des 16. Jahrhunderts bis zum Westfälischen Frieden (1580–1648)* (Berlin, 1912), pp. 67–123.

10. Ibid., pp. 119–20.

11. Merchants Adventurers to Privy Council, undated, *c.* 1584, SP 12/175/93.

12. Idem to idem, July 1584, SP 12/157/81.

13. Ibid.

14. For this point see K. R. Andrews, *Elizabethan Privateering* (Cambridge, 1964), pp. 16–18.

15. Merchants Adventurers to Privy Council, November 1586, SP 12/195/36.

16. 'The manner of the proceeding with the Merchants Adventurers', May 1584, SP 12/170/83.

17. Rudolph II to Lübeck, 4 July 1584, *Kölner Inventar*, no. 2179.

18. 'The Proposition of the Alderman of the Steelyard', 6 September 1584. BL. Add. MS. 48009, pp. 605–6.

19. Discussed by G. D. Ramsay, *The City of London in International Politics at the Accession of Elizabeth Tudor* (Manchester, 1975), pp. 158–62.

20. Hansa instructions, 15 November 1584, *Kölner Inventar*, no. 2244, printed in full at pp. 785–8. See also *CSPF, 1584–85*, p. 140; Schulte to Burghley, 8 October 1585. BL. Lansdowne MS. 45/23.

21. Evidence for a much fuller account is in existence with the printing of the despatches of the Hansa envoy Liseman in *Kölner Inventar*, pp. 855–7. See also BL. Add. MS. 48009, pp. 585–733, and 48010, *passim*.

22. Liseman to Suderman, December 1585, *Kölner Inventar*, no. 2368; 'A breviate of the late negotiation', *c.* November 1585, *CSPF, 1585—86*, p. 73f. For the difficulties in conducting negotiations with the Hansa commissioners see Beale to Walsingham, 29 August 1585, SP 12/181/73. For Liseman see P. Simson, 'Der Londoner Kontorsekretär Georg Liseman aus Danzig', *Hansische Geschichtsblätter*, XVI (1910), pp. 441–87.

23. Elizabeth to Lübeck, Bremen, Hamburg and Lüneburg, 5 November 1585 (four letters), *Kölner Inventar*, p. 851. The conclusion of the negotiations was explained by Walsingham to Willoughby, 9 November 1585. BL. Add. MS. 48009, pp. 725–6.

24. Leicester to Burghley, 18 February 1586, *CSPF, 1585–86*, p. 385; idem to idem, 18 June 1586, *CSPF, 1586–87*, pp. 27–8; decree of States General, 9 January 1587, ibid., pp. 289–90.

25. Merchants Adventurers to Privy Council, undated, *c.* September 1586, ibid., pp. 102–3; memorandum of Milward, 9 August 1586, ibid., pp. 118–19.

26. Magistrates and Senate of Hamburg to Elizabeth, 6 March 1586; also Schulte to Burghley, 6 March 1586, *CSPF, 1585–86*, pp. 420–5; further messages dated 19 and 20 August 1586, ibid., pp. 67–70, 73–6.

27. *A[cts of the] P[rivy] C[ouncil], 1585–87*, p. 40; Elizabeth to Hamburg, 1 April 1586, *Kölner Inventar*, no. 2409.

28. *APC, 1585–87*, p. 93. See also the letter of the Gloucestershire clothmakers calendared in *Danziger Inventar*, ed. P. Simson (*Inventare hansischer Archive des sechzehnten Jahrhunderts*, III) (Munich/Leipzig, 1913), no. 9668.

29. Ibid., pp. 272–4. The existence of the detailed study by J. D. Gould, 'The Crisis in the Export Trade, 1586–7', *English Historical Review*, LXXI (1956), pp. 212–22 makes it possible to deal briefly with the topic.

30. Burghley to Hatton, 12 May 1587, SP 12/201/15, printed in N. H. Nicolas, *Memoirs of the Life and Times of Sir Christopher Hatton* (London, 1847), pp. 470–2; Walsingham to Burghley, 14 May 1587, SP 12/201/1; Burghley to Walsingham, also 14 May 1587, SP 12/201/18.

31. *Tudor Royal Proclamations*, ed. P. L. Hughes and J. F. Larkin, vol. II (New Haven/London, 1969), no. 690.

32. For the instructions probably drafted at this time to Governor Saltonstall and Robert Beale see BL. Cotton MS. Nero B IX, no. 56. They may well relate to this mission, with Fletcher replacing Beale soon afterwards. Both Fletcher and Beale are recorded in the *Dictionary of National Biography* and in P. W. Hasler (ed.), *The House of Commons, 1558–1603* (London, 1981).

33. This paragraph is based upon the evidence in the despatch of Saltonstall and Fletcher to the Merchants Adventurers, 19 June 1587, *CSPF, 1586–88*, pp. 313–15. For the dissuasion by Lübeck see Lübeck to Hamburg, 6 August 1587, *Kölner Inventar*, no. 2491, full text p. 898; message of Hamburg Senate, 22 August 1587, ibid., no. 2493, full text p. 899.

34. Burghley to Hatton, 12 May 1587, as at note 30 above.

35. Lübeck to Westendorp, 20 July 1587, ibid., no. 2488; Hamburg to Westendorp, 22 July 1587, ibid. in full pp. 894–8, erroneously calendared under 1589 as no. 2636; Westendorp to Danzig, 11 July 1587, *Danziger Inventar*, no. 9686.

36. H. Kellenbenz, *Unternehmerkräfte im Hamburger Portugal- und Spanienhandel, 1590–1625* (Hamburg, 1954), pp. 100–4.

37. Individual trading families are discussed, ibid., pp. 105–76.

38. Wohltmann, *Stadt Stade*, pp. 75–6.

39. E. Weise, 'Neue Aktenfunde zur Geschichte der Merchants Adventurers im Staatsarchiv zu Hannover', *Stader Jahrbuch*, 1954, p. 84.

40. Bodley to Walsingham, 27 July 1585, *CSPF, 1584–85*, p. 631.

41. Frederick II, King of Denmark, to Elizabeth, 17 May 1585, *Kölner Inventar*, no. 2299.

42. One of them was Richard Sheppard, probably to be identified with the future father-in-law of Lionel Cranfield, first Earl of Middlesex. See letter of Nicholas Warner, 20 June 1587, *CSPF, 1586–88*, p. 315.

43. Saltonstall and Fletcher to Merchants Adventurers, 5 August 1587, *CSPF, 1587*, p. 225.

44. Idem to idem, 29 June 1587, *CSPF, 1586–88*, p. 320. The letter of the Merchants Adventurers to the Privy Council in favour of settlement at Stade, undated August 1587, is at SP 12/203/26.

45. Declaration of the Senate of Hamburg, 12/22 August 1587, *CSPF, 1586–88*, p. 352.

46. The text has been printed, from a copy in the Cologne archives, in Leptien, 'Stade als Hansestadt', pp. 177–97. Another copy exists at BL. Add. MS. 48010, fos. 559–99.

47. Soame is noted in *The House of Commons* (as n. 32). See also Saltonstall to Walsingham, 19 December 1589, SP 12/229/36.

48. Country clothiers to Burghley, 11 October 1587. BL. Lansdowne MS. 52/34.

49. Merchants Adventurers to Privy Council, 18 December 1587 (?), SP 12/144/51. Misdated in calendar to 1580.

50. London Port Book, 1587–88, E 190/7/8, entries for 28 November to 7 December.

51. Reasons for continuance at Stade, 27 December 1587, *CSPF, 1586–88*, pp. 457–8.

52. Edzard to Elizabeth, 13/23 October 1587, *CSPF, 1586–88*, p. 393.

53. Frederick II of Denmark to Elizabeth, 28 February 1588, ibid., pp. 230–1. This has been misdated a year earlier in the calendar: see the entry in *Kölner Inventar*, no. 2546, dated 19/29 February 1588.

54. Rudolph II to Dean and Chapter, 21/31 January 1589, *CSPF, 1589*, pp. 51–2. See also Dean and Chapter to Parma, 5 January/4 February 1590, *L[ist and] A[nalysis of] S[tate] P[apers Foreign]*, vol. I, no. 721.

55. Reasons for continuance, 27 December 1587 (as n. 51), p. 458.

56. Hamburg to Westendorp, 22 July 1587, *Kölner Inventar*, Appendix no. 236.

57. Elizabeth to Hamburg, 30 April 1588, ibid., no. 2552: seemingly identical with the 'Heads of a letter to Hamburg', *CSPF, 1586–88*, p. 429.

58. *APC, 1588*, pp. 91–2.

59. The evidence of what exactly happened is not quite consistent. See Ehrenberg, *Hamburg und England*, p. 188 (using Hamburg municipal records); Hamburg to governor Peacock, 28 June/8 July 1588, *CSPF, 1586–88*, pp. 652–3; Nicholas Pierson to Merchants Adventurers, 11 May 1588, ibid., pp. 611–12; *Kölner Inventar*, p. 294, n. 4.

60. William Milward to Burghley, 28 April 1589, *CSPF, 1589*, pp. 241–2.
61. *APC, 1588*, pp. 77–87.
62. Instructions to Bodley, 11 August 1588. BL. Harleian MS. 36/53.
63. Steelyard to Hamburg, October 1588, *Danziger Inventar*, no. 9809.
64. English reply to Dutch request, August 1584, *CSPF, 1584–85*, p. 700.
65. Stafford to Walsingham, 18 December 1584, ibid., p. 191; Burghley to Davison, 14 January 1585, ibid., p. 241; 'A note of such ships', 29 March 1585, ibid., p. 385.
66. Elizabeth to Hamburg, 5 November 1585, printed in E. I. Kouri (ed.), *Elizabethan England and Europe (Bulletin of the Institute of Historical Research*, Special Supplement XII) (London, 1982), no. 24; cf. BL. Add. MS. 48009, p. 724.
67. Willoughby to Elizabeth, 25 December 1585, *CSPF, 1585*, p. 238; but they were later reported all the same, Tenneker to Walsingham, 18 May 1587, *CSPF, 1586–88*, pp. 300–1.
68. News from Portugal, 26 December 1585, *CSPF, 1585-87*, p. 241; Steelyard to Danzig, 9 March/28 February 1588, *Danziger Inventar*, no. 9729.
69. Elizabeth to Hamburg, undated summer 1587, ibid., no. 9694.
70. Advertisements from Hamburg, 12 March 1586, *CSPF, 1585–86*, p. 437, and similar subsequent items.
71. Advertisements from Flushing, 29 November 1588, *CSPF, 1588*, pp. 350–1; Robert Peacock to Burghley, 1 December 1588, ibid., p. 360; newsletter, 10 November 1588, ibid., p. 310.
72. Milward to Walsingham, 4 April 1589, *CSPF, 1589*, pp. 197–8.
73. Milward to Burghley, 27 April 1589, ibid., p. 232, and 28 April, ibid., p. 241.
74. The progress of the expedition as recounted by R. B. Wernham, 'Queen Elizabeth and the Portugal Expedition of 1589', *English Historical Review*, LXVI (1951), pp. 3–26, 194–218 is taken for granted.
75. *APC, 1589*, p. 192.
76. Discourse of Colonel Anthony Wingfield, in R. Hakluyt, *The principall navigations, voiages and discoveries of the English nation*, ed. W. Raleigh (Glasgow, 1903–5), vol. VI, p. 510.
77. See for a recent verdict R. B. Wernham, *After the Armada* (Oxford, 1984), pp. 126–30.
78. *LASP*, vol. III, no. 906. The losses of the Danzig merchants are detailed at no. 905. The admiralty commission is at SP 12/227/49.
79. Requests of Steelyard, 22 February 1590, SP 12/222/86, misdated in *C[alendar of] S[tate] P[apers] D[omestic], 1581–90*, p. 580.
80. Undated draft, corrections in Burghley's hand, SP 12/235/10. The suggested reference to the Merchants Adventurers at *CSPD, 1581–90*, p. 707 is unwarranted.
81. *A declaration of the causes which moved the chief commanders of the Navy ...* (London, 1589). *Short Title Catalogue*, nos. 9196 and 9197. The Latin version of this remarkable state paper was reprinted by K. Höhlbaum, 'Königin Elisabeth und die Hansestädte im Jahre 1589. Eine englische Staatsschrift', *Hansische Geschichtsblätter*, X (1903),

pp. 136–62, from a copy in the Cologne archives. It does not appear that the English version has ever been reprinted, though it deserves to be.

82.   Various despatches from him are summarised in *LASP*; see particularly those of 27 June and 31 December 1590 in vol. II, nos. 729–32, and vol. III, no. 877; also his oration of 30 June 1590, vol. I, no. 746.

83.   Fynes Morison, *An Itinerary* (Glasgow, 1907–8), vol. I, pp. 3, 5, 78.

84.   Kellenbenz, *Unternehmerkräfte*, pp. 333–4.

85.   This has been investigated in the fine study by L. Beutin, *Hanse und Reich im handelspolitischen Endkampf gegen England* (Berlin, 1929), which has regrettably been allowed to go out of print.

22 Two Revolutions in Early Modern Denmark*

E. Ladewig Petersen and Knud J. V. Jespersen

Probably only die-hards would today contest the significance of the 'Tudor revolution in government'. It has become a well-established, almost venerable fact that 'the 1530s (represent) a period of revolutionary reorganisation in the fundamentals and details of government', the essential ingredient of which 'was the concept of national sovereignty' – the notion of 'the King-in-Parliament', established by the statute of the realm of 1534. The revolution did not involve 'the systematic and entire destruction of what was before'; it 'grew from roots which can be traced well back in time, and it was peculiarly the utmost show of legality and constitutional propriety': in spite of – or perhaps because of – its conservative look the revolution ensured its 'permanency and its ready acceptance'.[1]

Can this concept of a revolution – constitutional, conservative or otherwise – be extended to the continent, or did the continent remain isolated? Symptomatically, both Scandinavian powers Sweden Finland as well as Denmark–Norway – passed through 'contemporary revolutions', and both England and Denmark resettled again following revolutions in 1660, in the case of the former in spite of the 'notorious incompetence of the Stuarts'. And in the case of the latter? In short, at first sight contemporaneity seems to suggest a rewarding field for comparative study. This paper does not pretend to present new empirical results; it aims more modestly at bringing the constitutional, financial and political developments of Denmark during 'the age of aristocratic rule' (*adelsvaeldet*) into line with those of England and the continent.

This certainly does not imply any attempt to gloss over the idiosyncracies of the Danish case. In both Scandinavian countries aristocratic rule seems to have emerged during the fifteenth century, as in England, on the basis of a constitutionalist interpretation of late medieval populist theory, vehemently opposed by the expanding Oldenburg monarchy. In Sweden the early Vasa monarchy succeeded in arresting this trend, not simply by the establishment of hereditary monarchy in 1544 (which did not rule out constitutional guarantees), but most effectively by the creation of the distinctive 'state of Estates' (*ständerstat*), which made it possible for the Vasas to play off the aristocratic council against the noble and non-noble Estates of the Swedish diet (*riksdag*). In contrast, Denmark remained a society of Estates (*standssamfund*). The state council (*rigsråd*) – since 1536 representing all four Estates – remained the only body constitutionally entitled to share with the king the sovereignty of the Danish crown; the crisis point was not reached until the mid-seventeenth century, when external factors made this exclusive system of checks and balances inoperable.[2]

Perhaps this elaborate organisation merits a few words of introduction. Constitutionally, a coronation charter (*håndfaestning*) laid down the framework of each individual reign. The charter of 1536 could be said to provide a model constitution, since it fundamentally regulated the Danish diarchy after a period of more or less unrestricted reactionary rule (since the expulsion in 1523 of Christian II), of religious and social tension, and of civil war (1534–36). It should be borne in mind, however, that the drafting of a new coronation charter before the coronation of a new king (even when king-elect) served the council as a convenient means of settling accounts with the encroachment of the late king. This was apparently the case in 1513 and in 1523 after the reigns of expansive monarchs like John and Christian II.

In spite of the fact that the coronation charter of 1536 became by and large the standard for the entire period of aristocratic rule, the one following in 1559 – that of Frederick II – revised several important details to the benefit of the political status of the state council.[3] On the other hand the coronation of Christian IV in 1596 repeated that of his father *verbatim*, which, however, does not rule out the possibility that political or other relations had changed within the institutional framework. The absence of revision would suggest that the diarchy – the king-in-council, as it were – had worked in practice, and that the assumption of an axiomatic conflict between monarchy and aristocracy, so close to the hearts of earlier historians, cannot be maintained unreservedly. But the 'emancipation' of Christian IV and financial needs created by the internationalisation of Scandinavian conflicts since the 1620s, called for severe restrictions to be imposed upon his successor Frederick III in 1648 – at a crossroads when the constitutional issues had degenerated into an impasse that could apparently be resolved only by the authoritarian rule established in 1660.

A further feature requires introductory emphasis: the coronation charter seems Janus-faced. Institutionally it not only defined the exercise or limitations of constitutional authority and power (and prescribed the maintenance of the Lutheran church); conversely it also specified the privileges of the nobility, in theory shared by all nobles equally, which, although still neglected by international research, were almost the most extensive of the entire European orbit. The non-noble Estates, summoned only in cases of national emergency, had to content themselves with general royal guarantees of security and just rule. But in spite of its exclusivity the Danish aristocratic regime would still fit the early modern European pattern of a 'libertarian constitution' – just as the process of disintegration in the seventeenth century seems to follow European currents.

The well-known fact that Danish absolutism turned out to be the most extreme (as well as one of the most obnoxious) cannot simply be explained in terms of reaction against the exclusivity of the preceding aristocratic rule, though perhaps this was a contributory factor. The severe and far from undeserved censure of Danish absolutism, marked by dubious revolutionary origins and systematic suppression, served the English Whig politician Robert Molesworth as an appalling and ominous model;[4] and a generation later Montesquieu pointed out that Danish absolutism differed only from Persian despotism by the fact that it had been codified by the *Lex Regia* (1665). In contrast to more 'pragmatic' absolutist regimes Danish monocracy was based on solid theoretical foundations. The paradox remains: two unbloody 'revolutions' usher in, symbolically, two extreme constitutional systems, each in its way radical even by contemporary European standards.

The Revolution of 1536 and its Aftermath, the Domain State

E. Ladewig Petersen

I

According to late medieval aristocratic theory – inspired by the Bartoline principles of *regimen ad politicum – dominium* resided in the council, which represented all Estates. The king, strictly bound by his *juramentum*, should function only as a '*rex statutarius, usufructuarius et administrator regni non rerum dominus*'. Election of a successor *vivente rege* might, if done repeatedly, decline into a bad habit or lead to hereditary monarchy, which ought to be avoided at all costs, since it would inevitably reduce the council and the populace to serfdom. In his capacity as servant of the realm the king had to content himself with such means as were allocated to him to carry out his job.[5] In short, it was the council which disposed of the sovereignty of the state, symbolically expressed by the allegiance of those in charge of the castles of the realm (*slotslovene*).

In 1513 little more than a quarter of the crown lands was allocated to the royal household, the rest being either pledged or reserved to noble lords-lieutenant (*lensmaend*), freely or on favourable terms, in order that they might 'avert the damage and corruption of the realm'. This applies particularly to territorial fiefs involving the civil and military administration of a substantial district, while numerous small fiefs – a single manor or a cluster of peasant tenancies – served to reward petty nobles or servants.[6]

Such unfavourable conditions were of course insufficient to support an emerging modern monarchy, as was the principle of direct remuneration at the discretion of an avaricious aristocracy. Remarkably enough, in the course of the interregnum which followed the decision of the council in 1533 to postpone the election of a new king, and which was the prelude to civil war, Mogens Goye, the Lord Constable, had protested that 'anyone in possession of a crown fief is obliged to preserve the rights, the rents and the prerogative of the crown' until such time as 'God assigns us again a master and a king'.[7] The passage merits attention, revealing as it does that medieval notions were being replaced by a more modern and impersonal concept of the prerogative of the crown.

Following two years of civil war Copenhagen surrendered on 6 August 1536 to the new king-elect, Christian III. Early on the morning of 12 August the king imprisoned those bishops who were in Copenhagen at the time, and the rest followed later. Evidence suggests that this *coup d'état* had been planned by the king together with his closest councillors (including Mogens Goye and the new chancellor Johan Friis), and some of the Holsteiners who had both marshalled forces and contributed financial backing in the king's brutal campaign of reconquest.[8] Several details remain obscure, but

the king evidently faced two pressing problems: the future constitutional framework and the debts incurred in the war.

On 12 August the king presented his bill. When the council met,
protests were apparently still voiced at his Lutheran beliefs, but the
lay councillors were obliged to yield to the king's demand for the
secularisation of church property and his insistence that good government in future could be safeguarded only by the rule of the king and
his lay councillors, to the exclusion of the bishops.[9] At all events
confiscation of church property had become inescapable; taxation
alone could not suffice to meet the burden of the king's debts, but the
prospect of his disposing over ecclesiastical funds served to convince
his creditors that the debts could be met. Constitutional issues were to
be settled by a diet, to which all four Estates were summoned, and
which met in October 1536. If the king had contemplated establishing
a hereditary monarchy with the consent of the diet on the ostensible
grounds of preventing future 'disorder' (as the evidence suggests he
did), he was not successful.[10] On the contrary, the ambiguous statement passed when the diet was prorogued on 30 October that it had
been established in an unorthodox manner actually served to legitimate the fact that under the 'new' constitution the council still
functioned as the 'parliamentary' representatives of all the Estates of
the realm. On the other hand, authority over the castles encompassed
by the *slotslov* was to be exercised by king and council in common and
only in the case of a vacancy by the council alone. Accordingly the
prorogation declaration states that

> since the supreme authority of the realm resides mostly in the
> person of the king, (and since) he cannot be supposed to exercise it
> alone, he is obliged at all times to appoint a lord seneschal, a
> chancellor and a lord constable . . . to assist the king and the council
> of the realm in maintaining His Majesty's [that is the crown's]
> exercise of power in the business and affairs of the state.[11]

Finally, the coronation charter issued on the same day guaranteed the
nobility the monopoly of the great fiefs, the exclusive right of the
council to vote extraordinary taxation, as well as its right to sanction
war.

For all its narrower, artistocratic basis this 'new constitution'
resembles in principle the English concept of 'King-in-Parliament', in
both judicial terms and in its supposition that the king worked within
the framework of law and custom. In fact, both prorogation declara-

tion and coronation charter of 1536 provided the foundation of the Danish *monarchia mixta*, sometimes termed diarchy, over the next 125 years. None the less, recent research has demonstrated that the modernised constitution provided the springboard for important reforms, supported by both the king and council.

These reforms, initiated during the 1540s, proceeded along two or three different lines. First, sequestered church property had to be incorporated into the existing framework of the crown lands. Next, most of the petty fiefs – more than two-thirds of a total of around 220 – were abolished or incorporated into the larger units, and finally, but most importantly, the territorial fiefs were subjected to a process of concentration and the imposition of terms much more profitable to the crown. Admittedly during the reign of Christian III the government had to devote a great deal of effort to paying off its war debts, largely by way of extraordinary taxation and administrative retrenchment. These efforts succeeded, with the balance in the ordinary budget re-established by 1559, although only to be disturbed once more by the Scandinavian Seven Years War of 1563–70 and its equally painful aftermath.

These reforms naturally encountered opposition from conservatives mourning the loss of the golden age, but by 1588 on the death of Frederick II the situation had changed radically. Reform had made the holding of fiefs a prize to be competed for by noble careerists, a way of distinguishing the 'ins' from the 'outs'.[12] As in England, aristocratic attitudes had changed; the aristocratic elite had become a social group who were well-trained officials, as well as landowners. In principle four to five hundred adult nobles had to share between them some sixty territorial fiefs; in practice, however, these were monopolised by a few (extremely rich) families, who also dominated the council. The latter had come to serve and share the interests of the crown financially, administratively and politically.

II

According to the lists of the sins of the bishops presented in the royal proposal of 1536, the bishop-elect of Roskilde had boasted that he would 'admit or suffer no king into the realm, but to his own will and ends'. In his opinion 'no king ought to be awarded more than 15,000 guilders annually besides the services of a loose and dishonest woman'.[13] Leaving aside its scurrility remarkable for a man of the cloth, this alleged declaration reaches to the core of late medieval constitutional and fiscal principles. No records survive from which to ascertain the scope of the royal finances. An isolated memorandum from the chancellor in 1523 puts royal income during the reign of King John (1481–1513) at 59,000 marks (20–29,000 Rhenish guilders, including municipal taxes at 6500 marks, but omitting casual revenue – tolls, fines, etc.).[14] These figures are probably not far off the mark as regards net royal income after the deduction of local expenditure and the fees of lords-lieutenant. Customs revenue cannot be calculated, but the earliest extant rolls indicate that Sound dues (tolls from the passage of ships through Öresund) brought in approximately 4500–5900 Rhenish guilders.[15]

Of more significance is what might be termed fiscal typology. In 1502–5 Henry VII derived some 30 per cent of his income from crown lands, although parliamentary grants of taxation and customs, and, eventually, loans assumed rapidly increasing importance. At all events, Edward IV's solemn declaration 'to live upon mine own, and not to charge my subjects but in great causes and urgent necessity' would make little sense on the accession of Henry VIII.[16] At the other end of the scale the domain income of the French crown at the end of the Hundred Years War had declined to 3 per cent and was even less – despite Sully's reforms – by 1600; the situation was similar in Spain.[17] In contrast to this His Danish Majesty received some 75 per cent of his net revenue from crown lands in 1500. Admittedly the policy of royal imperialism up to the collapse of the Union of Kalmar in 1523 would have been inconceivable without substantial grants of extraordinary taxation, as would the defence measures taken against the exiled Christian II. Nevertheless, despite important reforms and changes in the course of the sixteenth century Denmark remained a domain state until the turbulent 1620s, an anomaly in the European context.

Secularisation of church property trebled the domain resources of the Danish crown, from 100,000 to 300,000 barrels of grain[18] (*tonder hartkorn*).[19] In 1650 the crown owned half the country's land (nobles 44 per cent) and there is reason to believe that this balance had not changed since the Reformation. Secularisation of church property – perhaps one-third of all land – made the crown the largest landowner, sharing the vested landed interests of the aristocracy. To make another comparison, secularisation in Sweden proper increased the crown's share of the land from about 5 per cent to about 28 per cent (nobles 22 per cent) although tax-paying freeholders at 50 per cent remained the largest group (they held 6 per cent in Denmark in 1650).[20] In England, the crown's share likewise amounted to about 5 per cent at the end of the Middle Ages; secularisation probably added 20 to 25 per cent, the better part of which (65 to 75 per cent) had, however, been sold by the accession of Elizabeth I.[21]

In spite of the fact that land values increased sixfold over the latter half of the sixteenth century[22] the Danish crown did not capitalise its assets. To a certain extent administrative and financial reforms served ends similar to the English crown's adroit adaption of fines, rents and capitalisation rates, but this is far from the whole story. As a result of the price revolution and managerial reforms, the increase in proceeds from the crown lands far exceeded the trebling warranted by their enlarged territorial extent. The 17–26,000 Rhenish guilders tentatively assumed for 1500 had risen to 173,000 *daler* by 1600, still accounting for 50 per cent of the crown's net income.[23] Sales of crown lands were insignificant until the mid-seventeenth century, and were likewise of minor importance in Sweden until the large-scale alienations of Gustavus Adolphus. In England, while Thomas Cromwell might advocate the retention of monastic property, domain income was no longer sufficient to sustain the medieval principles of Edward IV. Hard facts – a militant monarch and the financial crisis of 1536 – undermined Cromwell's principles: war in France and Scotland in the 1540s consumed £2.2 million, and sales of monastic lands raised £0.8 million in the last nine years of the reign of Henry VIII.[24] England had to succumb to the imperative of royal expenditure, as the major continental monarchies had already done.

III

There is no need to stress the importance of war as the fulcrum of development, but there is still room for the operation of secondary factors such as the availability of constitutional alternatives, of economic, fiscal or political priorities. There is no need, either, to analyse the origins of the secularisation of ecclesiastical property; in both England and Scandinavia the prevailing tension between the needs of the crown and the greed of the lay aristocracy made legislation inevitable. In Denmark the domains had become a relatively far more valuable asset than elsewhere, but the situation was more than a question of not killing the goose that laid the golden eggs.

It might be suspected that the profit motive and the crown's obligation to support noble lords-lieutenant would have combined to facilitate alienation, need and greed working together. But it could also be plausibly argued that the domain structure was inherent in the very foundations of the constitutional system through the weight of tradition. In principle a regular and reliable crown revenue made constitutional control simple and stable, and enabled the government to enforce a modernised version of the medieval programme which was invoked right down to the middle of the seventeenth century. Finally a limitation of (invariably extraordinary) taxation would tend, according to the prevailing economic doctrines of *oeconomia* to encourage economic and fiscal prosperity.[25]

The basic ideal of the Danish diarchy was achieved in 1559 and 1588 with the ordinary budget balanced after the distortions of wartime. Such an ideal presupposed in effect non-involvement in European conflict and the absence of standing forces (the navy excepted) – things would hardly have worked the other way round. A blessing or not, neutrality combined with military and financial expediency in the event of war did postpone the need to reform financial structures and military organisation.

One might, if a brief counter-factual argument is permissible, have expected the council to have been prepared to supply controllable taxation and customs, annually or for some specified period – as did the English parliament. Given the actual social system, far less permeable than those of England and Sweden, taxation of landed wealth was out of the question. Even regular municipal taxation remained as its medieval level, and by 1600 customs did not account for more than 10 per cent of the crown's gross revenue. No attempts were yet made to make fiscal ends match commercial prosperity, as in England, and it is doubtful if fiscal imposition would have proved adequate in the event of a financial emergency.

Whether due to the financial genius of Peder Oxe, the Lord Seneschal, or to someone else's ingenuity, the introduction of lastage to supplement the ancient ship dues at Elsinore in 1567 raised the proceeds of the Sound tolls at a stroke from 45,000 *daler* to 132,000 *daler*. But the stark reality that the treasurer's accounts, though far from exhaustive, register military spending over the years 1564–70 at about 4.2 million *daler* warrants the conclusion that without counter-productive abuse the customs could not under the circumstances be raised to meet wartime demands.[26] War had to be financed by taxation, credit and loans; it left debts of at least 1.75 million *daler* which had to be met before the ordinary balance could be restored in the late 1580s.

In 1563 Frederick II had probably expected to be able to subdue

Sweden by a blitzkrieg, a tactic that had worked back in 1520. In one lucid moment on New Year's Day 1570 the king acknowledged that he might have been ill advised or that he had lent a deaf ear to his councillor's warning, but he still refused to assume responsibility for the war.[27] Despite the king's conviction that 'we should have had peace today, had we been allowed to have our own way', the war had reached deadlock and had trapped the realm financially.

Whether this was a constitutional crisis or not, the council ignored the king's offer to resign, but pointed out that in a *monarchia mixta* both the head, His Majesty, and the limbs, the council, were necessary; it had no intention whatsoever of sacrificing this fundamental balance. Financial exertion and diplomatic skill restored peace with the Treaty of Stettin. Paradoxically the next royal adventure, the Kalmar War of 1611–13, left fewer scars, financially or constitutionally. This war cost 2 million *daler*, 30 per cent of which Christian IV had been able to meet from his own treasury; a further 30 per cent had been provided by the Kiel money market and the wealthy Queen Dowager.[28] In military terms this war followed the old beaten path of raising a mercenary army at the opening of hostilities, but financially new trends emerged. Backed by considerable royal funds, the king in 1611 could bring to bear the threat of declaring war in his capacity as Duke of Holstein, if the council refused to comply. Several other factors induced the council to yield, including increasing tensions among the German states, although in fact this war did little seriously to disturb the balance of power.

IV

If war, diplomacy and court expenditure were the principal agents in the formation of quasi-absolutist monarchy after the onset of the Italian dynastic wars, later aggravated by religious conflict, then Denmark, still no negligible quantity, remained until the early seventeenth century the exception which proved the rule, as did Sweden to some degree. Neither became sucked into the vortex of international conflict. Since the Danish–imperial peace settlement of Speyer in 1544 Denmark held aloof from continental embroilments, her main international interests being confined to Protestant Germany. It was symptomatic that only France maintained a resident envoy at the Danish court (1541), who was supposed to watch over peace in the Baltic and to ensure benevolent neutrality in the rear of the territories subject to Habsburg domination.[29]

The persistent conflicts over dynastic hegemony in Scandinavia which were spiced in due course by the struggle for naval and commercial supremacy in the Baltic remained largely outside the scope of the European contest, as did the second, related sphere of conflict, the Russian–Polish–Swedish embroglios from 1558 onwards. The inter-Scandinavian treaties of Brömsebro in 1541 and Stettin in 1570 even aimed at preventing further eruption. In contrast to most European treaties of concord, the regular border meetings established under their clauses between state councillors did prevent clashes for many decades, until the institution disintegrated under the pressure of royal sabotage and external stimuli in the early seventeenth century.[30]

If Wittenberg was the political and confessional Mecca of Denmark, and if her relations with the Protestant money and matrimonial markets had to some extent served to isolate the early Vasas, things changed on the accession of Christian IV. Dynastic policies and the pursuit of secularised bishoprics in northern Germany became major concerns of His Majesty's foreign policy, for both dynastic and strategic reasons, to provide for younger sons and to check Swedish expansionism, which was turning towards the south from the peace settlement of Stolbova in 1617, at the latest. Other factors may also have contributed: the need of the western powers in the early 1620s for proxies to prosecute continental wars, to prevent Habsburg hegemony, and, in a wider perspective, probably to nurse their own overseas interests. Finally, the increasing dependence of maritime powers on the metals, timber and other materials it supplied brought the Baltic area within the sphere of international concern. Altogether the early seventeenth century represents a watershed of great political, financial and constitutional significance.

The changes did not of course escape the attention of foreign observers. In an extensive report the French envoy, Charles de Dançay, examined the Scandinavian political systems and the balance of power in 1575.[31] A few years later an English envoy stressed in his reports the affluence of Danish society and the not unconnected aristocratic structure of the constitution. The nobles were determined to 'meintein their libertie' as well as electoral monarchy, 'by which the kingdom of Denmark consisteth'. On the other hand, Dançay had whispered in his ear that the crown 'is one of the richest in Europe'; it was burdened with no debts, and had substantial revenues from customs.[32]

So far, nothing would appear to have been rotten in the state of Denmark. And a few years later in 1606 a French diplomat noted Sweden's poverty, political isolation and internal political tensions, whereas by contrast Denmark's affluence and financial strength, coupled with the king's close political and matrimonial connections with Protestant Germany might well make Sweden an easy prey, and even perhaps make Christian IV a force to be reckoned with in the German lands. The envoy may have exaggerated the king's annual revenue, but he rightly pointed out that restrictive policies of expenditure enabled the king to hoard 'une notable somme du revenue'.[33]

A glance at the earliest 'balances of the realm's revenue and expenditure' from 1600 is sufficient to convince us that Denmark remained a domain state. Sixty-seven per cent of the crown's gross revenue (or 50 per cent of its net revenue after deduction of local costs) derived from crown lands, and 33 per cent from Sound dues. Substantial surpluses – in 1608 no less than 49 per cent of the gross income – were the direct result of restrictive financial policies, although it is true that favourable balance sheets such as these were achieved thanks solely to the Sound dues; net domain income did no more than match expenditure on the royal household, fixed naval costs and so on.[34]

Contrary to the accepted view, Sound tolls were not paid exclusively to the king's chamber in accordance with the royal prerogative; payments from the coffers at Elsinore or from the royal chamber to the treasurers of the realm – or vice-versa – occur regularly, obviously depending upon prevailing constitutional balances. The Sound dues had become the margin between the ordinary and extraordinary outgoings of the realm, as well as facilitating the king's remarkable hoarding of treasure. The annual revenue of the royal chamber can tentatively be put at 0.3–0.4 million *daler*, to which must be added the Swedish war indemnity of 1 million *daler* in 1616–19; in spite of conspicuous expense His Majesty's fortune seems to have passed the one million *daler* mark by 1618, and to have reached 1.5 million *daler* by the early 1620s.[35]

Financial emancipation, once achieved, enabled the king to pursue unfettered his own political ends, the pursuit of secularised bishoprics as well as the military and diplomatic preparation for entry into the continental conflict (under the very nose of Gustavus Adolphus). And the constraints upon him became positively elastic through ample use of the devious device of converting his personal expenditure into expenditure on behalf of the realm, to be met through the voting of taxation. In brief, the king's manoeuvres effectively paralysed financially and politically the council's avenues of control. Its final effort to check royal activity in 1623–24 came too late to avert disaster.[36]

V

The insistence upon a balanced ordinary budget and the policy of neutrality both contributed to the preservation of the domain structure of Danish public finance and of the country's archaic methods of military organisation in the event of war. Indeed, Denmark's affluence enabled her to bear the burdens and even the reverses of warfare by means of taxation, loans and credit – that is, on the basis of her landed wealth – well into the seventeenth century.

In 1600 Danish material and financial resources could probably still match those of Sweden, but the Danish and Swedish budgetary systems differed to the degree of almost defying comparison, as did the key factors of financial structure.[37] In Sweden 80–90 per cent of the crown's ordinary income still derived from its rents and economic activities, but in general income had been assigned to meet expenses at both central and local level. By contrast, in Denmark, as in England, local expenditure for administrative, social or other purposes (some 48 per cent of the crown's gross domain income) was met locally, leaving a net surplus in money or kind at governmental disposal. Allocation to central or national expenditure of specific sources of revenue did not occur until the period of acute crisis in the 1650s.

As a rule, however, Swedish governmental expenditure exceeded ordinary income by 40–55 per cent as early as 1573 and 1582, largely as a result of military spending. Two main problems thus faced the early Vasa rulers: how to transform crown revenue into cash or military material to supply its armies, and the need to raise substantial supplementary funds. As elsewhere, credit and loans played a key role; in 1573 national debts can be estimated at 1 million *daler*, and they had risen to an estimated 7 million *daler* on the eve of the German war in 1629, even though important money markets such as Kiel (controlled by the Danish king) seem to have remained out of Sweden's reach.

Sweden's almost permanent commitment to war from 1558 onwards thus forced her into fertile experiments to finance and supply her war effort. Royal monopolies in trade in important commodities played a significant role (metals, for example, and fur, supposedly a royal prerogative, and latterly attempts were made to monopolise the Baltic grain trade). The same applies to the levying of customs in the Baltic ports, and onerous extraordinary taxation expanded rapidly, effectively becoming regular taxation by the turn of the century. Indeed, the eternal problem of raising funds and fiscal considerations became the immanent corollary of territorial, dynastic and religious expansion until Gustavus Adolphus' German campaign.[38] The revolution in the financing of war had been brought about by a long and ingenious process, eventually to be completed by Gustavus Adolphus and Wallenstein; the military *perpetuum mobile* had become a dynamic force that took Europe by surprise and caught Denmark and Poland napping.

The meteoric rise of Sweden does not quite fit the general European pattern; most major powers had acquired the characteristics of a tax state necessary to prosecute their wars by 1500. The fact remains, however, that Sweden forced its way to the status of a military and tax state decades before Denmark. All European ramifications apart, this circumstance might help explain the shifting balance of power in Scandinavia. In a way, the constitutional, financial and (non-)military organisation of sixteenth-century Denmark had been an extension of medieval domain state principles, a subtle refinement of the *monarchia mixta*, and incidentally also highly centralised, in contrast, for example, to Poland. For several reasons a system, which seems in general to have worked throughout the classical period of economic prosperity and political non-commitment, had become hopelessly outdated by 1620. Denmark had to face confrontation with Sweden's supreme power, as well as the hard facts of the European environment: her ancient structures could not possibly survive challenges of such magnitude.

The Revolution of 1660 and its Precondition, the Tax-State
Knud J. V. Jespersen

I

On 14 November 1665 Frederick III, the absolute King of Denmark, signed the *Lex Regia*, thereby redeeming a promise given to the delegates of the diet of 1660, which had bestowed upon him his absolute power. This fundamental statute of the absolute regime – for many years kept a state secret – provided the formal constitutional basis of Danish absolutism, which thus differed from every other absolute regime in Europe by being not only the most absolute but also by being equipped with a formal constitution.

In the preamble to this statute the circumstances surrounding the transfer of power to the king were described in the manner the new régime wished them to be understood by posterity.[39] It avers that the entire process was the work of Almighty God, in whose hands the king was but a humble tool. The transfer of power from subjects to king was due only to the will of God, and the foundation of the new régime was thus both firm and legal.

It was further stated that God in his endless mercy and omnipotence had, to start with, saved Denmark from the imminent danger of total annihilation in the last war with Sweden (1657–60), but had then gone a step further by inducing the Estates of the realm to abstain from their ancient right of electing the king, and had inspired the aristocratic state council to the perfectly voluntary act of cancelling and ceding to the king the coronation charter, the council's most important constitutional guarantee. The Almighty had finally prevailed upon the king's subjects to release him from his oath according to the old constitution and had prompted the same subjects to cede to the king and his house full hereditary right to the throne, together with 'all *Iura Majestatis*, absolute power, sovereignty, and all attributes and regalities appertaining to the royal crown'. With the exception of only three points this total delegation of power was unconditional. These were that the kingdom should never be divided; that the form of government should remain Christian; and that the king should issue a fundamental statute defining the constitutional framework of the new regime. The *Lex Regia* was the fulfilment of the last condition.

As may be observed even from this summary account the royal author went out of his way to stress the totally voluntary character of the power delegation of 1660: only genuinely divine inspiration had moved the king's subjects, and this of course conformed perfectly to the preamble's description of the régime as strictly legal. It is not altogether surprising therefore that the very transfer of power itself was described as a perfectly harmonious act, in which the king was only the passive receiver and God the real mover and source of inspiration. In this way a very close relationship between God and the absolute monarch – the king by God's grace – was established by the statute. At the same time the distance between this semi-divine ruler and his subjects was correspondingly increased.

The picture drawn in the *Lex Regia* of the constitutional revolution of 1660 is of course no more than an element of the régime's propaganda for its own legality. The political realities beneath this harmonious picture are, as one might expect, an entirely different matter, and as such justify the use of the term revolution about the events in the autumn of 1660.

II

In a sense the events leading up to the constitutional revolution can be said to have begun on 27 May 1660. This was the day on which representatives of the Danish and Swedish governments signed the peace treaty concluding an exhausting three-year war which during its most critical moments had threatened the very existence of Denmark as an independent nation.

Denmark narrowly escaped this fate, but had none the less to cede all the Danish provinces east of the Oresund, except the small island of Bornholm, whose inhabitants two years earlier had thrown out single-handed the Swedish occupying forces. Now peace was at last a blessed reality, but hardly had the clouds of gunsmoke drifted away before the serious problems of the peace loomed on the horizon. In the course of the war the Danish government's debts had swollen to the formidable amount of more than five million *rigsdaler*, and a large army of mercenary soldiers waited with growing impatience for their demobilisation – and their pay.

The financial problems were aggravated by the fact that this time it was not possible simply to give the tax-screw some extra turns. The taxpayers – the non-noble Estates – were unable to pay heavy new taxes on top of the extensive systematic devastation inflicted by the occupying Swedish forces. So, once peace finally broke out, the government was faced with a financial problem which could be solved only by involving much larger sections of the population than was normal in the necessary political decisions.

In this tricky situation the government resorted to an exceptional expedient: the summoning of a diet representing the nobility, the clergy, and the towns. No one thought it necessary, however, to invite representatives of the country's largest group of taxpayers, the peasants. The summons was issued on 5 August, and on 8 September the delegates met for the first time in Copenhagen. In this assembly the foundation for the later political changes was laid. But at the beginning of September very few, if any, of the delegates foresaw this subsequent course of events. They had after all gathered in order to solve the urgent financial problems – not with a view to revising the constitution.

III

The strange chain of events which transformed the Danish constitution from an elective, constitutional monarchy to a hereditary absolute régime can conveniently be divided into three distinct phases. The first was the establishment of the hereditary monarchy during the period from the opening of the diet until Saturday, 13 October. In this phase the delegates of the diet played a decisive role. The second was the revocation of the coronation charter and its deliverance into the king's hands, which lasted until Wednesday, 17 October. During this stage only an inner circle of prominent politicians was involved. The third, during which the final decision to grant the king absolute power was made, began on 18 October and ended on 10 January 1661, when an act of sovereignty codifying the new political reality was issued. In this last phase only a few royal advisers and courtiers were active.

In many respects the first phase is the most remarkable and, at the same time, the most puzzling. The delegates started as stipulated by debating how to dispose of the large public debts. It was quickly agreed that two courses of action had to be taken: cut-backs on expenditure and the imposition of new taxes. The saving on expenditure was to be achieved by a drastic and immediate reduction of the armed forces, and revenue increased by a new tax on consumption. So far everything had progressed smoothly.

Indeed, serious problems did not arise until the nobility demanded exemption from the new tax by pointing to their old privileges which granted them freedom from taxation. This rather unwise step provoked great indignation among the non-noble delegates, who feared rightly enough that they would once again be left to bear the full burden of taxation. In order to prevent such an outcome they combined their forces to form an entirely new political pressure-group. This new political party, comprising an alliance between clergy and citizens, styled itself 'The Conjugated under the Liberty of Copenhagen', thus indicating that both the clergy and the provincial towns wished to be treated on equal terms with Copenhagen. The citizens of the capital had only a few months earlier been granted aristocratic privileges as a reward for their spirited defence of the city during the Swedish siege the year before. Now the spokesmen of this powerful political grouping – Hans Svane, the bishop of Zealand, and Hans Nansen, the mayor of Copenhagen – demanded that the new tax should apply to all inhabitants of the country regardless of rank, Estate and privileges. Otherwise the negotiations would be broken off. As the noble delegates still refused to yield, a solution within the existing political framework seemed impossible. The negotiations had reached deadlock.

On 4 October, however, events took an entirely new direction. On that day some members of the new party introduced a proposal including extensive reforms of the existing political system, whose main clause was the introduction of a hereditary monarchy and the abolition of the old elective system which had favoured the noble Estate. This reform bill was nothing short of revolutionary. Hereditary rights would almost automatically mean the cancellation of the king's coronation charter, and thus the annulment of the nobility's extensive privileges. If carried out, the bill would place the nobility on equal terms with the non-noble Estates, including rights of taxation.

How sincere the men behind the reform bill really were is extremely difficult to assess. Indeed, there is nothing else to indicate a serious interest among the 'conjugated' in bringing about radical changes in the constitution itself. But many non-noble delegates, on the other hand, were clearly anxious to press the nobility as hard as possible to make it yield on the question of taxation. The reform bill is therefore probably best understood as a tactical threat designed to break noble resistance, once normal bargaining had failed.

Sincere or not, the bill, once brought forward, changed the entire character of the diet proceedings at a stroke from a rather traditional discussion of tax policy and the distribution of financial burdens into a unique debate on the most fundamental principles of the constitution. And during the following days courtiers from the king's immediate entourage further stirred the waters by engaging in busy, but strictly unofficial, lobbying among the 'conjugated' to make them stick to the proposal. Meanwhile the official debate dragged on without any real aim, the real decisions having been removed elsewhere out of the public eye.

This energetic political spade-work succeeded so well that the lines of demarcation were drawn very sharply in the course of the next few days. Nearly all the non-noble delegates rallied behind the ever more determined efforts aimed at changing the constitution into a hereditary monarchy, while the nobility and the aristocratic state council were subjected to steadily increasing pressure to make them accept the proposal. Tax questions now dropped totally out of the discussions: they were tacitly taken off the agenda by the clandestine political manoeuvres outside the diet.

While his political advisors were extremely active, the king himself initially carefully avoided any official comment, a precaution which is perfectly understandable: premature royal consent to the bill without the unanimous recommendation of all Estates, the nobility included, would be a manifest violation of the constitution. The numerous unofficial contacts with the 'conjugated' politicians during the days after 4 October, and the confidence that the citizen-militia as well as the regular army units in Copenhagen were his loyal allies, nevertheless soon convinced the king that the last remnants of noble resistance would collapse if threats of physical violence were added to the political pressure.

Therefore, on 10 October, the king finally threw his weight into the scales on behalf of the 'conjugated' party. When darkness fell martial law was proclaimed in the capital. The guards on the ramparts were doubled, the city gates were closed, and all ships in the harbour were sailed into open water so that no one could leave the city without royal permission. At the same time military garrisons throughout the country received orders to quell any attempt at disturbances or anti-royal activity. The king finally set afoot the rumour that he was now ready to let himself be declared hereditary king by the non-noble Estates alone, should the nobility and the state council still not yield.

Confronted with such massive pressure and trapped in a hostile capital the delegates of the nobility and the members of the state council at last gave in. Reluctantly they joined their non-noble colleagues, and on 13 October delegates from all the Estates and the members of the defeated council gathered in the great hall of the royal palace where they unanimously offered the king full hereditary rights for himself and his royal house. The king's answer, not very surprisingly, was a graceful acceptance of this generous offer. From this moment hereditary monarchy was a constitutional reality in Denmark, while more than a century of uninterrupted aristocratic rule was terminated – wiped out by the alliance between king and non-noble Estates, thus demonstrating a political determination and a tactical flexibility which in the last resort overcame their political opponents, the old aristocratic régime. The road to still more radical constitutional changes was now wide open. The second phase – the removal of the remaining constitutional restraints upon the king's power – was about to begin.

Having received the standing ovation of the delegates crowded into the royal hall the king immediately appointed a constitutional committee charged with the task of scrutinising the constitution and proposing adjustments necessitated by the new status of the king. The committee of twenty-one members, only eight of whom represented noble and state council interests, met once the following morning, but even the initial discussions revealed a disagreement so fundamental that it was unlikely any results could be achieved. In this situation

Bishop Hans Svane brutally cut through all futile discussion with the suggestion that the coronation charter be totally cancelled and the king asked to formulate a new constitution himself, compatible with the hereditary principle. This radical move was obviously inspired by the king himself or his immediate entourage. Aware of this provenance the committee, despite emphatic protests from its noble members, rapidly concluded its work with a recommendation that the king be released from his oath according to the old constitution, and that the coronation charter be delivered into his hands with the request that he himself should lay down a new fundamental constitutional code.

Obviously influenced by the events of the previous days and pressed by a daily more determined king, the constitutional committee chose in other words the easy, but for its own influence invalidating, way out: shirking its responsibilities and leaving to the king alone the formulation of the new constitution. The recommendation subsequently received the approval of the diet, and on 17 October the revoked coronation charter was handed over to the king in a short, but solemn ceremony in the palace.

Everything was now left in the king's hands. The only conditions were some vaguely formulated wishes that privileges be maintained, that the kingdom should not be divided, and that the régime should remain Christian. All this, however, was quite vague and the fact of the matter was that by its recommendation the constitutional committee, followed by the diet, had removed all the checks imposed on royal power by the old constitution. All the cards had been played into the hands of the king.

He took swift action, and the revolution moved on to its third and last phase. The most immediate needs of the new hereditary king were to make sure of his subjects' loyalty and to establish the legality of the new régime. To meet these he at once arranged a grandiose ceremony, which took place the very next day, Thursday, 18 October, in front of the royal palace. Sitting on top of a hurriedly built platform covered with a red cloth the king received the homage of his people, and representatives of the four Estates made a solemn vow of fidelity and obedience to the king on behalf of all subjects. This ceremony over, the king and his train strode back to the palace to celebrate the victory over the aristocracy in the company of a few selected politicians of the 'conjugated' party. Meanwhile, down in the square, the onlookers fell upon the beautiful red cloth covering the now deserted platform, and during the subsequent scuffle a few people were slightly hurt. But they were, typically enough, the only ones to suffer actual physical harm during the entire revolution – one of the greatest in Danish history.

With this public ceremony concluded, hereditary royal absolutism was established *de facto*, even if not yet formalised. Such a status was not achieved until 10 January 1661, when the king issued a constitutional document on sovereignty. It took the form of a declaration from the subjects to the king, stating that he, besides his hereditary rights, was accorded absolute power and full authority to decide the order of succession as well as the constitution of the realm. The subjects at the same time renounced every right of criticism of or opposition to the king and his rule. The document was thus a summing-up and codification of the earlier constitutional changes, and in the course of the winter it was circulated in the country for signature by the representatives of the Estates. Once this procedure was completed royal absolutism was more than a fact: it was a formal constitutional reality which found its final form four years later in the *Lex Regia*.

The hereditary and absolute régime was the product of an extremely astute and purposeful exploitation by the king of the new political forces released during the diet. Admittedly, not a few people had had from the start a foreboding of some political co-operation between the clergy and the citizens to force the nobility to yield on the tax question, but only very few had at that time the imagination to visualise the dynamic alliance which emerged between the 'conjugated' party and the king. It was precisely this alliance, combined with the king's well-timed and well-calculated military pressure in the critical days around 10 October, that caused the collapse of noble resistance. Once this was accomplished it was an easy matter for the cunning tactician Frederick III to bring himself into a position which in the first place gave him freedom of political action, and in the second place enabled him to force through radical constitutional changes almost over the heads of the Estates. The course of events had certainly demonstrated that the king and his advisors were gifted with an extrordinary capability to derive maximum advantage from a fluid political situation. The same events disclosed a corresponding lack of political manoeuvrability on the part of the nobility and the state council. Their political inflexibility left them in a trap which in the autumn of 1660 led ultimately to the definitive breakdown of aristocratic rule in Denmark.

At only a single but none the less decisive point did events more or less assume the character of a *coup d'état*, namely when martial law was proclaimed on 10 October. But it was the exception which proved the rule, and in the *Lex Regia* the king could therefore raise his eyes towards heaven and insist that the good God was the sole creator of the change in government without being burdened with too bad a conscience. Indeed, the régime was legal not only in the narrow sense, but in every sense – even if it is necessary to add that at the decisive moment not legality but the crude threat of military action tipped the scales in favour of the king.

IV

The revolution of 1660 was the start of 189 years of royal absolutism in Denmark. And after the busy detective work of many generations of historians no important disagreement any longer exists as far as the course of events is concerned, even if it is still an open question who was the real architect of the revolution – if there was one.

Greater disagreement is discernible on the question of *why* things happened as they did, that is, when the political events of the autumn of 1660 are seen in a wider context. The central issue, of course, is what caused such a weakening of the nobility and the state council that they had to give up almost without resistance when they were confronted in 1660 with the alliance between king and non-noble forces – an alliance easily defeated on earlier occasions; or, conversely, what trends in the historical process had strengthened the king so far that he who only twelve years earlier had been obliged to sign the most disabling coronation charter ever signed by a Danish king was able in 1660 to break the back of aristocratic rule and assume absolute power without being met by active resistance, or even protests.

The answers to these questions have followed roughly two lines. The first, which could be labelled the 'monarchical school', interprets the *coup d'état* in 1536 and the subsequent Reformation as a decisive victory for the king.[40] Accordingly the entire period from 1536 to 1660 is perceived as one long period of the gradual strengthening of royal power with the 1660 revolution as the logical and unavoidable outcome of this development. Typically the historians of this school were specialists in the history of the sixteenth century, whilst their knowledge of the seventeenth century was only superficial. That may explain why they never succeeded in giving a satisfactory explanation for the many setbacks in royal power in the course of that century. For instance, they failed to explain why this strong, victorious king allowed the aristocratic state council to dictate history's most severe coronation charter in 1648.

In contrast, the other line of research, which could be labelled the 'school of aristocratic rule', interpreted the *coup* of 1536 and the subsequent secularisation as a massive strengthening of aristocratic power.[41] In opposition to the monarchical school whose interpretation had an evolutionary tone, this line of research was inclined to perceive the events of 1660 as a genuine revolution, representing a radical break with the political power structure of the past.

For these historians it was a principal task, therefore, not to explain how or why the king was strengthened during the preceding century, but to point out trends which caused a weakening of the king's political adversaries, the once so powerful aristocracy – a weakening so grave that the regime collapsed almost without resistance when it was put under pressure in 1660.

For this reason their research centred on the uncovering of features within the noble Estate itself that could help explain the loss of power. Most famous among such theories was that of degeneration, which effectively dominated the scene from its initial formulation in the nineteenth century until the Second World War. Put very simply, the basic idea of this theory was that the Danish nobility, as an ever more inbred race, went through a serious physical and moral degeneration during the seventeenth century. The inevitable consequence was weak and debilitated issue, soon leading to the rapid extinction of entire families. Obviously this weak, sickly and expiring group was soon unable to sustain its political power, and was therefore an easy victim when the vital alliance of king and non-noble Estates in 1660 finally decided to oust it from the centre of power. This simplistic theory was accepted as the historical truth for several generations. It was not, in fact, abandoned until recent research on the basis of new and extensive demographic evidence was able to demonstrate that the chain of cause and effect ran in exactly the opposite direction.[42] Modern scholars were able to prove that the numerical decline of the aristocracy did not, in fact, take place until after 1660. The phenomenon of the declining aristocracy had therefore to be interpreted as an effect of the new regime's systematic undermining of the old aristocracy's social and economic conditions rather than the precondition of its establishment.

In the 1920s the theory of degeneration was supplemented by a theory of misadministration – evidently inspired by historians of the absolute monarchy's propaganda.[43] The argument was that the aristocracy, which had a *de facto* monopoly of all influential administrative posts in the government, misgoverned the realm from about the 1640s to such an extent that by 1660 the state council simply had to give up. It was the only solution left. It was pointed out, as a weighty piece of evidence, that one of the new regime's very first acts was a thorough reorganisation of the entire administrative system. Against this sweeping interpretation one has to point out, however, that modern administrative research has now revealed that the theory is at best much too simple and at all events too isolated in its view.

A final theory, which cannot unequivocally be assigned to either established school, deserves mention.[44] It maintains, in greatly simplified terms, that the real force behind the 1660 revolution was the crown's largest creditors, mainly the rich merchants of Copenhagen, who wanted to secure their loans to an insolvent government by enabling the king to break the noble monopoly of the possession of free landed property and thus to make it available to the creditors. No matter how interesting this theory of some sort of commercial-financial power complex as the real holder of political power might be, it suffers nevertheless from the essential weakness of being extremely difficult either to prove or to refute.

With very few exceptions these standard interpretations were insular in the sense that their scope was specifically Danish. Only seldom was international research in similar fields taken into account. Realising the obvious flaws in such an isolated approach recent Danish scholarship now considers the old problem from a new and broader angle which seeks to incorporate international research with the weight it deserves.[45]

The point of departure for the current interpretation is the perception of the 1536 revolution and its consequences outlined above by Professor Ladewig Petersen. The central argument in this interpretation is that the stable political system, the diarchy, typical of the domain state of the sixteenth century, remained stable only while this domain state really existed. As the many wars made this special form of state finance insufficient from about 1620, it was gradually substituted by tax financing. However, this change in one of the state's most fundamental features caused a reorganisation and expansion of the government's role and tasks so radical that the old diarchy, created for the domain state, soon proved too inflexible and ineffective. The defects were further aggravated by the general development in military organisation, which by 1600 had transferred the monopoly of organised force from the nobility to the state. Nor could this formidable new state responsibility be effectively met within the existing archaic political structure. In other words, the rapidly increasing taxation and the new responsibility for a growing military organisation had by the mid-seventeenth century created a most acute need for a thorough-going reorganisation of the political system.

The negotiations concerning the coronation charter of 1648 strengthened the state council's position to such an extent that for a brief moment it looked as if this organ would succeed in acquiring an omnipotence enabling it to carry through the necessary reorganisation. But the state council nevertheless lost the contest with the king during the following decade. The explanation for this outcome may be found in three different fields.

There is first the circumstance that the council did not in fact succeed in its effort of reorganisation and modernisation. On the contrary, these efforts came to an abrupt halt during the Swedish wars (1657–60) which, if anything, paralysed its political initiative and energy. Secondly, the state council – regardless of its formal status as the political representative of all Estates – in fact represented only the interests of the tax-exempt nobility. Increasing taxation, therefore, soon trapped the council in the insoluble dilemma of either repeatedly granting taxes to which its otherwise tax-exempt fellow nobles had also to contribute, or, if they were exempted, of facing ever more furious protests from non-noble taxpayers without at the same time losing its political credibility. This dilemma grew with the increasing tax burdens, disclosing thereby the third factor which brought the council down in 1660: its problems with its constituency. Indeed, the increasing financing of state expenditure through direct taxes forced that state council to administer and defend a system which much too often ran contrary to the interests it represented, and this dichotomy created an ever increasing schism between council and nobility. The sad fact was that the state council in the end did not represent anyone but itself.

All these structural weaknesses can, in the last analysis, be traced back to the fact that while the state council was an adequate manifestation of the domain state's political structure, it became a structural anomaly in the emerging tax state. Therefore the foremost institution of aristocratic rule, the state council, was an easy victim when the political alliance between a determined non-noble opposition and a purposeful, cunning king became a reality in the autumn of 1660.

Its power demolished by the emerging tax state's prolonged and inevitable widening of the cleft between formal power structure and political reality, the state council – the rearguard of the domain state – almost voluntarily let itself be swept out of government office in the autumn of 1660. The new absolute regime's occupation of the positions of power was the political adjustment to the hard economic-financial facts of the tax state.

The emergence of the tax state on the ruins of the old domain state was a general European trend in the sixteenth century. With great simplification it can thus be argued that the 1660 revolution in Denmark was the ultimate product of the modernisation and Europeanisation of the Danish state's financial system. Fuelled by the many wars, this process had been under way for decades before its political consequences were drawn in 1660.

Notes

* Translated by Mrs Anne Kirsten Pettitt, MA.

1. G. R. Elton, *England under the Tudors*, 2nd edn (London, 1973), ch. ch. VII; quotations from pp. 160f, 479.

2. Aksel E. Christensen, 'Det danske staendersamfunds epoker', in Svend Ellehøj *et al.* (eds), *Festskrift til Astrid Friis* (Copenhagen, 1963), pp. 40–4.

3. P. Colding, *Studier i Danmarks politiske historie i slutningen af Christian III.s og begyndelsen af Frederik II.s tid* (Copenhagen, 1939), pp. 68–74.

4. See the revaluation of Molesworth's *Account* (1692) by Paul Ries, 'Robert Molesworths Analyse des dänischen Absolutismus', in D. Lohmann (ed.), *Studien zur Adelskultur des Barockzeitalters in Schweden, Dänemark und Schleswig-Holstein* (Neumünster, 1978), pp. 43–66; cf. also G. E. Aylmer, 'English Perceptions of Scandinavia in the Seventeenth Century', in G. Rystad (ed.), *Europe and Scandinavia: Aspects of the Process of Integration in the Seventeenth Century* (Lund, 1983), pp. 18–93.

5. *Aarsberetninger fra det kgl. Geheimarchiv*, vol. II (Copenhagen, 1856–60), p. 42f; *Kirkehistoriske Samlinger* (1972), pp. 33ff. Quotations from a responsum, probably by the pen of the archbishop of Lund in 1513.

6. Kr. Erslev, *Konge og lensmand i det sekstende århundrede* (Copenhagen, 1879; reprinted 1970), p. 27f.

7. *Danske Samlinger*, 2nd ser., vol II, p. 345f.

8. Astrid Friis in *Kirkehistoriske Samlinger*, 6th ser., vol. IV (1942), pp. 1–28.

9. *Monumenta historiae Danica*, vol. I, ed. H. F. Rørdam (Copenhagen, 1873), pp. 208–11.

10. Cf. ibid., p. 146, and *Kirkehistoriske Samlinger*, 6th ser., vol. III (1939–41), p. 544f; for the following see also Christensen, 'Staendersamfunds epoker', p. 41.

11.   *Gamle Danske Love*, vol. IV, ed. J. L. A. Kolderup-Rosenvinge
      (Copenhagen, 1824) p. 166f.
12.   K. J. V. Jespersen (ed.), *Rigsråd, adel og administration 1570–1648*
      (Odense, 1980), p. 123; cf. Elton, *England under the Tudors*, pp. 255,
      487.
13.   *Monumenta historiae Danica*, vol. I, p. 174.
14.   *Nye danske Magazin*, VI (1836) p. 290. By 1500 the Rhenish guilder
      equalled 2 marks. Debasement over the following decades reduced the
      rate to 1:3; the Rhenish guilder is roughly equivalent to the later
      continental and Danish *daler*.
15.   P. Enemark, *Studier i toldregnskabsmateriale i begyndelsen af det 16.
      århundrede*, vol. I (Århus, 1971), p. 120f.
16.   B. P. Wolfe, *The Crown Lands, 1461–1536* (London, 1970), pp. 47, 66,
      102; G. R. Elton, *The Tudor Revolution in Government* (Cambridge,
      1953/1966), pp. 231ff.
17.   M. Wolfe, *The Fiscal System of Renaissance France* (New Haven/
      London, 1972), p. 355; J. H. Elliott, *Imperial Spain* (London, 1963), pp.
      90, 196ff.
18.   The *tønde hartkorn* is a Danish unit of property-measurement, defined
      as the area of land that could rent one barrel of rye or barley annually.
19.   Erslev, *Konge og lensmand*, p. 109, appendix pp. xx–xxiv.
20.   M. Roberts, *The Early Vasas. A History of Sweden, 1523–1611*
      (Cambridge, 1968), p. 38.
21.   The estimate of D. C. Coleman in *The Economy of England, 1450–1750*
      (Oxford, 1977), pp. 43f, 189f.
22.   *Landbohistorisk Tidsskrift*, 2nd ser., IV (1982), pp. 50–60, 84.
23.   *Festskrift til Kristof Glamann* (Copenhagen, 1983), p. 295f.
24.   J. Thirsk (ed.), *The Agrarian History of England and Wales*, vol. IV
      (Cambridge, 1967), pp. 260, 324; Elton, *England under the Tudors*, p.
      140.
25.   B. Odén, *Rikets uppbörd och utgift* (Lund, 1955), pp. 30–2; E. Ladewig
      Petersen, 'From Domain State to Tax State', *Scandinavian Economic
      History Review*, XXIII (1975), pp. 122ff, 132–4.
26.   J. Grundtvig, *Frederik den Andens Statshusholdning* (Copenhagen, 1876),
      pp. 25, 84–8, 96; cf. *Festskrift Glamann*, p. 293.
27.   *Danske Magazin*, 3rd ser., V (1887), pp. 2–8; F. P. Jensen, *Danmarks
      konflikt med Sverige 1563–1570* (Copenhagen, 1982), ch. 18.
28.   *Festskrift Glamann*, p. 294; cf. for the following E. Ladewig Petersen,
      'Defence, War and Finance: Christian IV and the Council of the Realm
      1596–1629', *Scandinavian Journal of History*, VII (1982), p. 280.
29.   H. F. Rørdam, 'Résident français près de la cour de Danemark',
      Oversigt over det kgl. danske Videnskabernes Selskabs Forhandlinger
      (Copenhagen, 1898), pp. 619–68.
30.   G. Landberg, *Johan Gyllenstiernas nordiska forbundspolitik i belysning av
      den Skandinaviske diplomatins traditioner* (Uppsala, 1935), pp. 14–23.
31.   'Correspondance de Charles Dantzay, ministre de France a la cour de
      Danemark', *Handlingar rörande Skandinaviens historia*, vol. XI (Stock-
      holm, 1827), pp. 45–85.
32.   *Original Letters Illustrative of English History*, 2nd ser., vol. III, ed. H.

Ellis (London, 1827), pp. 143–56; *Calendar of State Papers Foreign*, vol. XXII, ed. R. B. Wernham (London, 1936), pp. 77–80.

33.   S. Andolf (ed.), *Relation du royaume de Suède par M. de Sainte-Cathérine 1606* (Gothenburg, 1980), *passim*, esp. pp. 53–7.

34.   Petersen, 'Domain State', pp. 134ff; idem, 'Defence, War and Finance', pp. 278, 282ff.

35.   Idem, 'Domain State', p. 138f; idem, 'Defence, War and Finance', pp. 287ff, 296–8; cf. G. Parker (ed.), *The Thirty Years War* (London, 1984), plate 2.

36.   Petersen, 'Defence, War and Finance', pp. 297–301; Rystad, *Europe and Scandinavia*, pp. 38–43.

37.   Ibid., p. 35 with references; see also B. Odén, *Kronohandel och finanspolitik, 1560–1595* (Lund, 1966).

38.   Despite Michael Roberts' objections (see *The Swedish Imperial Experience, 1560–1718* (Cambridge, 1979), ch. I) I have preferred the interpretation of Artur Attman.

39.   The standard edition of the *Lex Regia* is still A. D. Jørgensen (ed.), *Kongeloven og dens Forhistorie. Aktstykker Udgivne af de under Kirke- og Undervisningsministeriet samlede Arkiver* (Copenhagen, 1886), pp. 38–67; the preamble pp. 38–42; the quotation below p. 39. In an article addressed to readers to whom the Danish language is presumably inaccessible, there is no point in providing comprehensive references to literature and documents available only in that language. As this article in any case presents an interpretative essay, rather than the results of primary research, I have kept the notes to an absolute minimum. The following description and interpretation of the 1660 revolution is based on my booklet, *Statsomvaeltningen 1660. Forløb, forudsaetninger, fortolkning* (Copenhagen, 1983).

40.   This interpretation was preferred by the mentor of critical historical research in Denmark, Kr. Erslev, and put forward in his now classic standard work *Konge og Lensmand* (as n. 6). He was to some extent followed by his pupil, Knud Fabricius in *Kongeloven. Dens tilblivelse og Plads i Samtidens Natur- og Arveretlige Udvikling* (Copenhagen, 1920).

41.   The most intelligent and eloquent spokesman of this line of interpretation was J. A. Fridericia, *Adelsvaeldens sidste Dage* (Copenhagen, 1894). He was followed by several later historians, for example Gustav Bang and Erik Arup.

42.   The theory of degeneration was demolished by subsequent demographic research by Albert Fabritius, *Denmarks Riges Adel. Dens Tilgang og Afgang 1536–1935* (Copenhagen, 1946), and Sven Aage Hansen, *Adelsvaeldens grundlag* (Copenhagen, 1964).

43.   Cf. Knud Fabricius, 'Kollegiestyrets Gennembrud og Sejr 1660–1680', in Aage Sachs (ed.), *Den danske Centraladministration* (Copenhagen, 1921), pp. 115–251, and Knut Mykland, *Skiftet i forvaltningsordningen i Danmark og Norge i tiden fra omkring 1630 inntil Frederik den tredjes død* (Oslo, 1955).

44.   Johan Jørgensen, 'Bilantz 1660. Adelsvaeldens bo', in *Festskrift til Astrid Friis*, pp. 153–71; cf. also his *Rentemester Henrik Müller. En Studie over adelsvaeldens etablering i Danmark* (Copenhagen, 1966).

45.   An excellent summary of the present state of research in this field can be found in Leon Jaspersen's report to the 19th Scandinavian Historical Congress in Odense 1984, '1600-tallets danske magtstat', in E. Ladewig Petersen (ed.), *Magtstaten i Norden i 1600-tallet og dens sociale konsekvenser* (Odense, 1984), pp. 9–40; cf. Petersen, 'Domain State', pp. 116–48, and Knud J. V. Jespersen, 'Social Change and Military Revolution in Early Modern Europe: Some Danish Evidence', *Historical Journal*, XXVI (1983), pp. 1–13.

23 The European Powers and Sweden in the Reign of Gustav Vasa

Sven Lundkvist

When Gustav Vasa gained the Swedish throne in 1523 the country comprised what is now Sweden proper (with the exception of certain regions in the south and west) and Finland.* The northern border and the Russian border to the east were indeterminate in the vast wilderness, with only the Baltic Sea and the Gulf of Bothnia constituting clear boundaries. Of the total population of around one million, most pursued farming, stock-rearing, hunting and fishing. A few districts had some mining and metalworking, but the domestic economy was based on barter, with a few small towns and little foreign trade.

The reign of Gustav Vasa was to see the build-up of Sweden's economic, political and military strength. Despite many revolts against his authority at the outset of his reign the king was gradually able to gather more and more power in his hands by expanding the military, financial and administrative base of the country to the point where his financial strength became well-nigh unique in comparison with other contemporary European powers. Before the war of liberation of 1521–23 Sweden had been part of the Scandinavian Union of the northern kingdoms of Denmark, Norway and Sweden under the treaty of Kalmar in 1397. The union under a common monarch never became an integrated entity, for its members retained a great deal of internal autonomy. By 1523, however, a new situation had been created and the European powers, reluctant or otherwise, were forced to accept it. In many respects Sweden must have seemed backward and of no interest to the other European powers, yet in certain circumstances the country was to become more or less crucial to their policies. This paper deals with these problems by tackling three central questions: of what interest was Sweden to the European powers; how was this concern reflected in European politics; and how did those powers regard the Swedish king?

I. THE CONSTELLATION

The European powers' interest in Sweden can be explained along two lines of argument. The first recognises that the Baltic basin grew in significance for western Europe during the Middle Ages, which increased during the sixteenth century with the gradual shift of Europe's economic centre of gravity from Italy to the cities of southern Germany and the North Sea coast, with Antwerp to the fore. Thus the central European powers, especially the Holy Roman Emperor and the King of France, began to view the region through different eyes, with their interest chiefly focused on the Hanseatic League and its influence on the trade of the Baltic region. The other line of thought concerns the teachings of Martin Luther and their impact on northern Europe. Protestantism derived its strongest support from townsfolk and the lesser nobility, whereas in Scandinavia the peasantry initially held fast to established beliefs. With time, however, the role of ruling princes became decisive, and by taking over the governance and wealth of the church they created the conditions for a more active foreign policy and new political alliances. New dynastic ties were forged and older ones upset by these developments. Of course, interest in Scandinavia varied: France and the empire remained more concerned with the Mediterranean than with the Baltic, but Poland and Russia took quite another view, which the following analysis regards as the main reason for the changing constellation.

The Baltic

The character of Baltic trade changed during the fifteenth century, as the traditional export of furs, wax and metal gave way to other products such as grain, lumber, hides, linen and hemp. By 1500 the Netherlands had become greatly dependent on grain produced in the Baltic region and during the following century Baltic trade also acquired importance for other areas of western Europe. The expansion of the Dutch and English fleets would hardly have been possible, had it not been for the continuing supply of timber, hemp and pitch, while tallow and potash were needed for the expanding industries of Europe. Western Europe, in other words, gained vital raw materials from the Baltic in return for supplying them with consumer goods, both cheap cloth and rock salt as well as luxury items such as wine and silks. During the late Middle Ages Lübeck's monopoly of east-west trade from the Baltic was challenged; the stream of goods which earlier had been shipped via the so-called Trave route was increasingly carried by Dutch and English merchantmen through the Sound. Dutch cities, above all Amsterdam, were becoming dangerous competitors for Lübeck. In addition, it was faced with internal rifts with the Hansa. Danzig and the Livonian towns had a great commercial stake in trade with Dutch and English merchants, so that they objected to Lübeck's attempts to block their trade. Only the Wendish cities tended to support Lübeck. The result of this in-fighting was the break-up of the Hanseatic League. In the various wars between Lübeck and the Dutch in the sixteenth century, notably in 1510–12 and 1533–34, the city tried to persuade Denmark to close the Sound to Dutch shipping, but it remained unsuccessful as the Danes had no wish to promote Lübeck's commercial interests.

Denmark was in a strong political position in any case. Not only did it control the Sound, but the Great and Little Belts either side of Fünen as well. Danish policy was of concern not merely to Lübeck, the Dutch and the other Baltic powers but, through the dynastic link of King Christian II's marriage to a sister of Emperor Charles V, Denmark was drawn further into the web of European politics. The growing importance of Baltic trade created a strong political interest on the part of the mercantile powers with repercussions far beyond themselves, for closure of the Sound would cause food shortages in several European countries, above all the Netherlands. For these various reasons Denmark acquired a key role in north-western Europe.

Trade between the Hansa and the countries of western Europe rested upon the Russian market: control of this 'source of all prosperity' was therefore vital. During the fifteenth century Livonian Hansa towns began to squeeze out other Hansa members in an attempt to gain a monopoly of trade with Russia. The lead in opposing this policy was taken by Lübeck. During the latter part of the fifteenth century Russia began to expand its borders towards the Baltic, partly in the hope of establishing direct contact with the western European merchants; that sealed the fate of the Livonian cities as entrepots for Russian trade. In 1492 Ivangorod was established opposite the town of Narva, in 1510 Pskov was captured, and Smolensk soon followed in 1514. On reaching his majority Ivan IV mounted several expeditions towards the Baltic. Narva surrendered in 1558, thereby heralding the disintegration of the feudal state of the Teutonic Order. In 1553 the Englishman Richard Chancellor reached the mouth of the Dwina on the White Sea. Both the Russians and the

English had great hopes of this 'ice' route to the Russian market, the discovery of which made the Baltic powers nervous.

With the increasing importance of the Baltic and the emergence of strong new nation states on its shores commercial prospects in the region underwent a shift. Long before the collapse of the Teutonic Order in Livonia around 1560 the struggle for *dominium maris Baltici* was economically and politically in full swing. The European powers' reaction to Sweden's role in these developments will be examined later in this essay.

The Reformation

Because Luther and other reformers were backed by the majority of German princes who were in opposition to the emperor, the hope that a new order in the church would come about under the leadership of the emperor himself was crushed. As a result, opposition between Catholic and Protestant came to be connected with the political conflict between princes and emperor, and even caused tension between the Habsburgs and their enemies, the French Valois. The interests of the European powers, above all Charles V and Francis I, in the northern kingdoms should be seen in this light.

Apart from the appeal of Luther's ideas in principle, Sweden's conversion to the Reformation was influenced by the decision of the grand master of the Teutonic Order, Albert of Hohenzollern, to transform his territory into a secular Protestant duchy under Polish protection. That emerges from the Swedish king's decision to introduce the Reformation at the *Riksdag* at Västerås in 1527. Denmark was also fundamentally influenced by the Prussian decision, although direct pressure was also exerted by other Protestant German princes. By the end of the 1530s the northern kingdoms were all Protestant and acted as strong links in the chain of the European Reformation: Denmark even joined the Schmalkaldic League in 1538. On the other hand, Sweden failed to join the league, largely because of the vehement opposition of Berend von Mehlen, a former servant of the Vasas. Mehlen was by then a retainer of the Elector of Saxony, John Frederick, and intrigued against the Vasas to generate friction between King Gustav and other league members.

Dynastic connections

The dynastic connection between Charles V and Christian II of Denmark was another essential factor. In 1516 the latter had married

Maximilian's daughter Isabella, sister to the future Charles V. The heirs to Christian's dynastic claims were his daughters Dorothea, who married the Elector Palatine Frederick in 1535, and Christina, who became the barren widow of Francesco Sforza in 1535. Christian II and his heirs were to become a constant source of worry to the northern monarchs, with Elector Frederick proving particularly troublesome on account of the strong support for his claims which he received from the emperor. The fact that Gustav Vasa was not of royal blood, by contrast, was a decided handicap when dealing with other European princes. The remedy lay in marrying into a suitable princely family, and in 1531 he married Catherine of Saxony–Lauenburg, having been turned down as a suitor by several ruling houses, including the Polish. Negotiations with his future father-in-law were drawn out because the duke feared for the stability of Vasa's realm. This attitude was by no means atypical, since for many years Vasa was considered to be a usurper, especially by the emperor. His legitimacy grew in strength after his marriage, however, and was underpinned by the law passed by the Swedish Estates in 1544 that made the country into an hereditary monarchy. Thereafter the claims of the Vasa dynasty were accepted by other European ruling houses.

II. EUROPE AND SWEDEN: THE CONDUCT OF POLITICS

Though Sweden tried to gain a degree of independence in domestic policy during the late Middle Ages, the Swedish nobility had little interest in breaking away from the Scandinavian Union. At the end of the fifteenth century, however, the situation changed when several non-royal regents tried to secure a more independent position for the country. In order to be successful help had to be gained from powers who also opposed the king of the Union. Since Christian II pursued a very determined foreign policy in his dealings with Lübeck and the Hanseatic League, it was logical for King Gustav to turn to Lübeck for support.

Independence

Since the European powers were accustomed to viewing the king of the Union as a true ruler whose power derived from legitimate succession and Denmark's strong political position, an independent

Swedish kingdom was bound to be regarded as ruled by a usurper. On the other hand, there were powers who stood to benefit by the establishment of an independent Sweden. In those circumstances the support of Lübeck and the Hansa could be secured in return for certain favours. Lübeck contributed soldiers, warships and provisions of various kinds to the war effort. Then, in the spring of 1524, Lübeck demanded the sum of 120,871 marks from Sweden in compensation for its help. A few days after his election the new king issued a patent to Lübeck and Danzig containing trading concessions to the Hansa. Under its provisions they were granted exemption from tolls in a number of Swedish towns and a trading monopoly with Sweden, while Swedish trade westwards through the Sound and the Belts was to be suspended. These restrictions stemmed from the struggle to gain control over Baltic trade between Lübeck and the Netherlands. The events that were to lead to the deposal of Christian II, it is true, partly took place independently of the struggle for Baltic trade, and yet Lübeck was the moving force behind the revolt against Christian II. Though the new king of the Danes soon mastered the situation the struggle against the union monarchy continued, as Sweden and Denmark quarrelled over which was to have possession of the island of Gothland. This dispute was resolved through Hanseatic mediation, which decided in August 1524 that Denmark should retain control. The turn of events made Gustav Vasa believe that he had been duped, and resulted in an interesting change in the direction of Swedish policy.

As early as 1524 Sweden was in contact with the Netherlands. Negotiations continued into 1525, resulting in a treaty regulating commerce between the two countries which held a promise of future political co-operation. The Swedes, however, wanted to go further, with Vasa eager for a formal alliance. By 1527 talks had progressed to the point of 'a permanent and fast alliance' being sealed; the Dutch, led by Amsterdam, were also keen to reach an agreement, since the proposed pact would hinder the efforts of Lübeck and other Hanseatic cities to block Dutch shipping by arming men-of-war paid for out of the profits of Swedish trade. The Dutch regent Mary also favoured the continuation of the alliance in the form of an official treaty.

These negotiations broke down because of a reluctant Swedish royal council, but another diplomatic offensive against Lübeck was mounted when the king established contact with Prussia and Poland. In the first case the initiative came from Prussia; its transition to

Protestantism and the need for commercial partners culminated in a treaty of peace and commerce with Sweden in 1526. There were also plans, at least on the part of the Prussians, for a political and religious pact. Duke Albert of Prussia was even interested in promoting an alliance between Sweden and Poland in order to protect his territory from the Teutonic Order in Livonia, with whom he had just broken. Gustav Vasa had a like interest in such a pact, and in obtaining the hand of the Polish princess Hedvig, for marriage into the Polish royal house would confer an air of dynastic legitimacy upon his rule.

Swedish adherence to a Polish policy led to a desire for better relations with Danzig as a commercial alternative to Lübeck. Direct negotiations with Danzig were launched in consort with a Polish *demarche*, yet no alliance or marriage was forthcoming. The reasons for failure lay in Gustav Vasa's difficulties with a reluctant council and in domestic revolt. Sweden decided to withdraw from open confrontation with Lübeck, and over the next few years relations with the Hanseatic city improved.

Sweden's relations with Denmark were likewise far from cordial on account of the Gothland dispute. None the less, the two kings were forced to seek mutual aid in the face of the threatened invasion of Sweden by the deposed King Christian II and his henchman Berend von Mehlen, and they concluded a joint defence pact in 1528. With Christian II's capture in 1532 the Sound was re-opened to the Dutch by Sweden and Denmark, despite Lübeck's objections. The next year Lübeck declared war on the Dutch and appealed to Gustav Vasa for help. Since his domestic problems were not yet resolved, the Swedish monarch temporised; instead he called for the abolition of the special trade concessions which Lübeck enjoyed with Sweden and began to collect tolls. The Lübeckers did not give in easily, and retaliated by seizing Swedish goods. The break in relations was an accomplished fact when in July 1533 Vasa abolished Lübeck's privileges and confiscated her property in Sweden. The dispute, it appeared, could only be settled by war.

In the autumn Sweden approached the Dutch with the aim of taking concerted action against Lübeck. Although the Dutch and their regent Mary of Hungary were not disinclined, the soundings were overtaken by peace talks between Lübeck and the Dutch which led to a treaty the following spring. Thus Sweden lost a presumptive ally in the struggle against Lübeck. Meanwhile, the prospect of a Swedish–Dutch alliance against Lübeck had prompted Denmark to seek an accommodation with Sweden, with the result that a treaty of co-operation directed particularly against Lübeck was concluded in February 1534. But the treaty contained an even larger goal, that of lasting peace between the Scandinavian kingdoms, who were now preparing for Lübeck's response.

Trouble in the Baltic

In May 1534 Lübeck attacked Holstein and advanced into Denmark proper. With urban and rural unrest likely to play into Lübeck's hands, some of the nobility acclaimed the deposed Christian II while others rallied round the new king, Christian III. With the assistance of Swedish troops, who took Halland in late 1534 and Scania early the next year, Christian III was gradually able to regain control of Danish territory. The combined forces of Denmark, Sweden and Prussia inflicted a naval defeat on Lübeck in June 1535, which was accompanied by a land victory at the same time. Lübeck's ambitions were finally scotched and in February 1536 the city reached a peace treaty with Christian III.

Lübeck's design had been to foment a revolt in Sweden and mount an embargo of Swedish trade, but the other Hansa cities refused to join the blockade, notably Danzig and its eastern neighbours. The strength of the Swedish navy, aided by the Danish and Prussian fleets, thwarted Lübeck's strategy and, by the same token, prevented an invasion of its mainland. Lübeck tried to lure a variety of north German princes and even Henry VIII of England with the bait of the Swedish and Danish crowns, but only Duke Albert of Prussia succumbed to the promise of the Swedish throne: the other princes remained neutral.

Swedish diplomacy concentrated upon co-operation with Denmark, Prussia and Poland. In 1535 the Swedes wanted a pact with Poland, which was then at war with Russia, since both distrusted the latter's intentions in the Baltic. For his part, the emperor hoped to install the Elector Palatine as ruler of Scandinavia. This threat played a major role in bringing about co-operation between Sweden and Denmark. The Dutch, who had initially intervened to Elector Frederick's advantage by besieging Copenhagen, turned cool once the Sound was again closed to all traffic in April 1536, and the following May signed a three-year truce with Denmark which regulated commercial and other questions. Party to the agreement were Sweden and Prussia, as well as the dukes of Mecklenburg and the count of Oldenburg, and Gustav Vasa ratified it within a month. An agreement with Lübeck took much longer, for Sweden was diplomatically isolated. In order to secure a lasting agreement the king proposed new but more restricted concessions than those offered in 1523. Lübeck rejected the terms out-of-hand, however, and in August 1537 only signed a truce for five years.

Meanwhile, Denmark and Prussia began to drift apart from Sweden, which left King Gustav suspicious of their intentions. Late in the war Denmark signed a six-year alliance with various north German princes in the Schmalkaldic League which left Sweden isolated. Furthermore, von Mehlen was urging members of the league to attack Sweden, and when Vasa applied to join the league in 1538 he was turned down, despite the intervention of Christian III. Although von Mehlen made many energetic attempts to gather an invasion force and gained the support of the Saxon elector, by 1539 league members had cooled towards von Mehlen's plans, since they did not fancy the risk of war with the Swedes.

Relations between the former allies Denmark, Prussia and Sweden, therefore, had deteriorated sharply by the late 1530s. Despite the threat to all the northern Protestant powers presented by the emperor and the Elector Palatine, the Swedish king refused to soften his stand in discussions with the Danes. Within the Schmalkaldic League rumours were spread that Vasa had left Scandinavia for talks with the emperor and the French and Scottish kings. At a league meeting in Arnstadt in the fall of 1539 members discussed apprehensively the threat that an understanding between Sweden and the empire would pose.

Gustav Vasa's dilemma: Charles V or Francis I?

The background of Danish and Prussian anxiety as well as the worry of the league members was the international situation. Denmark's diplomatic position had deteriorated greatly around 1540 since the league's leader, Landgrave Philip of Hesse's, bigamous marriage had forced him into dependence on the emperor. With the expiry of its truce with the empire in May 1540 Denmark was obliged to fall back on Sweden, since its efforts to secure French support were vitiated by Charles V's *rapprochement* with Francis I. Attempts by Denmark to reach an agreement with the emperor and Elector Frederick had already foundered that spring.

Aware of the strained relations with its former allies, Sweden took diplomatic soundings in several directions. The Teutonic Order in

Livonia and Duke Albert of Mecklenburg were approached with the purpose of ensuring continuity of commercial links, were Sweden to attack Denmark and Prussia. Rumours that Sweden was in conclave with the emperor, however, were groundless. The negotiations between Denmark and Sweden which began late in 1540 proved hard going. The treaty of 1534 was resurrected and commercial relations re-established, but only a personal meeting between Christian III and Gustav Vasa could resolve the other points at issue. Despite the former's fears of a Swedish military build-up, both the Danes and the Schmalkaldic League were eager for such a meeting.

Eventually in the autumn of 1541 both sides put their name to the treaty of Brömsebro, which promised mutual aid in time of war and reciprocity in foreign policy. In a sub-clause the Danish king promised Sweden help against a first strike by Lübeck and action against Berend von Mehlen. As a consequence, Sweden was able to rebuff Lübeck's demands for fresh trade concessions. For their part, the Danes hoped for Swedish support in reaching an understanding with the emperor in order to avert the threat from Elector Frederick. The treaty of Brömsebro, which effectively wedded the two northern powers to a single foreign policy, strengthened Christian III's bargaining hand. Indeed, in November 1541 he openly joined Charles V's enemies by signing a treaty of mutual assistance with France. Seven months later Sweden followed. Although it had been courted by the emperor and offered both money and the prospect of territorial gains, Sweden embarked on talks with France during 1541 which culminated in a political and commercial alliance in July 1542. Its provisions envisaged mutual military and naval assistance and the widening of the pact to embrace Denmark, Scotland, the dukes of Prussia and Cleves, and even the English crown if it so chose. Therewith Sweden had come down decisively on France's side in the Habsburg–Valois struggle.

The result of Sweden's choice: peasant revolt and foreign intervention

The Scandinavian countries were affected in different ways by the war between France and the empire which began in mid-July 1542. That month the *Dackefejden* revolt, so called after its leader Nils Dacke, broke out in southern Sweden. The rebels made contact with Duke Albert of Brandenburg, who was planning to invade Sweden and seize the crown for himself. But the duke's plans were overtaken by Elector

Frederick's own attempts to exploit the situation. Early in 1543 Frederick urged the Catholic peasants under Dacke to support his cause, pointing out that the emperor was behind him. Charles V in fact through his secretary Granvelle that spring exhorted all Swedish subjects to recognise Frederick's claim to the throne through his marriage to Christian II's daughter Dorothea. But the willingness of the emperor and the Dutch regent Mary to back Frederick with arms was another matter. Charles V had already advised the Elector Palatine that his claim to the Danish throne would be best pursued by force, while Queen Mary argued that the Dutch were too hard pressed themselves to spare troops for a war against both Sweden and Denmark. Attempts by both Frederick and Duke Albert to enlist Lübeck and the Wendish cities in their cause foundered on the rock of commercial self-interest.

The Swedes, meanwhile, had not been idle. The king and nobility had broken the back of the peasant revolt in March, and Dacke himself was killed in the summer of 1543. The Swedish chancellor, Conrad von Pyhy, moreover, was recruiting mercenaries in Germany, and loans were raised from, among others, the Fugger banking house. A series of north German cities was won over by promises of trading concessions. Pyhy also managed to extract a declaration of intent from the Schmalkaldic League that Sweden might at last be admitted to membership. These efforts, coupled with intensive propaganda, helped Sweden overcome internal strife and foreign hostility. In April the chancellor at the head of between six and eight batallions drove Albert out of his Prussian duchy and thereby pre-empted the threat of invasion. In the summer Sweden promised cavalry and thirty thousand *dalers* to its Danish and French allies. Fears of an invasion were revived, however, by Charles V's victory over the Duke of Cleves, and only heavy pressure on the Wendish cities and the dukes of Mecklenburg prevented a reprise by Duke Albert.

The peace treaty between Denmark and the empire in May 1544, for which the Schmalkaldic League had so mightily striven, made provision for Sweden's inclusion as Denmark's ally, as a *quid pro quo* for Charles V's proposal to include England. Though the emperor undertook not to support any enterprise against King Christian III (with the deposed Christian II's claim being toned down), no such guarantee was extended to Sweden. Not only did the imperial commentary refer to Gustav Vasa as *occupator Sueciae*, it also revived a document of 1366 which contained Duke Albert's legal claim to the Swedish throne. For its part, Sweden would have preferred to negotiate a separate treaty with the empire, and tried instead to activate its alliance with France as a means of warding off invasion, the threat of which was increased by Sweden's assistance towards Duke Henry of Brunswick–Wolfenbüttel in the face of the fury of the Schmalkaldic League which had driven him out of his duchy.

Charles V's victories in early 1547 put Sweden under renewed pressure. On the one hand, King Gustav saw the need to settle the question of Christian II's dynastic claims with Denmark; on the other, he wanted an agreement with the emperor not to succour pretenders to the Swedish crown. But the emperor made any such accord conditional upon Sweden's ratification of the treaty of Speyer in 1544 between Denmark and the empire, which had kept the former out of European political involvements. In 1551 Sweden at last gave way and was rewarded with imperial support against any aggression by Lübeck. Although that promise was never delivered on account of shifting political fortunes within Germany, Sweden nevertheless contrived to sow dissension among members of the Hanseatic League.

The struggle for the Baltic

All the Baltic powers had a stake in the fate of the Teutonic Order in Livonia – Russia with its commercial expansion westwards, Poland with its interests in southern Livonia, Denmark with its long-standing claim to Estonia. Sweden, therefore, could not afford to stand aside in the struggle to seize the spoils of the disintegrating Order. Indeed, Swedish interference in Livonia, especially in Reval, was nothing new under Gustav Vasa, who had succeeded in asserting jurisdiction over Swedish subjects in that city. For Vasa the Livonian cities were unwelcome competitors in the trade with Russia: by direct trading he hoped to force Baltic commerce to use Sweden as an entrepot, and to that end Nylödöse (near present-day Gothenburg) was chosen as the storehouse for all goods shipped westwards. Swedish efforts to expand its Russian trade received a setback in the mid-1550s, however, when a serious border clash developed with Russia over control of the Carelian peninsula. Sweden's hopes of enlisting Polish aid in the dispute came to nothing in 1556 when the Poles signed a six-year truce with Russia, even though King Sigismund Augustus was well aware of possible arms shipments to Russia via the new route from England across the White Sea. The Swedes even sent a diplomatic mission to London themselves to stop English supplies being shipped to Russia along that route.

At that point civil war broke out in the territory of the Teutonic Order. For Sweden the timing was unfortunate, since the hostilities with Russia prevented it from taking full advantage of the disorder. Vasa's response was to offer to mediate in the war, an offer accepted by the Livonian towns who believed that arbitration would bind the hands of those involved. As the next priority the king then turned to peace with Russia. Although he was able to conclude a forty-year peace in 1557, the terms were unfavourable, but in the long term Sweden hoped to exploit Russia's underlying military weakness. As soon as the Russian–Swedish war ended, the struggle for *dominium maris Baltici* resumed. In it Livonia held the key. If controlled by Denmark, the Teutonic Order's lands posed a threat to Sweden on two flanks; if by Poland or Russia, either would gain a forward position which might endanger Swedish trade through the Gulf of Finland. These, therefore, were the strategic issues which the ageing king was to bequeath to his sons, who continued his ambitious policies.

III. THE EUROPEAN POWERS, GUSTAV VASA AND SWEDEN

The foregoing picture of Gustav Vasa shows an upstart who had seized the Swedish crown illegally and violently. Though contemporaries shared that view, it was to change with the establishment of a hereditary monarchy in 1544. By the 1550s his marriages and his long reign combined to lend him international recognition. Moreover, he gained vicarious prestige from the Protestant princes for having assisted Christian III of Denmark to oust Christian II. Internally, Vasa's rule was underpinned by a strong economy and military strength. The large loans extended to Christian III and to Duke Henry of Brunswick–Wolfenbüttel in 1544 gave credence to the rumours of the king's fortune, which were indeed true enough.

Gustav Vasa, on the other hand, was mistrusted by allies and enemies alike. At times he appeared indecisive and temporising; he cautiously avoided unnecessary risks. Some of his caution derived from his inability to rely upon the loyalty of his servants when acting on his behalf. His suspiciousness and duplicity increased with the onset of old age. Among his neighbours he counted as hot-tempered and awkward to deal with. In the mid-1530s a rumour circulated that he had beaten his wife to death. Former retainers who had fled the country to safety put about libellous pamphlets which portrayed him as an unscrupulous liar. It was these jibes which spurred Berend von Mehlen's intrigues against the Swedish king, and von Mehlen's words carried weight for his character and industry had been attested by Luther himself.

Yet there was an admirable side to this multifaceted monarch. He was a handsome and majestic man, a genial host, who looked after his guests well. Christian III of Denmark must have experienced this side of Gustav when, on several occasions, he was able to persuade the distrustful king to change his mind. It is also worth stressing that the bargains struck at Brömsebro were kept. In return, Christian remained true to the Swedish king, although he was of course obliged to rely upon Swedish financial backing since Denmark's economy left no room for extravagance. Although Vasa was an upstart, a monarch who was variously attacked by the clergy, nobles and peasants of his own realm, as well as by foreign powers backed by the emperor, he placed Sweden firmly on the European map. His policies had repercussions from Russia and the Tartars in the east to the western European countries, from the Arctic Circle to the Vatican. He took his place among the rulers of the new nation states, perhaps neither worse nor better than them, but with his own unmistakable style. He created the foundations upon which not only his sons but also his grandson, Gustavus Adolphus, were able to build Sweden into a great power.

*The sources for this essay are mainly based on my book *Gustav Vasa och Europa. Svensk handels- och utrikespolitik 1534–1557* (Studia historica Upsaliensia, II) (Uppsala, 1960). For a general picture of Swedish history in the sixteenth century see the excellent study by Michael Roberts, *The Early Vasas. A History of Sweden, 1523–1611* (Cambridge, 1968).

24 The Conclusive Years: The End of the Sixteenth Century as the Turning-Point of Polish History

Antoni Mączak

This essay stems from the continuing debate on the background to the partitions of Poland and from my own interest in the no-man's land between the economic and the constitutional development of that commonwealth. My assumptions are very simple. There are, roughly speaking, two extreme attitudes to the 'question of the partitions'. The one assumes that it is a nonsense to study the whole of the early modern period merely as an introduction to the final fate of the Republic, namely its dissolution in 1795. No Czech scholar would think that a book on Czech history before 1620 should merely be a prolegomenon to the White Mountain. To that the other school of thought on Poland's history would argue that the difference between the Czech and Polish cases lies in the fact that the White Mountain, not unlike the battle of Mohács in 1526 for Hungary, was a military contest, whereas the partitions of Poland were the very complex result not only of European international policy but of the country's long-term social and constitutional development as well. While its neighbours followed the general trend towards the centralisation of power and the establishment of a strong army, the Republic of Poland–Lithuania by contrast pursued decentralisation and exalted the civil liberties of the noble Estate.

So much historical and literary effort has been devoted to the partitions, and up to the early part of this century so much energy was expended on identifying certain individuals or social groups as the 'true villains', or rather on exculpating the Poles and indicting the foreign powers, that Polish historians are now reluctant to broach this subject at all. And yet it is not without importance for the course of

European history to understand what caused the disappearance of a state which once divided Russia and Prussia. Poland, as one particular example of a *Ständestaat*, deserves some attention on the part of students of early modern Europe. 'You make it sound as if Polish history were *normal*', a member of Norman Davies's seminar at Harvard remarked with astonishment.[1] This viewpoint has recently been advanced by a German historian of Eastern Europe, Gottfried Schramm, in his comparative study of pre-Mohács Hungary, Bohemia and Poland.[2] In the first two countries the might and the prerogatives of the Estates were crushed during the seventeenth century by the Habsburgs; in Poland they were developing undisturbed by the king. In a sense, the Polish–Lithuanian *Ständestaat* brought the political struggle to its logical conclusion: the Estates all but eliminated the king as a political factor and almost reduced him during the seventeenth century to one amongst many competing magnates. In the fifteenth century the upper echelons of the commons had already been manoeuvred out of the Estates' assemblies.[3] What remained as the ruling force was the nobility, while the clergy was represented in the Senate (the upper chamber) by the archbishops and bishops alone, who socially did not differ from the nobility.[4]

In another brilliant essay on the comparative history of eastern Central Europe Schramm argues that the political weakness of towns and their elites was not a decisive factor in Poland.[5] This was true, he suggests, for Brandenburg–Prussia as well, and it is difficult to find two more dissimilar lines of development than Poland and Prussia. To that my reply would be that in order to compare two neighbouring countries such as these one has to take into account other factors, as for instance their respective sizes, constitutional traditions, and the social and economic position of the aristocracy. Late medieval Poland – up to 1501/5 – may be studied as one of the best examples of a kingdom moulded by *Herrschaftsverträge*.[6] From 1374 the nobility extended its power and personal privileges at the expense of the king; the clergy followed, always viewed with distrust and often countered by the gentry.[7] As a very rough generalisation, the nobility at the close of the fifteenth century had at its disposal a tight network of assemblies, local, provincial and the *Sejm*.[8] By then the principal battlelines in the political and constitutional struggle were drawn between the magnates entrenched in the king's council (the Senate) and the gentry who dominated the Chamber of Deputies (*izba poselska*). The division of the *Sejm* into two separate chambers reflected separate interests and the social conflict which was to lead in

1501 to a privilege granted to the *domini consiliarii* just before his coronation by the future king, Alexander, whereby the sovereign's role was reduced to that of president of the royal council. The *turba malorum vel levium*, the gentry gathered in the Chamber of Deputies, had its day four years later in 1505 when the *Nihil Novi* Act was voted through by the *Sejm* and promulgated by the king: '*statuimus, ut deinceps futuris temporibus perpetuis nihil novi constitui debeat per nos et successores nostros sine communi consiliariorum et nuntiorum terrestrium consensu.*'[9]

Apart from the constitutional problems one might ask why the kings were not able to use the overt hostility between the two levels of the nobility to buttress their threatened position. Why was the lesser nobility, the gentry, in the long run incapable of preserving its political status over against the magnates? Why were the constitutional victories of the gentry during the entire sixteenth century scarcely matched by corresponding political success and increasing social independence of their richer neighbours?[10]

In the following analysis I contend that the impressive constitutional achievements of the gentry in the Chamber of Deputies, as well as the augmented competence of local nobles' assemblies, went hand-in-hand with the steep rise of the senatorial families as great landowners. So what was being won on the floor of the *Sejm* was being lost through economic competition. Furthermore, I argue that the sheer size of the country, together with its loose network of communications and low density of towns, proved advantageous to the upper and wealthier sections of the nobility. In these respects the close of the sixteenth as well as the early decades of the seventeenth century were of crucial importance. Any hope of establishing strong central power and a thick network of administration was in my opinion by then already doomed, so that the fate of the republic was all but sealed. However, it would be unwise to neglect several other features in a period already rich in significant issues.

Since the constitutional achievements of the second half of the sixteenth century are by now accessible to English-speaking readers, the acts of the *Sejm* sessions in the 1560s as well as the details of the Lublin Union with Lithuania will not be discussed here.[11] However, the principal goal of the politically conscious and active gentry – *executio iurium*, and in particular *executio bonorum regalium* – has rarely been compared with the vicissitudes of the administration of royal domains in other contemporary European countries. The relatively strict rules imposed by the *Sejm* on the leaseholders and stewards of the royal estates were intended to solve painful problems of the fisc, indirectly to free the gentry (or rather their tenants) from extraordinary taxation and, not least, to undermine the position of the magnates. One may surmise that for some gentry leaders the last issue was of most importance, but there are few testimonies to that effect. The first *revisio bonorum regalium* compiled in 1564/65 was a masterpiece of inquisitorial control on the part of the representatives of both Chambers and of the king, as the first Estate of the *Sejm*.[12] The next survey in 1569, however, hardly matched the quality of the first one. In the seventeenth century the income figures were more often than not largely of symbolic significance. When badly pressed by the Chamber of Deputies, the *starostowie*, or leaseholders of the royal estates, preferred to pay double or even higher multiples of their original dues rather than submit to some sort of serious survey.[13]

The documents relating to the royal estates have been preserved better than most other early modern archival records, and that is why they are thoroughly studied. However, relatively little has been done to compare the administration of royal estates and its reform in Poland and Lithuania with similar phenomena abroad. For the present argument it is of vital importance that Poland did not transform itself from a domain state to a tax state, to borrow the terminology of Joseph Schumpeter.[14] In that she did not follow Denmark (after 1660) but rather Brandenburg–Prussia and, to a certain extent, Sweden. But notwithstanding the deep differences between these states they were all, barring Poland, well endowed with civil servants and clerical services. In Denmark, Frederick II and Christian IV were able to undertake ambitious reforms of the royal domain. The *lensmand* (vassal) was transformed into a royal official and conditions of leasehold were altered to the benefit of the crown.[15] In Prussia under the rule of Duke Albert former estates of the Teutonic Order were distributed in various forms to the leading nobles and the duke drew little income from his own estates, which were often mortgaged to noble creditors.[16] The early Prussian bureaucracy, however, maintained the high standards of the Order's officialdom and the estate accounts and surveys make an excellent source for students of agrarian economy and administration.[17] Furthermore, the *reduktion* in Sweden in the 1680s was made possible because of the excellent job done by civil servants since the sixteenth century.

I wish to stress the administrative factor because in Poland it hardly applied. The study of Poland's administration and civil service from the Middle Ages to the eighteenth century is still in its infancy, reflecting both the historical situation and the current lack of understanding for this topic among Polish historians. Tax records used to be kept quite carelessly and no one normally dared inquire about tax declarations. In the seventeenth century, when a series of emergencies called for higher taxes, it was easier to change the taxation system from land tax to hearth tax and later to poll tax than to secure a reasonable degree of reliability on the part of noble taxpayers. All the instances of highly efficient and dependable civil servants date from the sixteenth century.[18] Whereas in most countries that embraced absolutism a network of civil servants had already developed in the fourteenth century (France is the best example), in Poland after 1388 the nobility struggled against the office of *iusticiarius* and succeeded in eliminating it altogether before 1481.[19] The function of the *iusticiarii* had been to arrest suspects and bring them before royal judges. It is therefore highly probable that the conflict between noble autonomy and central authority had already begun just after the extinction of the Piast dynasty in 1370.

But why were the nobles so successful against the monarchy? Numerous charters granted by Jagiełło (1386–1434) and his descendants were more often than not simply arrogated by various groups within the nobles' Estate. Historians have failed to analyse carefully which groups profited directly therefrom, but the crucial Statute of Nieszawa, extracted from the king under blackmail by the noble levy gathered for the campaign against the Teutonic Order in 1454, clearly shifted the political balance within Poland to the advantage of the middling gentry and so paved the way for its subsequent domination of the *Sejm*.[20] In the fifteenth and even in the early sixteenth century there was still no clear division between magnates and the rest of the nobility: the aristocracy as a whole was powerful in every public sphere from local assemblies to the *Sejm*. Nevertheless, between 1521 and 1538 the deputies tried to outlaw the prevailing custom which allowed senators to elect part of the deputies' number in the local nobles' assemblies. Yet the gentry still felt more at ease and less dependent when on their home territory.

In the mid-sixteenth century the situation changed sharply as the Chamber of Deputies became a refuge for politically conscious deputies who felt unsafe on their home territory. On the *Sejm* floor in 1563/64, the session which culminated in the formally decisive victory of the 'executionists', the palatine of Chełmno, Jan Działyński, in protesting against the *executio iurium*, which in his opinion was contrary to Prussian liberties,[21]

> most of all cursed those deputies from the Pomeranian lands who in addressing the Chamber exceeded their mandate, calling them light-minded and malign, who hide here behind the king's protection, but who back home keep silent and ought to remain silent and be ashamed of what they instigate here.[22]

Notwithstanding the impressive achievements of the deputies in the 1560s their cause had a fairly slim chance of success in the long run. In the first place the gentry was losing the economic battle with the great landowners; secondly, its members became increasingly enmeshed in relations of clientage with their mighty neighbours; thirdly, adherents of the *executio iurium* movement lacked adequate organisation: they could not form a faction because there was no powerful leader,[23] and each successful politician, if he did not scorn personal advancement, sooner or later was granted a senatorial title and so was lost to the movement.

The great boom in the grain trade in the second half of the sixteenth century, especially in the 1590s, could not be turned to direct account by all potential exporters. What we know about the distribution of market opportunities for various groups of grain producers may be summed up as follows:[24] in Baltic ports prices were usually much higher than in the hinterland. That has been demonstrated in detail for the whole Vistula basin, as well as for Danzig's hinterland. The only economical means of transport was river boats; road transport of bulky, heavy commodities (grain, timber, ashes, etc.) was very expensive, and large loads in any case imposed too great a strain on draft animals. Within Poland–Lithuania heavy tolls were not levied and for all practical purposes goods belonging to the nobility were exempt. However, feasible transport by no means came cheaply for every nobleman. The rafting or floating of goods was a relatively complex business which needed skilled and experienced managers and hands and was only worthwhile when a sufficient quantity of goods had been assembled. The quantitative sources available suggest that size and distance played a crucial role.

1. In the servile labour system the larger landed estates were more market-oriented than single farms belonging to the lesser gentry.

2. The further from Danzig the cheaper the grain and, in turn, the greater the relative profit from its sale.[25]
3. The further from Danzig the greater the share of large landowners in rafting local produce.
4. The further from Danzig the greater the annual fluctuations in grain exports, which meant that while the immediate hinterland brought its grain to the Danzig market each year the far-off provinces were able to send considerable quantities only in particularly fat years. As a consequence of the last two factors only the greater landlords were able to supply Danzig with grain from distant areas on a regular basis (see Tables 1 and 2).

The cumulative effect of all these variables redounded to the advantage of the magnates, and one may hazard that the further from the Baltic the more inequal became the opportunities of access to a profitable market. Active involvement in the grain, oxen or timber trade did not imply any diminution of status for the nobility. Records

Table 1 Landowners in the Vistula grain trade (1555–76)

Province of origin	Masovia		Little Poland		Ruthenia and Wolhynia	
Quality of harvest	High	Low	High	Low	High	Low
Average total transports*	35,648	17,144	18,505	6,092	14,813	1,845
Landowners' share (%)**	53	63	84	89	83	92
Percentage of landowners' share among:						
magnates	52	58	69	72	69	76
rich gentry	24	24	18	18	25	13
medium gentry	24	18	13	10	6	11

Note In order to show the contrast between fat and lean years four medium-harvest years for each province from the twelve years for which data are available have been disregarded. Masovia was nearest to, and Ruthenia–Wolhynia furthest from, Danzig.

*Commercial loads (for rye *circa* 2.2 metric tonnes).

**Other shares taken by merchants and the clergy.

Source A. Mączak, 'Export of Grain and the Problem of Distribution of National Income in the Years 1550–1650', *Acta Poloniae Historica*, XVIII (1968), p. 82.

Table 2 Assessment of gross profits from the grain trade by exporters from different provinces

Province of origin River shipments	Masovia		Little Poland		Ruthenia and Wolhynia	
	High	Low	High	Low	High	Low
Average price of rye in Danzig*	25,6	35,1	36,2	17,13	27,10	27,13
Gross profits of great landowners*	78,000	50,000	107,000	20,000	81,000	9,000
Gross profits of other vendors*	138,000	79,000	65,000	13,000	54,000	4,000

*In Prussian marks and groschen (20 groschen = 1 mark). In each case three years of high and low river shipments from the mid-sixteenth century have been chosen, when corresponding statistics of rye prices obtained by the royal estate of Malbork (Marienburg in Prussia) are available.
Source Mączak, 'Export of Grain', p. 83.

of the toll-house in Włocławek on the Vistula, where goods belonging to the nobility were duly registered but only in rare cases also charged, clearly reveal numerous partnerships buying up grain and other products from their localities in Masovia and sending them down to towns on the Lower Vistula in Royal Prussia or directly to Danzig.[26] That type of enterprise did not occur in the Upper Vistula basin. There, at least from the early seventeenth century onwards, great landowners offered space in their river boats to their lesser neighbours and oversaw their goods in Danzig. That practice went hand-in-hand with the buying-up of marketable goods at local markets or indeed from the lords of small estates direct.[27]

After 1579 even sample quantative data are lacking but the figures which we have for the total shipments of grain down the Vistula from beyond Warsaw show that they were rising fast. It is safe to assume that this increase was due primarily to the cumulative effect of the nobles' shift to domain farming at the expense of their tenants' holdings and to the increase in the number of great estates as a result of the purchase of gentry estates on a massive scale. Whatever evidence exists suggests that greater landlords were dominating the market and that they were spending money on consumption rather than on covering the operating costs of their estates (which were minimal), as well as developing their courts and buying land. The concentration of landed property during the late sixteenth and early seventeenth century was a very striking phenomenon (see Table 3). In his recent thesis on the land market in Greater Poland, a region beyond the immediate orbit of Danzig trade, Dr Andrzej Pośpiech has shown that this market became active during boom periods. Concentration of property required a nucleus of great estates, and that may be the reason why it did not occur in Masovia – the proverbial region of petty nobles – or in Royal Prussia, where local magnates at a provincial level rested their social standing and influence upon the royal estates which they held effectively by inheritance.[28] In the south and south-west of Poland, by contrast, the growth of estates owned by the leading magnate families was truly impressive: several noblemen launched their families in the space of one lifetime into the ranks of the highest aristocracy and richest landowners.

Among that group Sebastian and Stanisław Lubomirski increased their estates between 1581 and 1629 in the palatinate of Cracow alone from four to ninety-one villages (alongside twenty-three royal ones). Whoever was shrewd enough to strike roots in the Ukraine could be sure of multiplying his estates and revenues thanks to the rapid colonisation of that vast region. The extreme case was Prince Jeremi

Table 3 Distribution of noble property in the Palatinate of Cracow

Size of property	Percentage of owners		Percentage of villagers		Villages per owner	
	1581	1629	1581	1629	1581	1629
Less than 1 village	36.1	43.9	20.3	6.6	0.9	0.3
1	38.6	29.6	25.6	18.3	1.1	1.0
2–4	20.0	19.6	31.1	30.5	2.6	2.6
5–9	4.6	4.8	14.4	19.8	5.2	6.9
10 or more	0.7	2.1	8.7	24.8	20.3	19.9
Total (absolute figures)	849	771	1399	1268	1.7	1.7

Source A. Mączak, 'Zur Grundeigentumsstruktur in Polen im 16. bis 18. Jahrhundert', *Jahrbuch für Wirtschaftsgeschichte*, 1967, part IV, p. 148 (with corrections).

Wiśniowiecki who in 1630 according to inventories of his property owned six hundred hearths on the left bank of the Dnieper, which by 1647 had risen to the incredible figure of 38,460 (or around 230,000 souls).[29] The Wiśniowieckis originated from Ruthenia but several genuinely Polish families were also able to profit from the estate and colonisation boom in the wake of the incorporation into Poland of what had been the southern part of the grand duchy of Lithuania. The most interesting case of spectacular growth is that of Jan Zamoyski. '*Parvum parvo additur*' was his acquisitive principle, but from 1589 he was also able to acquire even large domains comprising fifteen or more villages. During his lifetime he increased his property from four villages in 1572 to over two hundred villages and eleven small towns. In addition, he administered six hundred royal villages and a dozen other towns.[30] The case of Zamoyski is especially important because he had been a very influential leader of the 'executionist' gentry and became the premier nobleman only on account of his role during the first interregna (1572–76) and because of the grace of King Stephen Báthory. As grand chancellor and grand hetman of Poland (there were counterparts for Lithuania) Zamoyski disposed of a large network of clients.[31]

While the chancellor-hetman (chief military commander; both posts held for life) was probably unique in his political career and general success, the establishment of clienteles was quite characteristic of Poland and Lithuania in these years. In that the republic was by no means unique in Europe, but generally patronage was changing its form wherever absolutism was on the rise, as in France and Spain, or where a rapid process of modernisation was involved, as with the Dutch United Provinces. At issue here is the traditional patronage exercised by the high nobility, a phenomenon which remained greatly in evidence wherever central power and modern bureaucracy could not reach.[32] Poland–Lithuania was to become the promised land of rural clientage and to remain so until the partitions of the late eighteenth century. That is the second reason, in my view, for the helplessness of any independent political movement of the gentry, and it leads on to the third.

How could a political party be run which set itself against the magnates? No network of communications existed comparable to that of the church, the king and the intensive personal contacts between high noble families which had emerged even before the sixteenth-century interregna when between sessions of the *Sejm* the leading senators were able to communicate much more quickly and easily than the squires. There was little prospect, therefore, of a balanced and efficient polity based upon true 'gentry democracy'. This explanation differs somewhat from the one advanced by Perry Anderson for what he defines as Polish 'anarchy, impotence and annexation'.[33] According to Anderson 'the paradoxical size of the *szlachta* and formal absence of titles within it produced a self-destructive caricature of a representative system proper within the gentry'. Neither the size of the privileged Estate nor the absence of formal titles by themselves explain anything: Denmark acquired its first counts only after the absolutist *coup* of Frederick III, while in the Spanish kingdoms *hidalgos* were roughly as numerous as the *szlachta* in Poland.[34] But Anderson is right that 'no immanent mediation of interest was practicable within the noble class' – at least on a scale of some 700,000 to 900,000 square kilometres. Another, though small, country with a relatively numerous and modestly endowed nobility, barely organised into 'a vertical hierarchy of ranks' – the Piedmont of Duke Emmanuel Philibert – became from 1559 onwards a model case of absolutism.[35]

It is not easy to pinpoint the overriding cause of a phenomenon so baffling as the Polish 'golden liberty'. Perhaps a solution to this dilemma will help resolve some more general questions about the possible relationships between rulers and their Estates in other European countries. The social fabric cannot be compared with molecular structures, so that historians would be well advised not to resort to the analytic principles governing chemical combinations which operate by the subtraction of individual components. There is no need to apologise, therefore, for the lack of a precise historical explanation.

Numerous and far-reaching fiscal and jurisdictional liberties were not uncommon in Europe before the era of absolutism. Bohemia–Moravia, Hungary, Sweden–Finland and Denmark–Norway all had elective monarchies. For Poland what mattered was that the 'normal' tug-of-war between the prince and the Estates was played out in such a vast country, and that the legacy of the Jagiellon dynasty – Lithuania – was in a sense a geopolitical liability: it brought little in rents and taxes, involved Poland in conflicts with Muscovy and the Tartars, and bequeathed an economic, social and seigneurial power structure which favoured the owners of immense estates. Despite such an obvious overstatement[36] the point serves to stress the difference between the situation of the Jagiellons and that of the Hohenzollerns, who were able to play off Brandenburg officials against Prussian subjects and vice-versa, or that of the Oldenburg dynasty who knew how to use the duchies of Schleswig and Holstein to strengthen their sway over Denmark.

It is too easy to say that Jagiełło and his descendants were weaklings, whereas the Hohenzollerns are commonly regarded as a particularly gifted dynasty. The Jagiellons found themselves in a precarious situation roughly determined by three central factors: they inherited and had to develop a society of Estates with poorly developed towns; as a consequence the money economy was primitive, which gave little scope for intensive taxation; and Poland's geopolitical position afforded little chance of concentrating their efforts in one direction, so for all practical purposes no important goal was attained during the sixteenth century. Moreover, there was little internal consensus about the priorities of domestic and international policy. For Greater Poland the Tartars were a very remote danger, while Prussia and Livonia were of little interest to Little Poland. All the same, it is easy to underestimate the role of various deeply-rooted customs in public life. Traditionally offices (including leaseholds of royal estates) were granted for life, which gave the king little opportunity of creating a truly dependable civil service. It was characteristic that once a *homo novus* had been appointed he did not usually feel any obligation of long-lasting loyalty towards his benefactor and sovereign. Sigismund III tried to be determined and peremptory in his appointments' policy,[37] but while he was able to disregard Protestant candidates after 1592 he could never introduce even minimal changes in the institutional and constitutional system.

After the first free election it was too late for any kind of *absolutum dominium*. Recently Professor Andrzej Wyczański has praised highly the movement for the execution of the laws, suggesting that it 'led not to a weakening but rather to a strengthening of royal power . . . and improved the efficiency of the central bureaucratic organs'. It also 'weakened the political influence' of lay and ecclesiastical magnates and 'gave the monarchy greater freedom of manoeuvre'.[38] I agree that the co-operation of the last Jagiellon, Sigismund Augustus (1548–72), with the Chamber of Deputies was for a time exemplary, but apart from changing the royal electoral system I do not see any real chance of establishing an efficient government based on the monarch and the gentry, but not on the magnates. It is difficult to overstate the gentry's disapproval of heavy taxation and the crown's active policy against Poland's neighbours. Were Polish nobles so distrustful of their monarchs only because of their poor experience with Henry of Valois?

It can be taken for granted that since those years royal authority had greatly diminished. If the Reformation provided a chance for an independent political movement of the gentry (and most of its parliamentary activists before 1572 were Protestants of various denominations), no acceptable Protestant candidates for the throne could be put forward. Nothing was done, moreover, to institutionalise co-operation between the king and the deputies. This leads me back to certain social changes that were taking place in the nobles' Estate. Its upper stratum – senatorial families – was never a closed caste; outstanding members of the gentry were acceptable as marriage partners and thus they were able to enter the more exclusive circles of the high aristocracy. A recent study of deputies from Báthory's reign (1576–86) has shown that a relatively large number would become senators under Sigismund III.[39] The sharp conflict between both chambers in the 1550s and 1560s was to be forgotten. During the *rokosz* of 1606–9 some radical overtones against the magnates could still be heard, but sixty years later, when the nobility once more took up arms against the monarch, those voices were silent. The *populus nobilium* was unable to keep what may be called the balance of social powers. Its internal cohesion was nationally provided almost entirely by its topmost stratum, the magnates. Genuine grass-roots gentry activity after 1600 was no longer possible and with it any long-term alliance with the king.

Dr Anna Sucheni-Grabowska, who has rightly stressed the last Jagiellon's skill in government and his sound choice of political allies, points out the crucial weakness of his situation: Sigismund Augustus lacked any close ties with financiers.[40] However, that obviously did not derive from personal neglect on his part but from the country's general situation. Poland's financial centre was Danzig, which remained beyond the king's sphere of influence. What is more, Danzig had good reason to distrust any Polish efforts towards administrative centralisation and was perfectly satisfied to co-operate politically and economically with individual magnates.[41]

To envisage the Polish Commonwealth run by true servants of the crown remains entirely conjectural. In Sigismund Augustus and Báthory's day royal secretaries had been both efficient and competent, and many of them enjoyed glittering careers.[42] But in Poland 'rule by secretaries', as in Sweden under Eric XIV, John III and Charles IX, was out of the question. By the time it was technically possible both the aristocratic elite and the politically conscious gentry had become too powerful. And, last but not least, Polish towns, which had already been ignored as allies by the early Jagiellons, never produced potential royal counsellors. Nothing was ever simple in Polish affairs. But in seeking to determine the latest date at which the fate of the state was still in balance I would draw particular attention to the 1560s. A free-for-all by foreign princes vying for the Polish throne from 1572 onwards must have been detrimental to any sensible reform, even if the Vasas were able to survive for more than eighty years. The decentralisation of power and administration which was already under way under Báthory was likely to destroy any effective financial reforms. But at the root of the structure of the state lay the distribution of property throughout the vast countryside. The power of the local lords was much more real than that of the distant king. They were both patrons and the only available power brokers. And since the king was to be freely elected, was his person or rather the particular patron the proper mainstay of security and stability? In a kingdom without hereditary monarchy the true dynasties were those of the magnates.

Notes

1. N. Davies, *God's Playground. A History of Poland*, vol. I (Oxford, 1982), p. xi.
2. G. Schramm, 'Polen – Böhmen – Ungarn: Übernationale Gemeinsamkeiten in der politischen Kultur des späten Mittelalters und der frühen Neuzeit', *Przegląd Historyczny* (forthcoming). Paper read at the 3rd Conference of Polish and West German historians, Mainz, July 1984.
3. J. Bardach, 'La formation des assemblées polonaises au XVe siècle et la taxation', *Standen en Landen*, LXX (1977), p. 281. Royal towns took their stand on their particular charters, but the privileges granted by King Casimir to the noble Estate in 1454 formally prejudiced the fiscal immunities of the towns, and the *Sejm* did not hesitate to tax them without their consent.
4. In formal terms no 'upper' and 'lower' House existed in Poland, and the gentry strongly objected to such epithets. There were, on the other hand, numerous procedural similarities between the respective relationships of both Houses of Parliament at Westminster and of the Senate and Chamber of Deputies in Poland.
5. G. Schramm, 'Adel und Staat. Ein Vergleich zwischen Brandenburg und Polen-Litauen im 17. Jahrhundert', in M. Biskup and K. Zernack (eds), *Schichtung und Entwicklung der Gesellschaft in Polen und Deutschland im 16. und 17. Jahrhundert. Parallelen, Verknüpfungen, Vergleiche (Vierteljahrschrift für Sozial- und Wirtschaftsgeschichte*, Beiheft LXXIV) (Wiesbaden, 1983), p. 61. The point in question comes out somewhat indirectly in the text, but it was stressed by Schramm in discussion.

6. Cf. collections of papers on *Herrschaftsverträge* which omit the Polish case, in *Schweizer Beiträge zur Allgemeinen Geschichte*, X (1952), and R. Vierhaus (ed.), *Herrschaftsverträge, Wahlkapitulationen, Fundamentalgesetze* (Veröffentlichungen des Max-Planck-Instituts für Geschichte, LVI) (Göttingen, 1977).

7. Cf. Bardach, 'Formation', p. 280, with full bibliography on early Polish parliamentarianism. Parallel to Bardach cf. S. Russocki, 'Le système représentatif de la république nobiliaire de Pologne', in K. Bosl (ed.), *Der moderne Parlamentarismus und seine Grundlagen in der ständischen Repräsentation* (Berlin, 1977); also cf. a series of papers in *Acta Poloniae Historica*, XXXVI (1977).

8. This is the point stressed by Bardach, 'Formation'. One may add that local assemblies were an excellent stage for noble, and particularly freshman, politicians; their traditions and conventions formed in the fifteenth and sixteenth centuries paved the way for the system of government and administration which prevailed in the later seventeenth and eighteenth centuries.

9. *Volumina legum*, vol. I, p. 299; cf. Bardach, 'Formation', p. 291.

10. The expression 'magnate' is a late coinage and rather pejorative. Recent discussions on the nature and definition of the magnates are of secondary importance; here the expression is used to describe great landowners, senators (with the exception of backbenchers or lesser castellans) and members of their families.

11. Cf. Davies, *God's Playground*; J. K. Fedorowicz (ed.), *A Republic of Nobles. Studies in Polish History to 1864* (Cambridge, 1982); A. Mączak, H. Samsonowicz, and P. Burke (eds), *East–Central Europe in Transition from the Fourteenth to the Seventeenth Century* (Cambridge, 1985), chs. 1 and 10.

12. The 1564/65 survey has been thoroughly analysed by Jan Rutkowski in his *opus* on income distribution in early modern Poland *Badania nad podziałem dochodów w Polsce w czasach nowożytnych*, vol. I (Cracow, 1938).

13. A. Sucheni-Grabowska, 'Walka o wymiar i przeznaczenie kwarty w końcu XVI i na początku XVII wieku', *Przegląd Historyczny*, LVI (1965). Recently K. Chłapowski has assessed the overall results of the *executio bonorum regalium* in *Realizacja reform egzekucji dóbr, 1563–1665* (Warsaw, 1984), concentrating on estates pawned in Little Poland.

14. E. Ladewig Petersen, 'From Domain State to Tax State', *Scandinavian Economic History Review*, XXIII (1975).

15. Idem, *Fra standssamfund til rangssamfund, 1500–1700* (Copenhagen, 1980), pp. 219, 291.

16. H. Schweichler, 'Das Domänenwesen unter Herzog Albrecht in Preußen (1525–1568)', *Mitteilungen der Literarischen Gesellschaft Masovia*, XVII (1911), pp. 119–20. On fraud cf. C. von Nostitz, *Haushaltungsbuch des Fürstenthums Preußen 1578*, ed. K. Lohmeyer (Leipzig, 1893), p. 155.

17. M. North, *Die Amtswirtschaften von Osterode und Soldau* (Berlin, 1982).

18. Much has been done and is being done on this subject by Professor Andrzej Wyczański. Cf. his general conclusions in both edited volumes *cit.* n. 11.

19. J. Bardach, *Historia państwa i prawa Polski*, vol. I, 2nd edn (Warsaw, 1964), p. 476f.

20. This was the conclusion of S. Roman in his *Przywileje nieszawskie* (Wrocław, 1957).

21. Since 1466 the western part of the former territory of the Teutonic Order belonged directly to the Polish kings and with the Union of Lublin in 1569 was incorporated into Poland.

22. A. T. Działiński (ed.), *Zródlopisma de dziejów Unii Korony Polskiej i Wielkiego Księstwa Litewskiego*, vol. II, part 1 (Poznań, 1856–61), p. 386.

23. Cf. D. J. Roorda, *Partij en factie* (Groningen, 1961), pp. 1–36.

24. Cf. W. Kula, *An Economic Theory of the Feudal System. Towards a Model of the Polish Economy, 1500–1800* (London, 1976). Lack of space prevents the inclusion of adequate evidence on prices and market conditions.

25. Comparable evidence has been collected from the first survey of royal estates in 1564/65. Cf. A. Mączak, 'Preise, Löhne und Lebenshaltungs-kosten in Europa des 16. Jahrhunderts. Ein Beitrag zur Quellenkritik', in I. Bog *et al.* (eds), *Wirtschaftliche und soziale Strukturen im säkularen Wandel. Festschrift für Wilhelm Abel zum 70. Geburtstag*, vol. II (Hanover, 1974), pp. 322–5, 340–1.

26. S. Kutrzeba and F. Duda (eds), *Regestra thelonei aquatici Wladis-laviensis saeculi XVI* (Cracow, 1915), *passim*.

27. The same practice was used by the Radziwiłłs in Lithuania, but probably only later.

28. A. Mączak in G. Labuda (ed.), *Historia Pomorza*, vol. II, part 1 (Poznań, 1976), p. 204. Eight leading noble families between 1526 and 1657 held 44% of royal estates (four of them as much as 32%); Bratian remained in the hands of a single family for 123 years; another family held Sztum (Stuhm) for over 106 years. Dr Pośpiech's thesis is on the property market in the county of Kalisz in the 16/17 c., University of Warsaw, 1984.

29. W. Tomkiewicz, *Jeremi Wiśniowiecki (1612–1651)* (Warsaw, 1933), ch. 5.

30. A. Tarnawski, *Działalność gospodarcza Jana Zamoyskiego, kanclerza i hetmana wielkiego koronnego* (Lwów, 1935).

31. W. Tygielski, 'A Faction that could not lose'. Paper read at a conference on *Patronat-Klientel-Beziehungen in der frühen Neuzeit*, Historisches Kolleg, Munich, October 1985 (forthcoming).

32. On various types of clientage in early modern Europe see the papers presented to the conference, above, n. 31.

33. P. Anderson, *Lineages of the Absolutist State* (London, 1974), p. 298.

34. M.-C. Gerbet, *La noblesse dans le royaume de Castille* (Paris, 1979), pp. 149–53. Cf. also J. Meyer, *Noblesses et pouvoirs dans l'Europe d'ancien régime* (Paris, 1973), pp. 28–9 and *passim*.

35. Recent publications by Professor Enrico Stumpo suggest that there is

much misunderstanding about the numbers and economic potential of the Piedmont nobility. Cf. his *Finanza e stato moderno nel Piemonte del seicento* (Rome, 1979), pp. 278, 290; idem, 'I ceti dirigenti in Italia nell' età moderna. Due modelli diversi: nobilità piemontese e patriziato toscano', in A. Tagliaferri (ed.), *I ceti dirigenti in Italia in età moderna e contemporanea* (Udine, 1984), pp. 167–8.

36. I cannot here embark upon the knotty subject of the long-term consequences of the Polish–Lithuanian unions. However, having recently read numerous examination papers by students on roughly this topic, I detect the blossoming in present-day Poland of a stereotyped argument which goes: Lithuania was the mainstay of the magnates: the latter were detrimental to Poland's fate: *ergo*, Lithuania was somewhat of a curse for Poland. Only a few candidates ventured, for instance, that without the Lithuanian buffer Poland would have been swallowed by Russia even earlier.

37. On royal power cf. Wyczański's papers in the edited collections *cit.* n. 11, and below, n. 38. Greater detail on Sigismund III is given by W. Czapliński, 'Rządy oligarchii w Polsce nowożytnej', *Przegląd Historyczny*, LII (1961); A Kersten, 'Problem władzy w Rzeczypospolitej czasu Wazów', in *O naprawę Rzeczypospolitej XVII–XVIII wieku* (Warsaw, 1965).

38. A. Wyczański, 'The Problem of Authority in Sixteenth-Century Poland. An Essay in Reinterpretation', in Fedorowicz, *Republic of Nobles* (as n. 11), p. 99. The author's final remark that 'these conclusions fly in the face of existing opinion' is not altogether accurate, for most students of the period agree that in Sigismund Augustus' reign both government and administration still worked well.

39. Witold Rodkiewicz's paper on deputies' careers is to appear in *Przegląd Historyczny*. Membership of the Chamber played different roles in the informal *cursus honorum* of the various strata of the nobility. For squires multiple membership was compatible with higher county offices and dignities; young magnates hardly bothered to run for it more than once, if at all.

40. A. Sucheni-Grabowska, 'Badania nad elitą władzy w latach 1551–1562', in A. Wyczański (ed.), *Społeczeństwo staropolskie*, vol. I (Warsaw, 1976), p. 96. This paper (with a French summary) is a thorough and balanced appreciation of Sigismund Augustus' government and administration.

41. For the role of Danzig in the Polish–Lithuanian Republic W. Czapliński's paper, 'Problem Gdańska w czasach Rzeczypospolitej szlacheckiej', *Przegląd Historyczny*, XLIII (1952) is still valid. Czapliński calls Danzig 'a collective magnate'.

42. A collective biography of Báthory's secretaries by Leszek Kieniewicz will appear in A. Wyczański (ed.), *Społeczeństwo staropolskie*, vol. IV (1986). On their predecessors from Sigismund Augustus' times cf. idem, 'Problem of Authority', pp. 106–7.

Part IV

25 The Reformation and the Modern World

Thomas Nipperdey

The leading figures of the Reformation – Luther, Zwingli, Calvin and the rest – are quite different from us. That is not a restatement of the rather trivial fact that people of the twentieth century are different from those of the sixteenth. The figures of the Reformation seem even more remote to us: they lived in direct contact with the reality of God, with the wrath of God which could kill, with the mercy of God which allowed men to live, and as often as not with the devil. For them, as for Luther, the crucial question was how to have a merciful God. It was a matter of life and death. Which of us could say that today? The men of the Reformation were concerned with salvation, we on the other hand are concerned with happiness. Ours is a secular, post-religious world. For this reason the Reformation strikes us as belonging to the past. It belongs in a museum. We can, of course, try to transfer the questions posed by the leading figures of the Reformation to our own time, for example: How can man so conduct his life and his life with others that he is able to live at peace with himself? Their answers, however, are different from our own. Ours bear the imprint of secularised religion, both individual and social, or at least of the dream or self-redemption. Here then, of course, lies the relevance of the distant world of the Reformation. It questions the self-assurance of our modern existence. For just because it is remote does not mean that it is necessarily totally outdated. That is, however, the purpose of our humane deliberations on the right way of life and the concern of Christian teaching today and our response to it, not the interest of scholarly reflection. My interest as an historian is more modest. I am concerned with the position of the Reformation in the course of world history and the role it plays in the origins of our modern world. Yet this is again, of course, closely related to the question of the existential modernity of the leading thinkers of the Reformation. For if they do indeed belong to the modern era, then they also belong to us.

In the first two and a half centuries after the Reformation nobody would have dreamed of positing a relationship between the leading figures of the Reformation and the modern world. Either they had

535

brought about a re-evaluation, a re-discovery of Truth, or they had been the undoing of the church. They were considered from a dogmatic stand-point, not a historical one; they belonged to the history of salvation and not to the secular history of humanity. And the messianic-soteriological ring to the expression 'the modern era' just did not exist. That all changed in the eighteenth century. The Pietists were the first to see the Reformation as something incomplete, something to be continued. The Enlightenment, idealistic philosophy and Liberalism all took up this idea and secularised it. Luther, Zwingli and Calvin were seen as champions against tradition, authority and hierarchy, against monasticism and the domination of the priesthood, as apostles of intellectual veracity who were opposed to all dogma and as advocates of self-determination, the autonomy of the individual, his emancipation and his coming of age. They were the ones who, having released the world, work, family, state, culture and society from the grip of the clerics, allowed these to assume responsibility for themselves. Luther, for example, is seen as a hero in the history of emancipation. So thought the Liberals, the Kulturprotestants, the elitist wing of the Protestant church, the Modernists. So too thought Marx, despite all his anti-religious sentiments, and so too thought the Catholics, though now of course in the completely negative sense. The leading figures of the Reformation were, for better or for worse, the fathers of the modern world.

This interpretation is ideological and has already been overturned by scholars during the early part of this century. The theologians were the first to discover the true Luther who was no humanistic believer in culture and progress. And historians have, in their own way, brought out the different nature of the sixteenth century and the difference between the Reformation and the modern age. It was Ernst Troeltsch who in 1906 first demonstrated with delight the break between the Reformation and modern times: the Reformation belonged to the Middle Ages; the modern world with its rationality, its cult of the individual and its democracy, grew up in the eighteenth century and here lay the great dividing-line in world history; and social history showed that only then (around the year 1800) was there a fundamental change in peoples' way of life and mode of thinking.

So the men of the Reformation are not the fathers of the modern world, it can make no such claims on them. I shall now briefly go over the arguments advanced by the historians on this point, as they are important for my later considerations. We can no longer see history to such an extent in terms of individuals, a new epoch does not begin with a handful of men; even the Reformation, the split in the church, was not simply brought about by Luther or Zwingli on their own: their contemporaries only partially understood and took over their theology. There were many reasons why the Reformation started with them, and indeed several for which they were not responsible. Moreover, the great turning-points in history cannot be traced back to one particular set of causes, for example to the history of the church or the history of ideas. To the modern age, which begins in the sixteenth century, belong discoveries, colonisation, the origins of capitalism, the gaining of power by the state and the origins of a system of competing power states in Europe, and to it also belong Renaissance culture and an individualising of the attitude to life and of thought, in other words a host of factors, which affect each other, but which are independent of one another. If indeed there are any fathers of the modern age from that period, then Columbus, Copernicus, Erasmus and the Medici bankers must be numbered among them.

Thus the more one has to do with the Reformation and its leading figures the more the medieval aspects become clear. That is particularly apparent in the case of Luther. Luther is a child of the Middle Ages and in some ways its chief representative. He is responding to a crisis of the late Middle Ages and his answers are new ones, but his questions and the categories he uses and his view of the world are rooted in the Middle Ages. One sees this most clearly when one compares him with his contemporaries; Luther was more medieval, less modern, than others who had an answer to the crisis of the times: humanists with their idea of undogmatic piety and a rational-humane ethic, mystics and spiritualists with their leanings towards individualism and subjectivism, and bourgeois sceptics, the advocates of an autonomous Renaissance culture or a secularisation of state and society. It is true that in the sixteenth century one cannot separate clearly the medieval from the modern, but these stirrings of modernity in the late Middle Ages are alien to Luther. His rebellion against the Middle Ages has its roots in pre-modern times and goes back beyond the medieval world to St Augustine and St Paul. Indeed, one can say that Luther succeeded in blocking the trend towards modernity which existed around 1500. He once again brought to the fore, with all its original force, the question of mercy and salvation, the question, in fact, of a medieval monk and one which flew in the face of all the rational, humanistic and secular trends of the times, whose emergence Luther managed to stall for another two and a half centuries. Of course other leading figures of the Reformation were by comparison less medieval and therefore, one could say, more modern (and therefore are still considered more modern today). Zwingli, who was less dogmatic and more a burgher moralist, Calvin, who was more rational and humanistic, and the Anabaptists and Spiritualists, who were opposed to an institutionalised, all-embracing church and its dogmatic resolutions and who were, in the last resort, advocates of individual piety and tolerance. The development of Swiss and Anglo-Saxon Protestantism seems to confirm this greater modernity. However, what the leading figures had in common seems to me of greater importance: they were all opposed to the radical wing of the Reformation, opposed to the urban sceptics and opposed to all the secular trends of the period. Their life support was archaic, religious, primeval rock.

Finally, we come to the effects of the Reformation. Certainly it was the beginning of a new age, but it was an age of different denominations, and then of absolutism. Church and dogma held on to their key position; the enforced culture of the church, which embraced all aspects of life and which bound the individual to new traditions and authority, remained. The Protestant churches were in many respects more old-fashioned than the leaders of the Reformation themselves; in as far as they did show initial signs of modernity these signs did not develop or, rather, remained isolated incidents. People lived in the static, closed pre-modern world of medieval Estates; there was no emancipation. In political terms the destruction of religious unity had placed the state in a more powerful position because it was now more responsible for religion and peace, and the various denominations were neutralised, which in turn formed the basis for absolutism. The new age, the sixteenth and the seventeenth century, and to some extent the eighteenth century, had its own character, distinct from that of the Middle Ages and of modern times. Of course, as is nearly always the case in history, so too was it the case in the Reformation that the actions of certain individuals turned out differently from the way they were intended. That the Lutheran churches in Germany became part of the authoritarian state, and the Calvinist ones in the Anglo-Saxon, Swiss and Dutch worlds the precursors of the modern liberal and democratic movements, had less to do with the theologians, Luther and Calvin, than with political circumstances. Other aspects were not so much the result of the Reformation as the result of its failure – the splitting of the church and its subsequent foundering on the rock of political circumstances. This is why, for example, it is precisely the Lutheran states which are more old-fashioned than

Luther's theory of the state and more old-fashioned than the Catholic and Calvinist states of the period. But when we look at the real effects of the Reformation as a whole and the new era it heralded, then it is the pre- and un-modern aspects which we must stress.

To be sure, the Reformation greatly intensified the plurality and divisions within Europe, for now there were competing churches, and this provided the basis for new dynamic impulses, the basis for the emancipation of states, of scholarship, of culture, of individuals, and the basis of liberty and freedom. If Europe had been a unified world, like the oriental cultures, then the modern world would not have grown up in Europe. In increasing the plurality within Europe the Reformation created favourable conditions for the growth of the modern world. But this cannot now be seen as a paternal relationship, paternity cannot sensibly be ascribed to the Reformation here; rather it is more a causal relationship, applicable generally to the world at large. In other words, every age helps to determine the next.

The men of the Reformation are thus not the fathers of the modern age, nor the standard bearers of the modern world. Today historians say that they wish to understand the Reformation and its time for its own sake, and do not want to degrade it and its foreignness to a piece of pre-history of our own time or to monopolise it for their own historical-philosophical speculations, wishes and ideas. The Reformation remains, in the first instance, the Reformation, and its relationship to modern times is misleading. Historians have a need for modesty.

After so much introduction I have at last arrived at my main point. For with these arguments based on specialist knowledge, indeed, we could say, based on historicity, the question of the connection between the Reformation and the modern era, the question of the course of world history over a period of five hundred years, is not finally cleared up once and for all. Perhaps the Reformation leaders were the grandfathers of the modern world? Let us give a different slant to the question. Let us not first ask what was modern about the leading figures of the Reformation or the Reformation itself, because that is not being very fair to them, but let us rather ask what are the roots of our own modernity. Here we come up against the Reformation and its leading figures. Max Weber's famous thesis points out the connection between the Protestant ethic and the essential spirit of capitalism. We misunderstand the thesis if, in response to it, we insist on discussing endlessly the question of religion and economics. I interpret the question more broadly, as Weber intended it to be understood: the modern world, that is the world of scholarship, of economics, of work and achievement, of dynamism, of democracy, has been more strongly influenced by Protestantism than by Catholicism. In societies of mixed denomination Protestants produce from their ranks a greater number of entrepreneurs and professors, and a greater number of people with the vision and ability to get things done. Is there some inner, and not just chance, connection here? Let me outline Weber's basic thesis, according to which religion is the dominant influence on human impulses and conduct and determines those attitudes in which the direct causes of our behaviour, i.e. interests, find expression. Taking this idea further, we could say that this disenchantment with the world and this rationalisation of our way of life did not come into being in the face of religion but, rather, because of it. These hypotheses are not only valid when applied to the particular form of Calvinist puritanism, but can also be applied to the beginnings of the Reformation, to Luther and Zwingli. The leaders of the Reformation created new themes of life, and injected into the world new social-moral norms, even new modes of behaviour, which persisted in all branches of the Protestant church. It is precisely the intensification of religion during the Reformation which is one of the most important roots of the modern world and of modern man. As we have seen, the leading figures of the Reformation are not the fathers of the modern world. But they and the Reformation created something which we can describe in Eisenstadt's term as the 'potential for modernisation', a mentality which created favourable conditions for the formation of the modern world from the latter part of the eighteenth century onwards, and which, when other circumstances came into play – such as economic, political, institutional – helped bring about modernisation, as the pre-modern elements of the world and of early Protestantism became weaker. In a second phase of Protestantism this potential for modernisation is actually realised.

Let me now, in a terribly condensed form, recall some of the ways in which the figures of the Reformation had an effect on religion in their own time. I freely admit that here I will be concentrating more on Luther than on other figures of the Reformation, but this is because it all began with him and because many of their basic views are identical – and where there are deviations from these they will be mentioned separately. Luther's Reformation, the revolution against the old church, begins with the revolt against abuses in the sale of indulgences, against the commercialisation and predictability of God's mercy, it begins with a prophetic protest against a church which is inextricably bound up with and adapted to the world. Luther and the Reformation recognised the Bible as the sole authority, as opposed to the authority of the church and tradition: *sola scriptura*. They made salvation dependent on mercy and faith alone: *sola gratia, sola fide*; and the prospect of salvation was no longer dependent upon the performing of good works, those pious, moral feats with which men justified themselves. It was above all Luther who radicalised the transcendent nature of God just as he radicalised man's sinfulness and damnation, leaving nothing in between. The reformers deprived the sacrament of its central position in the process of salvation and did away with this sacramental, concretised grace with its essentially supernatural nature and its quasi-magical effects. There was no longer a special status for priests who officiated at the mass, and no special ethical position reserved for monks, which in turn led to a breaking down of the hierarchy within the church, indeed it meant that the church ceased to be a sacramental institution for salvation. Finally, the Reformation put an end to the great Catholic middle-world which intervened between God and man, put an end to the world of the saints, indeed, put an end to the Catholic system of mediation and compromise between nature and grace, man and God, faith and the world, the system of analogies and syntheses and the system of 'both .. and'. Luther was a man who believed in 'either . . . or', and in this the other figures of the Reformation are indebted to him.

Having set the scene let us move on. Now, at last, we can change the direction of our questions. At this point I would like to set out some of the guiding principles of the modern world and explore their roots in religion and the Reformation.

1. The modern world is individualistic: rights, freedom, happiness, the self-fulfilment of the individual are what count, and society is based on a contract and made up of individuals who are now no longer fettered by the old restrictions of a non-individualistic society. Modernising means individualising, modernity means subjectivism. The history of this goes back a long way – to the Greeks, to the Jews and above all to early Christians. For after all, is not Christian religion concerned with the salvation of the individual soul? But here the Reformation marks the beginning of a new era and it has given a great impetus to this process. Luther (and here we must stress that it is above all Luther whom we mean at this point) is no modern individualist, no subjectivist, but he does believe in the personality of the individual. It is the individual who stands before God without support from tradition, institutions, nature or personal achievement:

there is nothing identifiable for him to cling on to. Luther conceived of religion as something completely personal, it is not something based on the supernatural–natural sacrament, but is something spiritual, invisible and internal. The individual no longer believes in what the church believes but he believes for its own sake, and believing is not synonymous with considering a metaphysical truth to be true, but means inward conviction, personal trust, in other words, *fides fiducialis*. Believing means, in contrast to everything metaphysical, believing that God created 'me', that Christ died for 'me'. In contradiction to tradition, Luther does not speak of sin as something distinct from 'myself' but talks of sin (egoism) as something which makes up 'my' person, indeed is 'my' person. This is the meaning of his writings on Original Sin. It is precisely this which is so offensive to the modern world, namely that it is sin which creates the individual personality. Or in other words: our life is based on conscience, and conscience is an individual matter. It determines behaviour. Behaviour is thus 'directed from within', norms and casuistic rules lose their force in the face of this personal conscience.

This process of personalisation – this 'personalism' – is also directed against the power of tradition and against the intervention of other authorities in the interpretation of the holy scriptures: it is the individual who stands in direct contact with the Bible and he who interprets it afresh each time. This personalisation process also modifies the influence of the church as an institution. The men of the Reformation did not transform the church into some sort of private club for the pious, into some kind of sect, but the church is now invisible, it is no longer an institution in a position of authority over and above the individual, with the task of supporting and protecting him. The critical attitude of the Protestant Christian towards the institution of the church has, since Pietism and the Enlightenment, left its mark even on daily life.

This personalised religion, this inner freedom remains central to the whole of the Reformation movement, even for those who differ with Luther. It has made the individual permanently responsible for himself, and established the modern principle of life being guided from within. It was not esoteric, elite humanism but this religious belief alone which produced this landmark in world history, this mass phenomenon, even in its secular forms. Of course, and one must not lose sight of this, the personalisation process brought about by the Reformation is founded on the existence of the individual face to face with God, whereas this is just what secular individualisation has got away from; for Luther, for example, freedom means being bound to God, whereas by freedom we mean something different.

In Germany, if I may interpolate for a moment, this personalisation has, within the specific framework of the Lutheran Church, developed into a particular phenomenon which we call German–Lutheran inwardness. The central issue for Luther and Lutheran Christians is God and the soul, not, as for Calvinists, God and the world. Inwardness and a Christian outlook are placed above the external forces of the world, the world of institutions, laws and deeds. The secular ideal of Germans since 1800, namely that of education as a process of self-improvement, self-cultivation and self-realisation grew up as a consequence of this approach to life. Another consequence was the tendency towards quietism and resignation, a surrendering to the existing state of affairs, to suffering and injustice, and towards unpolitical passivity. This has been the subject of strong criticism and self-criticism for a long time and rightly so. But the Lutheran concentration upon the individual and his soul, in other words, upon inwardness has actually a relevance for modern times, something which is worthy of further consideration. A man does not prove himself through his achievements, he is more than the product of himself, and he can and should resist the tremendous pressure of our times to strive towards conformity and the socialisation of his being. That is one of Luther's legacies to us.

2. The modern world is one of reflection and knowledge. This, no doubt, belongs to the Christian tradition, but again it was the Reformation which, long before the Enlightenment, immensely intensified this process. This also holds true for Luther, although he, unlike Zwingli and Calvin, fought vehemently to exclude reason from playing any part in religion and theology. The churches of the Reformation are churches based on the word, whether read, spoken, preached or sung, and not churches based on the sacrament and liturgy; the word conveys the sense and not an image. Protestant culture is a culture of the ear, not of the eye. Books and writings are not the concern of the priest alone but the concern of all. It is words which convey the meaning of life, and the concentration on the word trains intellectual awareness and powers of reflection; unlike confession, which is reduced to the level of ritual, it teaches man to say 'I', it teaches him the distance between his own ego and the world, the distance even between ego and the self. The word makes man more independent in the face of tradition and convention; behaviour which is guided from within is based on reflection. To this belong popular

education, elementary schooling, literacy, and it is the Protestant countries, particularly where compulsory education has been implemented by the state, which lead Europe in this. The ability to read and write, coming from the church of 'the Word', is a step towards emancipation, with tremendous consequences for secular culture as well. Their training in inwardness predestines Protestants for education. In Europe since the eighteenth century and especially in countries of mixed confession Protestants have been at an advantage in the sphere of education, and Catholics at a disadvantage, a 'deficit'. Reflection and the word, this is what Protestant churches have in common. Specific to continental Protestantism and in particular Central European Protestantism is the particular attitude to university and scholarship. Luther – to start with him again – was a teacher of the holy scriptures; the pulpit and the lectern were his domain. He made his theological discovery that man is justified by grace alone as a scholar working on the philological-hermeneutical interpretation of the texts. Unlike his colleague Karlstadt, for example, he did not rely on the uneducated simplicity of the peasants and fishermen, but linked conscience to knowledge and linked the existential concern of the believer to a searching and scientific interpretation of the Bible, to theology as a scholarly discipline. Zwingli and Calvin essentially went about things in the same way, though theirs was perhaps a more humanistic-rational approach. In Germany it was now the professors who, in the place of the pope or the church council, provided the correct teaching, which was accepted even by the princes. This remains a legacy of the continental church of the Reformation. Protestant churches are churches of the pastor, and the pastors are university educated theologians. Faith remains inextricably linked to the basic driving force of all knowledge, to doubting, namely to doubting whether one is interpreting the authoritative bible texts correctly, in other words, from the point of view of Christ. The practice of taking a critical look at tradition becomes the permanent driving force of scholarly study. The Bible, it is true, appears to be the new decisive authority, but because theologians constantly refer back directly to the Bible it is always possible, or even necessary, to reinterpret faith. This is the permanent unrest in Protestant theology as a scholarly discipline. The pastors were also scholars; and the other pupils of the universities, particularly the lawyers and the civil servants, were taught and educated in the shadow of theology. That was especially the case in Germany, where a close symbiosis developed between church, university, and the state of the bureaucrats and the princes. And because Germany was not a centralised country, but consisted of many states, many professors and many schools vying with one another, a diversity in intellectual matters developed here, and also a certain amount of freedom of choice for the individual, which reinforced the link between conscience and knowledge. Thus the intellectual trends towards modernisation since the early Enlightenment, and all free scholarly and intellectual reflection, have been worked out in, and not in opposition to or alongside, theology. The modern world has lived off precisely those problems first faced by theology. This generally holds true for Swiss Protestantism as well. The increase in reflection of a scholarly nature in modern culture is essentially rooted in the Reformation, as is the susceptibility of Protestants, who believe in all things academic and scientific, for any number of half-sciences. In Germany, one of the extreme consequences of this religious culture has been that professors have played such a leading role, and, further, that to hold strong convictions and points of view, above all to have a specific *Weltanschauung*, belongs to the German socio-cultural character. Marxism, with its theoretical passions and arguments between the orthodox Marxists on the one hand and the heterodox ones on the other, is a very German product of the Reformation. But enough of these asides on the subject of developments which are specifically German. One can generalise and say that, since the seventeenth century, the Protestant countries have led the way in the modern sciences. It is true that this has not been determined by religion alone – the Protestant countries have not made a particularly great contribution to modern natural sciences – but religion has been an important factor. The transcendent nature of God and the human personality of man do not leave much room for the influence of supernatural forces in nature, but take the process of disenchantment a step further. The unrecognisability of God gives more room to the recognisability of the world, the breaking away of theology from metaphysics, the differentiation between the order of salvation and the order of nature, between faith and knowledge, the critical attitude to tradition, the freedom of belief and the direct contact with God: these all allow the scientific explanation of the world and the natural sciences greater freedom. The new ideal of piety to be applied to the world directs the energies of those engaged in contemplative reflection to the scientific penetration of the world, releases curiosity and legitimises it. And ever since the rule of celibacy was lifted, the sons of pastors have been the ideal people to engage in this. The fact that there is no institutional church to define limits, defend tradition, force consensus and condemn Galileo, creates favourable conditions for the sciences to flourish. It is possible, with good reason, to criticise Protestant intellectuality, its faith in letters, just as its scientism. However, our world is a world of schools, of science, of reflection and of the word and this, to a large extent, stems from the Reformation.

3. The modern world is a world of work, achievement, discipline and efficiency. This is, no doubt, in part a consequence of the technical and industrial revolution and of the capitalist market economy; but it also has socio-moral roots, not only in later Calvinism, but also generally in the basic ideas of the early Reformation. Luther invested 'calling' and work in general with a new meaning, and all the others followed suit. The Reformation did away with monasticism, in other words, with a religious elite engaging in pious, ascetic deeds for the afterlife. The religious life was, thereafter, no longer a means of escape from the world, religious asceticism was an innerworldly asceticism. Everyday work, and not special acts of piety, was what God now demanded of us: work was a way of serving God in the real world, as well as being a service to one's fellow men at the same time. And all work was considered equal. There was no privileged position for the contemplative life, poverty was no longer a religious quality, the beggar was no longer, as in Catholicism, given a religious seal of approval; but also unearned income was – in principle – discredited, and all work had a right to be rewarded. The idleness of monks, beggars and nobility alike was frowned upon. Work became one of the duties of religious socio-moral education. This determined the everyday application of all the legacies of the Reformation and cultivated discipline, hard work, a sense of duty and conscientiousness. Luther, in addition, described the calling (*Beruf*) as an occupation which one first learnt and then practised all one's life, as something to which one was individually called by God, and this description gained acceptance within the common Protestant tradition.

Of course, one must stress an important distinction here between Luther and Lutheranism, on the one hand, and Anglo-Saxon Calvinism, on the other. For Luther and his church work is first and foremost an act of service to one's fellow men and in this sense it is completely at home in the old moral economy of pre-capitalist and pre-socialist days. Work is therefore not primarily tied to success and achievement. Man's individual standing with God is not dependent on his achievements in the sphere of work, for all work done in the faith of God and out of service to fellow human beings has the same worth. For this reason work is not so restless, so intent on growth and so much in the grip of asceticism, as with the puritans – there are more breaks from work, more small pleasures and more, modest, satisfaction. The modern idea of self-redemption and self-justification through work is not something which started with Luther. But Luther, like all the leaders of the Reformation, tied man's fulfilment in life to work and profession and linked purpose and meaning in life to work. And this similarity is more significant than the differences. This was a foundation of the modern world; this made it easier for Protestants to enter the dynamic world of industry and intensified their participation. (The Reformation also invested the institutions of family and marriage with new meaning and its re-appraisal of these institutions is closely linked to the demise of monasticism, but this can only be mentioned in passing.)

4. The modern world is different from the old world in that it is a dynamic world, constantly changing and shifting, a world of growth, of innovation, of unrest and, of course, instability. Men of energy and vision play a crucial role in it. This is just as much a result of the industrial and democratic revolutions, of the Enlightenment and of secularisation, certainly. But religious forces are at work here also. Protestants have a greater share in this modern dynamic force than Catholics. There is an aspect of their psyche which I would call Protestant unrest. We have already mentioned the revolution brought about when the Reformation turned against tradition and authority, and asserted personal responsibility over against all institutionalised norms. Both caused unrest. But in two respects we must give this idea greater precision. First, let us consider the intellectual aspect. The Protestants – the Lutherans here slightly more than the Calvinists – are opposed to systems, doubt attends any statement about faith, everything is provisional, nothing can be identified with God, the Bible is constantly being reinterpreted at any given time and the church lives, without the competence to decide, in and with the disagreements of the theologians. Catholics live according to an imperative: so be it! (*Roma locuta, causa finita*); Protestants, however, in doubt and question, ask: is it really so? Man is not born and nurtured enclosed by definitive views of the world and doctrines which are guaranteed by the church, but is always breaking out of the bounds. Hence the unrest. But this unrest is also existential. It stems from the continual uncertainty of man in the matter of his salvation. God and his mercy and faith cannot be objectified. The things which

would normally unburden, comfort and sustain man are now lacking, for example, trust in nature, tradition, good works, institutions, rituals, and the sacrament. Max Weber has talked a good deal about Calvinist unrest, but Lutheran unrest must be stressed just as much. For, indeed, Luther excluded that which is so important in Calvinist practice, namely the perfection or sanctification of the justified according to a rigid plan, his progress in the Christian shaping of his life, and the security he derives therefrom. For Luther the justification of salvation is never completely certain, salvation has to be justified over and over again, man remains what he is, *simul justus et peccator*. There is no progress. Therefore there exist no guidelines, no set patterns of behaviour to enable him to prove his worth and no church discipline for man to hold on to. Man is supposed to act inwardly and freely, but this makes him feel uncertain and isolated. Of course there is a carefree, relaxed trusting in God, but the other emotion keeps on surfacing. But more than anything, despite the differences, this unrest is a common Protestant legacy from, and a child of, the Reformation. The relief provided by the Catholic church does not exist, the conscience remains uneasy. Carefreeness, naivety, a willingness to take things for granted and *joie de vivre* are gnawed away at by Protestant seriousness and introspection. The normality of the sinful weekday and the Sunday of absolution and mercy does not exist. Protestants are not as happy as Catholics, life is a burden and a task, man lives in a state of anxiety and conflict, caught between the absolute demands and the encouragement of the Gospel, he lives on the edge of an abyss which is forever yawning wide open. Life is more akin to an experiment than a matter of carrying on acceptingly. This is the last reason for Protestant unrest. Because Protestants stand before God in isolated loneliness, this is the reason why, since the eighteenth century, they have taken such an active part in forming the world, the inward uneasiness makes them grasp at the world.

5. The modern world is a secular, profane world, no longer under the guardianship of faith and the church. Our more recent history is the history of secularisation. That has many roots, from Machiavelli to the Enlightenment, but one of its strongest roots lies in Christian religion, which has stripped the world of gods and sanctity, destroyed the understanding for magic, desacralised and disenchanted the world. The Reformation signals the beginning of a new era and in this nudges the world on a stage further. If monks and priests no longer hold privileged positions then the world of work, family and the state becomes the actual sphere of Christian life. If saints no longer exist,

and there is no procession through the fields with the priest and the sacrament, then heaven and earth become separated once and for all. The individual chosen from out of the world to stand before God keeps his position in the world. And if the church is no longer made up of a hierarchy of custodians of the sacrament then it no longer has any claim to a say in the direction of world affairs. The world is divested of clerics and clerical influence. Here we must, of course, recognise a fundamental difference between the Lutheran and the Reformed church: in the theological sense between Luther's doctrine of the two realms and the Reformed doctrine of the kingdom of Christ, the differing forms of differentiation, of the separation and the combining of religion and politics, church and state. Both have determined the nature of the modern world. For the Reformed Calvinist tradition this is well enough known and undisputed, especially in its Anglo-Saxon lineage: for instance, the quasi-republican constitution, the pathos of freedom and resistance, which in western Europe grew precisely out of the opposition to monarchs and states, the stronger links between the religious authorities and the community and, finally, the specific combination of the original theocratic desire to change the world, and then, after the demise of theocracy, the commitment to non-clerical, secular change in the name of the Gospel and God's righteousness right up to the social gospel of our century. It is more difficult and problematic with Luther and his churches (to which belong, of course, not just the German Lutheran churches but the Scandinavian churches as well). Luther fundamentally severed the Constantine connection between church and state, the amalgamation of the church and state hierarchy, and he was against a clericalisation of the world, because it would result in a more worldly church, and against the Calvinist leaning towards theocracy, towards the setting up of God's kingdom in this world. His pessimism was too strong for this: he believed that the world was a vale of tears and that Christians were an invisible minority, that man was a continually straying and sinful being. And he thought that the Christian standardisation of the world turned invisible faith into a law, perverted it and led to hypocrisy. It was impossible to make the world perfect. Here he distinguished between the two realms, that of God and the invisible church and that of the ordinary world. The world is not entrusted to the church, but rather to the natural reasonableness of man and the practical love of the Christian. This is the Reformation's general rejection of clericalism, and Luther's specific rejection of theocracy. This too is one of the foundations of the modern coming of age of rational man in his practical dealings with the world.

We know how problematic this has become. Naturally, Luther, as a product of the sixteenth century, assumed that the state with its princes and officials fitted into an essentially Christian framework and that they too were under God's jurisdiction. Therefore his teaching on the two different realms is difficult and sometimes contradictory. And in practical terms the theological division of worldly rulers and the church led, paradoxically, to a new union between church and state and led to the inclusion of precisely these German Lutheran churches in the authoritarian state, led to the instilling generally of obedience and subservience, and to resignation. An enormous amount has been said on the subject since Karl Barth's pronouncement on German Lutheranism, above all by way of criticism and self-criticism. However, one must still insist that the Lutheran theology of the two realms has made a positive contribution to modernity and has contributed to the relinquishing of the political sphere to responsible and rational beings who stand outside the world of the clerics and who come from the secular world. This has led to two distinct opposed human-political views. On the one hand to a sober realism: because Christian beliefs cannot be identified with a political programme, there can be no political doctrine of salvation, no Christian politics, merely Christians in politics, only painfully slow, realistic, piecemeal reforms dictated by compassion for one's fellow men. Lutherans are not hostile to the authority of the secular world, the secular world is not – as the Catholics felt for long enough and as Calvinists often feel – a godless world. The other consequence in the Lutheran sphere is in complete contrast: because there is no special spiritual sphere the involvement of the Christian in the world is his way of serving God within the world. As the old Protestant forms of religion and life dissolve, the secular things, family, work, nation, culture gain a new spirituality, they are a part of God on earth and they assume a transcendental quality within the world. The original separation of the two realms re-emerges as a new sanctification of worldly activity. Therefore Lutheran Protestants are sensitive to the spirit of the age, they do not wish to be considered behind the times, they pay homage to metaphysical opportunism, they identify with nationalism, socialism, pacifism, they take note of history, psychology, sociology, they represent the ethos of working and saving in the period of industrialisation and the ethos of consuming today. But in these respects the differences between the Lutheran and the Reformed churches have been smoothed out. Psychologically speaking one can say: Protestants, unlike Catholics, are not bound by institutions, norms and blind acceptance of old traditions; this can manifest itself in a general hunger for conviction and in a tendency to commit oneself to political and social involvement. In a situation where the influence of the church has been modified and religion personalised there develops a tendency for people to turn to substitute religions, such as modern social religions. Protestants are quite capable of becoming 'trendier than thou'. This is another form of Protestant secularity.

But if one is clear that the beginnings of the secular world go back to the Reformation, then one can take seriously the Christian potential of the secular world and at the same time criticise modern secularism, anarchic individualism, totalitarianism or indifference.

6. The modern world is one of loss brought about by modernisation, a world of new constraints, new restrictions to our freedom, new wounds and new miseries, a world, for example, of growth crises and a world where nature is plundered and exploited. It is a world of uncertainty and instability, of dangers and destructive tendencies. This, too, has something to do with religion. In Germany, for example, there are, among Protestants, not only more professors but also more cases of suicide and more users of sleeping tablets, in short, more successful people and more unhappy ones. Protestantism does not offer as much by way of external support through institutions and tradition and does not mediate between what is absolute and what is conditional, achievement counts for nought in the last resort, constant introspection subverts. For this reason Protestants have greater difficulty coming to terms with life, with happiness even. They are more prone than Catholics to anxiety and stress, less balanced and · less relaxed. This is the reverse side of dynamism and involvement.

What relevance does this contemplation have for us today? We learn that all of us, Christians and atheists, Protestants and Catholics, Lutherans and members of the Reformed churches, are the direct descendents of, and inherit from, our forefathers of the sixteenth century and we also learn what a gulf there is between us. We are reminded of the religious foundations of our culture and the secular consequences of events in the history of the church. Both are related, and it is of benefit to both if we bear this in mind. The leaders of the Reformation were, historically speaking, better at getting things moving and better at anticipating events than the modernists of that period, precisely because they went back to the nub of Christian religion. Being aware of the religious basis of the modern world lends legitimacy to our modernity and questions it at the same time. But this remains a matter for contemporary humane debate, once historians have had their say.

Index